PASCAL BRESSON & SYLVAIN DORANGE

FOR JUSTICE
THE SERGE & BEATE KLARSFELD STORY

Adapted from the book *Mémoires* by Serge and Beate Klarsfeld

W9-BGS-097

Date: 3/26/21

BIO KLARSFELD
Bresson, Pascal,
For justice : the Serge &
Beate Klarsfeld story /

PALM BEACH COUNTY
LIBRARY SYSTEM
3650 Summit Boulevard
West Palm Beach, FL 33406-4198

Life Drawn
by Humanoids

PASCAL BRESSON
Writer

SYLVAIN DORANGE
Artist

*

NANETTE McGUINNESS
Translator

MARK WAID
English Language Adaptation

*

VICTORIA PIERCE
US Edition Editor

VINCENT HENRY
Original Edition Editor

JERRY FRISSEN
Senior Art Director

RYAN LEWIS
Junior Designer

MARK WAID
Publisher

*

Rights and Licensing - licensing@humanoids.com
Press and Social Media - pr@humanoids.com

FOR JUSTICE. This title is a publication of Humanoids, Inc. 8033 Sunset Blvd. #628, Los Angeles, CA 90046. Copyright © 2021 Humanoids, Inc., Los Angeles (USA). All rights reserved. Humanoids and its logos are ® and © 2021 Humanoids, Inc.

Library of Congress Control Number: 2020942924

Life Drawn is an imprint of Humanoids, Inc.

Adapted from the book "Mémoires" by Serge and Beate Klarsfeld, World copyright ©Flammarion / Librairie Arthème Fayard, 2015

First published in France under the title *Beate et Serge Klarsfeld: un combat contre l'oubli* Copyright ©2020 La Boîte à Bulles & Pascal Bresson and Sylvain Dorange. All rights reserved. All characters, the distinctive likenesses thereof and all related indicia are trademarks of La Boîte à Bulles Sarl and / or of Pascal Bresson and Sylvain Dorange. No portion of this book may be reproduced by any means without the express written consent of the copyright holder except for artwork used for review purposes. Printed in Latvia.

PREFACE

In October of 1944, I was nine years old, and I had just come back to Paris after a journey of four long years across France, being hunted by the Vichy[1] police and by the Gestapo[2]—just like all the Jewish families in our country that was now conquered by Nazis. Right when we were freed after the war, that's when I joyfully discovered graphic novels and comics like *Les Pied Nickelés*, *Buffalo Bill*, *Charlot*, *Fantomas*...I was delighted. I used to live—and I still live—at Porte de Saint-Cloud[3], and when I could, I would run to Marcel Sembat[4] in Boulogne. Right when I turned on the Jean Jaurès Avenue, I could see a huge table with hundreds of comics. I only had a few pennies, stolen from my poor mother, and I needed to make a choice... What torture!

This passion lasted about two years. It slowly faded the more I gained interest in the classic authors, whose words were so right that the images escaped from them quite naturally, and comics would form in my head. With that in mind, during my teenage years, I was not interested in *Tintin* or *Lucky Luke*[5]. Once an adult, I really liked *Blueberry*, as I had also collaborated with Jean-Michel Charlier while he was looking for interesting topics for the series *Les Dossiers Noirs* (the Black Folders) for the ORTF[6], which dealt with historical characters that weren't famous but still played a big role in history. I suggested Otto Strasser and Menahem Begin, and ended up writing the screenplay for the show "Begin and the Irgoun". I also participated on set for the film on "Begin". He was the first Israeli political leader to have talked to Beate, a German in Israel. He soon became a close friend of ours, and three years later he became Prime Minister.

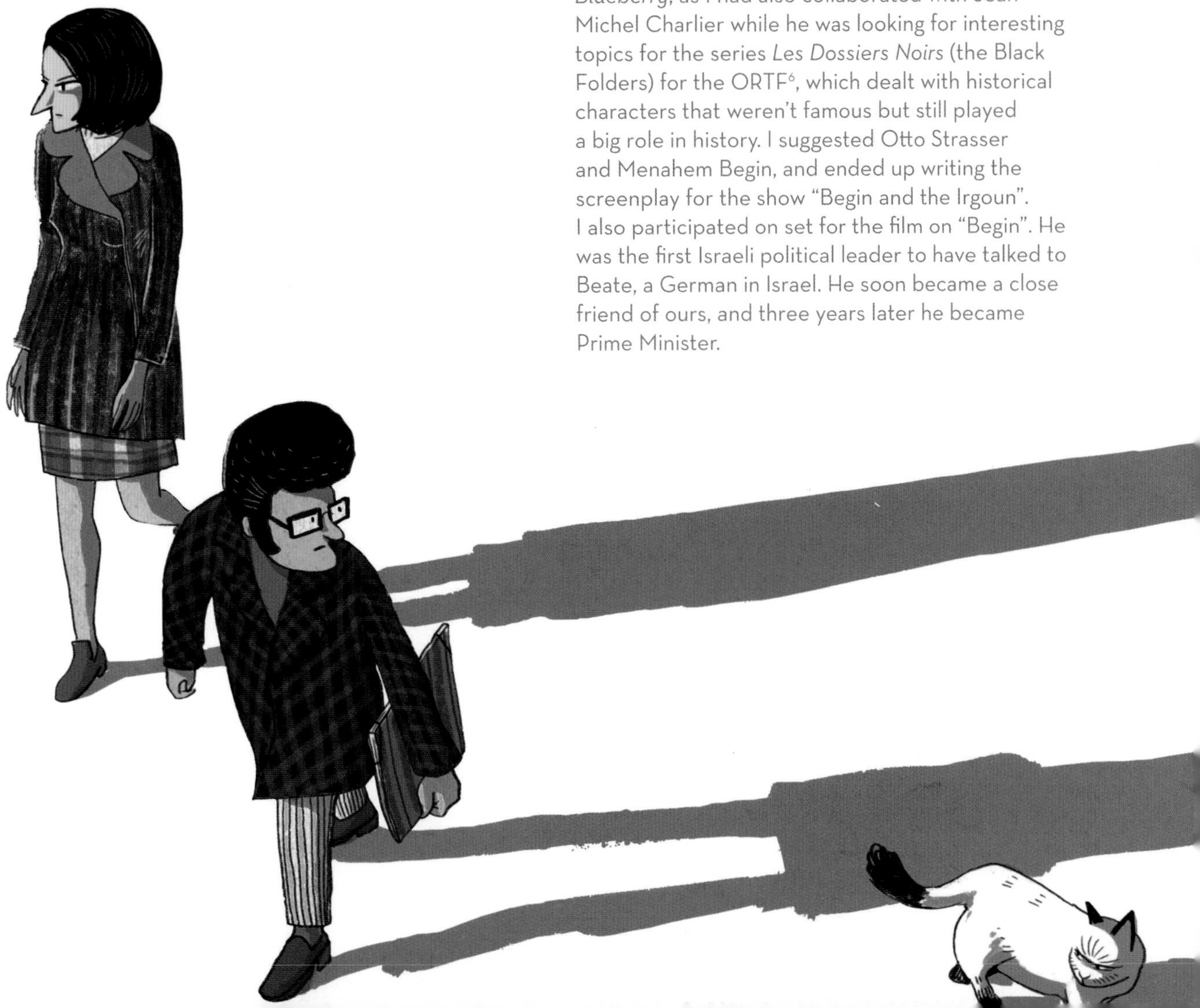

Little by little, I started really enjoying political graphic novels: I've always dreamed of a graphic novel, with many volumes, that would present the rich history of Jews in France, whose presence preceded the Romans and Asterix[7]. Students might enjoy history a little more if it was told through graphic novels. I've written some prefaces for graphic novels on the persecution of gypsies, as well as young Jewish girls living in Poland and France. I consider graphic novels, just like crime or sci-fi novels, as an authentic genre of literature, where amazing authors have created remarkable art with illustrations that could be sold for high prices.

But our family (mom, dad, the kids, the dogs, the cats, and no cleaning lady), the unexpected encounter that was probably programmed by destiny of a French Jewish man and a Lutheran German woman, Beate & Serge's fight to make sure all Nazi criminals went to trial and to change the memory of Vichy's role during WWII, the travels all around the world, the prisons, the attacks with the hidden bombs but also the attacks on the family's happiness, two kids that are so close and devoted to their parents, cute grandchildren, not forgetting the animals which were always a source of unconditional love and comfort...could all this be transcribed into a graphic novel? We were skeptical, but we trusted Pascal Bresson's enthusiasm and his respect for the truth. We recognized ourselves through Sylvan Dorange's characters and the settings that he draws.
Here we are, in a historical graphic novel that our grandchildren can read through page by page before reading our memoirs and see that even if Grandpa and Omi weren't Superman and Superwoman, they still did a hell of a job.

Serge Klarsfeld

Notes:

1: Vichy was the seat of the French State back then, with a pro-German collaborationist government.
2: German police that occupied Europe during WWII.
3: Right near the 15th and 16th arrondissements in Paris.
4: Known meeting point in Boulogne, which is a few streets away from Porte de Saint Cloud.
5: Two comics that everyone read at the time, very famous.
6: French national agency in charge of all public radio and television broadcast at the time, it was under strict control of the government until 1974.
7: Famous comedic French graphic novel character, known for fighting off the Romans in France.

Many thanks to the Memorial de la Shoah for their support

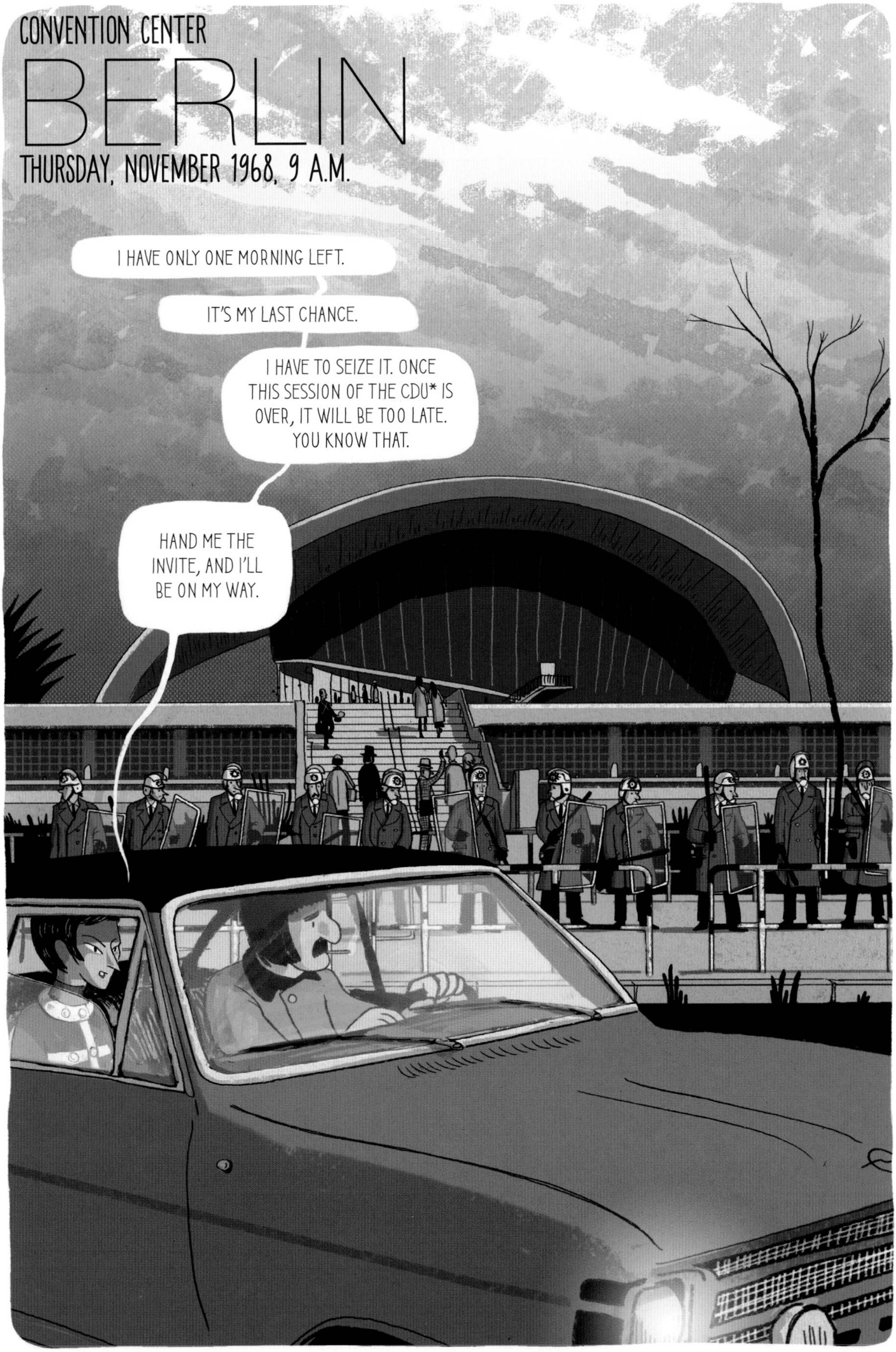
CONVENTION CENTER
BERLIN
THURSDAY, NOVEMBER 1968, 9 A.M.
I HAVE ONLY ONE MORNING LEFT.
IT'S MY LAST CHANCE.
I HAVE TO SEIZE IT. ONCE THIS SESSION OF THE CDU* IS OVER, IT WILL BE TOO LATE. YOU KNOW THAT.
HAND ME THE INVITE, AND I'LL BE ON MY WAY.

*CHRISTIAN DEMOCRATIC UNION OF GERMANY

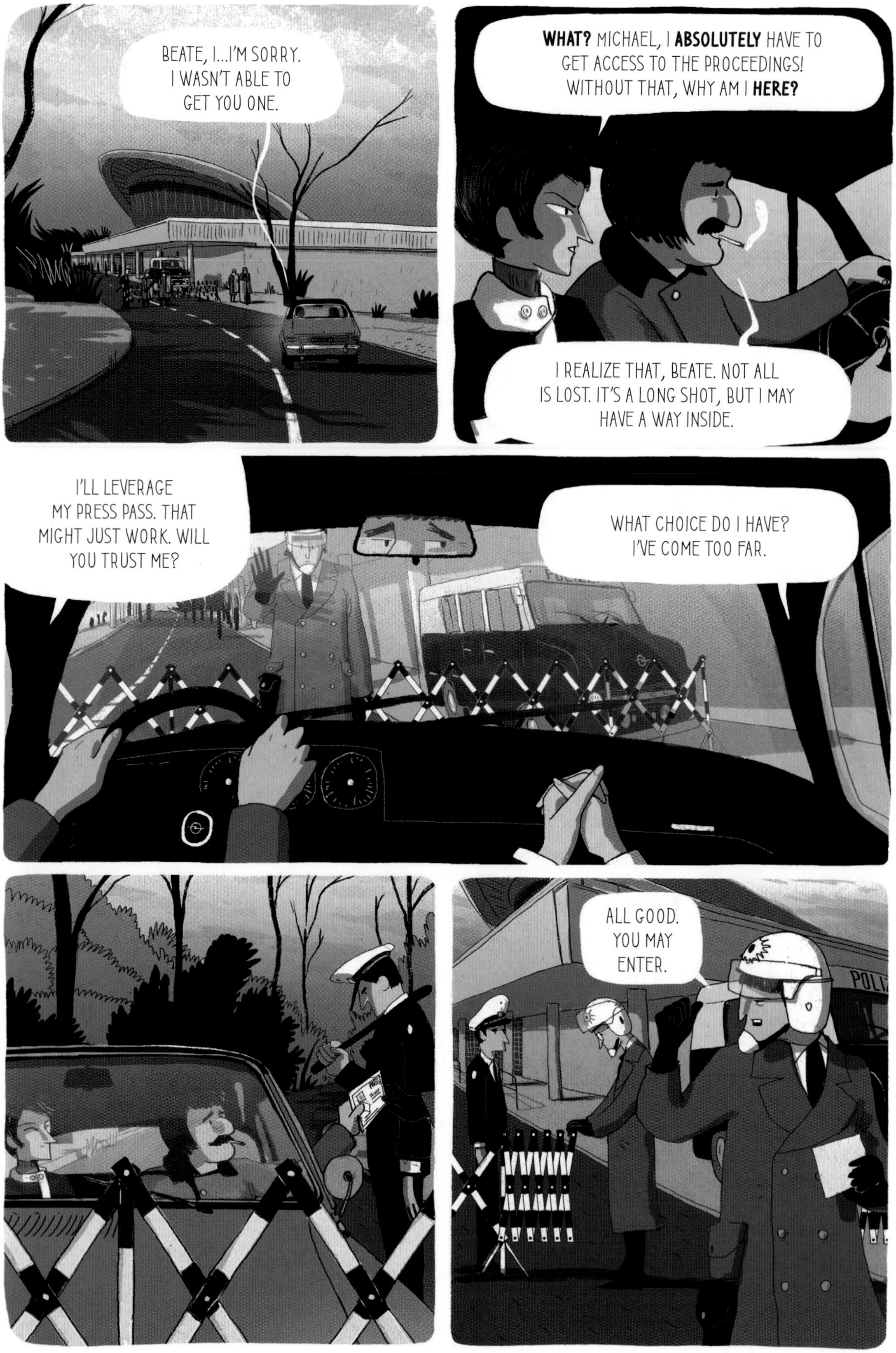

BEATE, I...I'M SORRY. I WASN'T ABLE TO GET YOU ONE.
WHAT? MICHAEL, I ABSOLUTELY HAVE TO GET ACCESS TO THE PROCEEDINGS! WITHOUT THAT, WHY AM I HERE?
I REALIZE THAT, BEATE. NOT ALL IS LOST. IT'S A LONG SHOT, BUT I MAY HAVE A WAY INSIDE.
I'LL LEVERAGE MY PRESS PASS. THAT MIGHT JUST WORK. WILL YOU TRUST ME?
WHAT CHOICE DO I HAVE? I'VE COME TOO FAR.
ALL GOOD. YOU MAY ENTER.

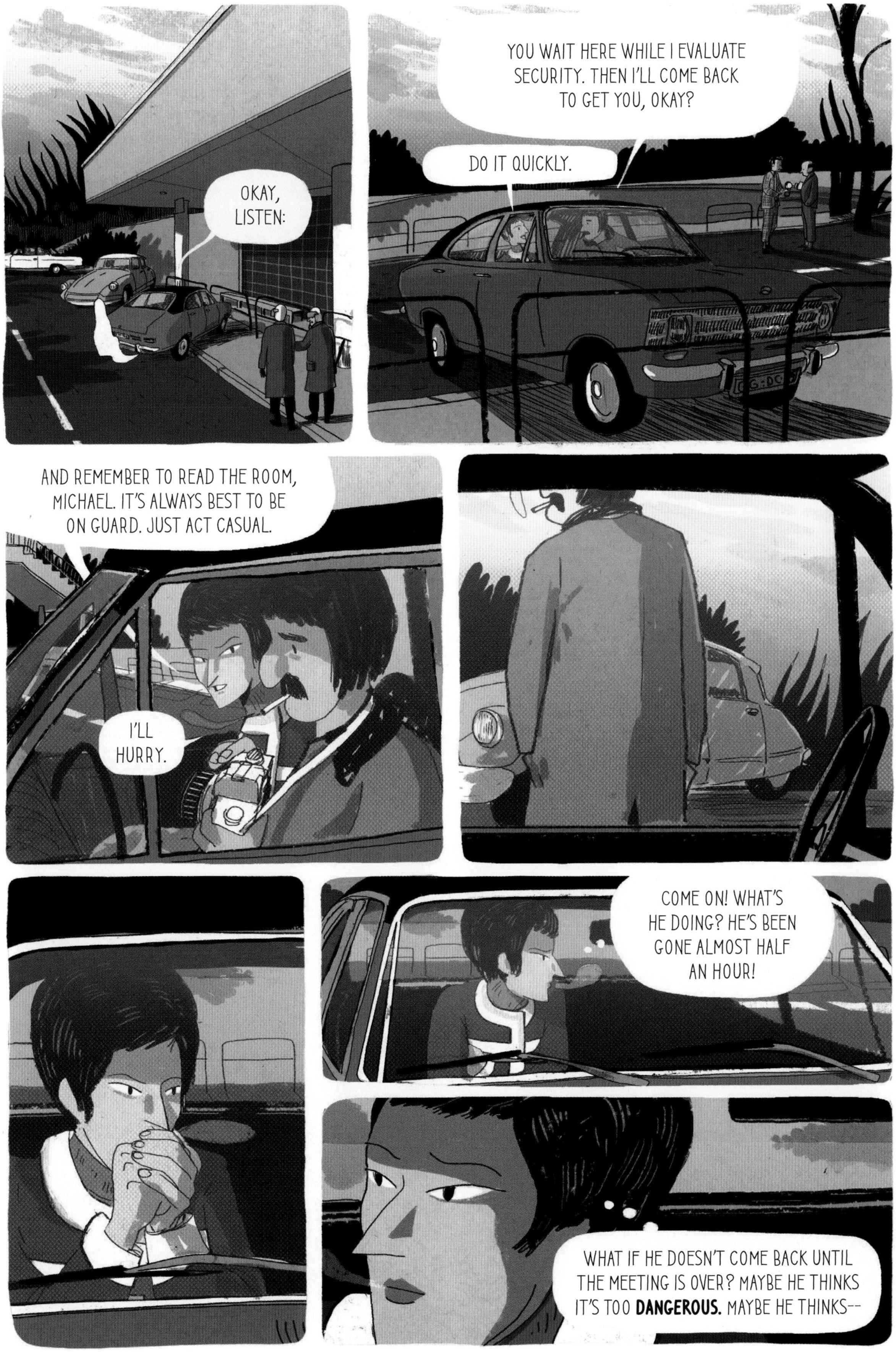
OKAY, LISTEN:
YOU WAIT HERE WHILE I EVALUATE SECURITY. THEN I'LL COME BACK TO GET YOU, OKAY?
DO IT QUICKLY.
AND REMEMBER TO READ THE ROOM, MICHAEL. IT'S ALWAYS BEST TO BE ON GUARD. JUST ACT CASUAL.
I'LL HURRY.
COME ON! WHAT'S HE DOING? HE'S BEEN GONE ALMOST HALF AN HOUR!
WHAT IF HE DOESN'T COME BACK UNTIL THE MEETING IS OVER? MAYBE HE THINKS IT'S TOO **DANGEROUS.** MAYBE HE THINKS--

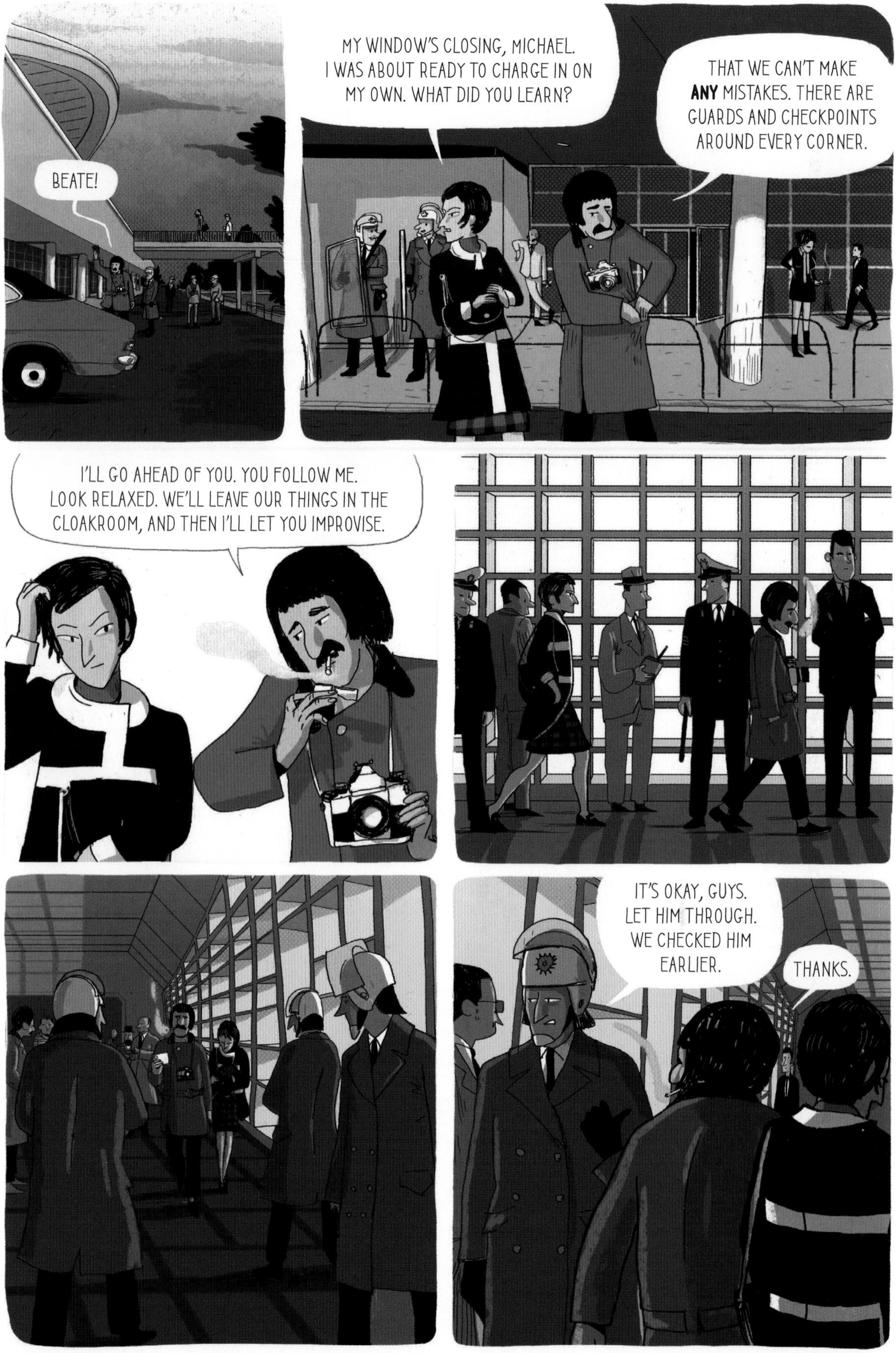
BEATE!
MY WINDOW'S CLOSING, MICHAEL. I WAS ABOUT READY TO CHARGE IN ON MY OWN. WHAT DID YOU LEARN?
THAT WE CAN'T MAKE **ANY** MISTAKES. THERE ARE GUARDS AND CHECKPOINTS AROUND EVERY CORNER.
I'LL GO AHEAD OF YOU. YOU FOLLOW ME. LOOK RELAXED. WE'LL LEAVE OUR THINGS IN THE CLOAKROOM, AND THEN I'LL LET YOU IMPROVISE.
IT'S OKAY, GUYS. LET HIM THROUGH. WE CHECKED HIM EARLIER.
THANKS.

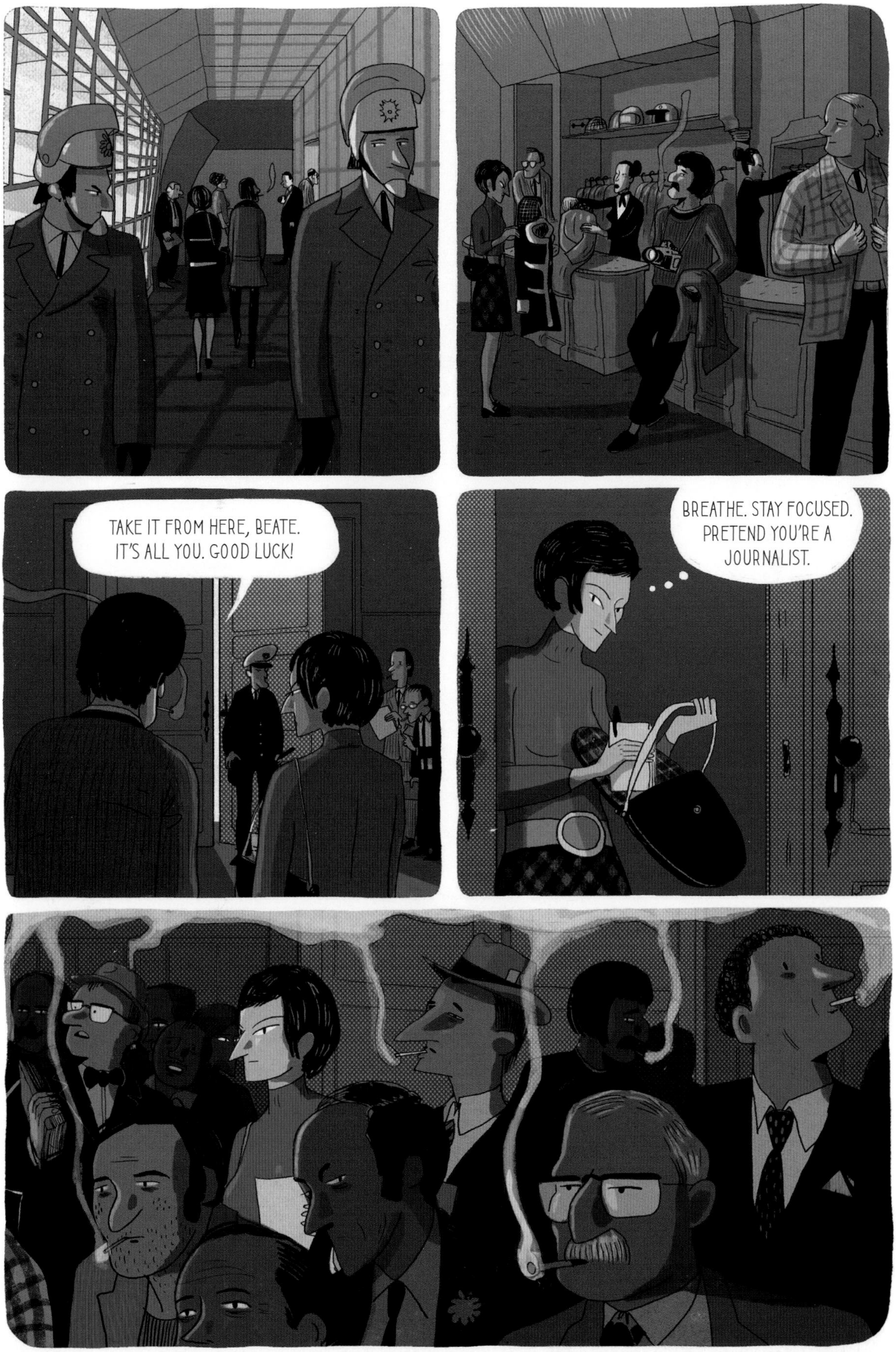
TAKE IT FROM HERE, BEATE. IT'S ALL YOU. GOOD LUCK!
BREATHE. STAY FOCUSED. PRETEND YOU'RE A JOURNALIST.

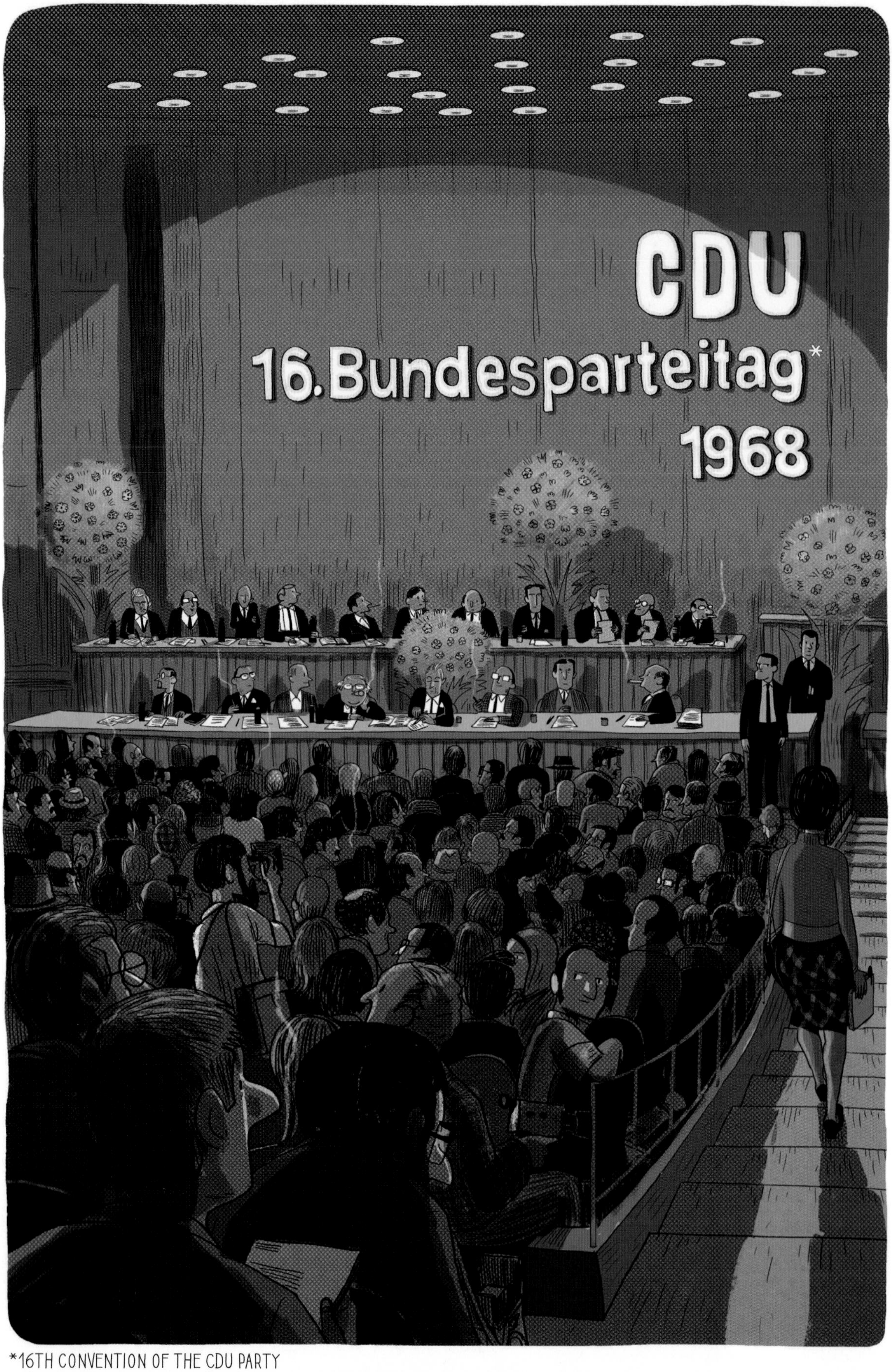

CDU
16. Bundesparteitag*
1968

*16TH CONVENTION OF THE CDU PARTY

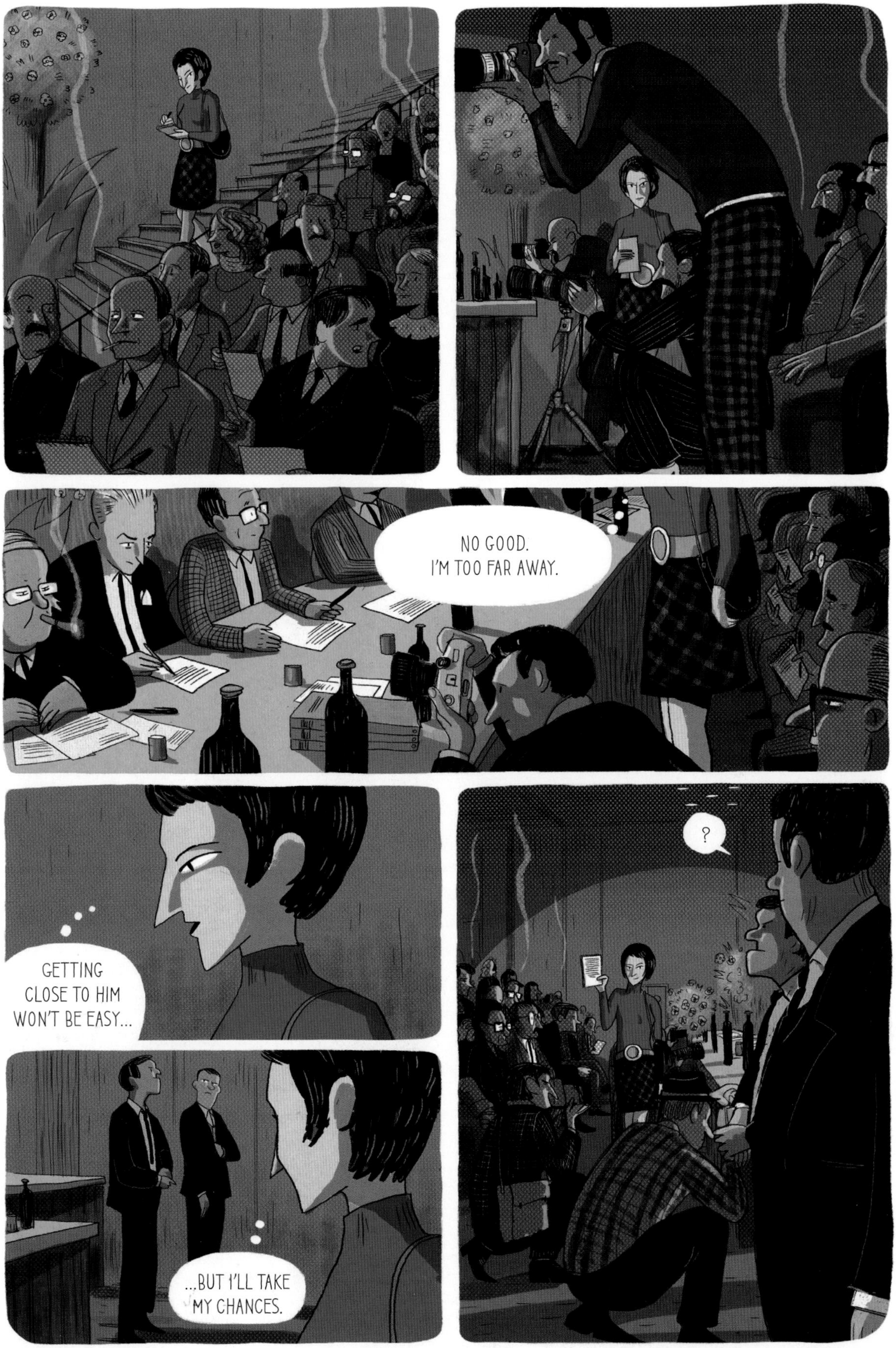
NO GOOD.
I'M TOO FAR AWAY.
GETTING CLOSE TO HIM WON'T BE EASY...
?
...BUT I'LL TAKE MY CHANCES.

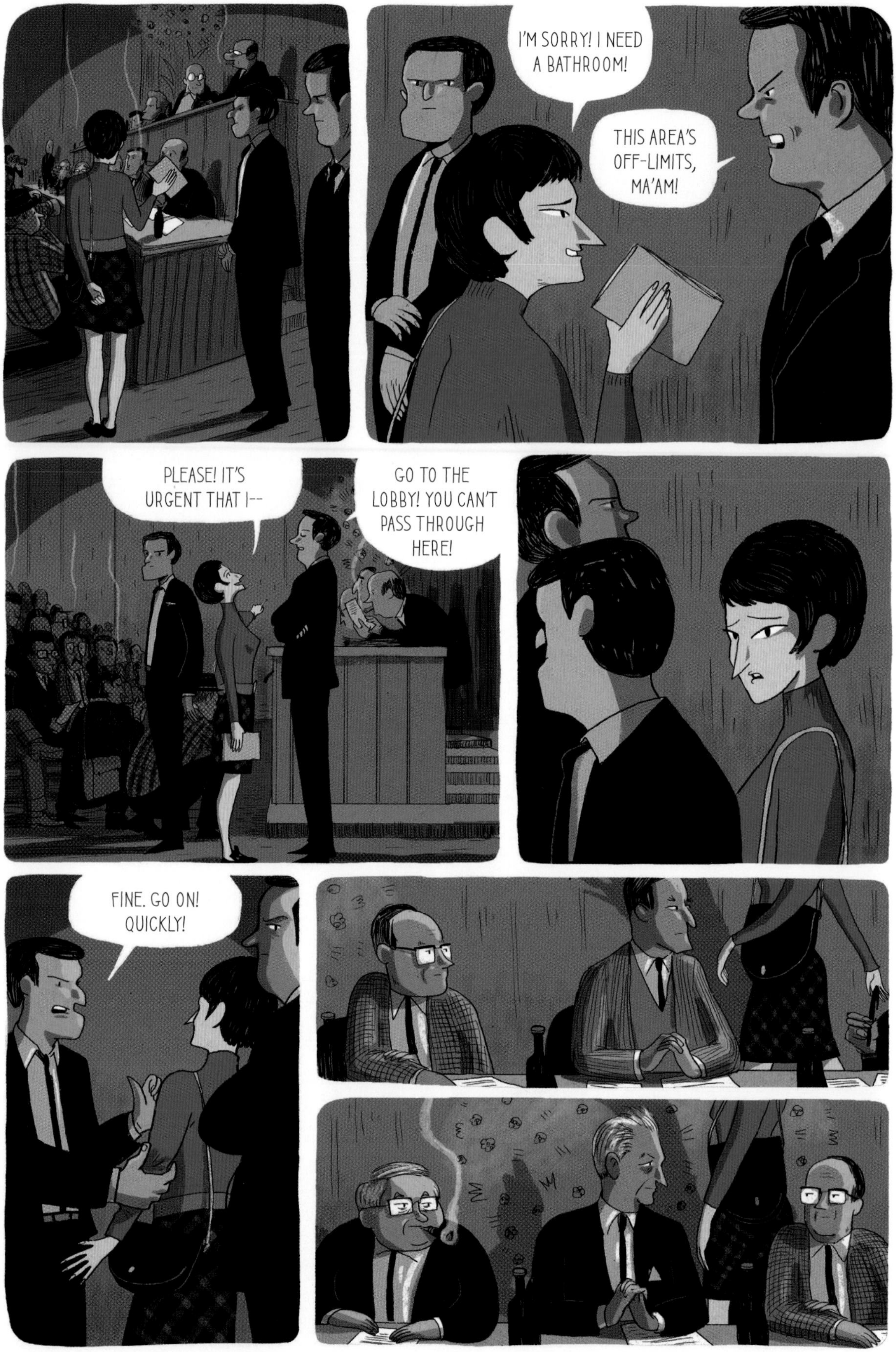
I'M SORRY! I NEED A BATHROOM!
THIS AREA'S OFF-LIMITS, MA'AM!
PLEASE! IT'S URGENT THAT I--
GO TO THE LOBBY! YOU CAN'T PASS THROUGH HERE!
FINE. GO ON! QUICKLY!

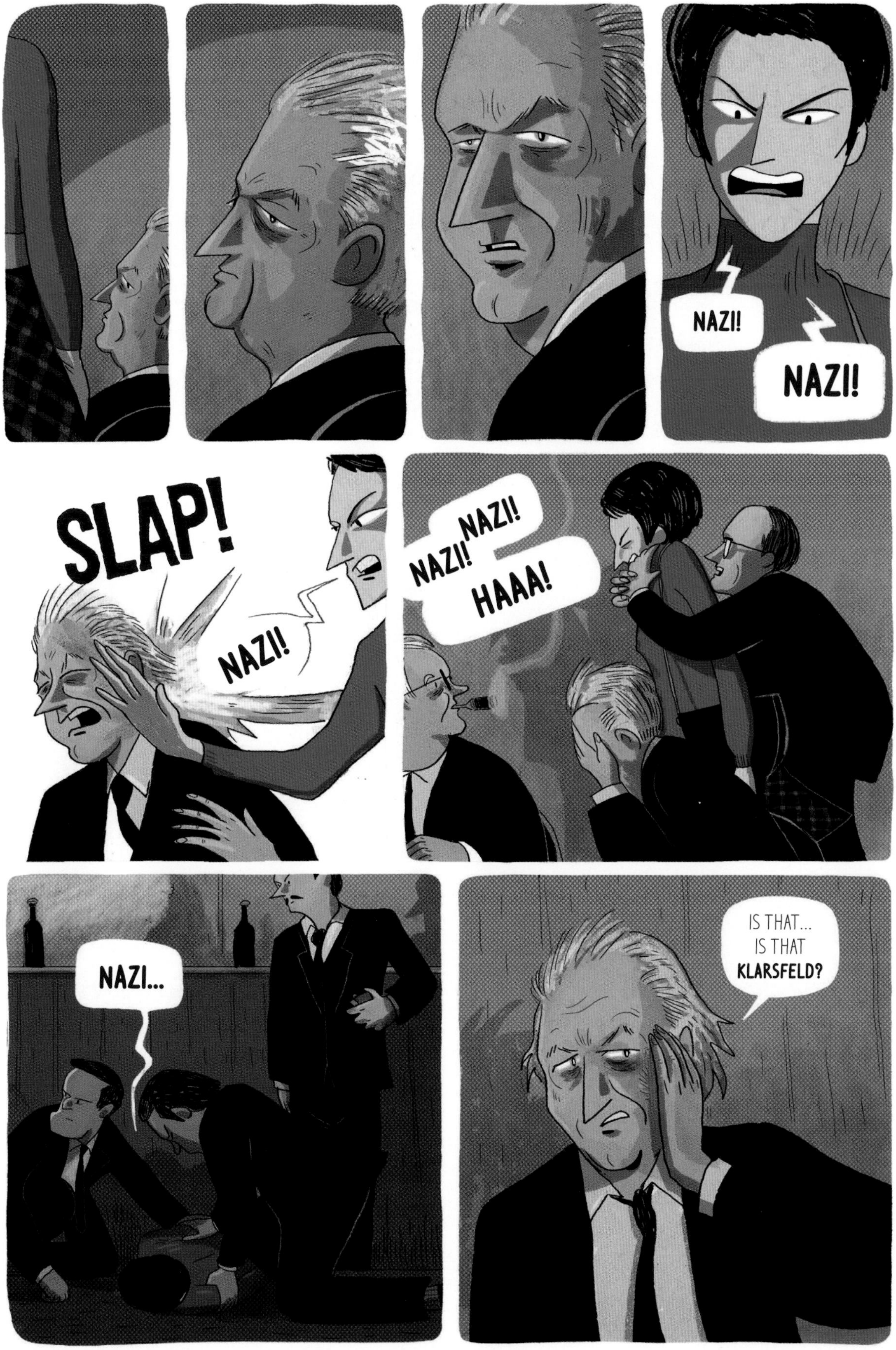
NAZI!
NAZI!
SLAP!
NAZI!
NAZI!
NAZI!
HAAA!
NAZI...
IS THAT...
IS THAT
KLARSFELD?

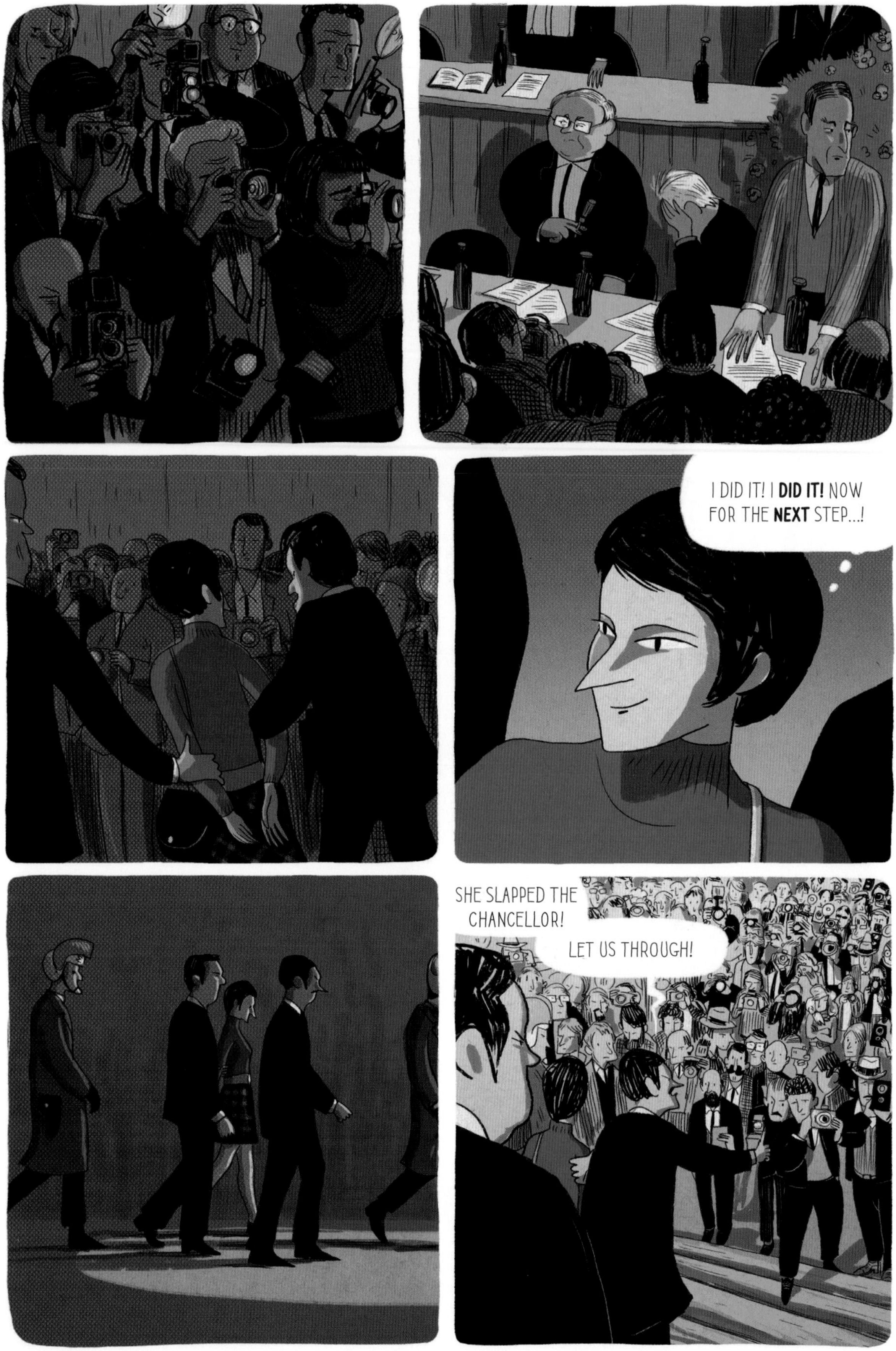
I DID IT! I **DID IT!** NOW FOR THE **NEXT** STEP...!
SHE SLAPPED THE CHANCELLOR!
LET US THROUGH!

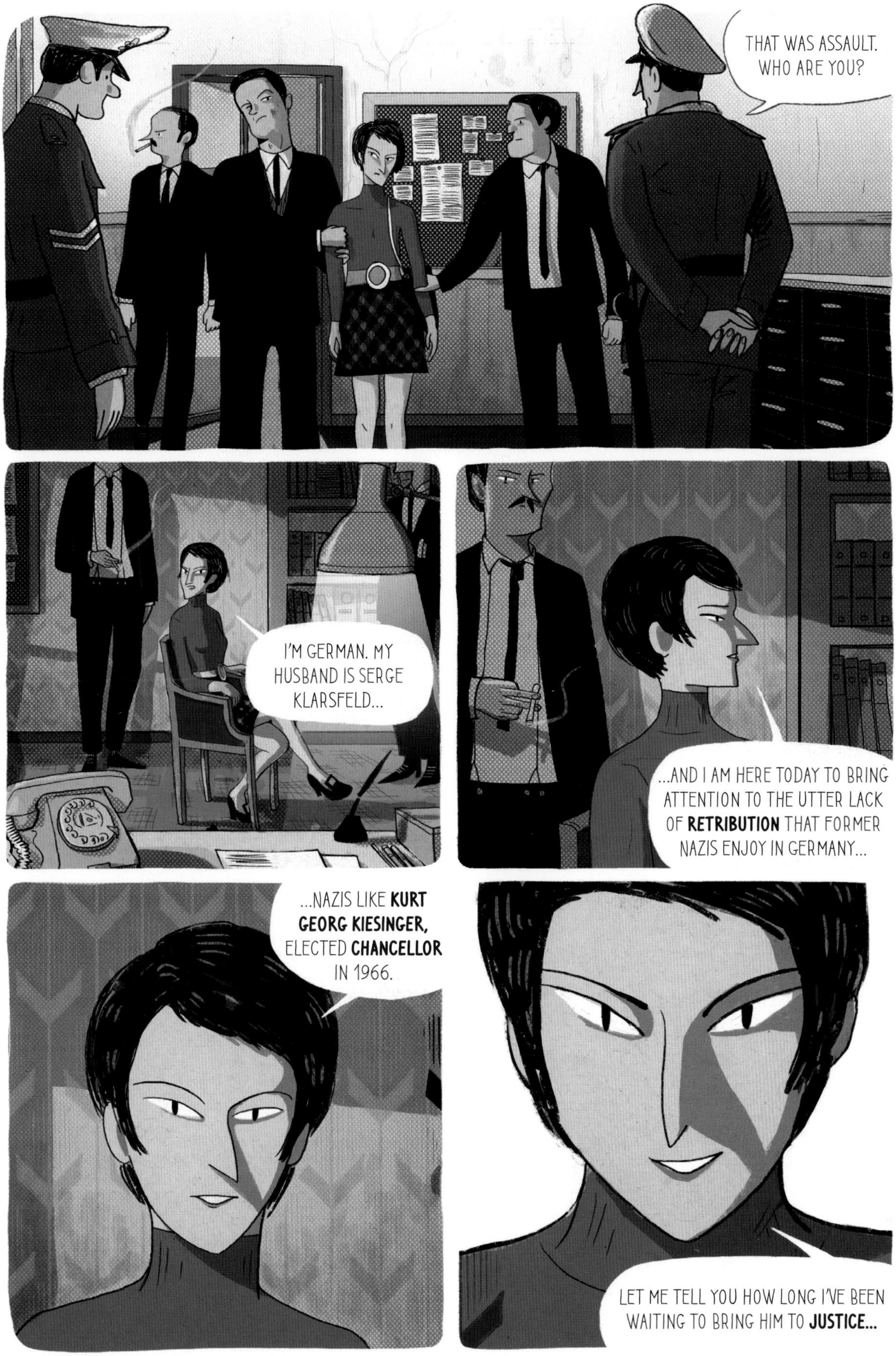
THAT WAS ASSAULT. WHO ARE YOU?
I'M GERMAN. MY HUSBAND IS SERGE KLARSFELD...
...AND I AM HERE TODAY TO BRING ATTENTION TO THE UTTER LACK OF **RETRIBUTION** THAT FORMER NAZIS ENJOY IN GERMANY...
...NAZIS LIKE **KURT GEORG KIESINGER,** ELECTED **CHANCELLOR** IN 1966.
LET ME TELL YOU HOW LONG I'VE BEEN WAITING TO BRING HIM TO **JUSTICE...**

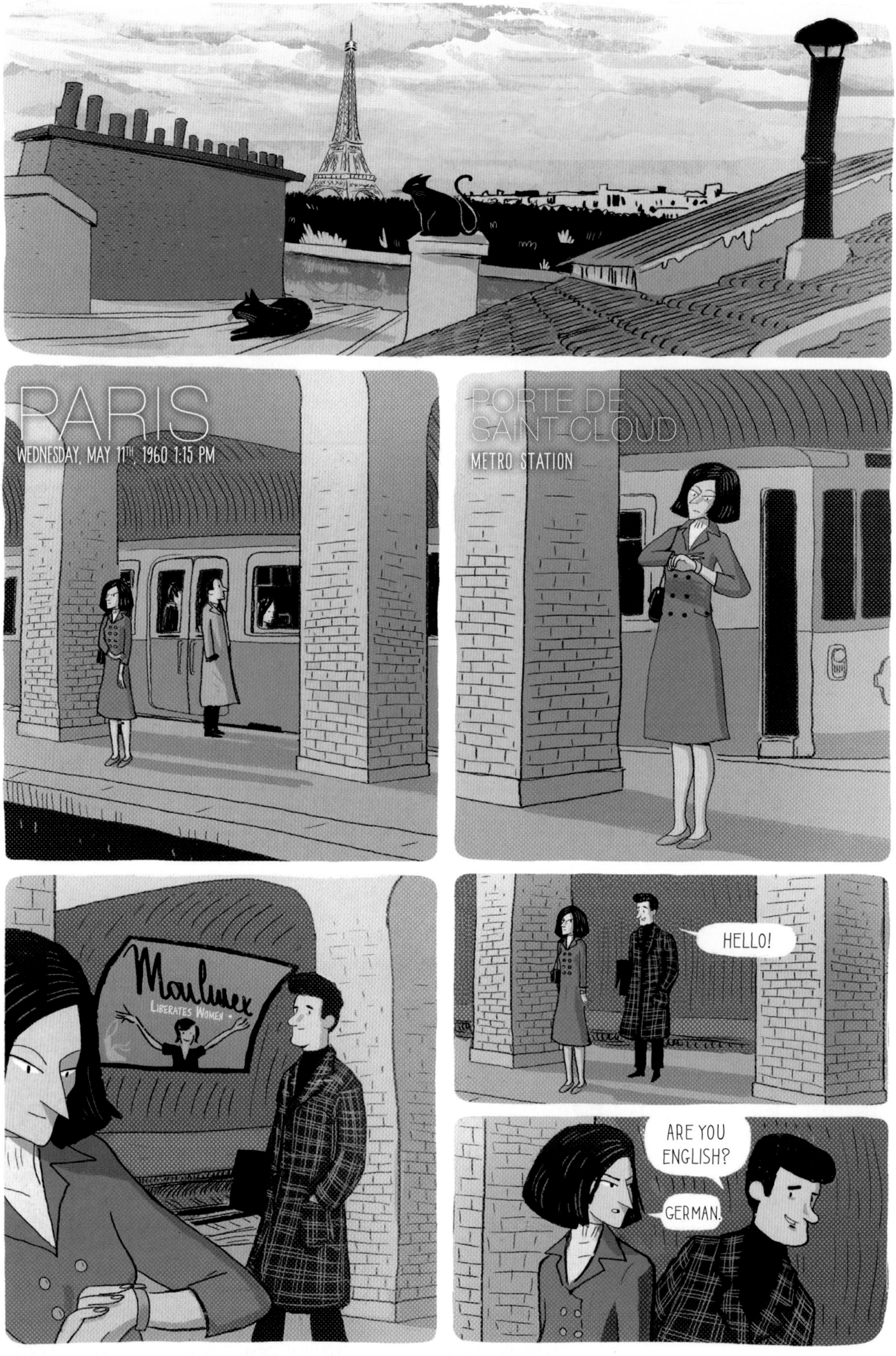
PARIS
WEDNESDAY, MAY 11TH, 1960 1:15 PM
PORTE DE SAINT-CLOUD
METRO STATION
Moulinex
LIBERATES WOMEN
HELLO!
ARE YOU ENGLISH?
GERMAN.

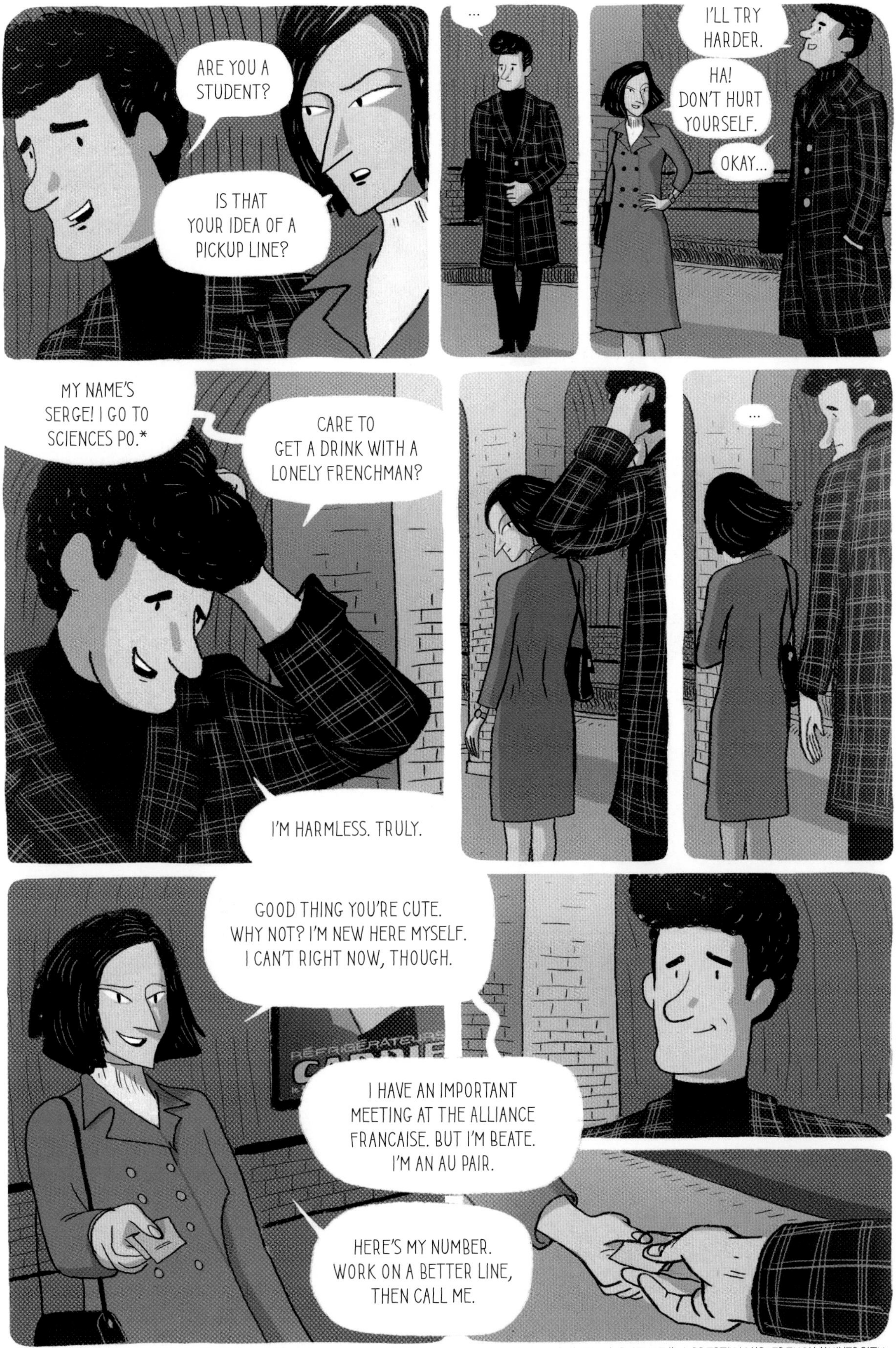
ARE YOU A STUDENT?
IS THAT YOUR IDEA OF A PICKUP LINE?
...
I'LL TRY HARDER.
HA! DON'T HURT YOURSELF.
OKAY...
MY NAME'S SERGE! I GO TO SCIENCES PO.*
CARE TO GET A DRINK WITH A LONELY FRENCHMAN?
I'M HARMLESS. TRULY.
...
GOOD THING YOU'RE CUTE. WHY NOT? I'M NEW HERE MYSELF. I CAN'T RIGHT NOW, THOUGH.
I HAVE AN IMPORTANT MEETING AT THE ALLIANCE FRANCAISE. BUT I'M BEATE. I'M AN AU PAIR.
HERE'S MY NUMBER. WORK ON A BETTER LINE, THEN CALL ME.

*SHORT FOR "THE PARIS INSTITUTE OF POLITICAL SCIENCE", A PRESTIGIOUS FRENCH UNIVERSITY

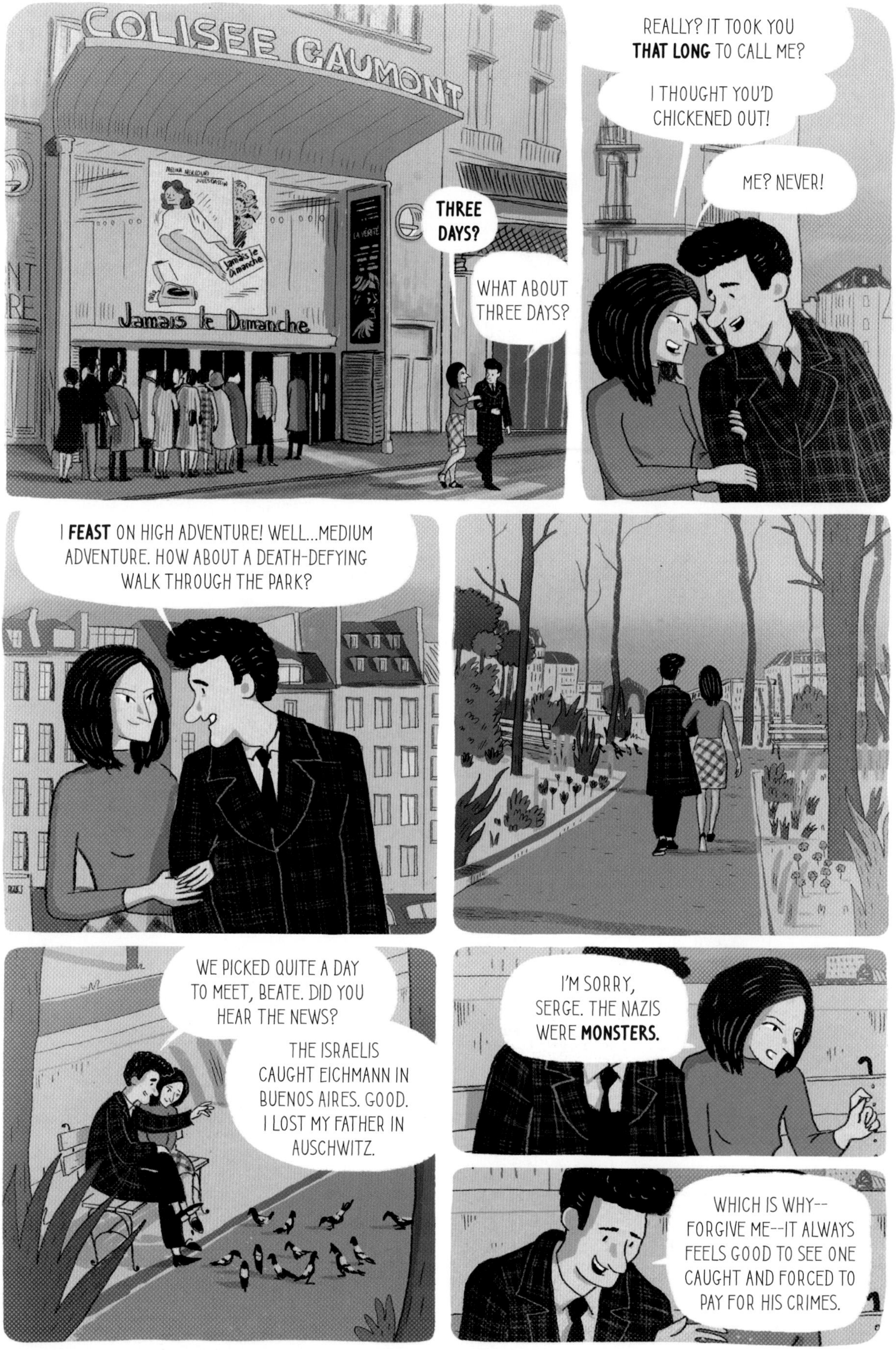
COLISEE GAUMONT
Jamais le Dimanche
THREE DAYS?
WHAT ABOUT THREE DAYS?
REALLY? IT TOOK YOU **THAT LONG** TO CALL ME?
I THOUGHT YOU'D CHICKENED OUT!
ME? NEVER!
I **FEAST** ON HIGH ADVENTURE! WELL...MEDIUM ADVENTURE. HOW ABOUT A DEATH-DEFYING WALK THROUGH THE PARK?
WE PICKED QUITE A DAY TO MEET, BEATE. DID YOU HEAR THE NEWS?
THE ISRAELIS CAUGHT EICHMANN IN BUENOS AIRES. GOOD. I LOST MY FATHER IN AUSCHWITZ.
I'M SORRY, SERGE. THE NAZIS WERE **MONSTERS.**
WHICH IS WHY--FORGIVE ME--IT ALWAYS FEELS GOOD TO SEE ONE CAUGHT AND FORCED TO PAY FOR HIS CRIMES.

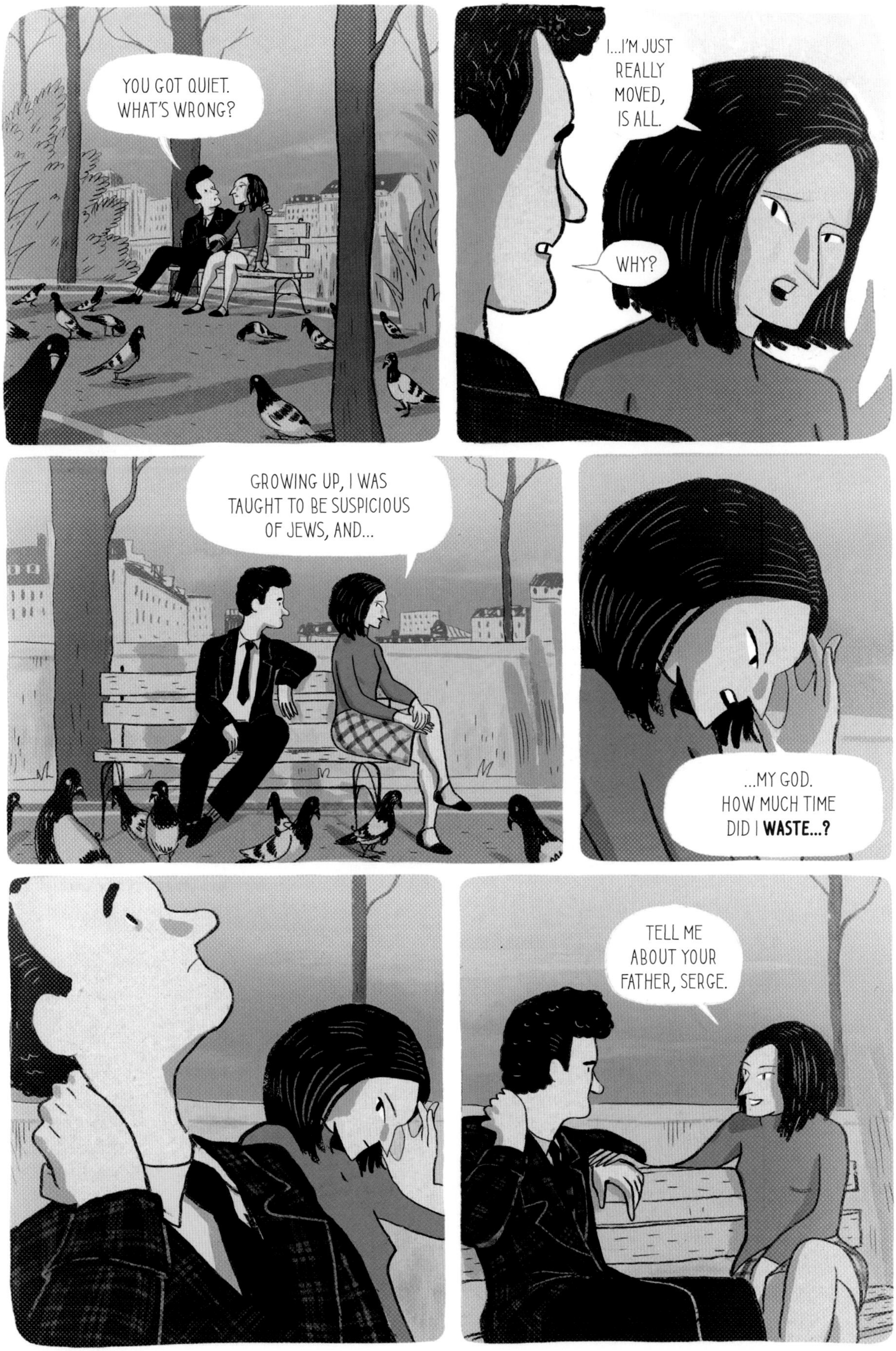
YOU GOT QUIET. WHAT'S WRONG?
I...I'M JUST REALLY MOVED, IS ALL.
WHY?
GROWING UP, I WAS TAUGHT TO BE SUSPICIOUS OF JEWS, AND...
...MY GOD. HOW MUCH TIME DID I **WASTE...?**
TELL ME ABOUT YOUR FATHER, SERGE.

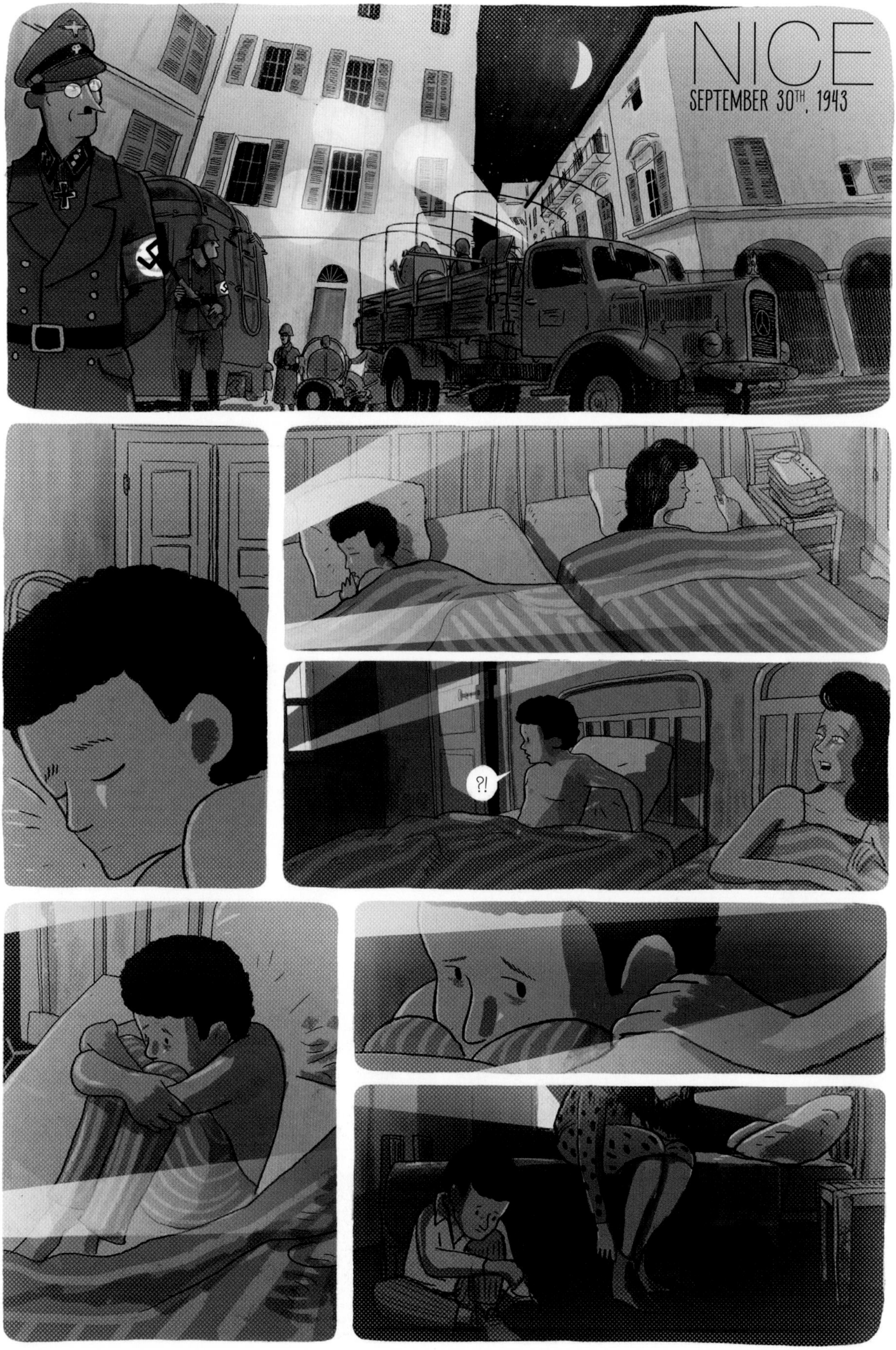
NICE
SEPTEMBER 30TH, 1943
?!

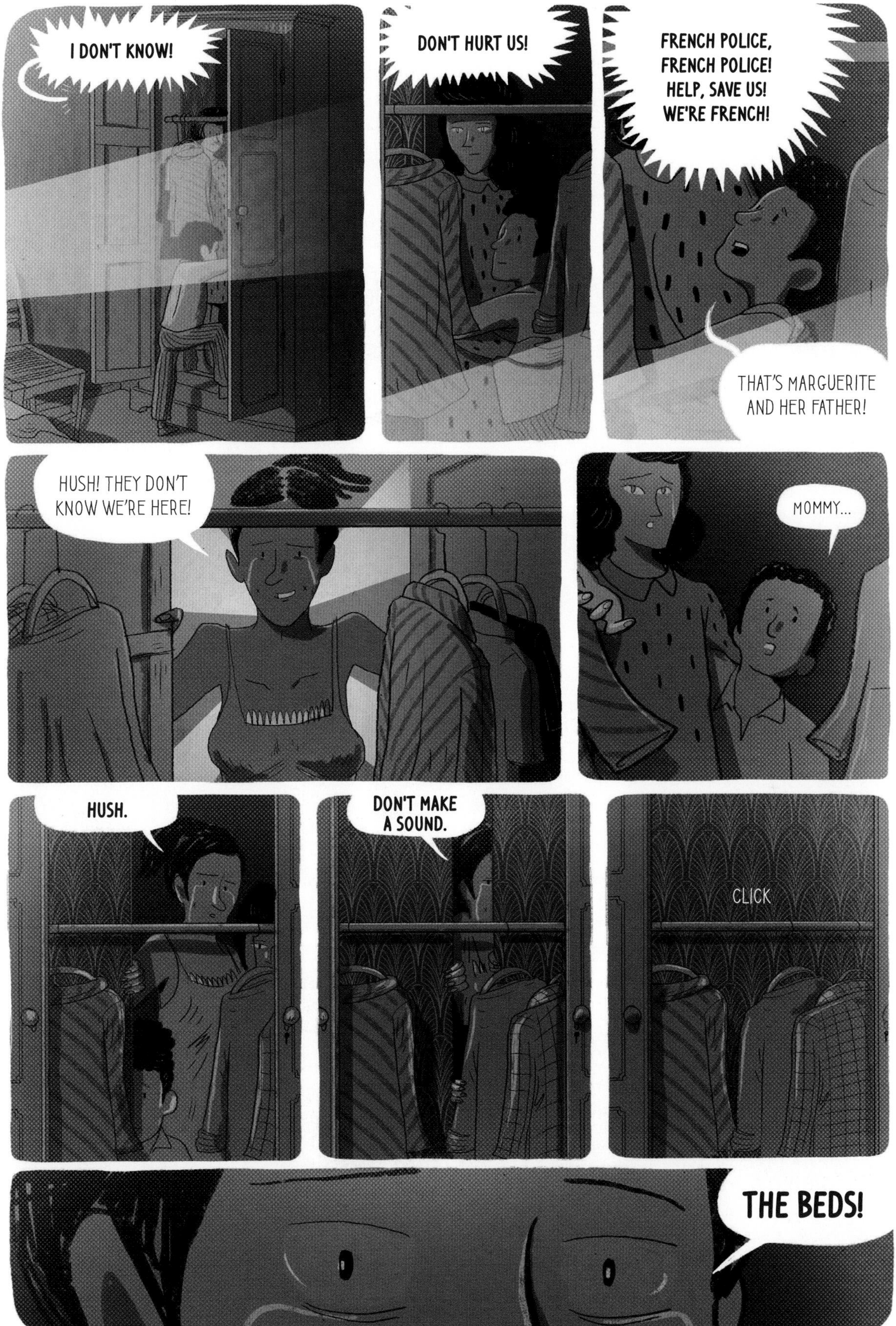
I DON'T KNOW!
DON'T HURT US!
FRENCH POLICE, FRENCH POLICE! HELP, SAVE US! WE'RE FRENCH!
THAT'S MARGUERITE AND HER FATHER!
HUSH! THEY DON'T KNOW WE'RE HERE!
MOMMY...
HUSH.
DON'T MAKE A SOUND.
CLICK
THE BEDS!

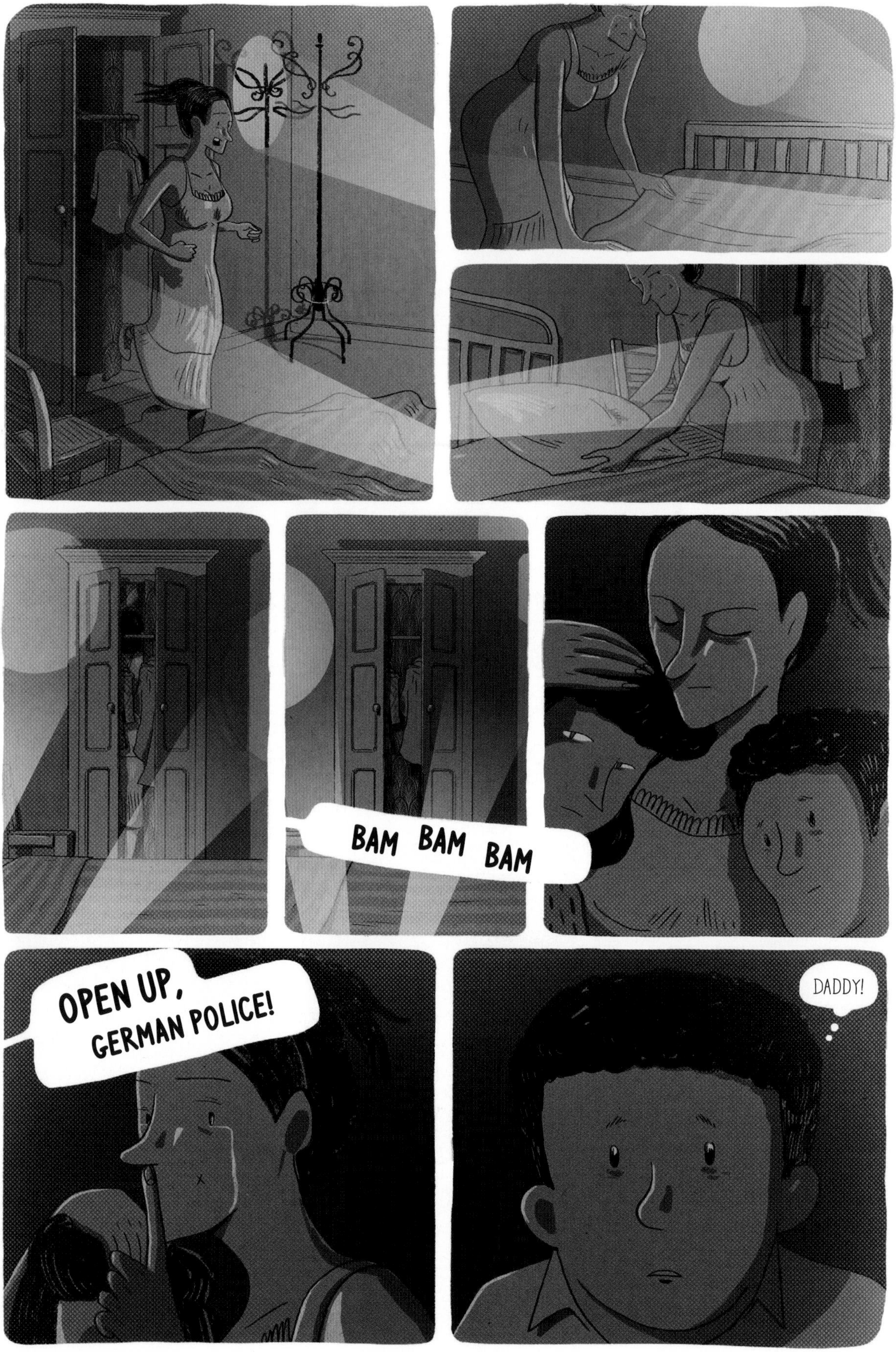
BAM BAM BAM
OPEN UP, GERMAN POLICE!
DADDY!

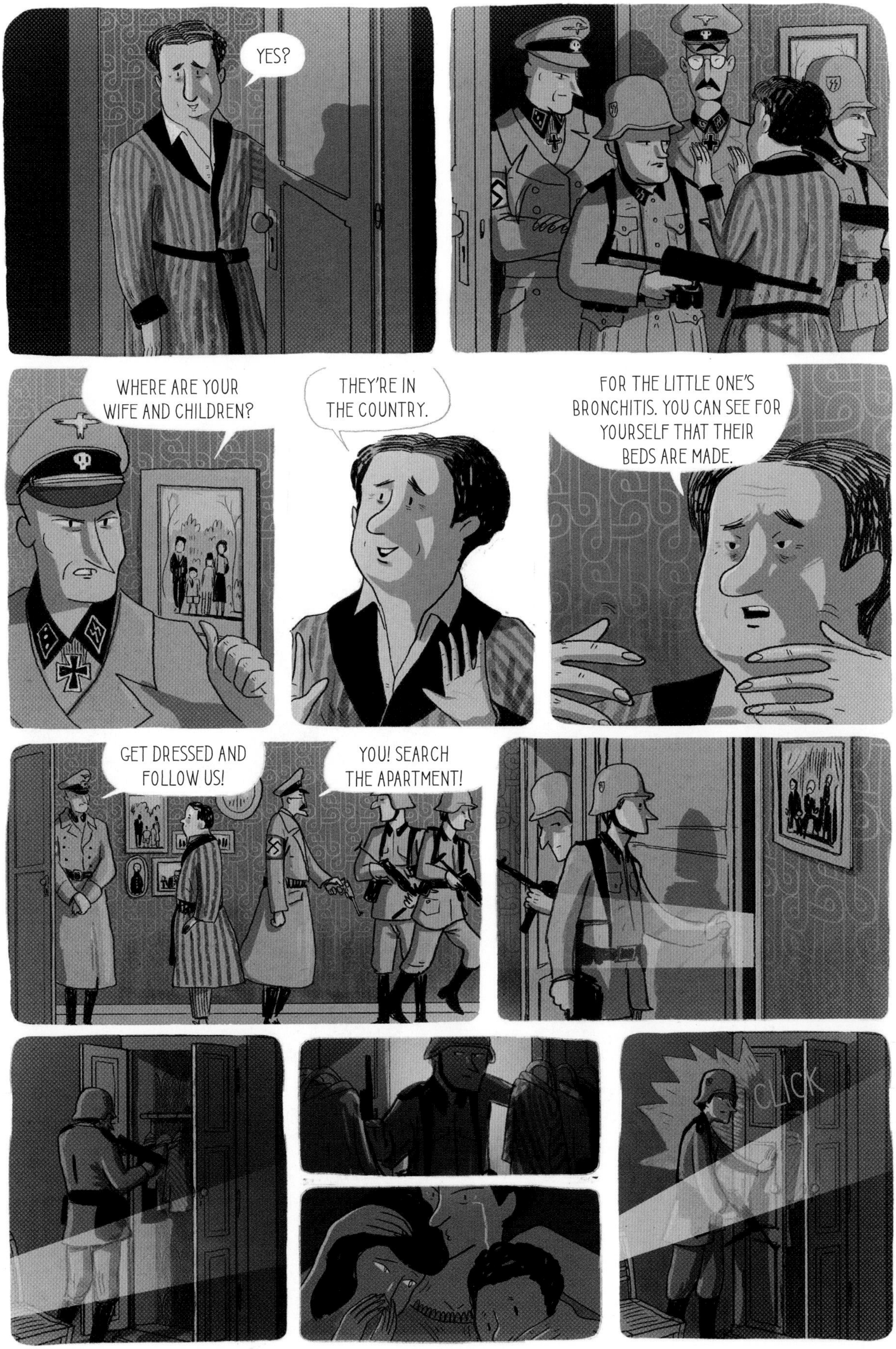
YES?
WHERE ARE YOUR WIFE AND CHILDREN?
THEY'RE IN THE COUNTRY.
FOR THE LITTLE ONE'S BRONCHITIS. YOU CAN SEE FOR YOURSELF THAT THEIR BEDS ARE MADE.
GET DRESSED AND FOLLOW US!
YOU! SEARCH THE APARTMENT!
CLICK

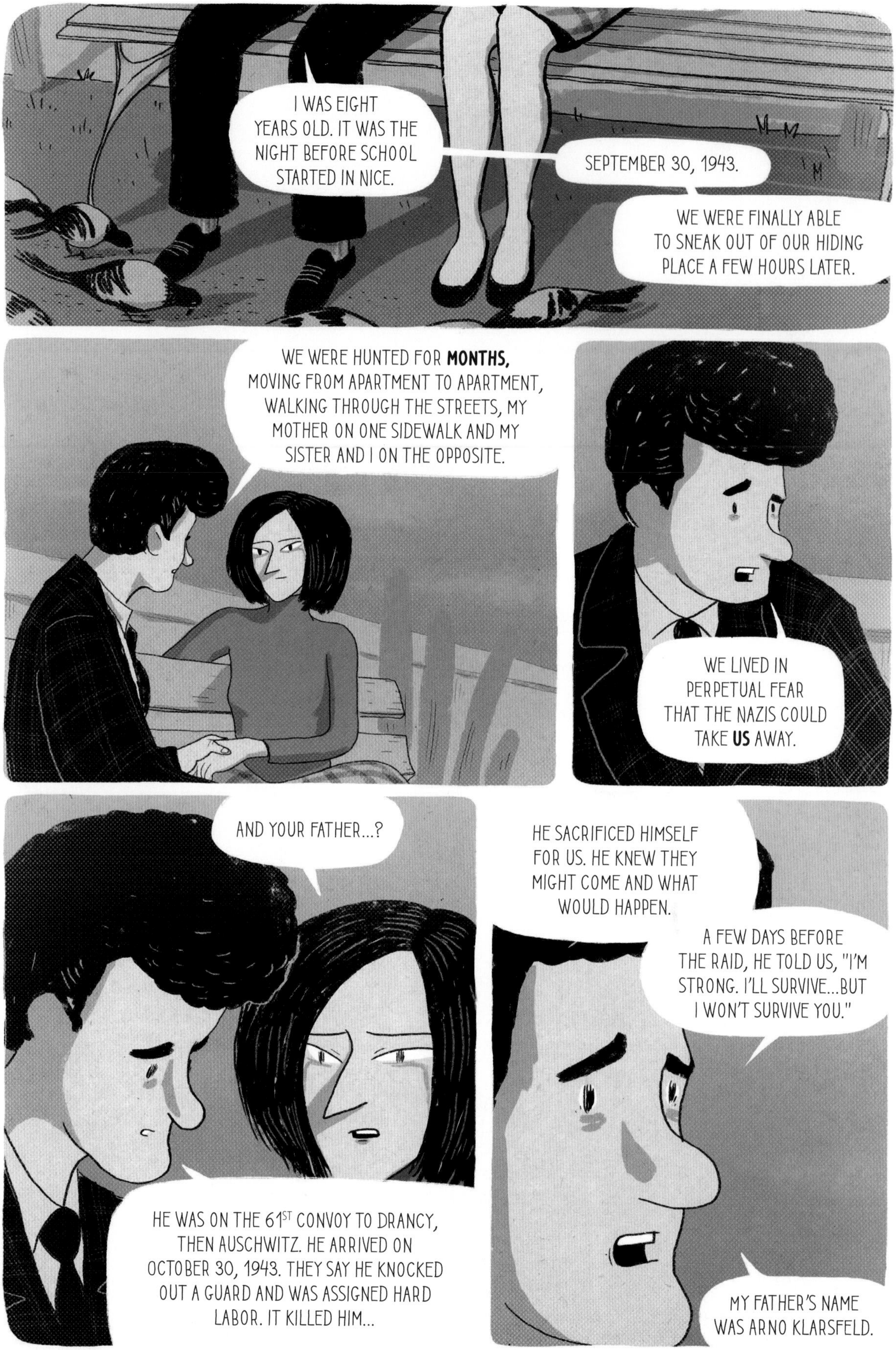
I WAS EIGHT YEARS OLD. IT WAS THE NIGHT BEFORE SCHOOL STARTED IN NICE.
SEPTEMBER 30, 1943.
WE WERE FINALLY ABLE TO SNEAK OUT OF OUR HIDING PLACE A FEW HOURS LATER.
WE WERE HUNTED FOR **MONTHS,** MOVING FROM APARTMENT TO APARTMENT, WALKING THROUGH THE STREETS, MY MOTHER ON ONE SIDEWALK AND MY SISTER AND I ON THE OPPOSITE.
WE LIVED IN PERPETUAL FEAR THAT THE NAZIS COULD TAKE **US** AWAY.
AND YOUR FATHER...?
HE WAS ON THE 61ST CONVOY TO DRANCY, THEN AUSCHWITZ. HE ARRIVED ON OCTOBER 30, 1943. THEY SAY HE KNOCKED OUT A GUARD AND WAS ASSIGNED HARD LABOR. IT KILLED HIM...
HE SACRIFICED HIMSELF FOR US. HE KNEW THEY MIGHT COME AND WHAT WOULD HAPPEN.
A FEW DAYS BEFORE THE RAID, HE TOLD US, "I'M STRONG. I'LL SURVIVE...BUT I WON'T SURVIVE YOU."
MY FATHER'S NAME WAS ARNO KLARSFELD.

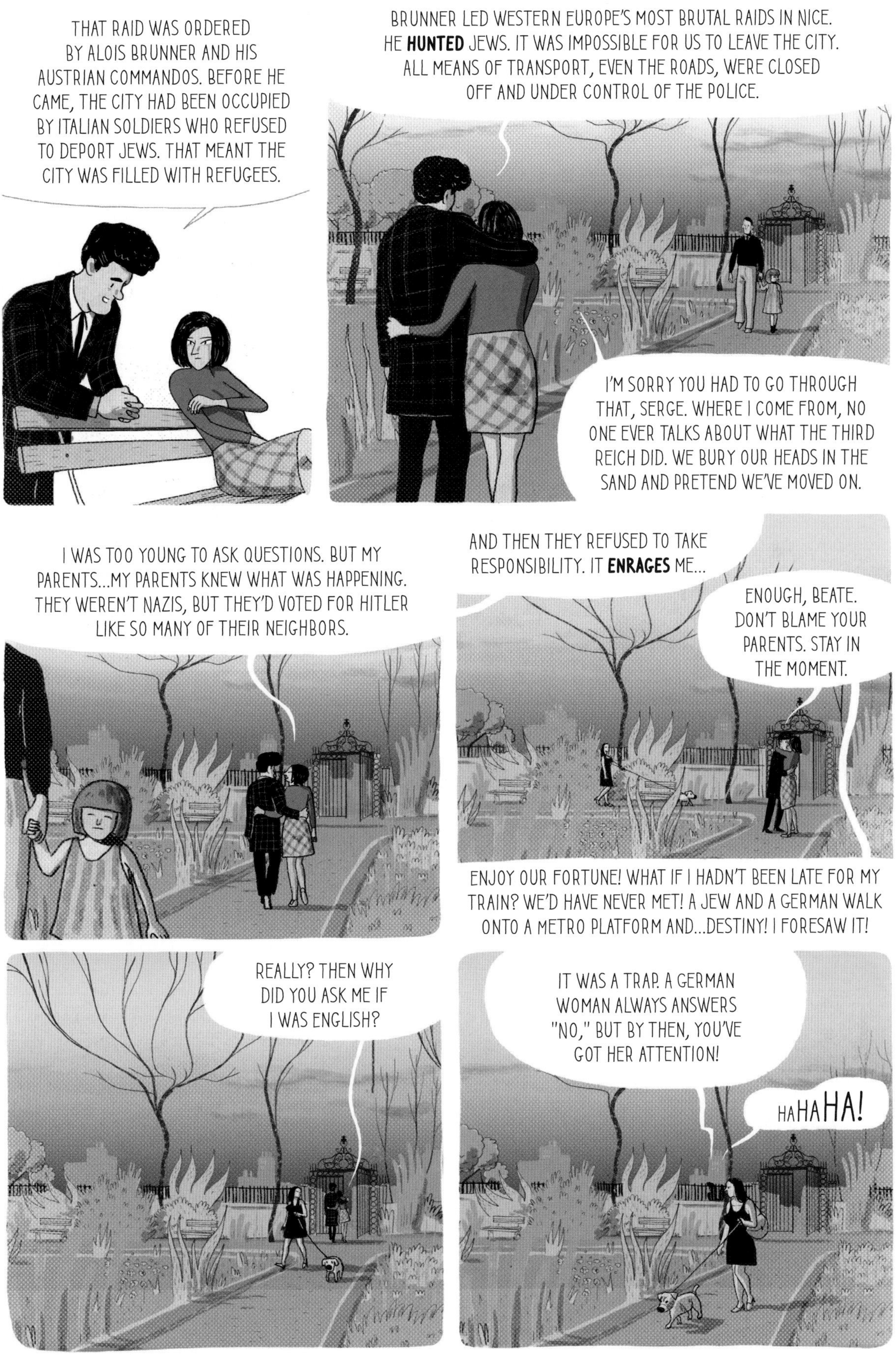
THAT RAID WAS ORDERED BY ALOIS BRUNNER AND HIS AUSTRIAN COMMANDOS. BEFORE HE CAME, THE CITY HAD BEEN OCCUPIED BY ITALIAN SOLDIERS WHO REFUSED TO DEPORT JEWS. THAT MEANT THE CITY WAS FILLED WITH REFUGEES.
BRUNNER LED WESTERN EUROPE'S MOST BRUTAL RAIDS IN NICE. HE **HUNTED** JEWS. IT WAS IMPOSSIBLE FOR US TO LEAVE THE CITY. ALL MEANS OF TRANSPORT, EVEN THE ROADS, WERE CLOSED OFF AND UNDER CONTROL OF THE POLICE.
I'M SORRY YOU HAD TO GO THROUGH THAT, SERGE. WHERE I COME FROM, NO ONE EVER TALKS ABOUT WHAT THE THIRD REICH DID. WE BURY OUR HEADS IN THE SAND AND PRETEND WE'VE MOVED ON.
I WAS TOO YOUNG TO ASK QUESTIONS. BUT MY PARENTS...MY PARENTS KNEW WHAT WAS HAPPENING. THEY WEREN'T NAZIS, BUT THEY'D VOTED FOR HITLER LIKE SO MANY OF THEIR NEIGHBORS.
AND THEN THEY REFUSED TO TAKE RESPONSIBILITY. IT **ENRAGES** ME...
ENOUGH, BEATE. DON'T BLAME YOUR PARENTS. STAY IN THE MOMENT.
ENJOY OUR FORTUNE! WHAT IF I HADN'T BEEN LATE FOR MY TRAIN? WE'D HAVE NEVER MET! A JEW AND A GERMAN WALK ONTO A METRO PLATFORM AND...DESTINY! I FORESAW IT!
REALLY? THEN WHY DID YOU ASK ME IF I WAS ENGLISH?
IT WAS A TRAP. A GERMAN WOMAN ALWAYS ANSWERS "NO," BUT BY THEN, YOU'VE GOT HER ATTENTION!
HAHAHA!

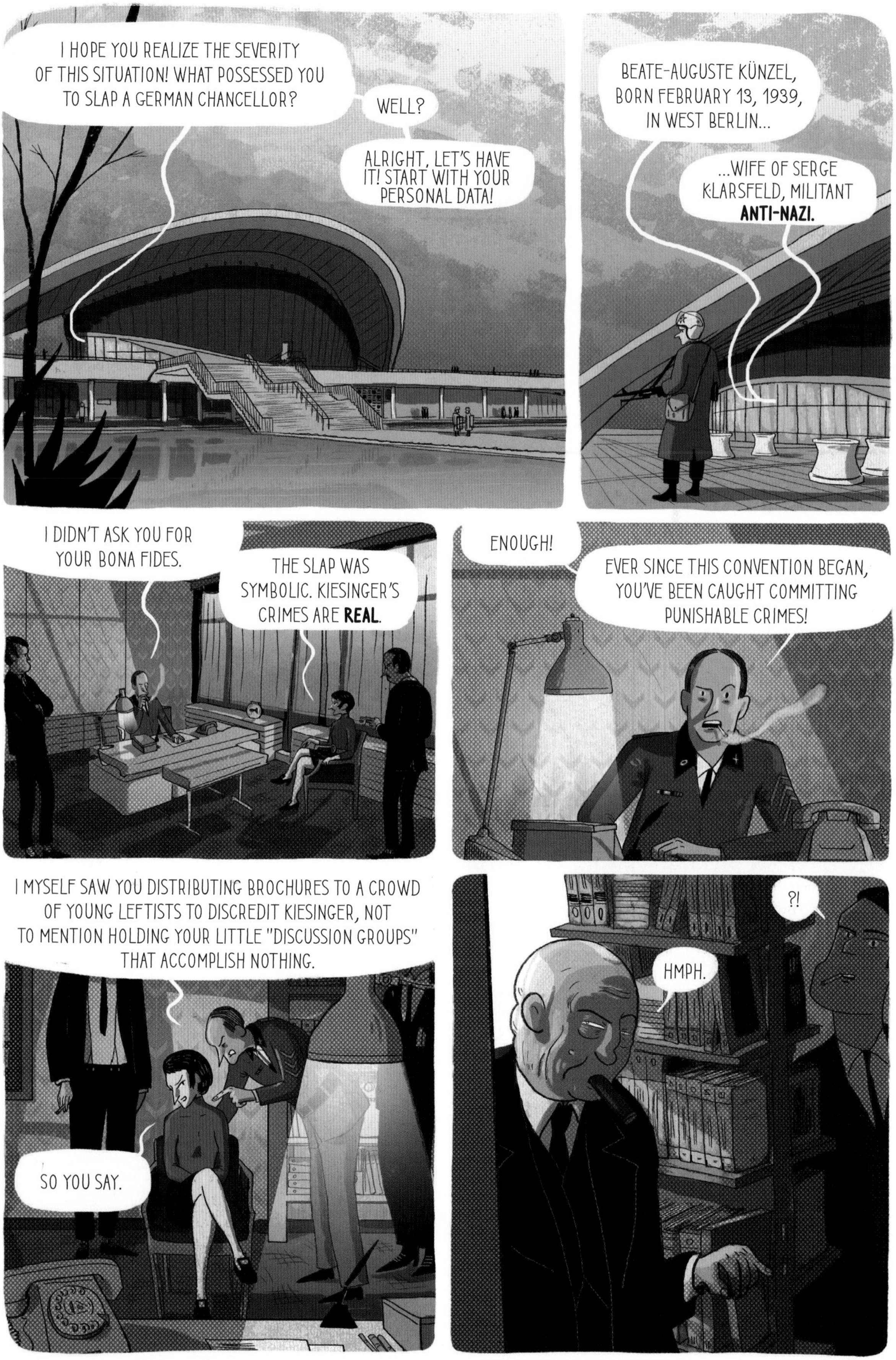
I HOPE YOU REALIZE THE SEVERITY OF THIS SITUATION! WHAT POSSESSED YOU TO SLAP A GERMAN CHANCELLOR?
WELL?
ALRIGHT, LET'S HAVE IT! START WITH YOUR PERSONAL DATA!
BEATE-AUGUSTE KÜNZEL, BORN FEBRUARY 13, 1939, IN WEST BERLIN...
...WIFE OF SERGE KLARSFELD, MILITANT **ANTI-NAZI.**
I DIDN'T ASK YOU FOR YOUR BONA FIDES.
THE SLAP WAS SYMBOLIC. KIESINGER'S CRIMES ARE **REAL**.
ENOUGH!
EVER SINCE THIS CONVENTION BEGAN, YOU'VE BEEN CAUGHT COMMITTING PUNISHABLE CRIMES!
I MYSELF SAW YOU DISTRIBUTING BROCHURES TO A CROWD OF YOUNG LEFTISTS TO DISCREDIT KIESINGER, NOT TO MENTION HOLDING YOUR LITTLE "DISCUSSION GROUPS" THAT ACCOMPLISH NOTHING.
SO YOU SAY.
?!
HMPH.

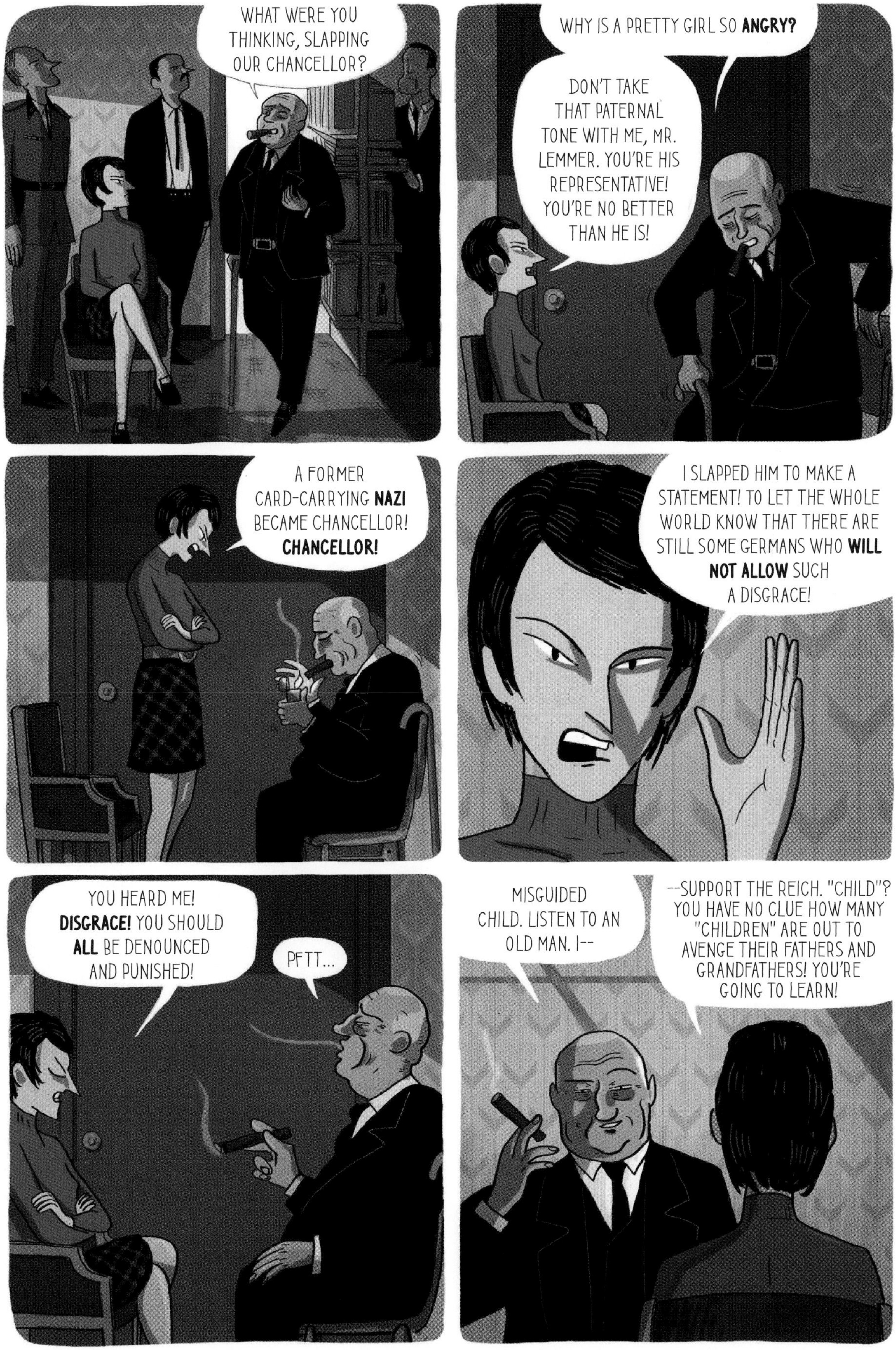
WHAT WERE YOU THINKING, SLAPPING OUR CHANCELLOR?
WHY IS A PRETTY GIRL SO **ANGRY?**
DON'T TAKE THAT PATERNAL TONE WITH ME, MR. LEMMER. YOU'RE HIS REPRESENTATIVE! YOU'RE NO BETTER THAN HE IS!
A FORMER CARD-CARRYING **NAZI** BECAME CHANCELLOR! **CHANCELLOR!**
I SLAPPED HIM TO MAKE A STATEMENT! TO LET THE WHOLE WORLD KNOW THAT THERE ARE STILL SOME GERMANS WHO **WILL NOT ALLOW** SUCH A DISGRACE!
YOU HEARD ME! **DISGRACE!** YOU SHOULD **ALL** BE DENOUNCED AND PUNISHED!
PFTT...
MISGUIDED CHILD. LISTEN TO AN OLD MAN. I--
--SUPPORT THE REICH. "CHILD"? YOU HAVE NO CLUE HOW MANY "CHILDREN" ARE OUT TO AVENGE THEIR FATHERS AND GRANDFATHERS! YOU'RE GOING TO LEARN!

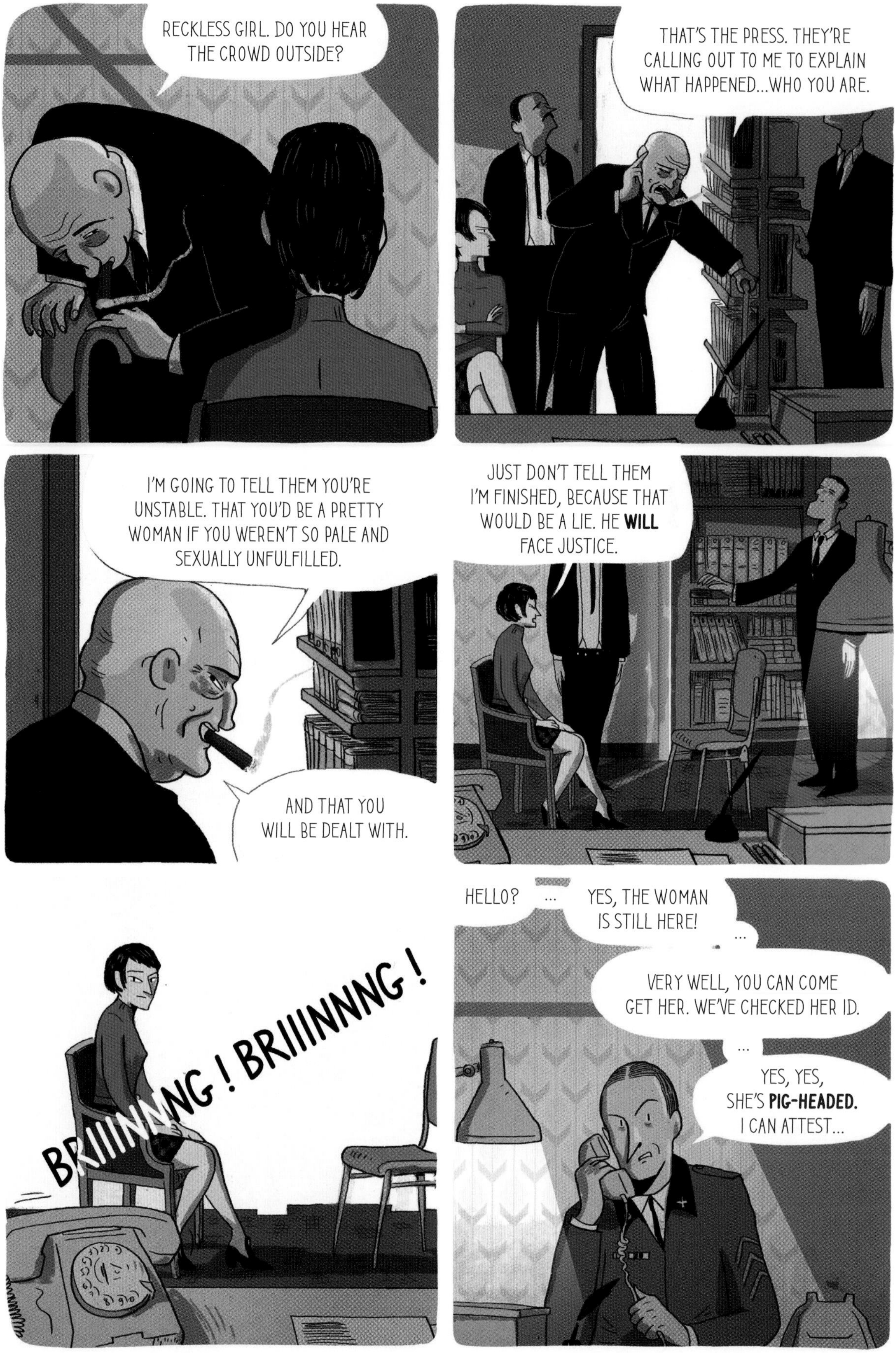
RECKLESS GIRL. DO YOU HEAR THE CROWD OUTSIDE?
THAT'S THE PRESS. THEY'RE CALLING OUT TO ME TO EXPLAIN WHAT HAPPENED...WHO YOU ARE.
I'M GOING TO TELL THEM YOU'RE UNSTABLE. THAT YOU'D BE A PRETTY WOMAN IF YOU WEREN'T SO PALE AND SEXUALLY UNFULFILLED.
AND THAT YOU WILL BE DEALT WITH.
JUST DON'T TELL THEM I'M FINISHED, BECAUSE THAT WOULD BE A LIE. HE **WILL** FACE JUSTICE.
BRIIINNNG! BRIIINNNG!
HELLO?
...
YES, THE WOMAN IS STILL HERE!
...
VERY WELL, YOU CAN COME GET HER. WE'VE CHECKED HER ID.
...
YES, YES, SHE'S **PIG-HEADED.** I CAN ATTEST...

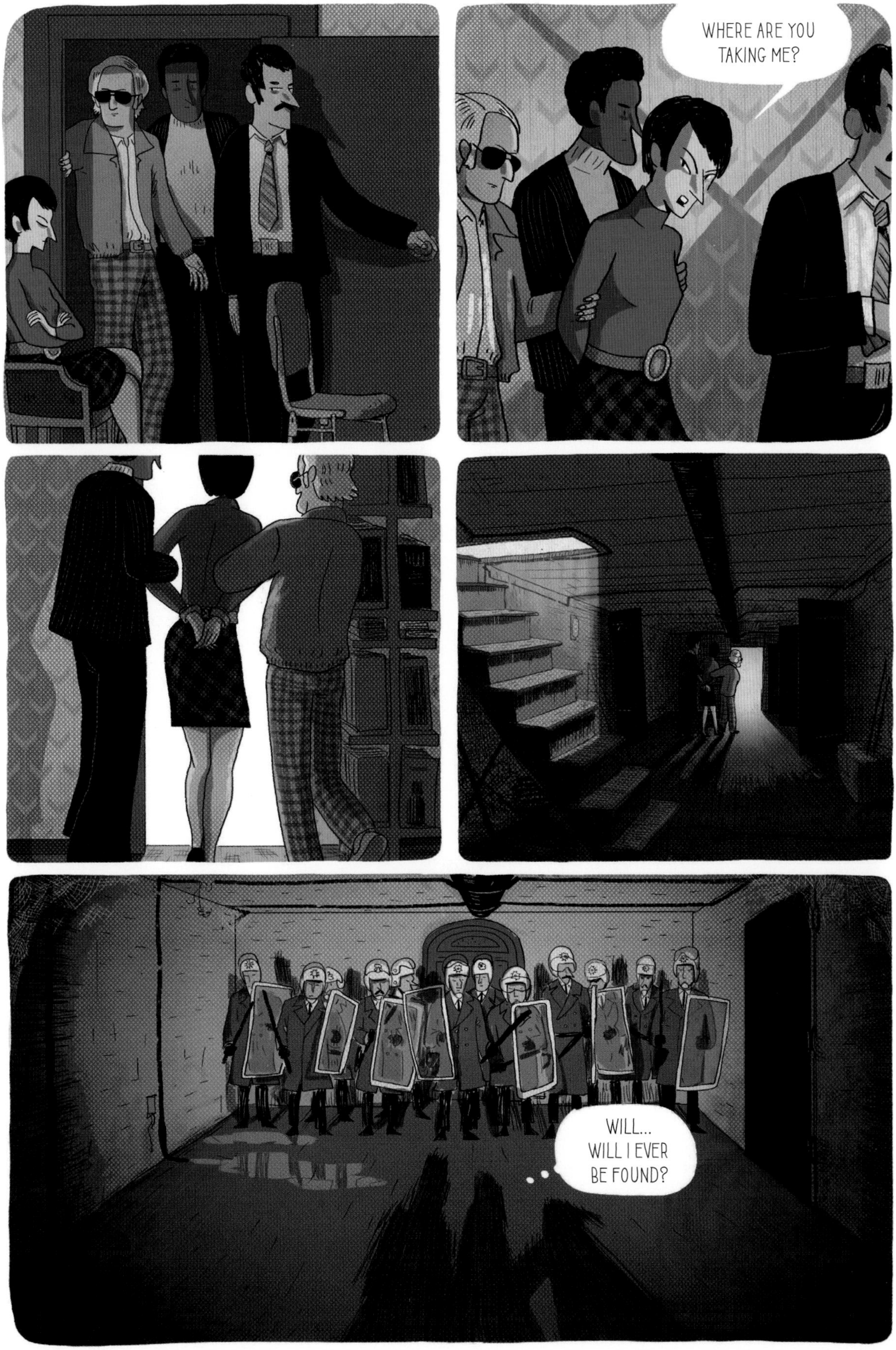
WHERE ARE YOU TAKING ME?
WILL... WILL I EVER BE FOUND?

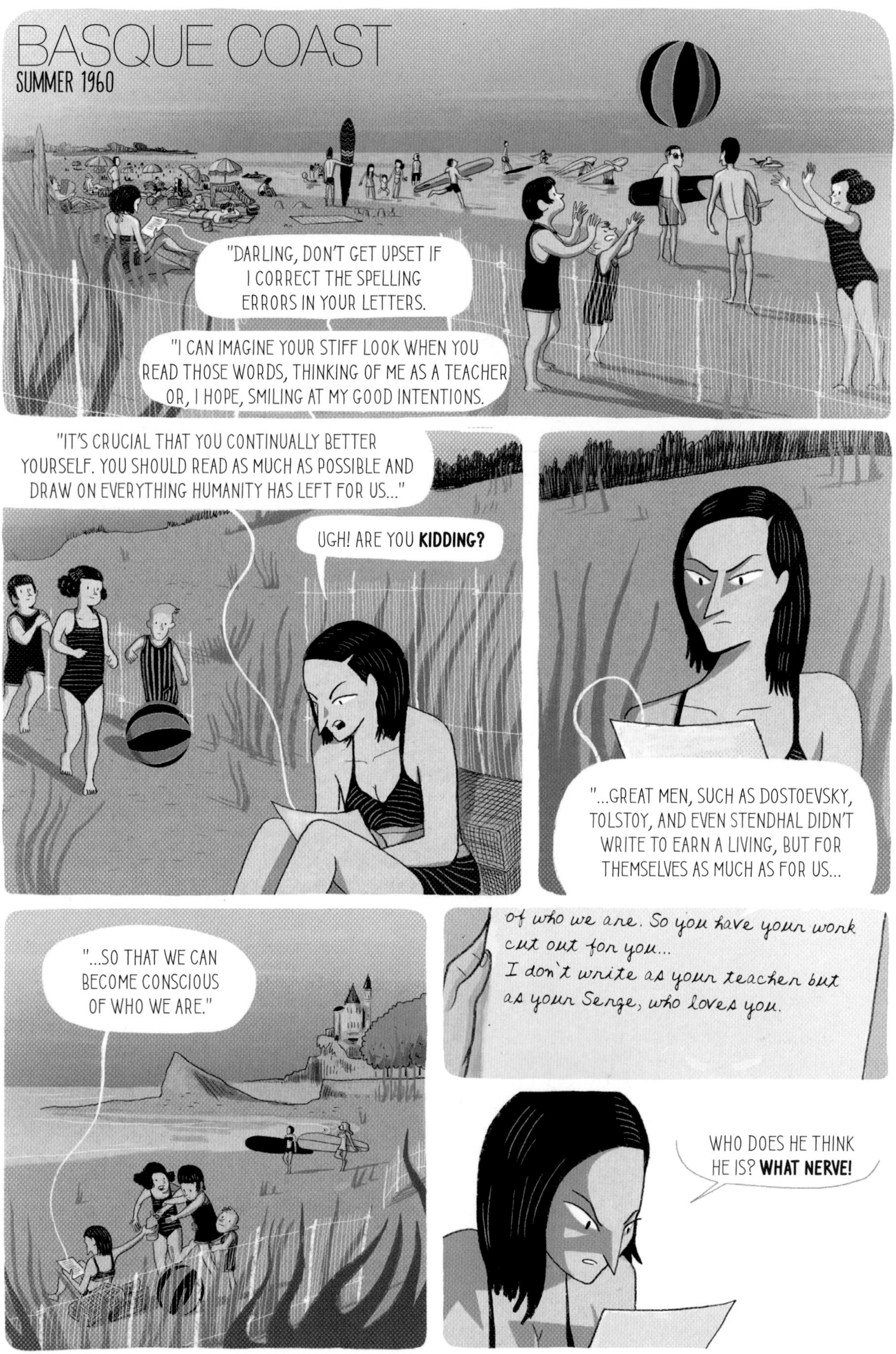
BASQUE COAST
SUMMER 1960
"DARLING, DON'T GET UPSET IF I CORRECT THE SPELLING ERRORS IN YOUR LETTERS.
"I CAN IMAGINE YOUR STIFF LOOK WHEN YOU READ THOSE WORDS, THINKING OF ME AS A TEACHER OR, I HOPE, SMILING AT MY GOOD INTENTIONS.
"IT'S CRUCIAL THAT YOU CONTINUALLY BETTER YOURSELF. YOU SHOULD READ AS MUCH AS POSSIBLE AND DRAW ON EVERYTHING HUMANITY HAS LEFT FOR US..."
UGH! ARE YOU **KIDDING?**
"...GREAT MEN, SUCH AS DOSTOEVSKY, TOLSTOY, AND EVEN STENDHAL DIDN'T WRITE TO EARN A LIVING, BUT FOR THEMSELVES AS MUCH AS FOR US...
"...SO THAT WE CAN BECOME CONSCIOUS OF WHO WE ARE."
of who we are. So you have your work cut out for you...
I don't write as your teacher but as your Serge, who loves you.
WHO DOES HE THINK HE IS? **WHAT NERVE!**

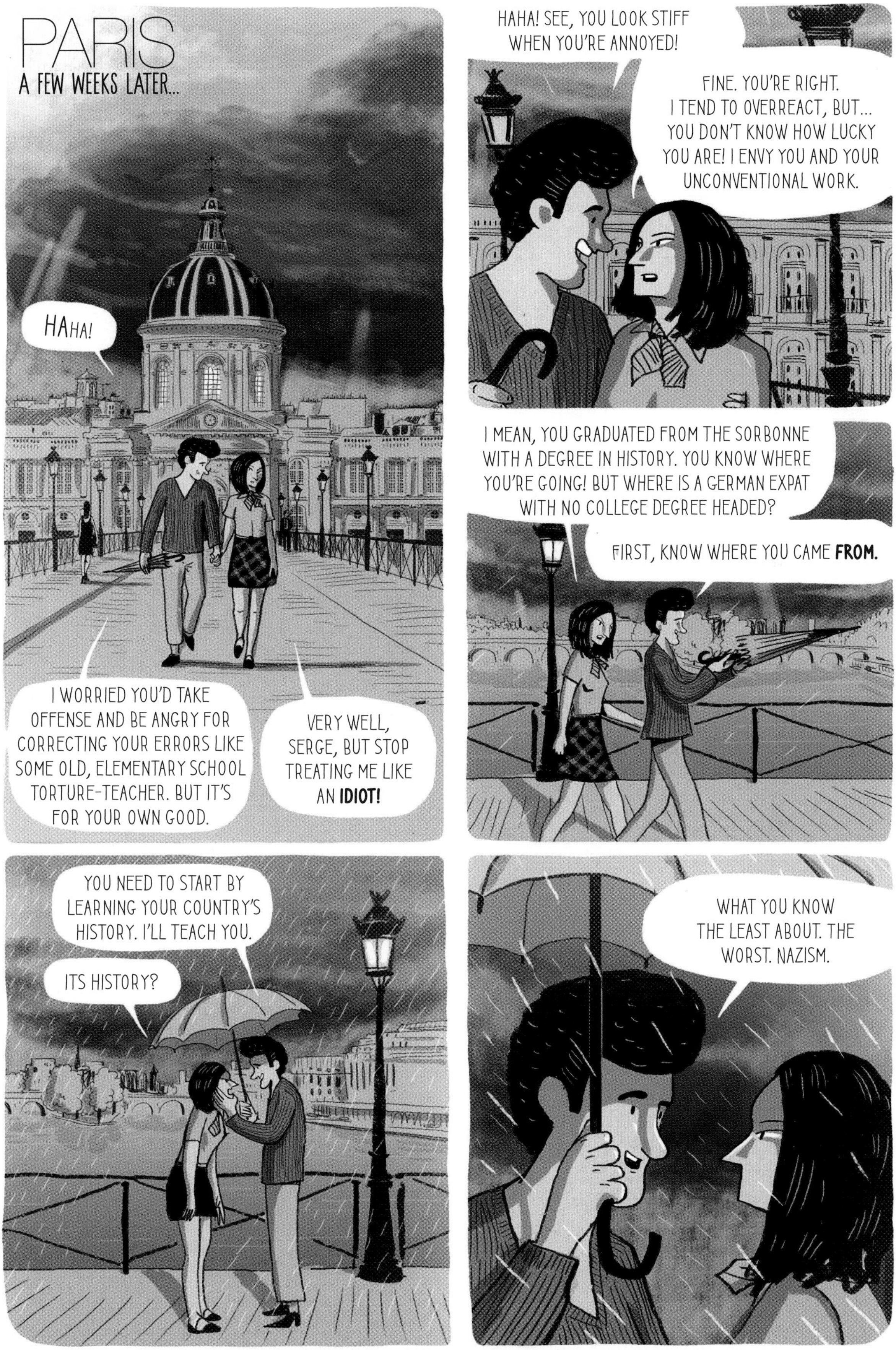
PARIS
A FEW WEEKS LATER...
HAHA!
I WORRIED YOU'D TAKE OFFENSE AND BE ANGRY FOR CORRECTING YOUR ERRORS LIKE SOME OLD, ELEMENTARY SCHOOL TORTURE-TEACHER. BUT IT'S FOR YOUR OWN GOOD.
VERY WELL, SERGE, BUT STOP TREATING ME LIKE AN **IDIOT!**
HAHA! SEE, YOU LOOK STIFF WHEN YOU'RE ANNOYED!
FINE. YOU'RE RIGHT. I TEND TO OVERREACT, BUT... YOU DON'T KNOW HOW LUCKY YOU ARE! I ENVY YOU AND YOUR UNCONVENTIONAL WORK.
I MEAN, YOU GRADUATED FROM THE SORBONNE WITH A DEGREE IN HISTORY. YOU KNOW WHERE YOU'RE GOING! BUT WHERE IS A GERMAN EXPAT WITH NO COLLEGE DEGREE HEADED?
FIRST, KNOW WHERE YOU CAME **FROM.**
YOU NEED TO START BY LEARNING YOUR COUNTRY'S HISTORY. I'LL TEACH YOU.
ITS HISTORY?
WHAT YOU KNOW THE LEAST ABOUT. THE WORST. NAZISM.

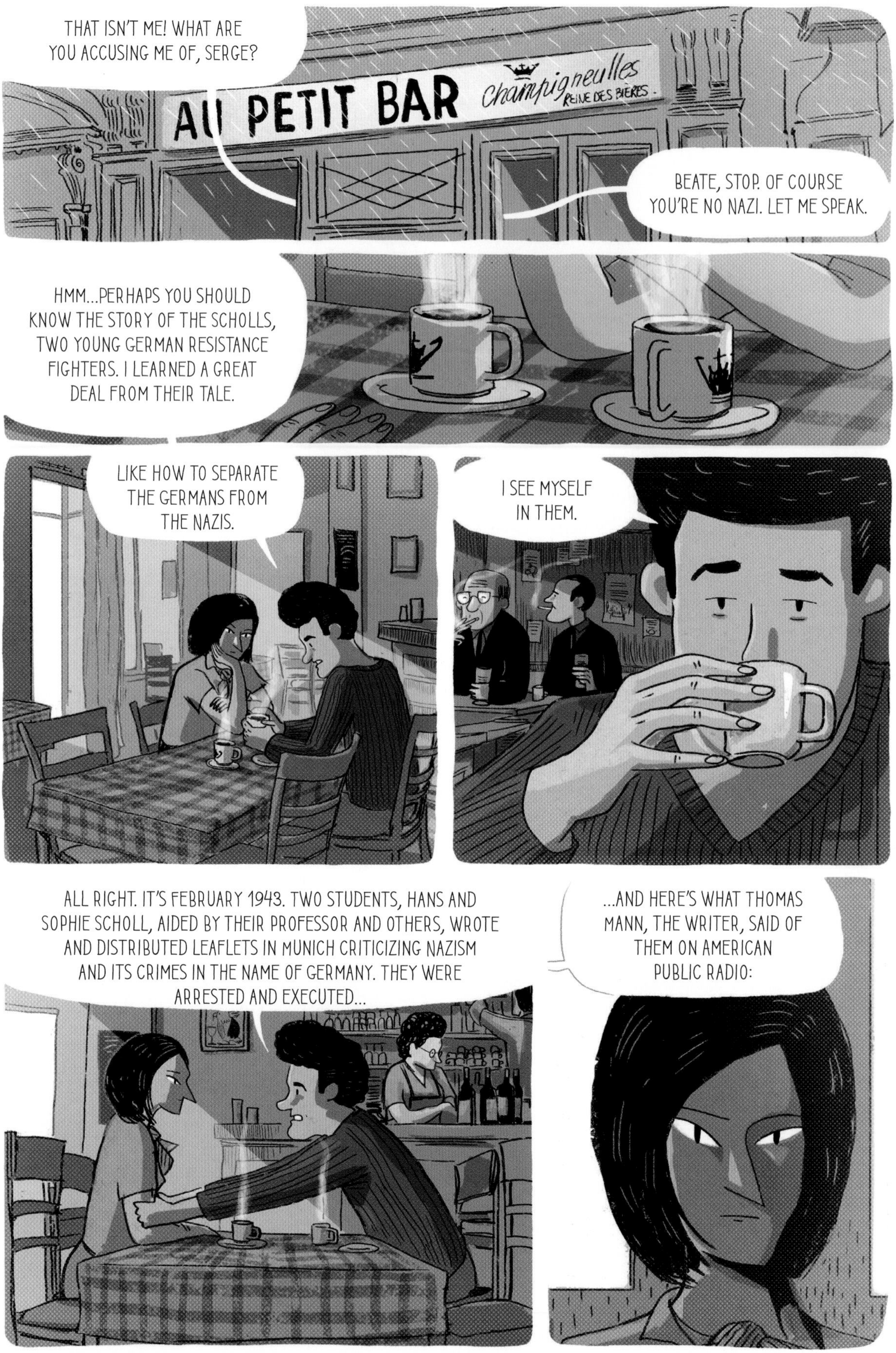
THAT ISN'T ME! WHAT ARE YOU ACCUSING ME OF, SERGE?
AU PETIT BAR
Champigneulles
REINE DES BIÈRES
BEATE, STOP. OF COURSE YOU'RE NO NAZI. LET ME SPEAK.
HMM...PERHAPS YOU SHOULD KNOW THE STORY OF THE SCHOLLS, TWO YOUNG GERMAN RESISTANCE FIGHTERS. I LEARNED A GREAT DEAL FROM THEIR TALE.
LIKE HOW TO SEPARATE THE GERMANS FROM THE NAZIS.
I SEE MYSELF IN THEM.
ALL RIGHT. IT'S FEBRUARY 1943. TWO STUDENTS, HANS AND SOPHIE SCHOLL, AIDED BY THEIR PROFESSOR AND OTHERS, WROTE AND DISTRIBUTED LEAFLETS IN MUNICH CRITICIZING NAZISM AND ITS CRIMES IN THE NAME OF GERMANY. THEY WERE ARRESTED AND EXECUTED...
...AND HERE'S WHAT THOMAS MANN, THE WRITER, SAID OF THEM ON AMERICAN PUBLIC RADIO:

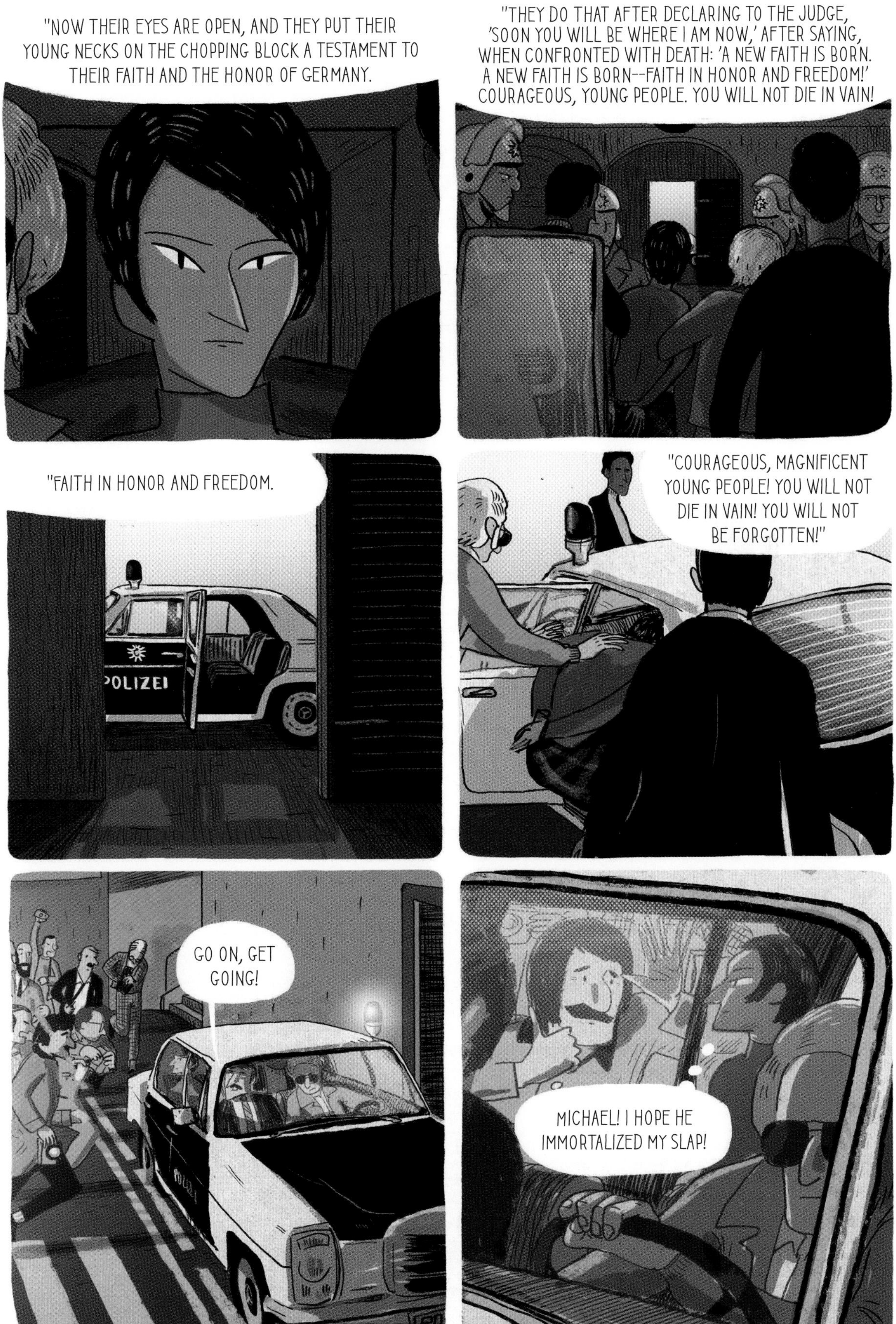
"NOW THEIR EYES ARE OPEN, AND THEY PUT THEIR YOUNG NECKS ON THE CHOPPING BLOCK A TESTAMENT TO THEIR FAITH AND THE HONOR OF GERMANY.
"THEY DO THAT AFTER DECLARING TO THE JUDGE, 'SOON YOU WILL BE WHERE I AM NOW,' AFTER SAYING, WHEN CONFRONTED WITH DEATH: 'A NEW FAITH IS BORN. A NEW FAITH IS BORN--FAITH IN HONOR AND FREEDOM!' COURAGEOUS, YOUNG PEOPLE. YOU WILL NOT DIE IN VAIN!
"FAITH IN HONOR AND FREEDOM.
POLIZEI
"COURAGEOUS, MAGNIFICENT YOUNG PEOPLE! YOU WILL NOT DIE IN VAIN! YOU WILL NOT BE FORGOTTEN!"
GO ON, GET GOING!
MICHAEL! I HOPE HE IMMORTALIZED MY SLAP!

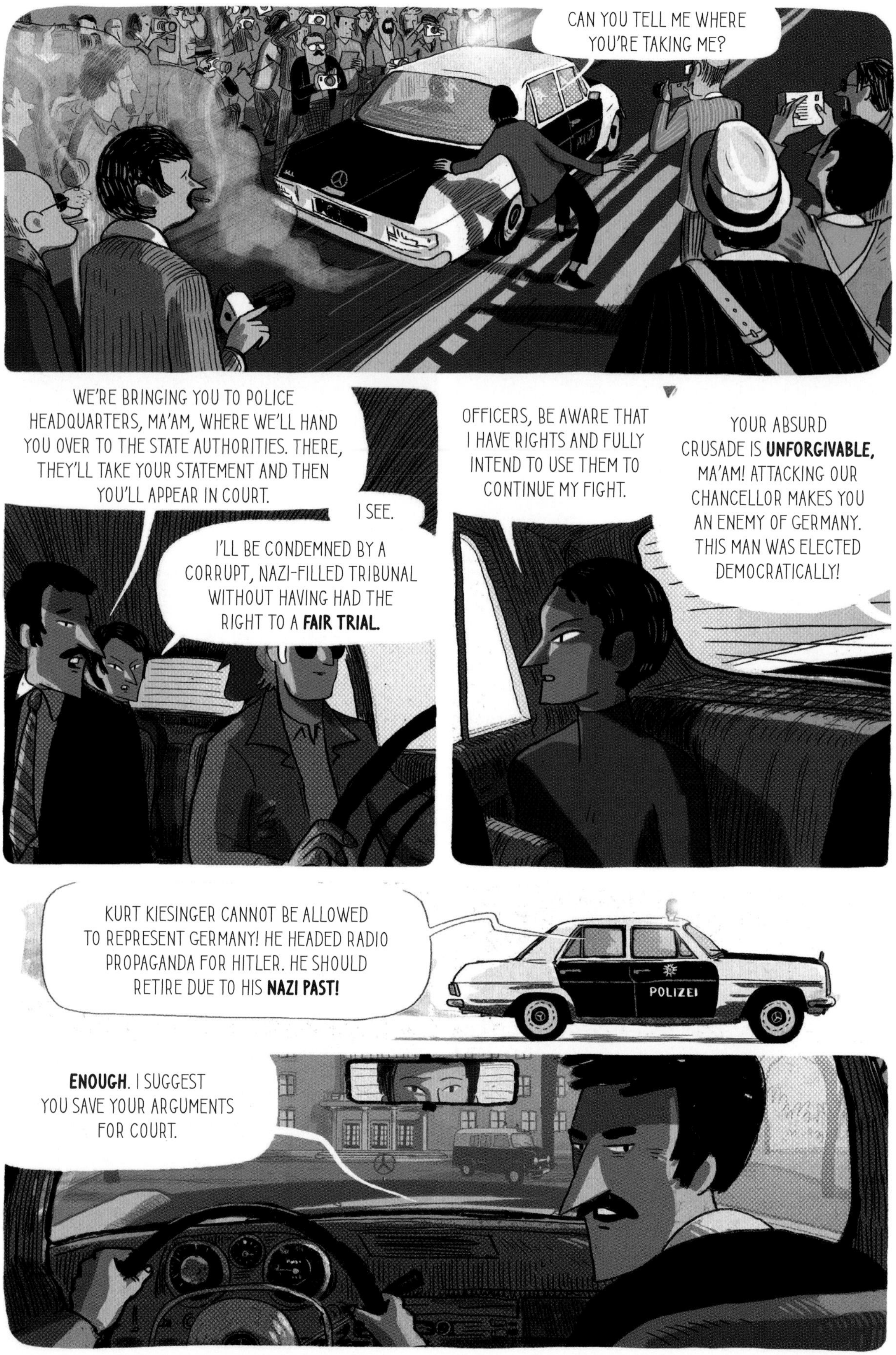
CAN YOU TELL ME WHERE YOU'RE TAKING ME?
WE'RE BRINGING YOU TO POLICE HEADQUARTERS, MA'AM, WHERE WE'LL HAND YOU OVER TO THE STATE AUTHORITIES. THERE, THEY'LL TAKE YOUR STATEMENT AND THEN YOU'LL APPEAR IN COURT.
I SEE.
I'LL BE CONDEMNED BY A CORRUPT, NAZI-FILLED TRIBUNAL WITHOUT HAVING HAD THE RIGHT TO A **FAIR TRIAL.**
OFFICERS, BE AWARE THAT I HAVE RIGHTS AND FULLY INTEND TO USE THEM TO CONTINUE MY FIGHT.
YOUR ABSURD CRUSADE IS **UNFORGIVABLE,** MA'AM! ATTACKING OUR CHANCELLOR MAKES YOU AN ENEMY OF GERMANY. THIS MAN WAS ELECTED DEMOCRATICALLY!
KURT KIESINGER CANNOT BE ALLOWED TO REPRESENT GERMANY! HE HEADED RADIO PROPAGANDA FOR HITLER. HE SHOULD RETIRE DUE TO HIS **NAZI PAST!**
POLIZEI
ENOUGH. I SUGGEST YOU SAVE YOUR ARGUMENTS FOR COURT.

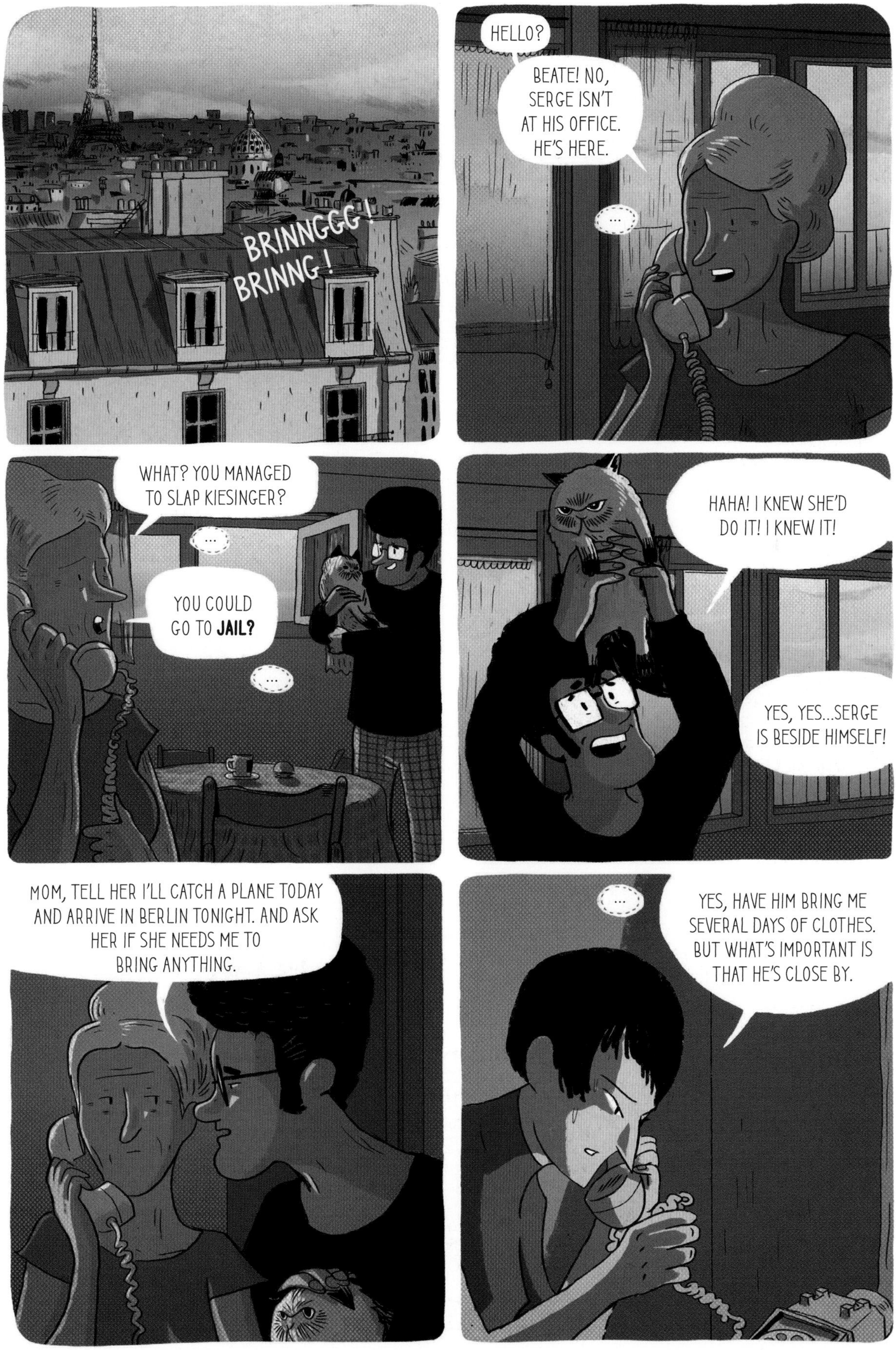
BRINNGGG!
BRINNG!
HELLO?
BEATE! NO, SERGE ISN'T AT HIS OFFICE. HE'S HERE.
...
WHAT? YOU MANAGED TO SLAP KIESINGER?
...
YOU COULD GO TO **JAIL?**
...
HAHA! I KNEW SHE'D DO IT! I KNEW IT!
YES, YES...SERGE IS BESIDE HIMSELF!
MOM, TELL HER I'LL CATCH A PLANE TODAY AND ARRIVE IN BERLIN TONIGHT. AND ASK HER IF SHE NEEDS ME TO BRING ANYTHING.
...
YES, HAVE HIM BRING ME SEVERAL DAYS OF CLOTHES. BUT WHAT'S IMPORTANT IS THAT HE'S CLOSE BY.

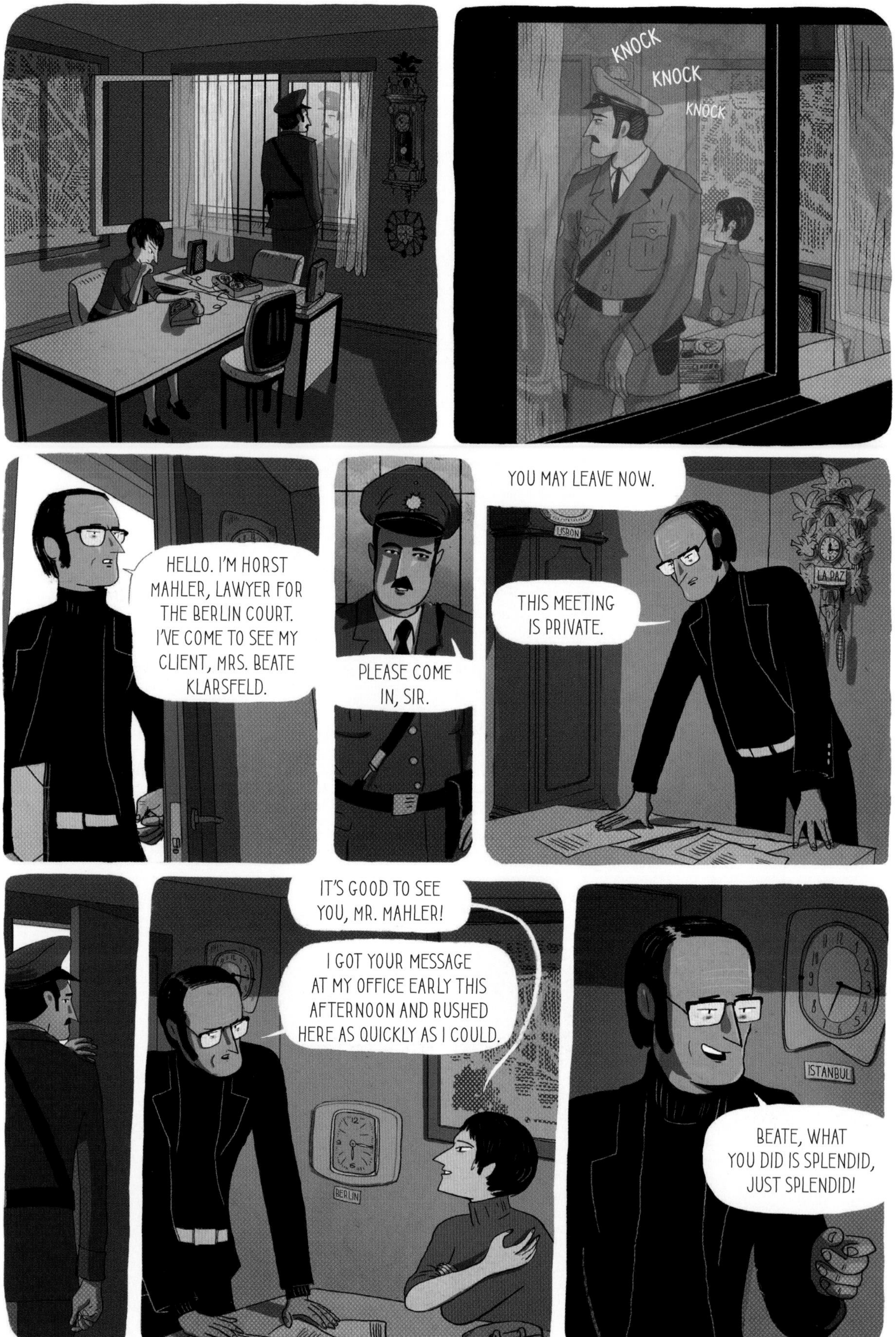
KNOCK
KNOCK
KNOCK
HELLO. I'M HORST MAHLER, LAWYER FOR THE BERLIN COURT. I'VE COME TO SEE MY CLIENT, MRS. BEATE KLARSFELD.
PLEASE COME IN, SIR.
YOU MAY LEAVE NOW.
LISBON
LA PAZ
THIS MEETING IS PRIVATE.
IT'S GOOD TO SEE YOU, MR. MAHLER!
I GOT YOUR MESSAGE AT MY OFFICE EARLY THIS AFTERNOON AND RUSHED HERE AS QUICKLY AS I COULD.
BERLIN
ISTANBUL
BEATE, WHAT YOU DID IS SPLENDID, JUST SPLENDID!

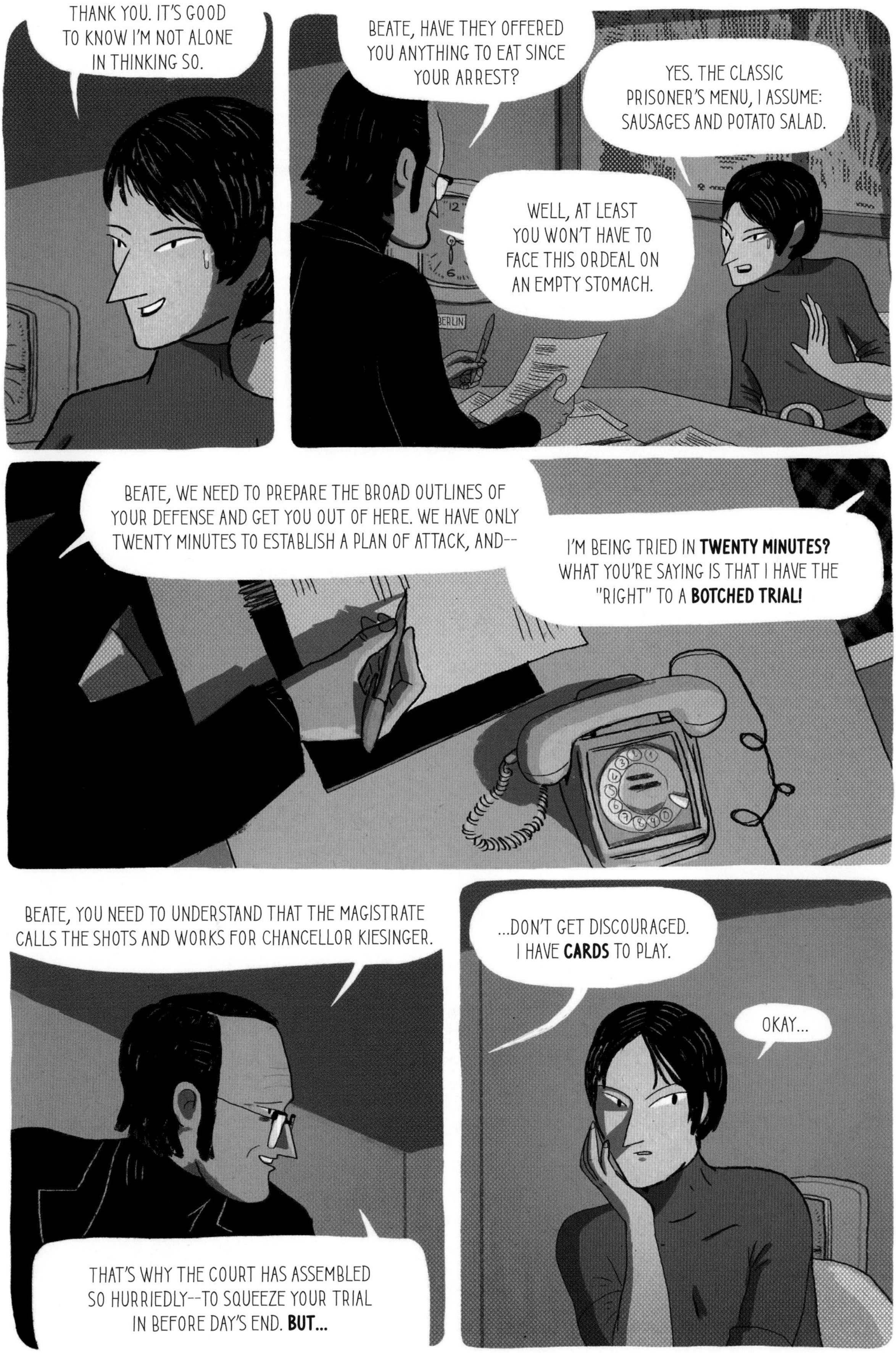
THANK YOU. IT'S GOOD TO KNOW I'M NOT ALONE IN THINKING SO.
BEATE, HAVE THEY OFFERED YOU ANYTHING TO EAT SINCE YOUR ARREST?
YES. THE CLASSIC PRISONER'S MENU, I ASSUME: SAUSAGES AND POTATO SALAD.
WELL, AT LEAST YOU WON'T HAVE TO FACE THIS ORDEAL ON AN EMPTY STOMACH.
BERLIN
BEATE, WE NEED TO PREPARE THE BROAD OUTLINES OF YOUR DEFENSE AND GET YOU OUT OF HERE. WE HAVE ONLY TWENTY MINUTES TO ESTABLISH A PLAN OF ATTACK, AND--
I'M BEING TRIED IN **TWENTY MINUTES?** WHAT YOU'RE SAYING IS THAT I HAVE THE "RIGHT" TO A **BOTCHED TRIAL!**
BEATE, YOU NEED TO UNDERSTAND THAT THE MAGISTRATE CALLS THE SHOTS AND WORKS FOR CHANCELLOR KIESINGER.
THAT'S WHY THE COURT HAS ASSEMBLED SO HURRIEDLY--TO SQUEEZE YOUR TRIAL IN BEFORE DAY'S END. **BUT...**
...DON'T GET DISCOURAGED. I HAVE **CARDS** TO PLAY.
OKAY...

FROM THE MEMOIRS OF SERGE KLARSFELD: BEATE HAS ALWAYS BEEN THE WOMAN OF MY DREAMS, WITH A BIT OF A "MARLENE DIETRICH" SIDE. WITH THE PASSAGE OF TIME, WE CEASED HAVING TO BE APART. SHE DIDN'T REMAIN AN AU PAIR FOR LONG, INSTEAD SEARCHING FOR A MORE FULFILLING POSITION. THE CREATION OF THE "FRANCO-GERMAN YOUTH OFFICE" IN 1963--WITH A PARISIAN BUREAU--ALLOWED HER TO BE HIRED AS A BILINGUAL SECRETARY IN DECEMBER, 1964. SHE SOON WROTE A MANIFESTO, "YOUNG GERMAN AU PAIRS IN PARIS," CALLING FOR THEIR BETTER TREATMENT.

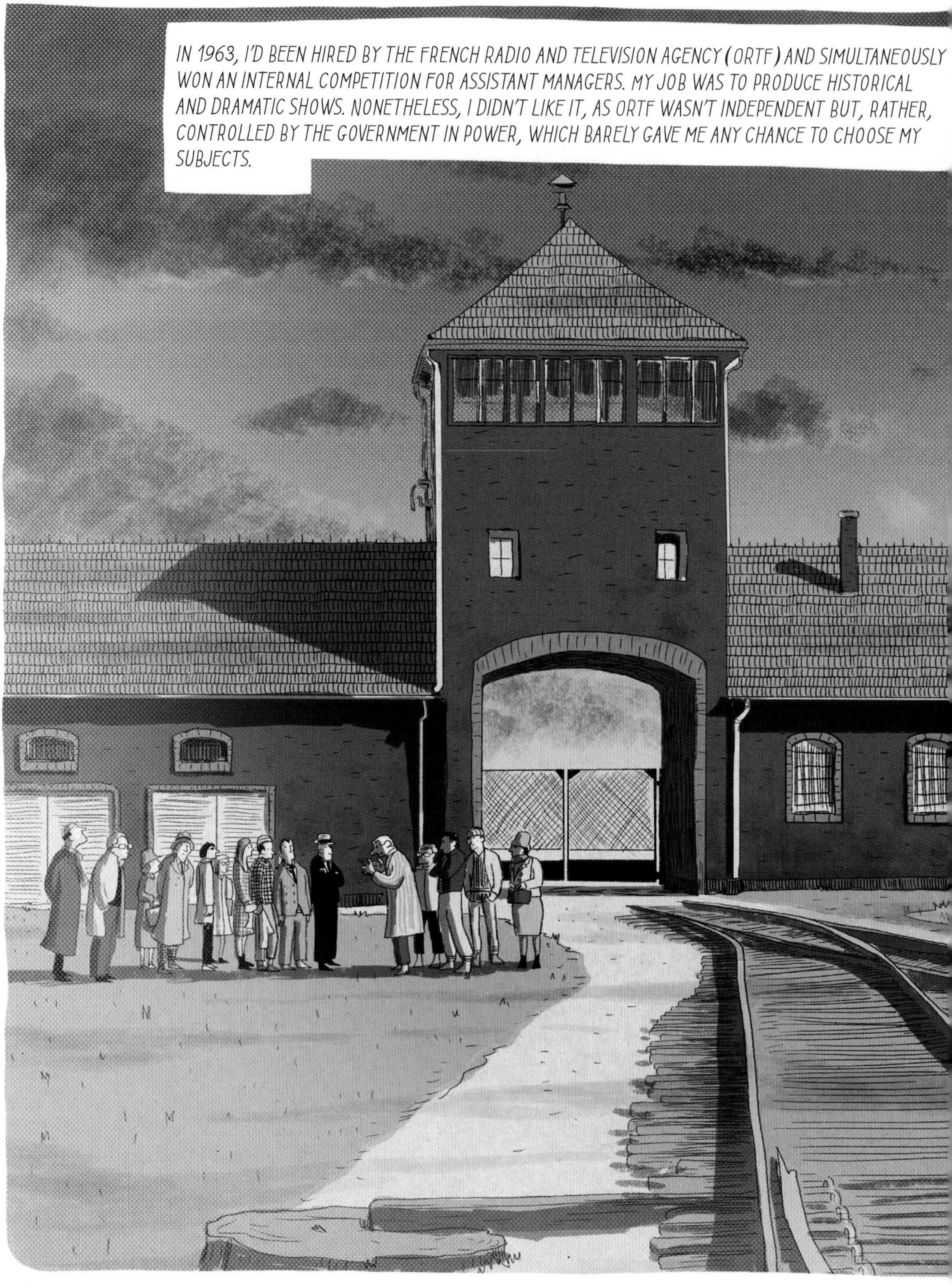
IN 1963, I'D BEEN HIRED BY THE FRENCH RADIO AND TELEVISION AGENCY (ORTF) AND SIMULTANEOUSLY WON AN INTERNAL COMPETITION FOR ASSISTANT MANAGERS. MY JOB WAS TO PRODUCE HISTORICAL AND DRAMATIC SHOWS. NONETHELESS, I DIDN'T LIKE IT, AS ORTF WASN'T INDEPENDENT BUT, RATHER, CONTROLLED BY THE GOVERNMENT IN POWER, WHICH BARELY GAVE ME ANY CHANCE TO CHOOSE MY SUBJECTS.

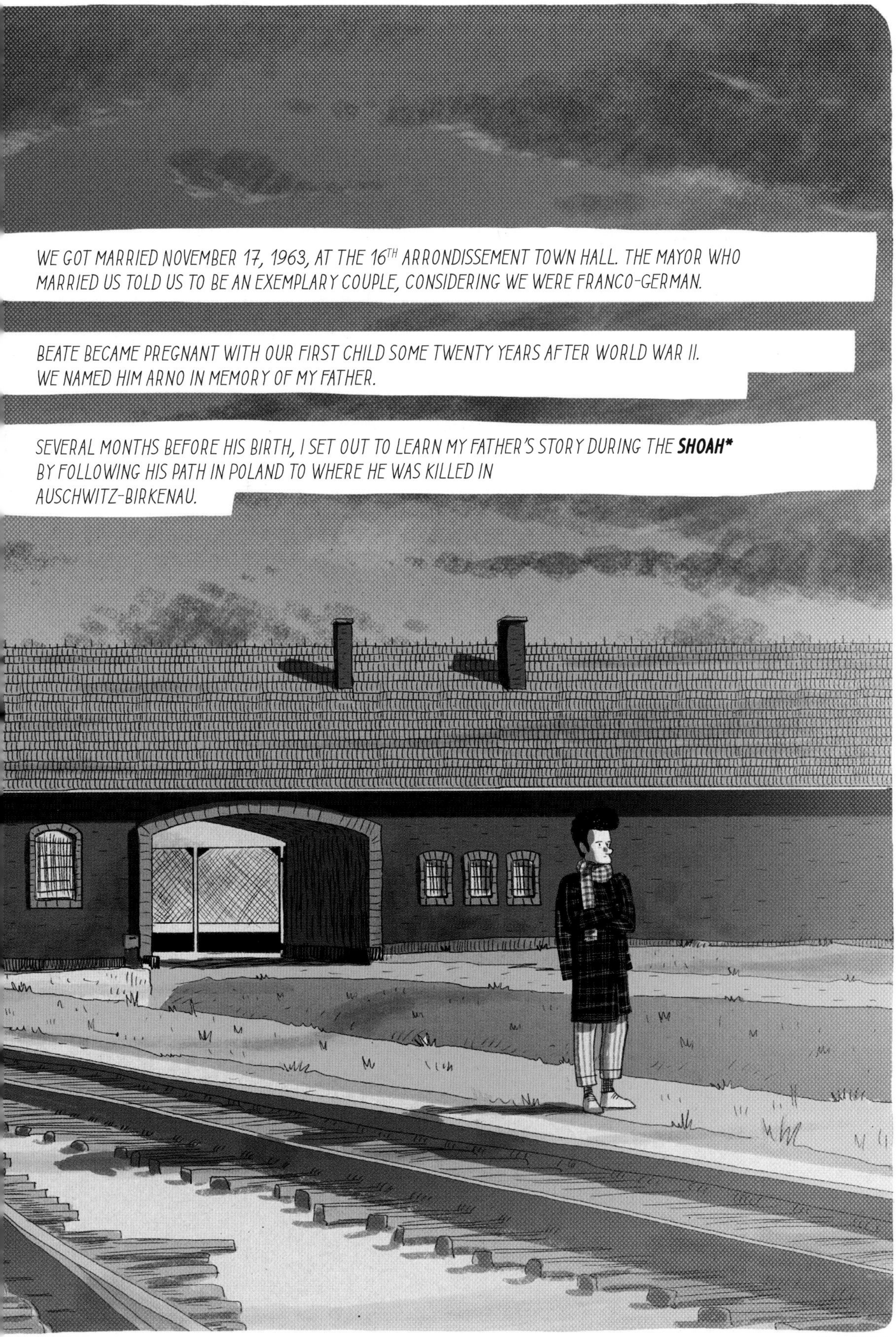
WE GOT MARRIED NOVEMBER 17, 1963, AT THE 16TH ARRONDISSEMENT TOWN HALL. THE MAYOR WHO MARRIED US TOLD US TO BE AN EXEMPLARY COUPLE, CONSIDERING WE WERE FRANCO-GERMAN.
BEATE BECAME PREGNANT WITH OUR FIRST CHILD SOME TWENTY YEARS AFTER WORLD WAR II. WE NAMED HIM ARNO IN MEMORY OF MY FATHER.
SEVERAL MONTHS BEFORE HIS BIRTH, I SET OUT TO LEARN MY FATHER'S STORY DURING THE **SHOAH*** BY FOLLOWING HIS PATH IN POLAND TO WHERE HE WAS KILLED IN AUSCHWITZ-BIRKENAU.

*HOLOCAUST

MY FEELING OF LOSS AROUND MY FATHER'S DEATH GREW DEEPER.

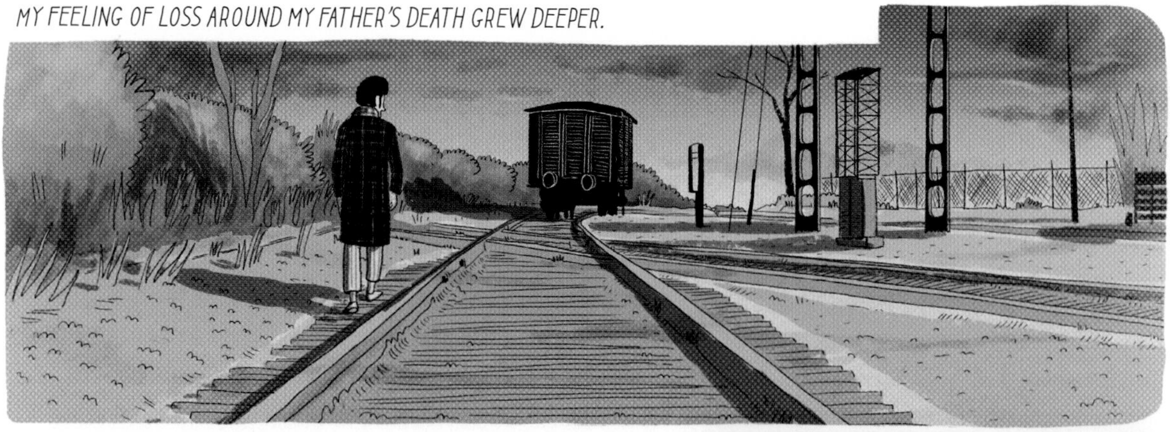

BEFORE MEETING MY FUTURE CHILD FOR THE FIRST TIME, IT FELT IMPORTANT TO FACE THE MEMORY OF A FATHER WHO DIED TOO SOON.

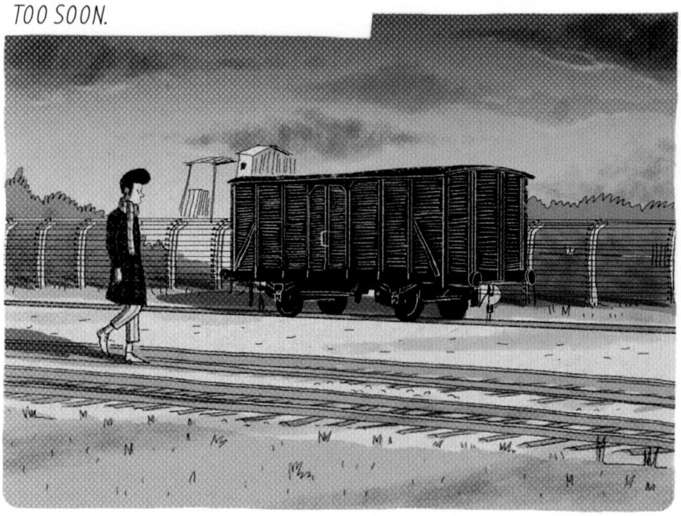

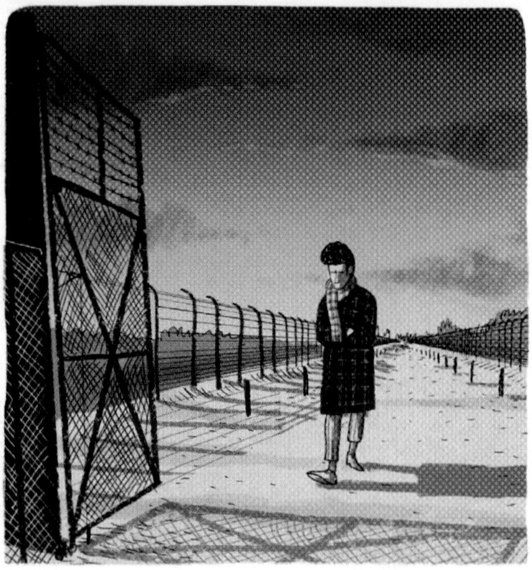

I SET OUT TO RETRACE THE LAST STAGES OF HIS LIFE...

...FROM THE TIME WHEN HE LEFT US IN NICE TO THE MOMENT HE DIED.

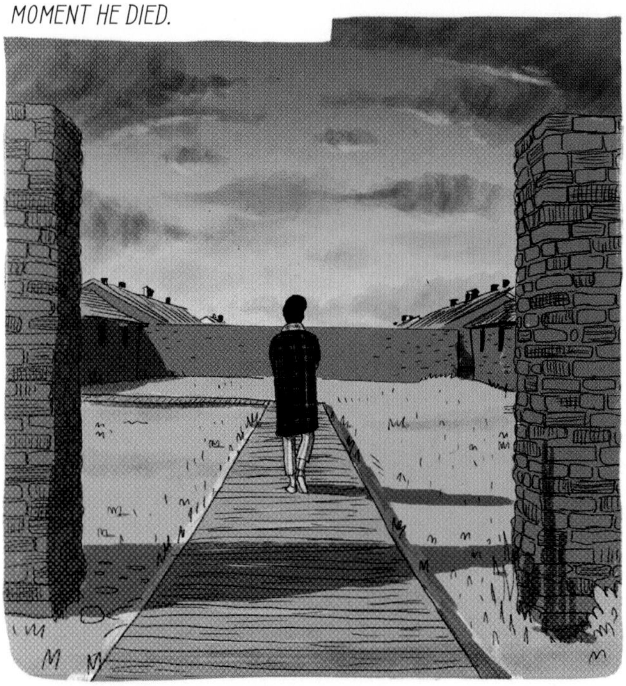

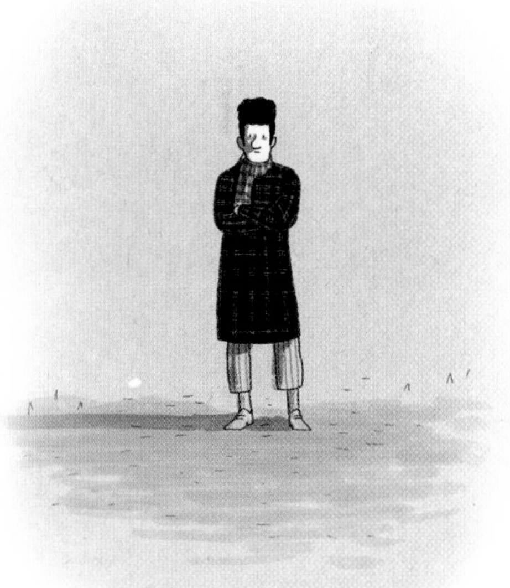

BIRKENAU WAS THE FINAL STOP FOR THE JEWISH PEOPLE. I FELT A STRONG CONNECTION.

I COULD ALMOST HEAR THE CRIES, THE SUFFERING AND THE ECHOES OF AGONY.

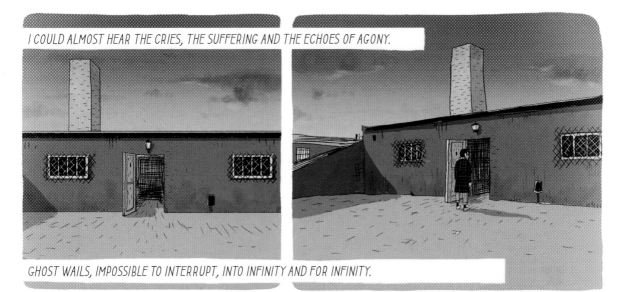

GHOST WAILS, IMPOSSIBLE TO INTERRUPT, INTO INFINITY AND FOR INFINITY.

I COULD NOT CLOSE MY EARS AND MY HEART TO THE SOUNDS OF THEIR LAMENTATIONS. HOW COULD I--THE MIRACULOUS SURVIVOR OF THIS GENOCIDE, SAVED BY MY FATHER'S SACRIFICE--REMAIN DEAF TO THEIR SUFFERING?

NO. THEIR PAIN CALLED OUT TO ME, URGING ME TO ASSUME MY RESPONSIBILITIES AS A JEW.

I COULDN'T TURN AWAY FROM MY HERITAGE. I WAS INDEBTED TO THEM ALL. MY ROLE AS A SURVIVOR WAS TO GIVE THEM BACK THEIR IDENTITY AND **SERVE JUSTICE.**

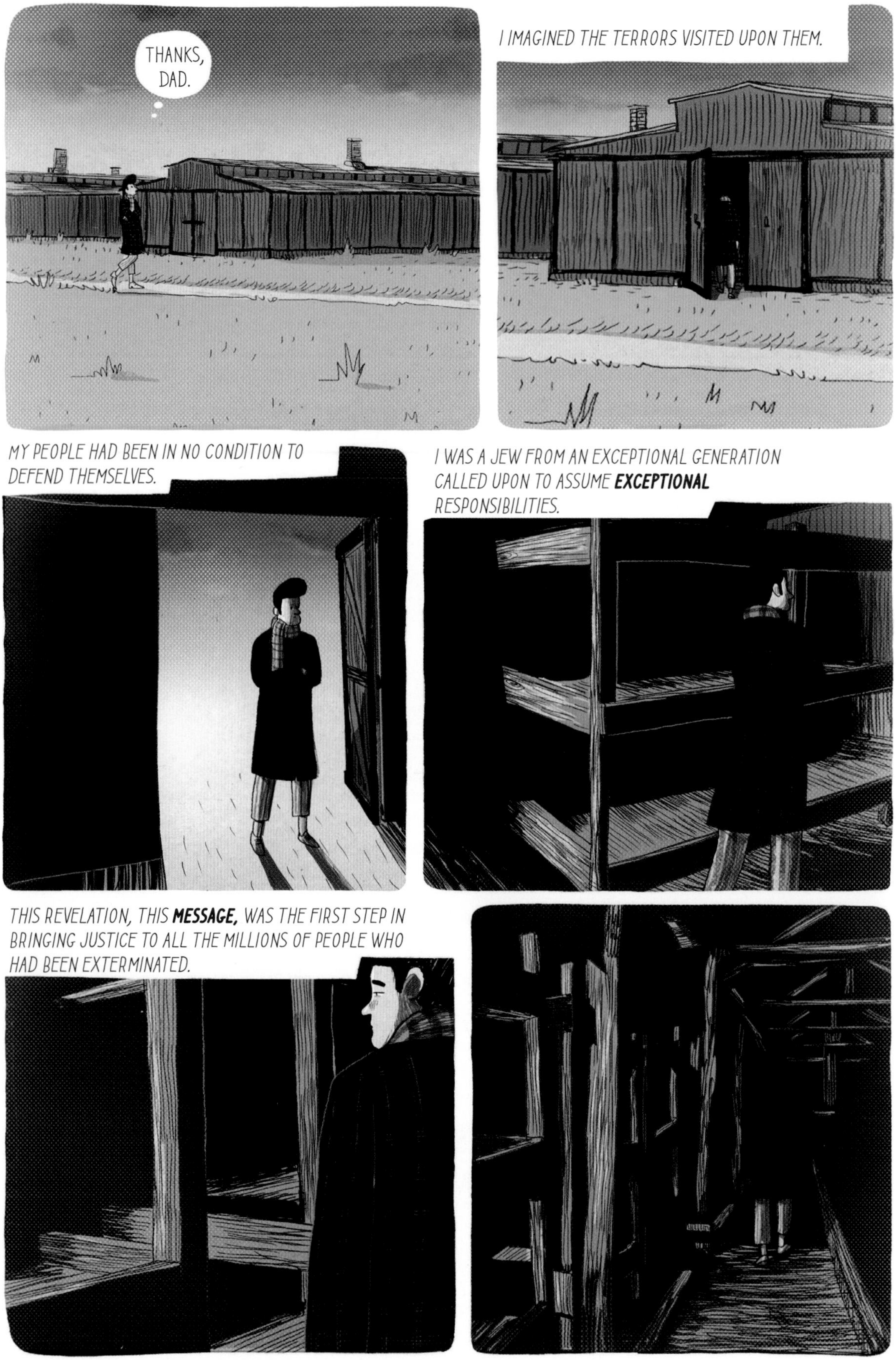
THANKS, DAD.
I IMAGINED THE TERRORS VISITED UPON THEM.
MY PEOPLE HAD BEEN IN NO CONDITION TO DEFEND THEMSELVES.
I WAS A JEW FROM AN EXCEPTIONAL GENERATION CALLED UPON TO ASSUME **EXCEPTIONAL** RESPONSIBILITIES.
THIS REVELATION, THIS **MESSAGE,** WAS THE FIRST STEP IN BRINGING JUSTICE TO ALL THE MILLIONS OF PEOPLE WHO HAD BEEN EXTERMINATED.

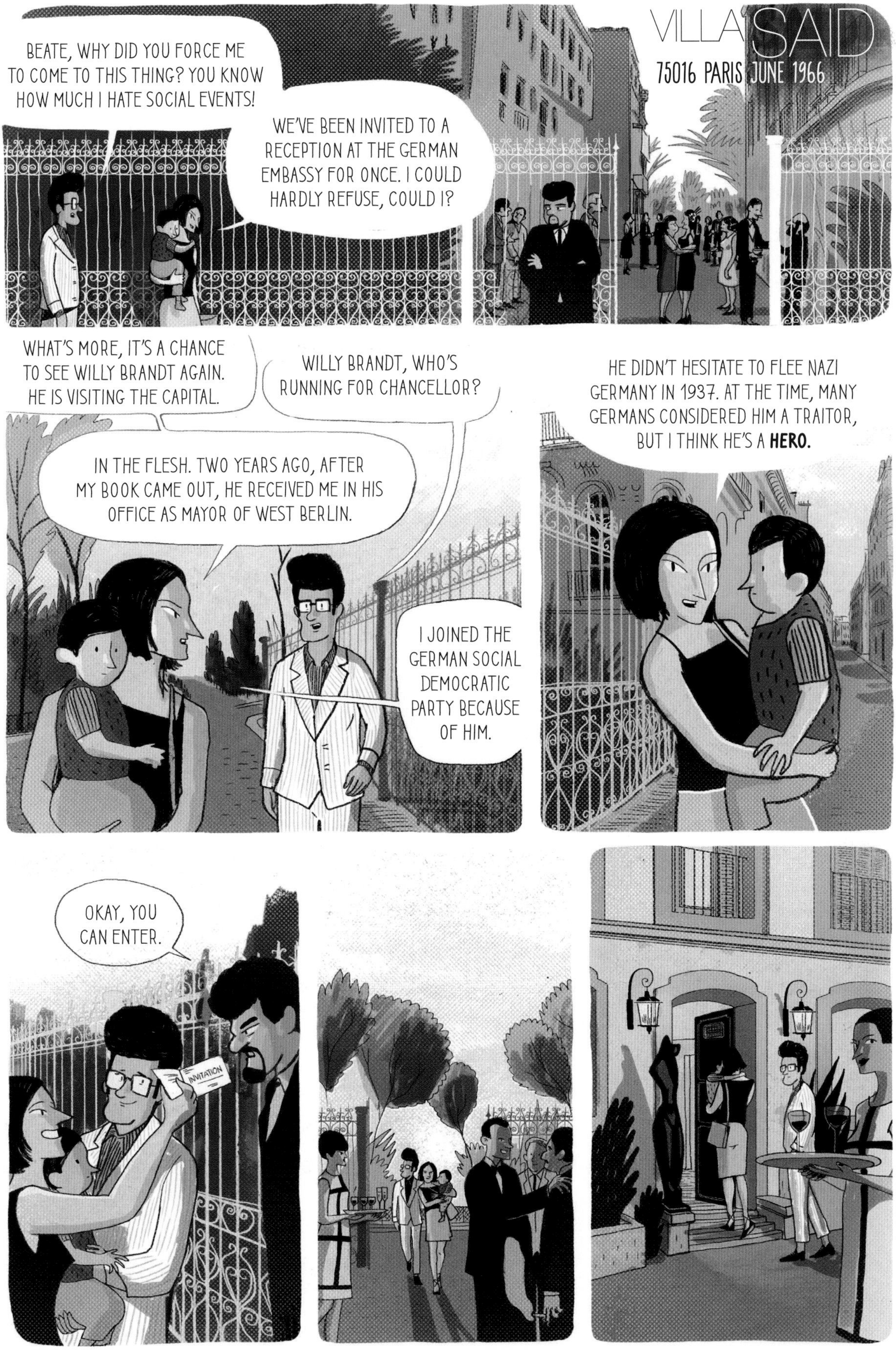
VILLA SAID
75016 PARIS JUNE 1966
BEATE, WHY DID YOU FORCE ME TO COME TO THIS THING? YOU KNOW HOW MUCH I HATE SOCIAL EVENTS!
WE'VE BEEN INVITED TO A RECEPTION AT THE GERMAN EMBASSY FOR ONCE. I COULD HARDLY REFUSE, COULD I?
WHAT'S MORE, IT'S A CHANCE TO SEE WILLY BRANDT AGAIN. HE IS VISITING THE CAPITAL.
WILLY BRANDT, WHO'S RUNNING FOR CHANCELLOR?
IN THE FLESH. TWO YEARS AGO, AFTER MY BOOK CAME OUT, HE RECEIVED ME IN HIS OFFICE AS MAYOR OF WEST BERLIN.
I JOINED THE GERMAN SOCIAL DEMOCRATIC PARTY BECAUSE OF HIM.
HE DIDN'T HESITATE TO FLEE NAZI GERMANY IN 1937. AT THE TIME, MANY GERMANS CONSIDERED HIM A TRAITOR, BUT I THINK HE'S A **HERO.**
OKAY, YOU CAN ENTER.
INVITATION

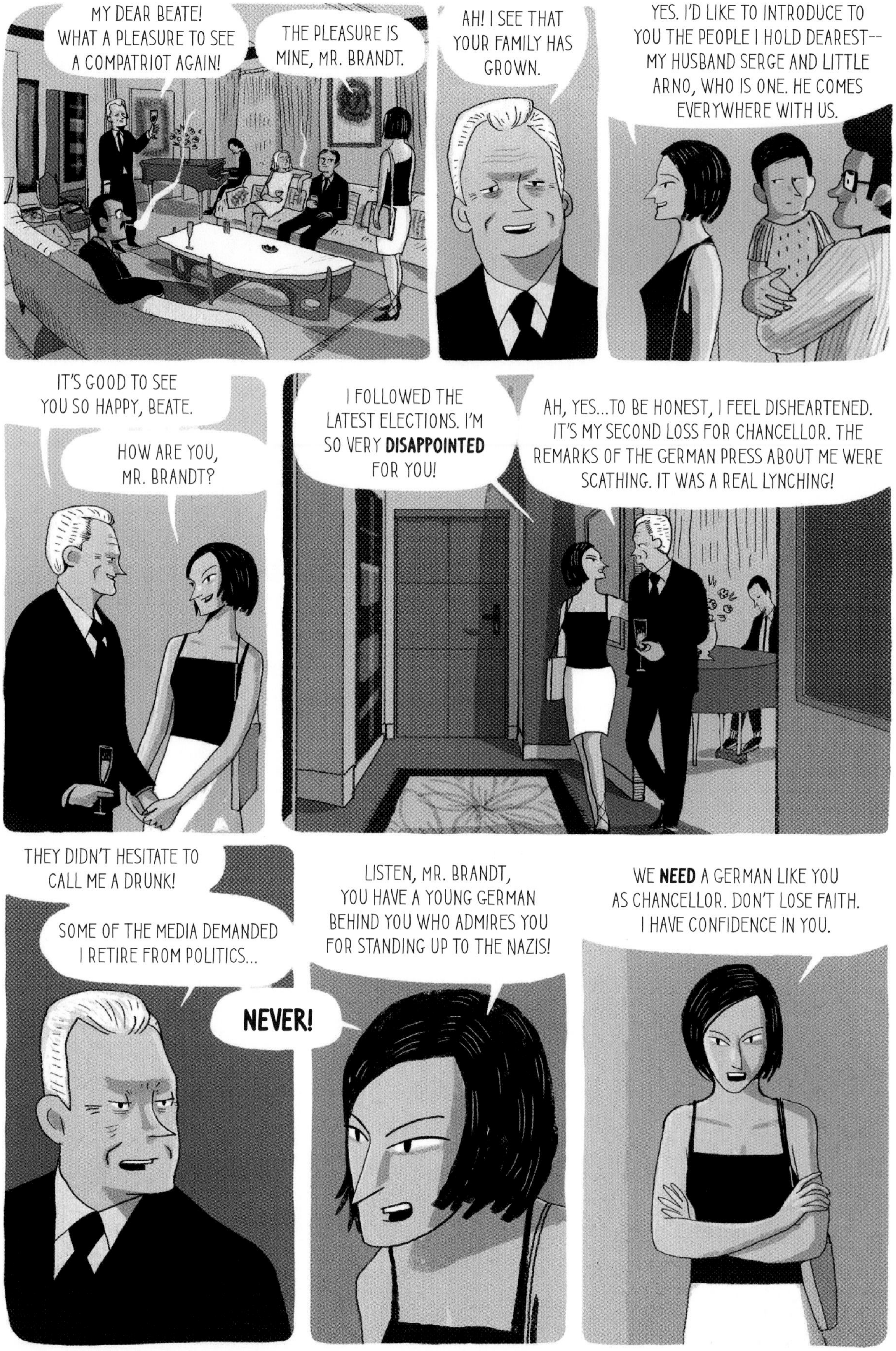
MY DEAR BEATE! WHAT A PLEASURE TO SEE A COMPATRIOT AGAIN!
THE PLEASURE IS MINE, MR. BRANDT.
AH! I SEE THAT YOUR FAMILY HAS GROWN.
YES. I'D LIKE TO INTRODUCE TO YOU THE PEOPLE I HOLD DEAREST-- MY HUSBAND SERGE AND LITTLE ARNO, WHO IS ONE. HE COMES EVERYWHERE WITH US.
IT'S GOOD TO SEE YOU SO HAPPY, BEATE.
HOW ARE YOU, MR. BRANDT?
I FOLLOWED THE LATEST ELECTIONS. I'M SO VERY **DISAPPOINTED** FOR YOU!
AH, YES...TO BE HONEST, I FEEL DISHEARTENED. IT'S MY SECOND LOSS FOR CHANCELLOR. THE REMARKS OF THE GERMAN PRESS ABOUT ME WERE SCATHING. IT WAS A REAL LYNCHING!
THEY DIDN'T HESITATE TO CALL ME A DRUNK!
SOME OF THE MEDIA DEMANDED I RETIRE FROM POLITICS...
NEVER!
LISTEN, MR. BRANDT, YOU HAVE A YOUNG GERMAN BEHIND YOU WHO ADMIRES YOU FOR STANDING UP TO THE NAZIS!
WE **NEED** A GERMAN LIKE YOU AS CHANCELLOR. DON'T LOSE FAITH. I HAVE CONFIDENCE IN YOU.

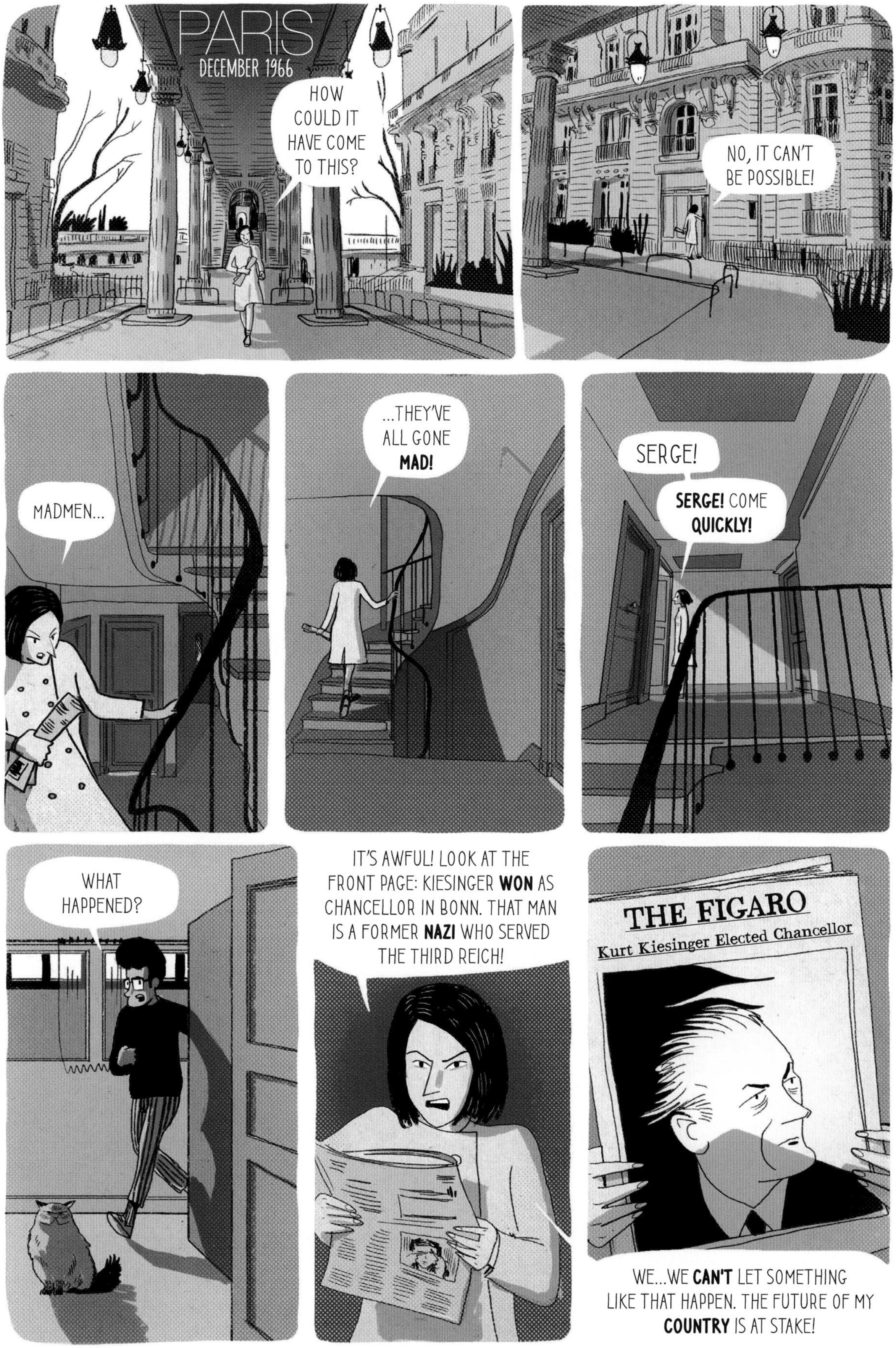
PARIS
DECEMBER 1966
HOW COULD IT HAVE COME TO THIS?
NO, IT CAN'T BE POSSIBLE!
MADMEN...
...THEY'VE ALL GONE **MAD!**
SERGE!
SERGE! COME **QUICKLY!**
WHAT HAPPENED?
IT'S AWFUL! LOOK AT THE FRONT PAGE: KIESINGER **WON** AS CHANCELLOR IN BONN. THAT MAN IS A FORMER **NAZI** WHO SERVED THE THIRD REICH!
THE FIGARO
Kurt Kiesinger Elected Chancellor
WE...WE **CAN'T** LET SOMETHING LIKE THAT HAPPEN. THE FUTURE OF MY **COUNTRY** IS AT STAKE!

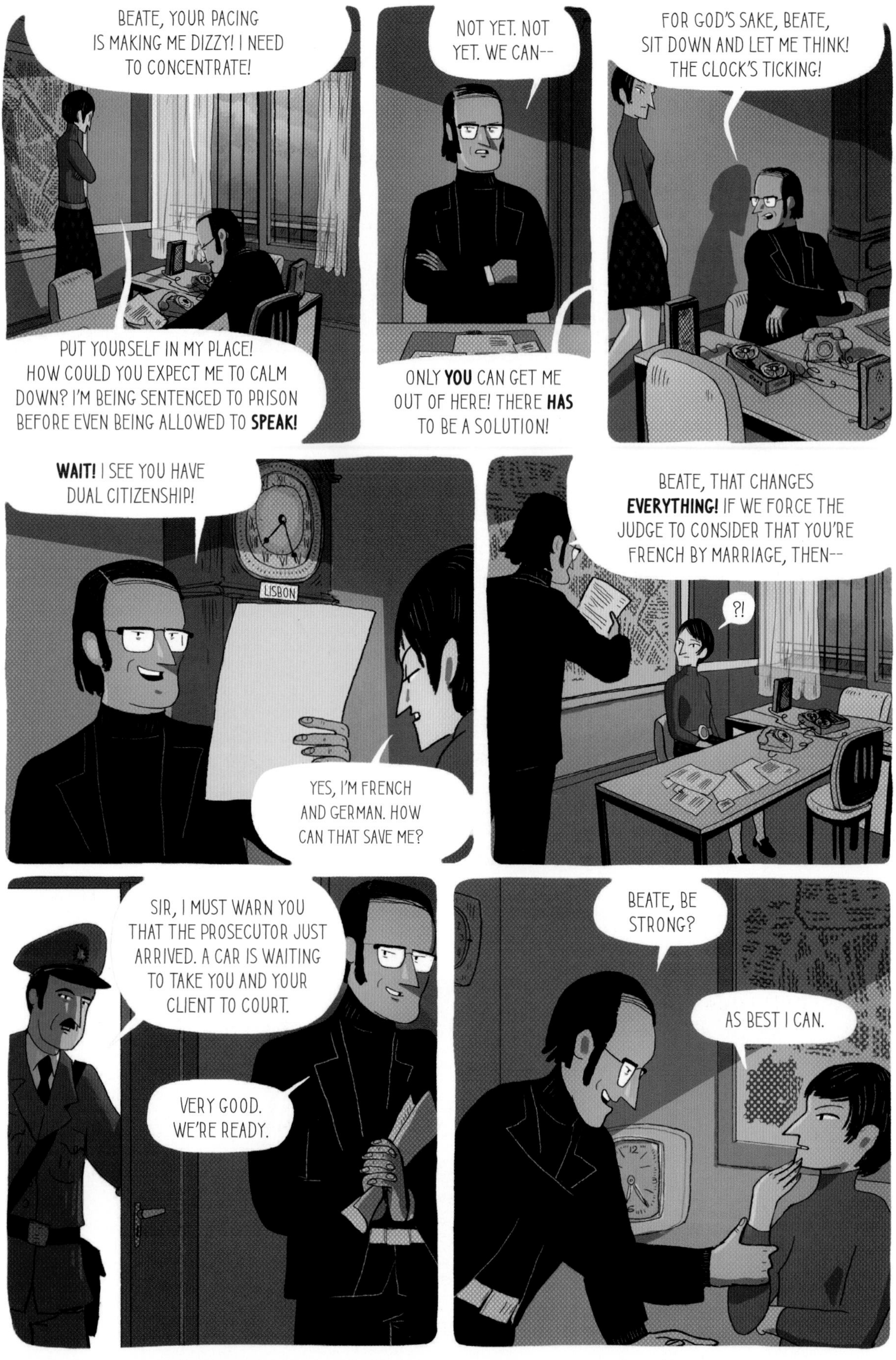
BEATE, YOUR PACING IS MAKING ME DIZZY! I NEED TO CONCENTRATE!
PUT YOURSELF IN MY PLACE! HOW COULD YOU EXPECT ME TO CALM DOWN? I'M BEING SENTENCED TO PRISON BEFORE EVEN BEING ALLOWED TO **SPEAK!**
NOT YET. NOT YET. WE CAN--
ONLY **YOU** CAN GET ME OUT OF HERE! THERE **HAS** TO BE A SOLUTION!
FOR GOD'S SAKE, BEATE, SIT DOWN AND LET ME THINK! THE CLOCK'S TICKING!
WAIT! I SEE YOU HAVE DUAL CITIZENSHIP!
LISBON
YES, I'M FRENCH AND GERMAN. HOW CAN THAT SAVE ME?
BEATE, THAT CHANGES **EVERYTHING!** IF WE FORCE THE JUDGE TO CONSIDER THAT YOU'RE FRENCH BY MARRIAGE, THEN--
?!
SIR, I MUST WARN YOU THAT THE PROSECUTOR JUST ARRIVED. A CAR IS WAITING TO TAKE YOU AND YOUR CLIENT TO COURT.
VERY GOOD. WE'RE READY.
BEATE, BE STRONG?
AS BEST I CAN.

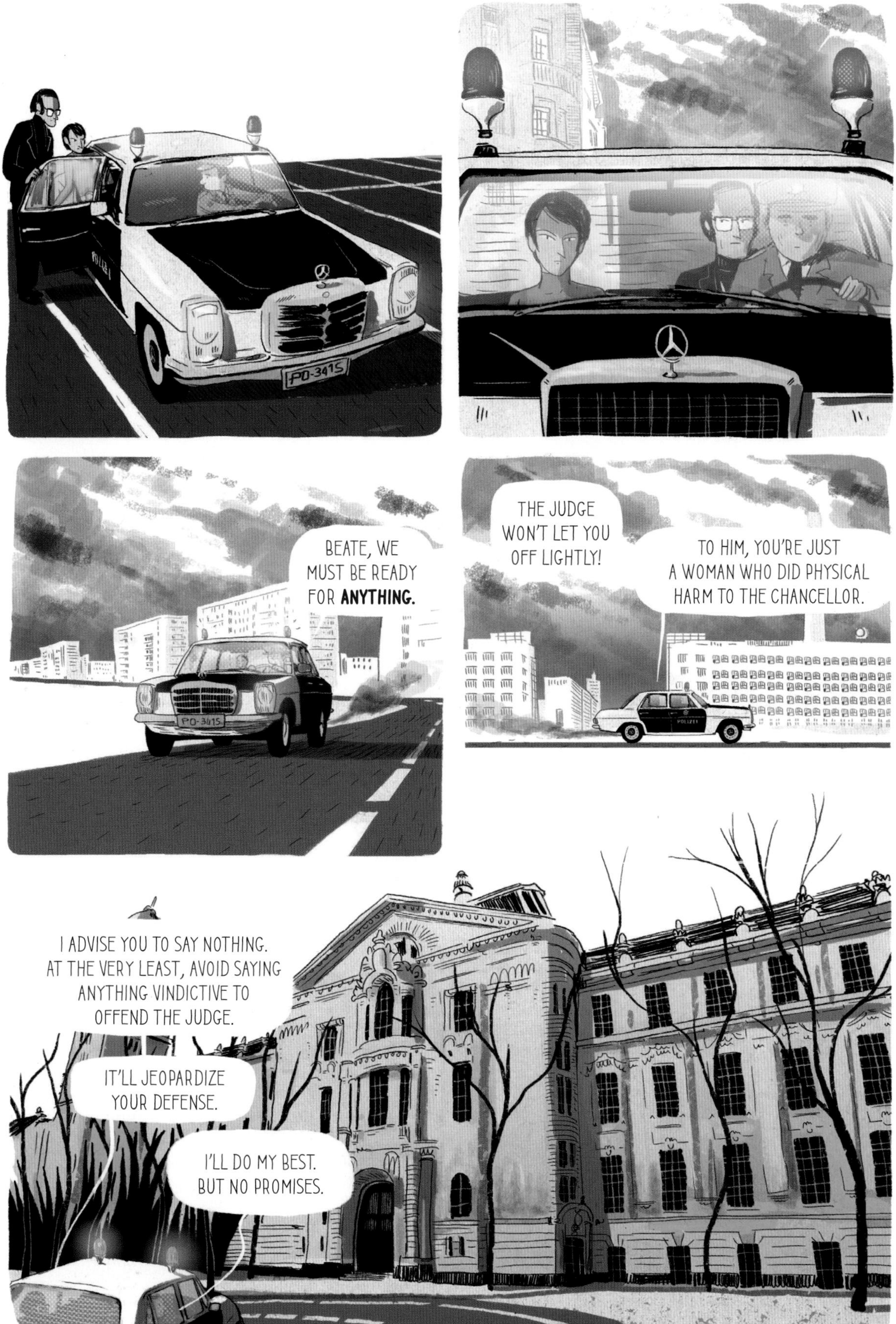
BEATE, WE MUST BE READY FOR **ANYTHING.**
THE JUDGE WON'T LET YOU OFF LIGHTLY!
TO HIM, YOU'RE JUST A WOMAN WHO DID PHYSICAL HARM TO THE CHANCELLOR.
I ADVISE YOU TO SAY NOTHING. AT THE VERY LEAST, AVOID SAYING ANYTHING VINDICTIVE TO OFFEND THE JUDGE.
IT'LL JEOPARDIZE YOUR DEFENSE.
I'LL DO MY BEST. BUT NO PROMISES.

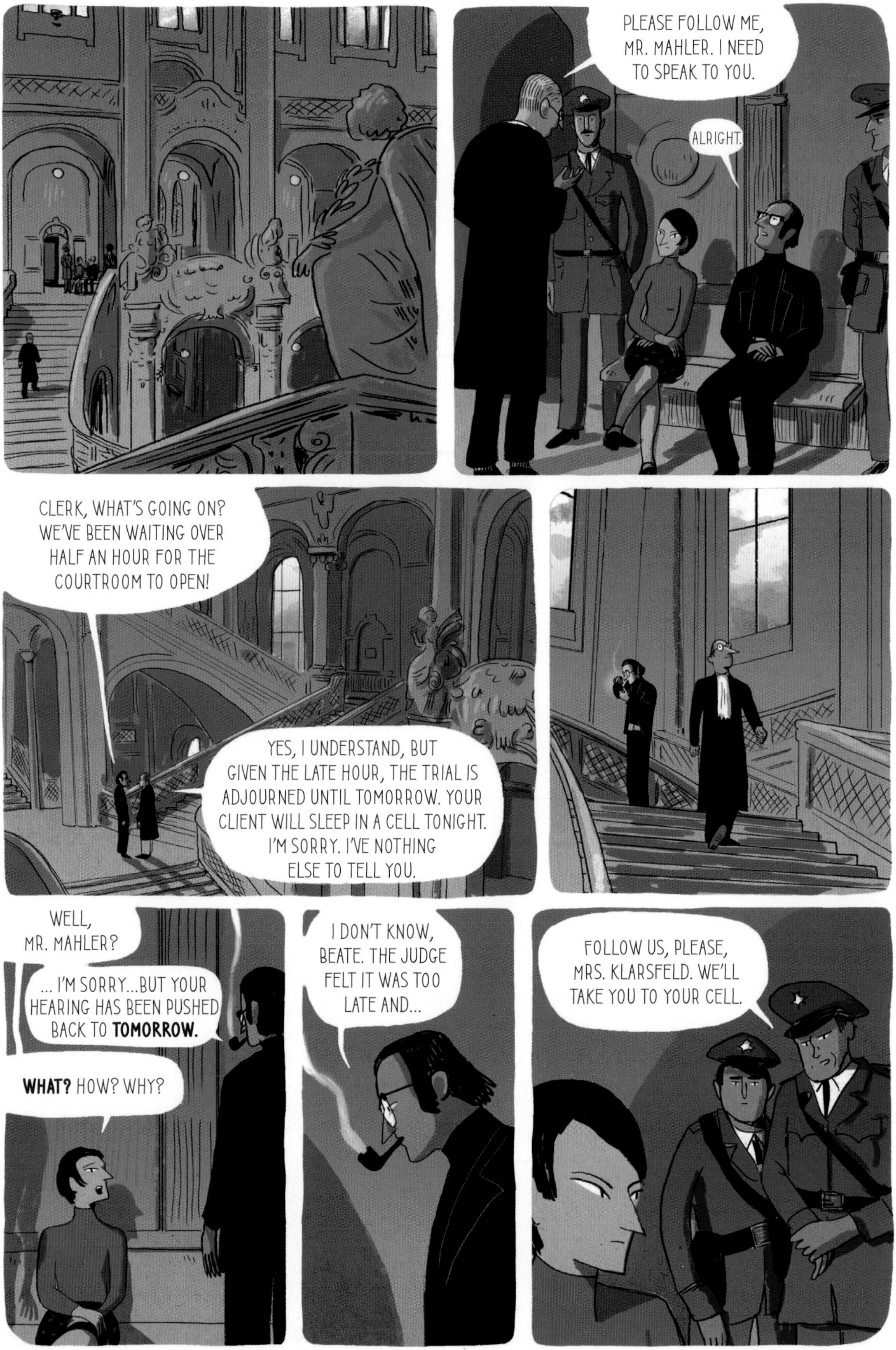
PLEASE FOLLOW ME, MR. MAHLER. I NEED TO SPEAK TO YOU.
ALRIGHT.
CLERK, WHAT'S GOING ON? WE'VE BEEN WAITING OVER HALF AN HOUR FOR THE COURTROOM TO OPEN!
YES, I UNDERSTAND, BUT GIVEN THE LATE HOUR, THE TRIAL IS ADJOURNED UNTIL TOMORROW. YOUR CLIENT WILL SLEEP IN A CELL TONIGHT. I'M SORRY. I'VE NOTHING ELSE TO TELL YOU.
WELL, MR. MAHLER?
... I'M SORRY...BUT YOUR HEARING HAS BEEN PUSHED BACK TO **TOMORROW.**
WHAT? HOW? WHY?
I DON'T KNOW, BEATE. THE JUDGE FELT IT WAS TOO LATE AND...
FOLLOW US, PLEASE, MRS. KLARSFELD. WE'LL TAKE YOU TO YOUR CELL.

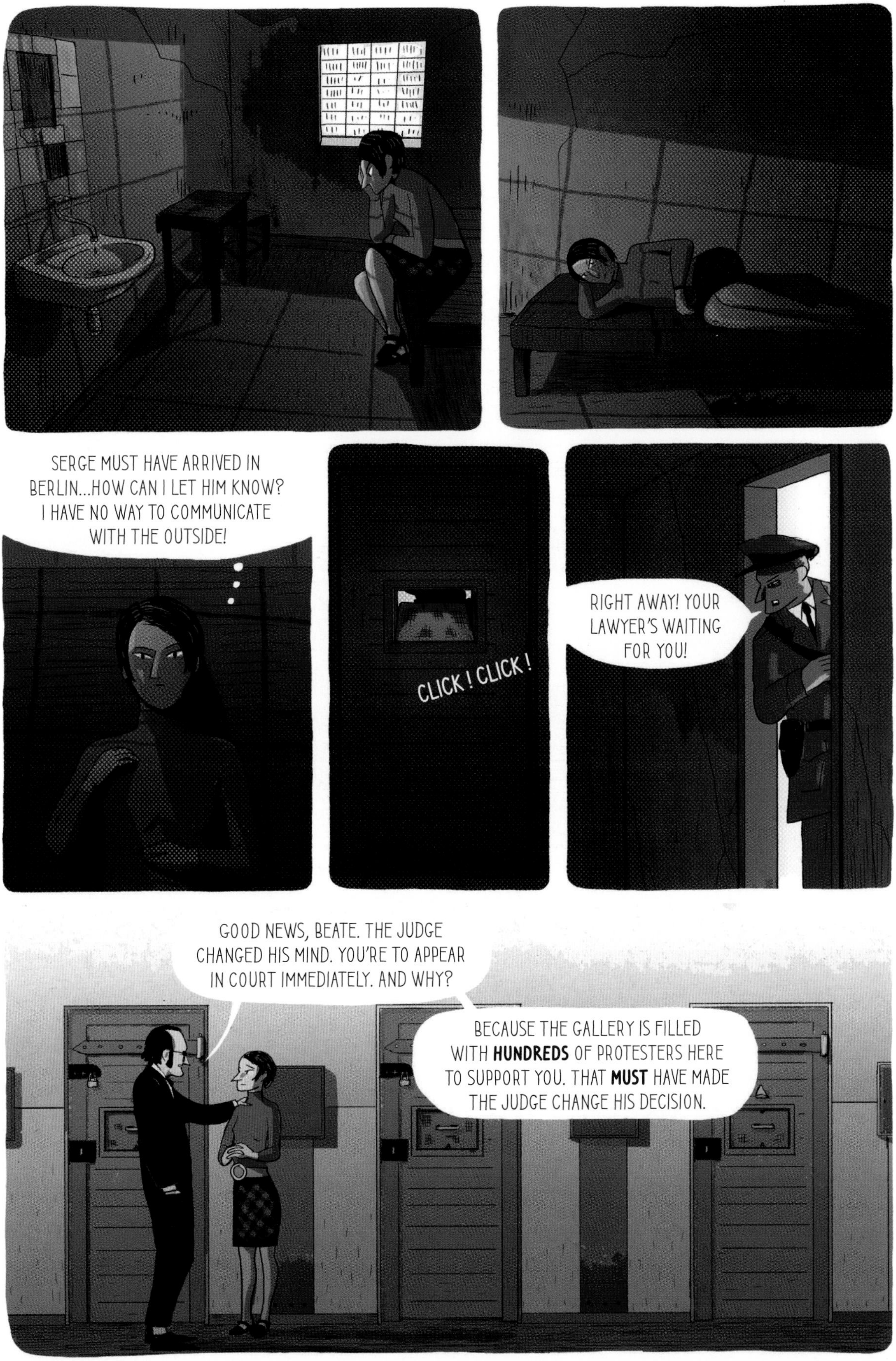
SERGE MUST HAVE ARRIVED IN BERLIN...HOW CAN I LET HIM KNOW? I HAVE NO WAY TO COMMUNICATE WITH THE OUTSIDE!
CLICK! CLICK!
RIGHT AWAY! YOUR LAWYER'S WAITING FOR YOU!
GOOD NEWS, BEATE. THE JUDGE CHANGED HIS MIND. YOU'RE TO APPEAR IN COURT IMMEDIATELY. AND WHY?
BECAUSE THE GALLERY IS FILLED WITH **HUNDREDS** OF PROTESTERS HERE TO SUPPORT YOU. THAT **MUST** HAVE MADE THE JUDGE CHANGE HIS DECISION.

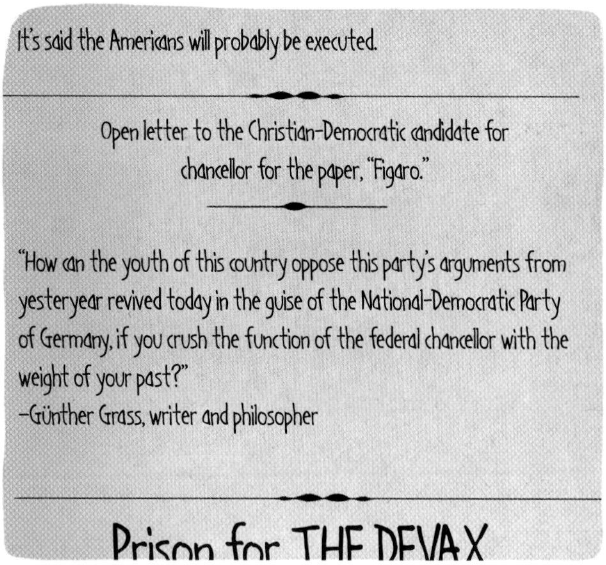

It's said the Americans will probably be executed.

Open letter to the Christian-Democratic candidate for chancellor for the paper, "Figaro."

"How can the youth of this country oppose this party's arguments from yesteryear revived today in the guise of the National-Democratic Party of Germany, if you crush the function of the federal chancellor with the weight of your past?"
–Günther Grass, writer and philosopher

Prison for THE DEVAX

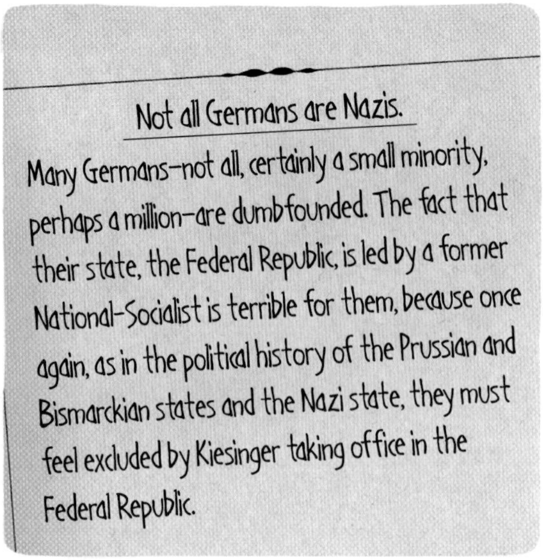

Not all Germans are Nazis.

Many Germans–not all, certainly a small minority, perhaps a million–are dumbfounded. The fact that their state, the Federal Republic, is led by a former National-Socialist is terrible for them, because once again, as in the political history of the Prussian and Bismarckian states and the Nazi state, they must feel excluded by Kiesinger taking office in the Federal Republic.

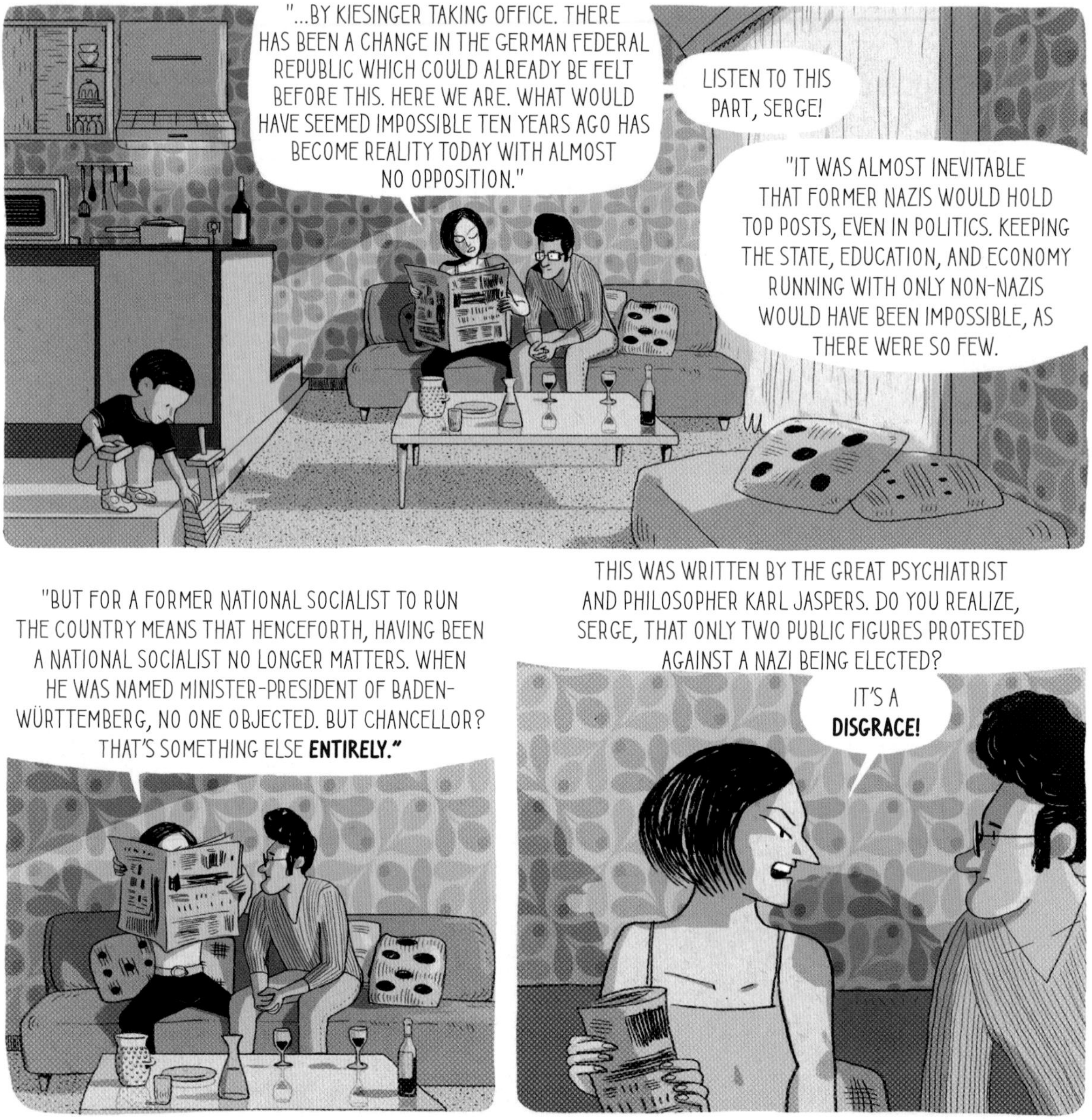
"...BY KIESINGER TAKING OFFICE. THERE HAS BEEN A CHANGE IN THE GERMAN FEDERAL REPUBLIC WHICH COULD ALREADY BE FELT BEFORE THIS. HERE WE ARE. WHAT WOULD HAVE SEEMED IMPOSSIBLE TEN YEARS AGO HAS BECOME REALITY TODAY WITH ALMOST NO OPPOSITION."
LISTEN TO THIS PART, SERGE!
"IT WAS ALMOST INEVITABLE THAT FORMER NAZIS WOULD HOLD TOP POSTS, EVEN IN POLITICS. KEEPING THE STATE, EDUCATION, AND ECONOMY RUNNING WITH ONLY NON-NAZIS WOULD HAVE BEEN IMPOSSIBLE, AS THERE WERE SO FEW.
"BUT FOR A FORMER NATIONAL SOCIALIST TO RUN THE COUNTRY MEANS THAT HENCEFORTH, HAVING BEEN A NATIONAL SOCIALIST NO LONGER MATTERS. WHEN HE WAS NAMED MINISTER-PRESIDENT OF BADEN-WÜRTTEMBERG, NO ONE OBJECTED. BUT CHANCELLOR? THAT'S SOMETHING ELSE **ENTIRELY.**"
THIS WAS WRITTEN BY THE GREAT PSYCHIATRIST AND PHILOSOPHER KARL JASPERS. DO YOU REALIZE, SERGE, THAT ONLY TWO PUBLIC FIGURES PROTESTED AGAINST A NAZI BEING ELECTED?
IT'S A **DISGRACE!**

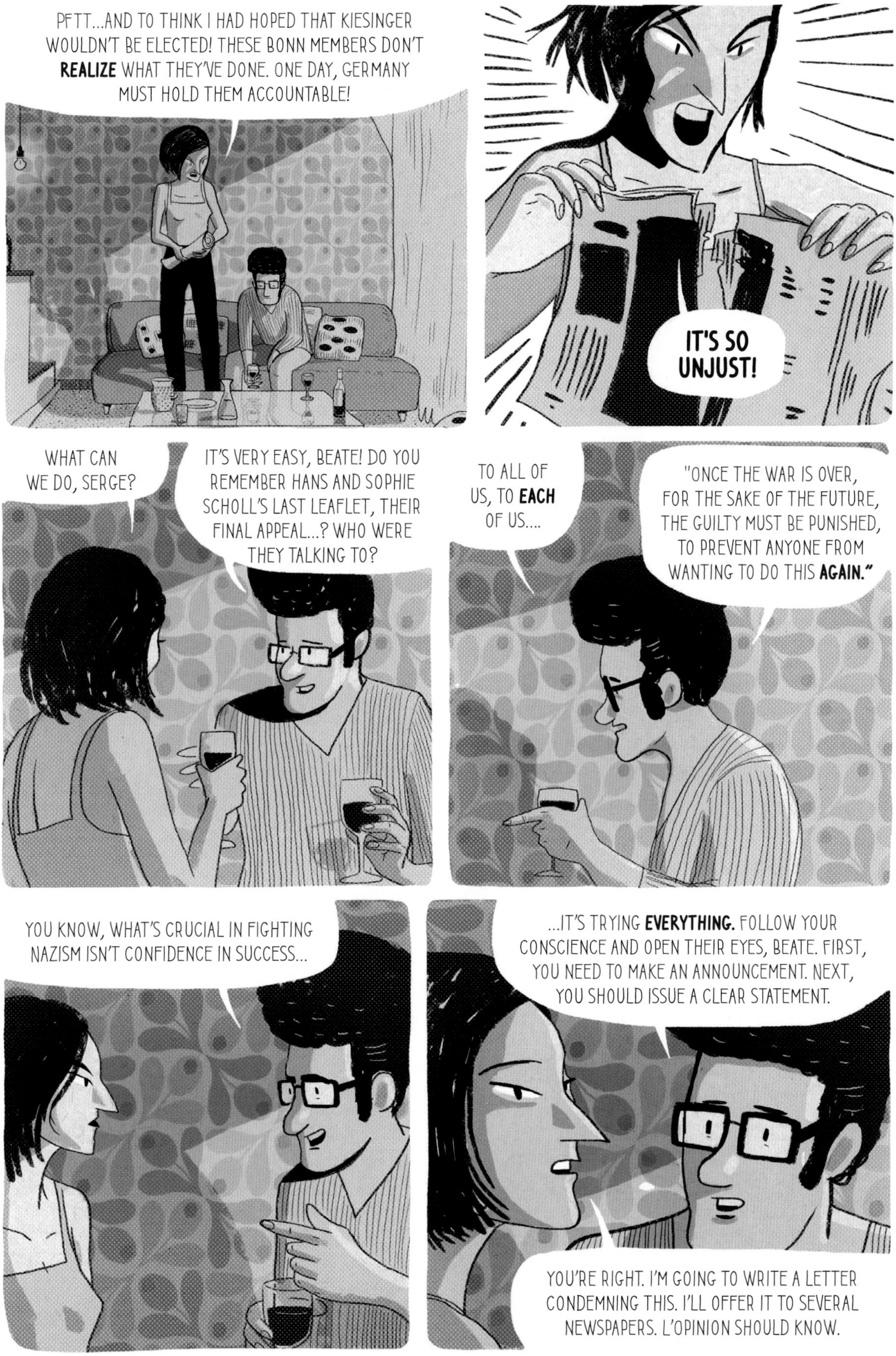
PFTT...AND TO THINK I HAD HOPED THAT KIESINGER WOULDN'T BE ELECTED! THESE BONN MEMBERS DON'T **REALIZE** WHAT THEY'VE DONE. ONE DAY, GERMANY MUST HOLD THEM ACCOUNTABLE!
IT'S SO UNJUST!
WHAT CAN WE DO, SERGE?
IT'S VERY EASY, BEATE! DO YOU REMEMBER HANS AND SOPHIE SCHOLL'S LAST LEAFLET, THEIR FINAL APPEAL...? WHO WERE THEY TALKING TO?
TO ALL OF US, TO **EACH** OF US....
"ONCE THE WAR IS OVER, FOR THE SAKE OF THE FUTURE, THE GUILTY MUST BE PUNISHED, TO PREVENT ANYONE FROM WANTING TO DO THIS **AGAIN.**"
YOU KNOW, WHAT'S CRUCIAL IN FIGHTING NAZISM ISN'T CONFIDENCE IN SUCCESS...
...IT'S TRYING **EVERYTHING.** FOLLOW YOUR CONSCIENCE AND OPEN THEIR EYES, BEATE. FIRST, YOU NEED TO MAKE AN ANNOUNCEMENT. NEXT, YOU SHOULD ISSUE A CLEAR STATEMENT.
YOU'RE RIGHT. I'M GOING TO WRITE A LETTER CONDEMNING THIS. I'LL OFFER IT TO SEVERAL NEWSPAPERS. L'OPINION SHOULD KNOW.

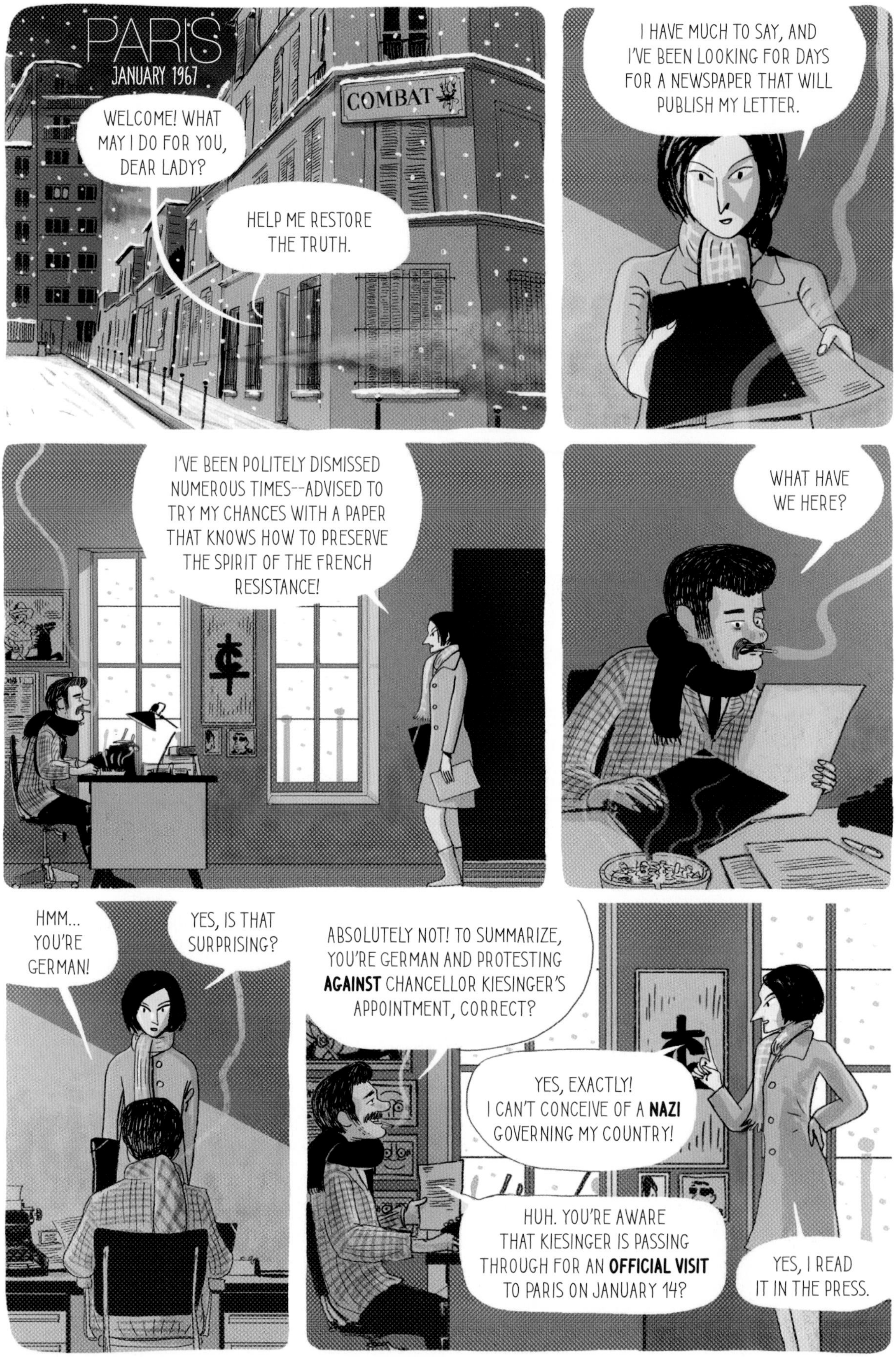
PARIS
JANUARY 1967
COMBAT
WELCOME! WHAT MAY I DO FOR YOU, DEAR LADY?
HELP ME RESTORE THE TRUTH.
I HAVE MUCH TO SAY, AND I'VE BEEN LOOKING FOR DAYS FOR A NEWSPAPER THAT WILL PUBLISH MY LETTER.
I'VE BEEN POLITELY DISMISSED NUMEROUS TIMES--ADVISED TO TRY MY CHANCES WITH A PAPER THAT KNOWS HOW TO PRESERVE THE SPIRIT OF THE FRENCH RESISTANCE!
WHAT HAVE WE HERE?
HMM... YOU'RE GERMAN!
YES, IS THAT SURPRISING?
ABSOLUTELY NOT! TO SUMMARIZE, YOU'RE GERMAN AND PROTESTING **AGAINST** CHANCELLOR KIESINGER'S APPOINTMENT, CORRECT?
YES, EXACTLY! I CAN'T CONCEIVE OF A **NAZI** GOVERNING MY COUNTRY!
HUH. YOU'RE AWARE THAT KIESINGER IS PASSING THROUGH FOR AN **OFFICIAL VISIT** TO PARIS ON JANUARY 14?
YES, I READ IT IN THE PRESS.

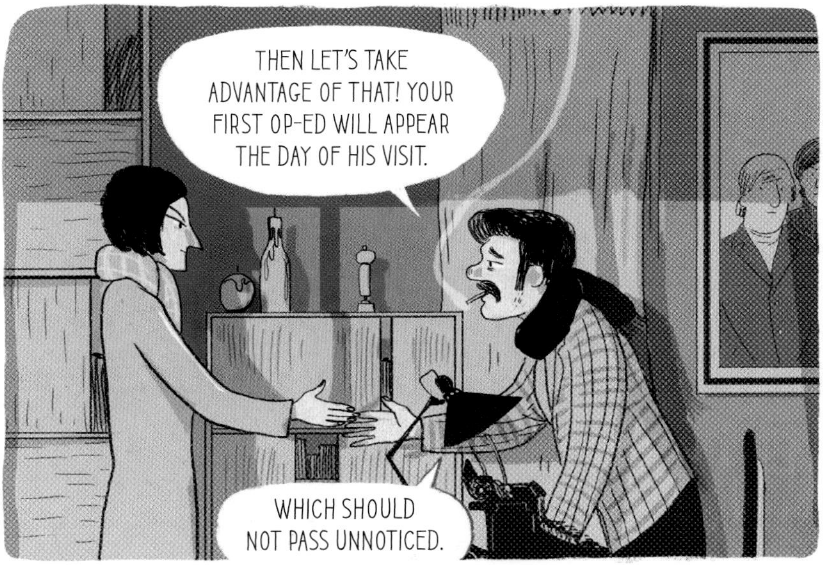
THEN LET'S TAKE ADVANTAGE OF THAT! YOUR FIRST OP-ED WILL APPEAR THE DAY OF HIS VISIT.
WHICH SHOULD NOT PASS UNNOTICED.

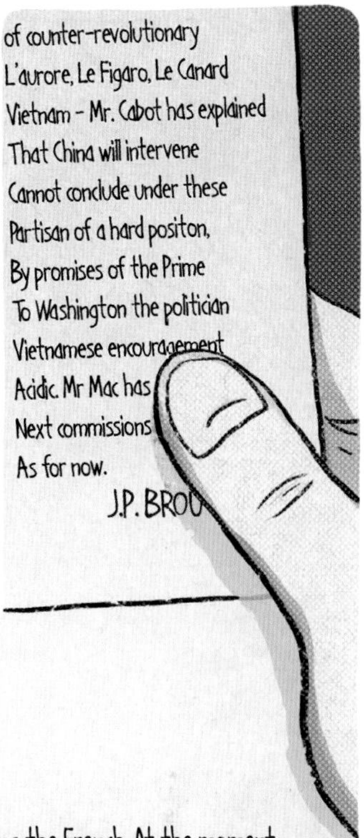
of counter-revolutionary
L'aurore, Le Figaro, Le Canard
Vietnam - Mr. Cabot has explained
That China will intervene
Cannot conclude under these
Partisan of a hard positon,
By promises of the Prime
To Washington the politician
Vietnamese encouragement
Acidic. Mr Mac has
Next commissions
As for now.
J.P. BROU

Opinion Column

"Willy Brandt has always gone against the tide..."

Official Germany has many faces: Willy Brandt's is the only one that won't arouse suspicion among the French. At the moment when Germany would rather recognize itself in the character of Mr. Kiesinger, fate grants, in counterpart, to Germany the chance of the accession of Willy Brandt to a prominent position in the government. Kiesinger has the opportunity to reassure his fellow older citizens.

He has always worked in concert with the German people. Like him, they were wrong for more than ten years, about adhering to the Nazi political party. Willy Brandt scares the Germans more than he attracts them, even if young people are looking up to him more and more. Because Willy Brandt always went against the current when it was necessary. He was wrong to have always been right in the great choices of his life and to have indissolubly linked morality to politics. We also blame Willy Brandt for his courage, and it took a German who was neither Jewish nor Communist, but who was a free German, to leave Germany whose troubled passions were embodied in Hitler.

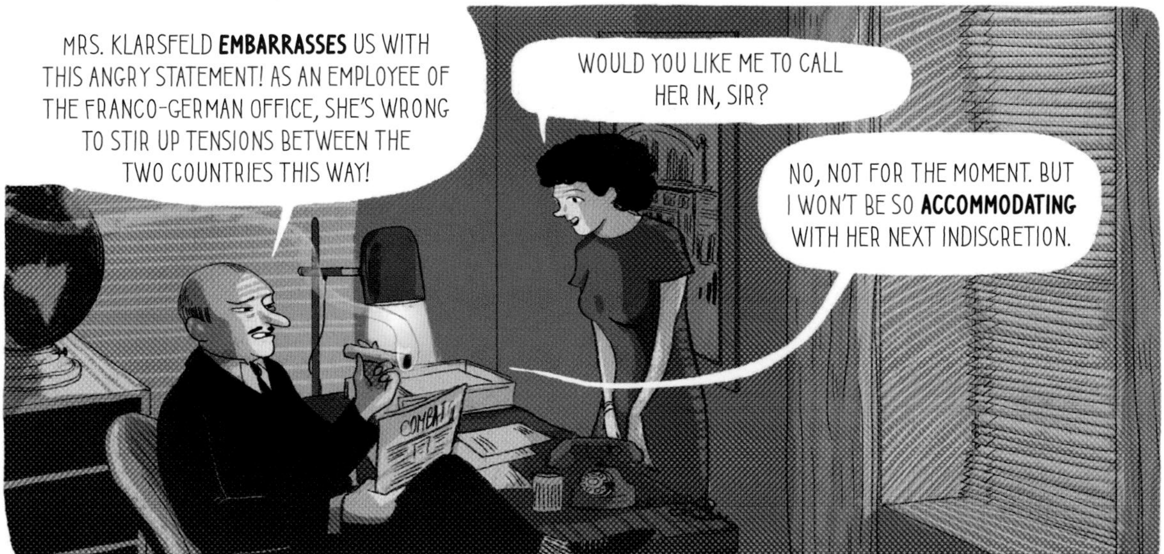
MRS. KLARSFELD EMBARRASSES US WITH THIS ANGRY STATEMENT! AS AN EMPLOYEE OF THE FRANCO-GERMAN OFFICE, SHE'S WRONG TO STIR UP TENSIONS BETWEEN THE TWO COUNTRIES THIS WAY!
WOULD YOU LIKE ME TO CALL HER IN, SIR?
NO, NOT FOR THE MOMENT. BUT I WON'T BE SO ACCOMMODATING WITH HER NEXT INDISCRETION.
COMBAT

TAP TAP TAP TAP TAP
TAP TAP TAP TAP TAP
TAP TAP TAP TAP TAP TAP
TAP TAP
TAP TAP TAP

"WHY WE MUST BET ON WILLY BRANDT." WITH A SLOGAN LIKE THAT, YOU'LL MAKE YOURSELF UNPOPULAR, SWEETHEART!

I NEED A **HARD-HITTING** TITLE FOR MY SECOND OP-ED!

HMM...READERS WILL THINK YOU'RE OBSESSED WITH THAT MAN! NOT TO MENTION, THERE'S A GOOD CHANCE THE FGYA* WON'T APPROVE OF THIS NEW ANNOUNCEMENT.

TOO BAD, SERGE. THEY CAN THROW ME OUT--I'LL RUN THAT RISK! I NEITHER HATE KIESINGER NOR DO I HAVE A MORBID FASCINATION WITH THE PAST...

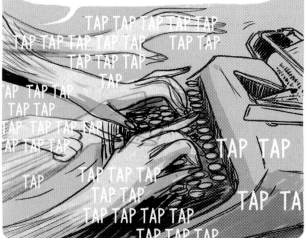

...BUT THERE'S A FUTURE FOR GERMANY WITHIN REACH. WILLY BRANDT IS THE ONLY ONE WHO WILL SAVE US FROM THE PAST'S **PUTRID YOKE.**

TAP TAP TAP TAP TAP
TAP TAP TAP TAP TAP TAP TAP
TAP TAP TAP
TAP
TAP TAP TAP
TAP TAP
TAP TAP TAP TAP
AP TAP TAP
TAP TAP TAP
TAP
TAP TAP TAP
TAP TAP
TAP TAP

"AS A GERMAN, I DEPLORE MR. KIESINGER'S ACCESSION AS CHANCELLOR. A FORMER MEMBER OF THE NAZI PARTY--EVEN IF ONLY OUT OF OPPORTUNISM--IN CHARGE OF GERMAN AFFAIRS? MIGHT AS WELL SAY THAT IT'S PUBLIC ABSOLUTION FOR A CERTAIN ERA AND ATTITUDE..."

TAP
TAP
TAP

TAP TAP
TAP TAP
TAP
TAP TAP

*FRENCH-GERMAN YOUTH OFFICE

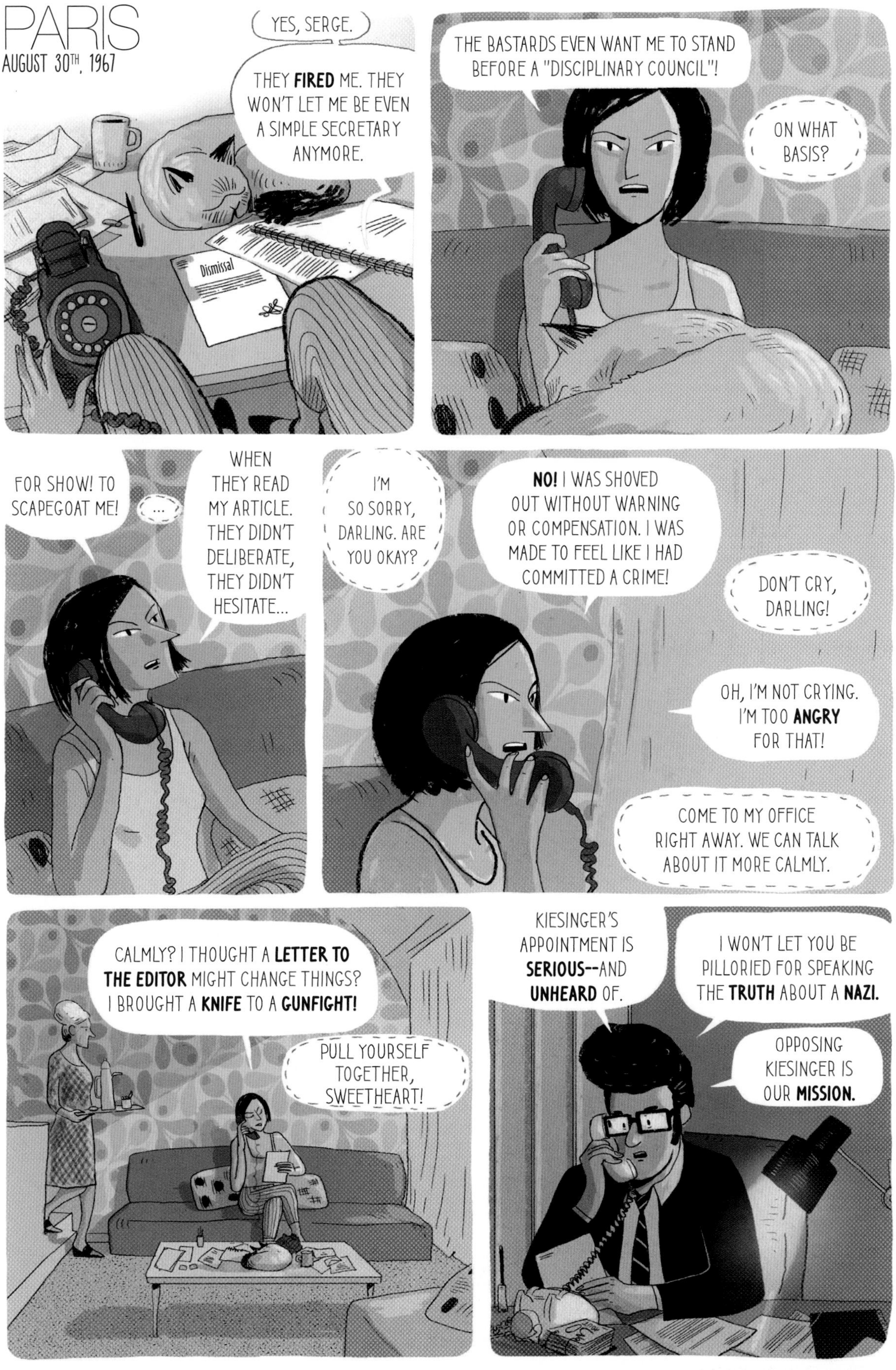
PARIS
AUGUST 30TH, 1967
YES, SERGE.
THEY FIRED ME. THEY WON'T LET ME BE EVEN A SIMPLE SECRETARY ANYMORE.
Dismissal
THE BASTARDS EVEN WANT ME TO STAND BEFORE A "DISCIPLINARY COUNCIL"!
ON WHAT BASIS?
FOR SHOW! TO SCAPEGOAT ME!
...
WHEN THEY READ MY ARTICLE. THEY DIDN'T DELIBERATE, THEY DIDN'T HESITATE...
I'M SO SORRY, DARLING. ARE YOU OKAY?
NO! I WAS SHOVED OUT WITHOUT WARNING OR COMPENSATION. I WAS MADE TO FEEL LIKE I HAD COMMITTED A CRIME!
DON'T CRY, DARLING!
OH, I'M NOT CRYING. I'M TOO ANGRY FOR THAT!
COME TO MY OFFICE RIGHT AWAY. WE CAN TALK ABOUT IT MORE CALMLY.
CALMLY? I THOUGHT A LETTER TO THE EDITOR MIGHT CHANGE THINGS? I BROUGHT A KNIFE TO A GUNFIGHT!
PULL YOURSELF TOGETHER, SWEETHEART!
KIESINGER'S APPOINTMENT IS SERIOUS--AND UNHEARD OF.
I WON'T LET YOU BE PILLORIED FOR SPEAKING THE TRUTH ABOUT A NAZI.
OPPOSING KIESINGER IS OUR MISSION.

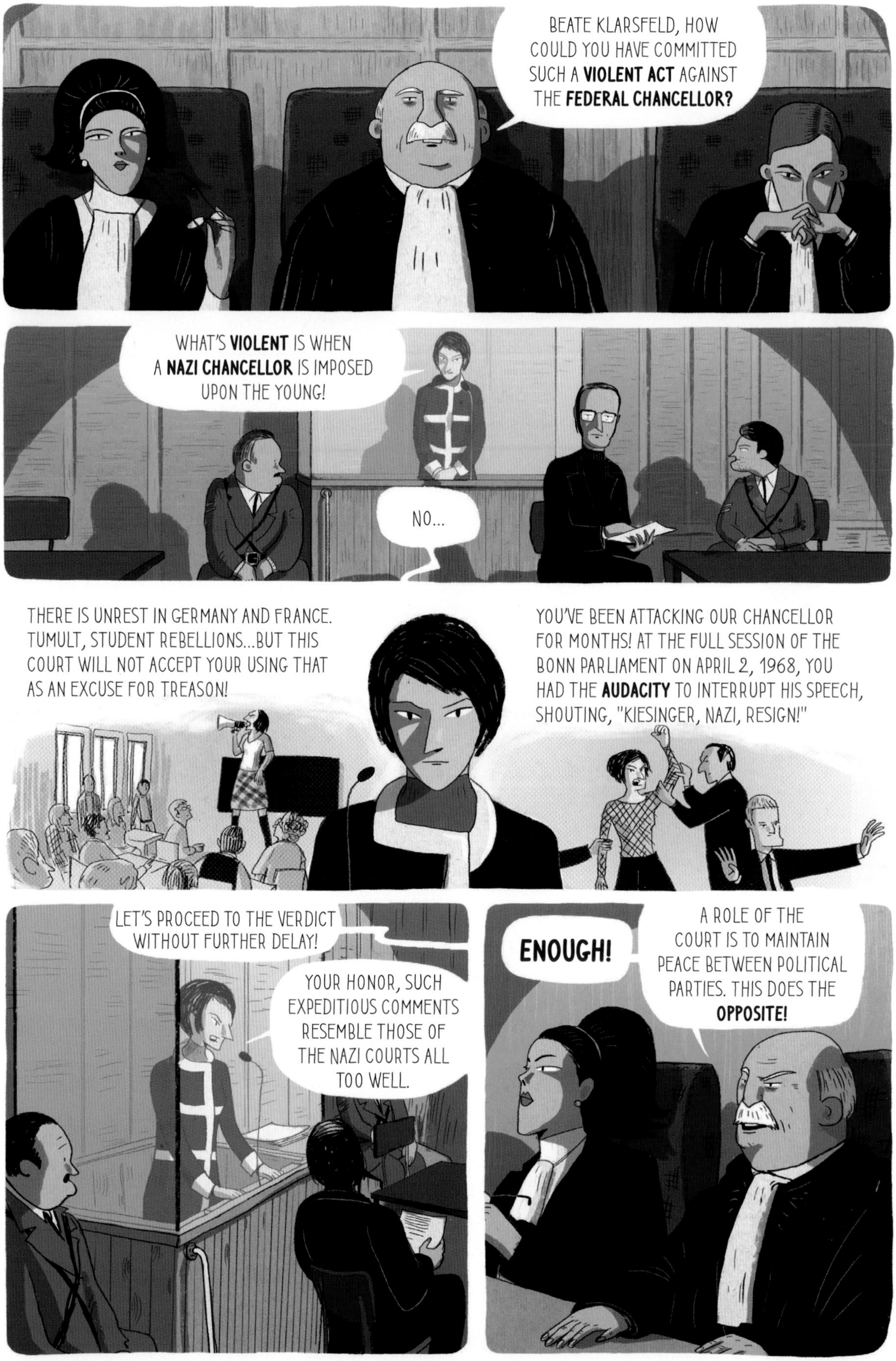

BEATE KLARSFELD, HOW COULD YOU HAVE COMMITTED SUCH A **VIOLENT ACT** AGAINST THE **FEDERAL CHANCELLOR?**
WHAT'S **VIOLENT** IS WHEN A **NAZI CHANCELLOR** IS IMPOSED UPON THE YOUNG!
NO...
THERE IS UNREST IN GERMANY AND FRANCE. TUMULT, STUDENT REBELLIONS...BUT THIS COURT WILL NOT ACCEPT YOUR USING THAT AS AN EXCUSE FOR TREASON!
YOU'VE BEEN ATTACKING OUR CHANCELLOR FOR MONTHS! AT THE FULL SESSION OF THE BONN PARLIAMENT ON APRIL 2, 1968, YOU HAD THE **AUDACITY** TO INTERRUPT HIS SPEECH, SHOUTING, "KIESINGER, NAZI, RESIGN!"
LET'S PROCEED TO THE VERDICT WITHOUT FURTHER DELAY!
YOUR HONOR, SUCH EXPEDITIOUS COMMENTS RESEMBLE THOSE OF THE NAZI COURTS ALL TOO WELL.
ENOUGH!
A ROLE OF THE COURT IS TO MAINTAIN PEACE BETWEEN POLITICAL PARTIES. THIS DOES THE **OPPOSITE!**

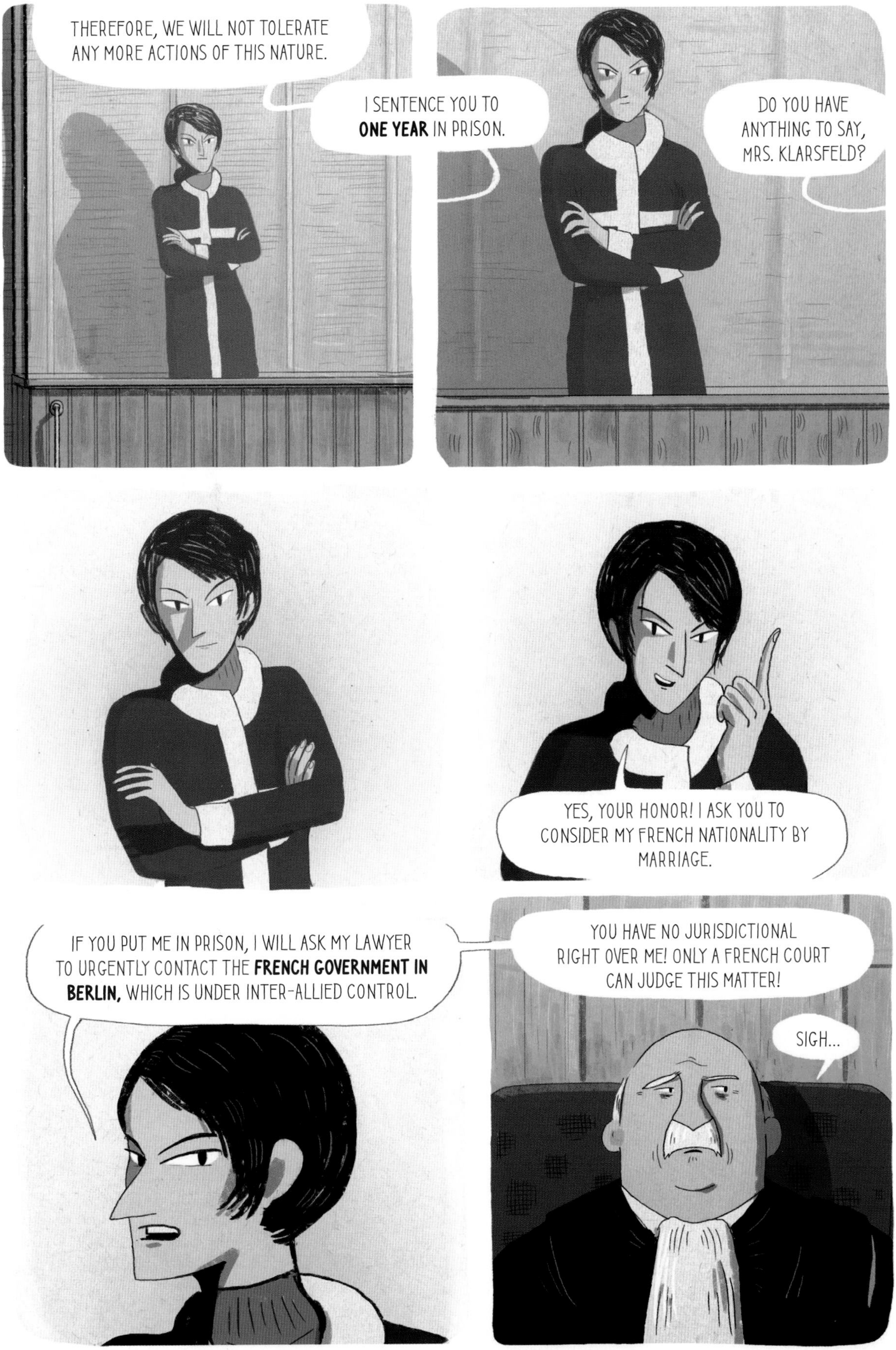
THEREFORE, WE WILL NOT TOLERATE ANY MORE ACTIONS OF THIS NATURE.
I SENTENCE YOU TO **ONE YEAR** IN PRISON.
DO YOU HAVE ANYTHING TO SAY, MRS. KLARSFELD?
YES, YOUR HONOR! I ASK YOU TO CONSIDER MY FRENCH NATIONALITY BY MARRIAGE.
IF YOU PUT ME IN PRISON, I WILL ASK MY LAWYER TO URGENTLY CONTACT THE **FRENCH GOVERNMENT IN BERLIN,** WHICH IS UNDER INTER-ALLIED CONTROL.
YOU HAVE NO JURISDICTIONAL RIGHT OVER ME! ONLY A FRENCH COURT CAN JUDGE THIS MATTER!
SIGH...

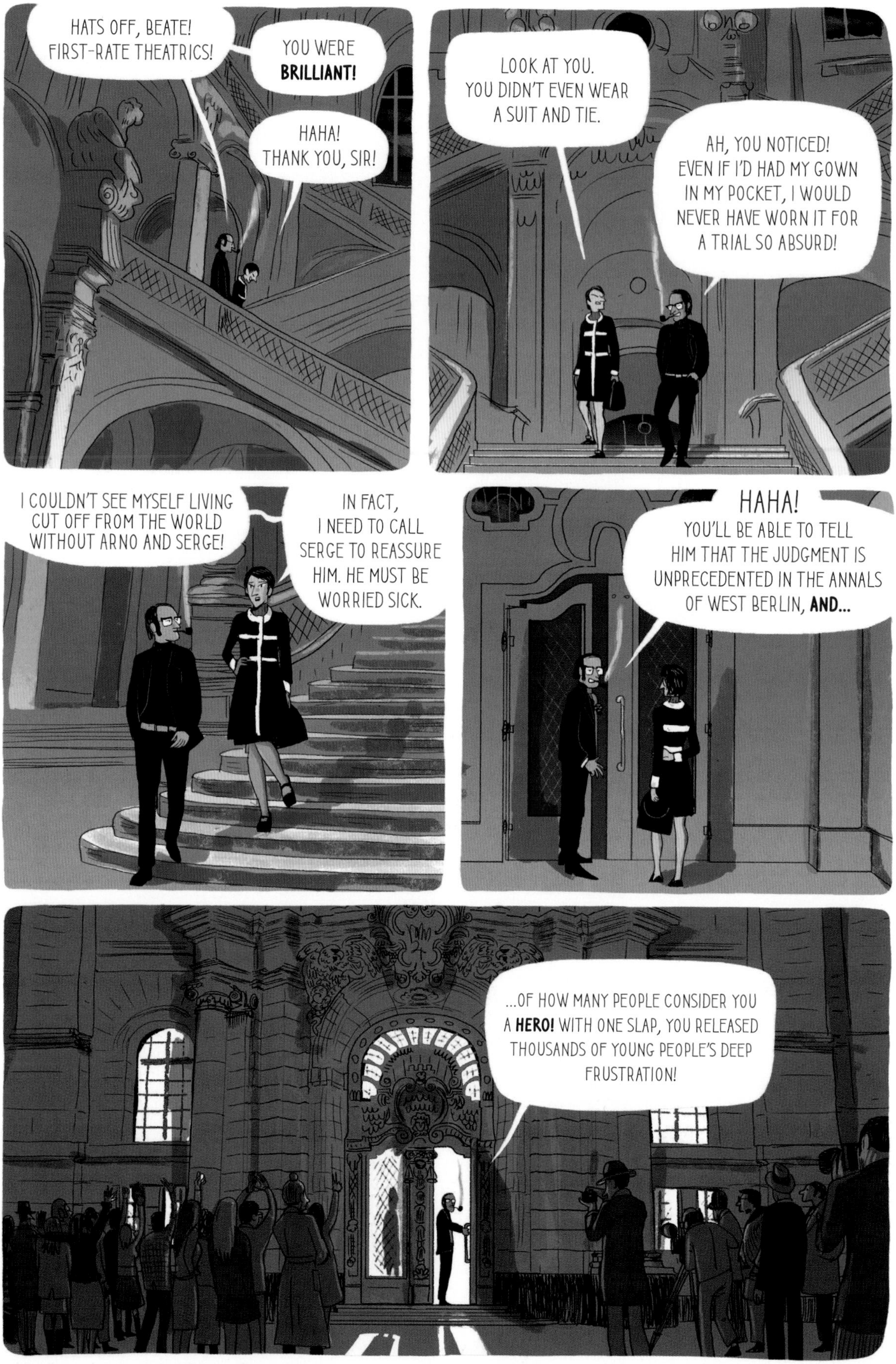
HATS OFF, BEATE! FIRST-RATE THEATRICS!
YOU WERE **BRILLIANT!**
HAHA! THANK YOU, SIR!
LOOK AT YOU. YOU DIDN'T EVEN WEAR A SUIT AND TIE.
AH, YOU NOTICED! EVEN IF I'D HAD MY GOWN IN MY POCKET, I WOULD NEVER HAVE WORN IT FOR A TRIAL SO ABSURD!
I COULDN'T SEE MYSELF LIVING CUT OFF FROM THE WORLD WITHOUT ARNO AND SERGE!
IN FACT, I NEED TO CALL SERGE TO REASSURE HIM. HE MUST BE WORRIED SICK.
HAHA! YOU'LL BE ABLE TO TELL HIM THAT THE JUDGMENT IS UNPRECEDENTED IN THE ANNALS OF WEST BERLIN, **AND...**
...OF HOW MANY PEOPLE CONSIDER YOU A **HERO!** WITH ONE SLAP, YOU RELEASED THOUSANDS OF YOUNG PEOPLE'S DEEP FRUSTRATION!

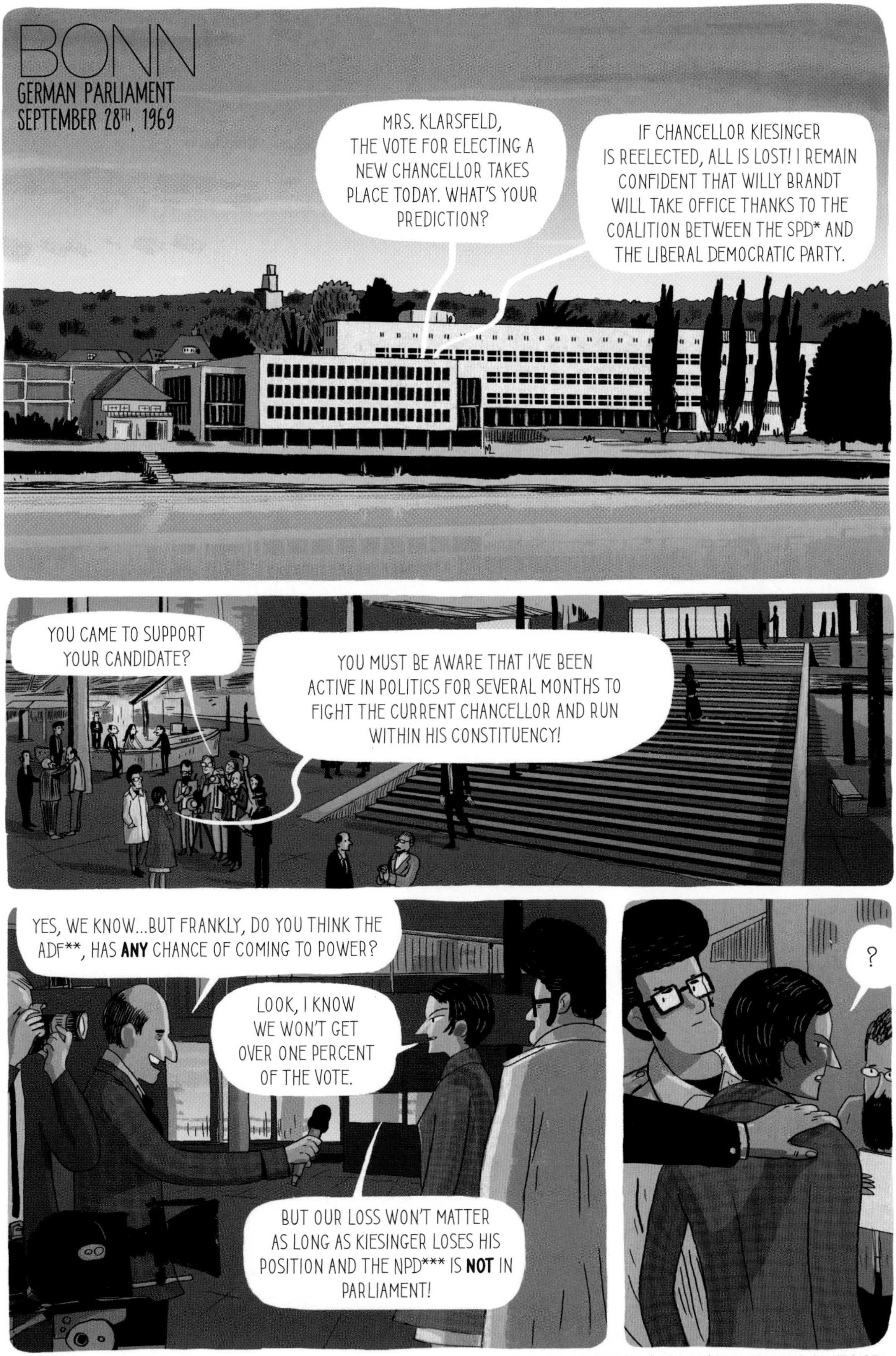
BONN
GERMAN PARLIAMENT
SEPTEMBER 28TH, 1969
MRS. KLARSFELD, THE VOTE FOR ELECTING A NEW CHANCELLOR TAKES PLACE TODAY. WHAT'S YOUR PREDICTION?
IF CHANCELLOR KIESINGER IS REELECTED, ALL IS LOST! I REMAIN CONFIDENT THAT WILLY BRANDT WILL TAKE OFFICE THANKS TO THE COALITION BETWEEN THE SPD* AND THE LIBERAL DEMOCRATIC PARTY.
YOU CAME TO SUPPORT YOUR CANDIDATE?
YOU MUST BE AWARE THAT I'VE BEEN ACTIVE IN POLITICS FOR SEVERAL MONTHS TO FIGHT THE CURRENT CHANCELLOR AND RUN WITHIN HIS CONSTITUENCY!
YES, WE KNOW...BUT FRANKLY, DO YOU THINK THE ADF**, HAS **ANY** CHANCE OF COMING TO POWER?
LOOK, I KNOW WE WON'T GET OVER ONE PERCENT OF THE VOTE.
BUT OUR LOSS WON'T MATTER AS LONG AS KIESINGER LOSES HIS POSITION AND THE NPD*** IS **NOT** IN PARLIAMENT!
?

*SOCIAL DEMOCRATIC PARTY **ACTION OF DEMOCRATIC PROGRESS PARTY (FAR LEFT) ***GERMAN FAR-RIGHT PARTY

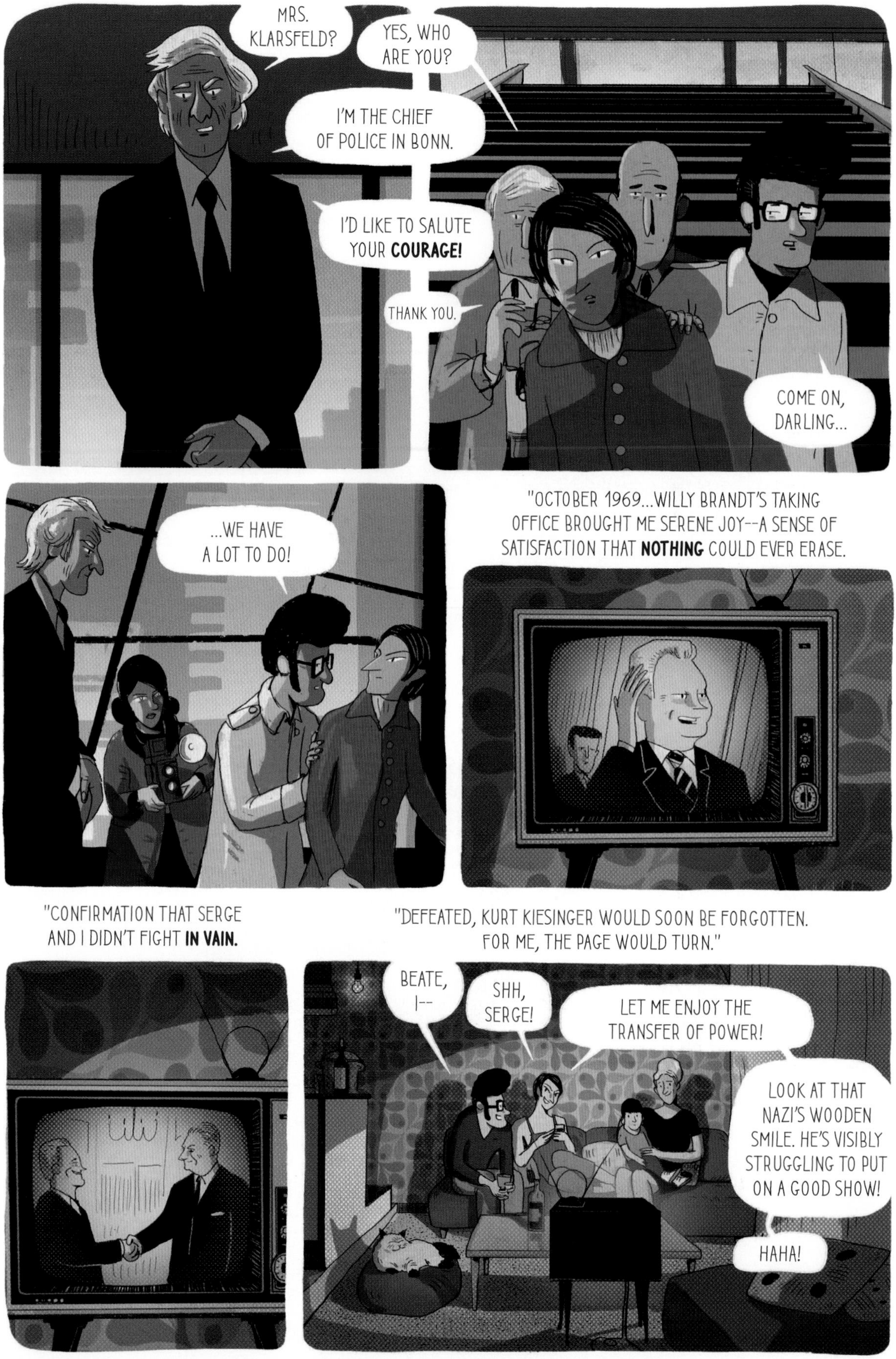

MRS. KLARSFELD?
YES, WHO ARE YOU?
I'M THE CHIEF OF POLICE IN BONN.
I'D LIKE TO SALUTE YOUR **COURAGE!**
THANK YOU.
COME ON, DARLING...
...WE HAVE A LOT TO DO!
"OCTOBER 1969...WILLY BRANDT'S TAKING OFFICE BROUGHT ME SERENE JOY--A SENSE OF SATISFACTION THAT **NOTHING** COULD EVER ERASE.
"CONFIRMATION THAT SERGE AND I DIDN'T FIGHT **IN VAIN.**
"DEFEATED, KURT KIESINGER WOULD SOON BE FORGOTTEN. FOR ME, THE PAGE WOULD TURN."
BEATE, I--
SHH, SERGE!
LET ME ENJOY THE TRANSFER OF POWER!
LOOK AT THAT NAZI'S WOODEN SMILE. HE'S VISIBLY STRUGGLING TO PUT ON A GOOD SHOW!
HAHA!

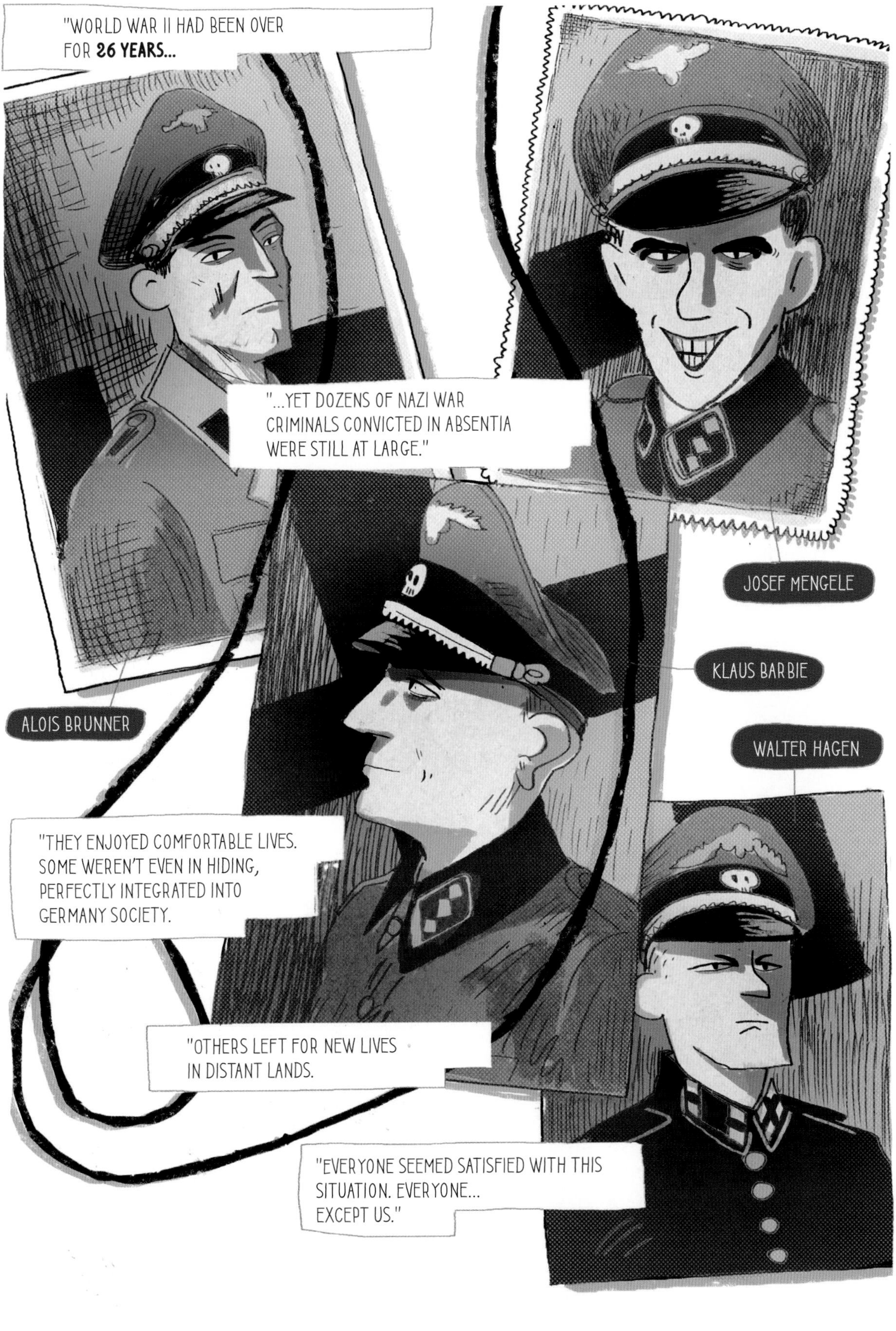
"WORLD WAR II HAD BEEN OVER FOR 26 YEARS...
"...YET DOZENS OF NAZI WAR CRIMINALS CONVICTED IN ABSENTIA WERE STILL AT LARGE."
JOSEF MENGELE
KLAUS BARBIE
ALOIS BRUNNER
WALTER HAGEN
"THEY ENJOYED COMFORTABLE LIVES. SOME WEREN'T EVEN IN HIDING, PERFECTLY INTEGRATED INTO GERMANY SOCIETY.
"OTHERS LEFT FOR NEW LIVES IN DISTANT LANDS.
"EVERYONE SEEMED SATISFIED WITH THIS SITUATION. EVERYONE... EXCEPT US."

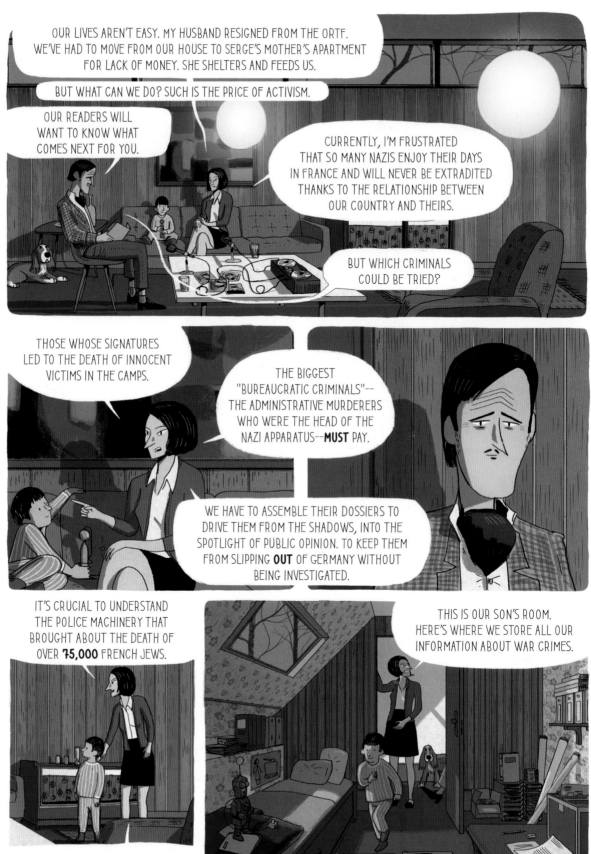

OUR LIVES AREN'T EASY. MY HUSBAND RESIGNED FROM THE ORTF. WE'VE HAD TO MOVE FROM OUR HOUSE TO SERGE'S MOTHER'S APARTMENT FOR LACK OF MONEY. SHE SHELTERS AND FEEDS US.

BUT WHAT CAN WE DO? SUCH IS THE PRICE OF ACTIVISM.

OUR READERS WILL WANT TO KNOW WHAT COMES NEXT FOR YOU.

CURRENTLY, I'M FRUSTRATED THAT SO MANY NAZIS ENJOY THEIR DAYS IN FRANCE AND WILL NEVER BE EXTRADITED THANKS TO THE RELATIONSHIP BETWEEN OUR COUNTRY AND THEIRS.

BUT WHICH CRIMINALS COULD BE TRIED?

THOSE WHOSE SIGNATURES LED TO THE DEATH OF INNOCENT VICTIMS IN THE CAMPS.

THE BIGGEST "BUREAUCRATIC CRIMINALS"-- THE ADMINISTRATIVE MURDERERS WHO WERE THE HEAD OF THE NAZI APPARATUS--**MUST** PAY.

WE HAVE TO ASSEMBLE THEIR DOSSIERS TO DRIVE THEM FROM THE SHADOWS, INTO THE SPOTLIGHT OF PUBLIC OPINION. TO KEEP THEM FROM SLIPPING **OUT** OF GERMANY WITHOUT BEING INVESTIGATED.

IT'S CRUCIAL TO UNDERSTAND THE POLICE MACHINERY THAT BROUGHT ABOUT THE DEATH OF OVER **75,000** FRENCH JEWS.

THIS IS OUR SON'S ROOM. HERE'S WHERE WE STORE ALL OUR INFORMATION ABOUT WAR CRIMES.

IF YOU'LL FOLLOW ME PLEASE, MR. LONDON, I HAVE SOMETHING TO SHOW YOU.

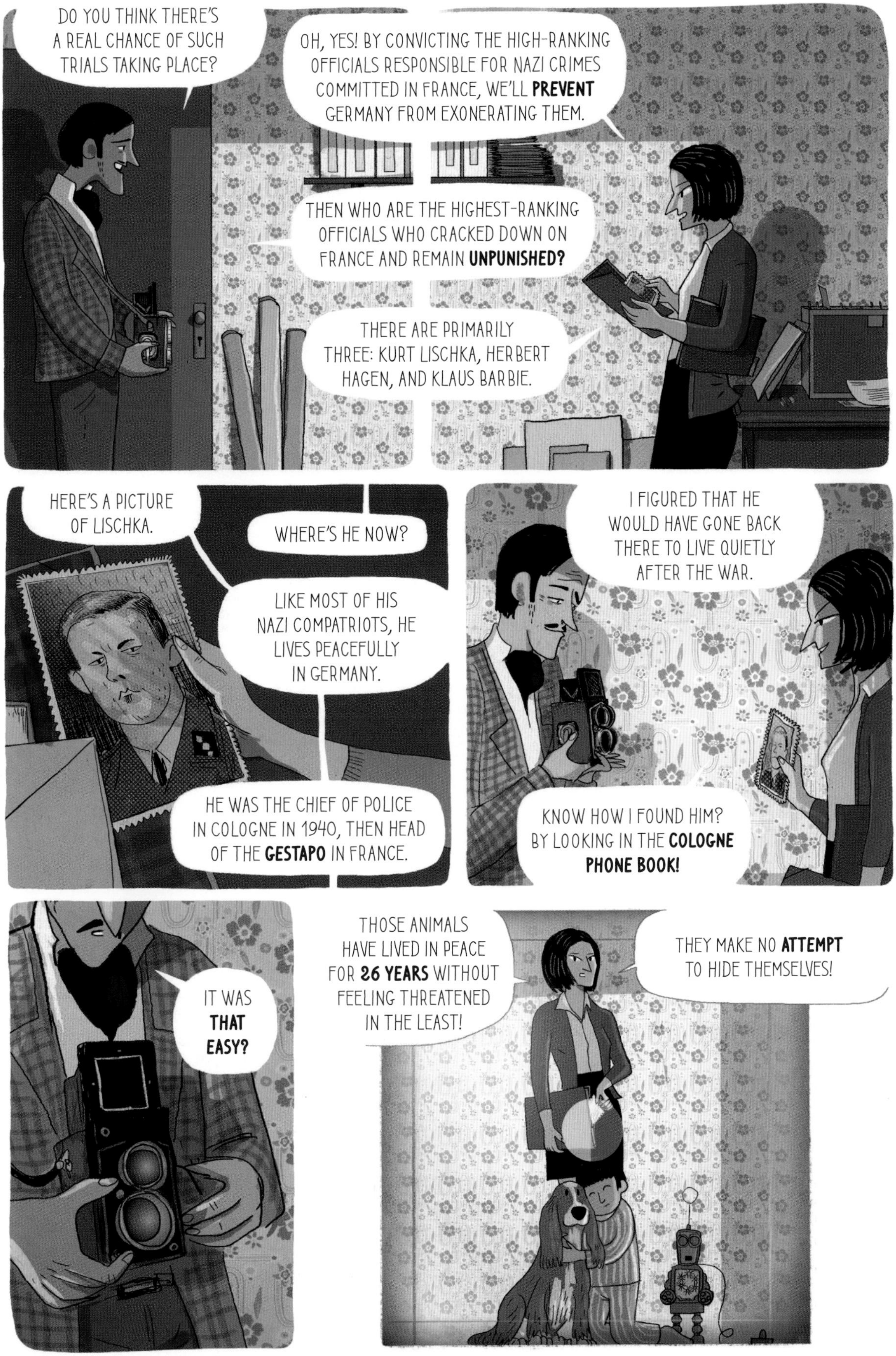
DO YOU THINK THERE'S A REAL CHANCE OF SUCH TRIALS TAKING PLACE?
OH, YES! BY CONVICTING THE HIGH-RANKING OFFICIALS RESPONSIBLE FOR NAZI CRIMES COMMITTED IN FRANCE, WE'LL **PREVENT** GERMANY FROM EXONERATING THEM.
THEN WHO ARE THE HIGHEST-RANKING OFFICIALS WHO CRACKED DOWN ON FRANCE AND REMAIN **UNPUNISHED?**
THERE ARE PRIMARILY THREE: KURT LISCHKA, HERBERT HAGEN, AND KLAUS BARBIE.
HERE'S A PICTURE OF LISCHKA.
WHERE'S HE NOW?
LIKE MOST OF HIS NAZI COMPATRIOTS, HE LIVES PEACEFULLY IN GERMANY.
HE WAS THE CHIEF OF POLICE IN COLOGNE IN 1940, THEN HEAD OF THE **GESTAPO** IN FRANCE.
I FIGURED THAT HE WOULD HAVE GONE BACK THERE TO LIVE QUIETLY AFTER THE WAR.
KNOW HOW I FOUND HIM? BY LOOKING IN THE **COLOGNE PHONE BOOK!**
IT WAS **THAT EASY?**
THOSE ANIMALS HAVE LIVED IN PEACE FOR **26 YEARS** WITHOUT FEELING THREATENED IN THE LEAST!
THEY MAKE NO **ATTEMPT** TO HIDE THEMSELVES!

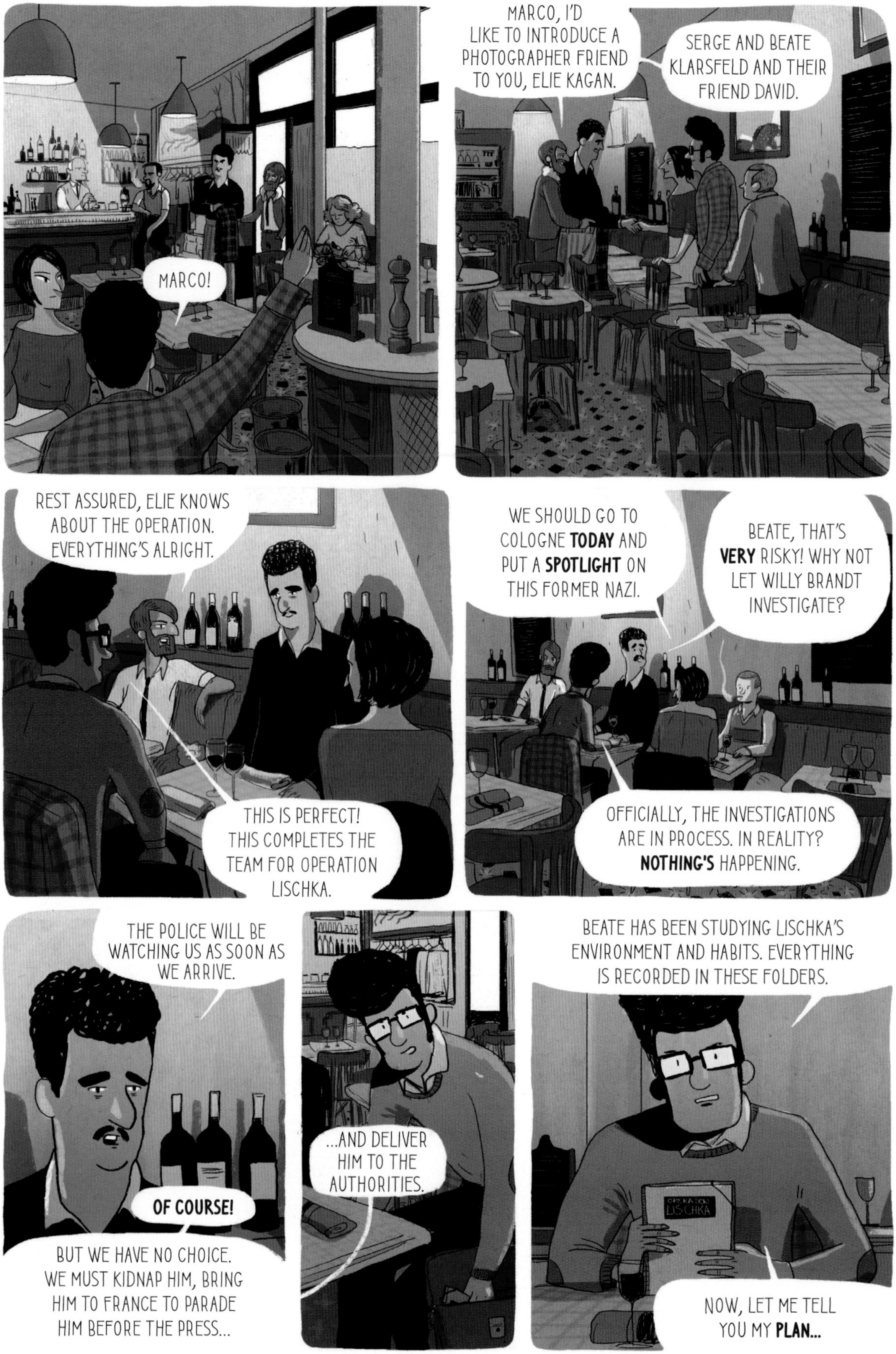
MARCO!
MARCO, I'D LIKE TO INTRODUCE A PHOTOGRAPHER FRIEND TO YOU, ELIE KAGAN.
SERGE AND BEATE KLARSFELD AND THEIR FRIEND DAVID.
REST ASSURED, ELIE KNOWS ABOUT THE OPERATION. EVERYTHING'S ALRIGHT.
THIS IS PERFECT! THIS COMPLETES THE TEAM FOR OPERATION LISCHKA.
WE SHOULD GO TO COLOGNE **TODAY** AND PUT A **SPOTLIGHT** ON THIS FORMER NAZI.
BEATE, THAT'S **VERY** RISKY! WHY NOT LET WILLY BRANDT INVESTIGATE?
OFFICIALLY, THE INVESTIGATIONS ARE IN PROCESS. IN REALITY? **NOTHING'S** HAPPENING.
THE POLICE WILL BE WATCHING US AS SOON AS WE ARRIVE.
OF COURSE!
BUT WE HAVE NO CHOICE. WE MUST KIDNAP HIM, BRING HIM TO FRANCE TO PARADE HIM BEFORE THE PRESS...
...AND DELIVER HIM TO THE AUTHORITIES.
BEATE HAS BEEN STUDYING LISCHKA'S ENVIRONMENT AND HABITS. EVERYTHING IS RECORDED IN THESE FOLDERS.
OPERATION LISCHKA
NOW, LET ME TELL YOU MY **PLAN...**

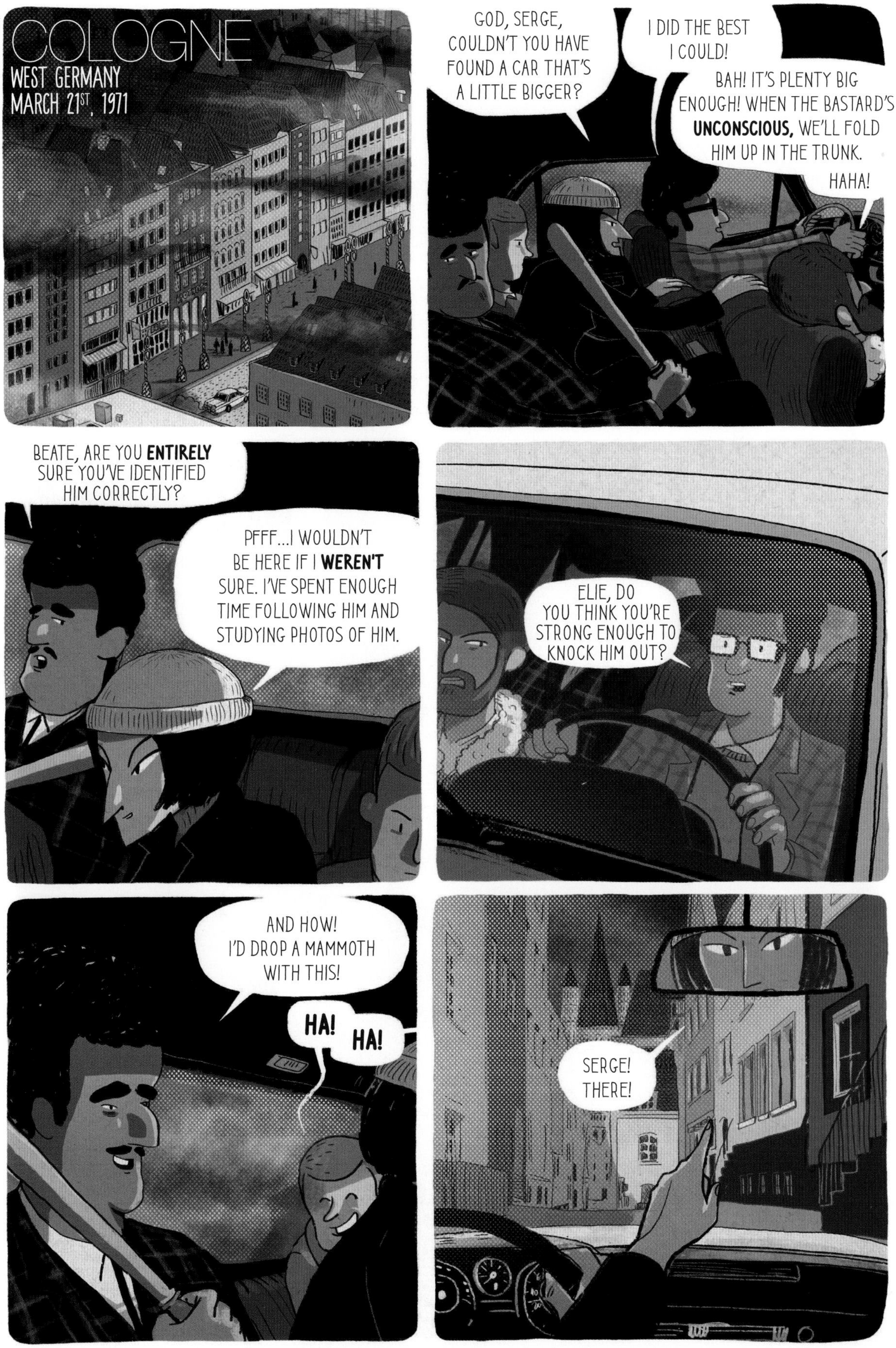

COLOGNE
WEST GERMANY
MARCH 21ST, 1971
GOD, SERGE, COULDN'T YOU HAVE FOUND A CAR THAT'S A LITTLE BIGGER?
I DID THE BEST I COULD!
BAH! IT'S PLENTY BIG ENOUGH! WHEN THE BASTARD'S **UNCONSCIOUS,** WE'LL FOLD HIM UP IN THE TRUNK.
HAHA!
BEATE, ARE YOU **ENTIRELY** SURE YOU'VE IDENTIFIED HIM CORRECTLY?
PFFF...I WOULDN'T BE HERE IF I **WEREN'T** SURE. I'VE SPENT ENOUGH TIME FOLLOWING HIM AND STUDYING PHOTOS OF HIM.
ELIE, DO YOU THINK YOU'RE STRONG ENOUGH TO KNOCK HIM OUT?
AND HOW! I'D DROP A MAMMOTH WITH THIS!
HA! HA!
SERGE! THERE!

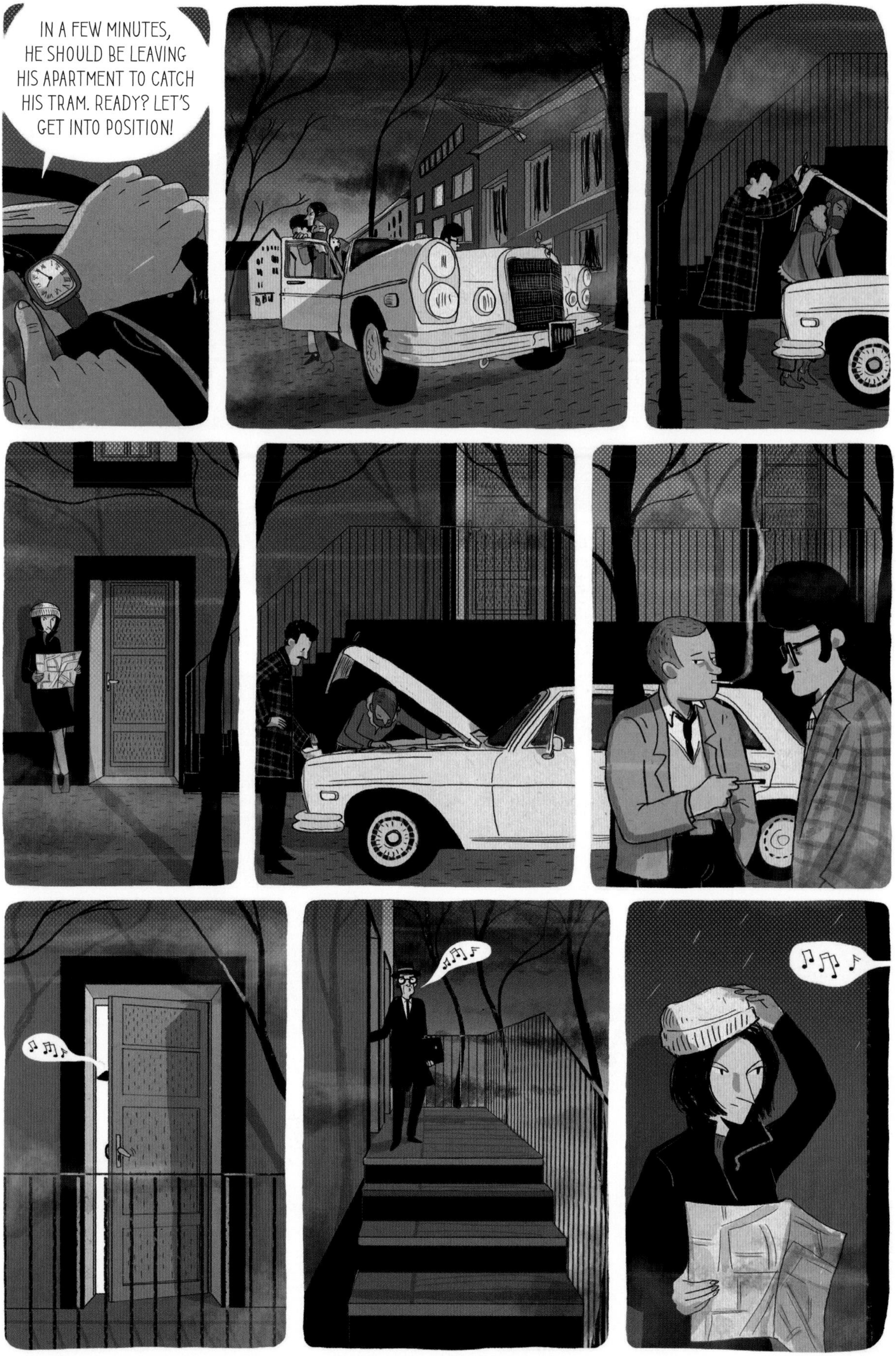
IN A FEW MINUTES, HE SHOULD BE LEAVING HIS APARTMENT TO CATCH HIS TRAM. READY? LET'S GET INTO POSITION!

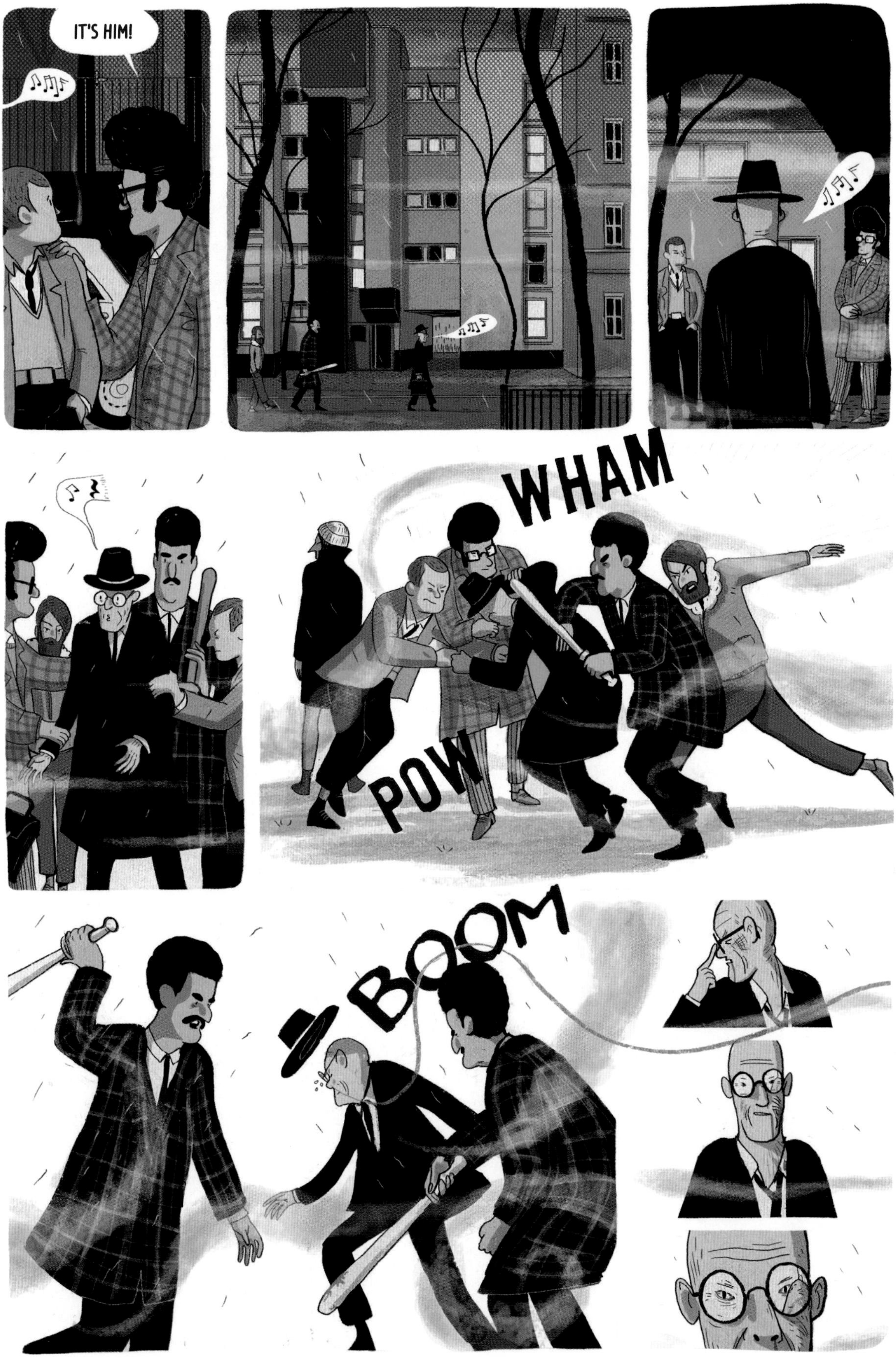
IT'S HIM!
WHAM
POW
BOOM

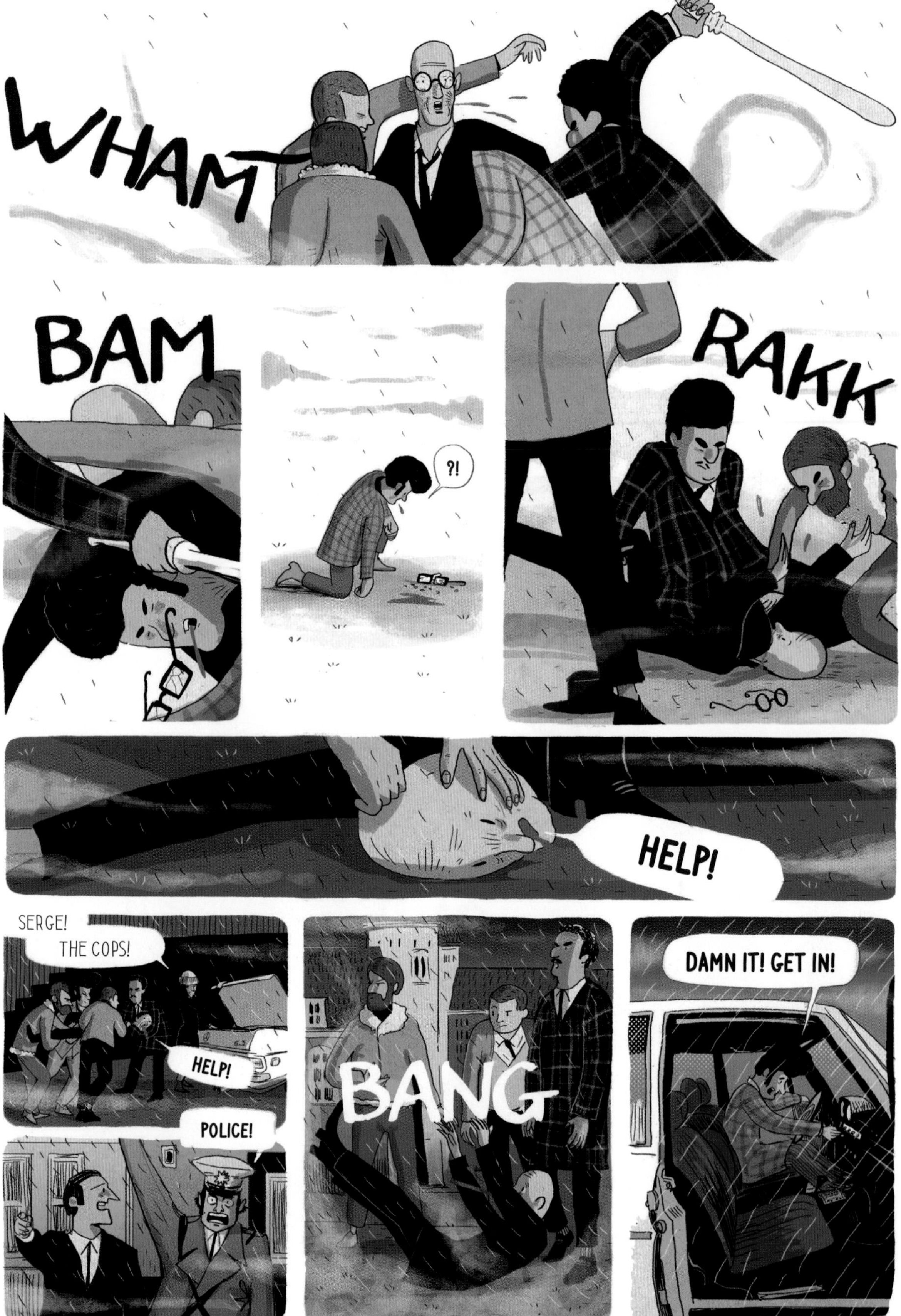
WHAM
BAM
?!
RAKK
HELP!
SERGE!
THE COPS!
HELP!
POLICE!
BANG
DAMN IT! GET IN!

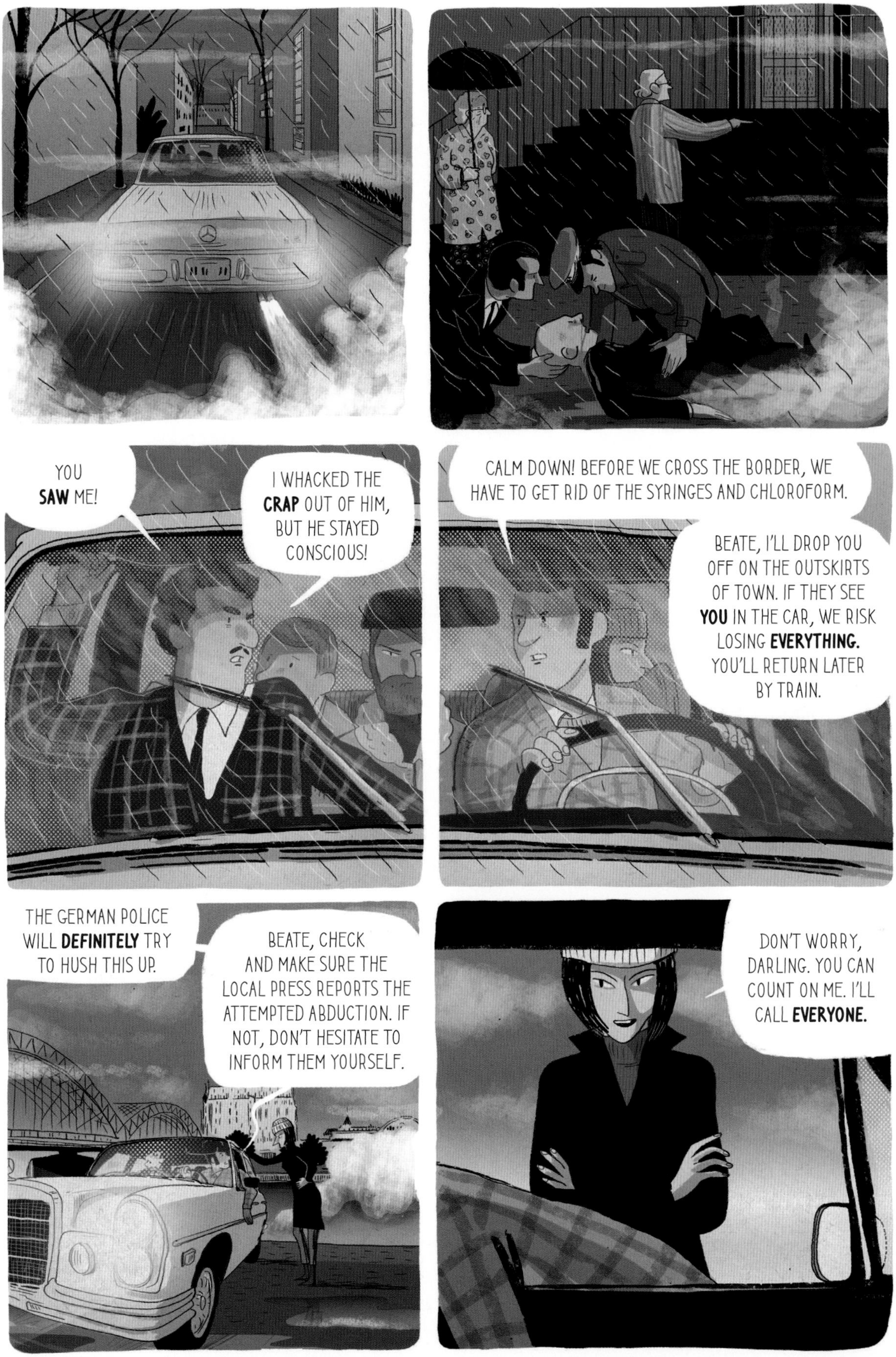

YOU SAW ME!
I WHACKED THE CRAP OUT OF HIM, BUT HE STAYED CONSCIOUS!
CALM DOWN! BEFORE WE CROSS THE BORDER, WE HAVE TO GET RID OF THE SYRINGES AND CHLOROFORM.
BEATE, I'LL DROP YOU OFF ON THE OUTSKIRTS OF TOWN. IF THEY SEE YOU IN THE CAR, WE RISK LOSING EVERYTHING. YOU'LL RETURN LATER BY TRAIN.
THE GERMAN POLICE WILL DEFINITELY TRY TO HUSH THIS UP.
BEATE, CHECK AND MAKE SURE THE LOCAL PRESS REPORTS THE ATTEMPTED ABDUCTION. IF NOT, DON'T HESITATE TO INFORM THEM YOURSELF.
DON'T WORRY, DARLING. YOU CAN COUNT ON ME. I'LL CALL EVERYONE.

THANKS!

HELLO, IS THIS THE **COLOGNE GAZETTE...?**

THIS IS MRS. SCHMIDT. I LIVE ON BERGISCH GLADBACHER ROAD.

I WITNESSED A **KIDNAPPING ATTEMPT** YESTERDAY! SOME YOUNG PEOPLE CLUBBED A MAN OUT OF THE BLUE!

LUCKILY, THE POLICE INTERVENED!

HOWEVER, THIS MORNING, I DON'T SEE **ANYTHING** IN THE PAPER ABOUT IT.

LOOK MORE CLOSELY, MA'AM. PAGE TWO, AT THE BOTTOM. THERE'S A SHORT REPORT.

his death. I think there are many others responsible. I accuse all of society: judges, middle-class parents. I would like this all to pass and for us to forget. But ultimately, I cannot forget...

Four unknown persons attacked an honest businessman before fleeing.

Five million viewers visit the galleries to see this love story.

In Germany the people who the monarchy is always availa elective; but the truth of th vereign use of political power ten of their own volition in to get elected. The Germa erit. The arrival of the tru princes, on the end of the of Otho, the duke of Nor of Thuringia, also known throne in 912 was given of Franconen, who represe house of the thousand together with everyo essor, HLenry [] whom the Fowler.

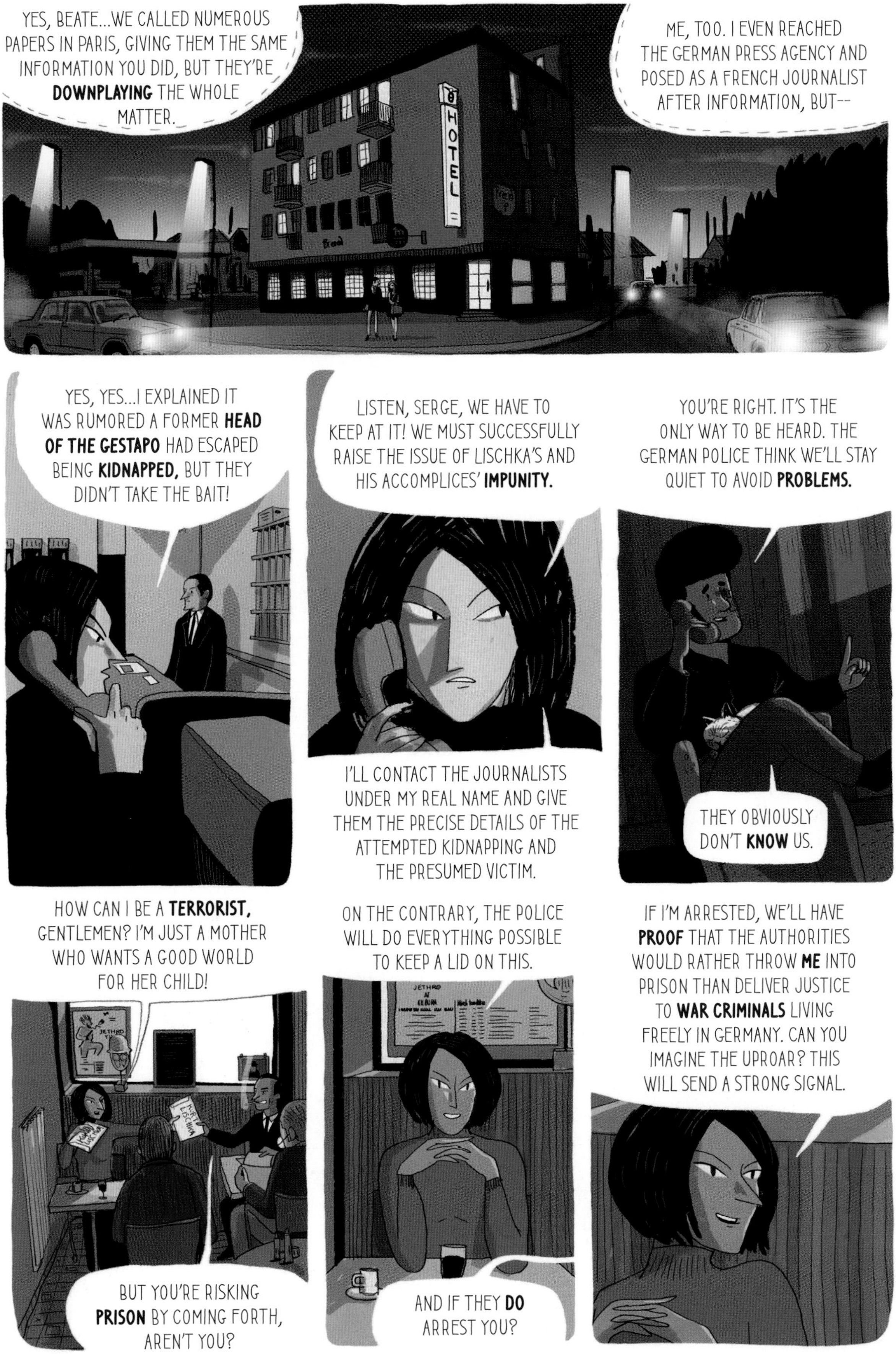
YES, BEATE...WE CALLED NUMEROUS PAPERS IN PARIS, GIVING THEM THE SAME INFORMATION YOU DID, BUT THEY'RE **DOWNPLAYING** THE WHOLE MATTER.
HOTEL
ME, TOO. I EVEN REACHED THE GERMAN PRESS AGENCY AND POSED AS A FRENCH JOURNALIST AFTER INFORMATION, BUT--
YES, YES...I EXPLAINED IT WAS RUMORED A FORMER **HEAD OF THE GESTAPO** HAD ESCAPED BEING **KIDNAPPED,** BUT THEY DIDN'T TAKE THE BAIT!
LISTEN, SERGE, WE HAVE TO KEEP AT IT! WE MUST SUCCESSFULLY RAISE THE ISSUE OF LISCHKA'S AND HIS ACCOMPLICES' **IMPUNITY.**
I'LL CONTACT THE JOURNALISTS UNDER MY REAL NAME AND GIVE THEM THE PRECISE DETAILS OF THE ATTEMPTED KIDNAPPING AND THE PRESUMED VICTIM.
YOU'RE RIGHT. IT'S THE ONLY WAY TO BE HEARD. THE GERMAN POLICE THINK WE'LL STAY QUIET TO AVOID **PROBLEMS.**
THEY OBVIOUSLY DON'T **KNOW** US.
HOW CAN I BE A **TERRORIST,** GENTLEMEN? I'M JUST A MOTHER WHO WANTS A GOOD WORLD FOR HER CHILD!
BUT YOU'RE RISKING **PRISON** BY COMING FORTH, AREN'T YOU?
ON THE CONTRARY, THE POLICE WILL DO EVERYTHING POSSIBLE TO KEEP A LID ON THIS.
AND IF THEY **DO** ARREST YOU?
IF I'M ARRESTED, WE'LL HAVE **PROOF** THAT THE AUTHORITIES WOULD RATHER THROW **ME** INTO PRISON THAN DELIVER JUSTICE TO **WAR CRIMINALS** LIVING FREELY IN GERMANY. CAN YOU IMAGINE THE UPROAR? THIS WILL SEND A STRONG SIGNAL.

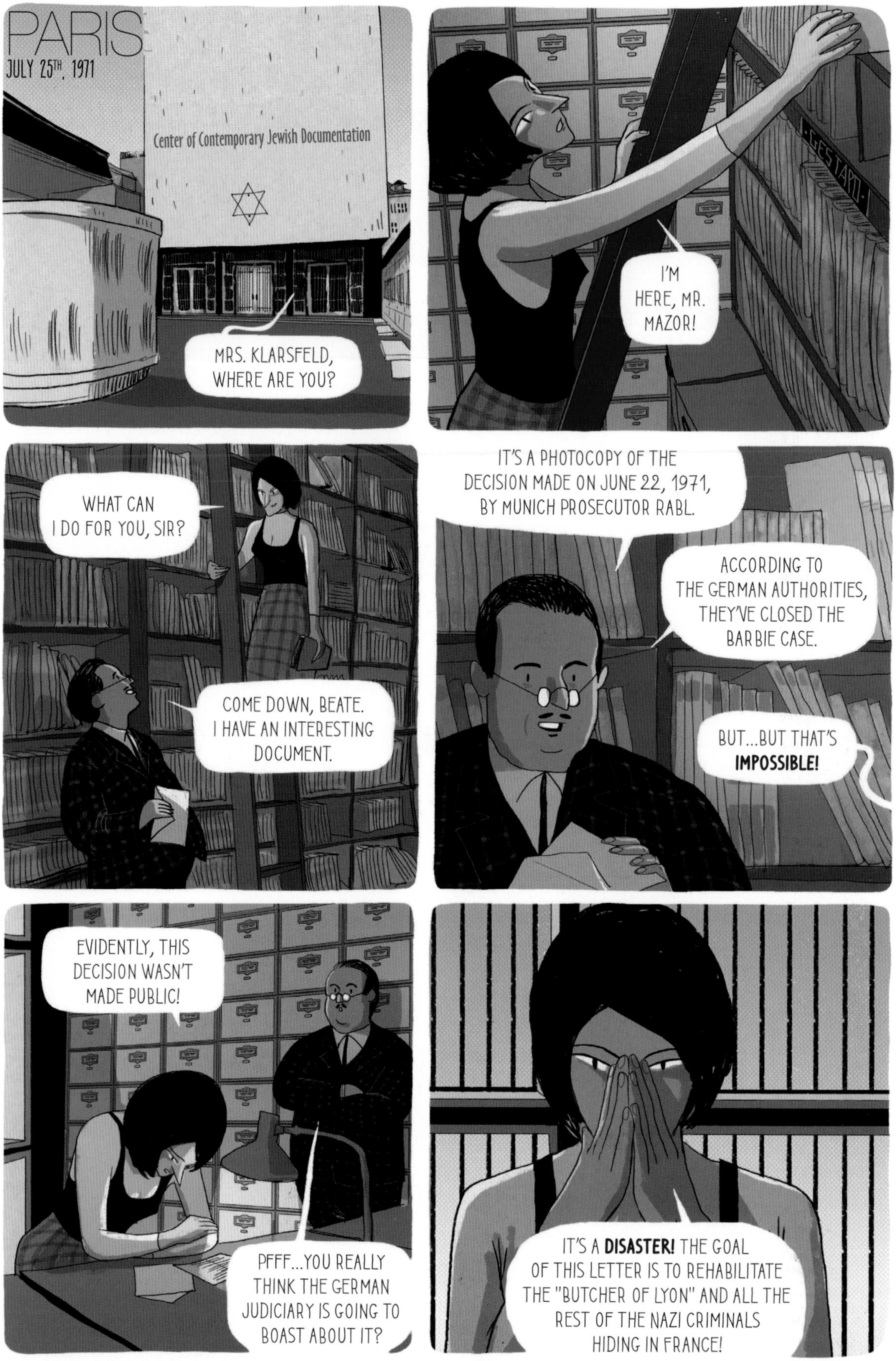
PARIS
JULY 25TH, 1971
Center of Contemporary Jewish Documentation
MRS. KLARSFELD, WHERE ARE YOU?
I'M HERE, MR. MAZOR!
GESTAPO
WHAT CAN I DO FOR YOU, SIR?
COME DOWN, BEATE. I HAVE AN INTERESTING DOCUMENT.
IT'S A PHOTOCOPY OF THE DECISION MADE ON JUNE 22, 1971, BY MUNICH PROSECUTOR RABL.
ACCORDING TO THE GERMAN AUTHORITIES, THEY'VE CLOSED THE BARBIE CASE.
BUT...BUT THAT'S **IMPOSSIBLE!**
EVIDENTLY, THIS DECISION WASN'T MADE PUBLIC!
PFFF...YOU REALLY THINK THE GERMAN JUDICIARY IS GOING TO BOAST ABOUT IT?
IT'S A **DISASTER!** THE GOAL OF THIS LETTER IS TO REHABILITATE THE "BUTCHER OF LYON" AND ALL THE REST OF THE NAZI CRIMINALS HIDING IN FRANCE!

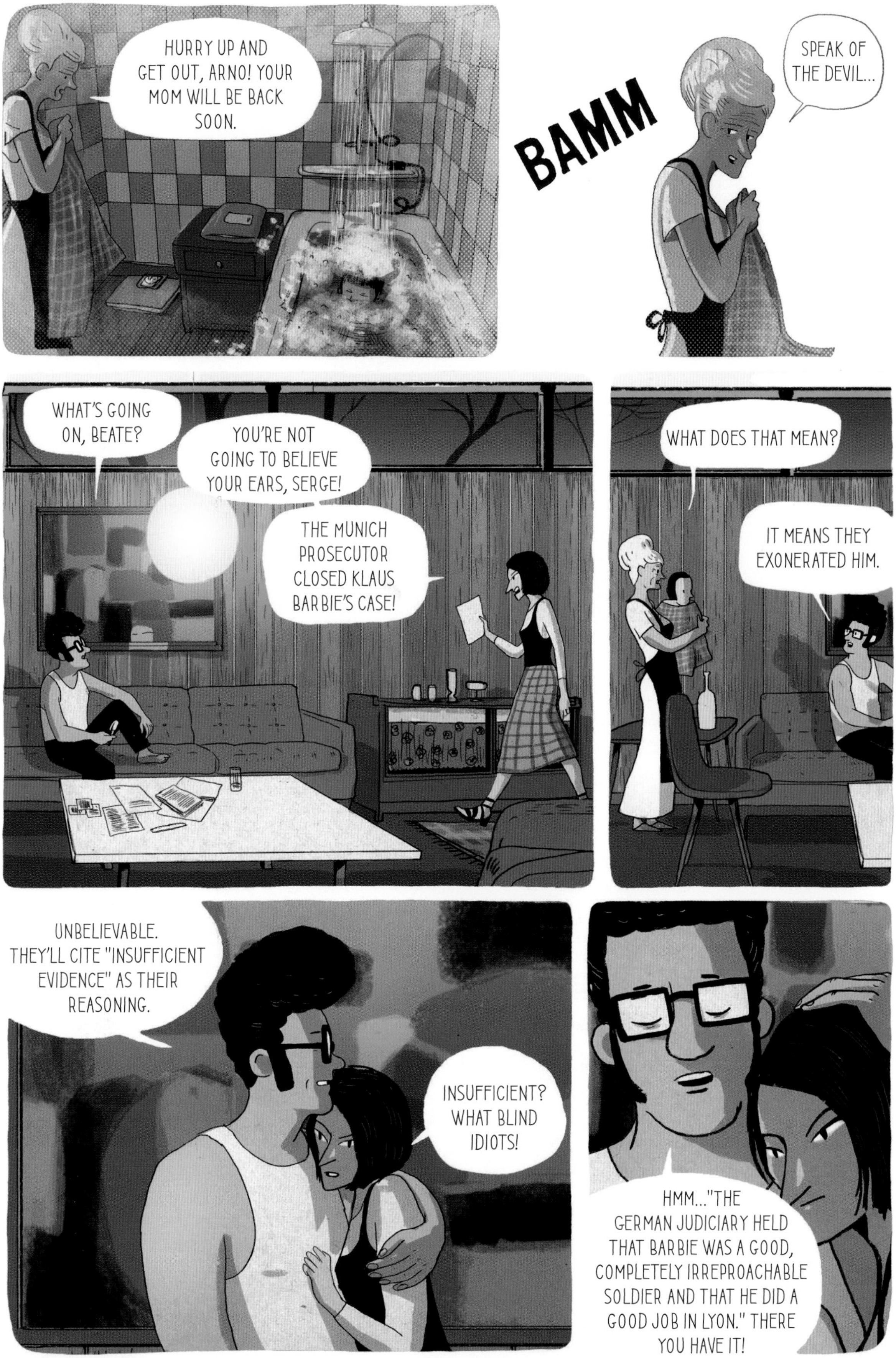
HURRY UP AND GET OUT, ARNO! YOUR MOM WILL BE BACK SOON.
BAMM
SPEAK OF THE DEVIL...
WHAT'S GOING ON, BEATE?
YOU'RE NOT GOING TO BELIEVE YOUR EARS, SERGE!
THE MUNICH PROSECUTOR CLOSED KLAUS BARBIE'S CASE!
WHAT DOES THAT MEAN?
IT MEANS THEY EXONERATED HIM.
UNBELIEVABLE. THEY'LL CITE "INSUFFICIENT EVIDENCE" AS THEIR REASONING.
INSUFFICIENT? WHAT BLIND IDIOTS!
HMM..."THE GERMAN JUDICIARY HELD THAT BARBIE WAS A GOOD, COMPLETELY IRREPROACHABLE SOLDIER AND THAT HE DID A GOOD JOB IN LYON." THERE YOU HAVE IT!

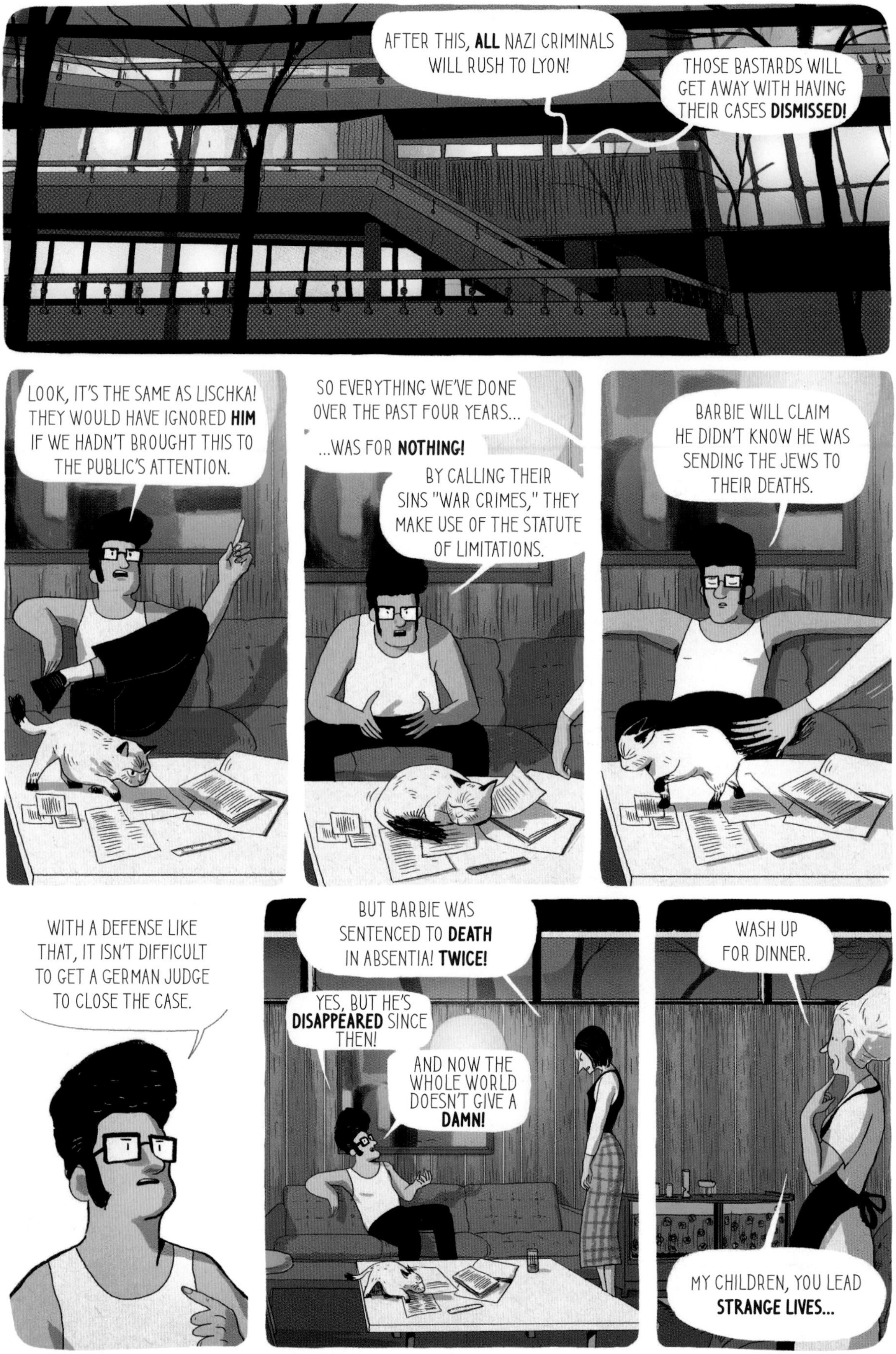
AFTER THIS, **ALL** NAZI CRIMINALS WILL RUSH TO LYON!
THOSE BASTARDS WILL GET AWAY WITH HAVING THEIR CASES **DISMISSED!**
LOOK, IT'S THE SAME AS LISCHKA! THEY WOULD HAVE IGNORED **HIM** IF WE HADN'T BROUGHT THIS TO THE PUBLIC'S ATTENTION.
SO EVERYTHING WE'VE DONE OVER THE PAST FOUR YEARS...
...WAS FOR **NOTHING!**
BY CALLING THEIR SINS "WAR CRIMES," THEY MAKE USE OF THE STATUTE OF LIMITATIONS.
BARBIE WILL CLAIM HE DIDN'T KNOW HE WAS SENDING THE JEWS TO THEIR DEATHS.
WITH A DEFENSE LIKE THAT, IT ISN'T DIFFICULT TO GET A GERMAN JUDGE TO CLOSE THE CASE.
BUT BARBIE WAS SENTENCED TO **DEATH** IN ABSENTIA! **TWICE!**
YES, BUT HE'S **DISAPPEARED** SINCE THEN!
AND NOW THE WHOLE WORLD DOESN'T GIVE A **DAMN!**
WASH UP FOR DINNER.
MY CHILDREN, YOU LEAD **STRANGE LIVES...**

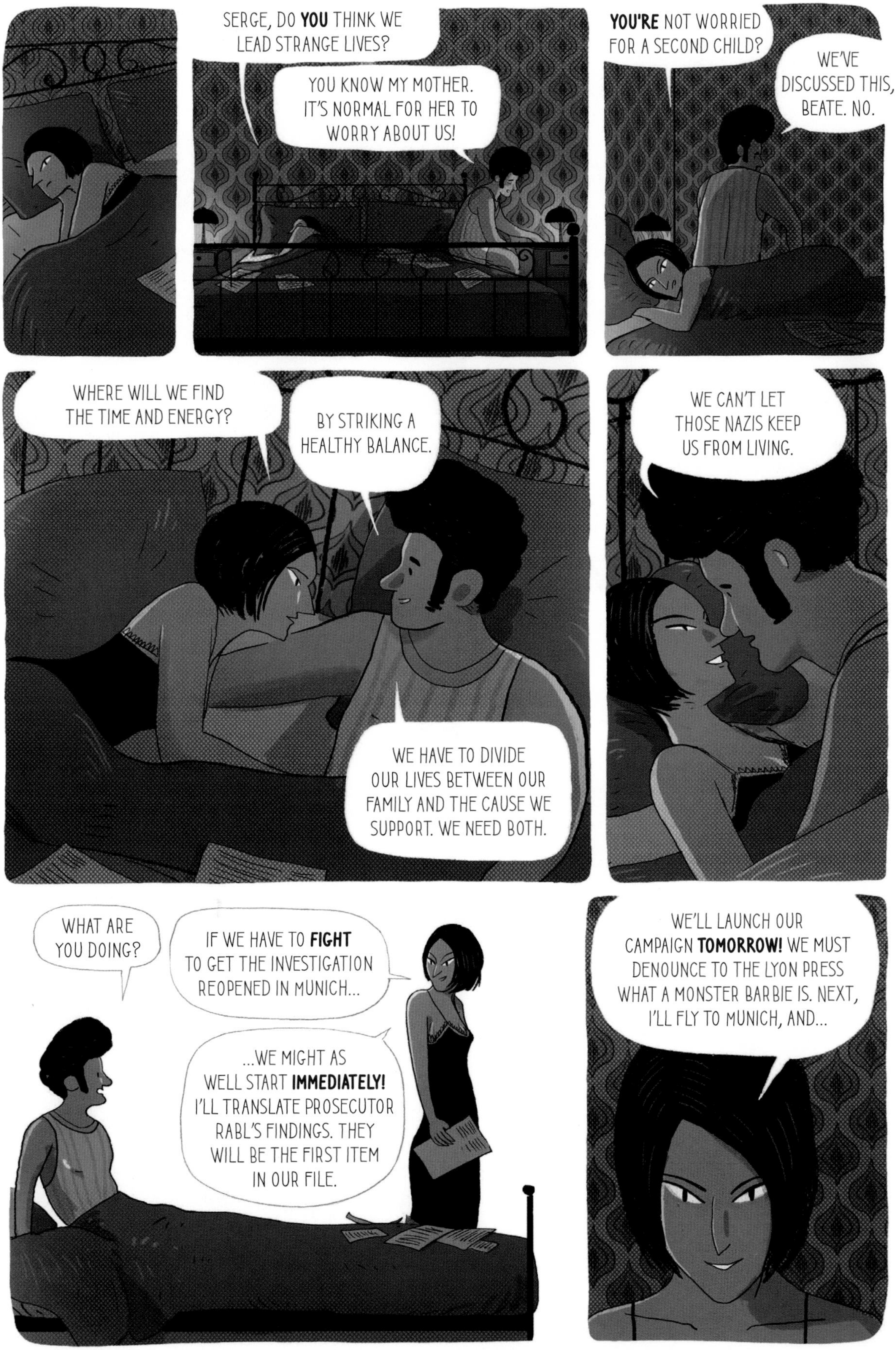
SERGE, DO **YOU** THINK WE LEAD STRANGE LIVES?
YOU KNOW MY MOTHER. IT'S NORMAL FOR HER TO WORRY ABOUT US!
YOU'RE NOT WORRIED FOR A SECOND CHILD?
WE'VE DISCUSSED THIS, BEATE. NO.
WHERE WILL WE FIND THE TIME AND ENERGY?
BY STRIKING A HEALTHY BALANCE.
WE HAVE TO DIVIDE OUR LIVES BETWEEN OUR FAMILY AND THE CAUSE WE SUPPORT. WE NEED BOTH.
WE CAN'T LET THOSE NAZIS KEEP US FROM LIVING.
WHAT ARE YOU DOING?
IF WE HAVE TO **FIGHT** TO GET THE INVESTIGATION REOPENED IN MUNICH...
...WE MIGHT AS WELL START **IMMEDIATELY!** I'LL TRANSLATE PROSECUTOR RABL'S FINDINGS. THEY WILL BE THE FIRST ITEM IN OUR FILE.
WE'LL LAUNCH OUR CAMPAIGN **TOMORROW!** WE MUST DENOUNCE TO THE LYON PRESS WHAT A MONSTER BARBIE IS. NEXT, I'LL FLY TO MUNICH, AND...

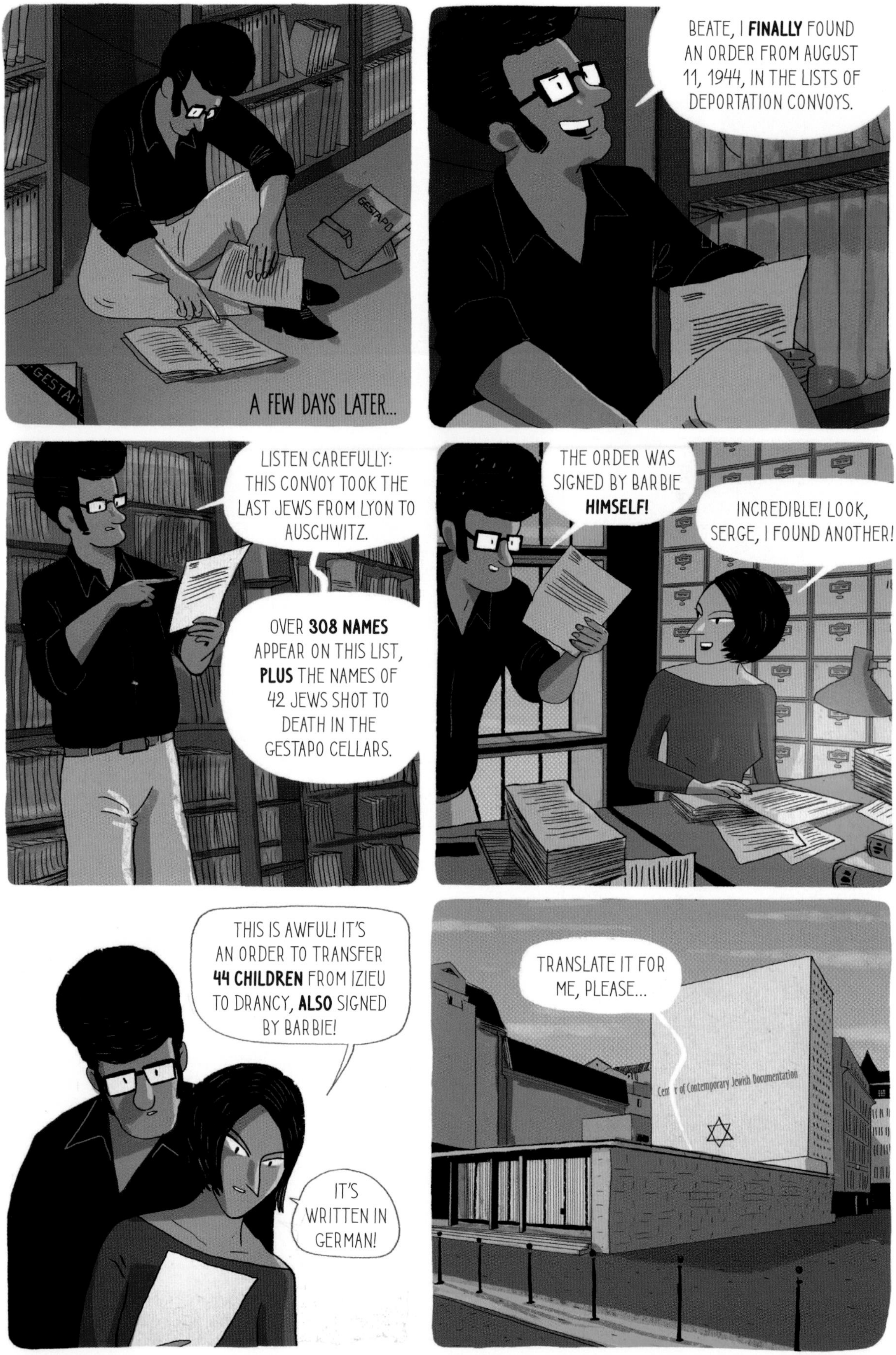
A FEW DAYS LATER...
GESTAPO
BEATE, I **FINALLY** FOUND AN ORDER FROM AUGUST 11, 1944, IN THE LISTS OF DEPORTATION CONVOYS.
LISTEN CAREFULLY: THIS CONVOY TOOK THE LAST JEWS FROM LYON TO AUSCHWITZ.
OVER **308 NAMES** APPEAR ON THIS LIST, **PLUS** THE NAMES OF 42 JEWS SHOT TO DEATH IN THE GESTAPO CELLARS.
THE ORDER WAS SIGNED BY BARBIE **HIMSELF!**
INCREDIBLE! LOOK, SERGE, I FOUND ANOTHER!
THIS IS AWFUL! IT'S AN ORDER TO TRANSFER **44 CHILDREN** FROM IZIEU TO DRANCY, **ALSO** SIGNED BY BARBIE!
IT'S WRITTEN IN GERMAN!
TRANSLATE IT FOR ME, PLEASE...
Center of Contemporary Jewish Documentation

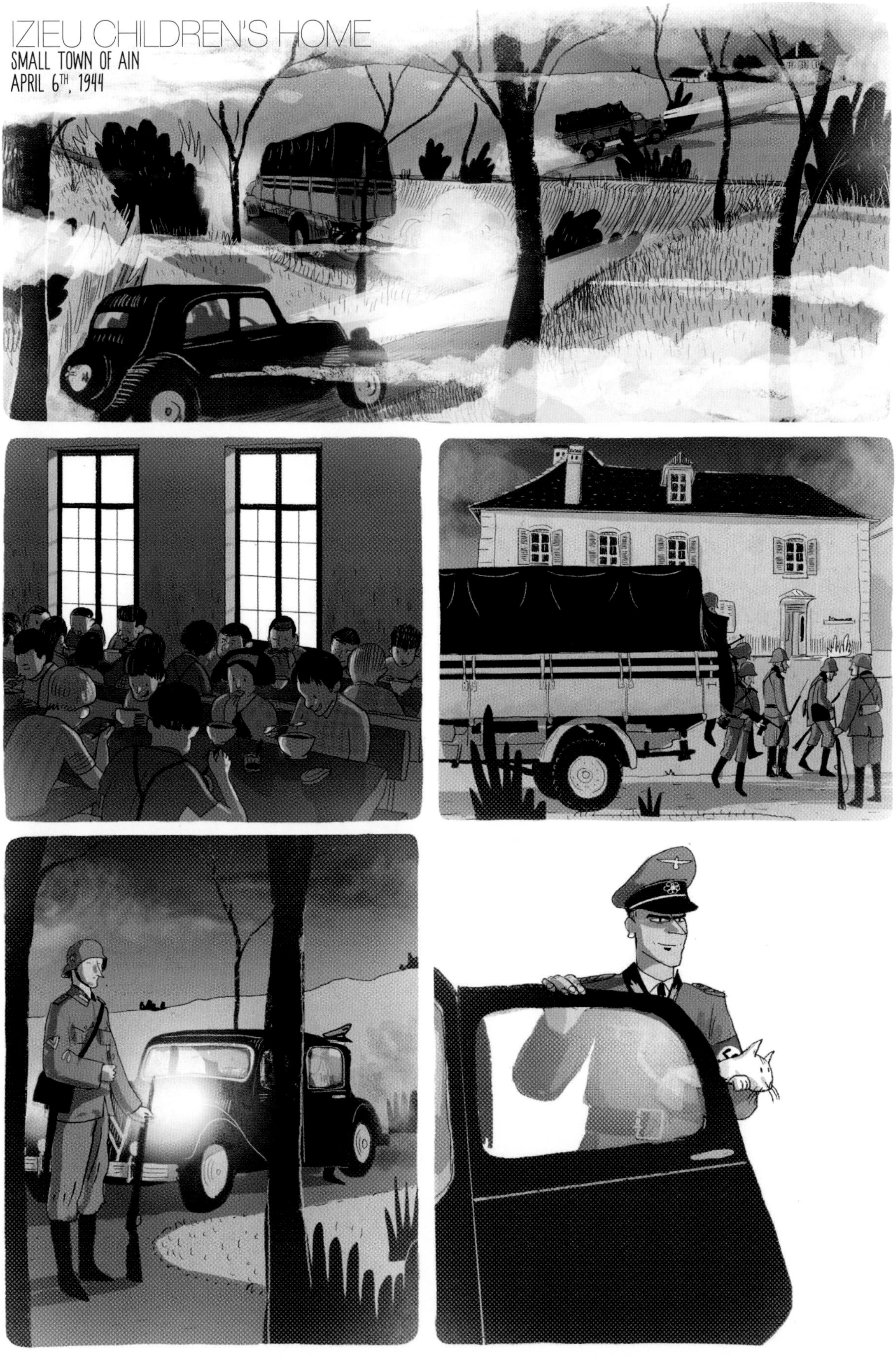
IZIEU CHILDREN'S HOME
SMALL TOWN OF AIN
APRIL 6TH, 1944

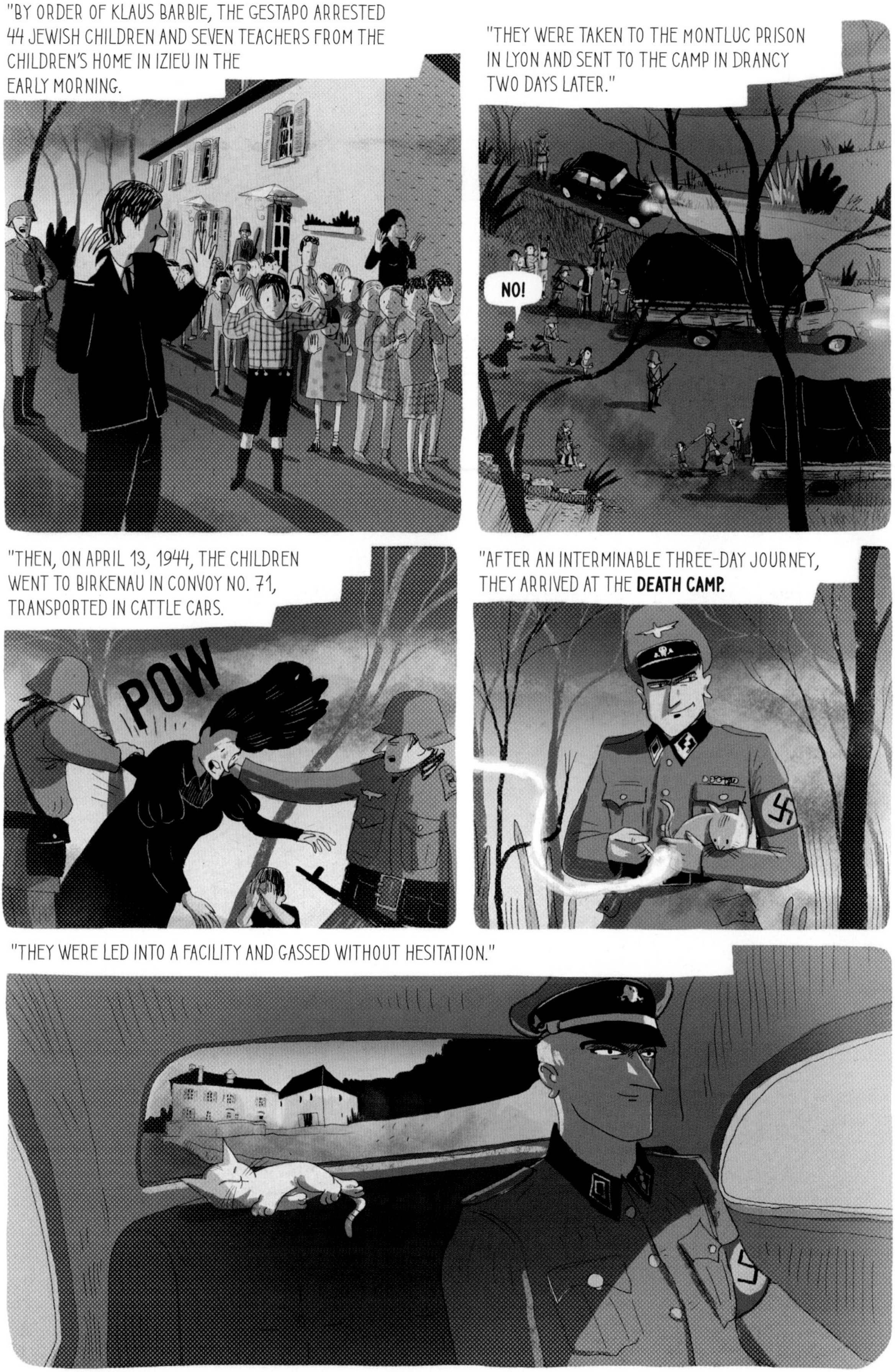
"BY ORDER OF KLAUS BARBIE, THE GESTAPO ARRESTED 44 JEWISH CHILDREN AND SEVEN TEACHERS FROM THE CHILDREN'S HOME IN IZIEU IN THE EARLY MORNING.
"THEY WERE TAKEN TO THE MONTLUC PRISON IN LYON AND SENT TO THE CAMP IN DRANCY TWO DAYS LATER."
NO!
"THEN, ON APRIL 13, 1944, THE CHILDREN WENT TO BIRKENAU IN CONVOY NO. 71, TRANSPORTED IN CATTLE CARS.
POW
"AFTER AN INTERMINABLE THREE-DAY JOURNEY, THEY ARRIVED AT THE **DEATH CAMP.**
"THEY WERE LED INTO A FACILITY AND GASSED WITHOUT HESITATION."

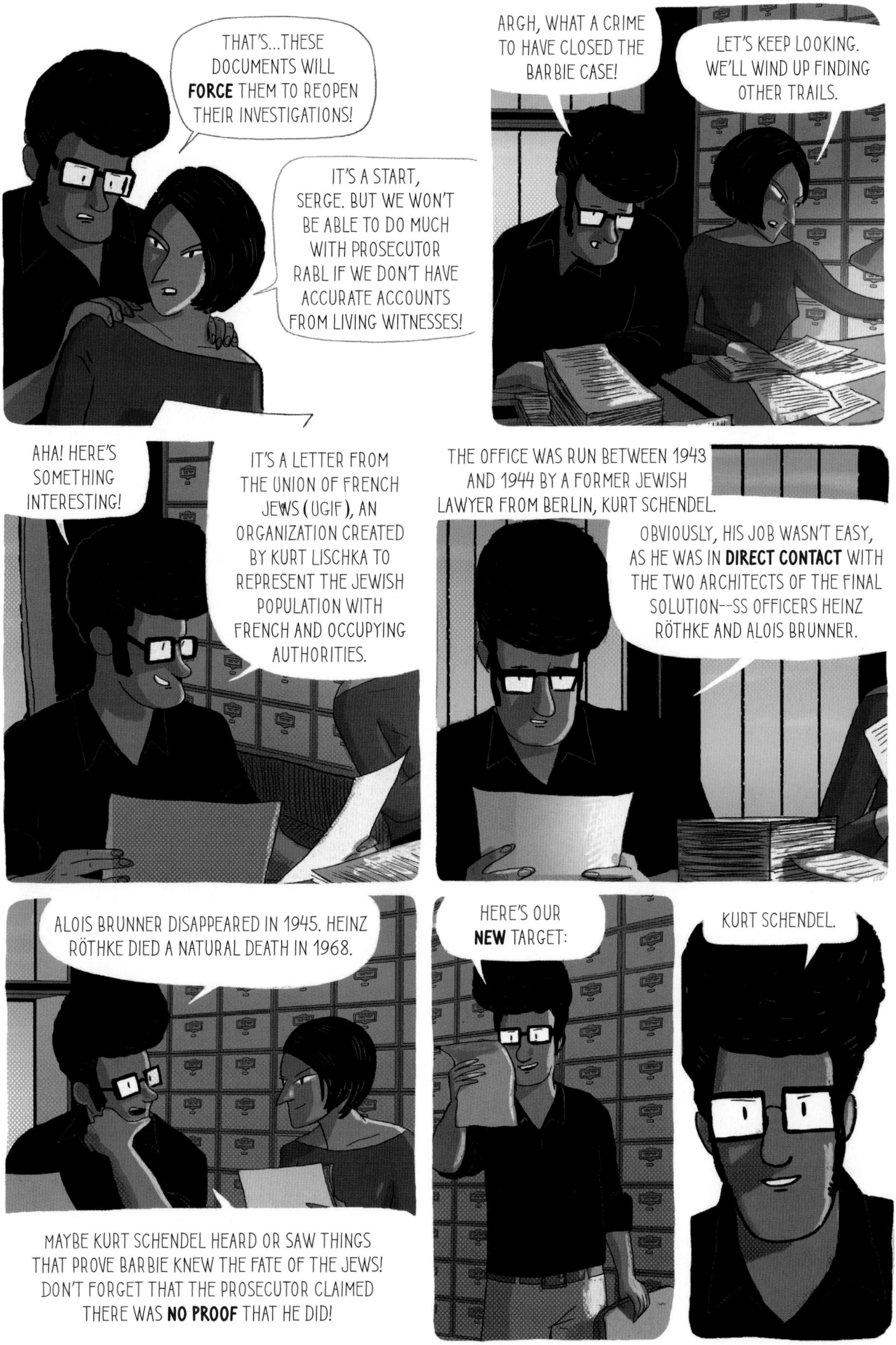

THAT'S...THESE DOCUMENTS WILL **FORCE** THEM TO REOPEN THEIR INVESTIGATIONS!
IT'S A START, SERGE. BUT WE WON'T BE ABLE TO DO MUCH WITH PROSECUTOR RABL IF WE DON'T HAVE ACCURATE ACCOUNTS FROM LIVING WITNESSES!
ARGH, WHAT A CRIME TO HAVE CLOSED THE BARBIE CASE!
LET'S KEEP LOOKING. WE'LL WIND UP FINDING OTHER TRAILS.
AHA! HERE'S SOMETHING INTERESTING!
IT'S A LETTER FROM THE UNION OF FRENCH JEWS (UGIF), AN ORGANIZATION CREATED BY KURT LISCHKA TO REPRESENT THE JEWISH POPULATION WITH FRENCH AND OCCUPYING AUTHORITIES.
THE OFFICE WAS RUN BETWEEN 1943 AND 1944 BY A FORMER JEWISH LAWYER FROM BERLIN, KURT SCHENDEL.
OBVIOUSLY, HIS JOB WASN'T EASY, AS HE WAS IN **DIRECT CONTACT** WITH THE TWO ARCHITECTS OF THE FINAL SOLUTION--SS OFFICERS HEINZ RÖTHKE AND ALOIS BRUNNER.
ALOIS BRUNNER DISAPPEARED IN 1945. HEINZ RÖTHKE DIED A NATURAL DEATH IN 1968.
MAYBE KURT SCHENDEL HEARD OR SAW THINGS THAT PROVE BARBIE KNEW THE FATE OF THE JEWS! DON'T FORGET THAT THE PROSECUTOR CLAIMED THERE WAS **NO PROOF** THAT HE DID!
HERE'S OUR **NEW** TARGET:
KURT SCHENDEL.

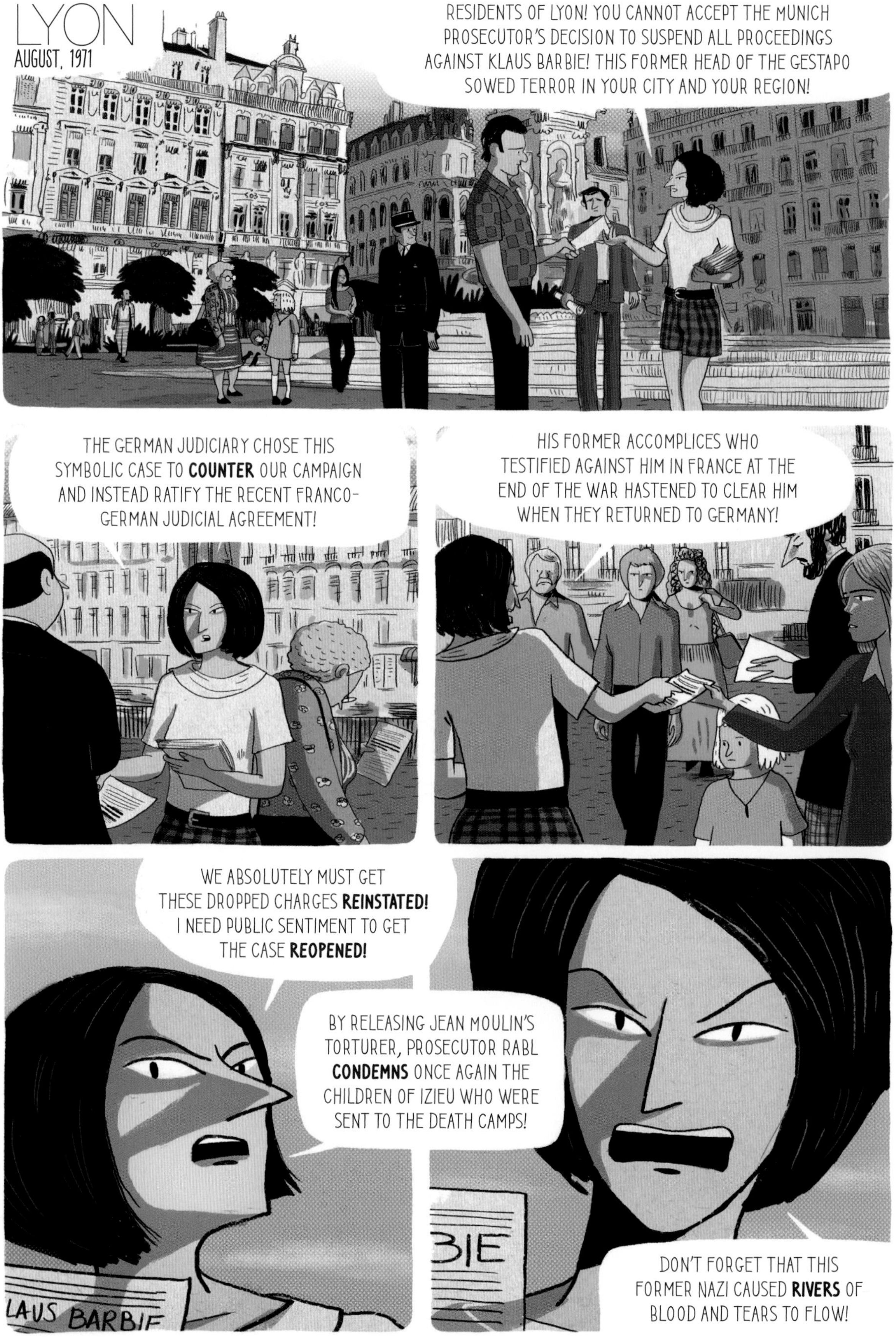
LYON
AUGUST, 1971
RESIDENTS OF LYON! YOU CANNOT ACCEPT THE MUNICH PROSECUTOR'S DECISION TO SUSPEND ALL PROCEEDINGS AGAINST KLAUS BARBIE! THIS FORMER HEAD OF THE GESTAPO SOWED TERROR IN YOUR CITY AND YOUR REGION!
THE GERMAN JUDICIARY CHOSE THIS SYMBOLIC CASE TO **COUNTER** OUR CAMPAIGN AND INSTEAD RATIFY THE RECENT FRANCO-GERMAN JUDICIAL AGREEMENT!
HIS FORMER ACCOMPLICES WHO TESTIFIED AGAINST HIM IN FRANCE AT THE END OF THE WAR HASTENED TO CLEAR HIM WHEN THEY RETURNED TO GERMANY!
WE ABSOLUTELY MUST GET THESE DROPPED CHARGES **REINSTATED!** I NEED PUBLIC SENTIMENT TO GET THE CASE **REOPENED!**
BY RELEASING JEAN MOULIN'S TORTURER, PROSECUTOR RABL **CONDEMNS** ONCE AGAIN THE CHILDREN OF IZIEU WHO WERE SENT TO THE DEATH CAMPS!
LAUS BARBIE
BIE
DON'T FORGET THAT THIS FORMER NAZI CAUSED **RIVERS** OF BLOOD AND TEARS TO FLOW!

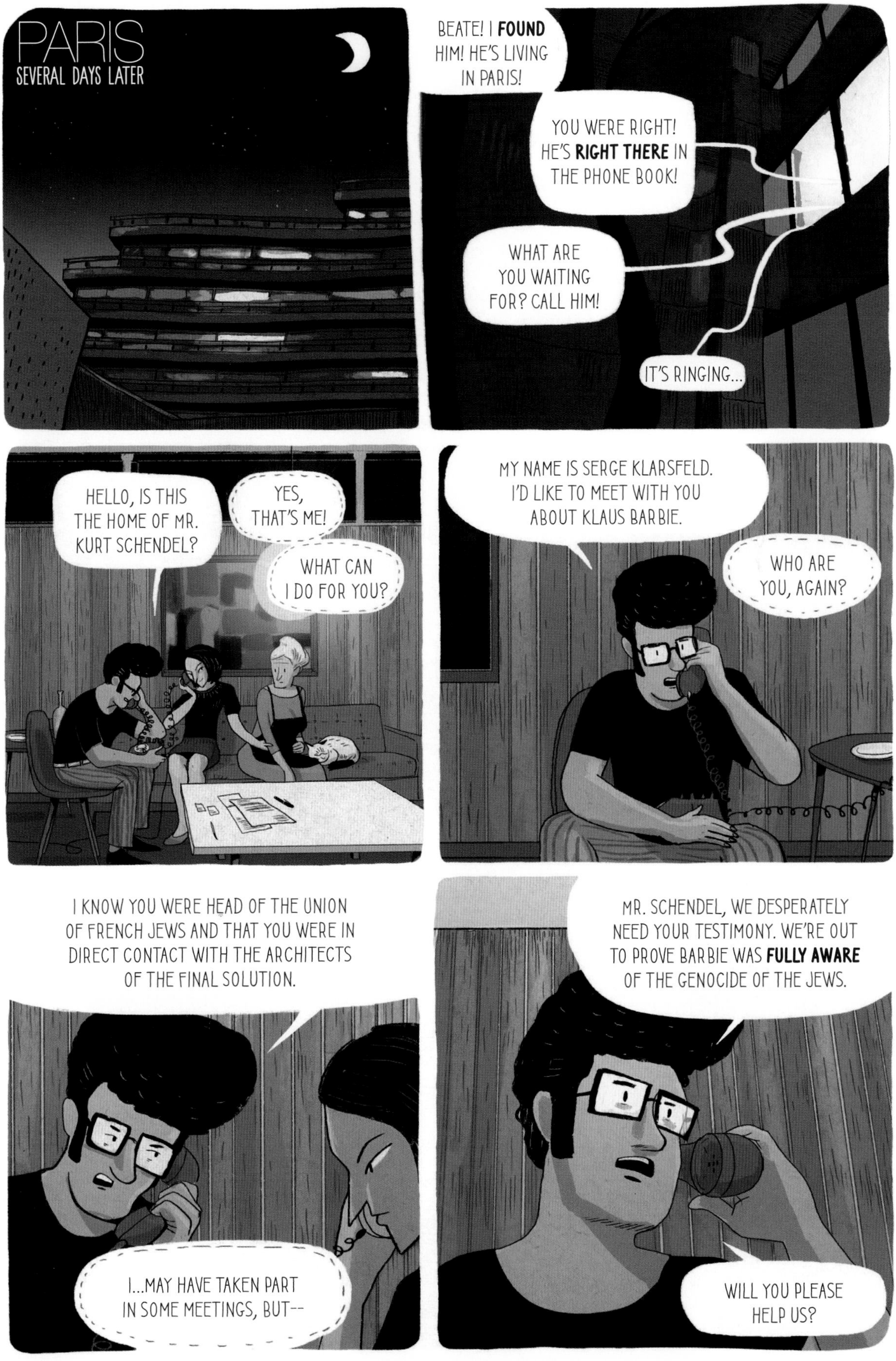
PARIS
SEVERAL DAYS LATER
BEATE! I **FOUND** HIM! HE'S LIVING IN PARIS!
YOU WERE RIGHT! HE'S **RIGHT THERE** IN THE PHONE BOOK!
WHAT ARE YOU WAITING FOR? CALL HIM!
IT'S RINGING...
HELLO, IS THIS THE HOME OF MR. KURT SCHENDEL?
YES, THAT'S ME!
WHAT CAN I DO FOR YOU?
MY NAME IS SERGE KLARSFELD. I'D LIKE TO MEET WITH YOU ABOUT KLAUS BARBIE.
WHO ARE YOU, AGAIN?
I KNOW YOU WERE HEAD OF THE UNION OF FRENCH JEWS AND THAT YOU WERE IN DIRECT CONTACT WITH THE ARCHITECTS OF THE FINAL SOLUTION.
I...MAY HAVE TAKEN PART IN SOME MEETINGS, BUT--
MR. SCHENDEL, WE DESPERATELY NEED YOUR TESTIMONY. WE'RE OUT TO PROVE BARBIE WAS **FULLY AWARE** OF THE GENOCIDE OF THE JEWS.
WILL YOU PLEASE HELP US?

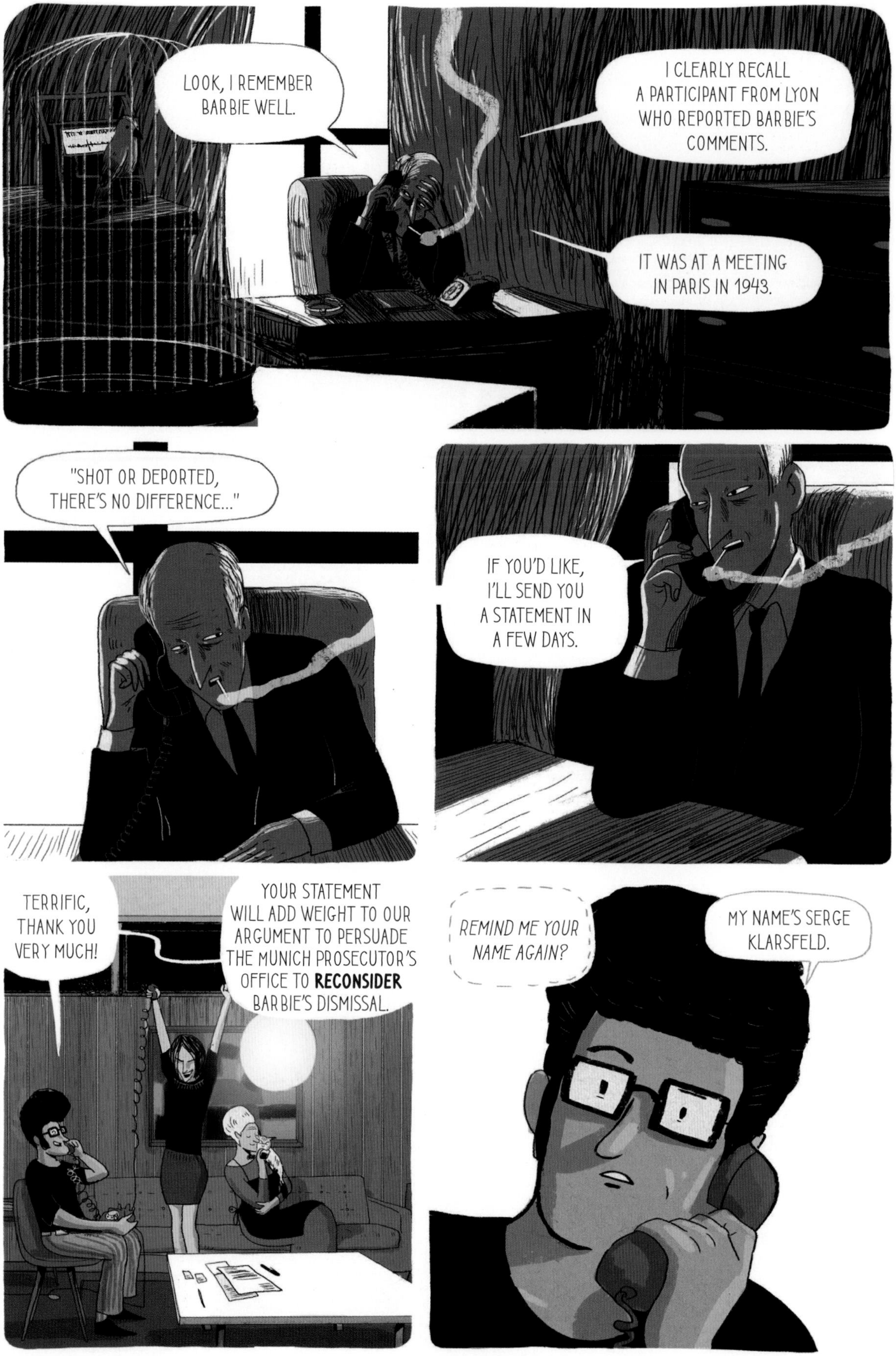
LOOK, I REMEMBER BARBIE WELL.
I CLEARLY RECALL A PARTICIPANT FROM LYON WHO REPORTED BARBIE'S COMMENTS.
IT WAS AT A MEETING IN PARIS IN 1943.
"SHOT OR DEPORTED, THERE'S NO DIFFERENCE..."
IF YOU'D LIKE, I'LL SEND YOU A STATEMENT IN A FEW DAYS.
TERRIFIC, THANK YOU VERY MUCH!
YOUR STATEMENT WILL ADD WEIGHT TO OUR ARGUMENT TO PERSUADE THE MUNICH PROSECUTOR'S OFFICE TO **RECONSIDER** BARBIE'S DISMISSAL.
REMIND ME YOUR NAME AGAIN?
MY NAME'S SERGE KLARSFELD.

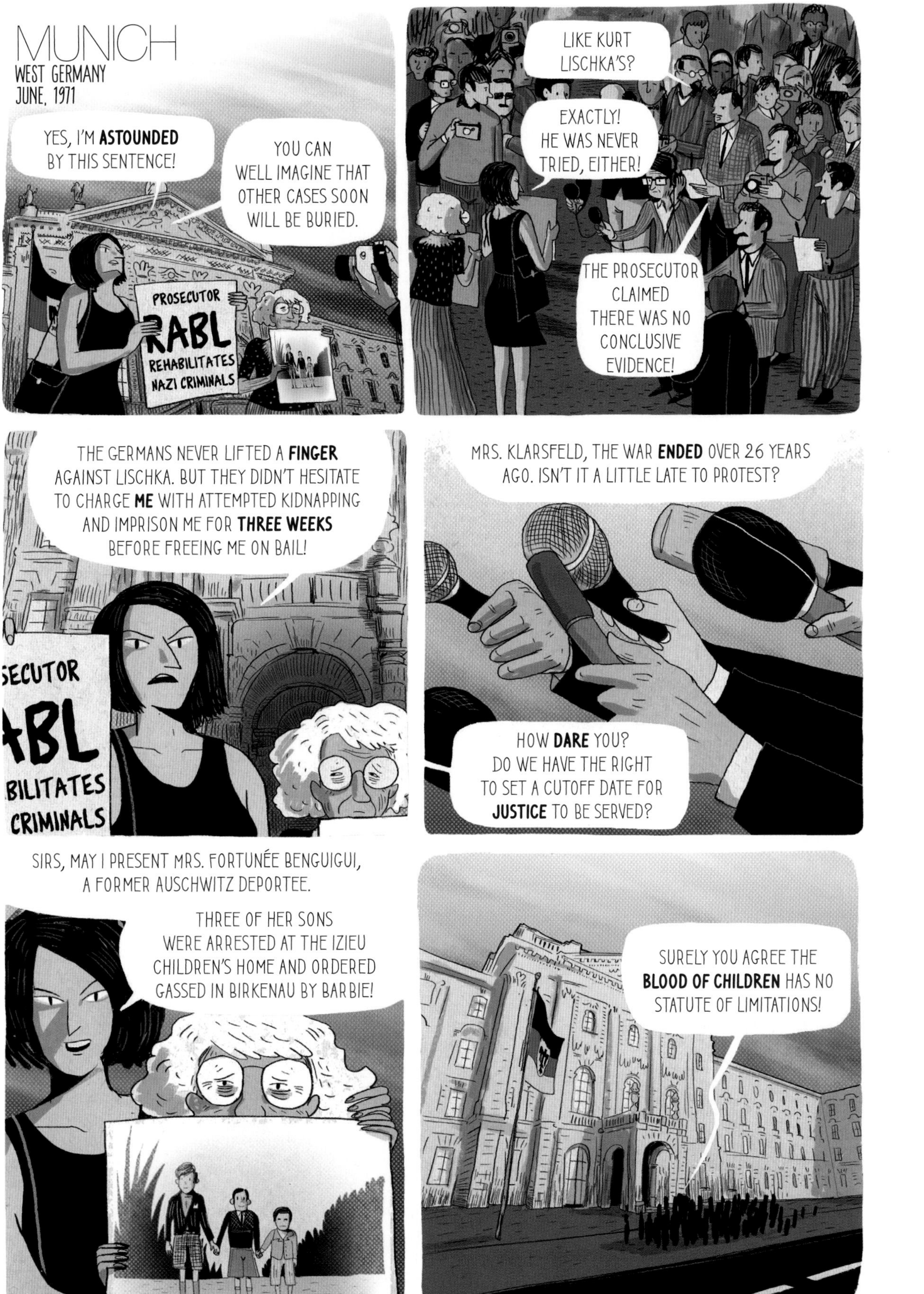
MUNICH
WEST GERMANY
JUNE, 1971
YES, I'M **ASTOUNDED** BY THIS SENTENCE!
YOU CAN WELL IMAGINE THAT OTHER CASES SOON WILL BE BURIED.
PROSECUTOR RABL REHABILITATES NAZI CRIMINALS
LIKE KURT LISCHKA'S?
EXACTLY! HE WAS NEVER TRIED, EITHER!
THE PROSECUTOR CLAIMED THERE WAS NO CONCLUSIVE EVIDENCE!
THE GERMANS NEVER LIFTED A **FINGER** AGAINST LISCHKA. BUT THEY DIDN'T HESITATE TO CHARGE **ME** WITH ATTEMPTED KIDNAPPING AND IMPRISON ME FOR **THREE WEEKS** BEFORE FREEING ME ON BAIL!
SECUTOR RABL BILITATES CRIMINALS
MRS. KLARSFELD, THE WAR **ENDED** OVER 26 YEARS AGO. ISN'T IT A LITTLE LATE TO PROTEST?
HOW **DARE** YOU? DO WE HAVE THE RIGHT TO SET A CUTOFF DATE FOR **JUSTICE** TO BE SERVED?
SIRS, MAY I PRESENT MRS. FORTUNÉE BENGUIGUI, A FORMER AUSCHWITZ DEPORTEE.
THREE OF HER SONS WERE ARRESTED AT THE IZIEU CHILDREN'S HOME AND ORDERED GASSED IN BIRKENAU BY BARBIE!
SURELY YOU AGREE THE **BLOOD OF CHILDREN** HAS NO STATUTE OF LIMITATIONS!

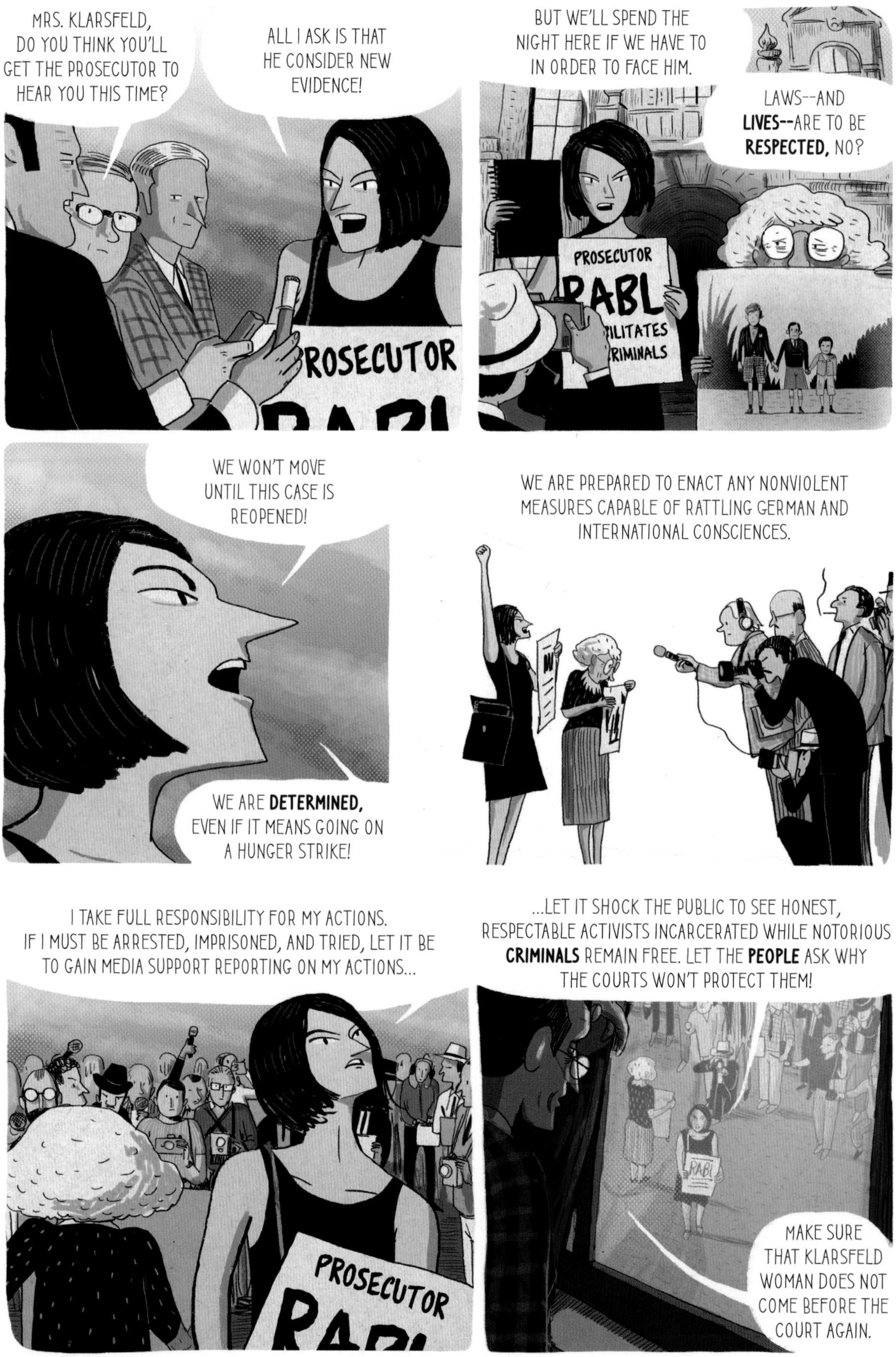

MRS. KLARSFELD, DO YOU THINK YOU'LL GET THE PROSECUTOR TO HEAR YOU THIS TIME?
ALL I ASK IS THAT HE CONSIDER NEW EVIDENCE!
PROSECUTOR
BUT WE'LL SPEND THE NIGHT HERE IF WE HAVE TO IN ORDER TO FACE HIM.
LAWS--AND **LIVES--**ARE TO BE **RESPECTED,** NO?
PROSECUTOR RABL
WE WON'T MOVE UNTIL THIS CASE IS REOPENED!
WE ARE **DETERMINED,** EVEN IF IT MEANS GOING ON A HUNGER STRIKE!
WE ARE PREPARED TO ENACT ANY NONVIOLENT MEASURES CAPABLE OF RATTLING GERMAN AND INTERNATIONAL CONSCIENCES.
I TAKE FULL RESPONSIBILITY FOR MY ACTIONS. IF I MUST BE ARRESTED, IMPRISONED, AND TRIED, LET IT BE TO GAIN MEDIA SUPPORT REPORTING ON MY ACTIONS...
PROSECUTOR
...LET IT SHOCK THE PUBLIC TO SEE HONEST, RESPECTABLE ACTIVISTS INCARCERATED WHILE NOTORIOUS **CRIMINALS** REMAIN FREE. LET THE **PEOPLE** ASK WHY THE COURTS WON'T PROTECT THEM!
RABL
MAKE SURE THAT KLARSFELD WOMAN DOES NOT COME BEFORE THE COURT AGAIN.

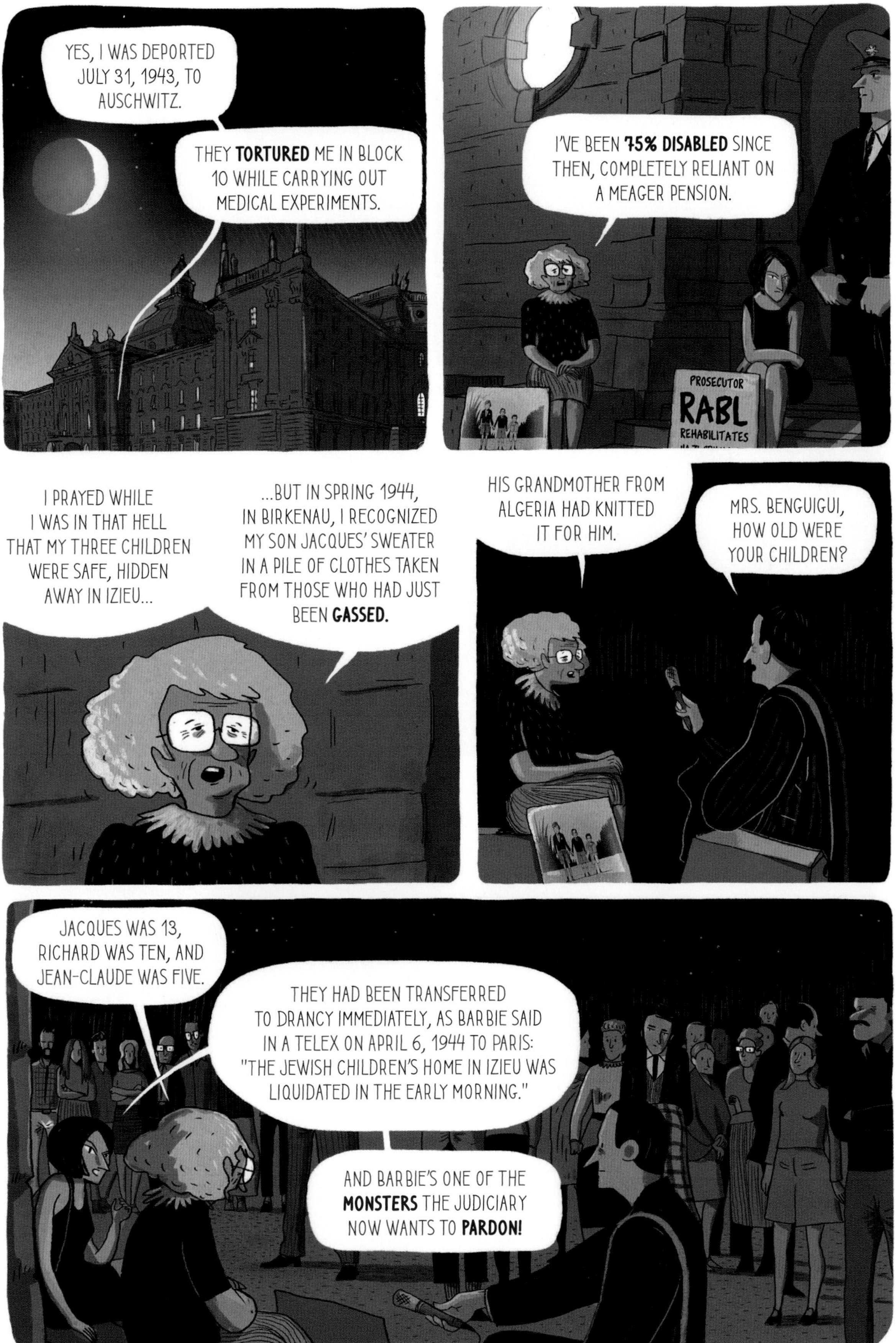
YES, I WAS DEPORTED JULY 31, 1943, TO AUSCHWITZ.
THEY **TORTURED** ME IN BLOCK 10 WHILE CARRYING OUT MEDICAL EXPERIMENTS.
I'VE BEEN **75% DISABLED** SINCE THEN, COMPLETELY RELIANT ON A MEAGER PENSION.
PROSECUTOR RABL REHABILITATES
I PRAYED WHILE I WAS IN THAT HELL THAT MY THREE CHILDREN WERE SAFE, HIDDEN AWAY IN IZIEU...
...BUT IN SPRING 1944, IN BIRKENAU, I RECOGNIZED MY SON JACQUES' SWEATER IN A PILE OF CLOTHES TAKEN FROM THOSE WHO HAD JUST BEEN **GASSED.**
HIS GRANDMOTHER FROM ALGERIA HAD KNITTED IT FOR HIM.
MRS. BENGUIGUI, HOW OLD WERE YOUR CHILDREN?
JACQUES WAS 13, RICHARD WAS TEN, AND JEAN-CLAUDE WAS FIVE.
THEY HAD BEEN TRANSFERRED TO DRANCY IMMEDIATELY, AS BARBIE SAID IN A TELEX ON APRIL 6, 1944 TO PARIS: "THE JEWISH CHILDREN'S HOME IN IZIEU WAS LIQUIDATED IN THE EARLY MORNING."
AND BARBIE'S ONE OF THE **MONSTERS** THE JUDICIARY NOW WANTS TO **PARDON!**

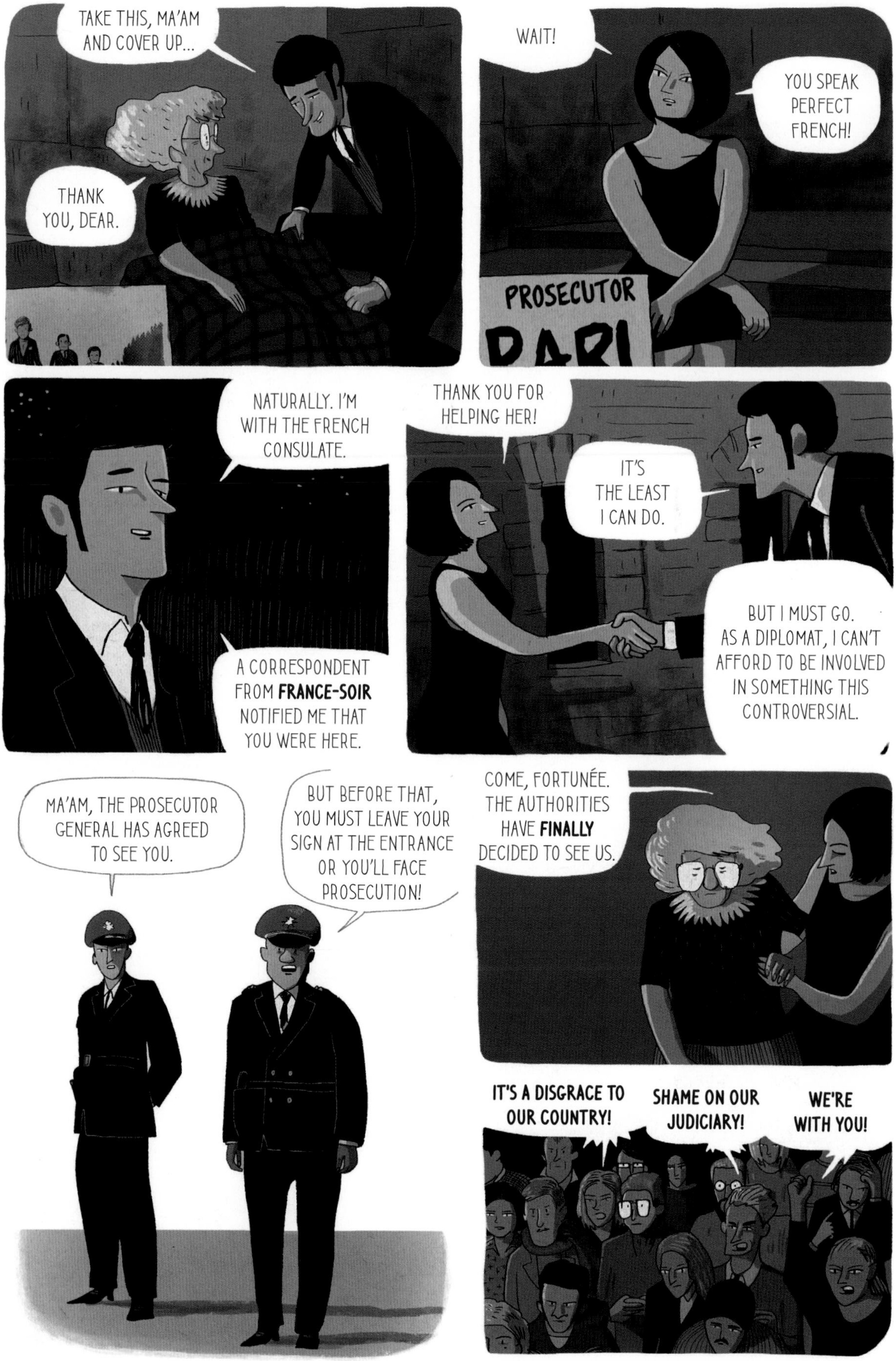
TAKE THIS, MA'AM AND COVER UP...
THANK YOU, DEAR.
WAIT!
YOU SPEAK PERFECT FRENCH!
PROSECUTOR
NATURALLY. I'M WITH THE FRENCH CONSULATE.
A CORRESPONDENT FROM FRANCE-SOIR NOTIFIED ME THAT YOU WERE HERE.
THANK YOU FOR HELPING HER!
IT'S THE LEAST I CAN DO.
BUT I MUST GO. AS A DIPLOMAT, I CAN'T AFFORD TO BE INVOLVED IN SOMETHING THIS CONTROVERSIAL.
MA'AM, THE PROSECUTOR GENERAL HAS AGREED TO SEE YOU.
BUT BEFORE THAT, YOU MUST LEAVE YOUR SIGN AT THE ENTRANCE OR YOU'LL FACE PROSECUTION!
COME, FORTUNÉE. THE AUTHORITIES HAVE FINALLY DECIDED TO SEE US.
IT'S A DISGRACE TO OUR COUNTRY!
SHAME ON OUR JUDICIARY!
WE'RE WITH YOU!

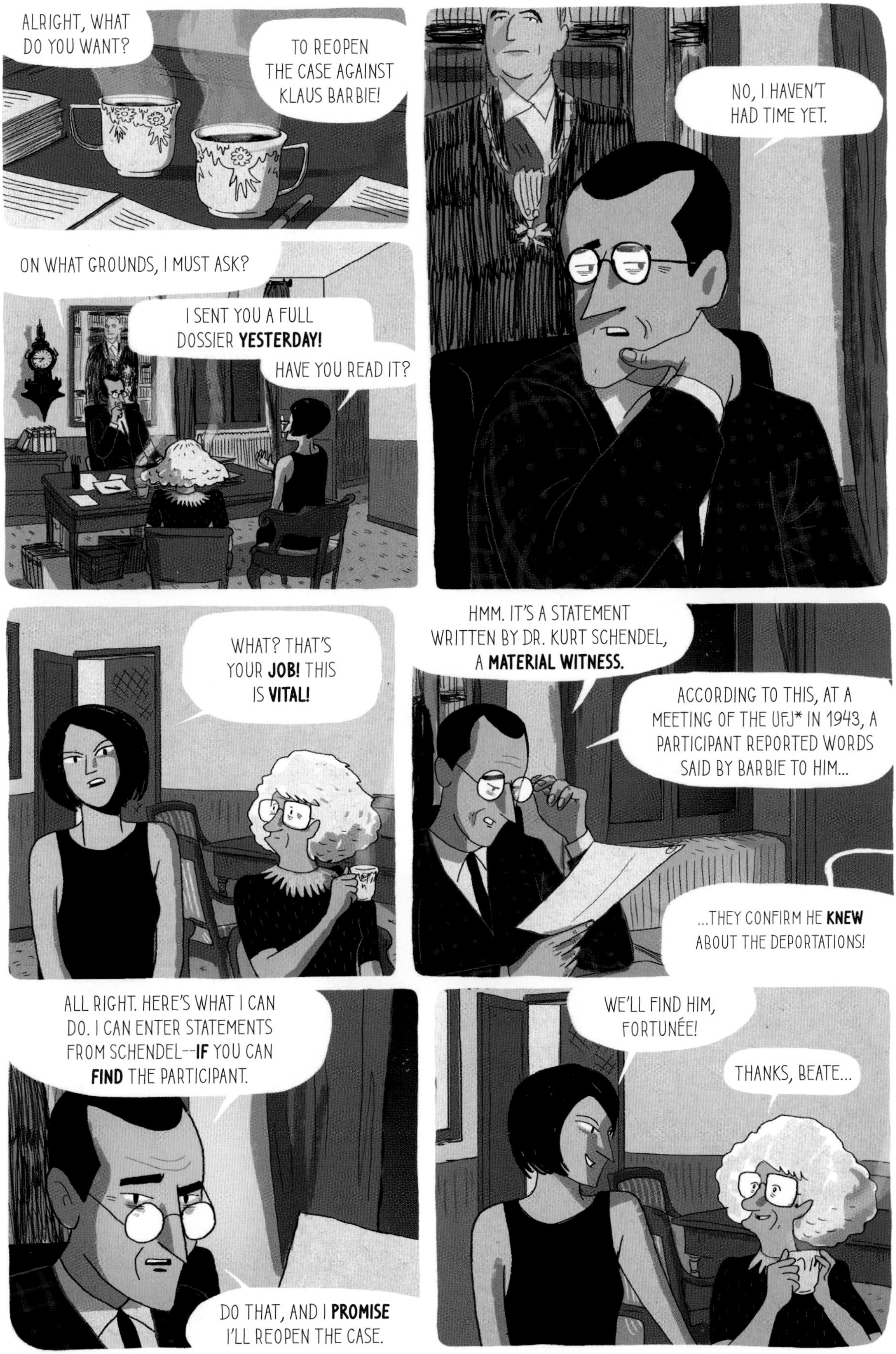

ALRIGHT, WHAT DO YOU WANT?
TO REOPEN THE CASE AGAINST KLAUS BARBIE!
ON WHAT GROUNDS, I MUST ASK?
I SENT YOU A FULL DOSSIER **YESTERDAY!**
HAVE YOU READ IT?
NO, I HAVEN'T HAD TIME YET.
WHAT? THAT'S YOUR **JOB!** THIS IS **VITAL!**
HMM. IT'S A STATEMENT WRITTEN BY DR. KURT SCHENDEL, A **MATERIAL WITNESS.**
ACCORDING TO THIS, AT A MEETING OF THE UFJ* IN 1943, A PARTICIPANT REPORTED WORDS SAID BY BARBIE TO HIM...
...THEY CONFIRM HE **KNEW** ABOUT THE DEPORTATIONS!
ALL RIGHT. HERE'S WHAT I CAN DO. I CAN ENTER STATEMENTS FROM SCHENDEL--**IF** YOU CAN **FIND** THE PARTICIPANT.
DO THAT, AND I **PROMISE** I'LL REOPEN THE CASE.
WE'LL FIND HIM, FORTUNÉE!
THANKS, BEATE...

*UNION OF FRENCH JEWS

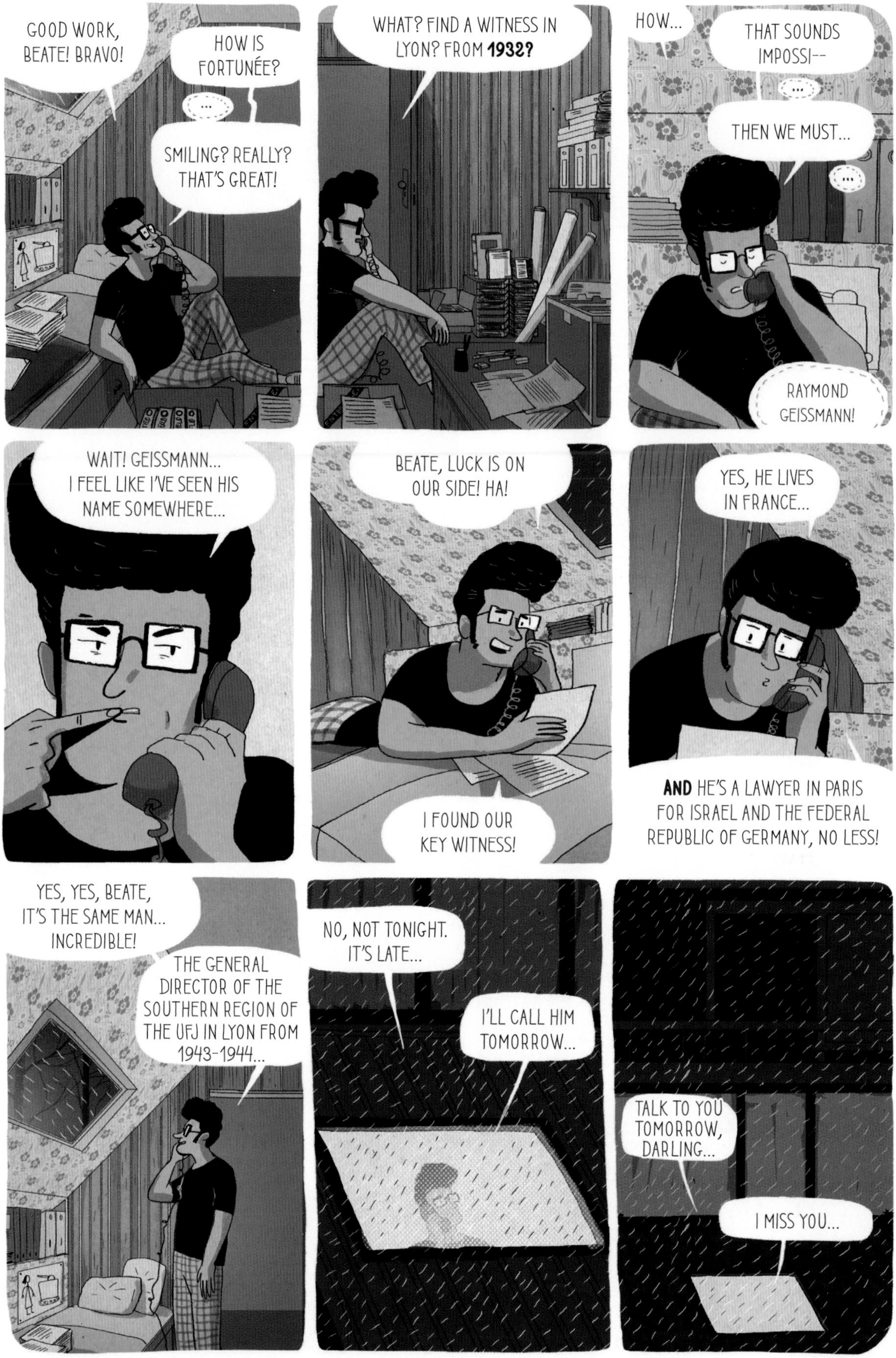

GOOD WORK, BEATE! BRAVO!
HOW IS FORTUNÉE?
...
SMILING? REALLY? THAT'S GREAT!
WHAT? FIND A WITNESS IN LYON? FROM **1932?**
HOW...
THAT SOUNDS IMPOSSI--
...
THEN WE MUST...
...
RAYMOND GEISSMANN!
WAIT! GEISSMANN... I FEEL LIKE I'VE SEEN HIS NAME SOMEWHERE...
BEATE, LUCK IS ON OUR SIDE! HA!
I FOUND OUR KEY WITNESS!
YES, HE LIVES IN FRANCE...
AND HE'S A LAWYER IN PARIS FOR ISRAEL AND THE FEDERAL REPUBLIC OF GERMANY, NO LESS!
YES, YES, BEATE, IT'S THE SAME MAN... INCREDIBLE!
THE GENERAL DIRECTOR OF THE SOUTHERN REGION OF THE UFJ IN LYON FROM 1943-1944...
NO, NOT TONIGHT. IT'S LATE...
I'LL CALL HIM TOMORROW...
TALK TO YOU TOMORROW, DARLING...
I MISS YOU...

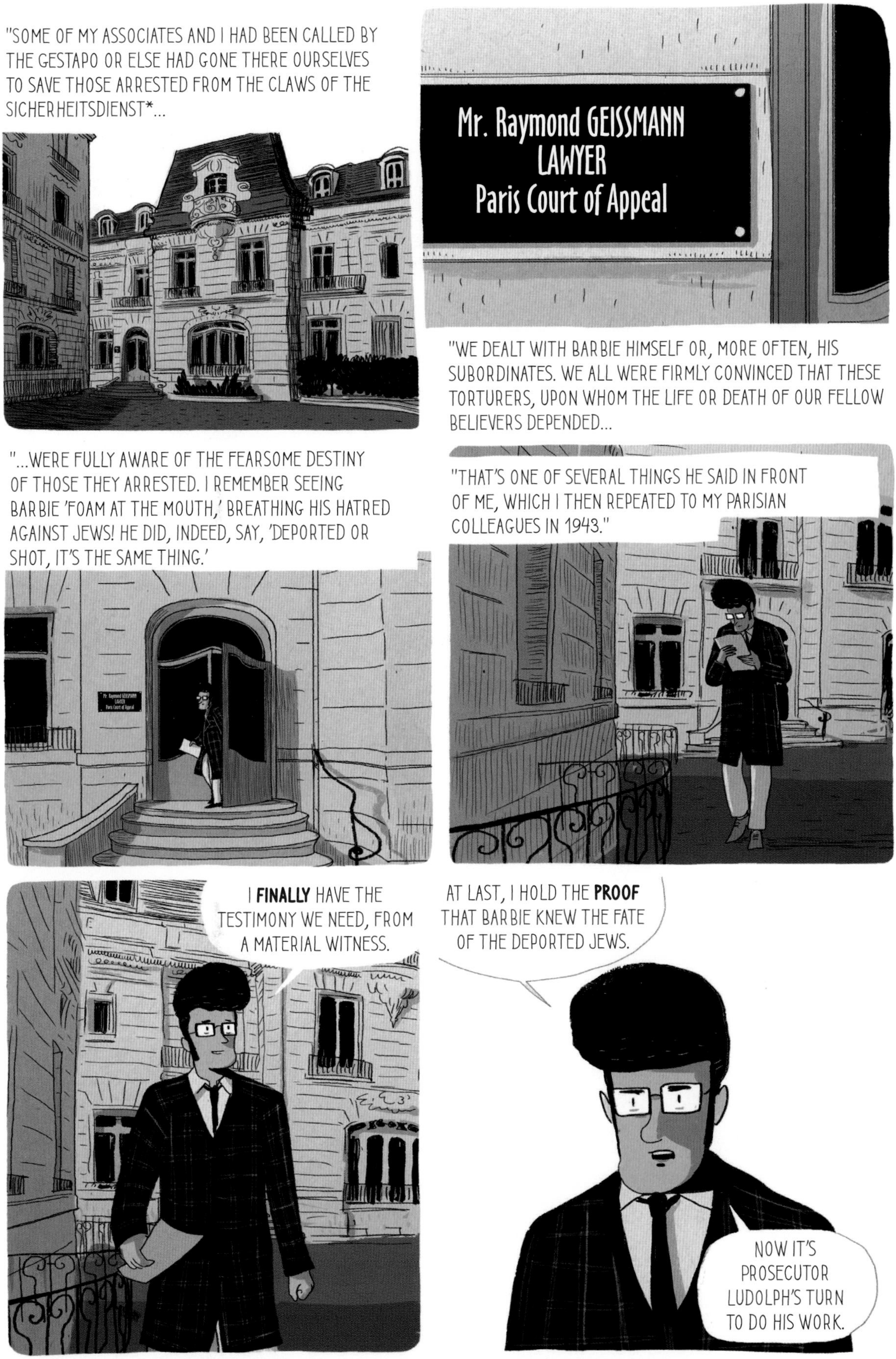
"SOME OF MY ASSOCIATES AND I HAD BEEN CALLED BY THE GESTAPO OR ELSE HAD GONE THERE OURSELVES TO SAVE THOSE ARRESTED FROM THE CLAWS OF THE SICHERHEITSDIENST*...
Mr. Raymond GEISSMANN
LAWYER
Paris Court of Appeal
"WE DEALT WITH BARBIE HIMSELF OR, MORE OFTEN, HIS SUBORDINATES. WE ALL WERE FIRMLY CONVINCED THAT THESE TORTURERS, UPON WHOM THE LIFE OR DEATH OF OUR FELLOW BELIEVERS DEPENDED...
"...WERE FULLY AWARE OF THE FEARSOME DESTINY OF THOSE THEY ARRESTED. I REMEMBER SEEING BARBIE 'FOAM AT THE MOUTH,' BREATHING HIS HATRED AGAINST JEWS! HE DID, INDEED, SAY, 'DEPORTED OR SHOT, IT'S THE SAME THING.'
"THAT'S ONE OF SEVERAL THINGS HE SAID IN FRONT OF ME, WHICH I THEN REPEATED TO MY PARISIAN COLLEAGUES IN 1943."
I **FINALLY** HAVE THE TESTIMONY WE NEED, FROM A MATERIAL WITNESS.
AT LAST, I HOLD THE **PROOF** THAT BARBIE KNEW THE FATE OF THE DEPORTED JEWS.
NOW IT'S PROSECUTOR LUDOLPH'S TURN TO DO HIS WORK.

*THE SECURITY SERVICE OF THE REICHSFÜHRER-SS

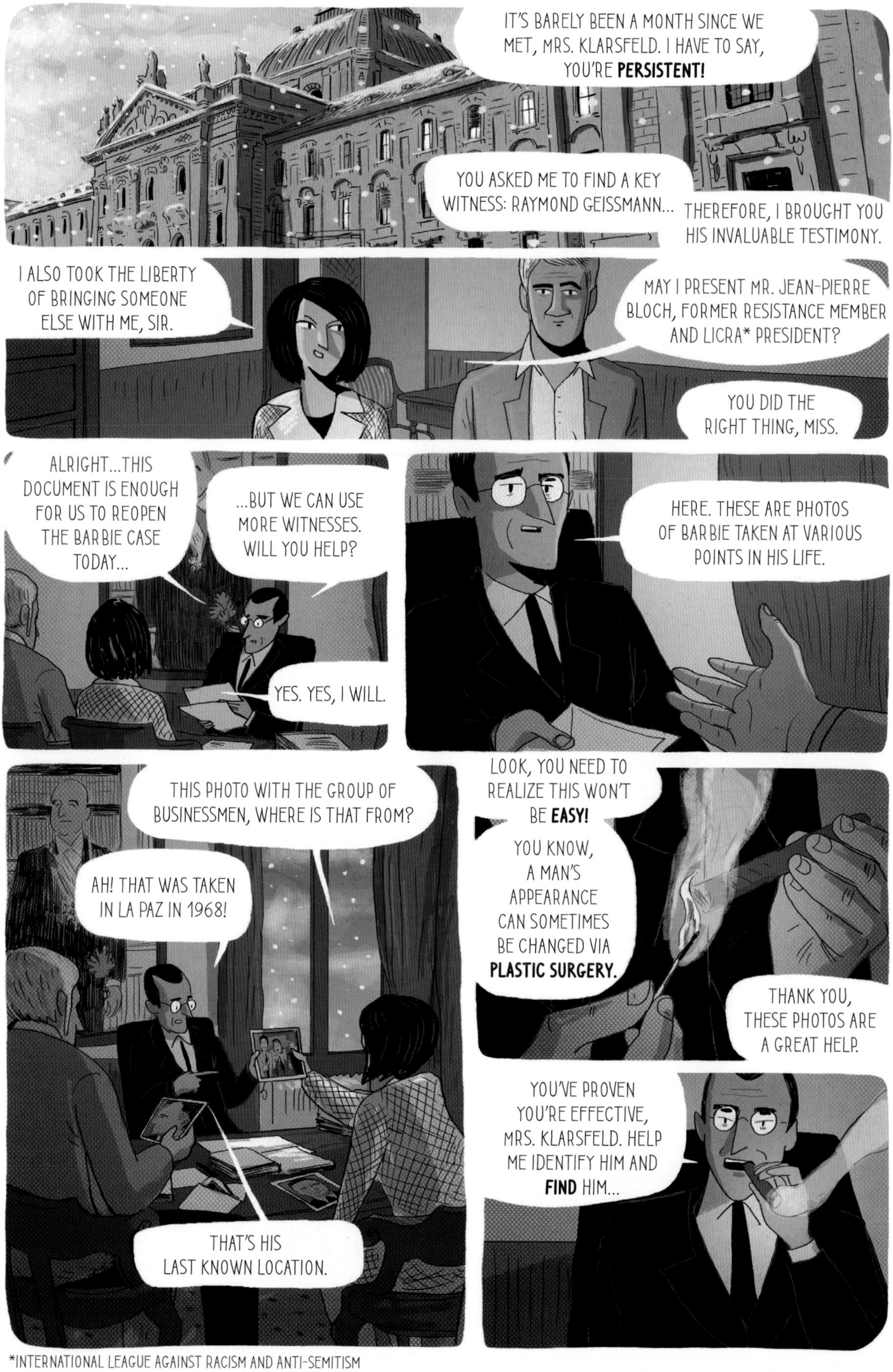
IT'S BARELY BEEN A MONTH SINCE WE MET, MRS. KLARSFELD. I HAVE TO SAY, YOU'RE **PERSISTENT!**
YOU ASKED ME TO FIND A KEY WITNESS: RAYMOND GEISSMANN...
THEREFORE, I BROUGHT YOU HIS INVALUABLE TESTIMONY.
I ALSO TOOK THE LIBERTY OF BRINGING SOMEONE ELSE WITH ME, SIR.
MAY I PRESENT MR. JEAN-PIERRE BLOCH, FORMER RESISTANCE MEMBER AND LICRA* PRESIDENT?
YOU DID THE RIGHT THING, MISS.
ALRIGHT...THIS DOCUMENT IS ENOUGH FOR US TO REOPEN THE BARBIE CASE TODAY...
...BUT WE CAN USE MORE WITNESSES. WILL YOU HELP?
YES. YES, I WILL.
HERE. THESE ARE PHOTOS OF BARBIE TAKEN AT VARIOUS POINTS IN HIS LIFE.
THIS PHOTO WITH THE GROUP OF BUSINESSMEN, WHERE IS THAT FROM?
AH! THAT WAS TAKEN IN LA PAZ IN 1968!
THAT'S HIS LAST KNOWN LOCATION.
LOOK, YOU NEED TO REALIZE THIS WON'T BE **EASY!**
YOU KNOW, A MAN'S APPEARANCE CAN SOMETIMES BE CHANGED VIA **PLASTIC SURGERY.**
THANK YOU, THESE PHOTOS ARE A GREAT HELP.
YOU'VE PROVEN YOU'RE EFFECTIVE, MRS. KLARSFELD. HELP ME IDENTIFY HIM AND **FIND** HIM...

*INTERNATIONAL LEAGUE AGAINST RACISM AND ANTI-SEMITISM

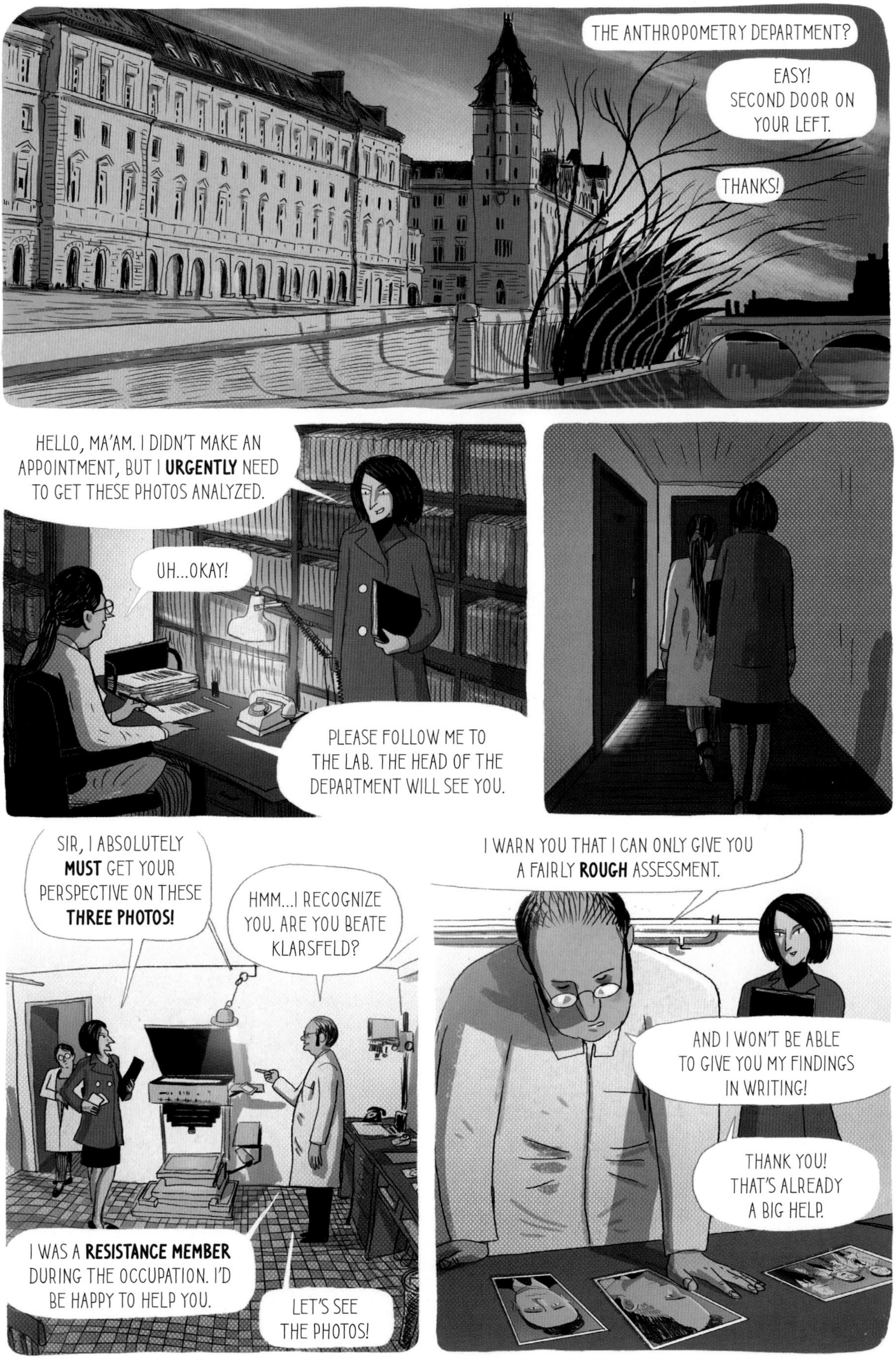
THE ANTHROPOMETRY DEPARTMENT?
EASY! SECOND DOOR ON YOUR LEFT.
THANKS!
HELLO, MA'AM. I DIDN'T MAKE AN APPOINTMENT, BUT I **URGENTLY** NEED TO GET THESE PHOTOS ANALYZED.
UH...OKAY!
PLEASE FOLLOW ME TO THE LAB. THE HEAD OF THE DEPARTMENT WILL SEE YOU.
SIR, I ABSOLUTELY **MUST** GET YOUR PERSPECTIVE ON THESE **THREE PHOTOS!**
HMM...I RECOGNIZE YOU. ARE YOU BEATE KLARSFELD?
I WAS A **RESISTANCE MEMBER** DURING THE OCCUPATION. I'D BE HAPPY TO HELP YOU.
LET'S SEE THE PHOTOS!
I WARN YOU THAT I CAN ONLY GIVE YOU A FAIRLY **ROUGH** ASSESSMENT.
AND I WON'T BE ABLE TO GIVE YOU MY FINDINGS IN WRITING!
THANK YOU! THAT'S ALREADY A BIG HELP.

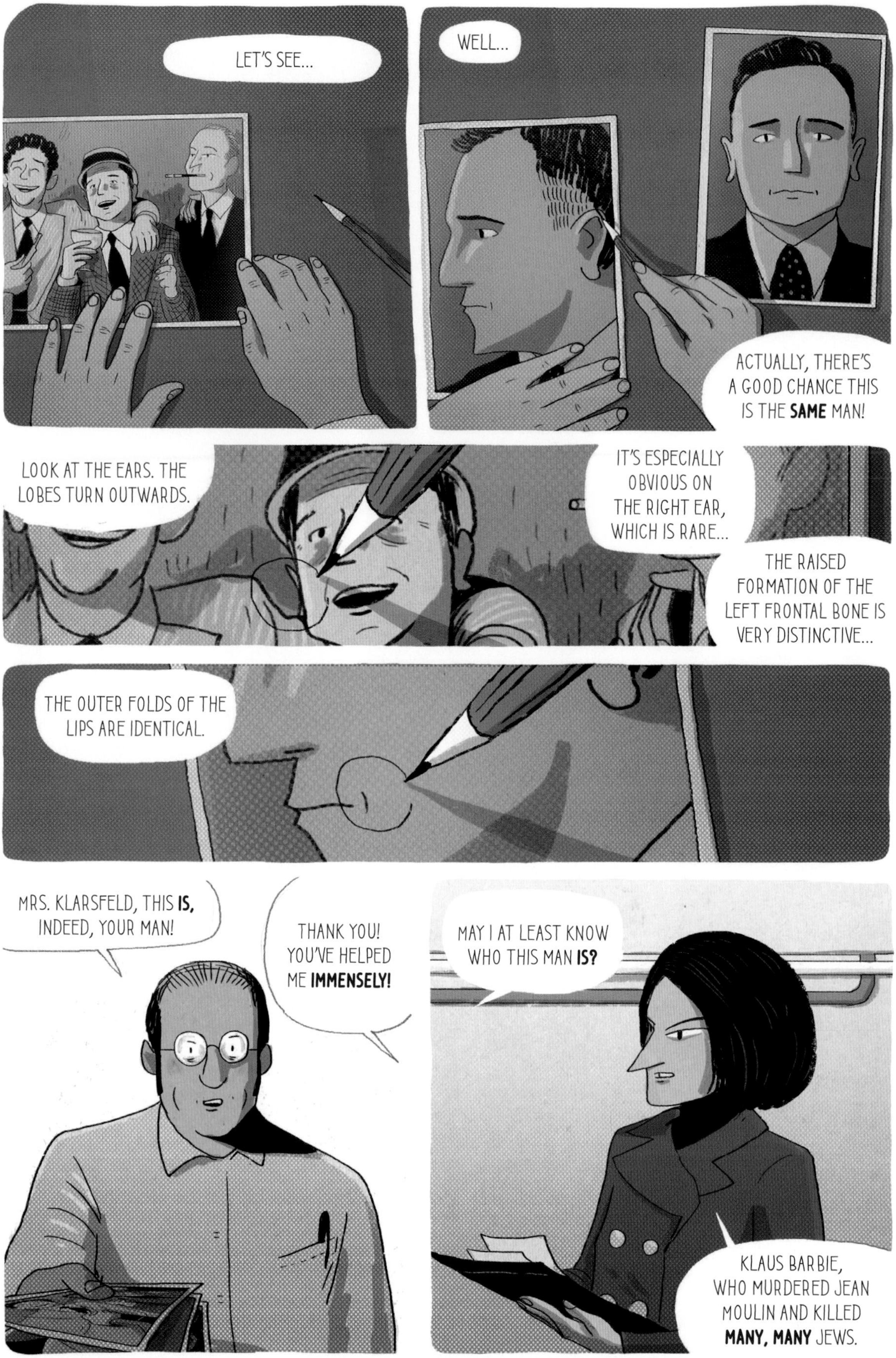
LET'S SEE...
WELL...
ACTUALLY, THERE'S A GOOD CHANCE THIS IS THE **SAME** MAN!
LOOK AT THE EARS. THE LOBES TURN OUTWARDS.
IT'S ESPECIALLY OBVIOUS ON THE RIGHT EAR, WHICH IS RARE...
THE RAISED FORMATION OF THE LEFT FRONTAL BONE IS VERY DISTINCTIVE...
THE OUTER FOLDS OF THE LIPS ARE IDENTICAL.
MRS. KLARSFELD, THIS **IS,** INDEED, YOUR MAN!
THANK YOU! YOU'VE HELPED ME **IMMENSELY!**
MAY I AT LEAST KNOW WHO THIS MAN **IS?**
KLAUS BARBIE, WHO MURDERED JEAN MOULIN AND KILLED **MANY, MANY** JEWS.

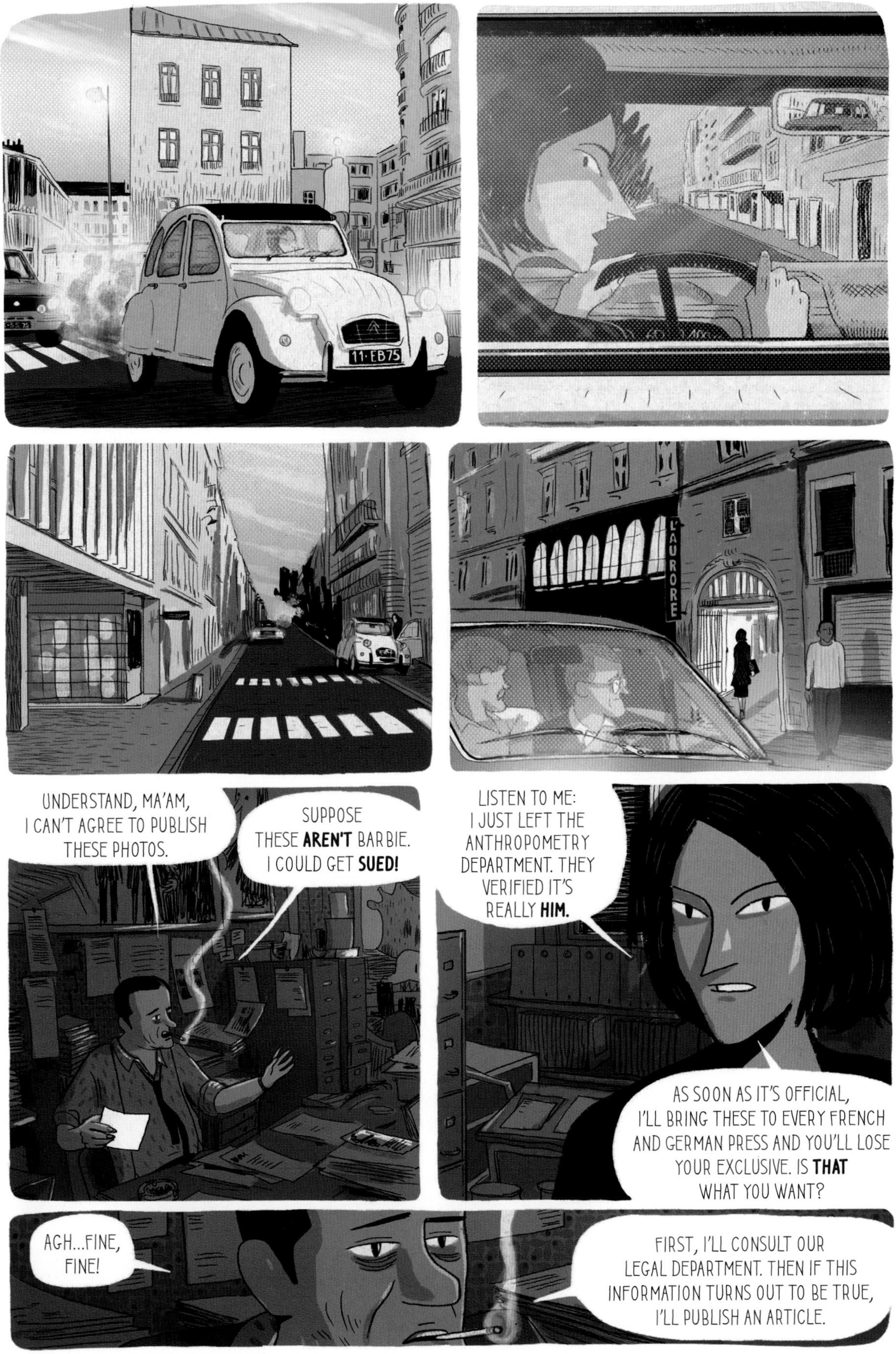
11·EB75
L'AURORE
UNDERSTAND, MA'AM, I CAN'T AGREE TO PUBLISH THESE PHOTOS.
SUPPOSE THESE **AREN'T** BARBIE. I COULD GET **SUED!**
LISTEN TO ME: I JUST LEFT THE ANTHROPOMETRY DEPARTMENT. THEY VERIFIED IT'S REALLY **HIM.**
AS SOON AS IT'S OFFICIAL, I'LL BRING THESE TO EVERY FRENCH AND GERMAN PRESS AND YOU'LL LOSE YOUR EXCLUSIVE. IS **THAT** WHAT YOU WANT?
AGH...FINE, FINE!
FIRST, I'LL CONSULT OUR LEGAL DEPARTMENT. THEN IF THIS INFORMATION TURNS OUT TO BE TRUE, I'LL PUBLISH AN ARTICLE.

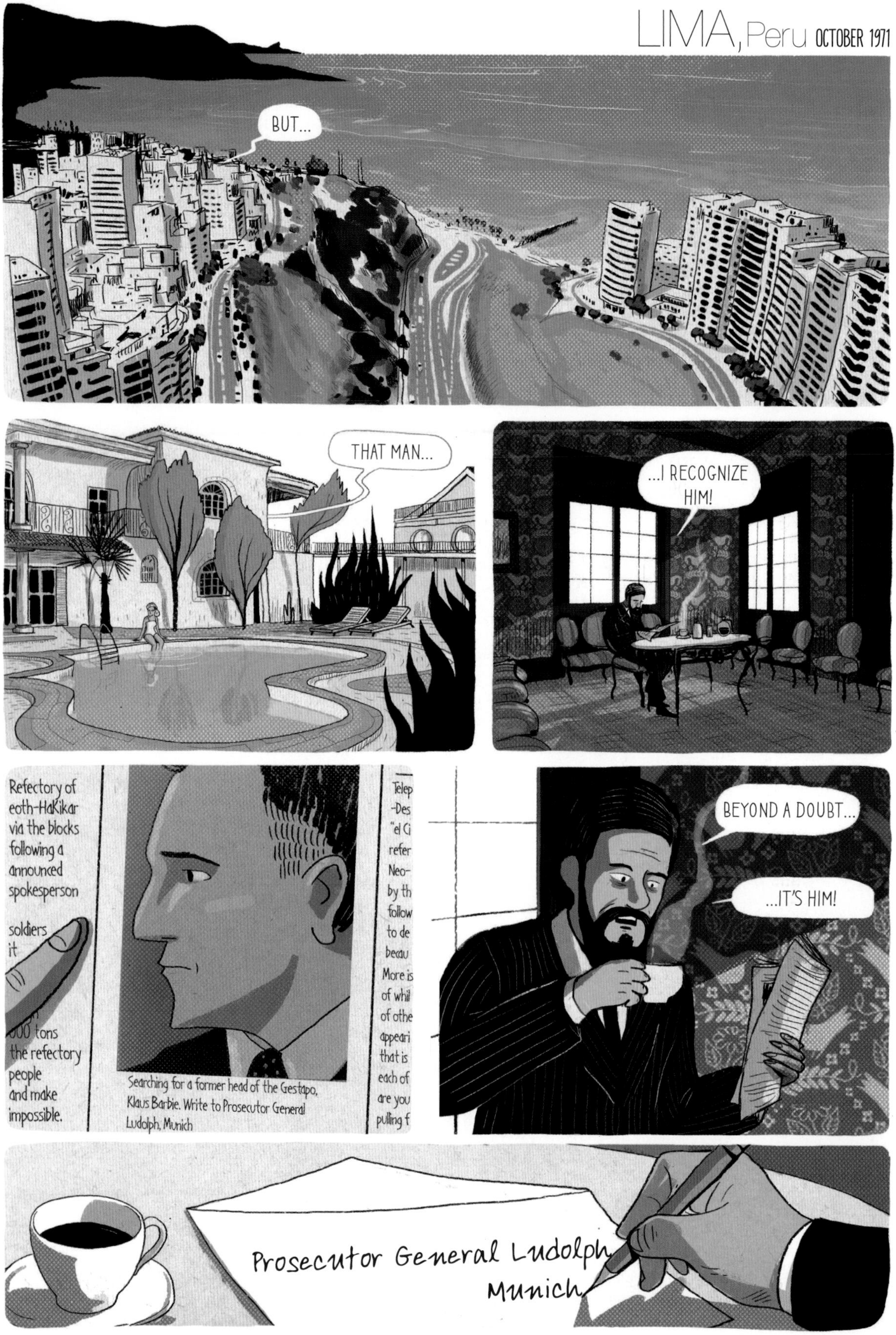
LIMA, Peru OCTOBER 1971
BUT...
THAT MAN...
...I RECOGNIZE HIM!
Refectory of eoth-HaKikar via the blocks following a announced spokesperson soldiers it 000 tons the refectory people and make impossible.
Searching for a former head of the Gestapo, Klaus Barbie. Write to Prosecutor General Ludolph, Munich
Telep -Des "el Ci refer Neo- by th follow to de becau More is of whi of othe appeari that is each of are you pulling f
BEYOND A DOUBT...
...IT'S HIM!
Prosecutor General Ludolph
Munich

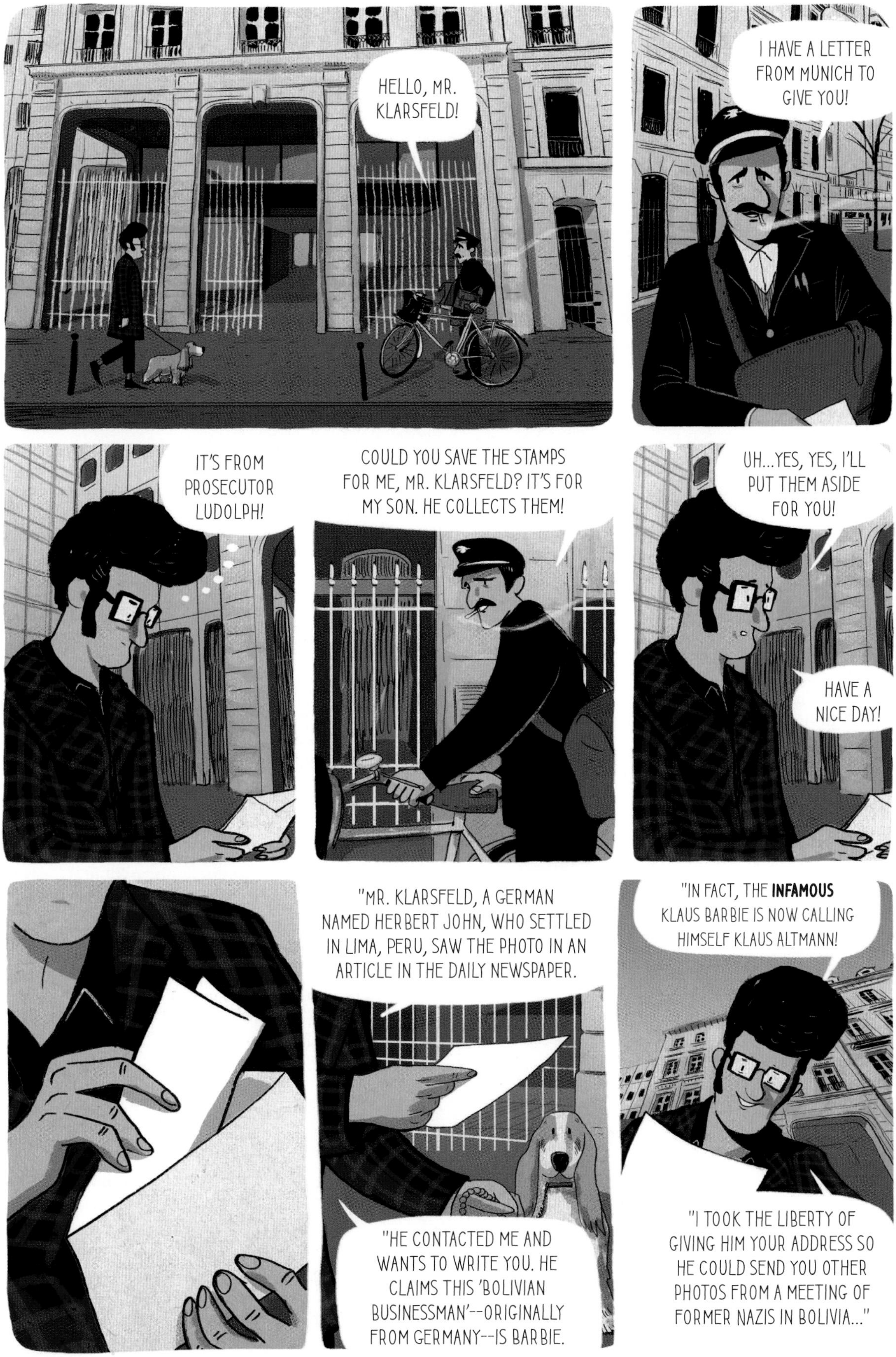
HELLO, MR. KLARSFELD!
I HAVE A LETTER FROM MUNICH TO GIVE YOU!
IT'S FROM PROSECUTOR LUDOLPH!
COULD YOU SAVE THE STAMPS FOR ME, MR. KLARSFELD? IT'S FOR MY SON. HE COLLECTS THEM!
UH...YES, YES, I'LL PUT THEM ASIDE FOR YOU!
HAVE A NICE DAY!
"MR. KLARSFELD, A GERMAN NAMED HERBERT JOHN, WHO SETTLED IN LIMA, PERU, SAW THE PHOTO IN AN ARTICLE IN THE DAILY NEWSPAPER.
"HE CONTACTED ME AND WANTS TO WRITE YOU. HE CLAIMS THIS 'BOLIVIAN BUSINESSMAN'--ORIGINALLY FROM GERMANY--IS BARBIE.
"IN FACT, THE **INFAMOUS** KLAUS BARBIE IS NOW CALLING HIMSELF KLAUS ALTMANN!
"I TOOK THE LIBERTY OF GIVING HIM YOUR ADDRESS SO HE COULD SEND YOU OTHER PHOTOS FROM A MEETING OF FORMER NAZIS IN BOLIVIA..."

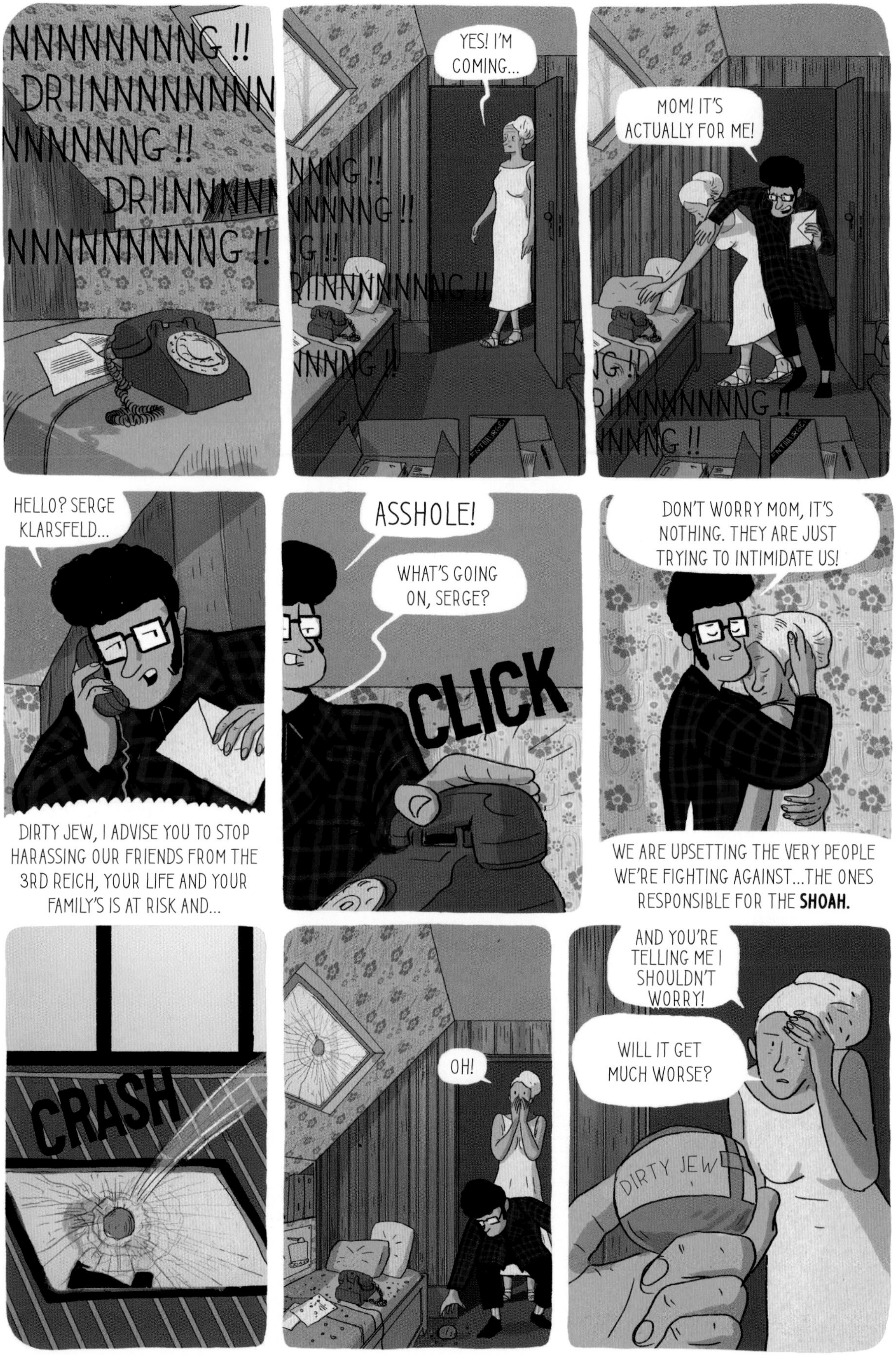
NNNNNNNNG!!
DRIINNNNNNNNN
NNNNNNG!!
DRIINNNNNN
NNNNNNNNNG!!
YES! I'M COMING...
MOM! IT'S ACTUALLY FOR ME!
HELLO? SERGE KLARSFELD...
DIRTY JEW, I ADVISE YOU TO STOP HARASSING OUR FRIENDS FROM THE 3RD REICH, YOUR LIFE AND YOUR FAMILY'S IS AT RISK AND...
ASSHOLE!
WHAT'S GOING ON, SERGE?
CLICK
DON'T WORRY MOM, IT'S NOTHING. THEY ARE JUST TRYING TO INTIMIDATE US!
WE ARE UPSETTING THE VERY PEOPLE WE'RE FIGHTING AGAINST...THE ONES RESPONSIBLE FOR THE **SHOAH.**
CRASH
OH!
AND YOU'RE TELLING ME I SHOULDN'T WORRY!
WILL IT GET MUCH WORSE?
DIRTY JEW

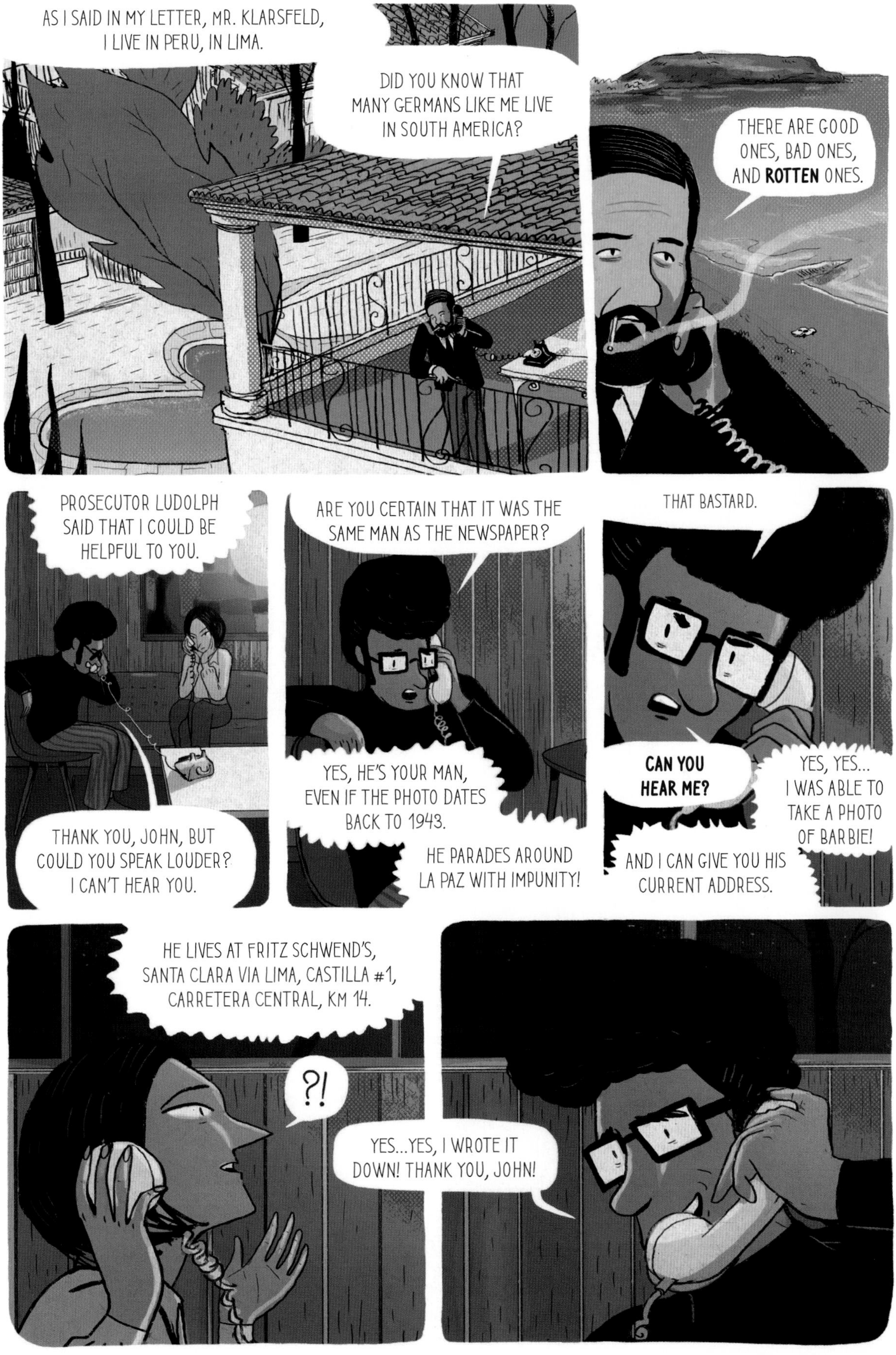

AS I SAID IN MY LETTER, MR. KLARSFELD, I LIVE IN PERU, IN LIMA.
DID YOU KNOW THAT MANY GERMANS LIKE ME LIVE IN SOUTH AMERICA?
THERE ARE GOOD ONES, BAD ONES, AND **ROTTEN** ONES.
PROSECUTOR LUDOLPH SAID THAT I COULD BE HELPFUL TO YOU.
THANK YOU, JOHN, BUT COULD YOU SPEAK LOUDER? I CAN'T HEAR YOU.
ARE YOU CERTAIN THAT IT WAS THE SAME MAN AS THE NEWSPAPER?
YES, HE'S YOUR MAN, EVEN IF THE PHOTO DATES BACK TO 1943.
HE PARADES AROUND LA PAZ WITH IMPUNITY!
THAT BASTARD.
CAN YOU HEAR ME?
YES, YES... I WAS ABLE TO TAKE A PHOTO OF BARBIE!
AND I CAN GIVE YOU HIS CURRENT ADDRESS.
HE LIVES AT FRITZ SCHWEND'S, SANTA CLARA VIA LIMA, CASTILLA #1, CARRETERA CENTRAL, KM 14.
?!
YES...YES, I WROTE IT DOWN! THANK YOU, JOHN!

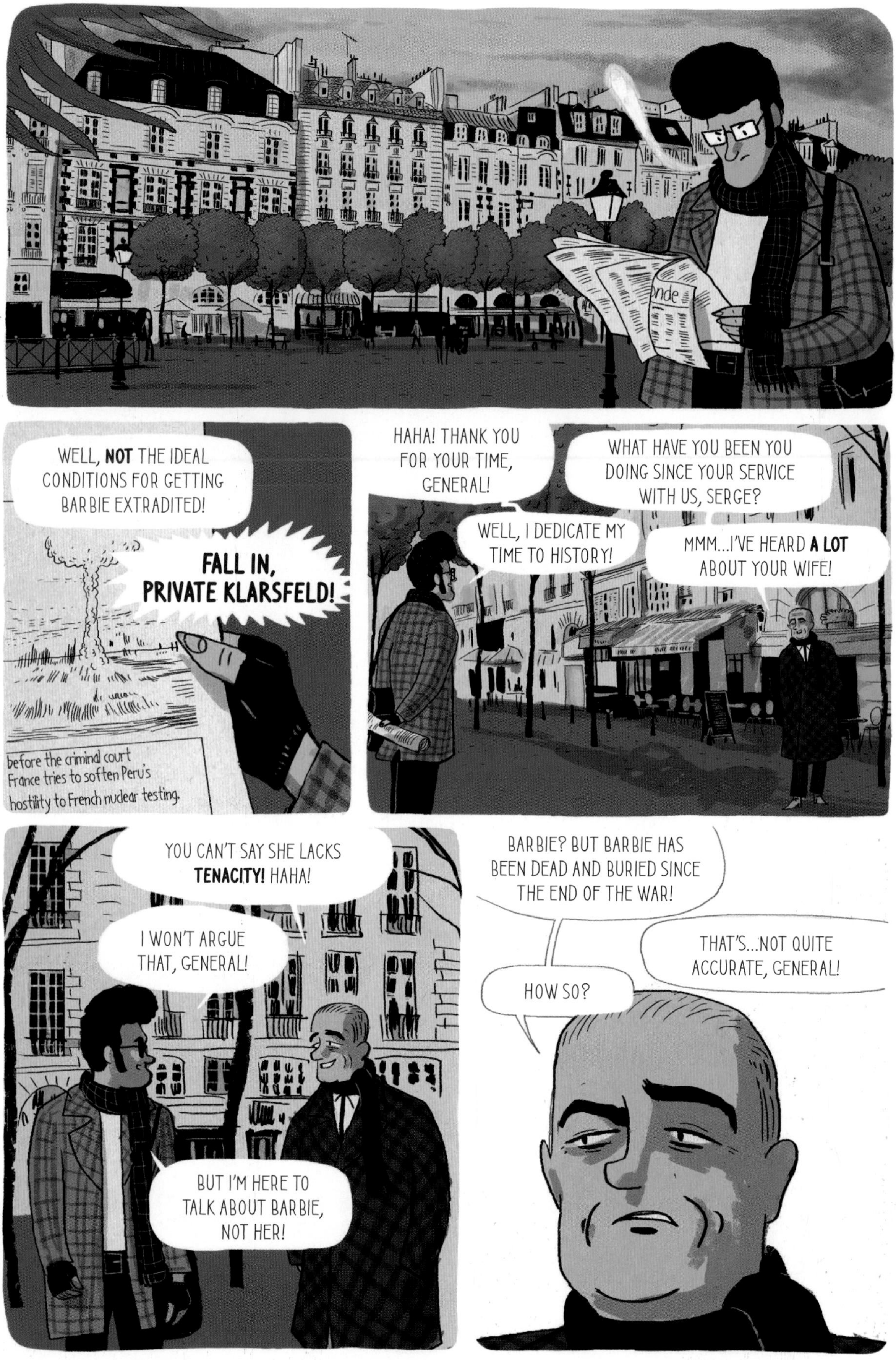

WELL, **NOT** THE IDEAL CONDITIONS FOR GETTING BARBIE EXTRADITED!
FALL IN, PRIVATE KLARSFELD!
before the criminal court
France tries to soften Peru's
hostility to French nuclear testing.
HAHA! THANK YOU FOR YOUR TIME, GENERAL!
WHAT HAVE YOU BEEN YOU DOING SINCE YOUR SERVICE WITH US, SERGE?
WELL, I DEDICATE MY TIME TO HISTORY!
MMM...I'VE HEARD **A LOT** ABOUT YOUR WIFE!
YOU CAN'T SAY SHE LACKS **TENACITY!** HAHA!
I WON'T ARGUE THAT, GENERAL!
BUT I'M HERE TO TALK ABOUT BARBIE, NOT HER!
BARBIE? BUT BARBIE HAS BEEN DEAD AND BURIED SINCE THE END OF THE WAR!
THAT'S...NOT QUITE ACCURATE, GENERAL!
HOW SO?

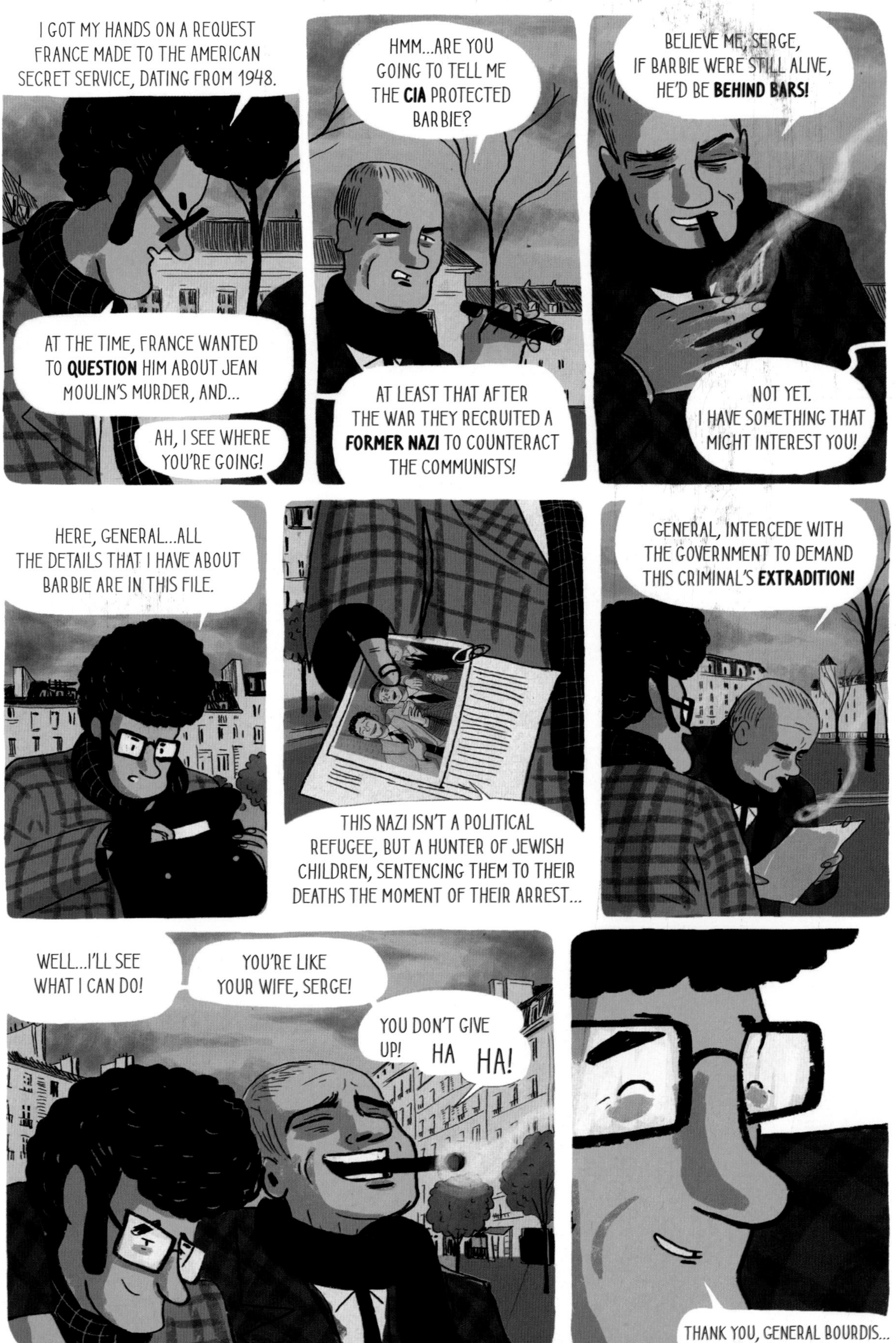
I GOT MY HANDS ON A REQUEST FRANCE MADE TO THE AMERICAN SECRET SERVICE, DATING FROM 1948.
AT THE TIME, FRANCE WANTED TO **QUESTION** HIM ABOUT JEAN MOULIN'S MURDER, AND...
AH, I SEE WHERE YOU'RE GOING!
HMM...ARE YOU GOING TO TELL ME THE **CIA** PROTECTED BARBIE?
AT LEAST THAT AFTER THE WAR THEY RECRUITED A **FORMER NAZI** TO COUNTERACT THE COMMUNISTS!
BELIEVE ME, SERGE, IF BARBIE WERE STILL ALIVE, HE'D BE **BEHIND BARS!**
NOT YET. I HAVE SOMETHING THAT MIGHT INTEREST YOU!
HERE, GENERAL...ALL THE DETAILS THAT I HAVE ABOUT BARBIE ARE IN THIS FILE.
THIS NAZI ISN'T A POLITICAL REFUGEE, BUT A HUNTER OF JEWISH CHILDREN, SENTENCING THEM TO THEIR DEATHS THE MOMENT OF THEIR ARREST...
GENERAL, INTERCEDE WITH THE GOVERNMENT TO DEMAND THIS CRIMINAL'S **EXTRADITION!**
WELL...I'LL SEE WHAT I CAN DO!
YOU'RE LIKE YOUR WIFE, SERGE!
YOU DON'T GIVE UP!
HA
HA!
THANK YOU, GENERAL BOURDIS...

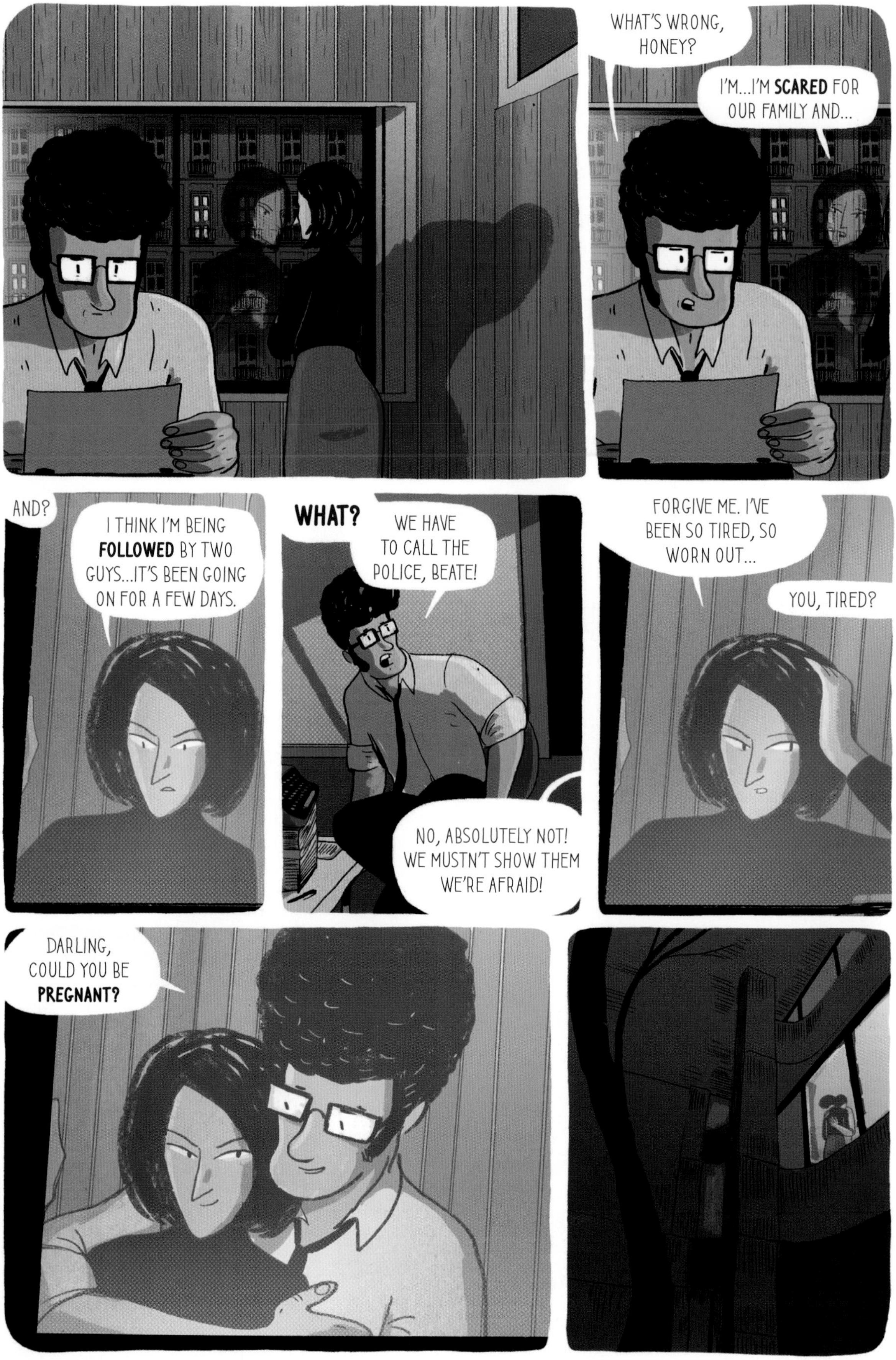
WHAT'S WRONG, HONEY?
I'M...I'M **SCARED** FOR OUR FAMILY AND...
AND?
I THINK I'M BEING **FOLLOWED** BY TWO GUYS...IT'S BEEN GOING ON FOR A FEW DAYS.
WHAT?
WE HAVE TO CALL THE POLICE, BEATE!
NO, ABSOLUTELY NOT! WE MUSTN'T SHOW THEM WE'RE AFRAID!
FORGIVE ME. I'VE BEEN SO TIRED, SO WORN OUT...
YOU, TIRED?
DARLING, COULD YOU BE **PREGNANT?**

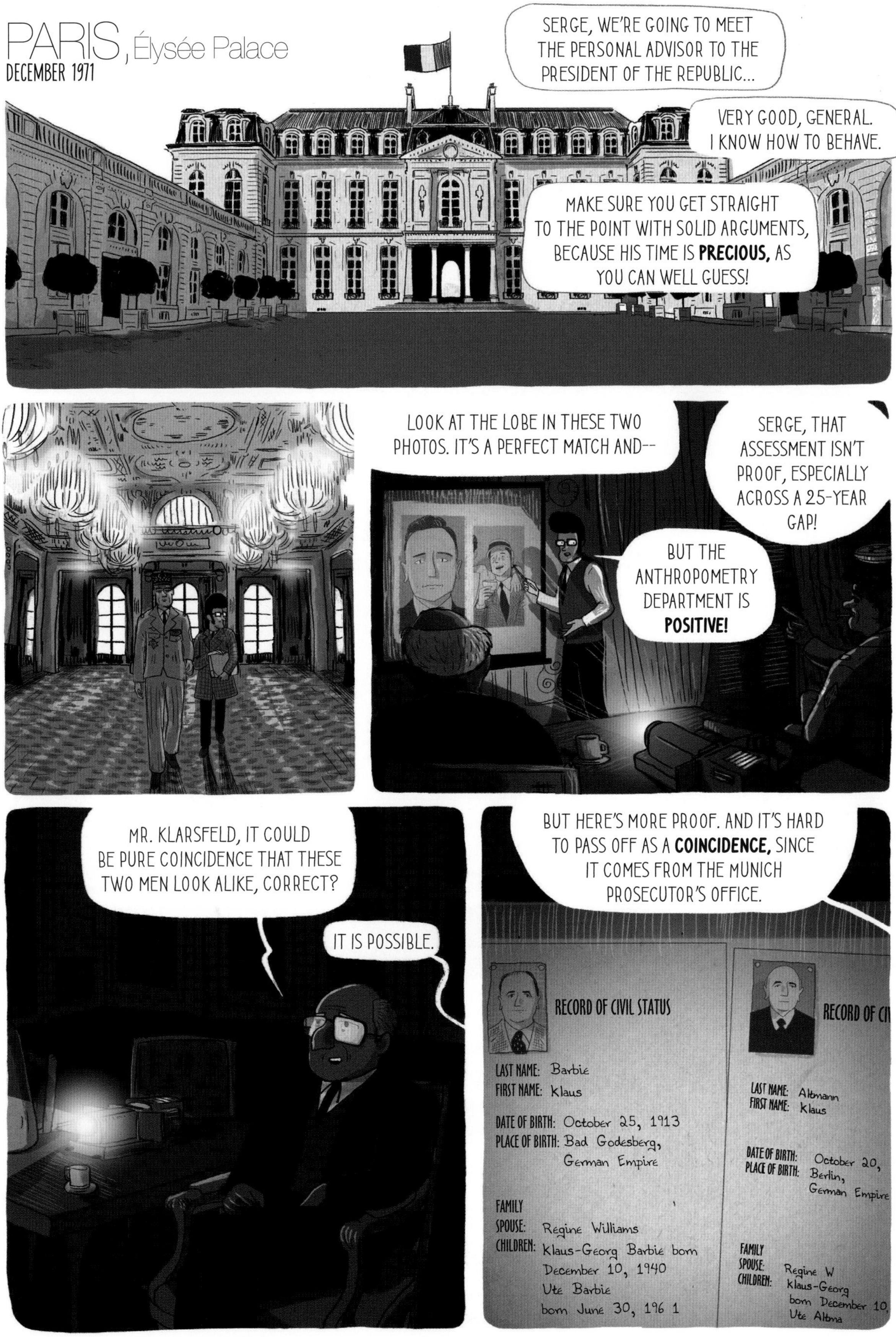
PARIS, Élysée Palace
DECEMBER 1971
SERGE, WE'RE GOING TO MEET THE PERSONAL ADVISOR TO THE PRESIDENT OF THE REPUBLIC...
VERY GOOD, GENERAL. I KNOW HOW TO BEHAVE.
MAKE SURE YOU GET STRAIGHT TO THE POINT WITH SOLID ARGUMENTS, BECAUSE HIS TIME IS **PRECIOUS,** AS YOU CAN WELL GUESS!
LOOK AT THE LOBE IN THESE TWO PHOTOS. IT'S A PERFECT MATCH AND--
SERGE, THAT ASSESSMENT ISN'T PROOF, ESPECIALLY ACROSS A 25-YEAR GAP!
BUT THE ANTHROPOMETRY DEPARTMENT IS **POSITIVE!**
MR. KLARSFELD, IT COULD BE PURE COINCIDENCE THAT THESE TWO MEN LOOK ALIKE, CORRECT?
IT IS POSSIBLE.
BUT HERE'S MORE PROOF. AND IT'S HARD TO PASS OFF AS A **COINCIDENCE,** SINCE IT COMES FROM THE MUNICH PROSECUTOR'S OFFICE.
RECORD OF CIVIL STATUS
LAST NAME: Barbie
FIRST NAME: Klaus
DATE OF BIRTH: October 25, 1913
PLACE OF BIRTH: Bad Godesberg, German Empire
FAMILY
SPOUSE: Regine Williams
CHILDREN: Klaus-Georg Barbie born December 10, 1940
Ute Barbie born June 30, 196 1
LAST NAME: Altmann
FIRST NAME: Klaus
DATE OF BIRTH: October 20,
PLACE OF BIRTH: Berlin, German Empire
FAMILY
SPOUSE: Regine W
CHILDREN: Klaus-Georg born December 10,

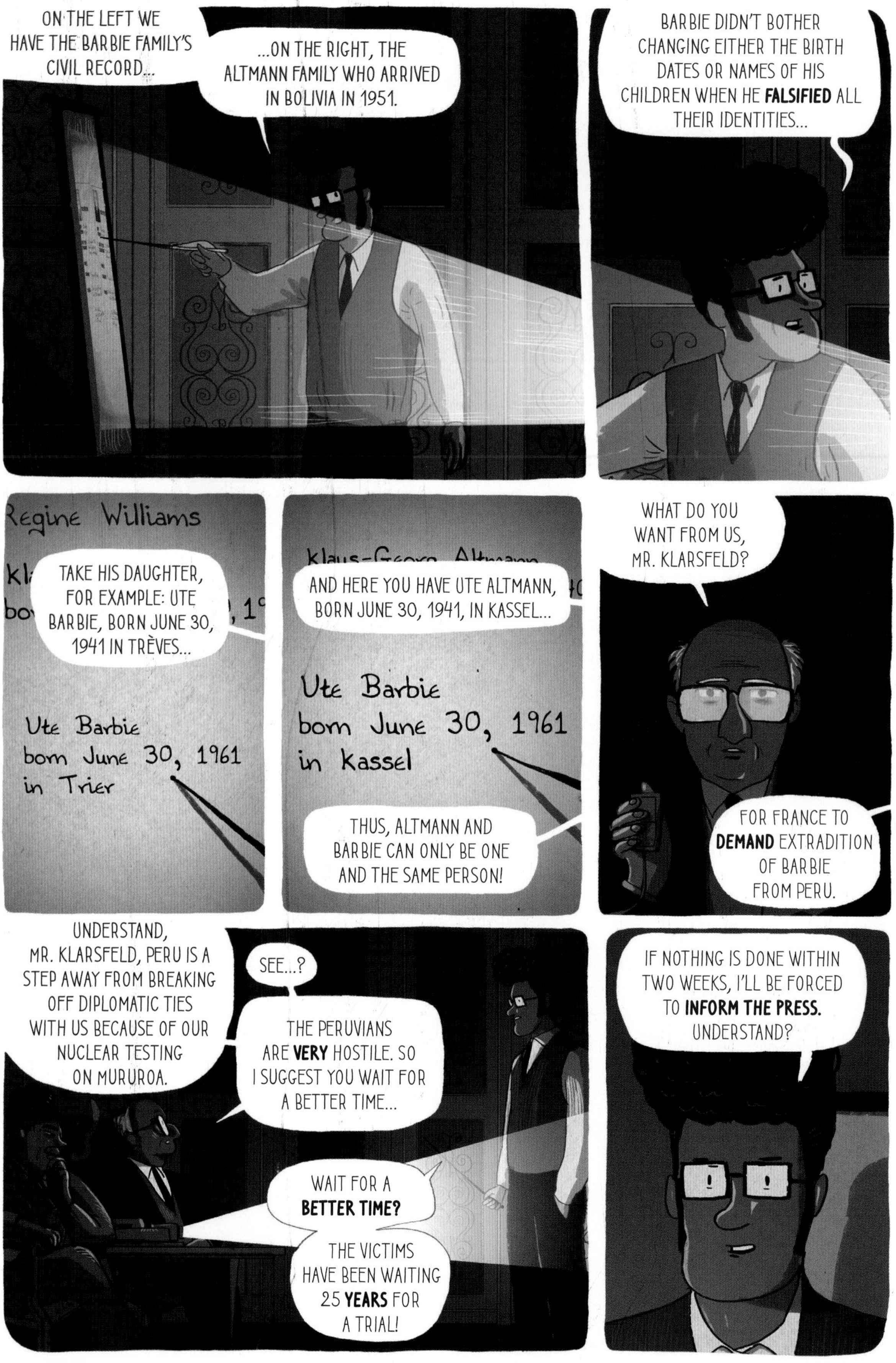
ON THE LEFT WE HAVE THE BARBIE FAMILY'S CIVIL RECORD...
...ON THE RIGHT, THE ALTMANN FAMILY WHO ARRIVED IN BOLIVIA IN 1951.
BARBIE DIDN'T BOTHER CHANGING EITHER THE BIRTH DATES OR NAMES OF HIS CHILDREN WHEN HE **FALSIFIED** ALL THEIR IDENTITIES...
Regine Williams
TAKE HIS DAUGHTER, FOR EXAMPLE: UTE BARBIE, BORN JUNE 30, 1941 IN TRÈVES...
Ute Barbie
born June 30, 1961
in Trier
AND HERE YOU HAVE UTE ALTMANN, BORN JUNE 30, 1941, IN KASSEL...
Ute Barbie
born June 30, 1961
in kassel
THUS, ALTMANN AND BARBIE CAN ONLY BE ONE AND THE SAME PERSON!
WHAT DO YOU WANT FROM US, MR. KLARSFELD?
FOR FRANCE TO **DEMAND** EXTRADITION OF BARBIE FROM PERU.
UNDERSTAND, MR. KLARSFELD, PERU IS A STEP AWAY FROM BREAKING OFF DIPLOMATIC TIES WITH US BECAUSE OF OUR NUCLEAR TESTING ON MURUROA.
SEE...?
THE PERUVIANS ARE **VERY** HOSTILE. SO I SUGGEST YOU WAIT FOR A BETTER TIME...
WAIT FOR A **BETTER TIME?**
THE VICTIMS HAVE BEEN WAITING 25 **YEARS** FOR A TRIAL!
IF NOTHING IS DONE WITHIN TWO WEEKS, I'LL BE FORCED TO **INFORM THE PRESS.** UNDERSTAND?

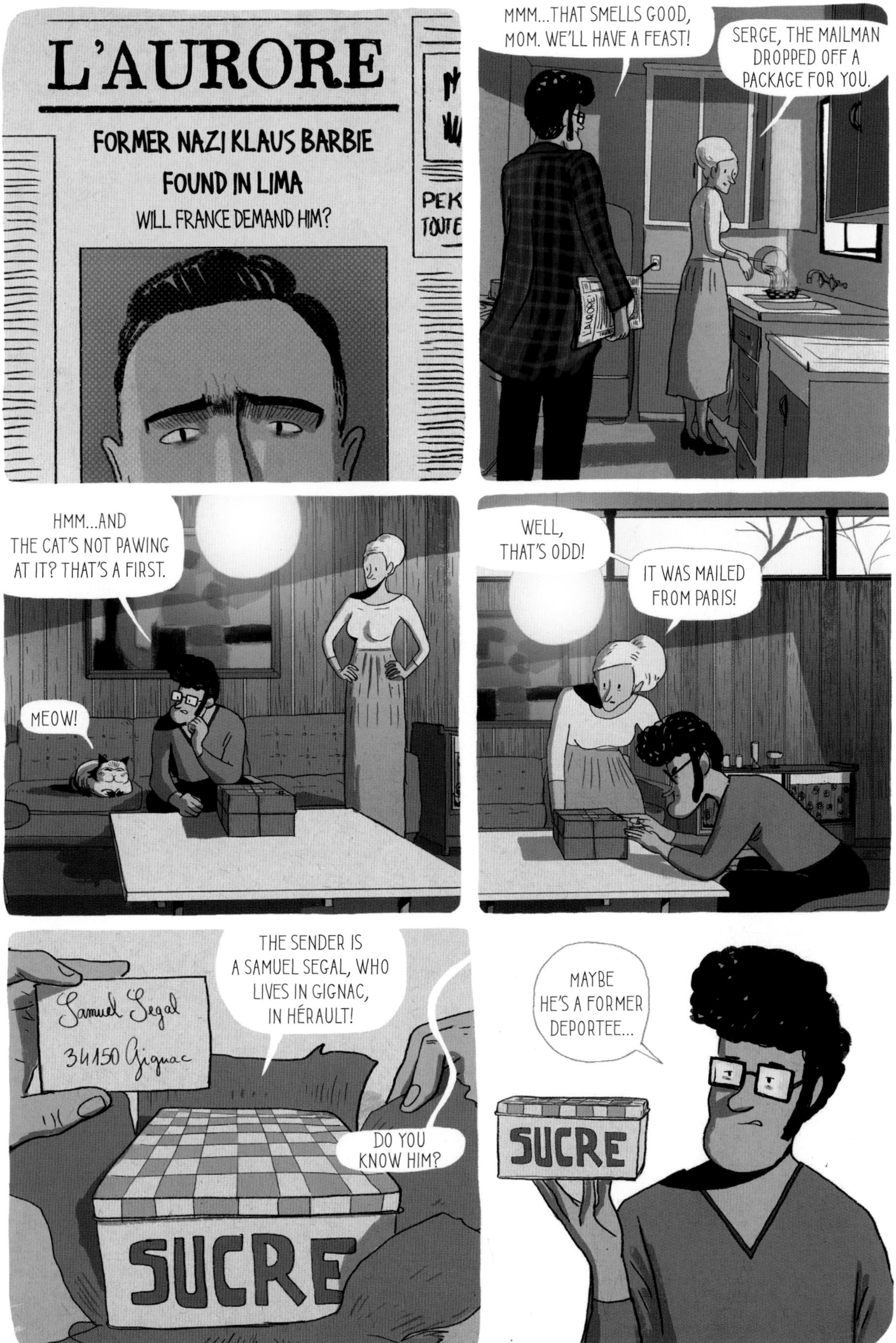
L'AURORE
FORMER NAZI KLAUS BARBIE
FOUND IN LIMA
WILL FRANCE DEMAND HIM?
MMM...THAT SMELLS GOOD, MOM. WE'LL HAVE A FEAST!
SERGE, THE MAILMAN DROPPED OFF A PACKAGE FOR YOU.
HMM...AND THE CAT'S NOT PAWING AT IT? THAT'S A FIRST.
MEOW!
WELL, THAT'S ODD!
IT WAS MAILED FROM PARIS!
Samuel Segal
34150 Gignac
THE SENDER IS A SAMUEL SEGAL, WHO LIVES IN GIGNAC, IN HÉRAULT!
DO YOU KNOW HIM?
SUCRE
MAYBE HE'S A FORMER DEPORTEE...
SUCRE

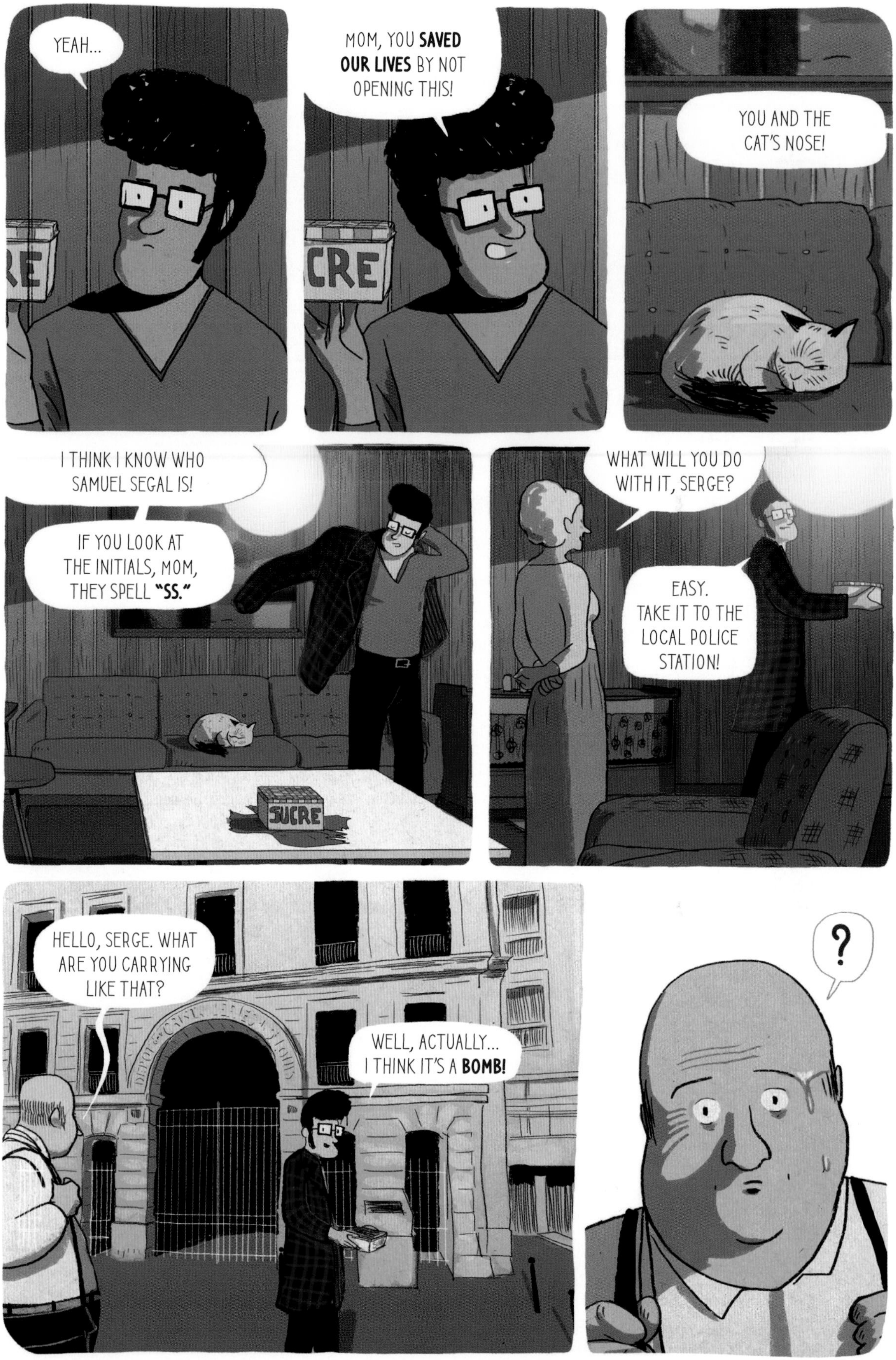
YEAH...
MOM, YOU **SAVED OUR LIVES** BY NOT OPENING THIS!
YOU AND THE CAT'S NOSE!
I THINK I KNOW WHO SAMUEL SEGAL IS!
IF YOU LOOK AT THE INITIALS, MOM, THEY SPELL **"SS."**
SUCRE
WHAT WILL YOU DO WITH IT, SERGE?
EASY. TAKE IT TO THE LOCAL POLICE STATION!
HELLO, SERGE. WHAT ARE YOU CARRYING LIKE THAT?
WELL, ACTUALLY... I THINK IT'S A **BOMB!**
?

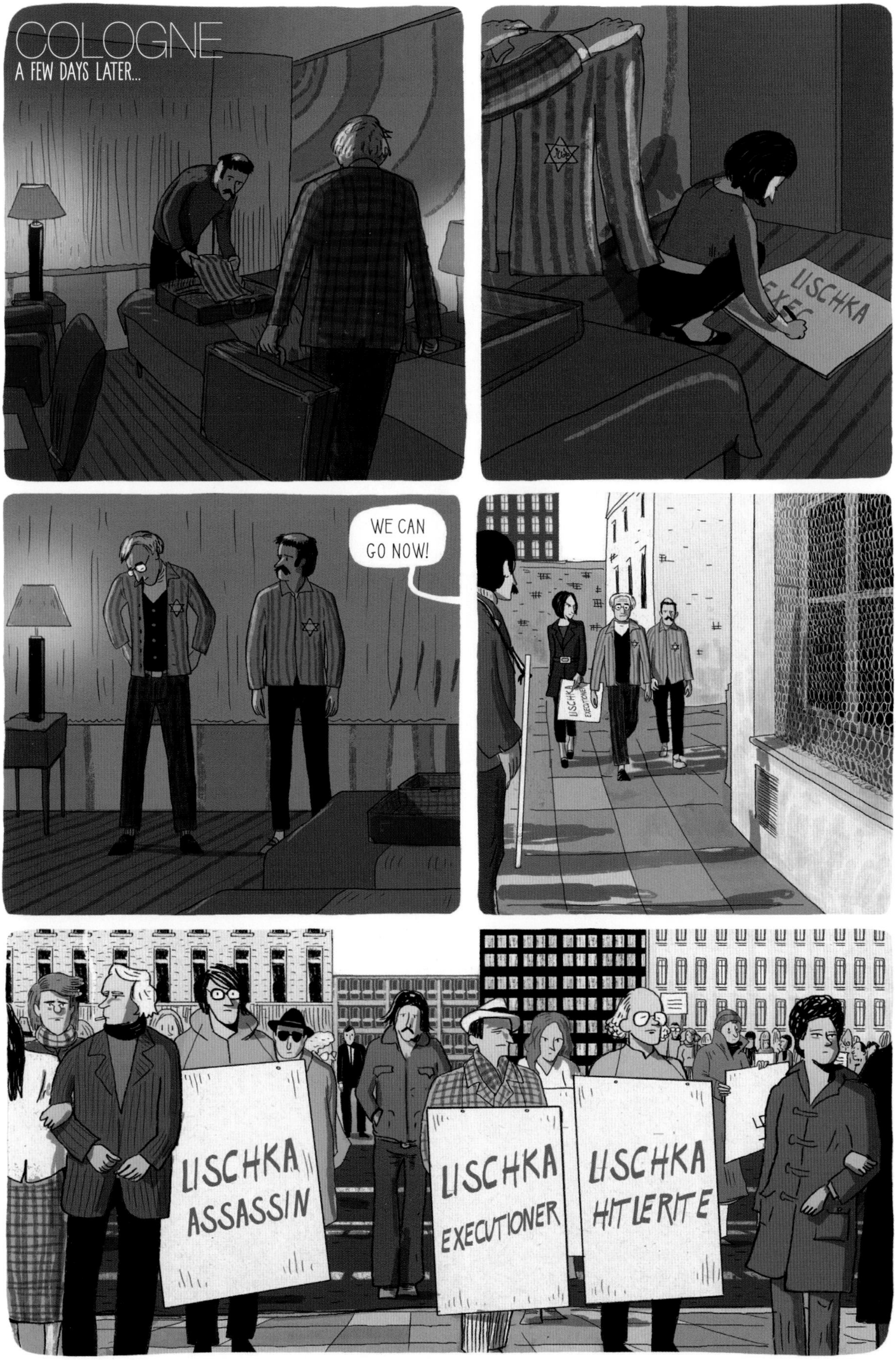
COLOGNE
A FEW DAYS LATER...
LISCHKA
EXEC
WE CAN GO NOW!
LISCHKA EXECUTIONER
LISCHKA ASSASSIN
LISCHKA EXECUTIONER
LISCHKA HITLERITE

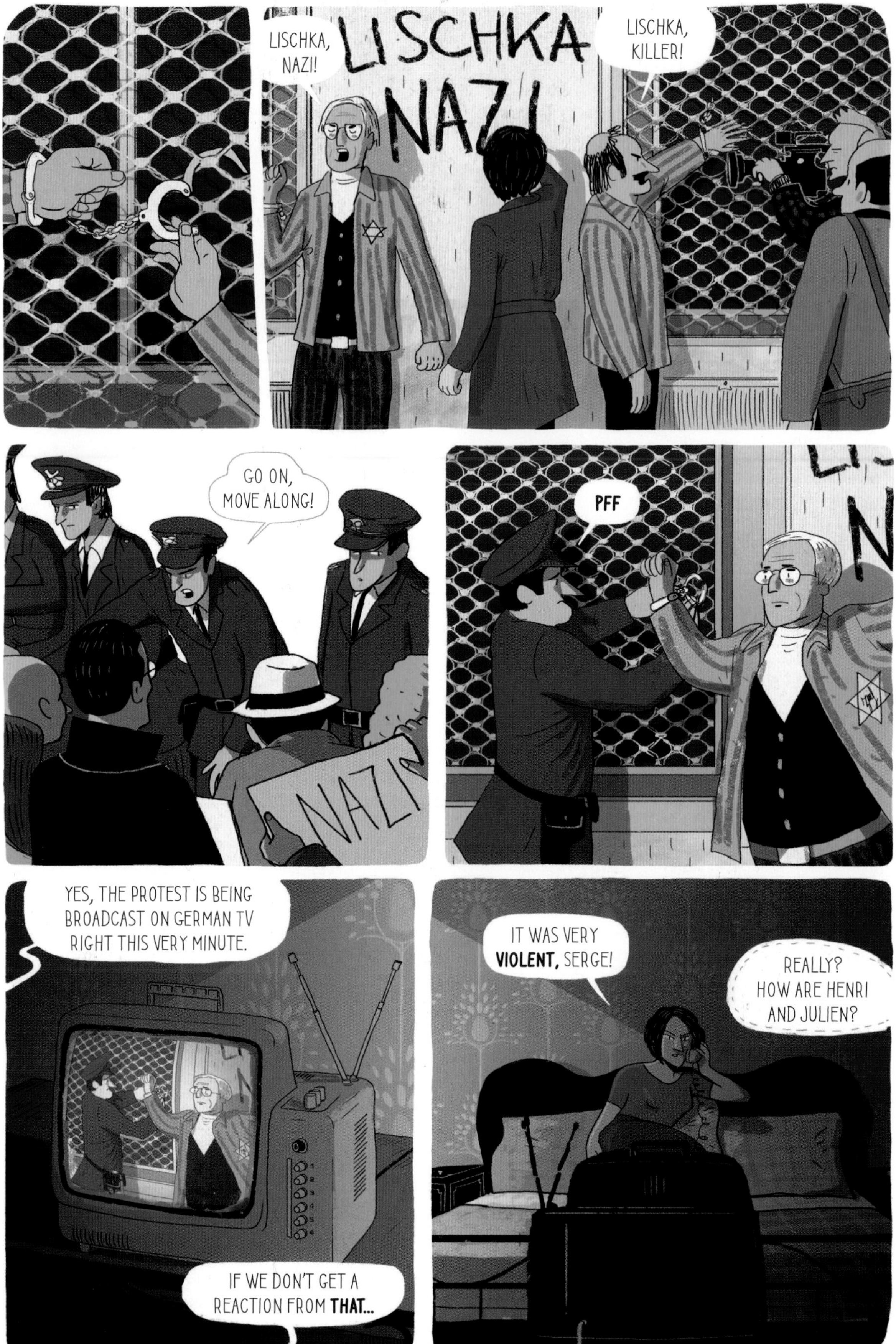
LISCHKA, NAZI!
LISCHKA NAZI
LISCHKA, KILLER!
GO ON, MOVE ALONG!
NAZI
PFF
YES, THE PROTEST IS BEING BROADCAST ON GERMAN TV RIGHT THIS VERY MINUTE.
IF WE DON'T GET A REACTION FROM **THAT...**
IT WAS VERY **VIOLENT,** SERGE!
REALLY? HOW ARE HENRI AND JULIEN?

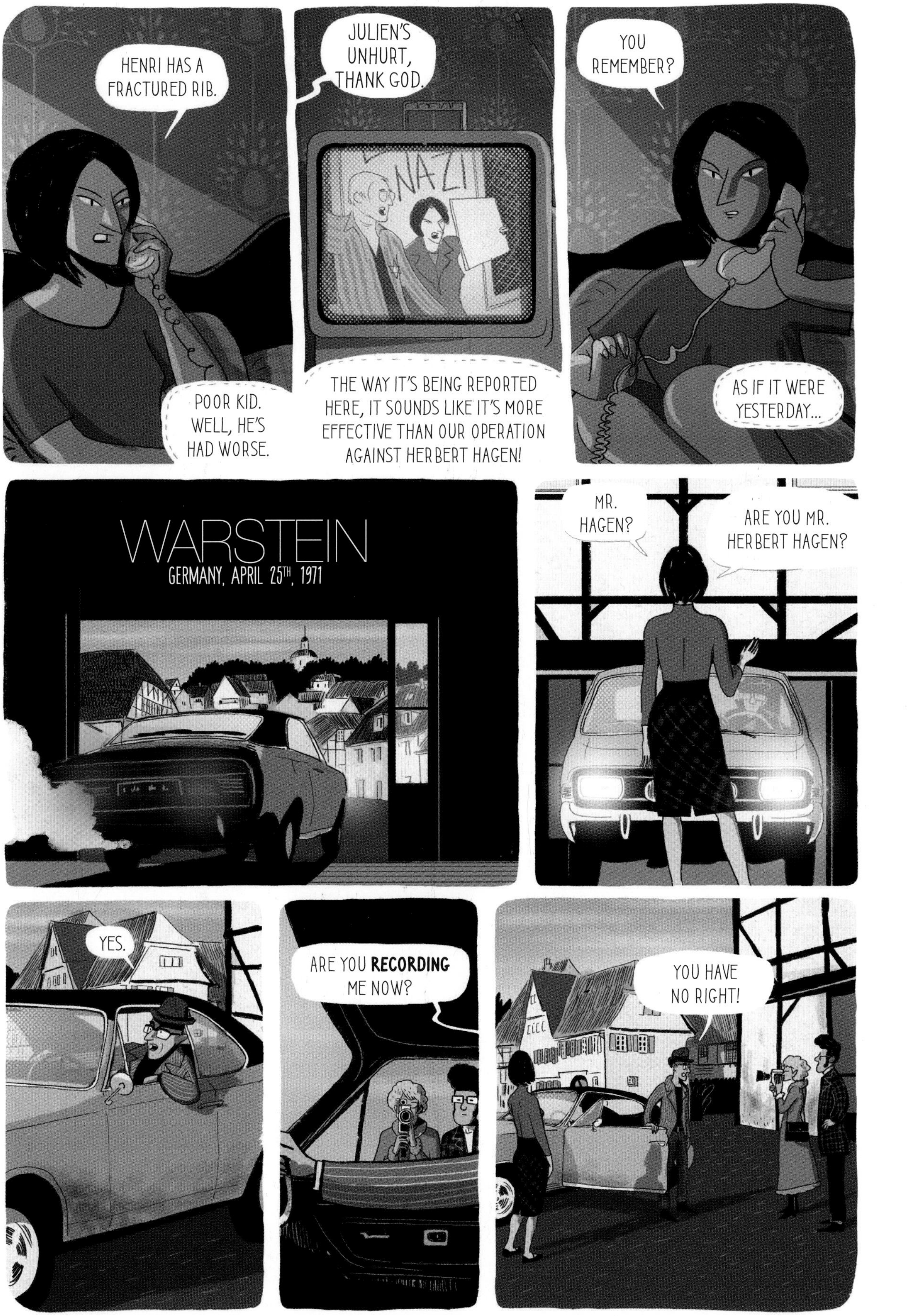
HENRI HAS A FRACTURED RIB.
POOR KID. WELL, HE'S HAD WORSE.
JULIEN'S UNHURT, THANK GOD.
NAZI
THE WAY IT'S BEING REPORTED HERE, IT SOUNDS LIKE IT'S MORE EFFECTIVE THAN OUR OPERATION AGAINST HERBERT HAGEN!
YOU REMEMBER?
AS IF IT WERE YESTERDAY...
WARSTEIN
GERMANY, APRIL 25TH, 1971
MR. HAGEN?
ARE YOU MR. HERBERT HAGEN?
YES.
ARE YOU **RECORDING** ME NOW?
YOU HAVE NO RIGHT!

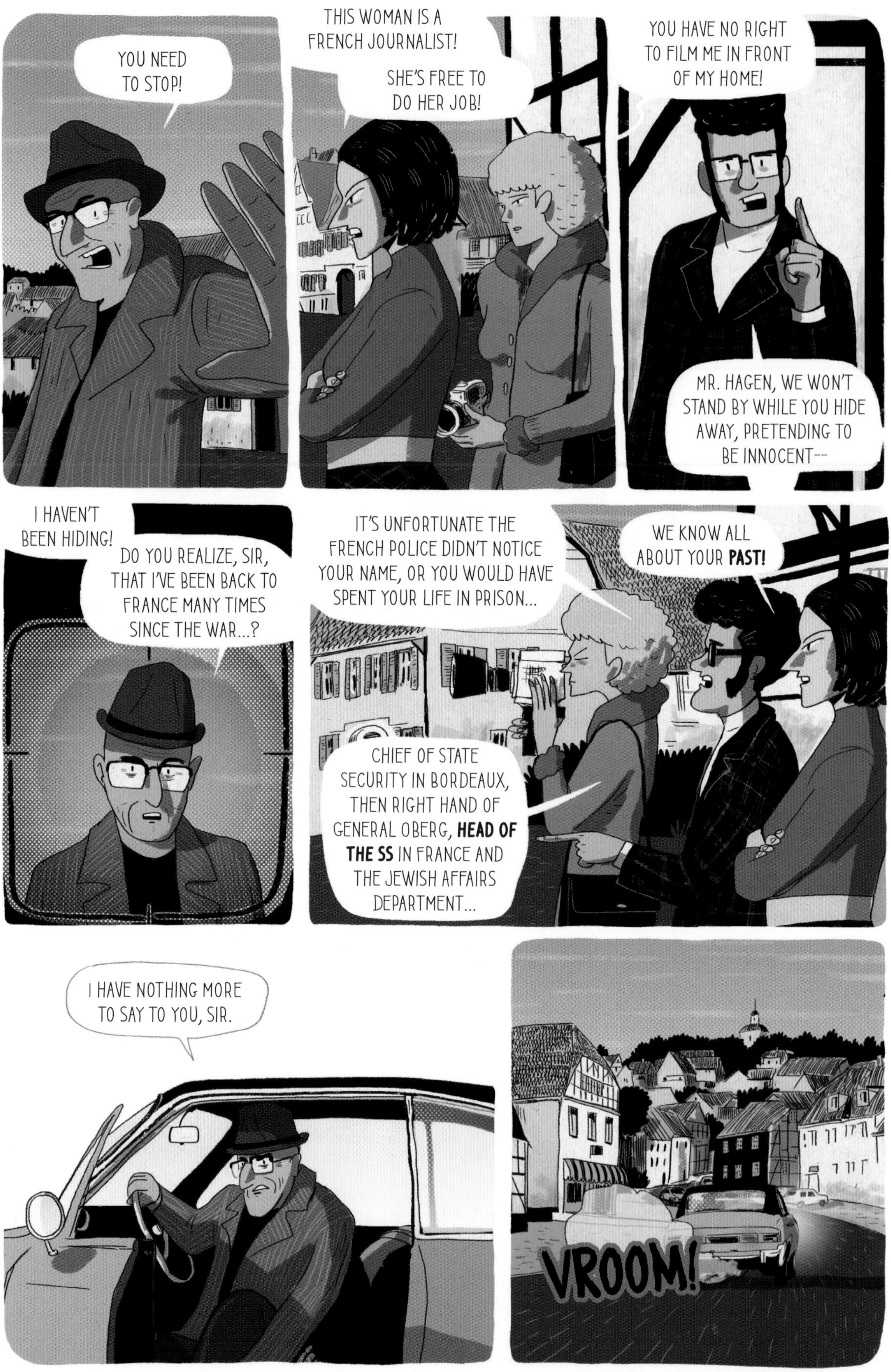
YOU NEED TO STOP!
THIS WOMAN IS A FRENCH JOURNALIST!
SHE'S FREE TO DO HER JOB!
YOU HAVE NO RIGHT TO FILM ME IN FRONT OF MY HOME!
MR. HAGEN, WE WON'T STAND BY WHILE YOU HIDE AWAY, PRETENDING TO BE INNOCENT--
I HAVEN'T BEEN HIDING!
DO YOU REALIZE, SIR, THAT I'VE BEEN BACK TO FRANCE MANY TIMES SINCE THE WAR...?
IT'S UNFORTUNATE THE FRENCH POLICE DIDN'T NOTICE YOUR NAME, OR YOU WOULD HAVE SPENT YOUR LIFE IN PRISON...
WE KNOW ALL ABOUT YOUR **PAST!**
CHIEF OF STATE SECURITY IN BORDEAUX, THEN RIGHT HAND OF GENERAL OBERG, **HEAD OF THE SS** IN FRANCE AND THE JEWISH AFFAIRS DEPARTMENT...
I HAVE NOTHING MORE TO SAY TO YOU, SIR.
VROOM!

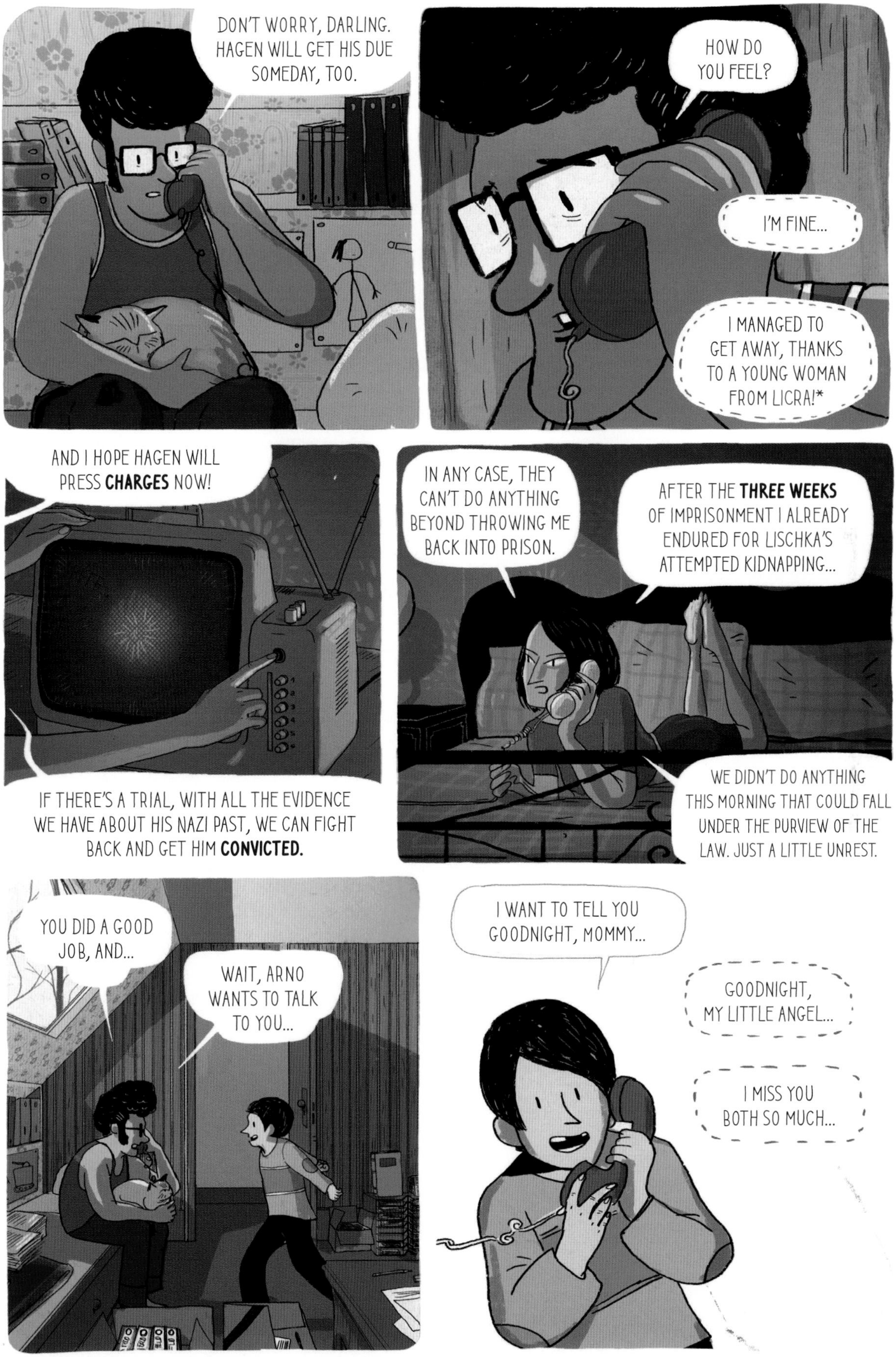
DON'T WORRY, DARLING. HAGEN WILL GET HIS DUE SOMEDAY, TOO.
HOW DO YOU FEEL?
I'M FINE...
I MANAGED TO GET AWAY, THANKS TO A YOUNG WOMAN FROM LICRA!*
AND I HOPE HAGEN WILL PRESS **CHARGES** NOW!
IF THERE'S A TRIAL, WITH ALL THE EVIDENCE WE HAVE ABOUT HIS NAZI PAST, WE CAN FIGHT BACK AND GET HIM **CONVICTED.**
IN ANY CASE, THEY CAN'T DO ANYTHING BEYOND THROWING ME BACK INTO PRISON.
AFTER THE **THREE WEEKS** OF IMPRISONMENT I ALREADY ENDURED FOR LISCHKA'S ATTEMPTED KIDNAPPING...
WE DIDN'T DO ANYTHING THIS MORNING THAT COULD FALL UNDER THE PURVIEW OF THE LAW. JUST A LITTLE UNREST.
YOU DID A GOOD JOB, AND...
WAIT, ARNO WANTS TO TALK TO YOU...
I WANT TO TELL YOU GOODNIGHT, MOMMY...
GOODNIGHT, MY LITTLE ANGEL...
I MISS YOU BOTH SO MUCH...

*THE INTERNATIONAL LEAGUE AGAINST RACISM AND ANTISEMITISM

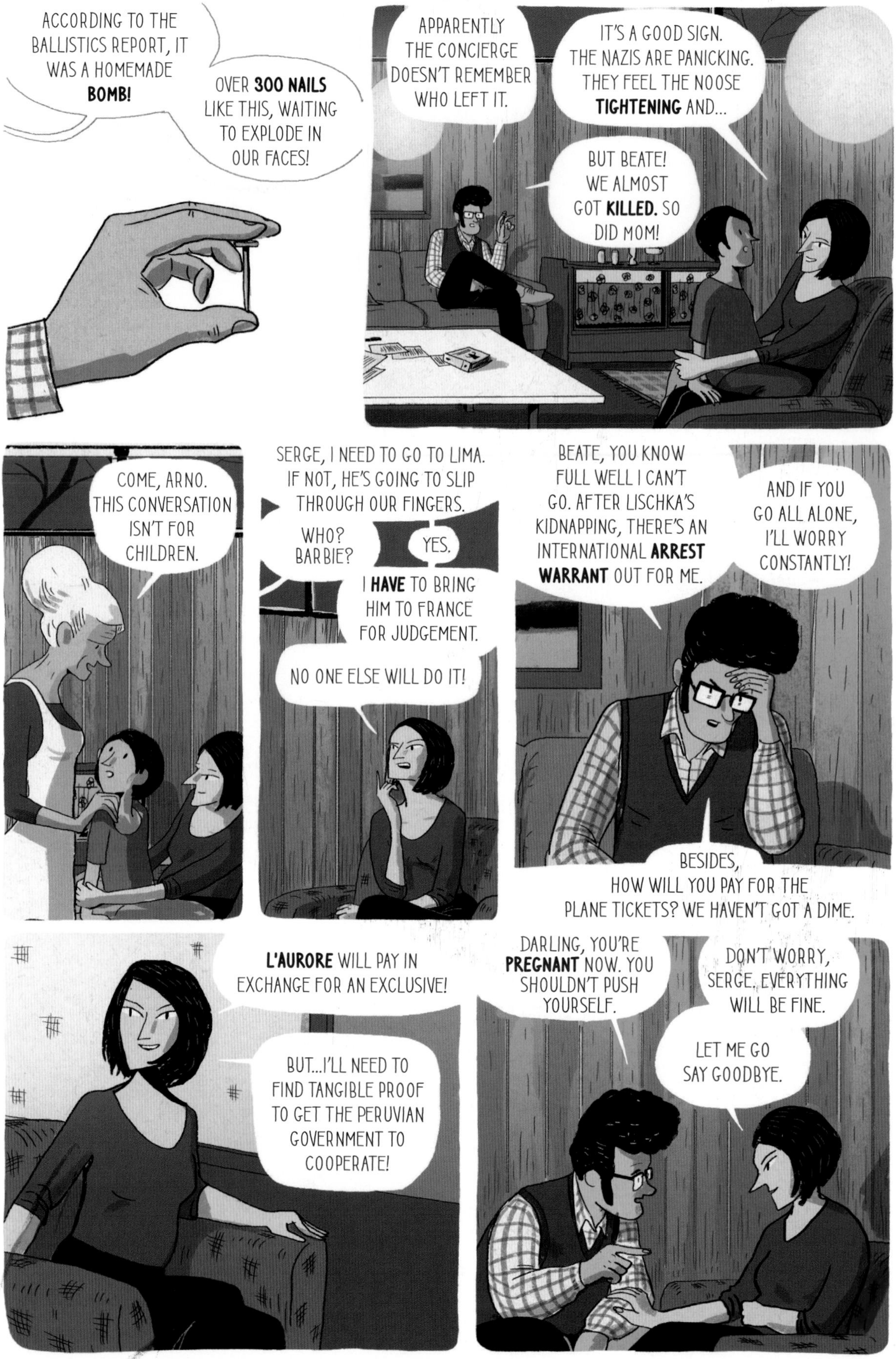
ACCORDING TO THE BALLISTICS REPORT, IT WAS A HOMEMADE **BOMB!**
OVER **300 NAILS** LIKE THIS, WAITING TO EXPLODE IN OUR FACES!
APPARENTLY THE CONCIERGE DOESN'T REMEMBER WHO LEFT IT.
IT'S A GOOD SIGN. THE NAZIS ARE PANICKING. THEY FEEL THE NOOSE **TIGHTENING** AND...
BUT BEATE! WE ALMOST GOT **KILLED.** SO DID MOM!
COME, ARNO. THIS CONVERSATION ISN'T FOR CHILDREN.
SERGE, I NEED TO GO TO LIMA. IF NOT, HE'S GOING TO SLIP THROUGH OUR FINGERS.
WHO? BARBIE?
YES.
I **HAVE** TO BRING HIM TO FRANCE FOR JUDGEMENT.
NO ONE ELSE WILL DO IT!
BEATE, YOU KNOW FULL WELL I CAN'T GO. AFTER LISCHKA'S KIDNAPPING, THERE'S AN INTERNATIONAL **ARREST WARRANT** OUT FOR ME.
AND IF YOU GO ALL ALONE, I'LL WORRY CONSTANTLY!
BESIDES, HOW WILL YOU PAY FOR THE PLANE TICKETS? WE HAVEN'T GOT A DIME.
L'AURORE WILL PAY IN EXCHANGE FOR AN EXCLUSIVE!
BUT...I'LL NEED TO FIND TANGIBLE PROOF TO GET THE PERUVIAN GOVERNMENT TO COOPERATE!
DARLING, YOU'RE **PREGNANT** NOW. YOU SHOULDN'T PUSH YOURSELF.
DON'T WORRY, SERGE. EVERYTHING WILL BE FINE.
LET ME GO SAY GOODBYE.

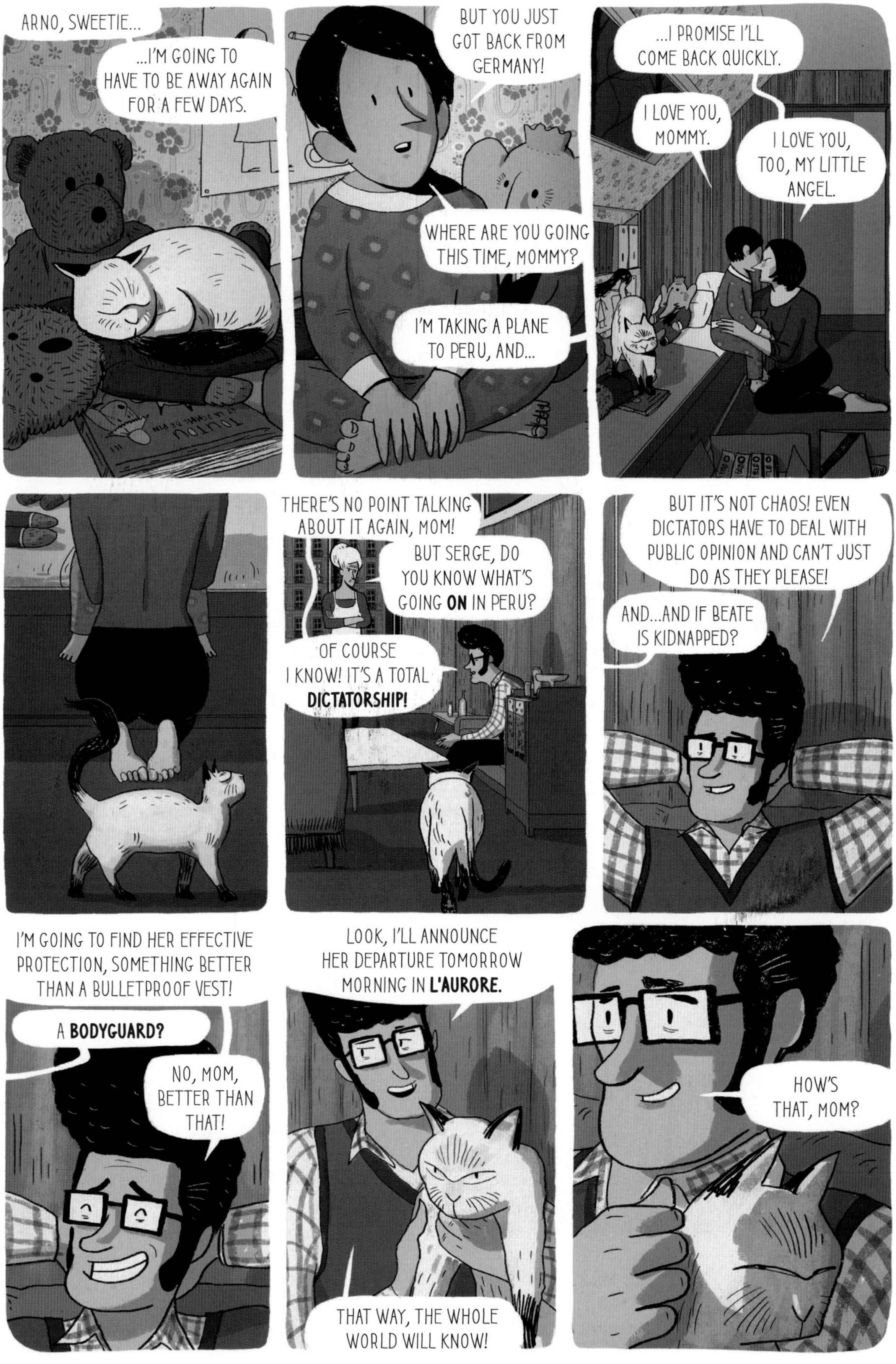
ARNO, SWEETIE...
...I'M GOING TO HAVE TO BE AWAY AGAIN FOR A FEW DAYS.
BUT YOU JUST GOT BACK FROM GERMANY!
WHERE ARE YOU GOING THIS TIME, MOMMY?
I'M TAKING A PLANE TO PERU, AND...
...I PROMISE I'LL COME BACK QUICKLY.
I LOVE YOU, MOMMY.
I LOVE YOU, TOO, MY LITTLE ANGEL.
THERE'S NO POINT TALKING ABOUT IT AGAIN, MOM!
BUT SERGE, DO YOU KNOW WHAT'S GOING **ON** IN PERU?
OF COURSE I KNOW! IT'S A TOTAL **DICTATORSHIP!**
BUT IT'S NOT CHAOS! EVEN DICTATORS HAVE TO DEAL WITH PUBLIC OPINION AND CAN'T JUST DO AS THEY PLEASE!
AND...AND IF BEATE IS KIDNAPPED?
I'M GOING TO FIND HER EFFECTIVE PROTECTION, SOMETHING BETTER THAN A BULLETPROOF VEST!
A **BODYGUARD?**
NO, MOM, BETTER THAN THAT!
LOOK, I'LL ANNOUNCE HER DEPARTURE TOMORROW MORNING IN **L'AURORE.**
THAT WAY, THE WHOLE WORLD WILL KNOW!
HOW'S THAT, MOM?

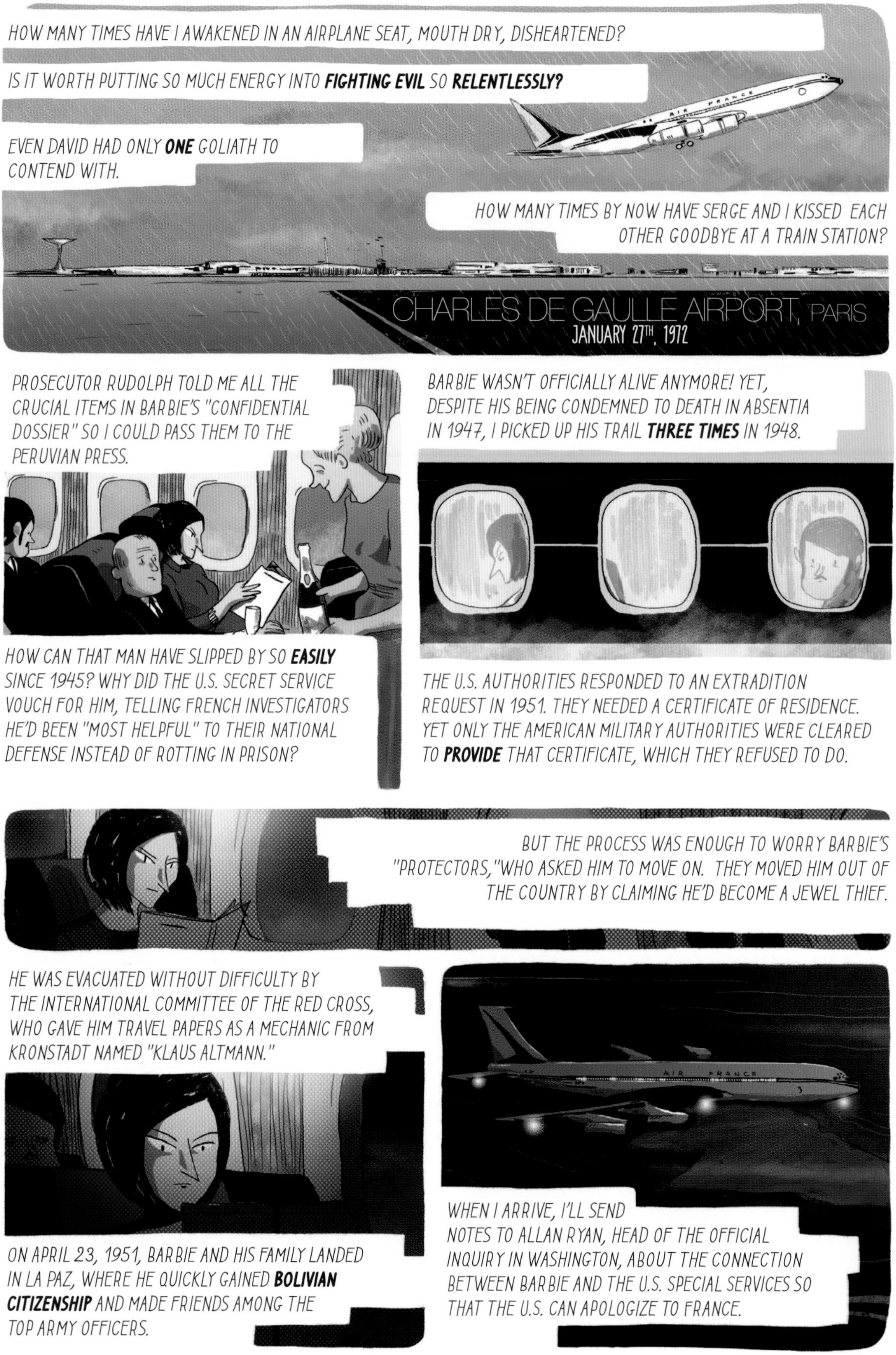
HOW MANY TIMES HAVE I AWAKENED IN AN AIRPLANE SEAT, MOUTH DRY, DISHEARTENED?
IS IT WORTH PUTTING SO MUCH ENERGY INTO **FIGHTING EVIL** SO **RELENTLESSLY?**
EVEN DAVID HAD ONLY **ONE** GOLIATH TO CONTEND WITH.
HOW MANY TIMES BY NOW HAVE SERGE AND I KISSED EACH OTHER GOODBYE AT A TRAIN STATION?
CHARLES DE GAULLE AIRPORT, PARIS
JANUARY 27TH, 1972
PROSECUTOR RUDOLPH TOLD ME ALL THE CRUCIAL ITEMS IN BARBIE'S "CONFIDENTIAL DOSSIER" SO I COULD PASS THEM TO THE PERUVIAN PRESS.
HOW CAN THAT MAN HAVE SLIPPED BY SO **EASILY** SINCE 1945? WHY DID THE U.S. SECRET SERVICE VOUCH FOR HIM, TELLING FRENCH INVESTIGATORS HE'D BEEN "MOST HELPFUL" TO THEIR NATIONAL DEFENSE INSTEAD OF ROTTING IN PRISON?
BARBIE WASN'T OFFICIALLY ALIVE ANYMORE! YET, DESPITE HIS BEING CONDEMNED TO DEATH IN ABSENTIA IN 1947, I PICKED UP HIS TRAIL **THREE TIMES** IN 1948.
THE U.S. AUTHORITIES RESPONDED TO AN EXTRADITION REQUEST IN 1951. THEY NEEDED A CERTIFICATE OF RESIDENCE. YET ONLY THE AMERICAN MILITARY AUTHORITIES WERE CLEARED TO **PROVIDE** THAT CERTIFICATE, WHICH THEY REFUSED TO DO.
BUT THE PROCESS WAS ENOUGH TO WORRY BARBIE'S "PROTECTORS," WHO ASKED HIM TO MOVE ON. THEY MOVED HIM OUT OF THE COUNTRY BY CLAIMING HE'D BECOME A JEWEL THIEF.
HE WAS EVACUATED WITHOUT DIFFICULTY BY THE INTERNATIONAL COMMITTEE OF THE RED CROSS, WHO GAVE HIM TRAVEL PAPERS AS A MECHANIC FROM KRONSTADT NAMED "KLAUS ALTMANN."
ON APRIL 23, 1951, BARBIE AND HIS FAMILY LANDED IN LA PAZ, WHERE HE QUICKLY GAINED **BOLIVIAN CITIZENSHIP** AND MADE FRIENDS AMONG THE TOP ARMY OFFICERS.
WHEN I ARRIVE, I'LL SEND NOTES TO ALLAN RYAN, HEAD OF THE OFFICIAL INQUIRY IN WASHINGTON, ABOUT THE CONNECTION BETWEEN BARBIE AND THE U.S. SPECIAL SERVICES SO THAT THE U.S. CAN APOLOGIZE TO FRANCE.

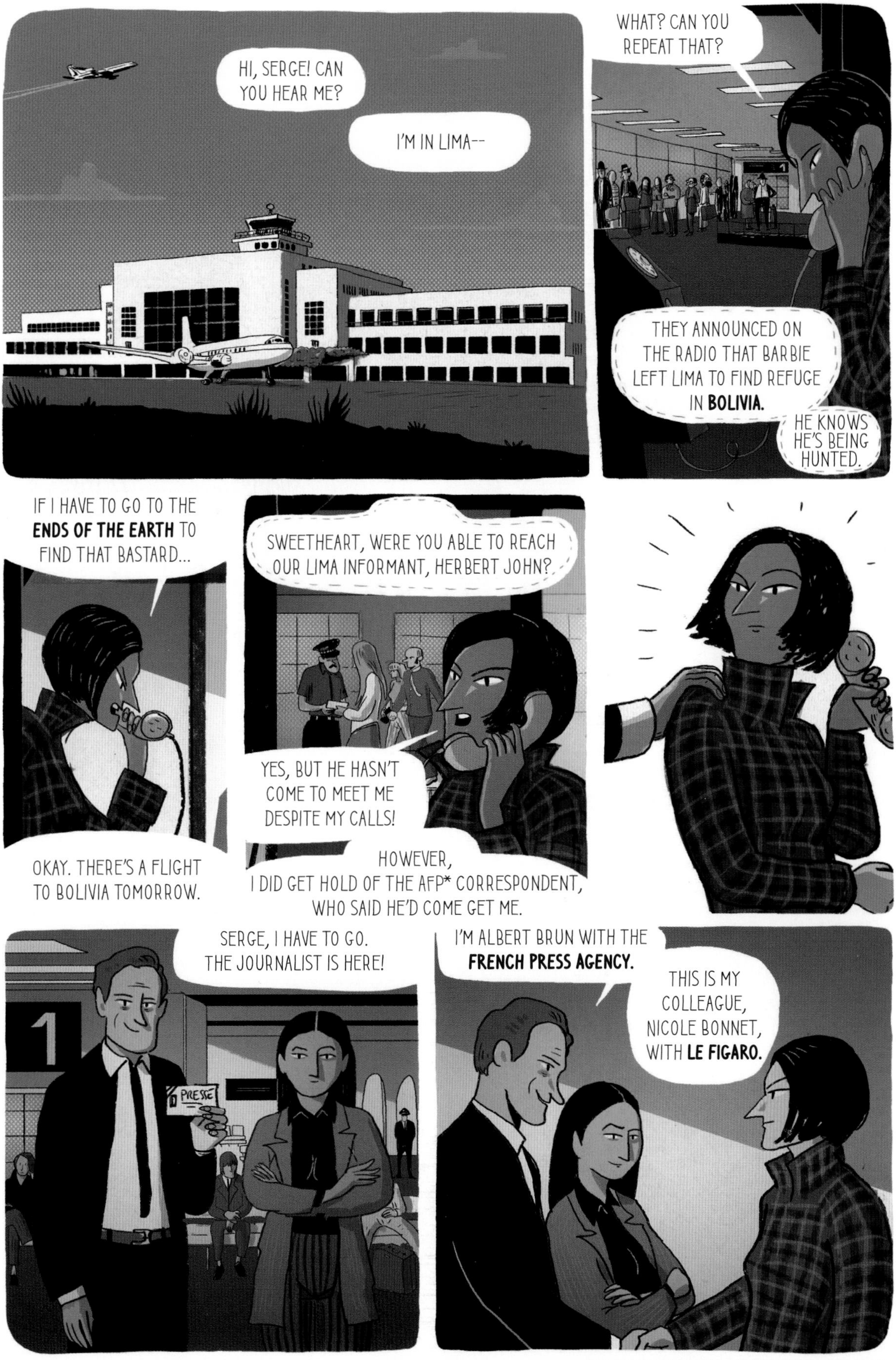
HI, SERGE! CAN YOU HEAR ME?
I'M IN LIMA--
WHAT? CAN YOU REPEAT THAT?
THEY ANNOUNCED ON THE RADIO THAT BARBIE LEFT LIMA TO FIND REFUGE IN **BOLIVIA.**
HE KNOWS HE'S BEING HUNTED.
IF I HAVE TO GO TO THE **ENDS OF THE EARTH** TO FIND THAT BASTARD...
OKAY. THERE'S A FLIGHT TO BOLIVIA TOMORROW.
SWEETHEART, WERE YOU ABLE TO REACH OUR LIMA INFORMANT, HERBERT JOHN?
YES, BUT HE HASN'T COME TO MEET ME DESPITE MY CALLS!
HOWEVER, I DID GET HOLD OF THE AFP* CORRESPONDENT, WHO SAID HE'D COME GET ME.
SERGE, I HAVE TO GO. THE JOURNALIST IS HERE!
PRESSE
I'M ALBERT BRUN WITH THE **FRENCH PRESS AGENCY.**
THIS IS MY COLLEAGUE, NICOLE BONNET, WITH **LE FIGARO.**

*AGENCE FRANCE PRESS, I.E., FRENCH PRESS AGENCY.

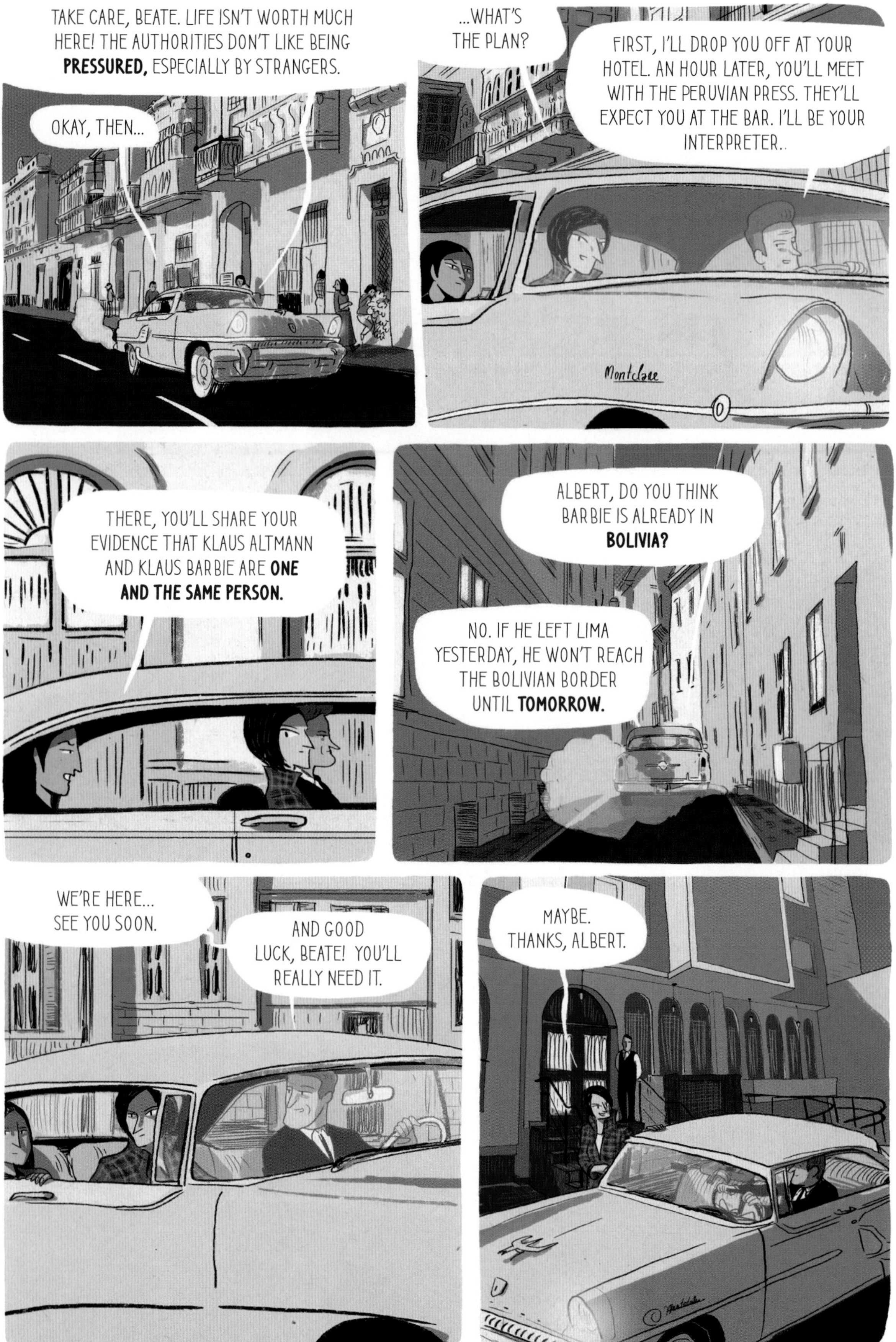
TAKE CARE, BEATE. LIFE ISN'T WORTH MUCH HERE! THE AUTHORITIES DON'T LIKE BEING **PRESSURED,** ESPECIALLY BY STRANGERS.
OKAY, THEN...
...WHAT'S THE PLAN?
FIRST, I'LL DROP YOU OFF AT YOUR HOTEL. AN HOUR LATER, YOU'LL MEET WITH THE PERUVIAN PRESS. THEY'LL EXPECT YOU AT THE BAR. I'LL BE YOUR INTERPRETER..
Montclare
THERE, YOU'LL SHARE YOUR EVIDENCE THAT KLAUS ALTMANN AND KLAUS BARBIE ARE **ONE AND THE SAME PERSON.**
ALBERT, DO YOU THINK BARBIE IS ALREADY IN **BOLIVIA?**
NO. IF HE LEFT LIMA YESTERDAY, HE WON'T REACH THE BOLIVIAN BORDER UNTIL **TOMORROW.**
WE'RE HERE... SEE YOU SOON.
AND GOOD LUCK, BEATE! YOU'LL REALLY NEED IT.
MAYBE. THANKS, ALBERT.

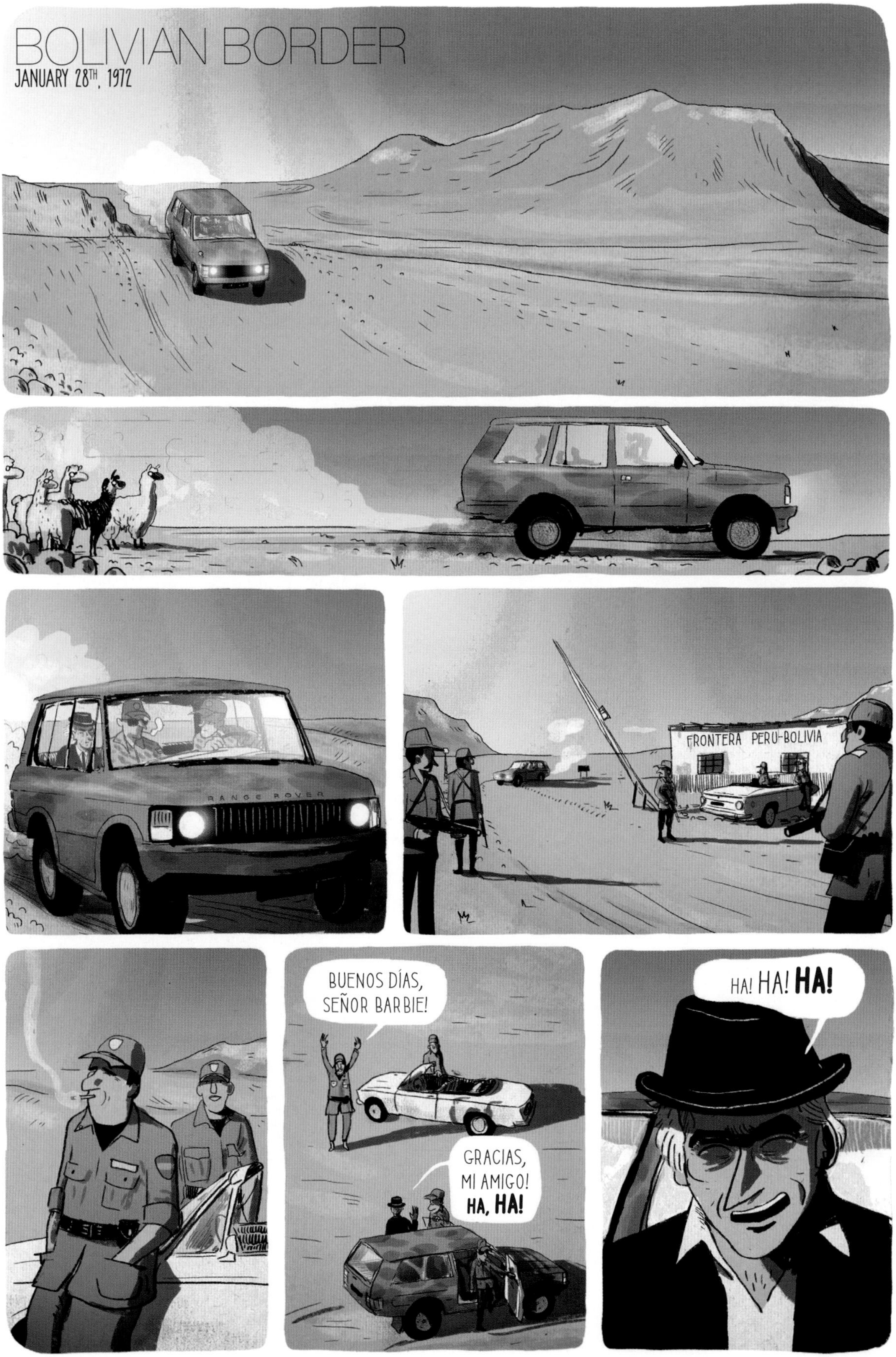
BOLIVIAN BORDER
JANUARY 28TH, 1972
FRONTERA PERU-BOLIVIA
RANGE ROVER
BUENOS DÍAS, SEÑOR BARBIE!
GRACIAS, MI AMIGO! HA, HA!
HA! HA! HA!

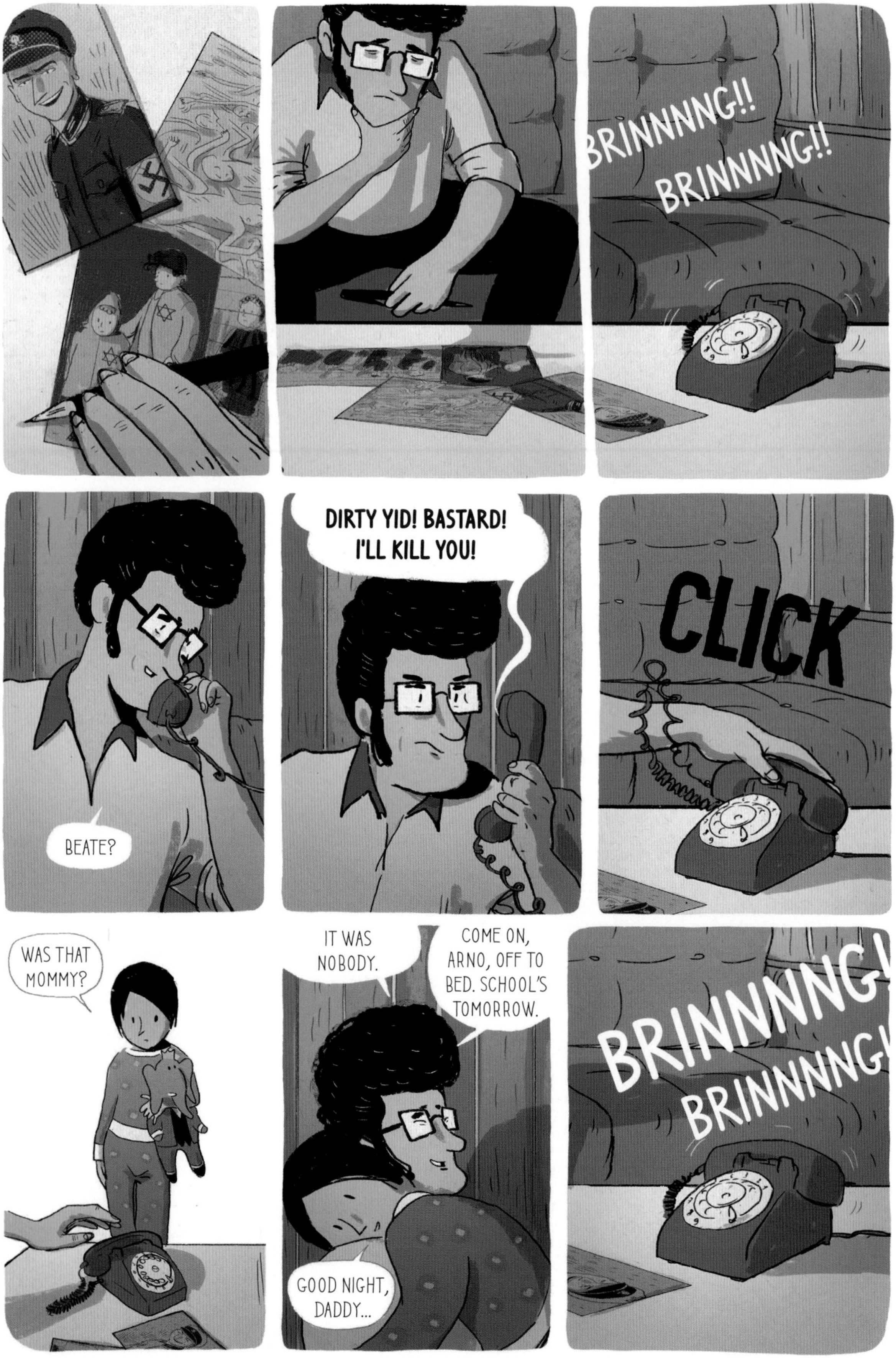

BRINNNNG!!
BRINNNNG!!
BEATE?
DIRTY YID! BASTARD! I'LL KILL YOU!
CLICK
WAS THAT MOMMY?
IT WAS NOBODY.
COME ON, ARNO, OFF TO BED. SCHOOL'S TOMORROW.
GOOD NIGHT, DADDY...
BRINNNNG!
BRINNNNG!

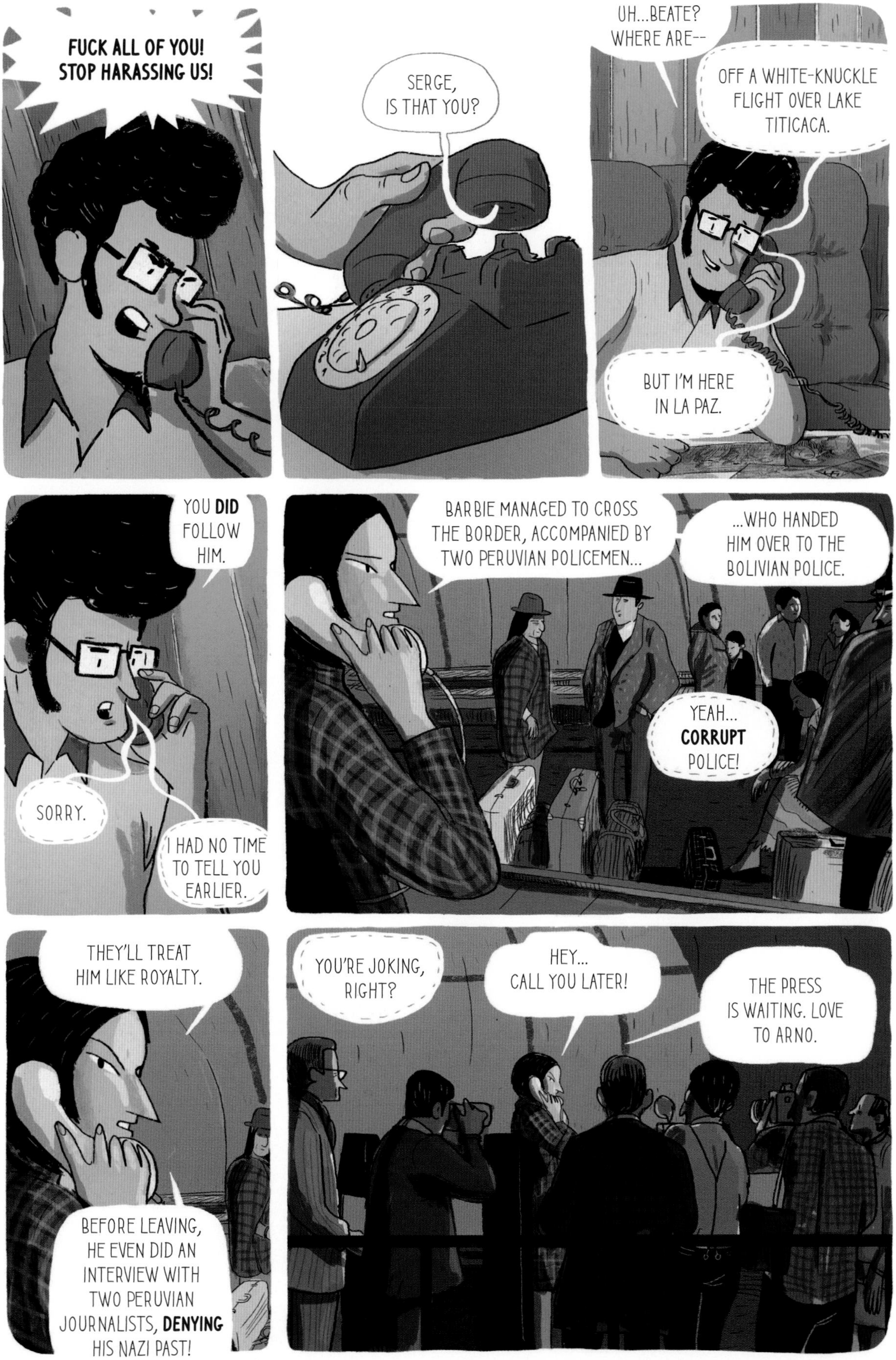
FUCK ALL OF YOU! STOP HARASSING US!
SERGE, IS THAT YOU?
UH...BEATE? WHERE ARE--
OFF A WHITE-KNUCKLE FLIGHT OVER LAKE TITICACA.
BUT I'M HERE IN LA PAZ.
YOU DID FOLLOW HIM.
SORRY.
I HAD NO TIME TO TELL YOU EARLIER.
BARBIE MANAGED TO CROSS THE BORDER, ACCOMPANIED BY TWO PERUVIAN POLICEMEN...
...WHO HANDED HIM OVER TO THE BOLIVIAN POLICE.
YEAH... CORRUPT POLICE!
THEY'LL TREAT HIM LIKE ROYALTY.
BEFORE LEAVING, HE EVEN DID AN INTERVIEW WITH TWO PERUVIAN JOURNALISTS, DENYING HIS NAZI PAST!
YOU'RE JOKING, RIGHT?
HEY... CALL YOU LATER!
THE PRESS IS WAITING. LOVE TO ARNO.

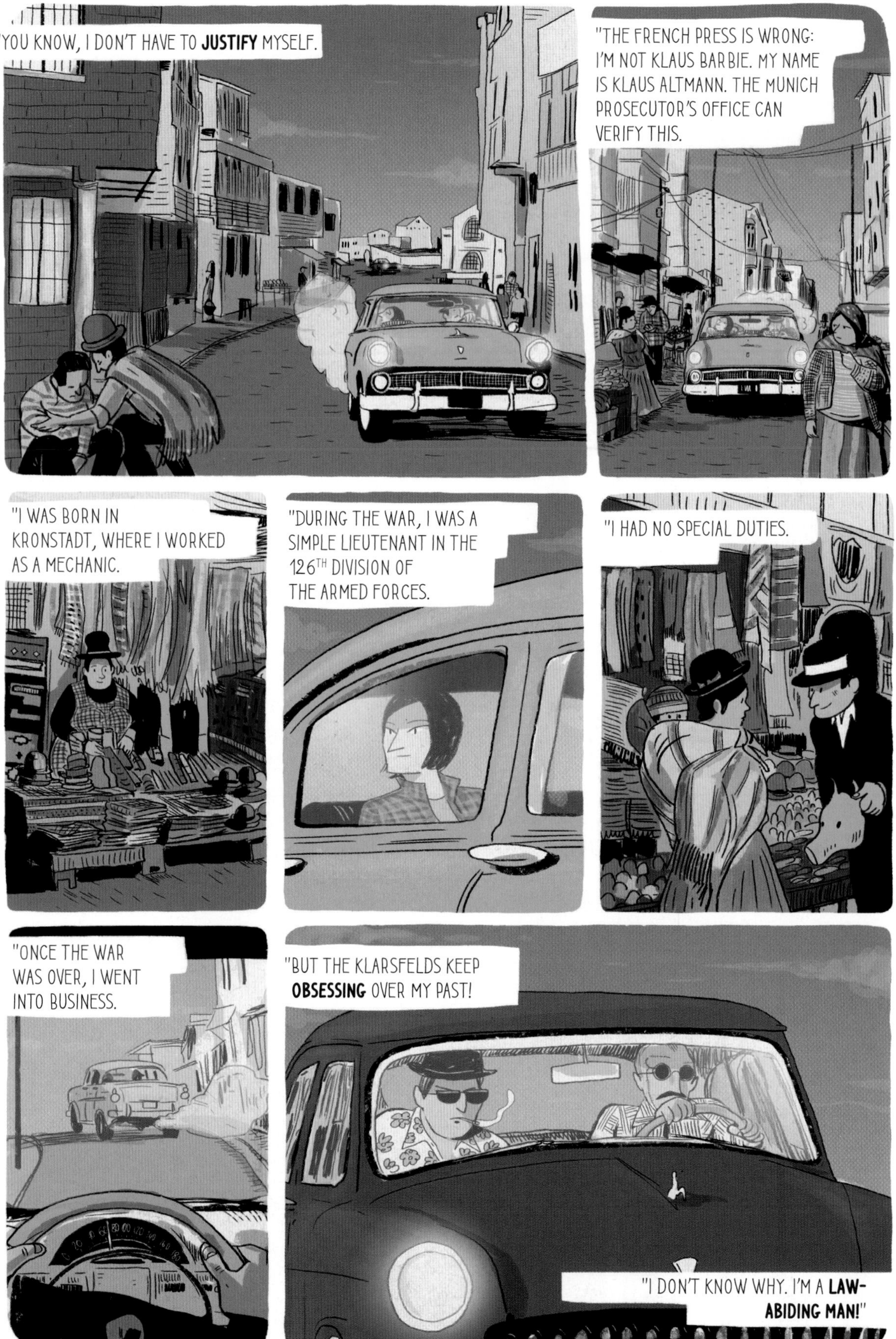
"YOU KNOW, I DON'T HAVE TO **JUSTIFY** MYSELF.
"THE FRENCH PRESS IS WRONG: I'M NOT KLAUS BARBIE. MY NAME IS KLAUS ALTMANN. THE MUNICH PROSECUTOR'S OFFICE CAN VERIFY THIS.
"I WAS BORN IN KRONSTADT, WHERE I WORKED AS A MECHANIC.
"DURING THE WAR, I WAS A SIMPLE LIEUTENANT IN THE 126TH DIVISION OF THE ARMED FORCES.
"I HAD NO SPECIAL DUTIES.
"ONCE THE WAR WAS OVER, I WENT INTO BUSINESS.
"BUT THE KLARSFELDS KEEP **OBSESSING** OVER MY PAST!
"I DON'T KNOW WHY. I'M A **LAW-ABIDING MAN!**"

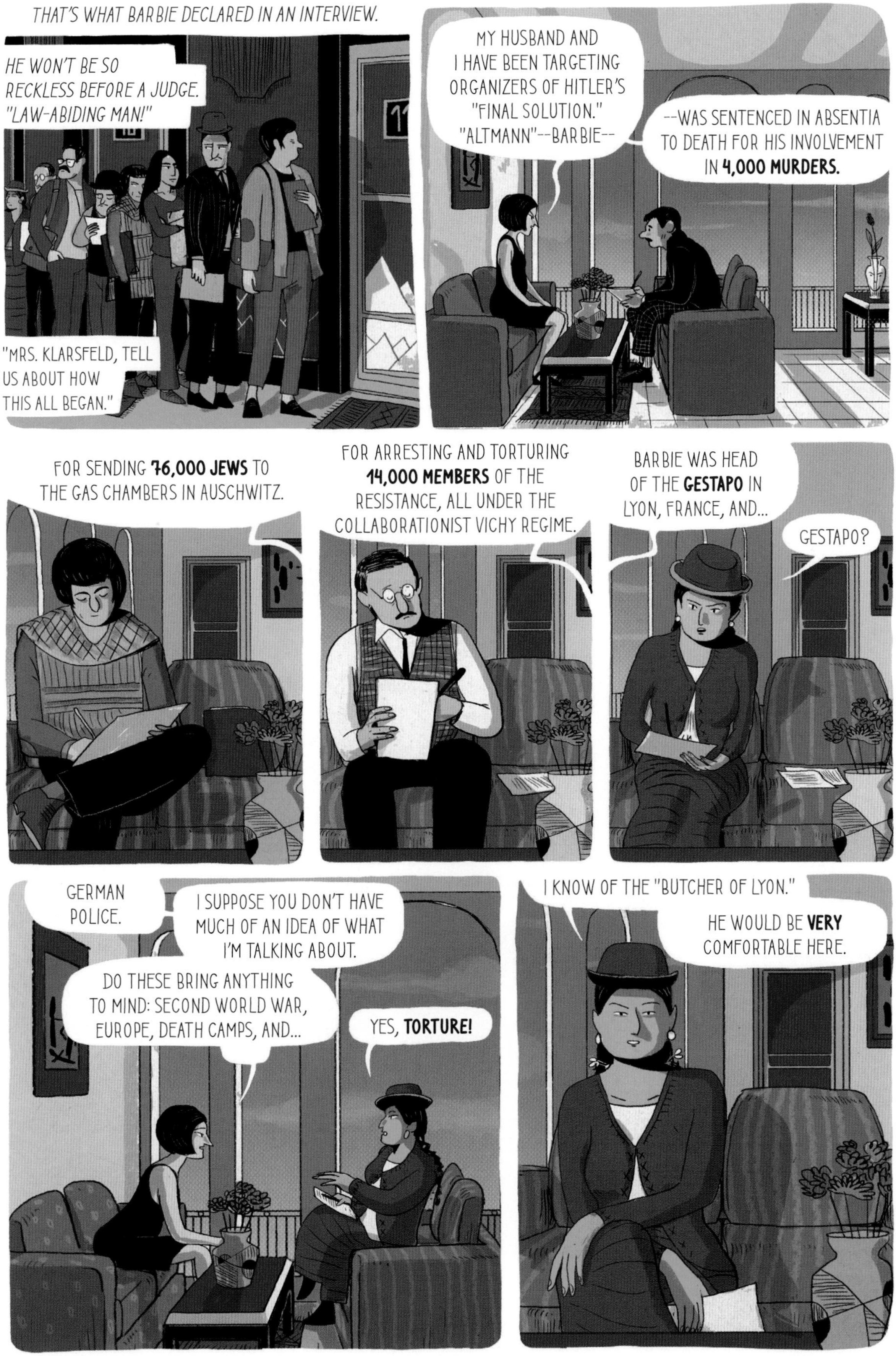
THAT'S WHAT BARBIE DECLARED IN AN INTERVIEW.
HE WON'T BE SO RECKLESS BEFORE A JUDGE. "LAW-ABIDING MAN!"
"MRS. KLARSFELD, TELL US ABOUT HOW THIS ALL BEGAN."
MY HUSBAND AND I HAVE BEEN TARGETING ORGANIZERS OF HITLER'S "FINAL SOLUTION." "ALTMANN"--BARBIE--
--WAS SENTENCED IN ABSENTIA TO DEATH FOR HIS INVOLVEMENT IN **4,000 MURDERS.**
FOR SENDING **76,000 JEWS** TO THE GAS CHAMBERS IN AUSCHWITZ.
FOR ARRESTING AND TORTURING **14,000 MEMBERS** OF THE RESISTANCE, ALL UNDER THE COLLABORATIONIST VICHY REGIME.
BARBIE WAS HEAD OF THE **GESTAPO** IN LYON, FRANCE, AND...
GESTAPO?
GERMAN POLICE.
I SUPPOSE YOU DON'T HAVE MUCH OF AN IDEA OF WHAT I'M TALKING ABOUT.
DO THESE BRING ANYTHING TO MIND: SECOND WORLD WAR, EUROPE, DEATH CAMPS, AND...
YES, **TORTURE!**
I KNOW OF THE "BUTCHER OF LYON."
HE WOULD BE **VERY** COMFORTABLE HERE.

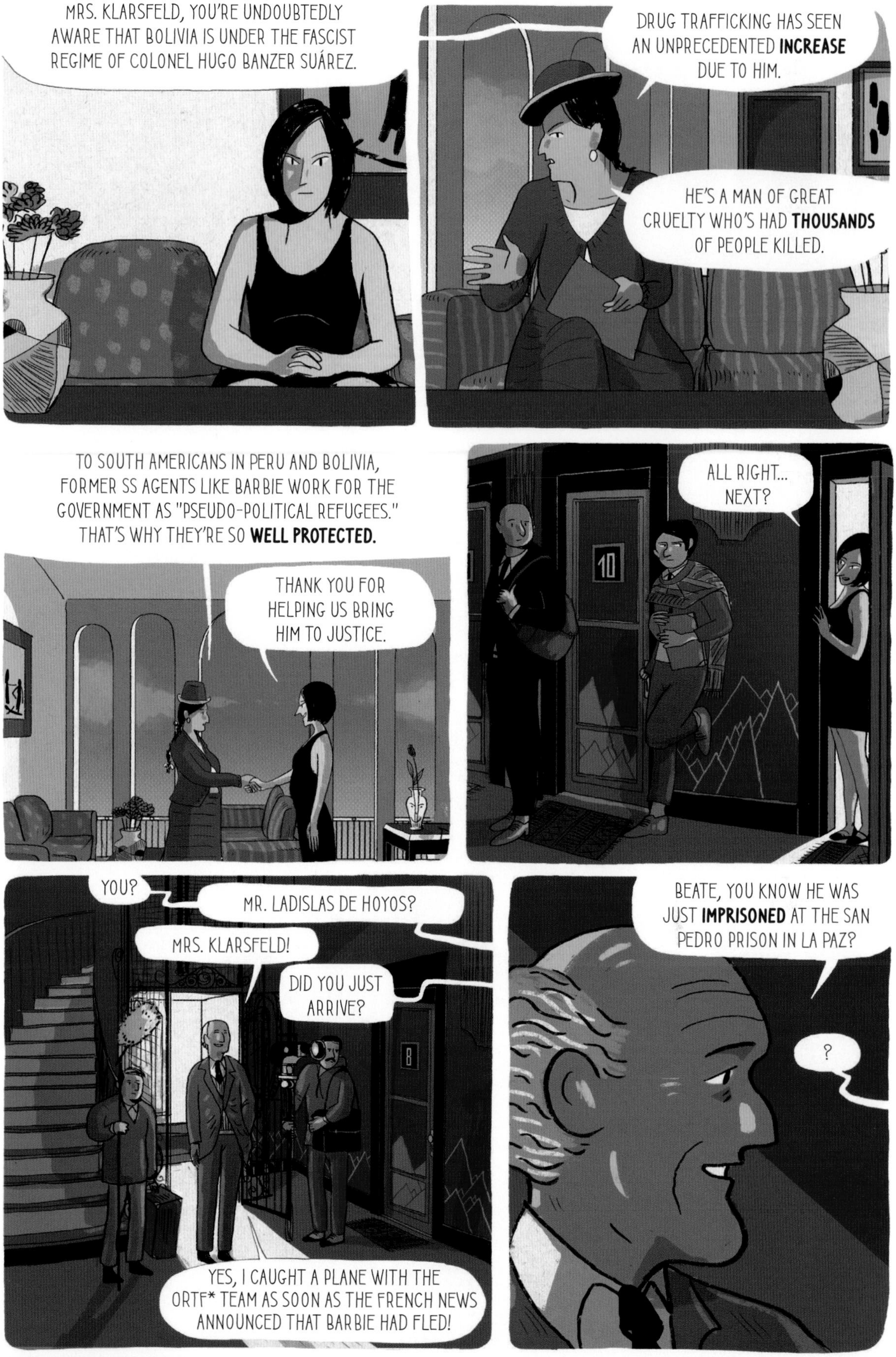
MRS. KLARSFELD, YOU'RE UNDOUBTEDLY AWARE THAT BOLIVIA IS UNDER THE FASCIST REGIME OF COLONEL HUGO BANZER SUÁREZ.
DRUG TRAFFICKING HAS SEEN AN UNPRECEDENTED **INCREASE** DUE TO HIM.
HE'S A MAN OF GREAT CRUELTY WHO'S HAD **THOUSANDS** OF PEOPLE KILLED.
TO SOUTH AMERICANS IN PERU AND BOLIVIA, FORMER SS AGENTS LIKE BARBIE WORK FOR THE GOVERNMENT AS "PSEUDO-POLITICAL REFUGEES." THAT'S WHY THEY'RE SO **WELL PROTECTED.**
THANK YOU FOR HELPING US BRING HIM TO JUSTICE.
ALL RIGHT... NEXT?
10
YOU?
MR. LADISLAS DE HOYOS?
MRS. KLARSFELD!
DID YOU JUST ARRIVE?
8
YES, I CAUGHT A PLANE WITH THE ORTF* TEAM AS SOON AS THE FRENCH NEWS ANNOUNCED THAT BARBIE HAD FLED!
BEATE, YOU KNOW HE WAS JUST **IMPRISONED** AT THE SAN PEDRO PRISON IN LA PAZ?
?

*FRENCH BROADCASTING SERVICE.

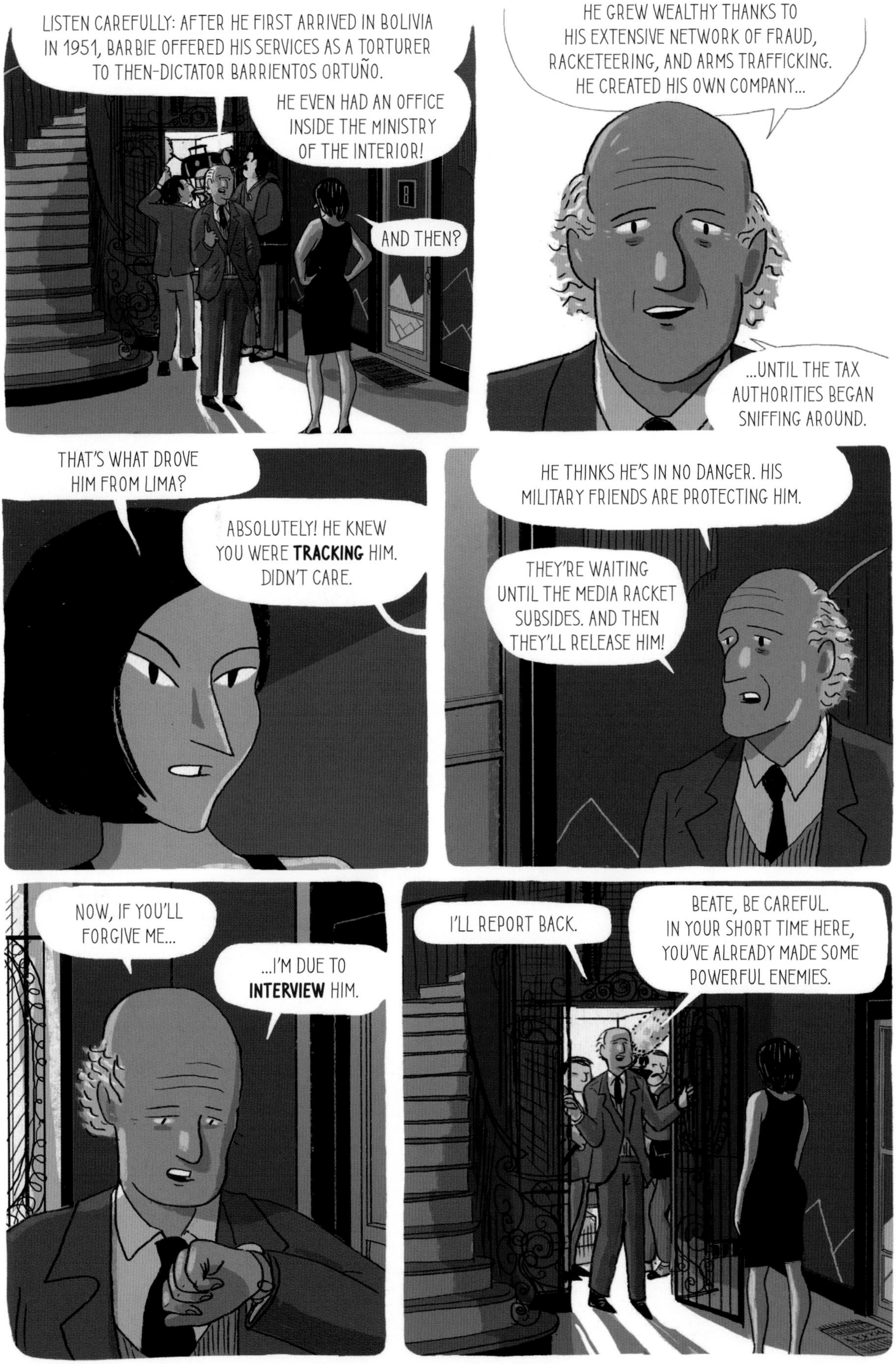
LISTEN CAREFULLY: AFTER HE FIRST ARRIVED IN BOLIVIA IN 1951, BARBIE OFFERED HIS SERVICES AS A TORTURER TO THEN-DICTATOR BARRIENTOS ORTUÑO.
HE EVEN HAD AN OFFICE INSIDE THE MINISTRY OF THE INTERIOR!
AND THEN?
HE GREW WEALTHY THANKS TO HIS EXTENSIVE NETWORK OF FRAUD, RACKETEERING, AND ARMS TRAFFICKING. HE CREATED HIS OWN COMPANY...
...UNTIL THE TAX AUTHORITIES BEGAN SNIFFING AROUND.
THAT'S WHAT DROVE HIM FROM LIMA?
ABSOLUTELY! HE KNEW YOU WERE **TRACKING** HIM. DIDN'T CARE.
HE THINKS HE'S IN NO DANGER. HIS MILITARY FRIENDS ARE PROTECTING HIM.
THEY'RE WAITING UNTIL THE MEDIA RACKET SUBSIDES. AND THEN THEY'LL RELEASE HIM!
NOW, IF YOU'LL FORGIVE ME...
...I'M DUE TO **INTERVIEW** HIM.
I'LL REPORT BACK.
BEATE, BE CAREFUL. IN YOUR SHORT TIME HERE, YOU'VE ALREADY MADE SOME POWERFUL ENEMIES.

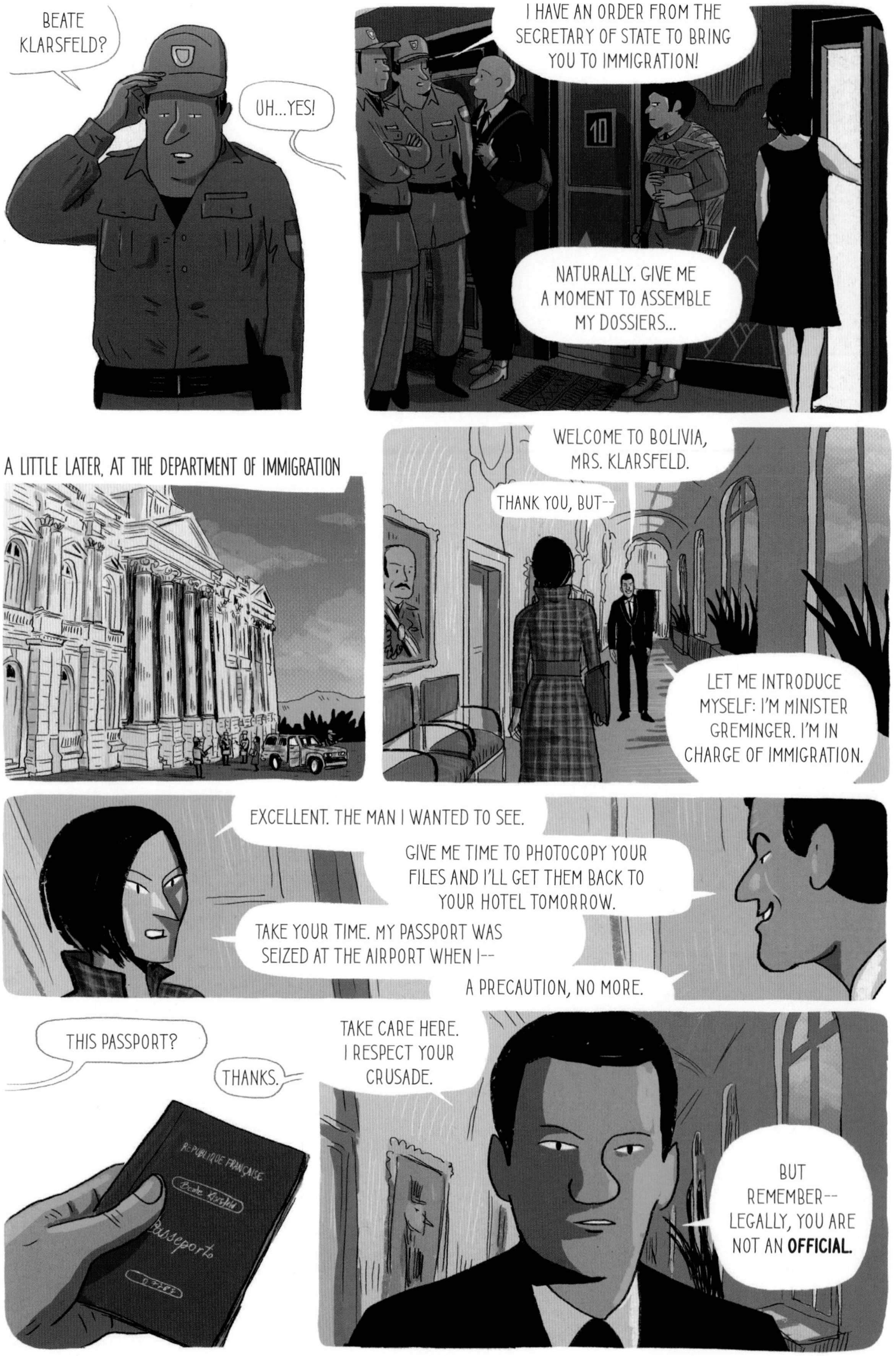
BEATE KLARSFELD?
UH...YES!
I HAVE AN ORDER FROM THE SECRETARY OF STATE TO BRING YOU TO IMMIGRATION!
NATURALLY. GIVE ME A MOMENT TO ASSEMBLE MY DOSSIERS...
A LITTLE LATER, AT THE DEPARTMENT OF IMMIGRATION
WELCOME TO BOLIVIA, MRS. KLARSFELD.
THANK YOU, BUT--
LET ME INTRODUCE MYSELF: I'M MINISTER GREMINGER. I'M IN CHARGE OF IMMIGRATION.
EXCELLENT. THE MAN I WANTED TO SEE.
GIVE ME TIME TO PHOTOCOPY YOUR FILES AND I'LL GET THEM BACK TO YOUR HOTEL TOMORROW.
TAKE YOUR TIME. MY PASSPORT WAS SEIZED AT THE AIRPORT WHEN I--
A PRECAUTION, NO MORE.
THIS PASSPORT?
THANKS.
TAKE CARE HERE. I RESPECT YOUR CRUSADE.
BUT REMEMBER-- LEGALLY, YOU ARE NOT AN **OFFICIAL.**

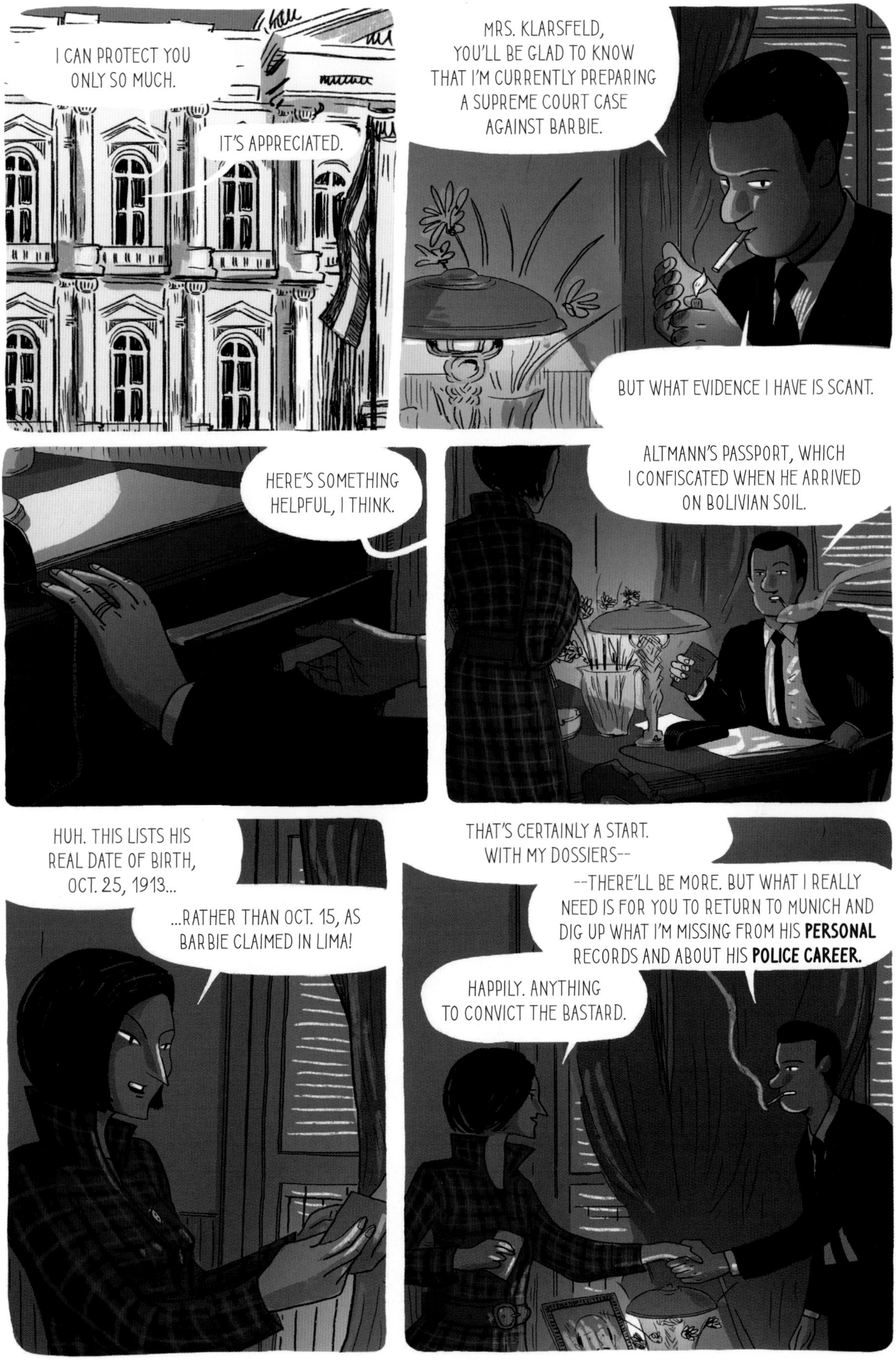
I CAN PROTECT YOU ONLY SO MUCH.
IT'S APPRECIATED.
MRS. KLARSFELD, YOU'LL BE GLAD TO KNOW THAT I'M CURRENTLY PREPARING A SUPREME COURT CASE AGAINST BARBIE.
BUT WHAT EVIDENCE I HAVE IS SCANT.
HERE'S SOMETHING HELPFUL, I THINK.
ALTMANN'S PASSPORT, WHICH I CONFISCATED WHEN HE ARRIVED ON BOLIVIAN SOIL.
HUH. THIS LISTS HIS REAL DATE OF BIRTH, OCT. 25, 1913...
...RATHER THAN OCT. 15, AS BARBIE CLAIMED IN LIMA!
THAT'S CERTAINLY A START. WITH MY DOSSIERS--
--THERE'LL BE MORE. BUT WHAT I REALLY NEED IS FOR YOU TO RETURN TO MUNICH AND DIG UP WHAT I'M MISSING FROM HIS **PERSONAL** RECORDS AND ABOUT HIS **POLICE CAREER.**
HAPPILY. ANYTHING TO CONVICT THE BASTARD.

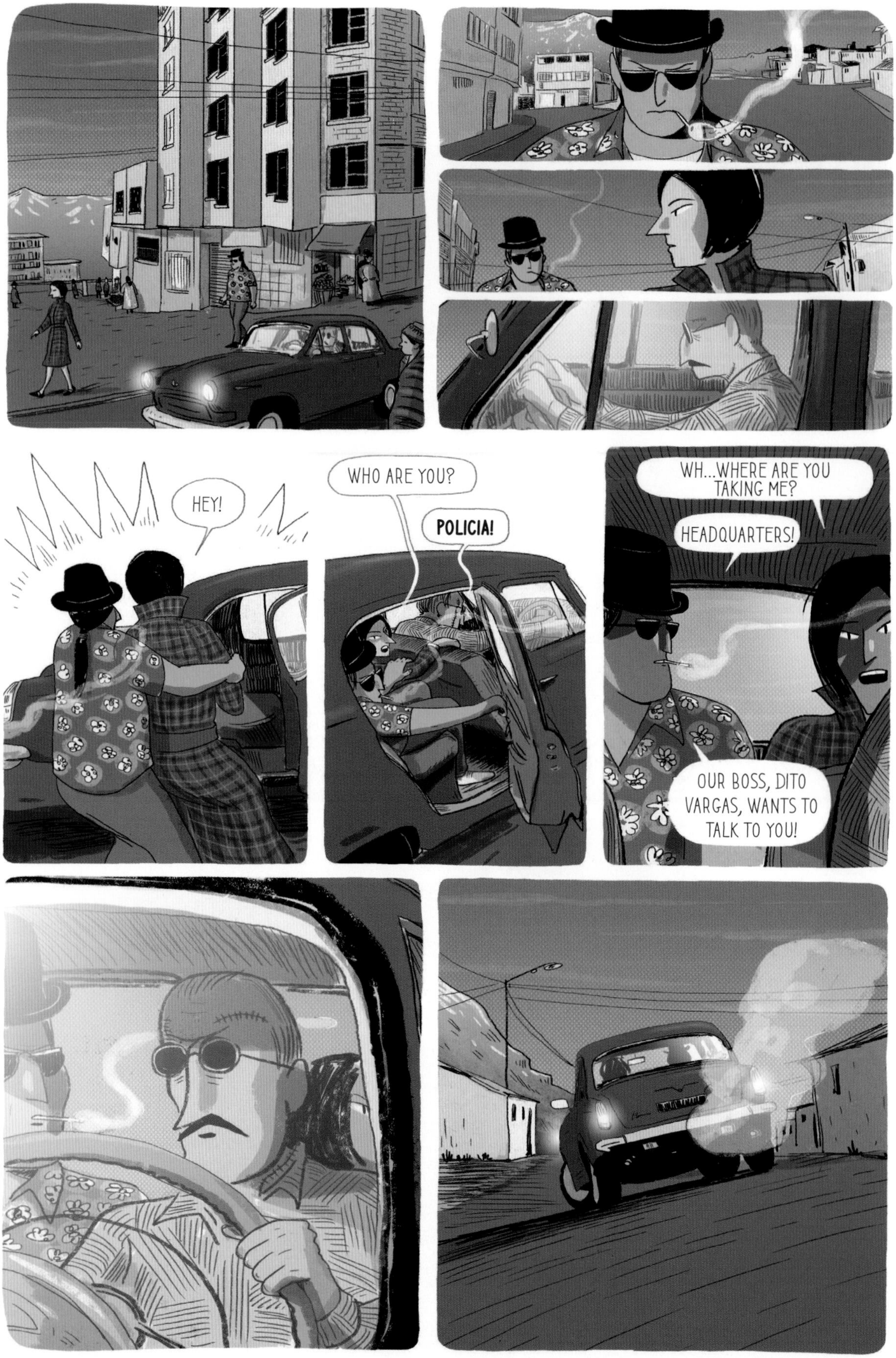

HEY!
WHO ARE YOU?
POLICIA!
WH...WHERE ARE YOU TAKING ME?
HEADQUARTERS!
OUR BOSS, DITO VARGAS, WANTS TO TALK TO YOU!

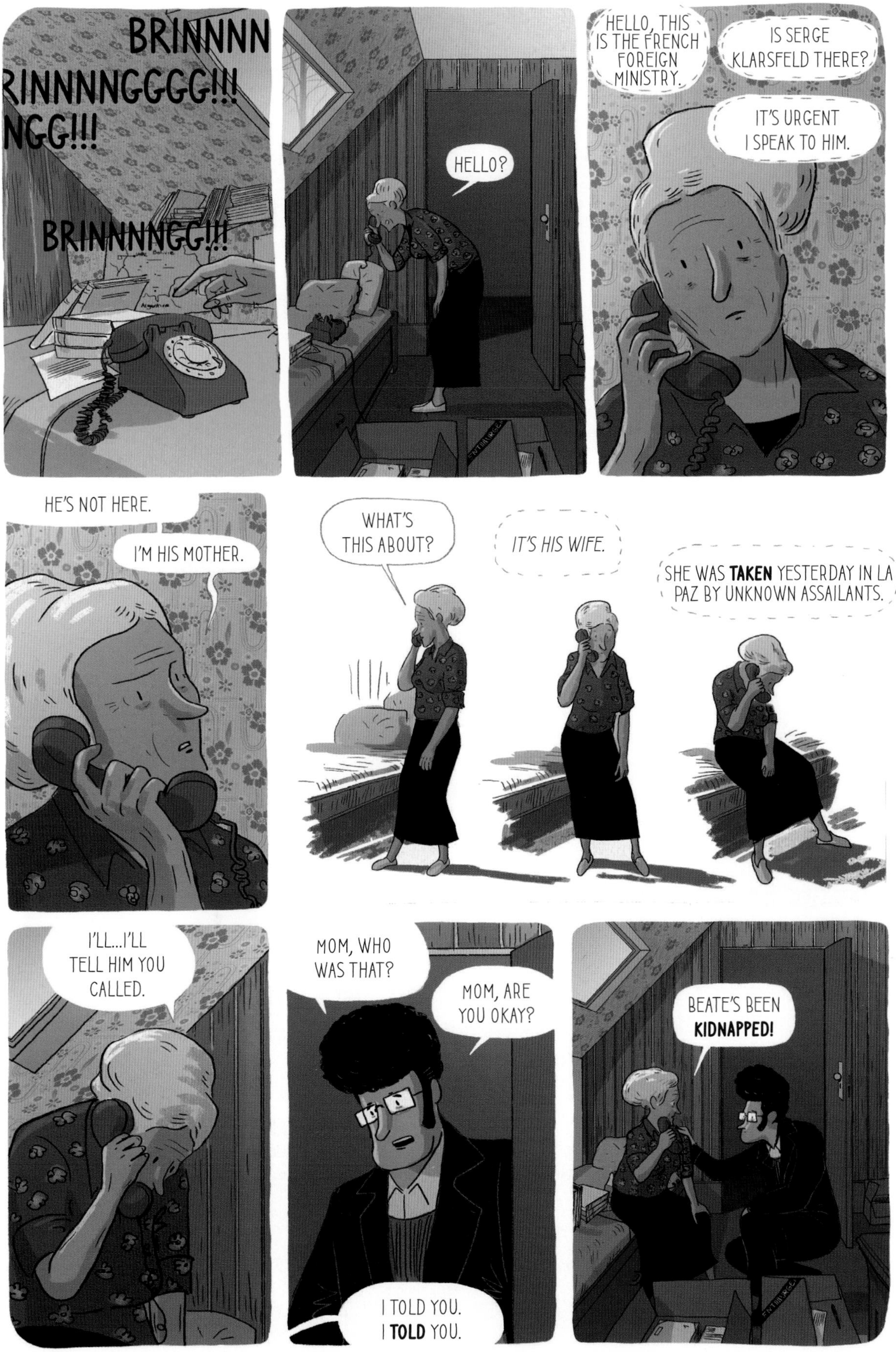
BRINNNN
RINNNNGGGG!!!
NGG!!!
BRINNNNGG!!!
HELLO?
HELLO, THIS IS THE FRENCH FOREIGN MINISTRY.
IS SERGE KLARSFELD THERE?
IT'S URGENT I SPEAK TO HIM.
HE'S NOT HERE.
I'M HIS MOTHER.
WHAT'S THIS ABOUT?
IT'S HIS WIFE.
SHE WAS **TAKEN** YESTERDAY IN LA PAZ BY UNKNOWN ASSAILANTS.
I'LL...I'LL TELL HIM YOU CALLED.
MOM, WHO WAS THAT?
MOM, ARE YOU OKAY?
I TOLD YOU. I **TOLD** YOU.
BEATE'S BEEN **KIDNAPPED!**

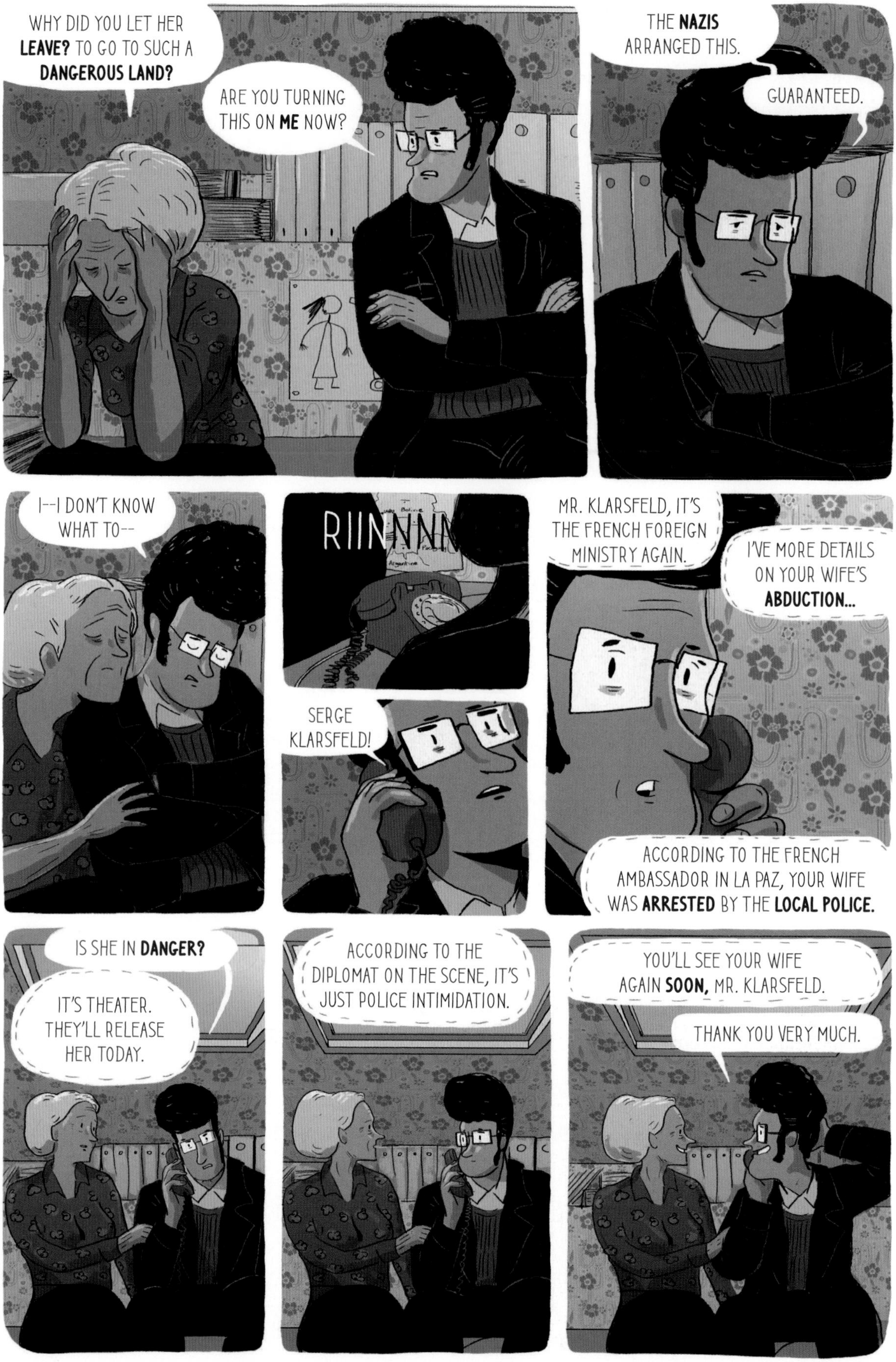
WHY DID YOU LET HER LEAVE? TO GO TO SUCH A DANGEROUS LAND?
ARE YOU TURNING THIS ON ME NOW?
THE NAZIS ARRANGED THIS.
GUARANTEED.
I--I DON'T KNOW WHAT TO--
RIINNNN
SERGE KLARSFELD!
MR. KLARSFELD, IT'S THE FRENCH FOREIGN MINISTRY AGAIN.
I'VE MORE DETAILS ON YOUR WIFE'S ABDUCTION...
ACCORDING TO THE FRENCH AMBASSADOR IN LA PAZ, YOUR WIFE WAS ARRESTED BY THE LOCAL POLICE.
IS SHE IN DANGER?
IT'S THEATER. THEY'LL RELEASE HER TODAY.
ACCORDING TO THE DIPLOMAT ON THE SCENE, IT'S JUST POLICE INTIMIDATION.
YOU'LL SEE YOUR WIFE AGAIN SOON, MR. KLARSFELD.
THANK YOU VERY MUCH.

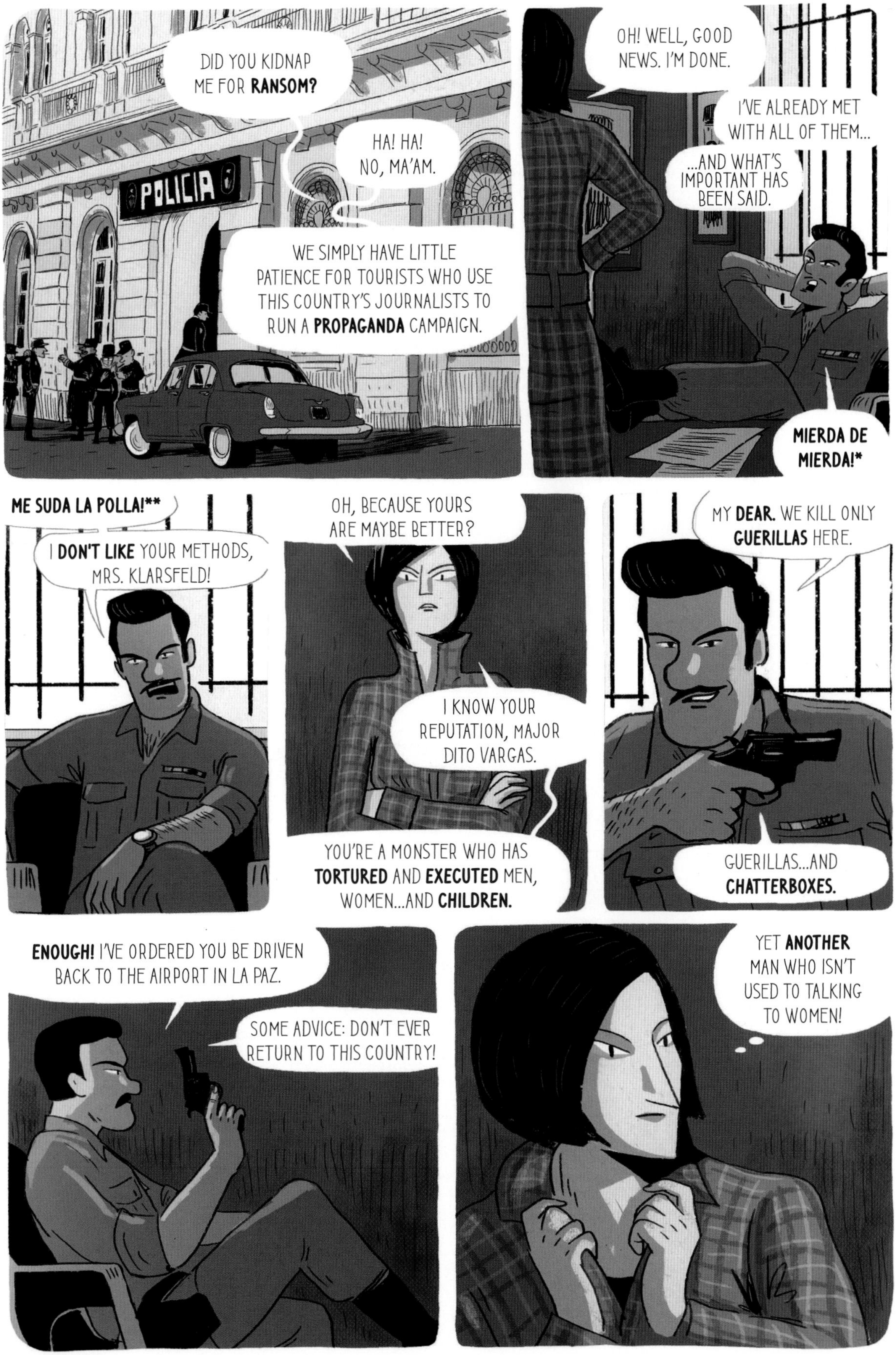

DID YOU KIDNAP ME FOR **RANSOM?**
HA! HA! NO, MA'AM.
WE SIMPLY HAVE LITTLE PATIENCE FOR TOURISTS WHO USE THIS COUNTRY'S JOURNALISTS TO RUN A **PROPAGANDA** CAMPAIGN.
POLICIA
OH! WELL, GOOD NEWS. I'M DONE.
I'VE ALREADY MET WITH ALL OF THEM...
...AND WHAT'S IMPORTANT HAS BEEN SAID.
MIERDA DE MIERDA!*
ME SUDA LA POLLA!**
I **DON'T LIKE** YOUR METHODS, MRS. KLARSFELD!
OH, BECAUSE YOURS ARE MAYBE BETTER?
I KNOW YOUR REPUTATION, MAJOR DITO VARGAS.
YOU'RE A MONSTER WHO HAS **TORTURED** AND **EXECUTED** MEN, WOMEN...AND **CHILDREN.**
MY **DEAR.** WE KILL ONLY **GUERILLAS** HERE.
GUERILLAS...AND **CHATTERBOXES.**
ENOUGH! I'VE ORDERED YOU BE DRIVEN BACK TO THE AIRPORT IN LA PAZ.
SOME ADVICE: DON'T EVER RETURN TO THIS COUNTRY!
YET **ANOTHER** MAN WHO ISN'T USED TO TALKING TO WOMEN!

*FUCKING HELL!
**I DON'T GIVE A SHIT!

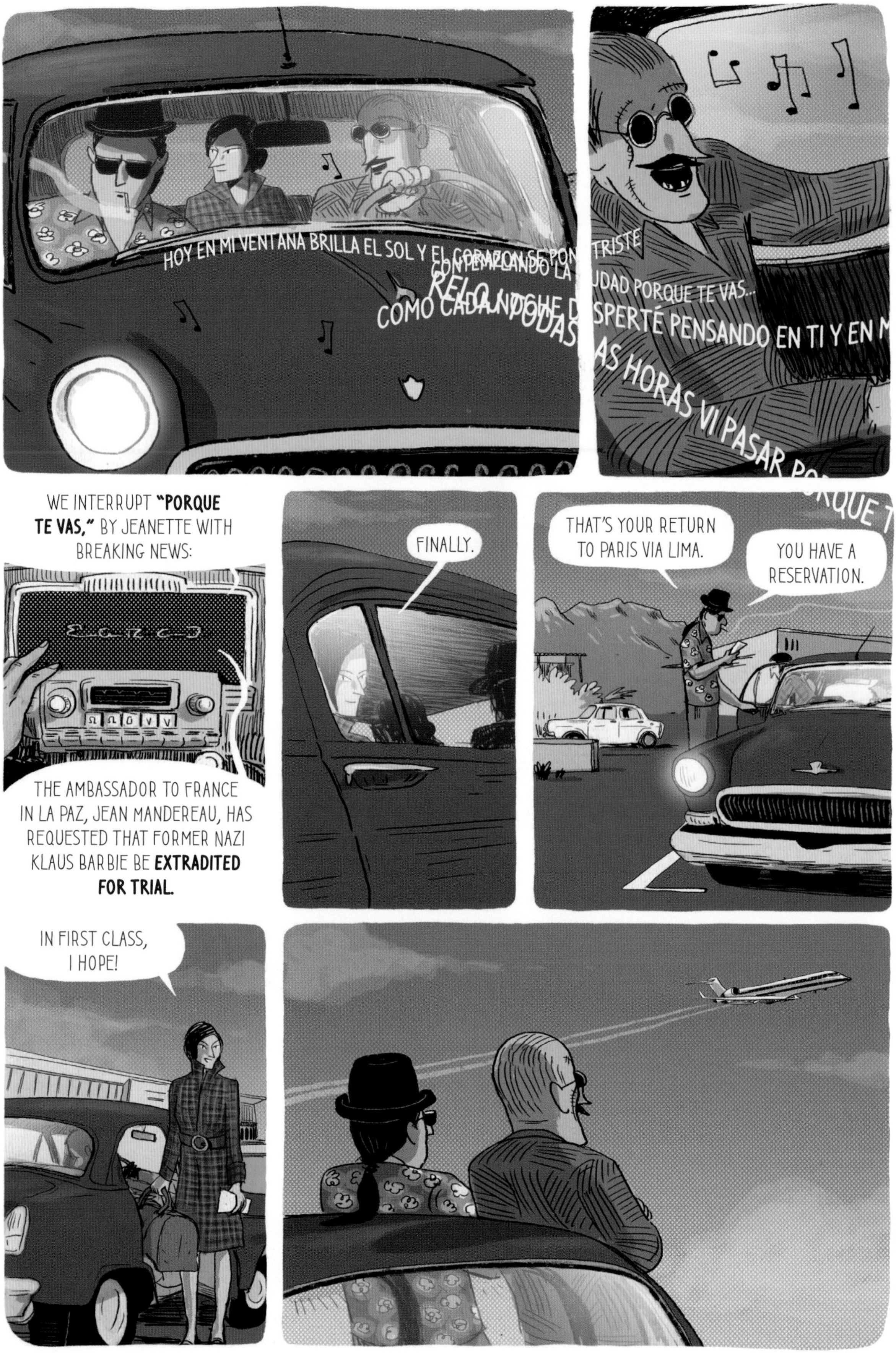

HOY EN MI VENTANA BRILLA EL SOL Y EL CORAZON SE PON TRISTE
CONTEMPLANDO LA UDAD PORQUE TE VAS...
COMO CADA NOCHE DESPERTÉ PENSANDO EN TI Y EN M
AS HORAS VI PASAR PORQUE T
WE INTERRUPT **"PORQUE TE VAS,"** BY JEANETTE WITH BREAKING NEWS:
THE AMBASSADOR TO FRANCE IN LA PAZ, JEAN MANDEREAU, HAS REQUESTED THAT FORMER NAZI KLAUS BARBIE BE **EXTRADITED FOR TRIAL.**
FINALLY.
THAT'S YOUR RETURN TO PARIS VIA LIMA.
YOU HAVE A RESERVATION.
IN FIRST CLASS, I HOPE!

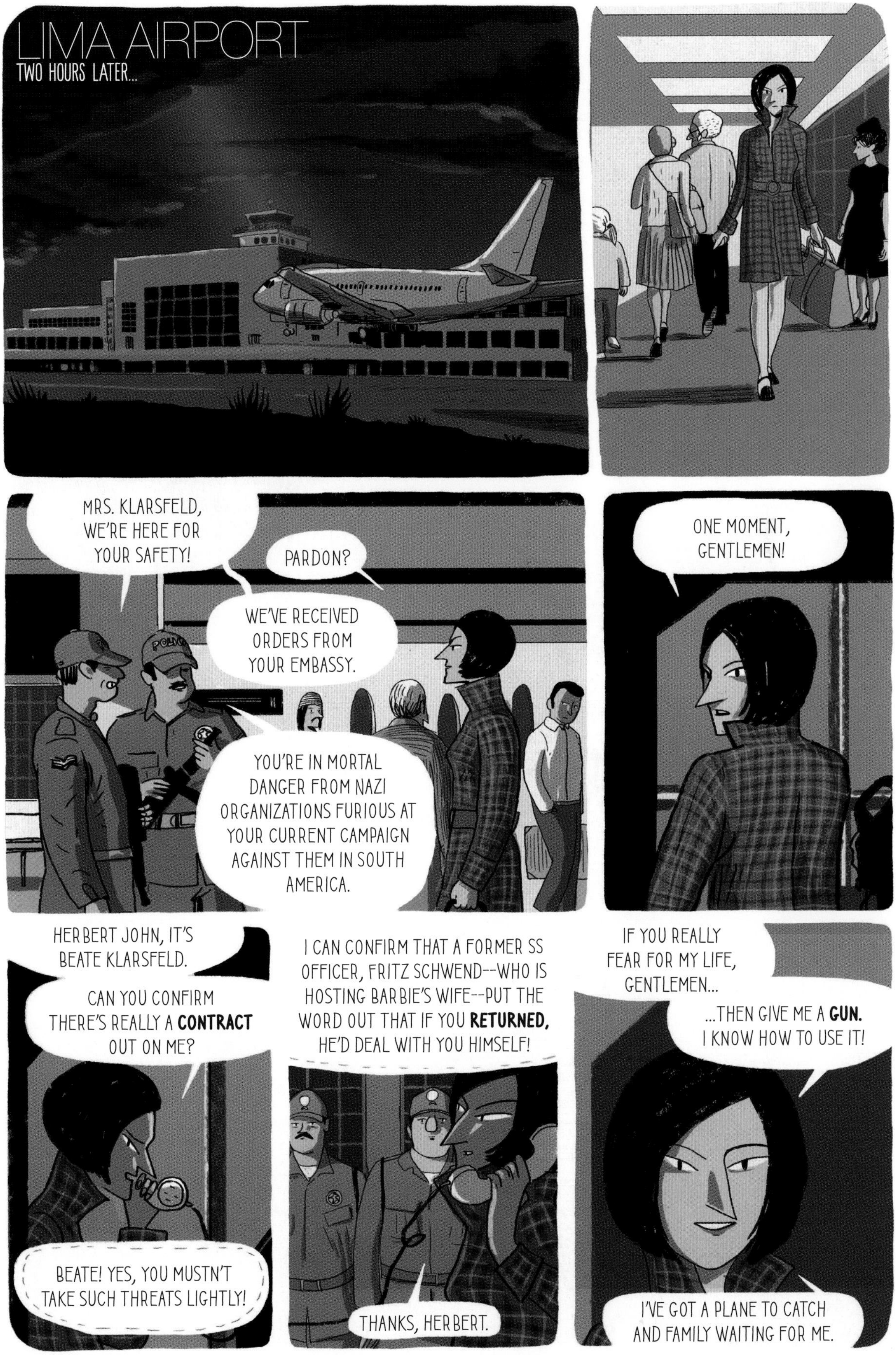
LIMA AIRPORT
TWO HOURS LATER...
MRS. KLARSFELD, WE'RE HERE FOR YOUR SAFETY!
PARDON?
WE'VE RECEIVED ORDERS FROM YOUR EMBASSY.
YOU'RE IN MORTAL DANGER FROM NAZI ORGANIZATIONS FURIOUS AT YOUR CURRENT CAMPAIGN AGAINST THEM IN SOUTH AMERICA.
ONE MOMENT, GENTLEMEN!
HERBERT JOHN, IT'S BEATE KLARSFELD.
CAN YOU CONFIRM THERE'S REALLY A CONTRACT OUT ON ME?
BEATE! YES, YOU MUSTN'T TAKE SUCH THREATS LIGHTLY!
I CAN CONFIRM THAT A FORMER SS OFFICER, FRITZ SCHWEND--WHO IS HOSTING BARBIE'S WIFE--PUT THE WORD OUT THAT IF YOU RETURNED, HE'D DEAL WITH YOU HIMSELF!
THANKS, HERBERT.
IF YOU REALLY FEAR FOR MY LIFE, GENTLEMEN...
...THEN GIVE ME A GUN. I KNOW HOW TO USE IT!
I'VE GOT A PLANE TO CATCH AND FAMILY WAITING FOR ME.

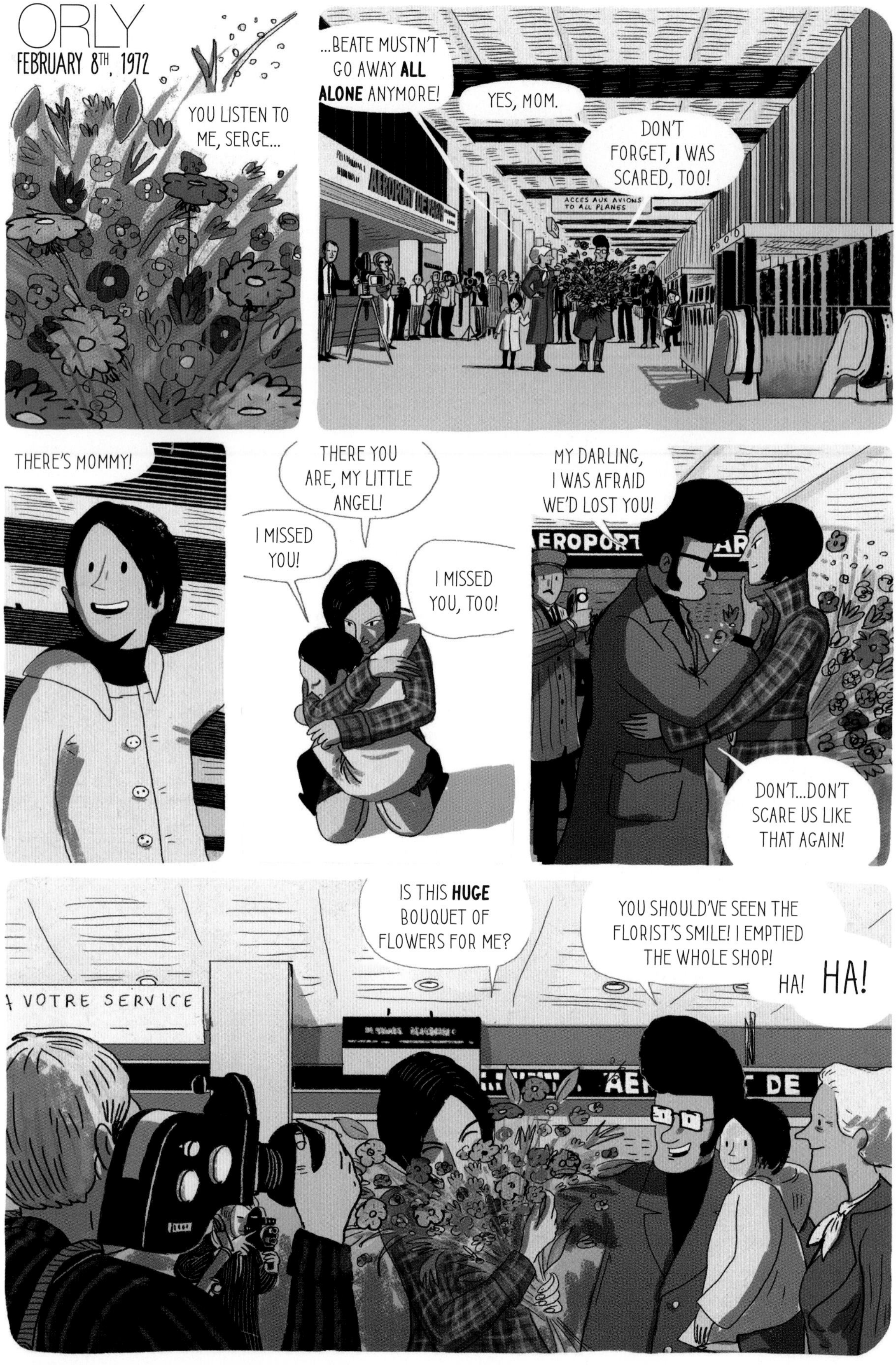
ORLY
FEBRUARY 8TH, 1972
YOU LISTEN TO ME, SERGE...
...BEATE MUSTN'T GO AWAY ALL ALONE ANYMORE!
YES, MOM.
DON'T FORGET, I WAS SCARED, TOO!
AEROPORT DE PARIS
ACCES AUX AVIONS
TO ALL PLANES
THERE'S MOMMY!
THERE YOU ARE, MY LITTLE ANGEL!
I MISSED YOU!
I MISSED YOU, TOO!
MY DARLING, I WAS AFRAID WE'D LOST YOU!
AEROPORT
DON'T...DON'T SCARE US LIKE THAT AGAIN!
IS THIS HUGE BOUQUET OF FLOWERS FOR ME?
YOU SHOULD'VE SEEN THE FLORIST'S SMILE! I EMPTIED THE WHOLE SHOP!
HA! HA!
A VOTRE SERVICE
DE

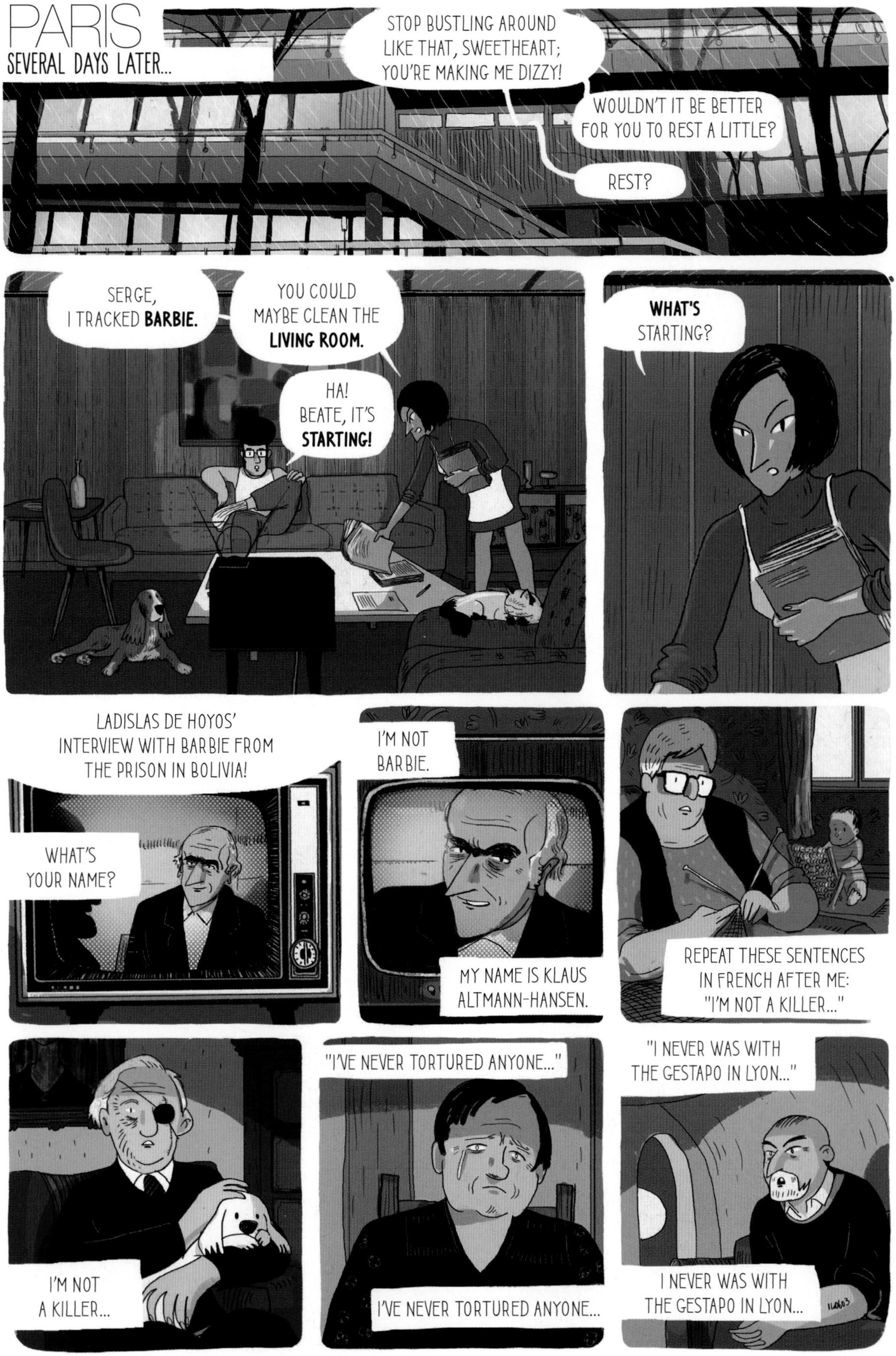
PARIS
SEVERAL DAYS LATER...
STOP BUSTLING AROUND LIKE THAT, SWEETHEART; YOU'RE MAKING ME DIZZY!
WOULDN'T IT BE BETTER FOR YOU TO REST A LITTLE?
REST?
SERGE, I TRACKED **BARBIE.**
YOU COULD MAYBE CLEAN THE **LIVING ROOM.**
HA! BEATE, IT'S **STARTING!**
WHAT'S STARTING?
LADISLAS DE HOYOS' INTERVIEW WITH BARBIE FROM THE PRISON IN BOLIVIA!
WHAT'S YOUR NAME?
I'M NOT BARBIE.
MY NAME IS KLAUS ALTMANN-HANSEN.
REPEAT THESE SENTENCES IN FRENCH AFTER ME: "I'M NOT A KILLER..."
I'M NOT A KILLER...
"I'VE NEVER TORTURED ANYONE..."
I'VE NEVER TORTURED ANYONE...
"I NEVER WAS WITH THE GESTAPO IN LYON..."
I NEVER WAS WITH THE GESTAPO IN LYON...

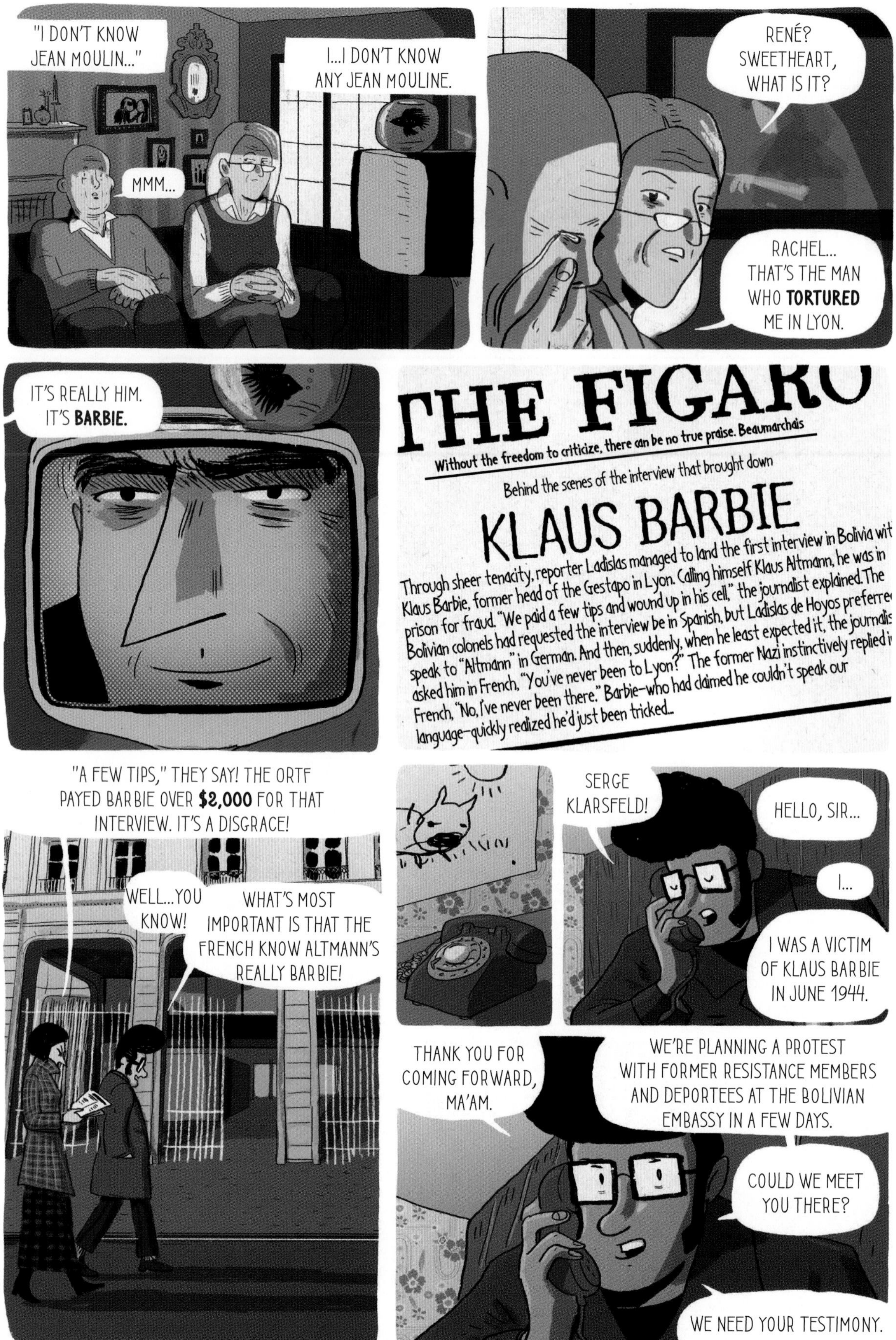

"I DON'T KNOW JEAN MOULIN..."
I...I DON'T KNOW ANY JEAN MOULINE.
MMM...
RENÉ? SWEETHEART, WHAT IS IT?
RACHEL... THAT'S THE MAN WHO **TORTURED** ME IN LYON.
IT'S REALLY HIM. IT'S **BARBIE.**
THE FIGARO
Without the freedom to criticize, there can be no true praise. Beaumarchais
Behind the scenes of the interview that brought down
KLAUS BARBIE
Through sheer tenacity, reporter Ladislas managed to land the first interview in Bolivia wit
Klaus Barbie, former head of the Gestapo in Lyon. Calling himself Klaus Altmann, he was in
prison for fraud. "We paid a few tips and wound up in his cell," the journalist explained. The
Bolivian colonels had requested the interview be in Spanish, but Ladislas de Hoyos preferre
speak to "Altmann" in German. And then, suddenly, when he least expected it, the journalis
asked him in French, "You've never been to Lyon?" The former Nazi instinctively replied i
French, "No, I've never been there." Barbie—who had claimed he couldn't speak our
language—quickly realized he'd just been tricked...
"A FEW TIPS," THEY SAY! THE ORTF PAYED BARBIE OVER **$2,000** FOR THAT INTERVIEW. IT'S A DISGRACE!
WELL...YOU KNOW!
WHAT'S MOST IMPORTANT IS THAT THE FRENCH KNOW ALTMANN'S REALLY BARBIE!
SERGE KLARSFELD!
HELLO, SIR...
I...
I WAS A VICTIM OF KLAUS BARBIE IN JUNE 1944.
THANK YOU FOR COMING FORWARD, MA'AM.
WE'RE PLANNING A PROTEST WITH FORMER RESISTANCE MEMBERS AND DEPORTEES AT THE BOLIVIAN EMBASSY IN A FEW DAYS.
COULD WE MEET YOU THERE?
WE NEED YOUR TESTIMONY.

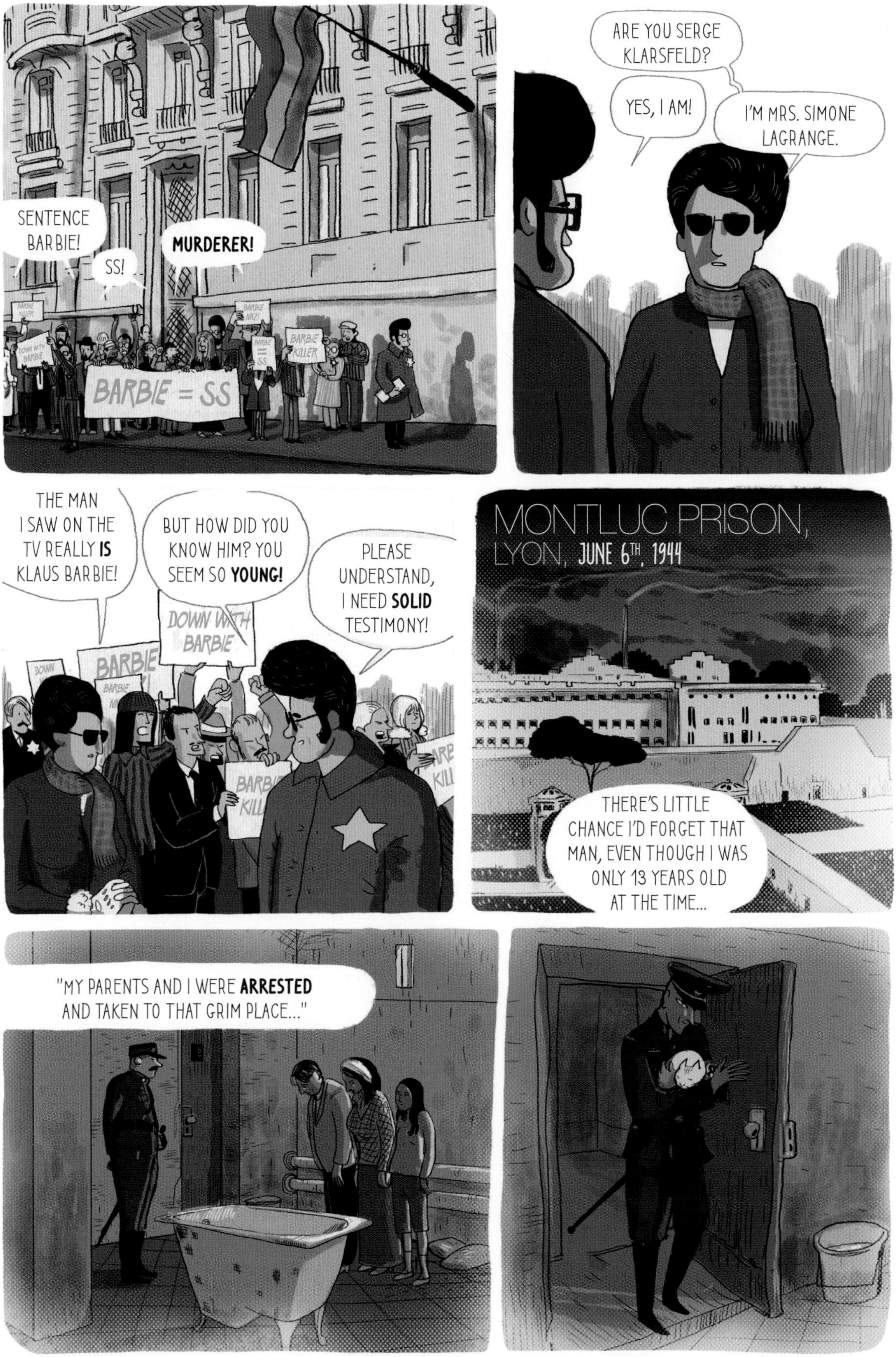

SENTENCE BARBIE!
SS!
MURDERER!
BARBIE = SS
BARBIE KILLER
ARE YOU SERGE KLARSFELD?
YES, I AM!
I'M MRS. SIMONE LAGRANGE.
THE MAN I SAW ON THE TV REALLY **IS** KLAUS BARBIE!
BUT HOW DID YOU KNOW HIM? YOU SEEM SO **YOUNG!**
DOWN WITH BARBIE
PLEASE UNDERSTAND, I NEED **SOLID** TESTIMONY!
MONTLUC PRISON, LYON, JUNE 6TH, 1944
THERE'S LITTLE CHANCE I'D FORGET THAT MAN, EVEN THOUGH I WAS ONLY 13 YEARS OLD AT THE TIME...
"MY PARENTS AND I WERE **ARRESTED** AND TAKEN TO THAT GRIM PLACE..."

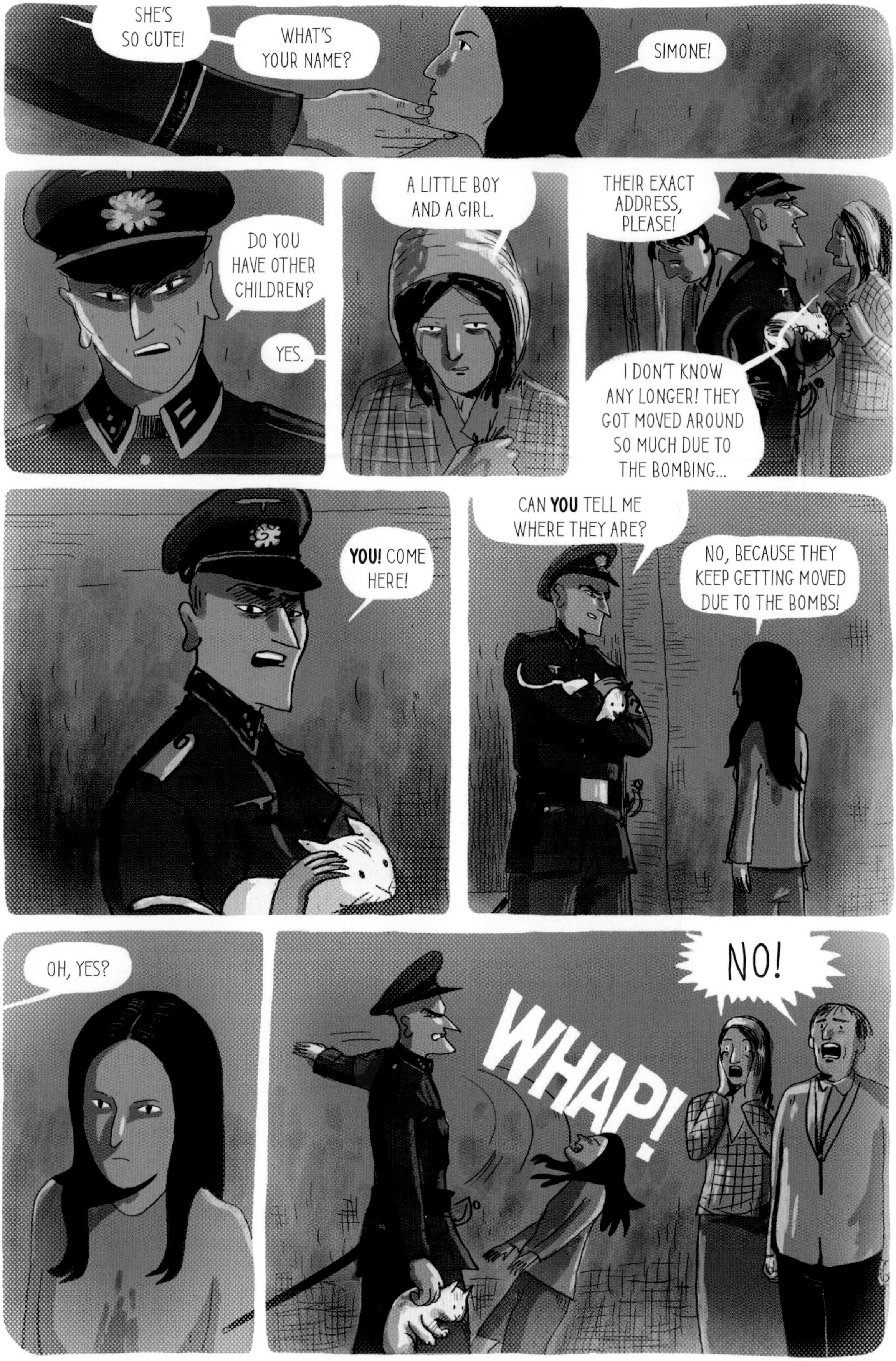
SHE'S SO CUTE!
WHAT'S YOUR NAME?
SIMONE!
DO YOU HAVE OTHER CHILDREN?
YES.
A LITTLE BOY AND A GIRL.
THEIR EXACT ADDRESS, PLEASE!
I DON'T KNOW ANY LONGER! THEY GOT MOVED AROUND SO MUCH DUE TO THE BOMBING...
YOU! COME HERE!
CAN YOU TELL ME WHERE THEY ARE?
NO, BECAUSE THEY KEEP GETTING MOVED DUE TO THE BOMBS!
OH, YES?
WHAP!
NO!

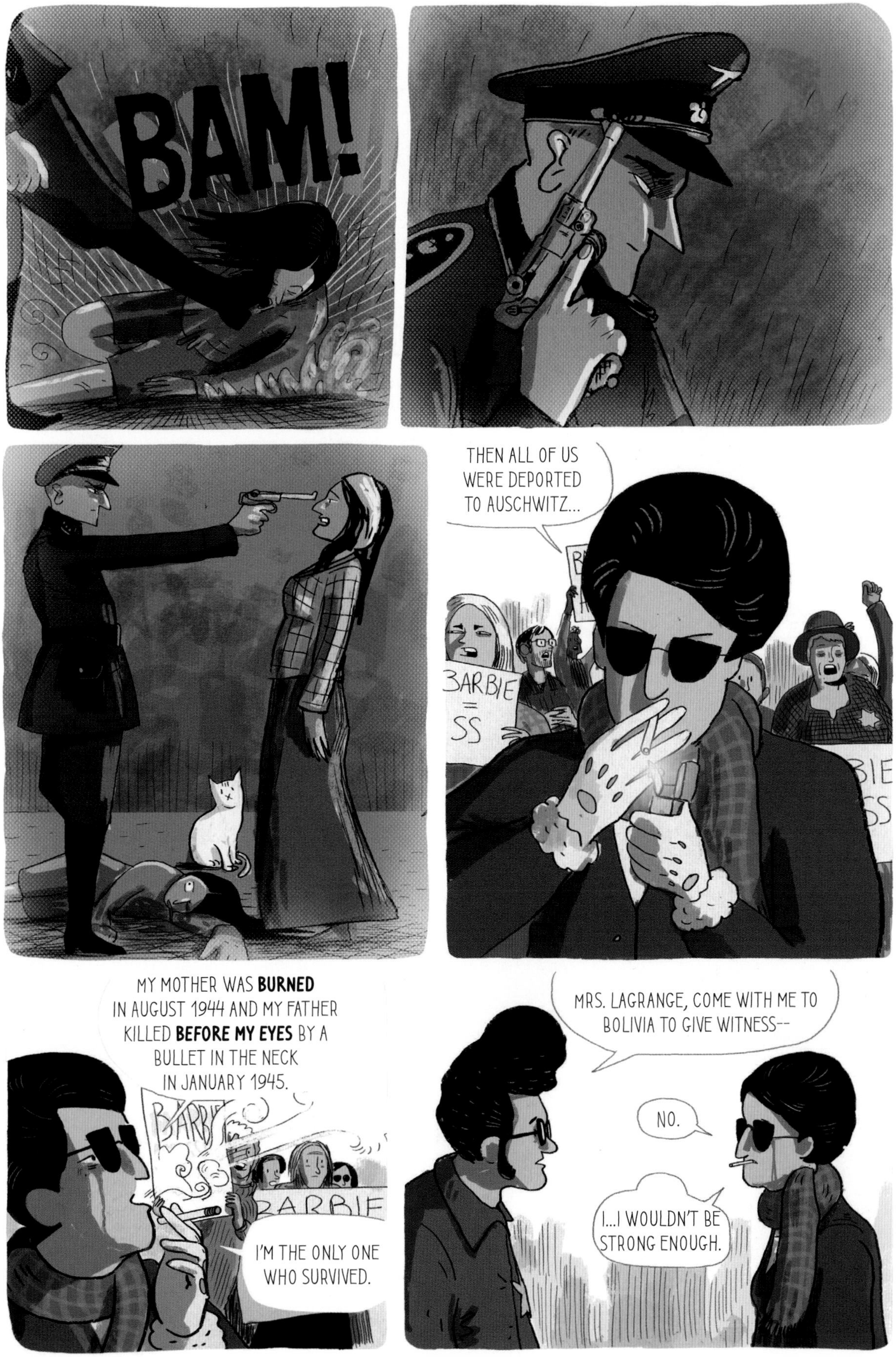
BAM!
THEN ALL OF US WERE DEPORTED TO AUSCHWITZ...
BARBIE = SS
MY MOTHER WAS **BURNED** IN AUGUST 1944 AND MY FATHER KILLED **BEFORE MY EYES** BY A BULLET IN THE NECK IN JANUARY 1945.
I'M THE ONLY ONE WHO SURVIVED.
MRS. LAGRANGE, COME WITH ME TO BOLIVIA TO GIVE WITNESS--
NO.
I...I WOULDN'T BE STRONG ENOUGH.

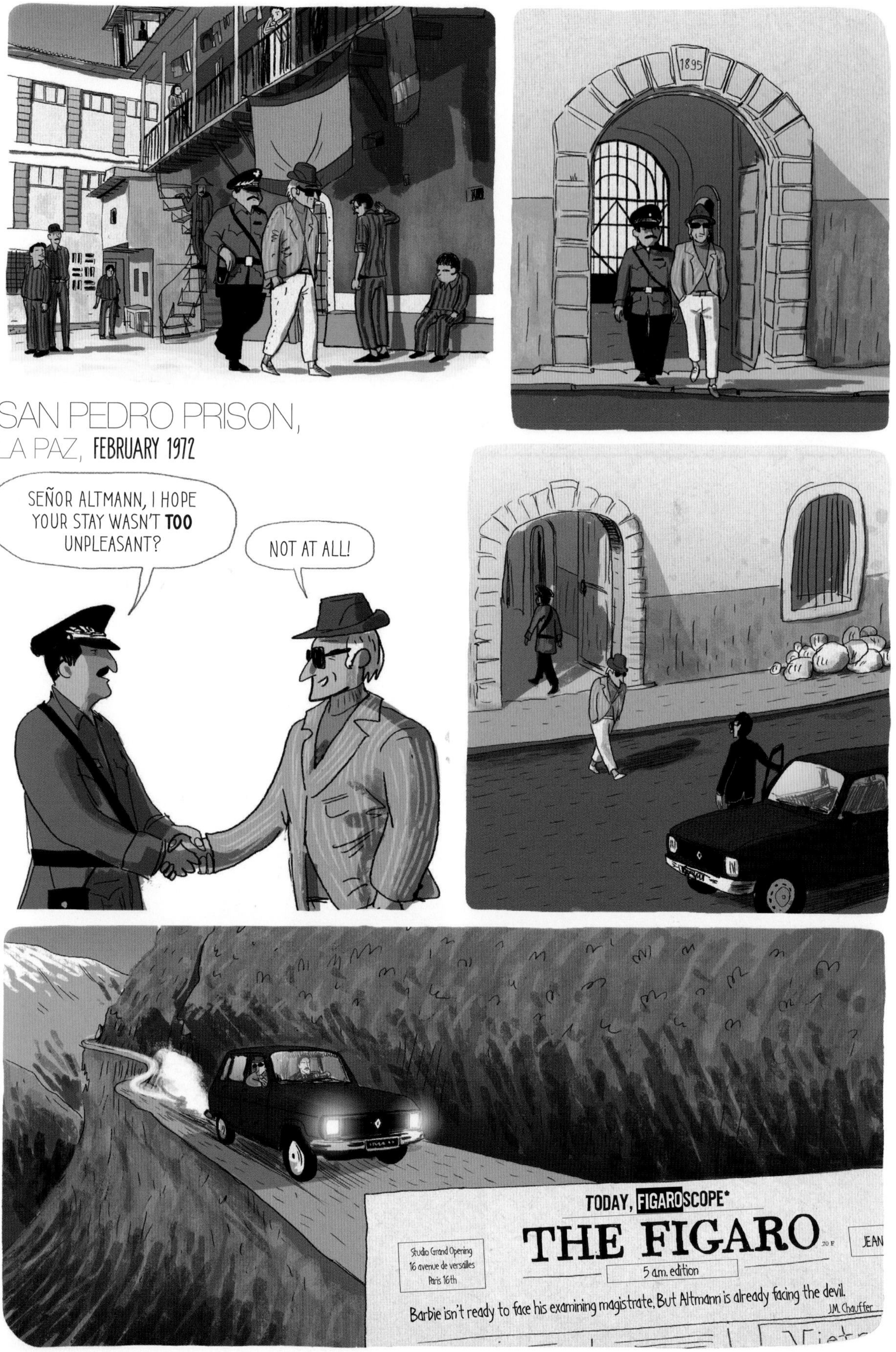
1895
SAN PEDRO PRISON,
LA PAZ, FEBRUARY 1972
SEÑOR ALTMANN, I HOPE YOUR STAY WASN'T **TOO** UNPLEASANT?
NOT AT ALL!
TODAY, FIGAROSCOPE*
THE FIGARO
5 a.m. edition
Studio Grand Opening 16 avenue de versailles Paris 16th
JEAN
Barbie isn't ready to face his examining magistrate, But Altmann is already facing the devil.
J.M. Chauffer

*SECTION OF LE FIGARO **FRANCS

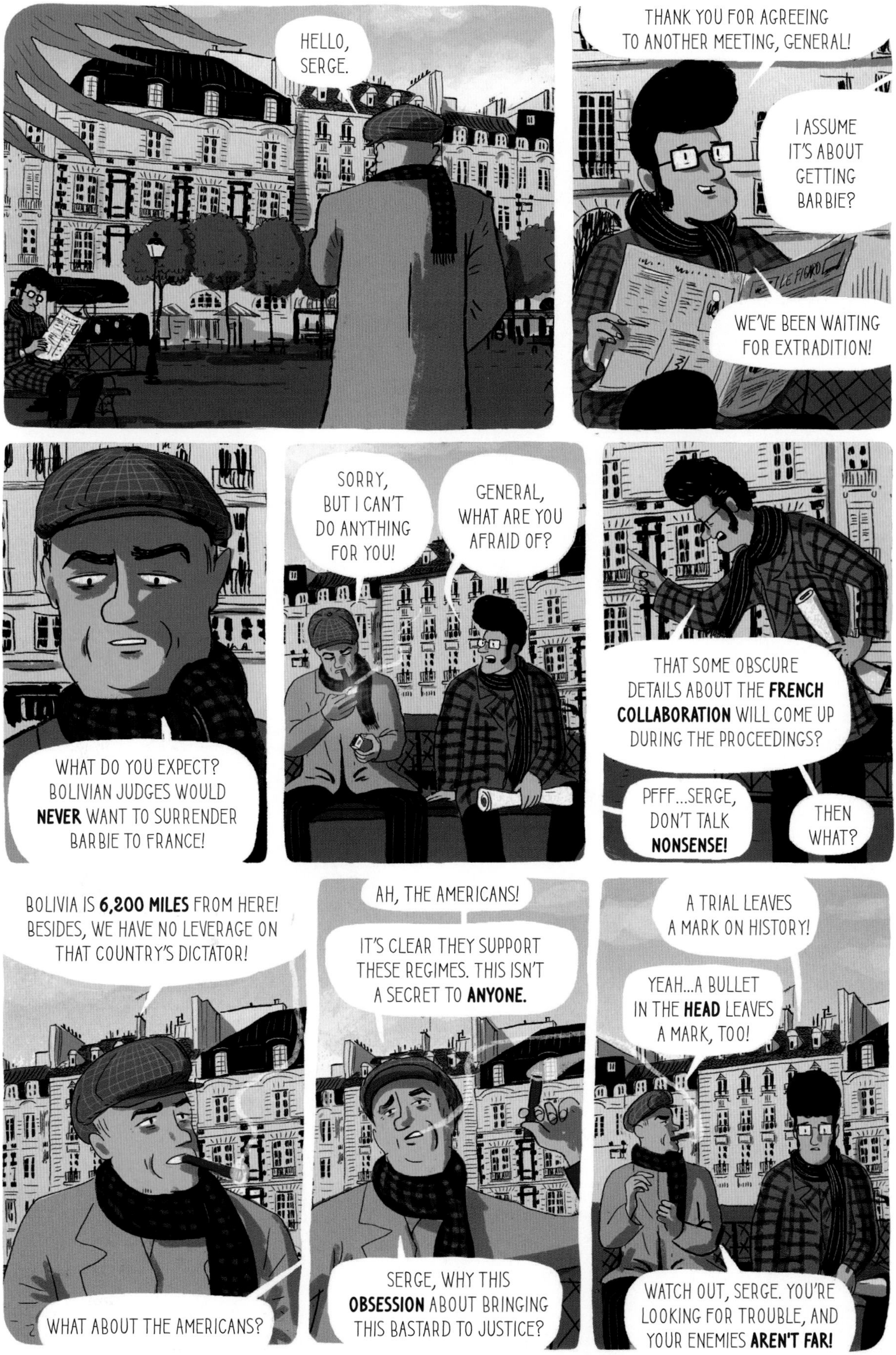
HELLO, SERGE.
THANK YOU FOR AGREEING TO ANOTHER MEETING, GENERAL!
I ASSUME IT'S ABOUT GETTING BARBIE?
LE FIGARO
WE'VE BEEN WAITING FOR EXTRADITION!
WHAT DO YOU EXPECT? BOLIVIAN JUDGES WOULD **NEVER** WANT TO SURRENDER BARBIE TO FRANCE!
SORRY, BUT I CAN'T DO ANYTHING FOR YOU!
GENERAL, WHAT ARE YOU AFRAID OF?
THAT SOME OBSCURE DETAILS ABOUT THE **FRENCH COLLABORATION** WILL COME UP DURING THE PROCEEDINGS?
PFFF...SERGE, DON'T TALK **NONSENSE!**
THEN WHAT?
BOLIVIA IS **6,200 MILES** FROM HERE! BESIDES, WE HAVE NO LEVERAGE ON THAT COUNTRY'S DICTATOR!
WHAT ABOUT THE AMERICANS?
AH, THE AMERICANS!
IT'S CLEAR THEY SUPPORT THESE REGIMES. THIS ISN'T A SECRET TO **ANYONE.**
SERGE, WHY THIS **OBSESSION** ABOUT BRINGING THIS BASTARD TO JUSTICE?
A TRIAL LEAVES A MARK ON HISTORY!
YEAH...A BULLET IN THE **HEAD** LEAVES A MARK, TOO!
WATCH OUT, SERGE. YOU'RE LOOKING FOR TROUBLE, AND YOUR ENEMIES **AREN'T FAR!**

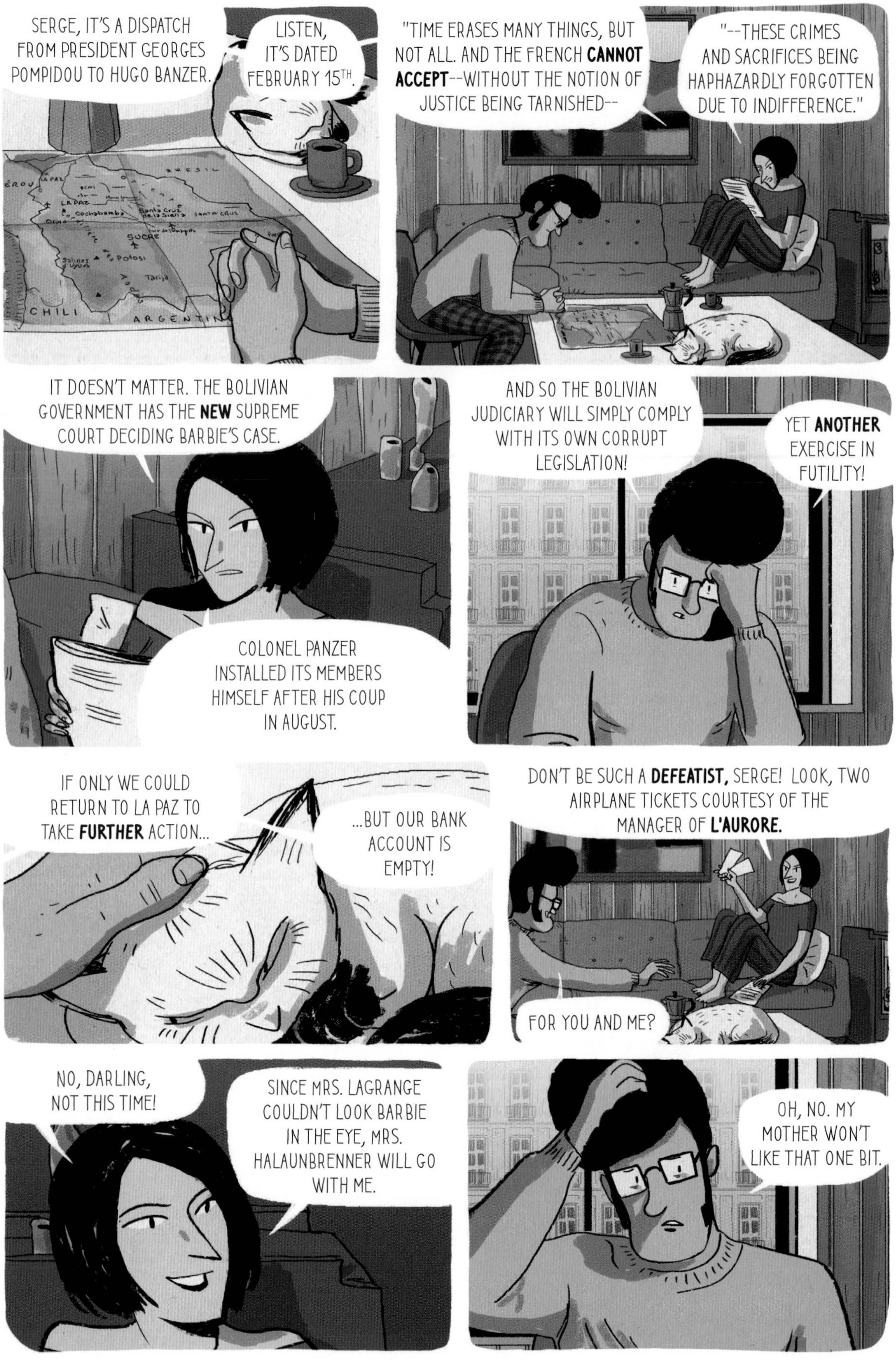
SERGE, IT'S A DISPATCH FROM PRESIDENT GEORGES POMPIDOU TO HUGO BANZER.
LISTEN, IT'S DATED FEBRUARY 15TH.
BRESIL
LA PAZ
Cochabamba
SUCRE
Potosi
Tarija
CHILI
ARGENTIN
"TIME ERASES MANY THINGS, BUT NOT ALL. AND THE FRENCH **CANNOT ACCEPT**--WITHOUT THE NOTION OF JUSTICE BEING TARNISHED--
"--THESE CRIMES AND SACRIFICES BEING HAPHAZARDLY FORGOTTEN DUE TO INDIFFERENCE."
IT DOESN'T MATTER. THE BOLIVIAN GOVERNMENT HAS THE **NEW** SUPREME COURT DECIDING BARBIE'S CASE.
COLONEL PANZER INSTALLED ITS MEMBERS HIMSELF AFTER HIS COUP IN AUGUST.
AND SO THE BOLIVIAN JUDICIARY WILL SIMPLY COMPLY WITH ITS OWN CORRUPT LEGISLATION!
YET **ANOTHER** EXERCISE IN FUTILITY!
IF ONLY WE COULD RETURN TO LA PAZ TO TAKE **FURTHER** ACTION...
...BUT OUR BANK ACCOUNT IS EMPTY!
DON'T BE SUCH A **DEFEATIST,** SERGE! LOOK, TWO AIRPLANE TICKETS COURTESY OF THE MANAGER OF **L'AURORE.**
FOR YOU AND ME?
NO, DARLING, NOT THIS TIME!
SINCE MRS. LAGRANGE COULDN'T LOOK BARBIE IN THE EYE, MRS. HALAUNBRENNER WILL GO WITH ME.
OH, NO. MY MOTHER WON'T LIKE THAT ONE BIT.

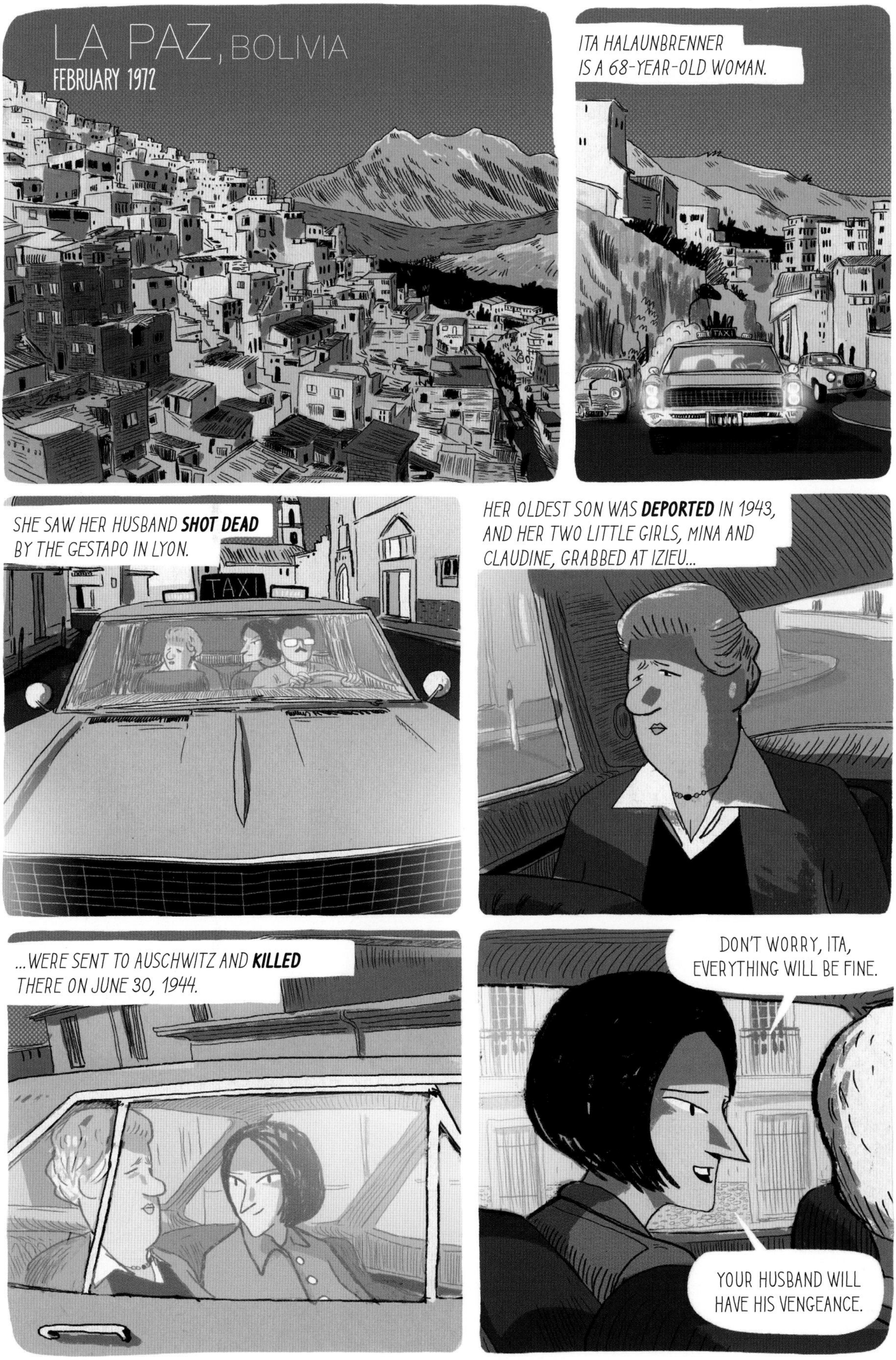
LA PAZ, BOLIVIA
FEBRUARY 1972
ITA HALAUNBRENNER IS A 68-YEAR-OLD WOMAN.
TAXI
SHE SAW HER HUSBAND **SHOT DEAD** BY THE GESTAPO IN LYON.
TAXI
HER OLDEST SON WAS **DEPORTED** IN 1943, AND HER TWO LITTLE GIRLS, MINA AND CLAUDINE, GRABBED AT IZIEU...
...WERE SENT TO AUSCHWITZ AND **KILLED** THERE ON JUNE 30, 1944.
DON'T WORRY, ITA, EVERYTHING WILL BE FINE.
YOUR HUSBAND WILL HAVE HIS VENGEANCE.

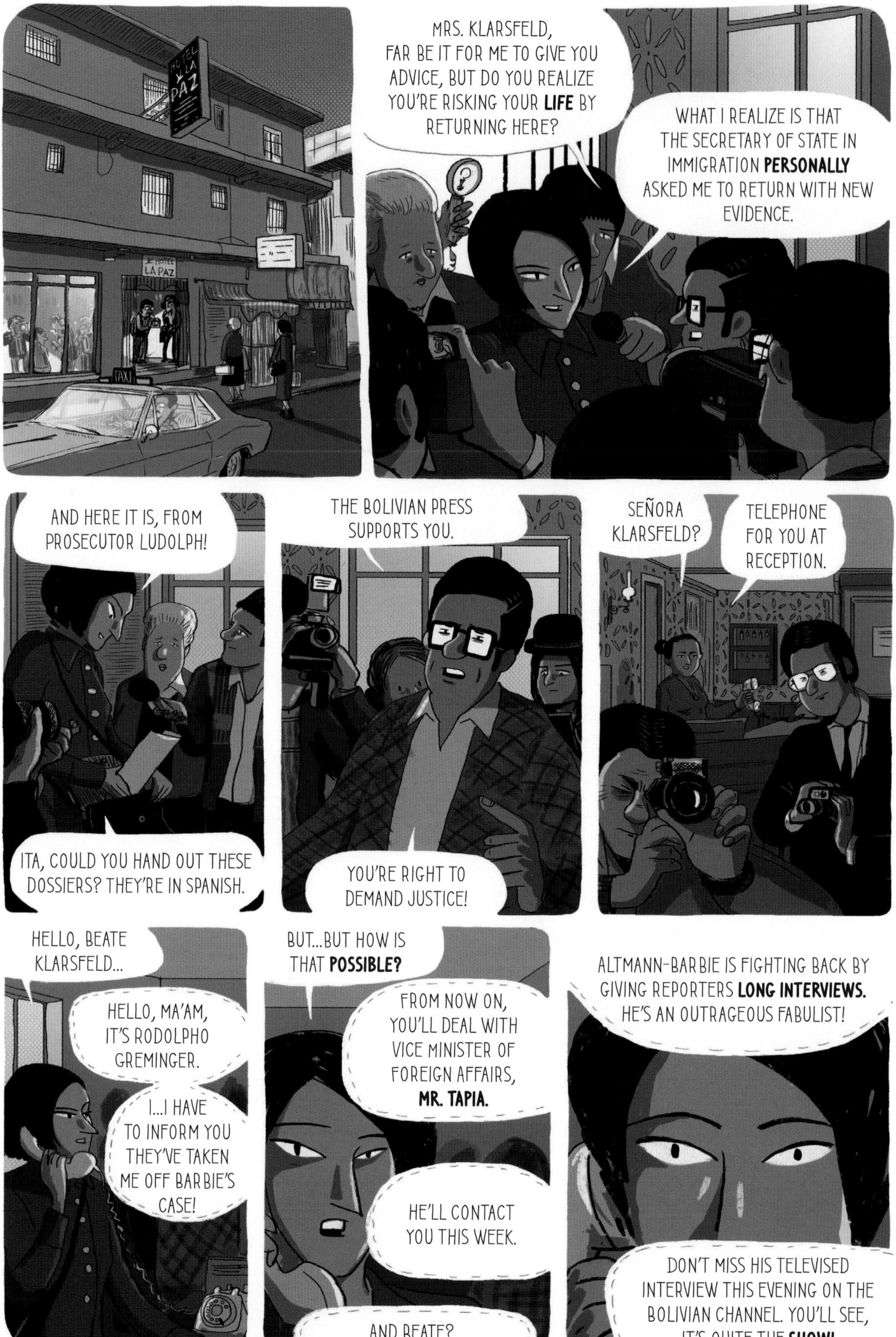
HOTEL LA PAZ
HOTEL LA PAZ
TAXI
MRS. KLARSFELD, FAR BE IT FOR ME TO GIVE YOU ADVICE, BUT DO YOU REALIZE YOU'RE RISKING YOUR **LIFE** BY RETURNING HERE?
WHAT I REALIZE IS THAT THE SECRETARY OF STATE IN IMMIGRATION **PERSONALLY** ASKED ME TO RETURN WITH NEW EVIDENCE.
AND HERE IT IS, FROM PROSECUTOR LUDOLPH!
ITA, COULD YOU HAND OUT THESE DOSSIERS? THEY'RE IN SPANISH.
THE BOLIVIAN PRESS SUPPORTS YOU.
YOU'RE RIGHT TO DEMAND JUSTICE!
SEÑORA KLARSFELD?
TELEPHONE FOR YOU AT RECEPTION.
HELLO, BEATE KLARSFELD...
HELLO, MA'AM, IT'S RODOLPHO GREMINGER.
I...I HAVE TO INFORM YOU THEY'VE TAKEN ME OFF BARBIE'S CASE!
BUT...BUT HOW IS THAT **POSSIBLE?**
FROM NOW ON, YOU'LL DEAL WITH VICE MINISTER OF FOREIGN AFFAIRS, **MR. TAPIA.**
HE'LL CONTACT YOU THIS WEEK.
AND BEATE?
ALTMANN-BARBIE IS FIGHTING BACK BY GIVING REPORTERS **LONG INTERVIEWS.** HE'S AN OUTRAGEOUS FABULIST!
DON'T MISS HIS TELEVISED INTERVIEW THIS EVENING ON THE BOLIVIAN CHANNEL. YOU'LL SEE, IT'S QUITE THE **SHOW!**

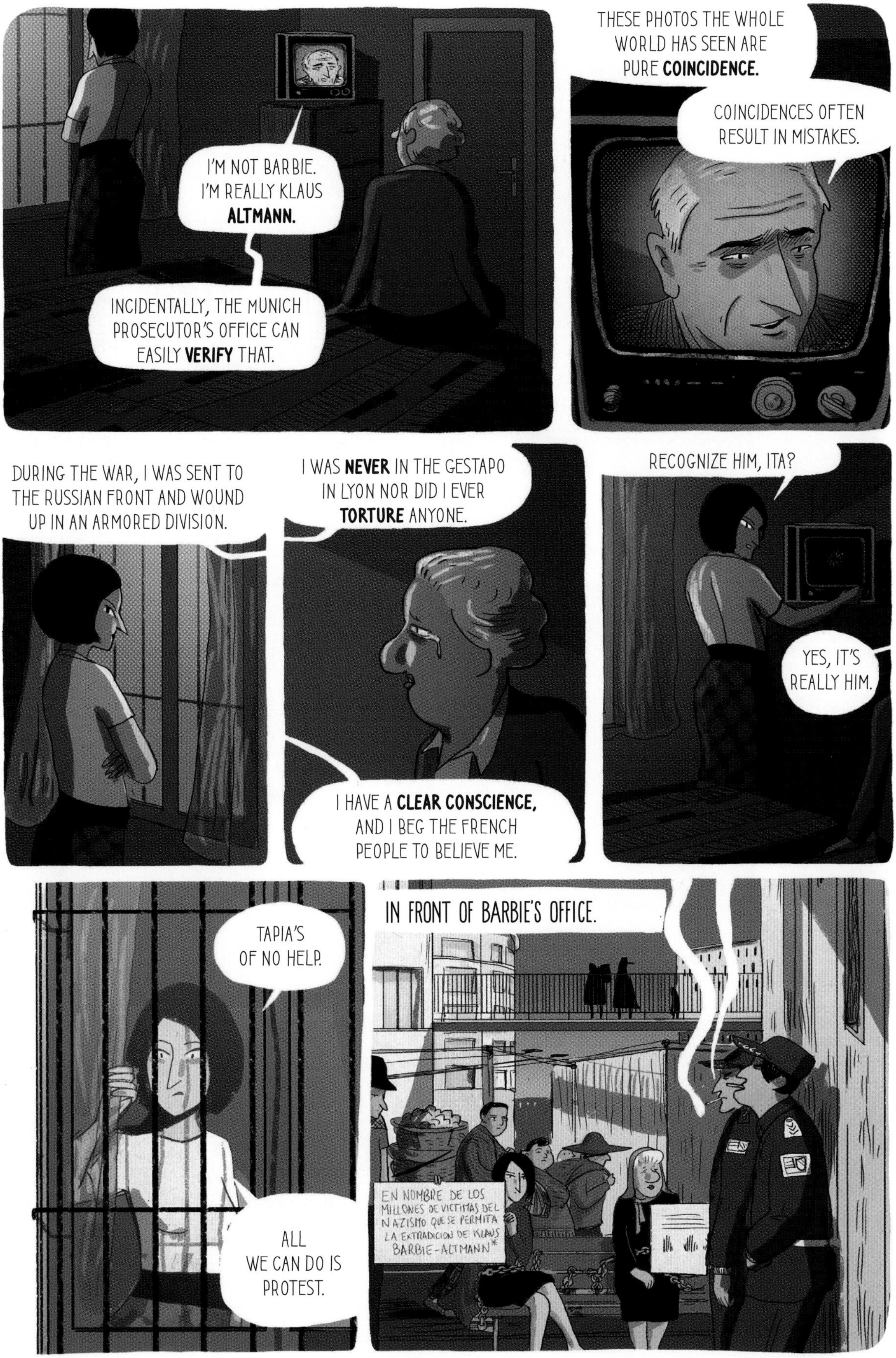
I'M NOT BARBIE. I'M REALLY KLAUS **ALTMANN.**
INCIDENTALLY, THE MUNICH PROSECUTOR'S OFFICE CAN EASILY **VERIFY** THAT.
THESE PHOTOS THE WHOLE WORLD HAS SEEN ARE PURE **COINCIDENCE.**
COINCIDENCES OFTEN RESULT IN MISTAKES.
DURING THE WAR, I WAS SENT TO THE RUSSIAN FRONT AND WOUND UP IN AN ARMORED DIVISION.
I WAS **NEVER** IN THE GESTAPO IN LYON NOR DID I EVER **TORTURE** ANYONE.
I HAVE A **CLEAR CONSCIENCE,** AND I BEG THE FRENCH PEOPLE TO BELIEVE ME.
RECOGNIZE HIM, ITA?
YES, IT'S REALLY HIM.
TAPIA'S OF NO HELP.
ALL WE CAN DO IS PROTEST.
IN FRONT OF BARBIE'S OFFICE.
EN NOMBRE DE LOS MILLONES DE VICTIMAS DEL NAZISMO QUE SE PERMITA LA EXTRADICION DE KLAUS BARBIE-ALTMANN*

*IN THE NAME OF THE MILLIONS OF NAZI VICTIMS,
LET KLAUS BARBIE-ALTMANN BE EXTRADITED.

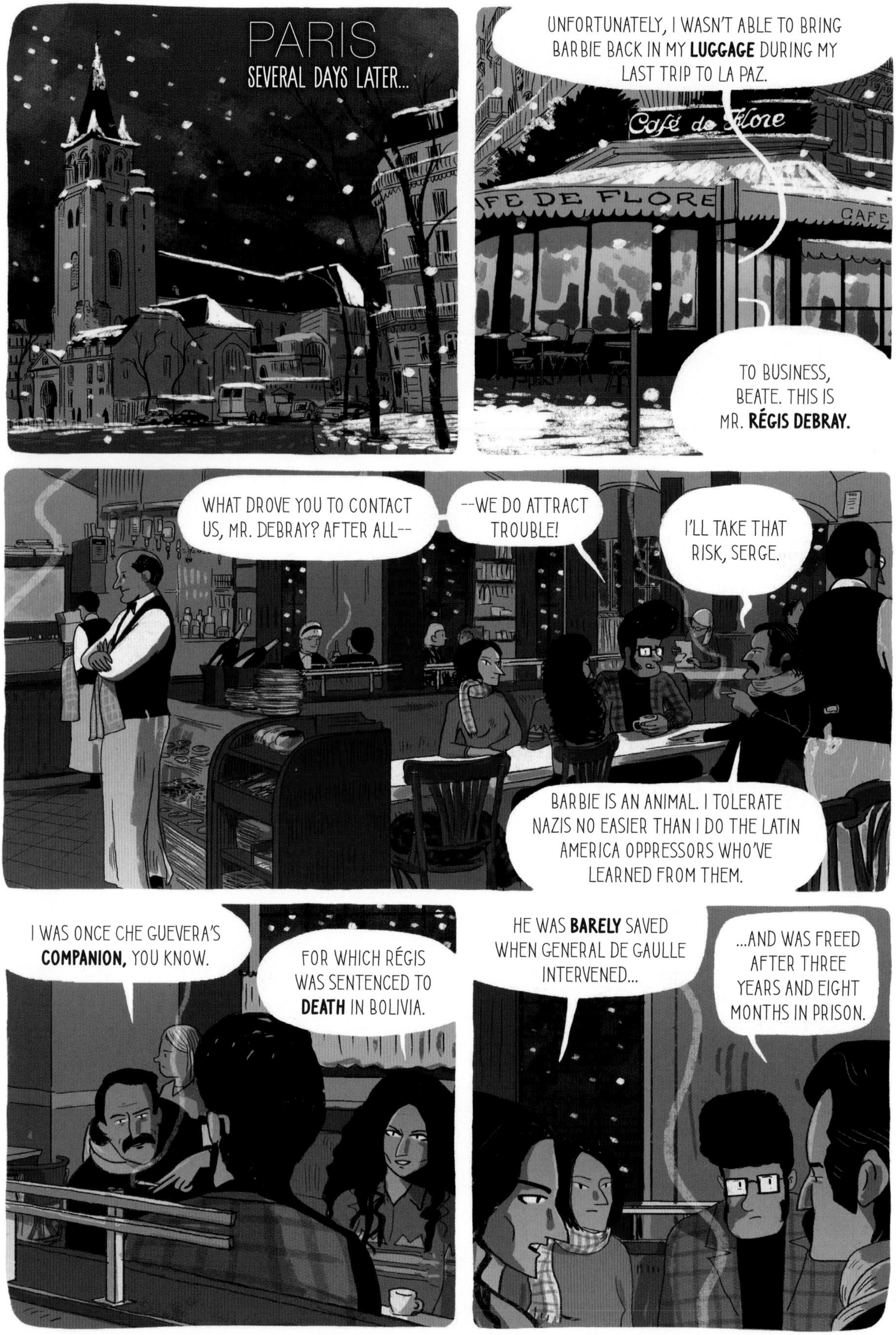
PARIS
SEVERAL DAYS LATER...
UNFORTUNATELY, I WASN'T ABLE TO BRING BARBIE BACK IN MY **LUGGAGE** DURING MY LAST TRIP TO LA PAZ.
Café de Flore
CAFE DE FLORE
CAFE
TO BUSINESS, BEATE. THIS IS MR. **RÉGIS DEBRAY.**
WHAT DROVE YOU TO CONTACT US, MR. DEBRAY? AFTER ALL--
--WE DO ATTRACT TROUBLE!
I'LL TAKE THAT RISK, SERGE.
BARBIE IS AN ANIMAL. I TOLERATE NAZIS NO EASIER THAN I DO THE LATIN AMERICA OPPRESSORS WHO'VE LEARNED FROM THEM.
I WAS ONCE CHE GUEVERA'S **COMPANION,** YOU KNOW.
FOR WHICH RÉGIS WAS SENTENCED TO **DEATH** IN BOLIVIA.
HE WAS **BARELY** SAVED WHEN GENERAL DE GAULLE INTERVENED...
...AND WAS FREED AFTER THREE YEARS AND EIGHT MONTHS IN PRISON.

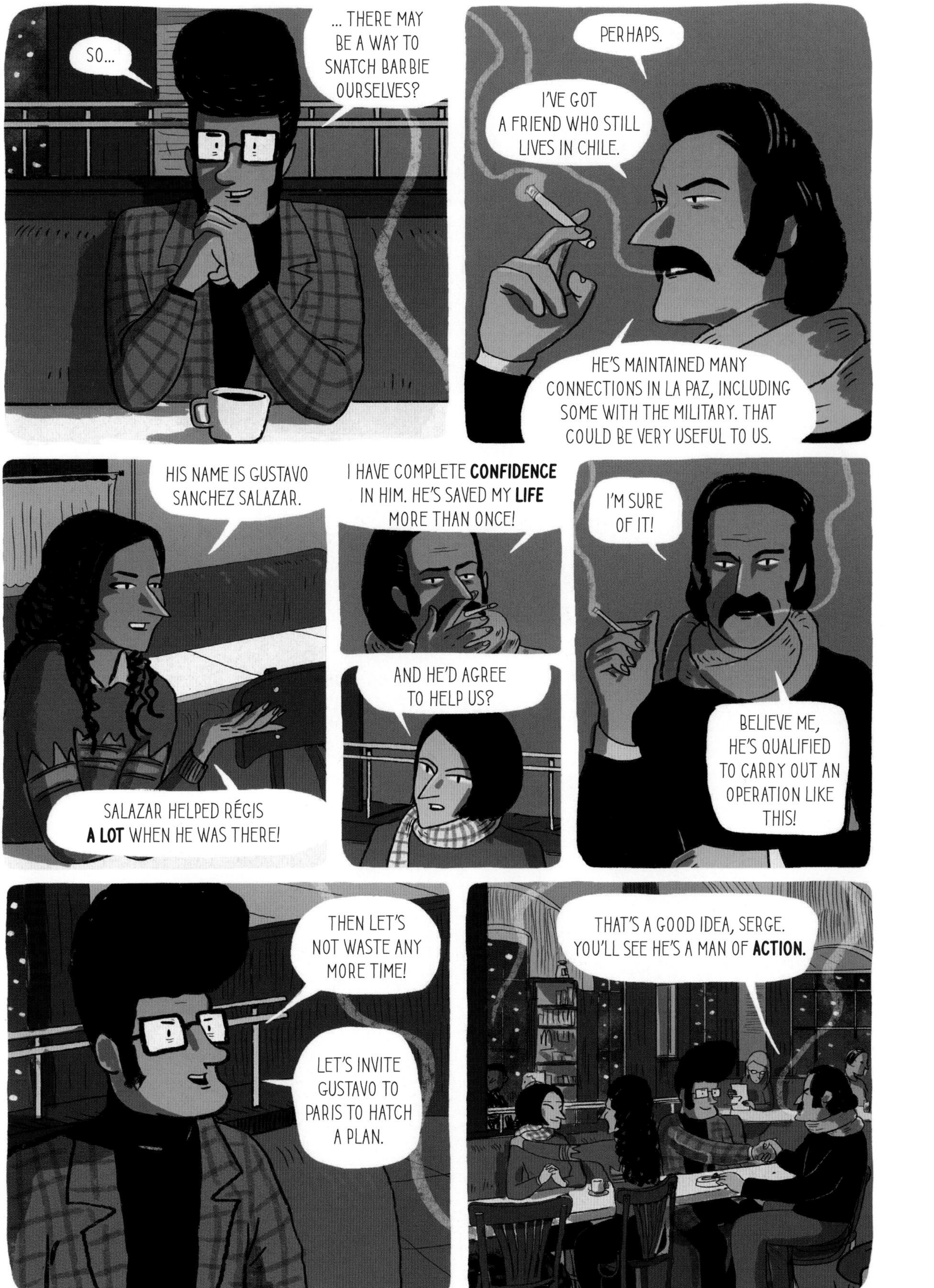
SO...
... THERE MAY BE A WAY TO SNATCH BARBIE OURSELVES?
PERHAPS.
I'VE GOT A FRIEND WHO STILL LIVES IN CHILE.
HE'S MAINTAINED MANY CONNECTIONS IN LA PAZ, INCLUDING SOME WITH THE MILITARY. THAT COULD BE VERY USEFUL TO US.
HIS NAME IS GUSTAVO SANCHEZ SALAZAR.
SALAZAR HELPED RÉGIS **A LOT** WHEN HE WAS THERE!
I HAVE COMPLETE **CONFIDENCE** IN HIM. HE'S SAVED MY **LIFE** MORE THAN ONCE!
AND HE'D AGREE TO HELP US?
I'M SURE OF IT!
BELIEVE ME, HE'S QUALIFIED TO CARRY OUT AN OPERATION LIKE THIS!
THEN LET'S NOT WASTE ANY MORE TIME!
LET'S INVITE GUSTAVO TO PARIS TO HATCH A PLAN.
THAT'S A GOOD IDEA, SERGE. YOU'LL SEE HE'S A MAN OF **ACTION.**

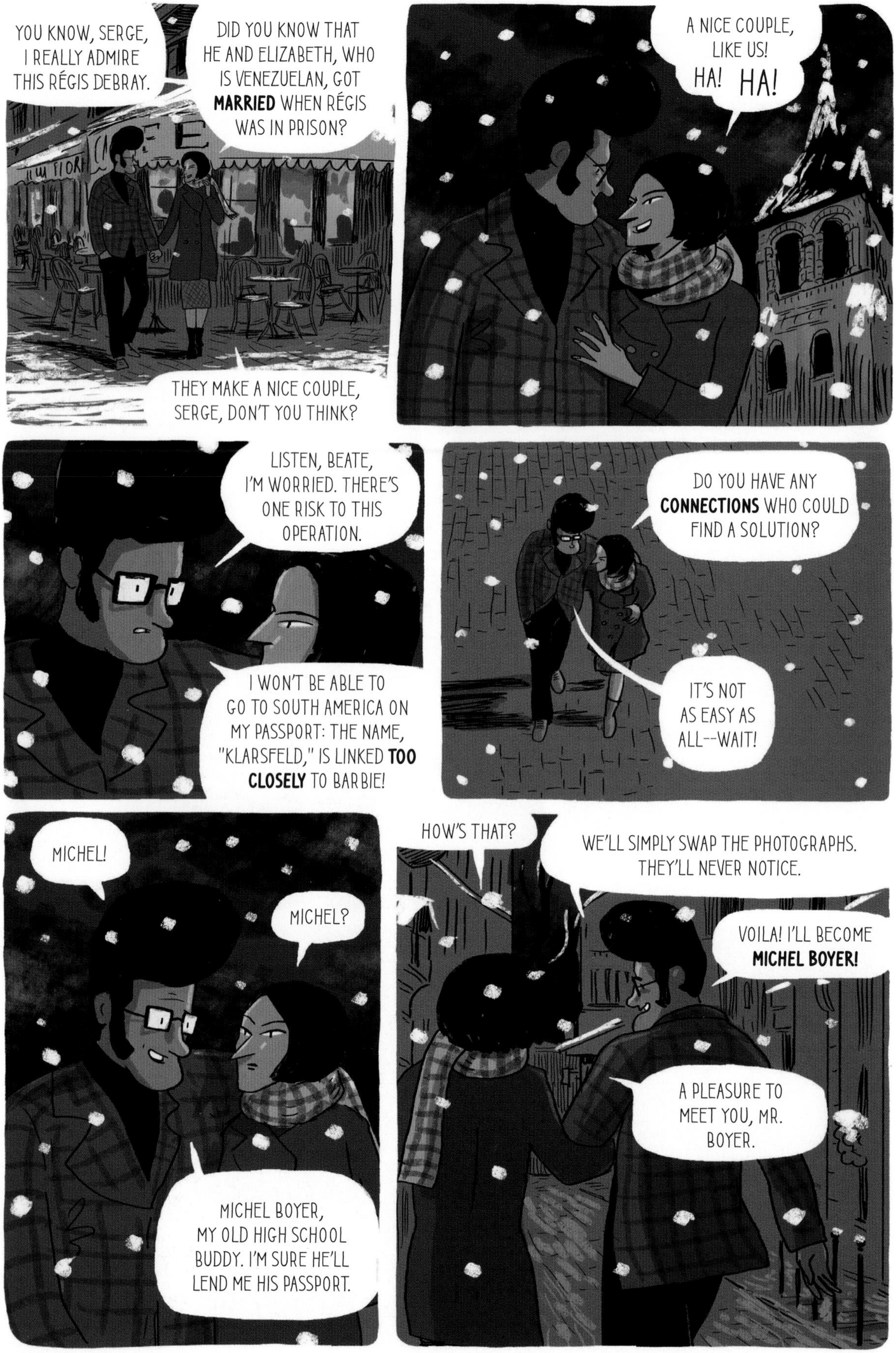
YOU KNOW, SERGE, I REALLY ADMIRE THIS RÉGIS DEBRAY.
DID YOU KNOW THAT HE AND ELIZABETH, WHO IS VENEZUELAN, GOT **MARRIED** WHEN RÉGIS WAS IN PRISON?
THEY MAKE A NICE COUPLE, SERGE, DON'T YOU THINK?
A NICE COUPLE, LIKE US! HA! HA!
LISTEN, BEATE, I'M WORRIED. THERE'S ONE RISK TO THIS OPERATION.
I WON'T BE ABLE TO GO TO SOUTH AMERICA ON MY PASSPORT: THE NAME, "KLARSFELD," IS LINKED **TOO CLOSELY** TO BARBIE!
DO YOU HAVE ANY **CONNECTIONS** WHO COULD FIND A SOLUTION?
IT'S NOT AS EASY AS ALL--WAIT!
MICHEL!
MICHEL?
MICHEL BOYER, MY OLD HIGH SCHOOL BUDDY. I'M SURE HE'LL LEND ME HIS PASSPORT.
HOW'S THAT?
WE'LL SIMPLY SWAP THE PHOTOGRAPHS. THEY'LL NEVER NOTICE.
VOILA! I'LL BECOME **MICHEL BOYER!**
A PLEASURE TO MEET YOU, MR. BOYER.

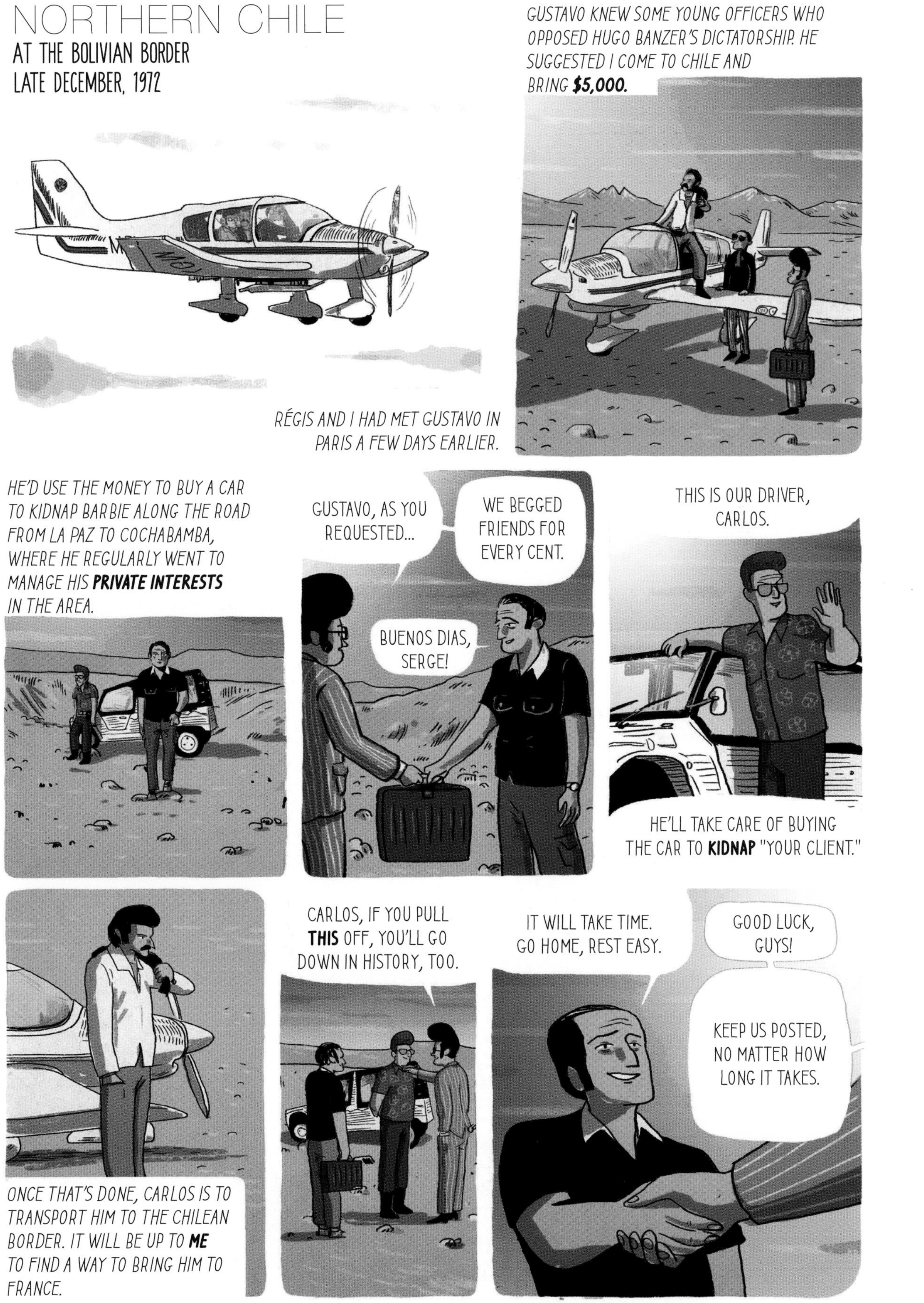
NORTHERN CHILE
AT THE BOLIVIAN BORDER
LATE DECEMBER, 1972
GUSTAVO KNEW SOME YOUNG OFFICERS WHO OPPOSED HUGO BANZER'S DICTATORSHIP. HE SUGGESTED I COME TO CHILE AND BRING $5,000.
RÉGIS AND I HAD MET GUSTAVO IN PARIS A FEW DAYS EARLIER.
HE'D USE THE MONEY TO BUY A CAR TO KIDNAP BARBIE ALONG THE ROAD FROM LA PAZ TO COCHABAMBA, WHERE HE REGULARLY WENT TO MANAGE HIS PRIVATE INTERESTS IN THE AREA.
GUSTAVO, AS YOU REQUESTED...
WE BEGGED FRIENDS FOR EVERY CENT.
BUENOS DIAS, SERGE!
THIS IS OUR DRIVER, CARLOS.
HE'LL TAKE CARE OF BUYING THE CAR TO KIDNAP "YOUR CLIENT."
ONCE THAT'S DONE, CARLOS IS TO TRANSPORT HIM TO THE CHILEAN BORDER. IT WILL BE UP TO ME TO FIND A WAY TO BRING HIM TO FRANCE.
CARLOS, IF YOU PULL THIS OFF, YOU'LL GO DOWN IN HISTORY, TOO.
IT WILL TAKE TIME. GO HOME, REST EASY.
GOOD LUCK, GUYS!
KEEP US POSTED, NO MATTER HOW LONG IT TAKES.

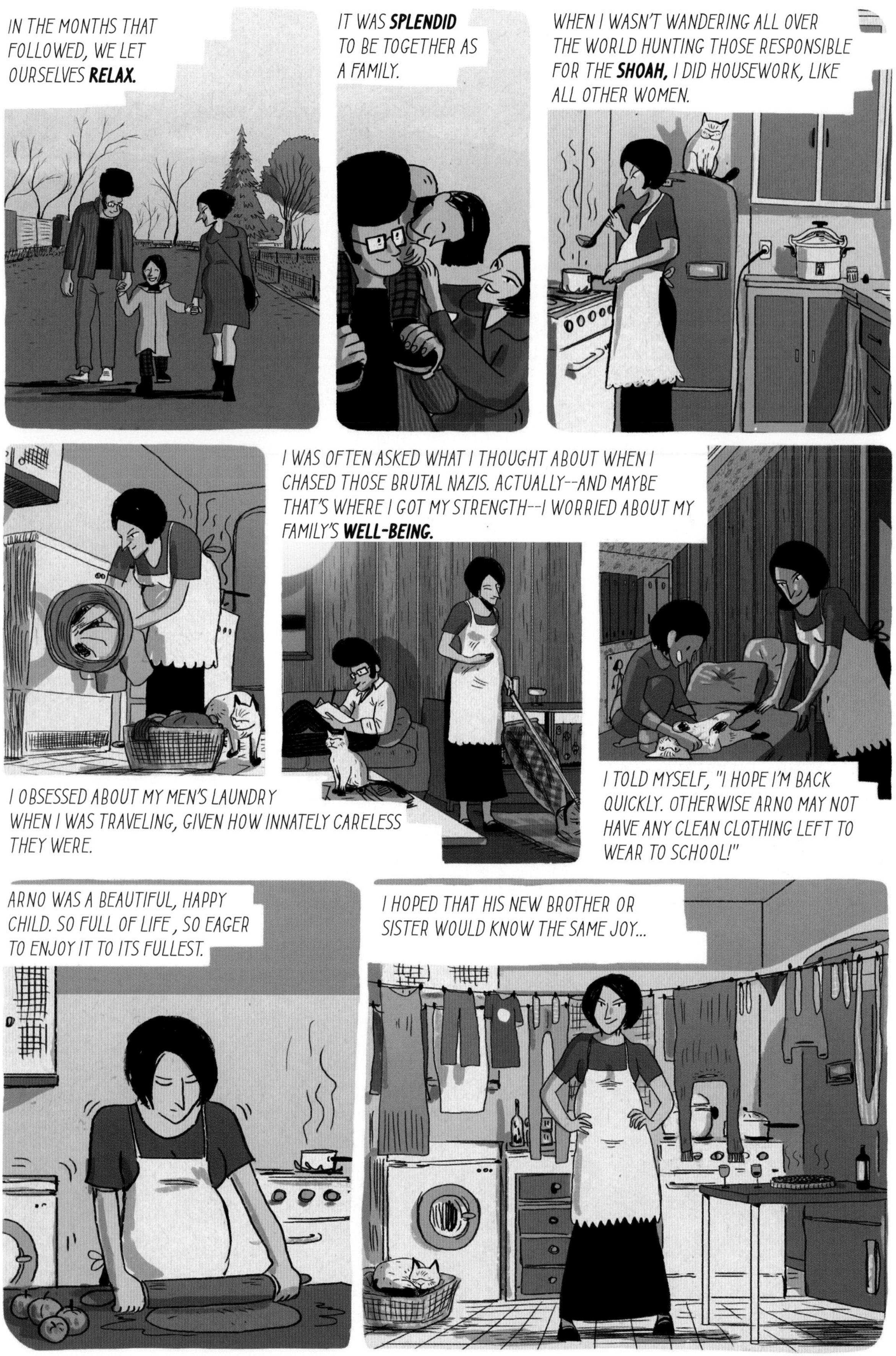
IN THE MONTHS THAT FOLLOWED, WE LET OURSELVES RELAX.
IT WAS SPLENDID TO BE TOGETHER AS A FAMILY.
WHEN I WASN'T WANDERING ALL OVER THE WORLD HUNTING THOSE RESPONSIBLE FOR THE SHOAH, I DID HOUSEWORK, LIKE ALL OTHER WOMEN.
I WAS OFTEN ASKED WHAT I THOUGHT ABOUT WHEN I CHASED THOSE BRUTAL NAZIS. ACTUALLY--AND MAYBE THAT'S WHERE I GOT MY STRENGTH--I WORRIED ABOUT MY FAMILY'S WELL-BEING.
I OBSESSED ABOUT MY MEN'S LAUNDRY WHEN I WAS TRAVELING, GIVEN HOW INNATELY CARELESS THEY WERE.
I TOLD MYSELF, "I HOPE I'M BACK QUICKLY. OTHERWISE ARNO MAY NOT HAVE ANY CLEAN CLOTHING LEFT TO WEAR TO SCHOOL!"
ARNO WAS A BEAUTIFUL, HAPPY CHILD. SO FULL OF LIFE, SO EAGER TO ENJOY IT TO ITS FULLEST.
I HOPED THAT HIS NEW BROTHER OR SISTER WOULD KNOW THE SAME JOY...

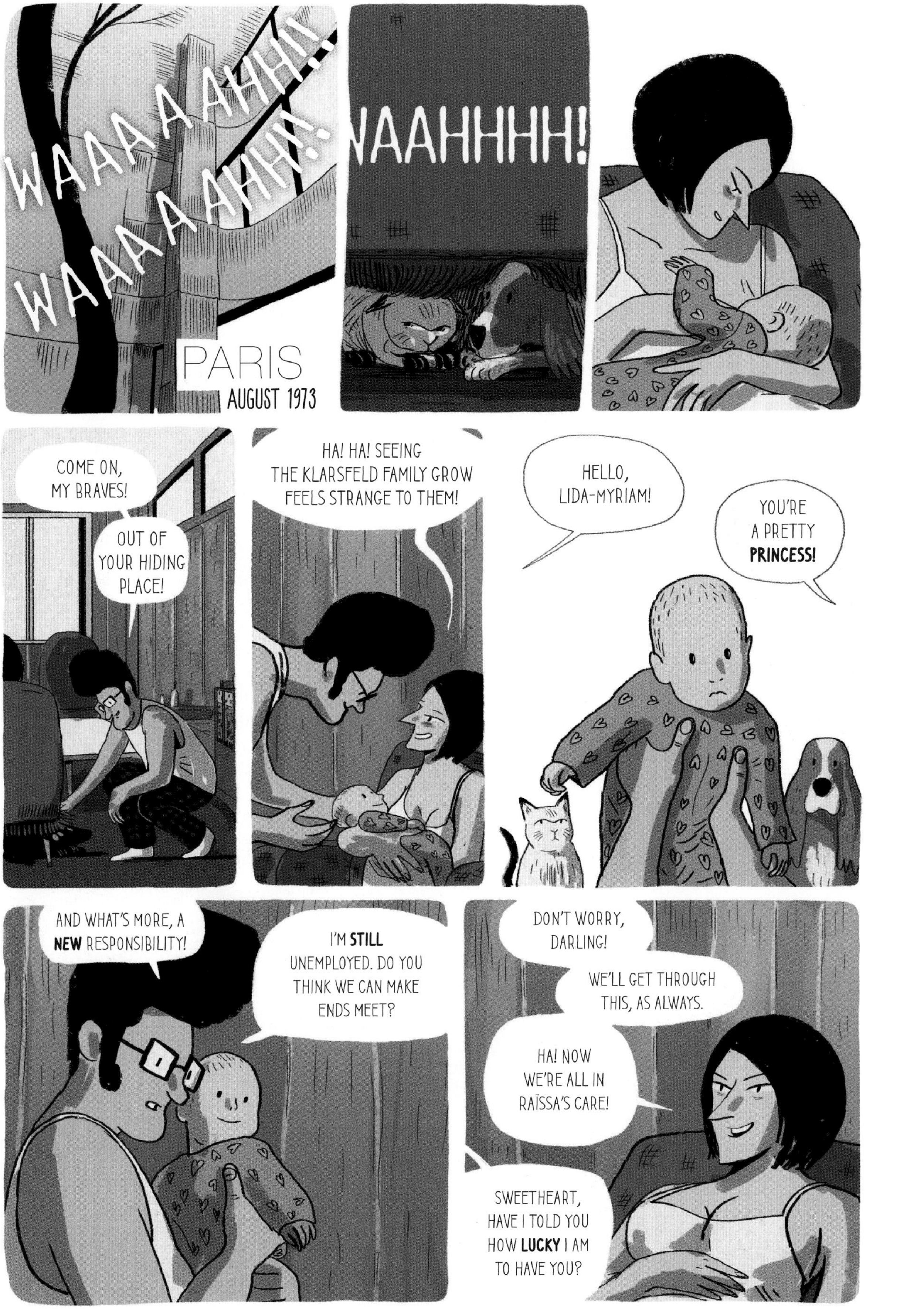
WAAAAAHH!!
WAAAAAHH!!
PARIS
AUGUST 1973
WAAHHHH!
COME ON, MY BRAVES!
OUT OF YOUR HIDING PLACE!
HA! HA! SEEING THE KLARSFELD FAMILY GROW FEELS STRANGE TO THEM!
HELLO, LIDA-MYRIAM!
YOU'RE A PRETTY **PRINCESS!**
AND WHAT'S MORE, A **NEW** RESPONSIBILITY!
I'M **STILL** UNEMPLOYED. DO YOU THINK WE CAN MAKE ENDS MEET?
DON'T WORRY, DARLING!
WE'LL GET THROUGH THIS, AS ALWAYS.
HA! NOW WE'RE ALL IN RAÏSSA'S CARE!
SWEETHEART, HAVE I TOLD YOU HOW **LUCKY** I AM TO HAVE YOU?

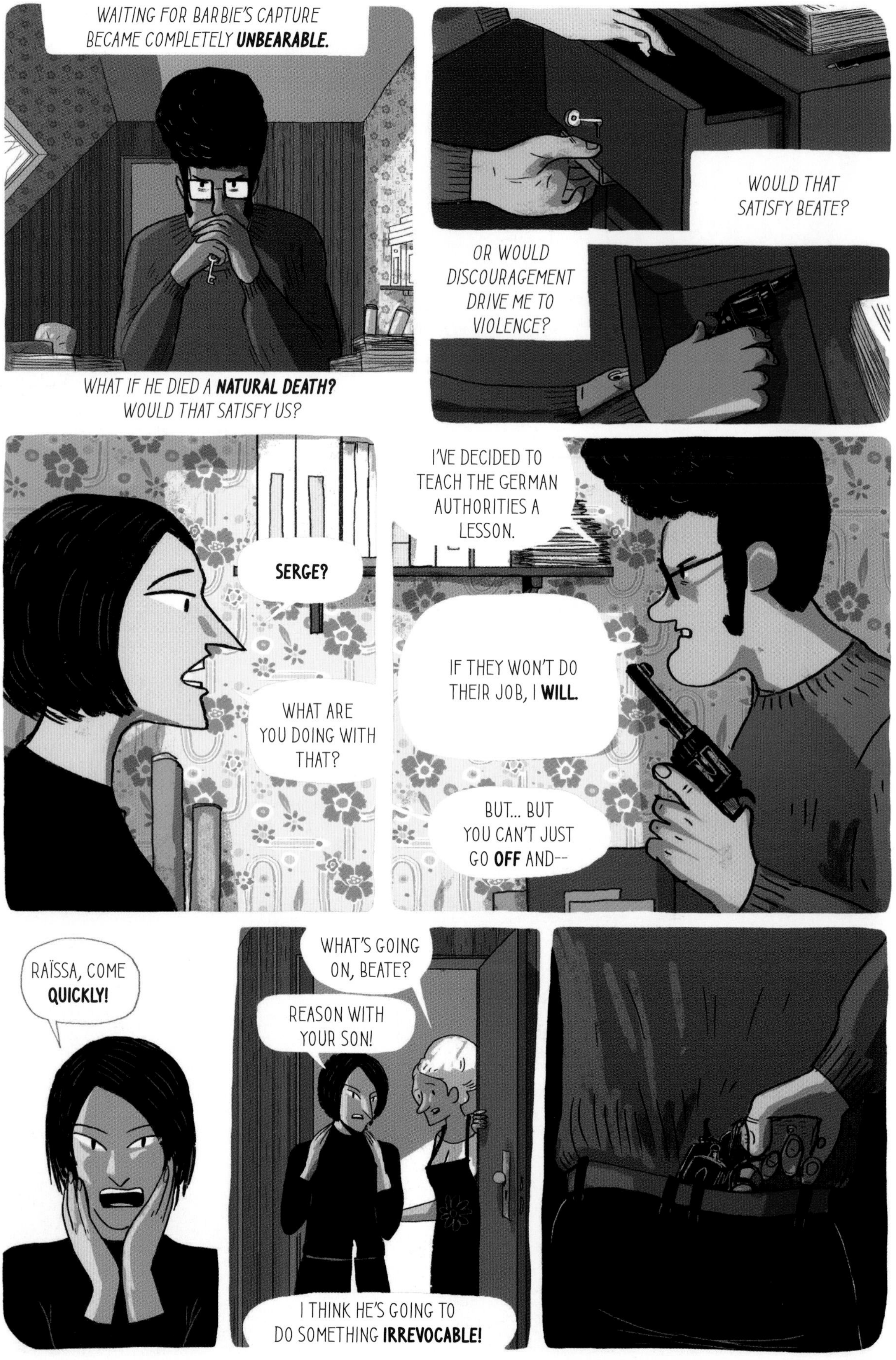
WAITING FOR BARBIE'S CAPTURE BECAME COMPLETELY **UNBEARABLE.**
WHAT IF HE DIED A **NATURAL DEATH?** WOULD THAT SATISFY US?
WOULD THAT SATISFY BEATE?
OR WOULD DISCOURAGEMENT DRIVE ME TO VIOLENCE?
I'VE DECIDED TO TEACH THE GERMAN AUTHORITIES A LESSON.
SERGE?
IF THEY WON'T DO THEIR JOB, I **WILL.**
WHAT ARE YOU DOING WITH THAT?
BUT... BUT YOU CAN'T JUST GO **OFF** AND--
RAÏSSA, COME **QUICKLY!**
WHAT'S GOING ON, BEATE?
REASON WITH YOUR SON!
I THINK HE'S GOING TO DO SOMETHING **IRREVOCABLE!**

COLOGNE
WEST GERMANY
DECEMBER 7TH, 1973

I'D FACE LISCHKA **MYSELF.**

SECRETLY.

NO ONE WOULD KNOW.

HE REMAINED BRAZENLY EASY TO FIND.

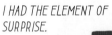

I HAD THE ELEMENT OF SURPRISE.

LISCHKA WAS ARMED AND HAD A GUN PERMIT...

...SO I HAD TO MOVE FAST.

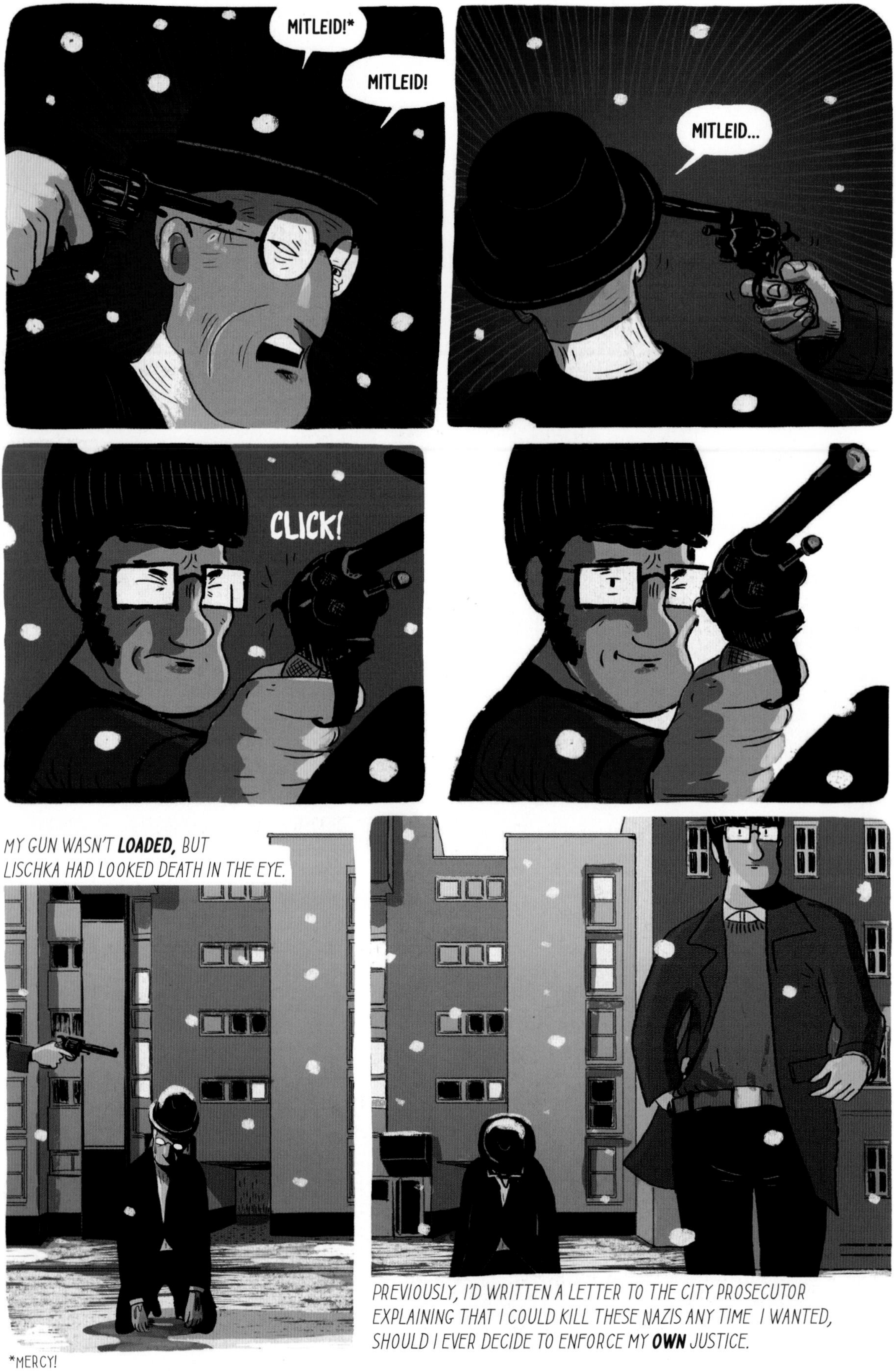
MITLEID!*
MITLEID!
MITLEID...
CLICK!
MY GUN WASN'T **LOADED,** BUT LISCHKA HAD LOOKED DEATH IN THE EYE.
PREVIOUSLY, I'D WRITTEN A LETTER TO THE CITY PROSECUTOR EXPLAINING THAT I COULD KILL THESE NAZIS ANY TIME I WANTED, SHOULD I EVER DECIDE TO ENFORCE MY **OWN** JUSTICE.
*MERCY!

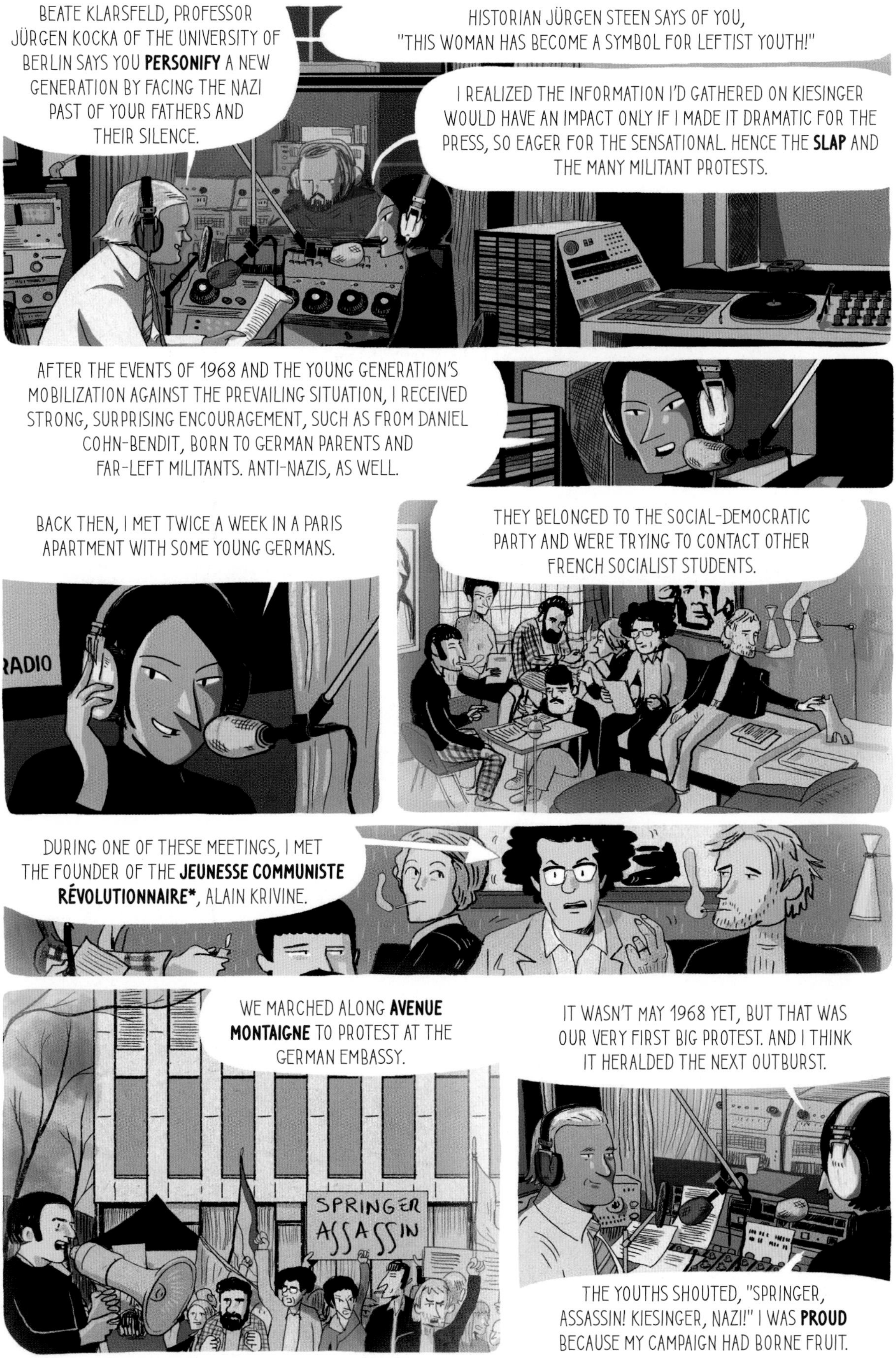
BEATE KLARSFELD, PROFESSOR JÜRGEN KOCKA OF THE UNIVERSITY OF BERLIN SAYS YOU **PERSONIFY** A NEW GENERATION BY FACING THE NAZI PAST OF YOUR FATHERS AND THEIR SILENCE.
HISTORIAN JÜRGEN STEEN SAYS OF YOU, "THIS WOMAN HAS BECOME A SYMBOL FOR LEFTIST YOUTH!"
I REALIZED THE INFORMATION I'D GATHERED ON KIESINGER WOULD HAVE AN IMPACT ONLY IF I MADE IT DRAMATIC FOR THE PRESS, SO EAGER FOR THE SENSATIONAL. HENCE THE **SLAP** AND THE MANY MILITANT PROTESTS.
AFTER THE EVENTS OF 1968 AND THE YOUNG GENERATION'S MOBILIZATION AGAINST THE PREVAILING SITUATION, I RECEIVED STRONG, SURPRISING ENCOURAGEMENT, SUCH AS FROM DANIEL COHN-BENDIT, BORN TO GERMAN PARENTS AND FAR-LEFT MILITANTS. ANTI-NAZIS, AS WELL.
BACK THEN, I MET TWICE A WEEK IN A PARIS APARTMENT WITH SOME YOUNG GERMANS.
RADIO
THEY BELONGED TO THE SOCIAL-DEMOCRATIC PARTY AND WERE TRYING TO CONTACT OTHER FRENCH SOCIALIST STUDENTS.
DURING ONE OF THESE MEETINGS, I MET THE FOUNDER OF THE **JEUNESSE COMMUNISTE RÉVOLUTIONNAIRE***, ALAIN KRIVINE.
WE MARCHED ALONG **AVENUE MONTAIGNE** TO PROTEST AT THE GERMAN EMBASSY.
SPRINGER ASSASSIN
IT WASN'T MAY 1968 YET, BUT THAT WAS OUR VERY FIRST BIG PROTEST. AND I THINK IT HERALDED THE NEXT OUTBURST.
THE YOUTHS SHOUTED, "SPRINGER, ASSASSIN! KIESINGER, NAZI!" I WAS **PROUD** BECAUSE MY CAMPAIGN HAD BORNE FRUIT.

* THE REVOLUTIONARY COMMUNIST YOUTH

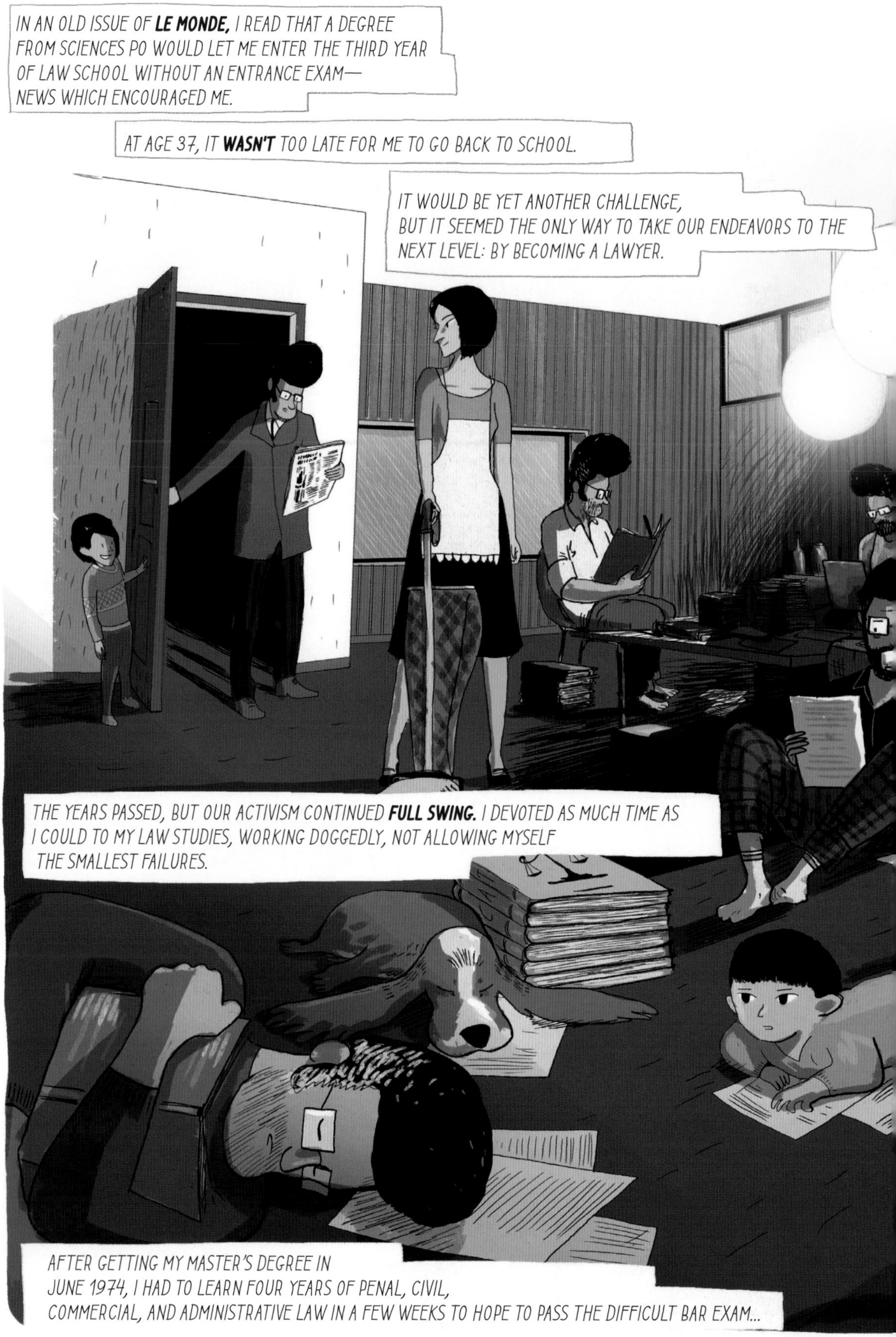
IN AN OLD ISSUE OF **LE MONDE,** I READ THAT A DEGREE FROM SCIENCES PO WOULD LET ME ENTER THE THIRD YEAR OF LAW SCHOOL WITHOUT AN ENTRANCE EXAM— NEWS WHICH ENCOURAGED ME.
AT AGE 37, IT **WASN'T** TOO LATE FOR ME TO GO BACK TO SCHOOL.
IT WOULD BE YET ANOTHER CHALLENGE, BUT IT SEEMED THE ONLY WAY TO TAKE OUR ENDEAVORS TO THE NEXT LEVEL: BY BECOMING A LAWYER.
THE YEARS PASSED, BUT OUR ACTIVISM CONTINUED **FULL SWING.** I DEVOTED AS MUCH TIME AS I COULD TO MY LAW STUDIES, WORKING DOGGEDLY, NOT ALLOWING MYSELF THE SMALLEST FAILURES.
AFTER GETTING MY MASTER'S DEGREE IN JUNE 1974, I HAD TO LEARN FOUR YEARS OF PENAL, CIVIL, COMMERCIAL, AND ADMINISTRATIVE LAW IN A FEW WEEKS TO HOPE TO PASS THE DIFFICULT BAR EXAM...

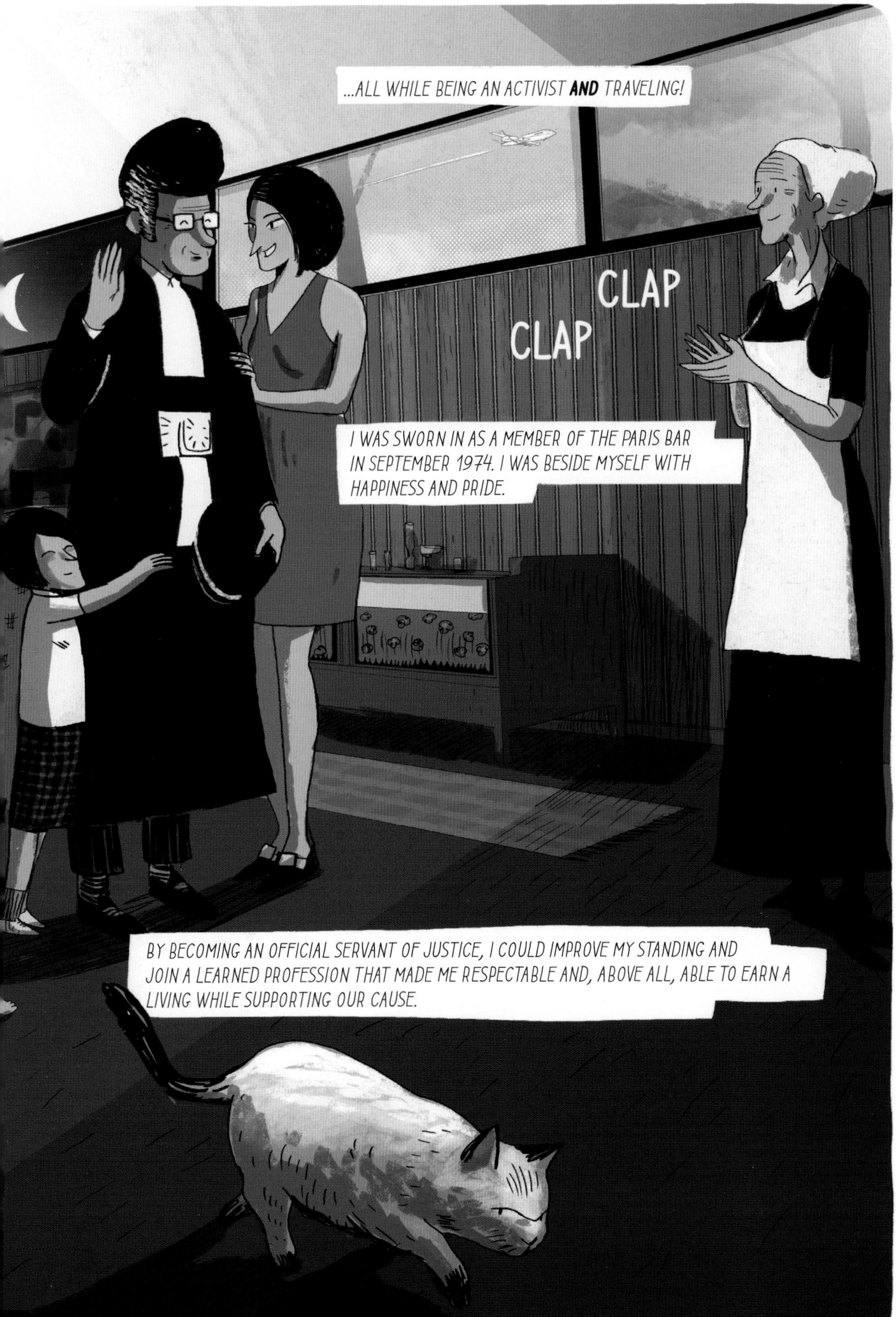
...ALL WHILE BEING AN ACTIVIST **AND** TRAVELING!
CLAP
CLAP
I WAS SWORN IN AS A MEMBER OF THE PARIS BAR IN SEPTEMBER 1974. I WAS BESIDE MYSELF WITH HAPPINESS AND PRIDE.
BY BECOMING AN OFFICIAL SERVANT OF JUSTICE, I COULD IMPROVE MY STANDING AND JOIN A LEARNED PROFESSION THAT MADE ME RESPECTABLE AND, ABOVE ALL, ABLE TO EARN A LIVING WHILE SUPPORTING OUR CAUSE.

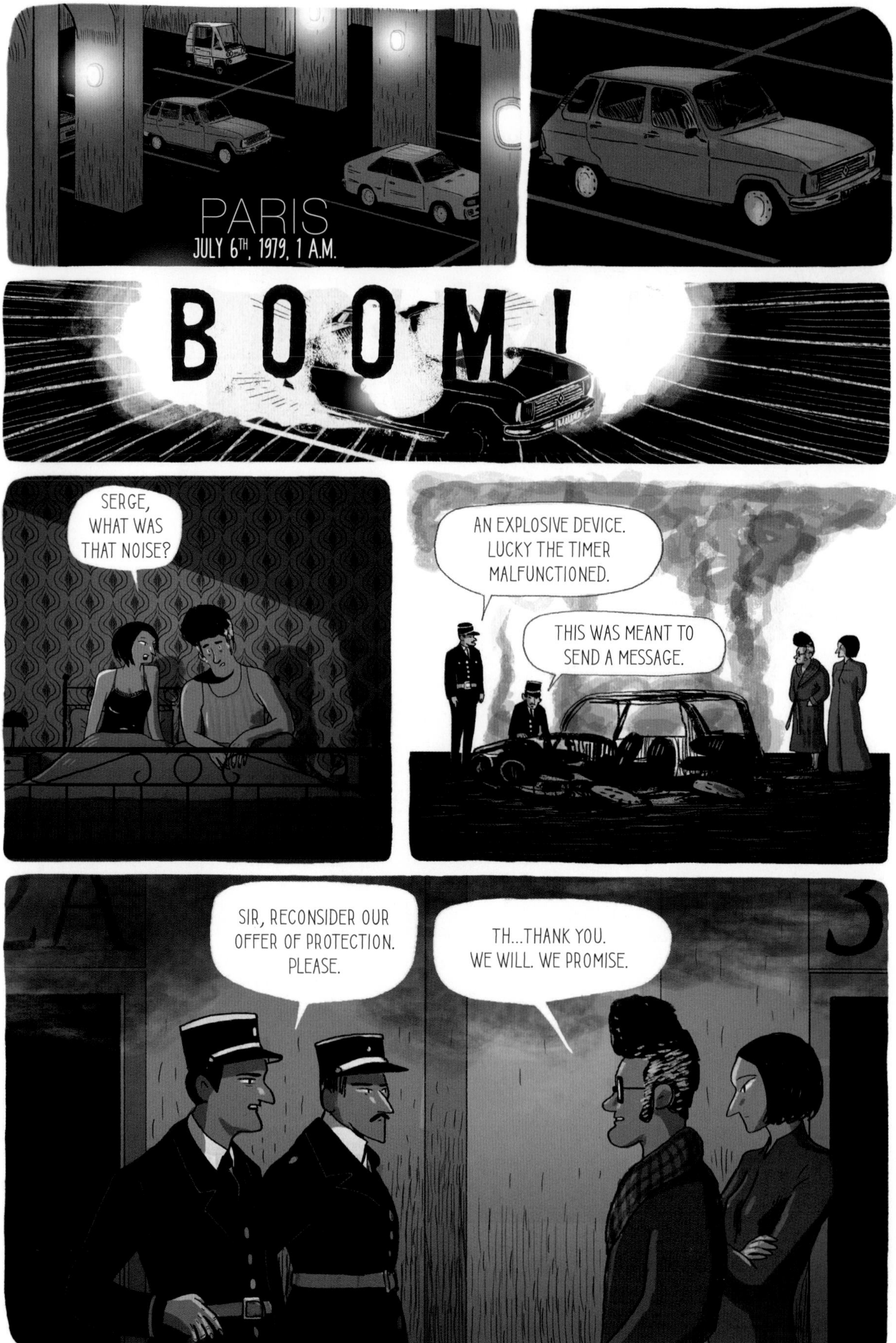
PARIS
JULY 6TH, 1979, 1 A.M.
BOOM!
SERGE, WHAT WAS THAT NOISE?
AN EXPLOSIVE DEVICE. LUCKY THE TIMER MALFUNCTIONED.
THIS WAS MEANT TO SEND A MESSAGE.
SIR, RECONSIDER OUR OFFER OF PROTECTION. PLEASE.
TH...THANK YOU. WE WILL. WE PROMISE.

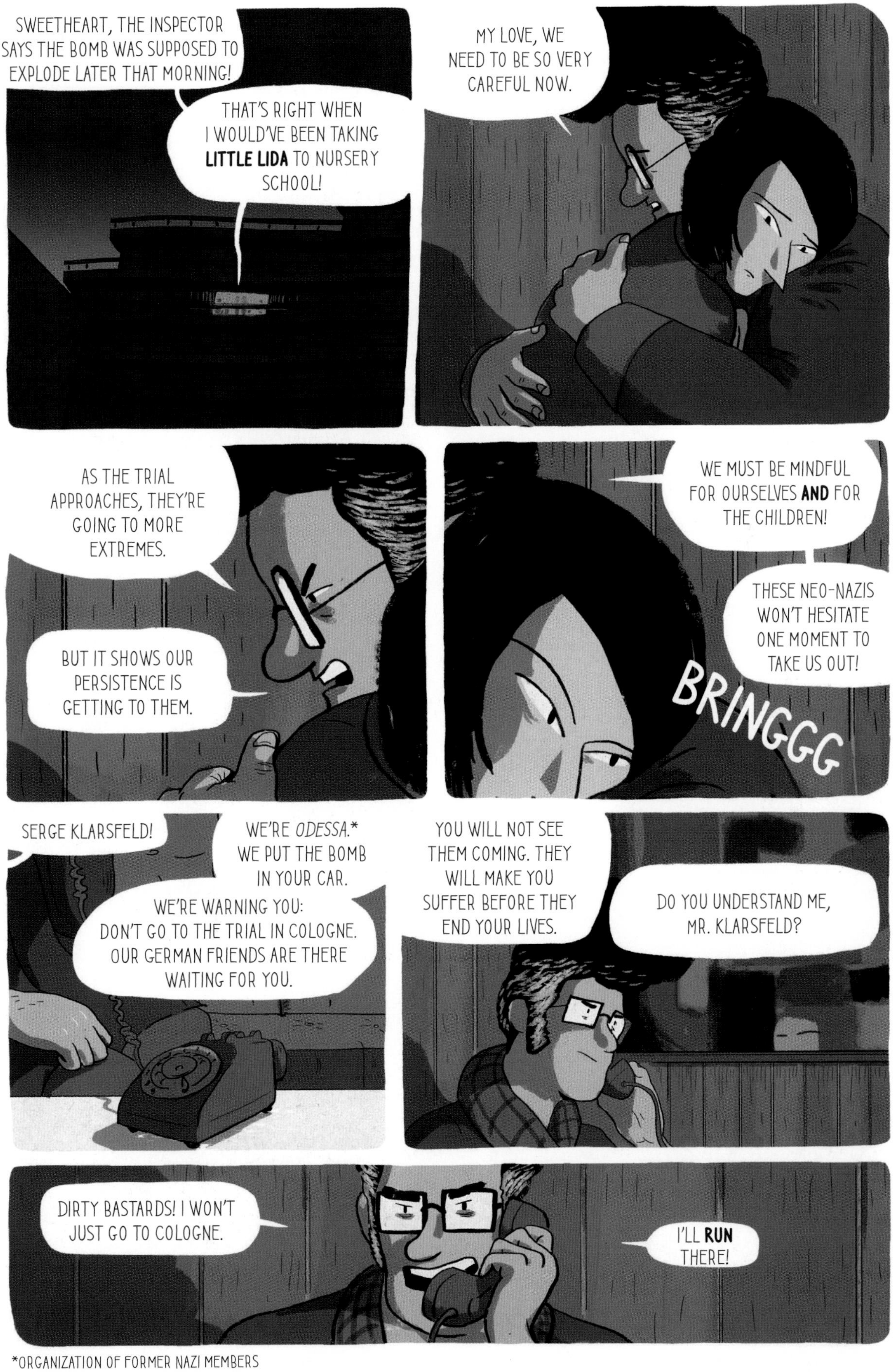
SWEETHEART, THE INSPECTOR SAYS THE BOMB WAS SUPPOSED TO EXPLODE LATER THAT MORNING!
THAT'S RIGHT WHEN I WOULD'VE BEEN TAKING **LITTLE LIDA** TO NURSERY SCHOOL!
MY LOVE, WE NEED TO BE SO VERY CAREFUL NOW.
AS THE TRIAL APPROACHES, THEY'RE GOING TO MORE EXTREMES.
BUT IT SHOWS OUR PERSISTENCE IS GETTING TO THEM.
WE MUST BE MINDFUL FOR OURSELVES **AND** FOR THE CHILDREN!
THESE NEO-NAZIS WON'T HESITATE ONE MOMENT TO TAKE US OUT!
BRINGGG
SERGE KLARSFELD!
WE'RE *ODESSA*.* WE PUT THE BOMB IN YOUR CAR.
WE'RE WARNING YOU: DON'T GO TO THE TRIAL IN COLOGNE. OUR GERMAN FRIENDS ARE THERE WAITING FOR YOU.
YOU WILL NOT SEE THEM COMING. THEY WILL MAKE YOU SUFFER BEFORE THEY END YOUR LIVES.
DO YOU UNDERSTAND ME, MR. KLARSFELD?
DIRTY BASTARDS! I WON'T JUST GO TO COLOGNE.
I'LL **RUN** THERE!

*ORGANIZATION OF FORMER NAZI MEMBERS

BOLIVIA A FEW DAYS LATER...

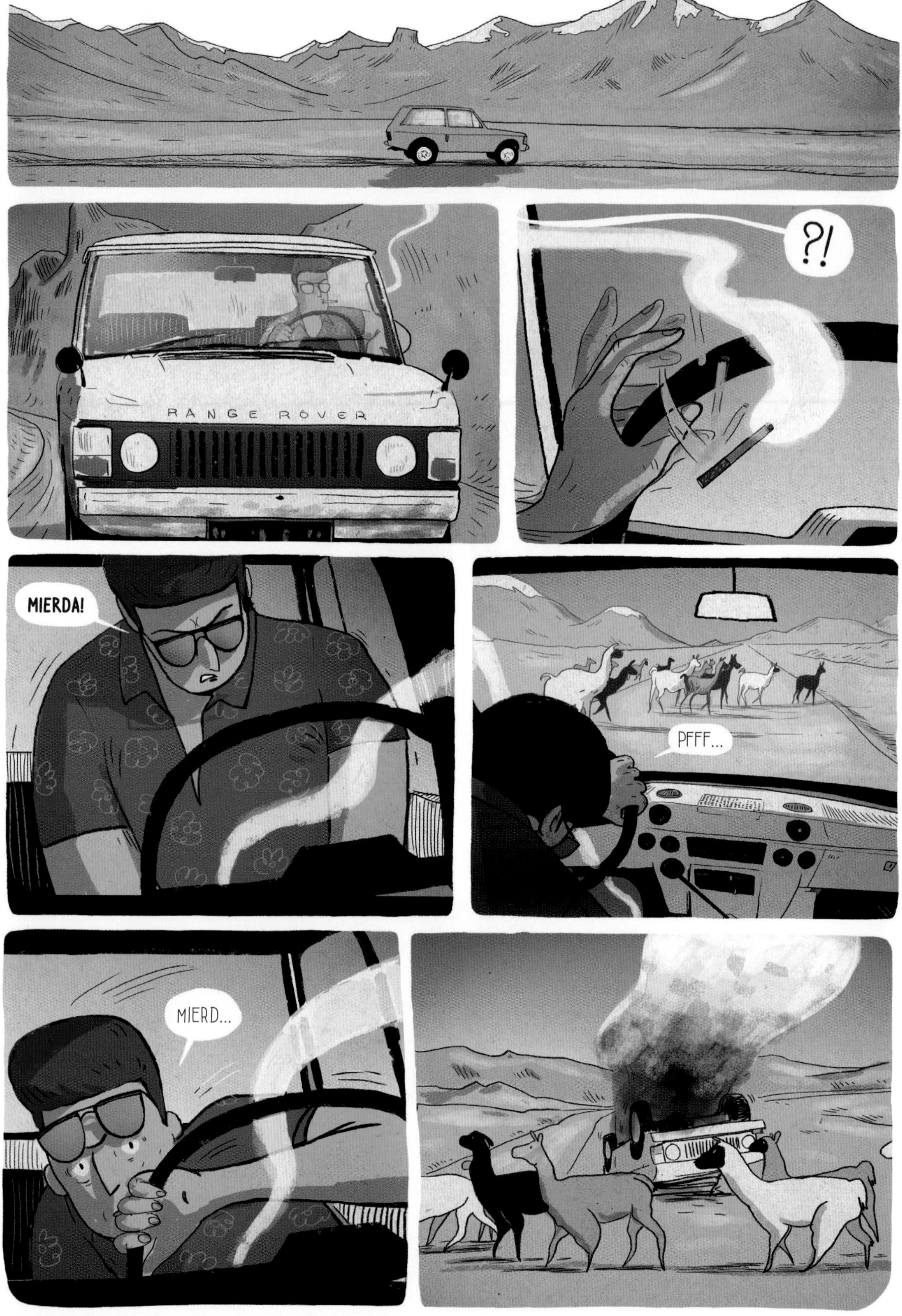
RANGE ROVER
?!
MIERDA!
PFFF...
MIERD...

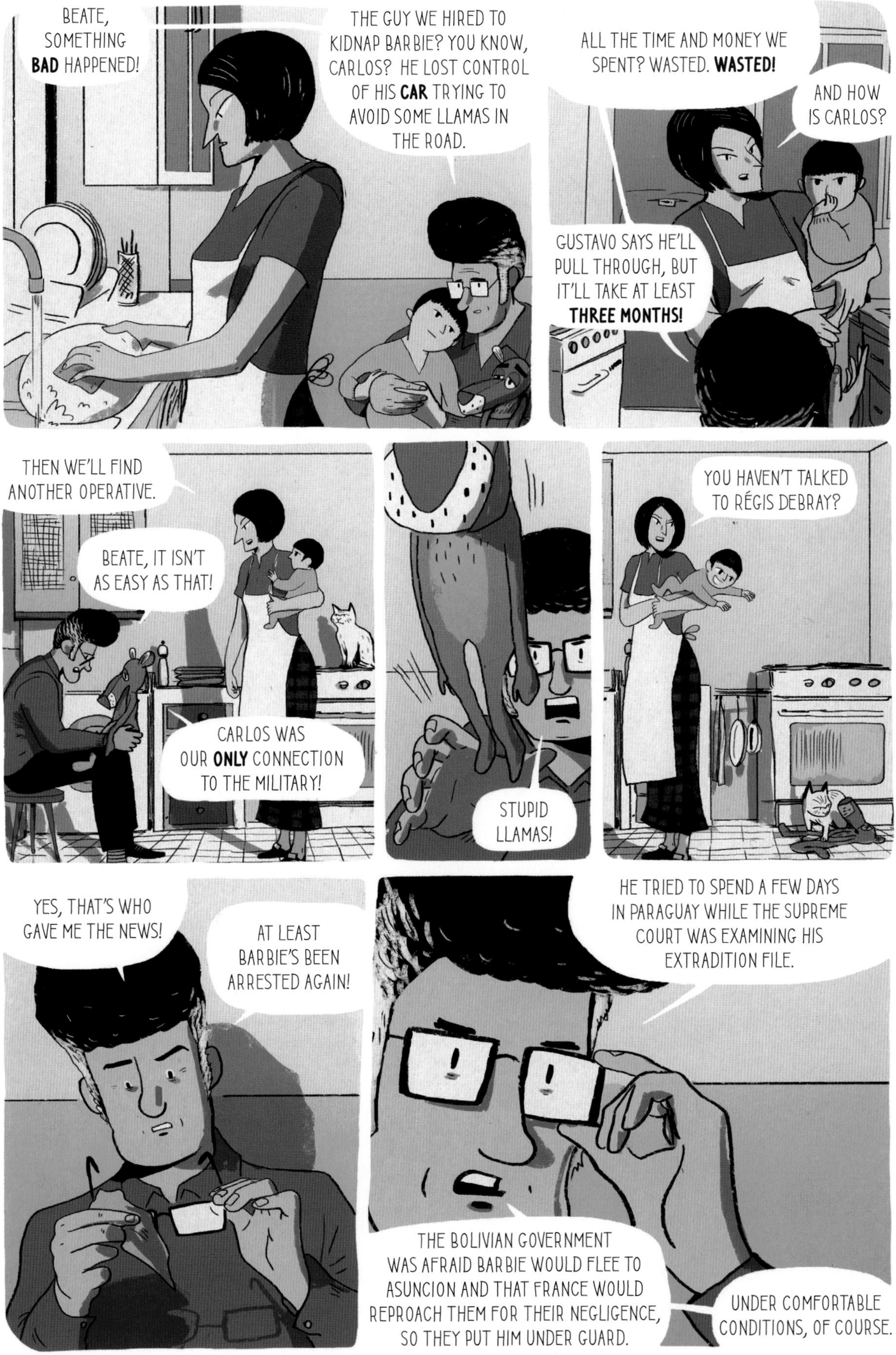
BEATE, SOMETHING BAD HAPPENED!
THE GUY WE HIRED TO KIDNAP BARBIE? YOU KNOW, CARLOS? HE LOST CONTROL OF HIS CAR TRYING TO AVOID SOME LLAMAS IN THE ROAD.
ALL THE TIME AND MONEY WE SPENT? WASTED. WASTED!
AND HOW IS CARLOS?
GUSTAVO SAYS HE'LL PULL THROUGH, BUT IT'LL TAKE AT LEAST THREE MONTHS!
THEN WE'LL FIND ANOTHER OPERATIVE.
BEATE, IT ISN'T AS EASY AS THAT!
CARLOS WAS OUR ONLY CONNECTION TO THE MILITARY!
STUPID LLAMAS!
YOU HAVEN'T TALKED TO RÉGIS DEBRAY?
YES, THAT'S WHO GAVE ME THE NEWS!
AT LEAST BARBIE'S BEEN ARRESTED AGAIN!
HE TRIED TO SPEND A FEW DAYS IN PARAGUAY WHILE THE SUPREME COURT WAS EXAMINING HIS EXTRADITION FILE.
THE BOLIVIAN GOVERNMENT WAS AFRAID BARBIE WOULD FLEE TO ASUNCION AND THAT FRANCE WOULD REPROACH THEM FOR THEIR NEGLIGENCE, SO THEY PUT HIM UNDER GUARD.
UNDER COMFORTABLE CONDITIONS, OF COURSE.

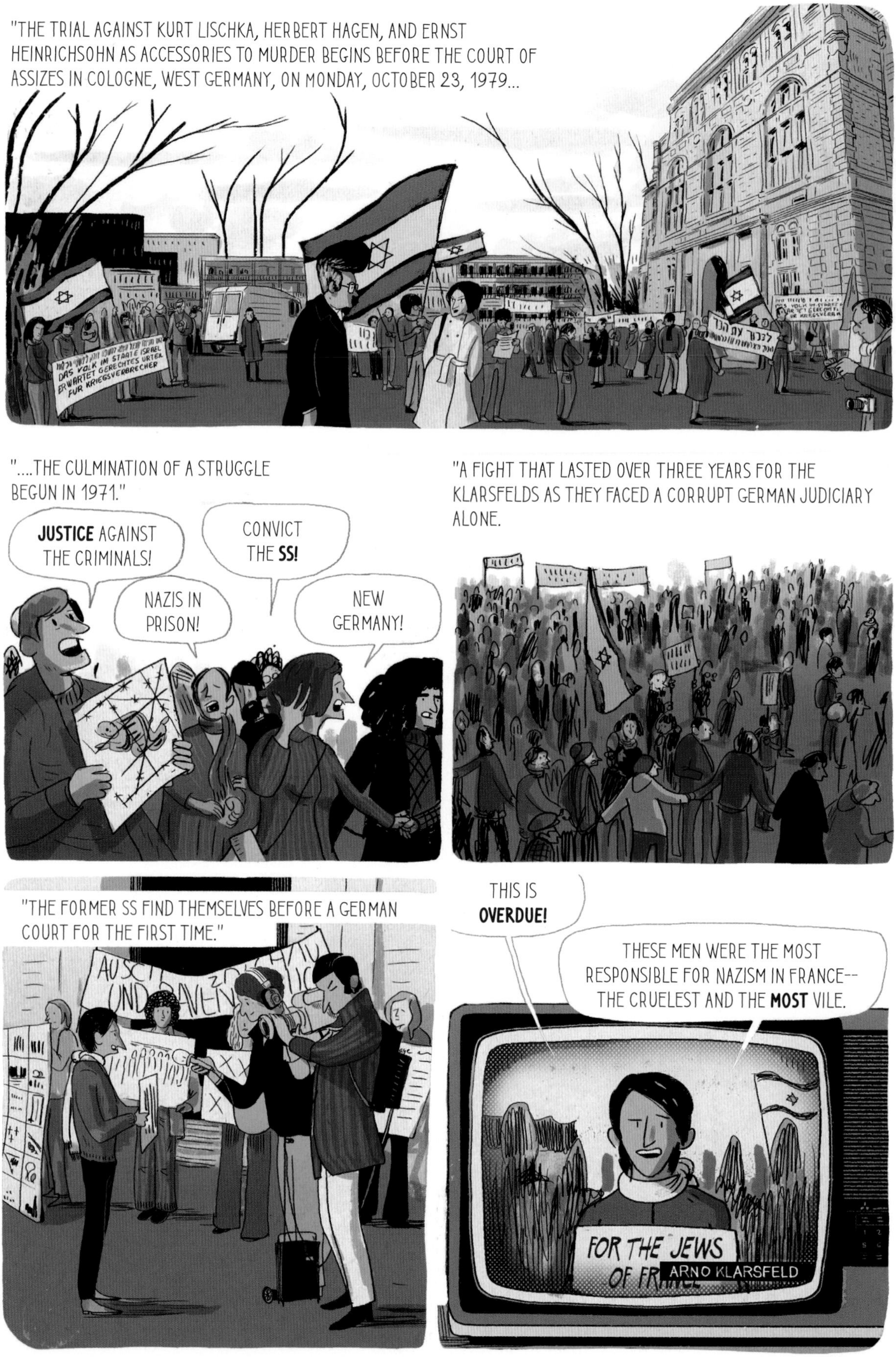
"THE TRIAL AGAINST KURT LISCHKA, HERBERT HAGEN, AND ERNST HEINRICHSOHN AS ACCESSORIES TO MURDER BEGINS BEFORE THE COURT OF ASSIZES IN COLOGNE, WEST GERMANY, ON MONDAY, OCTOBER 23, 1979...
"....THE CULMINATION OF A STRUGGLE BEGUN IN 1971."
JUSTICE AGAINST THE CRIMINALS!
CONVICT THE **SS!**
NAZIS IN PRISON!
NEW GERMANY!
"A FIGHT THAT LASTED OVER THREE YEARS FOR THE KLARSFELDS AS THEY FACED A CORRUPT GERMAN JUDICIARY ALONE.
"THE FORMER SS FIND THEMSELVES BEFORE A GERMAN COURT FOR THE FIRST TIME."
THIS IS **OVERDUE!**
THESE MEN WERE THE MOST RESPONSIBLE FOR NAZISM IN FRANCE-- THE CRUELEST AND THE **MOST** VILE.
FOR THE JEWS
ARNO KLARSFELD

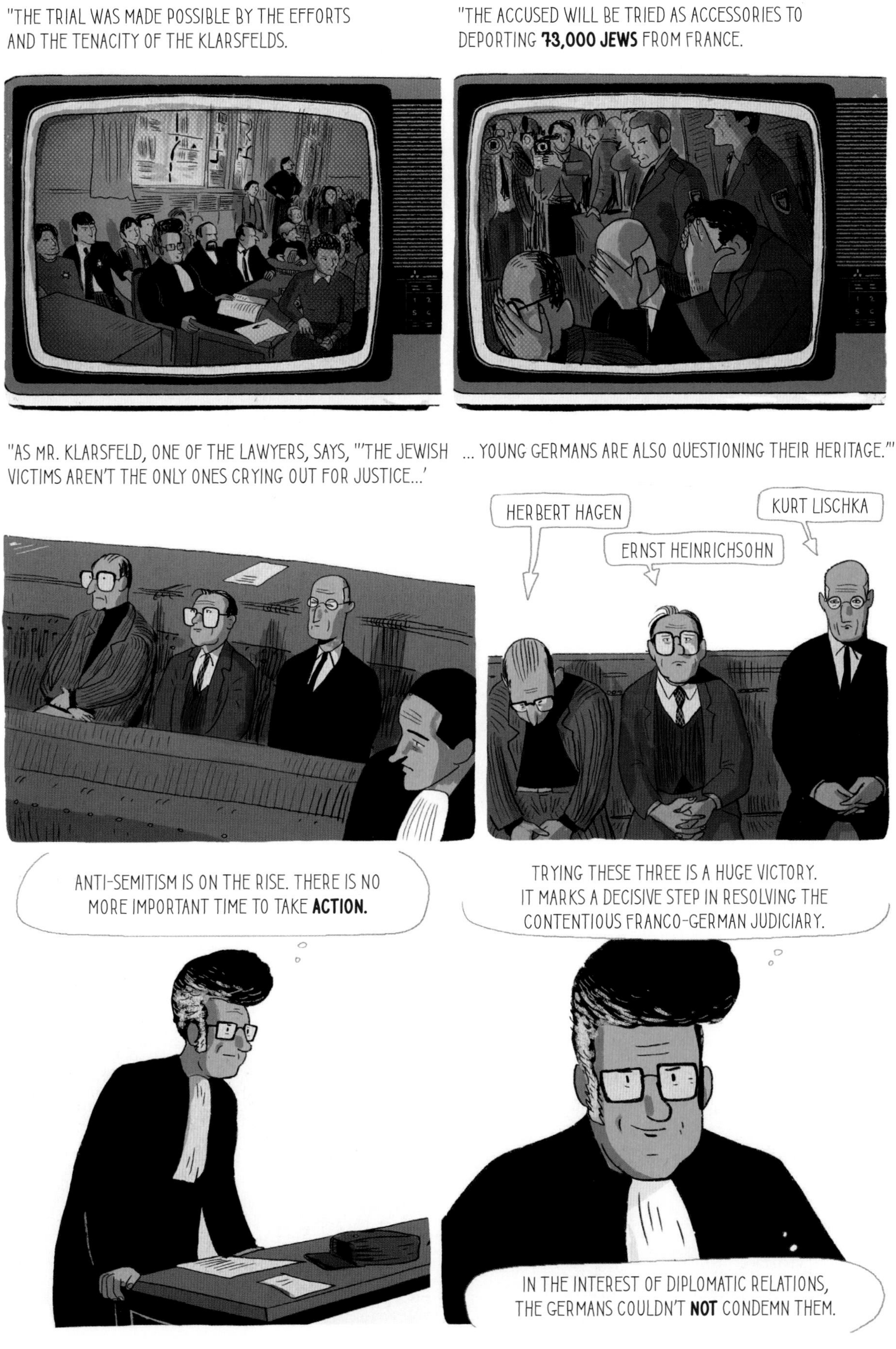
"THE TRIAL WAS MADE POSSIBLE BY THE EFFORTS AND THE TENACITY OF THE KLARSFELDS.
"THE ACCUSED WILL BE TRIED AS ACCESSORIES TO DEPORTING 73,000 JEWS FROM FRANCE.
"AS MR. KLARSFELD, ONE OF THE LAWYERS, SAYS, "'THE JEWISH VICTIMS AREN'T THE ONLY ONES CRYING OUT FOR JUSTICE...'
... YOUNG GERMANS ARE ALSO QUESTIONING THEIR HERITAGE."'
HERBERT HAGEN
ERNST HEINRICHSOHN
KURT LISCHKA
ANTI-SEMITISM IS ON THE RISE. THERE IS NO MORE IMPORTANT TIME TO TAKE ACTION.
TRYING THESE THREE IS A HUGE VICTORY. IT MARKS A DECISIVE STEP IN RESOLVING THE CONTENTIOUS FRANCO-GERMAN JUDICIARY.
IN THE INTEREST OF DIPLOMATIC RELATIONS, THE GERMANS COULDN'T NOT CONDEMN THEM.

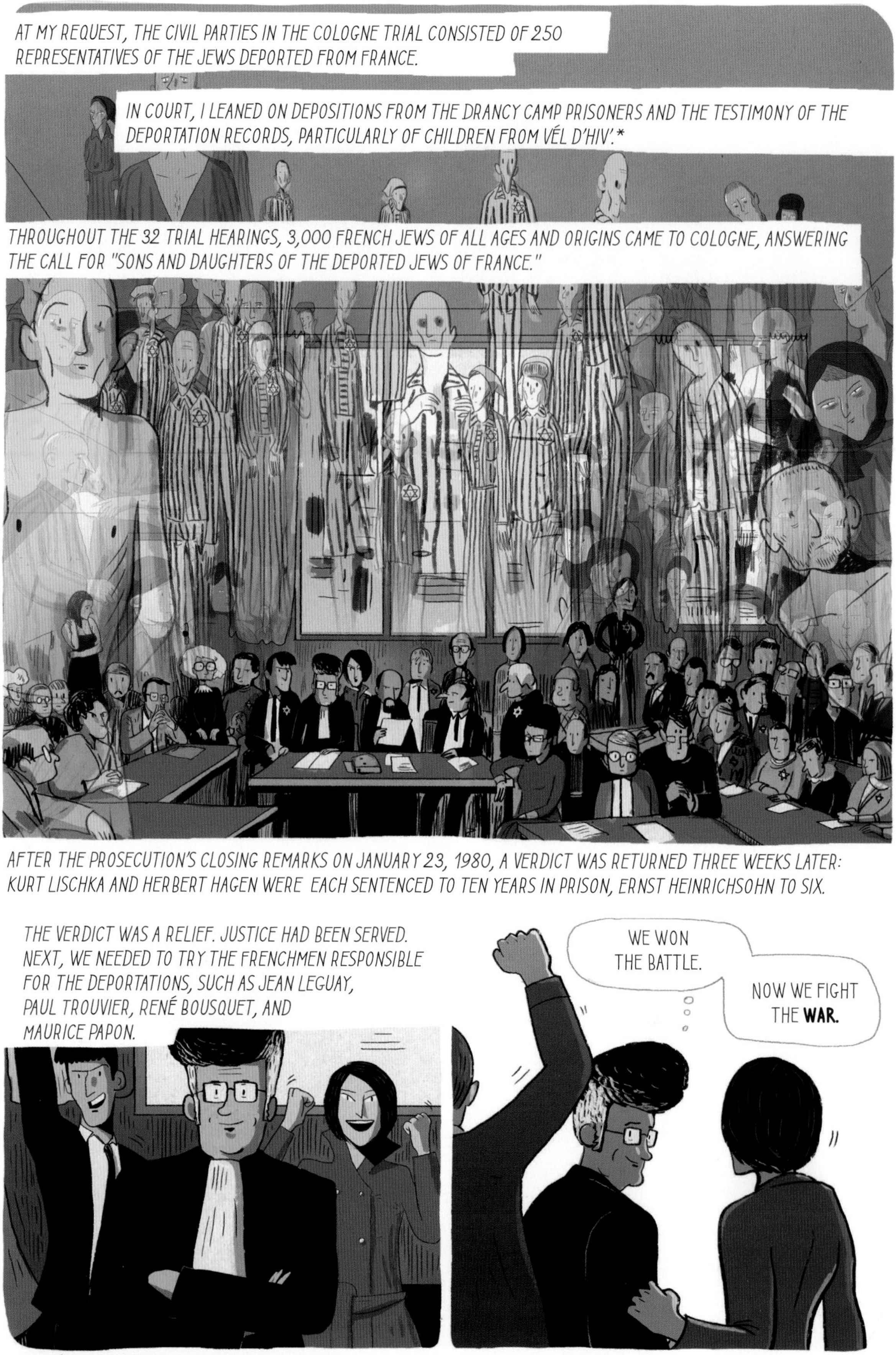
AT MY REQUEST, THE CIVIL PARTIES IN THE COLOGNE TRIAL CONSISTED OF 250 REPRESENTATIVES OF THE JEWS DEPORTED FROM FRANCE.
IN COURT, I LEANED ON DEPOSITIONS FROM THE DRANCY CAMP PRISONERS AND THE TESTIMONY OF THE DEPORTATION RECORDS, PARTICULARLY OF CHILDREN FROM VÉL D'HIV'.*
THROUGHOUT THE 32 TRIAL HEARINGS, 3,000 FRENCH JEWS OF ALL AGES AND ORIGINS CAME TO COLOGNE, ANSWERING THE CALL FOR "SONS AND DAUGHTERS OF THE DEPORTED JEWS OF FRANCE."
AFTER THE PROSECUTION'S CLOSING REMARKS ON JANUARY 23, 1980, A VERDICT WAS RETURNED THREE WEEKS LATER: KURT LISCHKA AND HERBERT HAGEN WERE EACH SENTENCED TO TEN YEARS IN PRISON, ERNST HEINRICHSOHN TO SIX.
THE VERDICT WAS A RELIEF. JUSTICE HAD BEEN SERVED. NEXT, WE NEEDED TO TRY THE FRENCHMEN RESPONSIBLE FOR THE DEPORTATIONS, SUCH AS JEAN LEGUAY, PAUL TROUVIER, RENÉ BOUSQUET, AND MAURICE PAPON.
WE WON THE BATTLE.
NOW WE FIGHT THE **WAR.**

* THE VÉL D'HIV' ROUNDUP WAS A MASS ARREST OF JEWS IN
PARIS IN JULY 1942 BY THE FRENCH POLICE

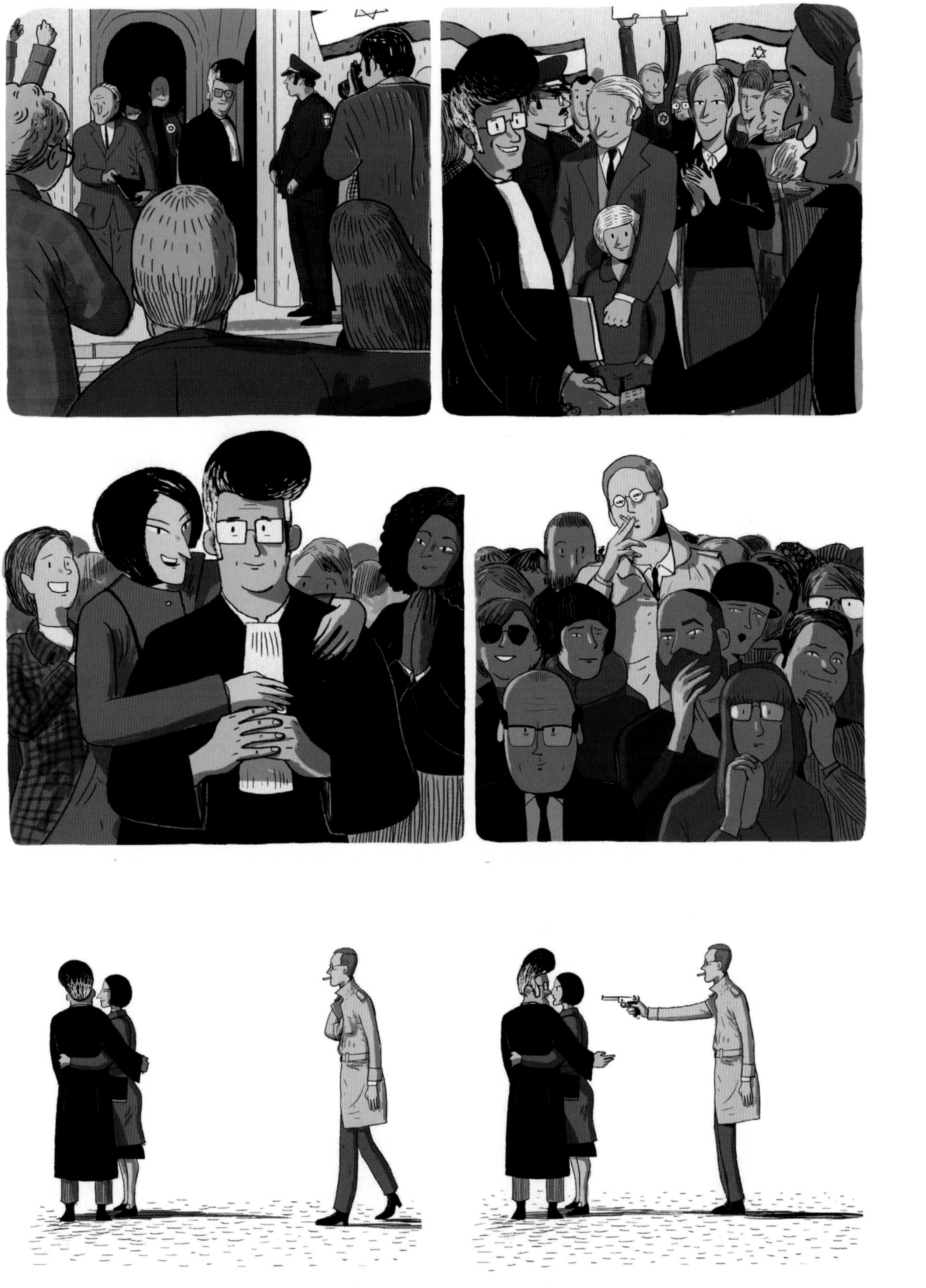

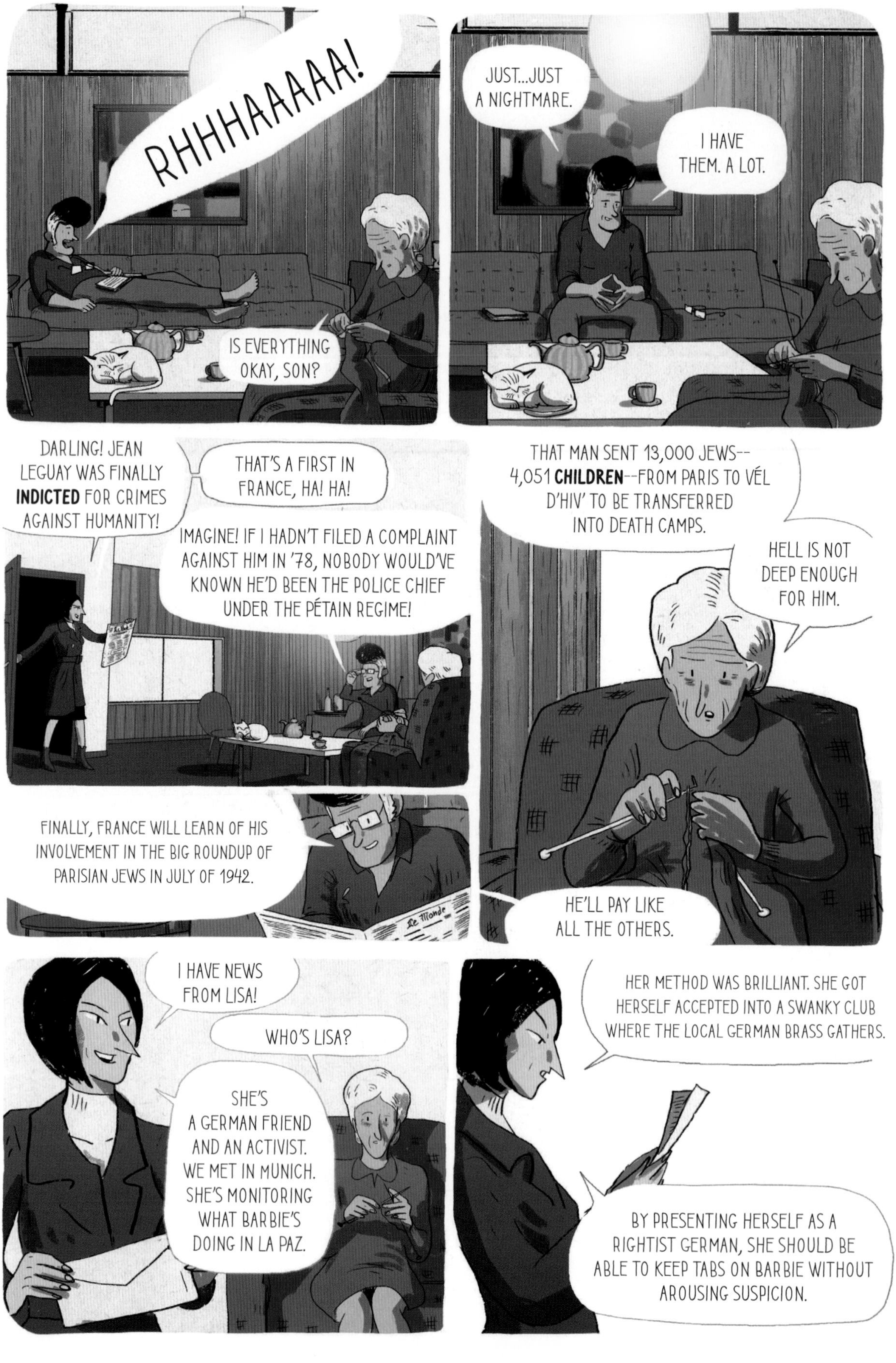

RHHHAAAAAA!
IS EVERYTHING OKAY, SON?
JUST...JUST A NIGHTMARE.
I HAVE THEM. A LOT.
DARLING! JEAN LEGUAY WAS FINALLY **INDICTED** FOR CRIMES AGAINST HUMANITY!
THAT'S A FIRST IN FRANCE, HA! HA!
IMAGINE! IF I HADN'T FILED A COMPLAINT AGAINST HIM IN '78, NOBODY WOULD'VE KNOWN HE'D BEEN THE POLICE CHIEF UNDER THE PÉTAIN REGIME!
FINALLY, FRANCE WILL LEARN OF HIS INVOLVEMENT IN THE BIG ROUNDUP OF PARISIAN JEWS IN JULY OF 1942.
Le Monde
THAT MAN SENT 13,000 JEWS--4,051 **CHILDREN**--FROM PARIS TO VÉL D'HIV' TO BE TRANSFERRED INTO DEATH CAMPS.
HELL IS NOT DEEP ENOUGH FOR HIM.
HE'LL PAY LIKE ALL THE OTHERS.
I HAVE NEWS FROM LISA!
WHO'S LISA?
SHE'S A GERMAN FRIEND AND AN ACTIVIST. WE MET IN MUNICH. SHE'S MONITORING WHAT BARBIE'S DOING IN LA PAZ.
HER METHOD WAS BRILLIANT. SHE GOT HERSELF ACCEPTED INTO A SWANKY CLUB WHERE THE LOCAL GERMAN BRASS GATHERS.
BY PRESENTING HERSELF AS A RIGHTIST GERMAN, SHE SHOULD BE ABLE TO KEEP TABS ON BARBIE WITHOUT AROUSING SUSPICION.

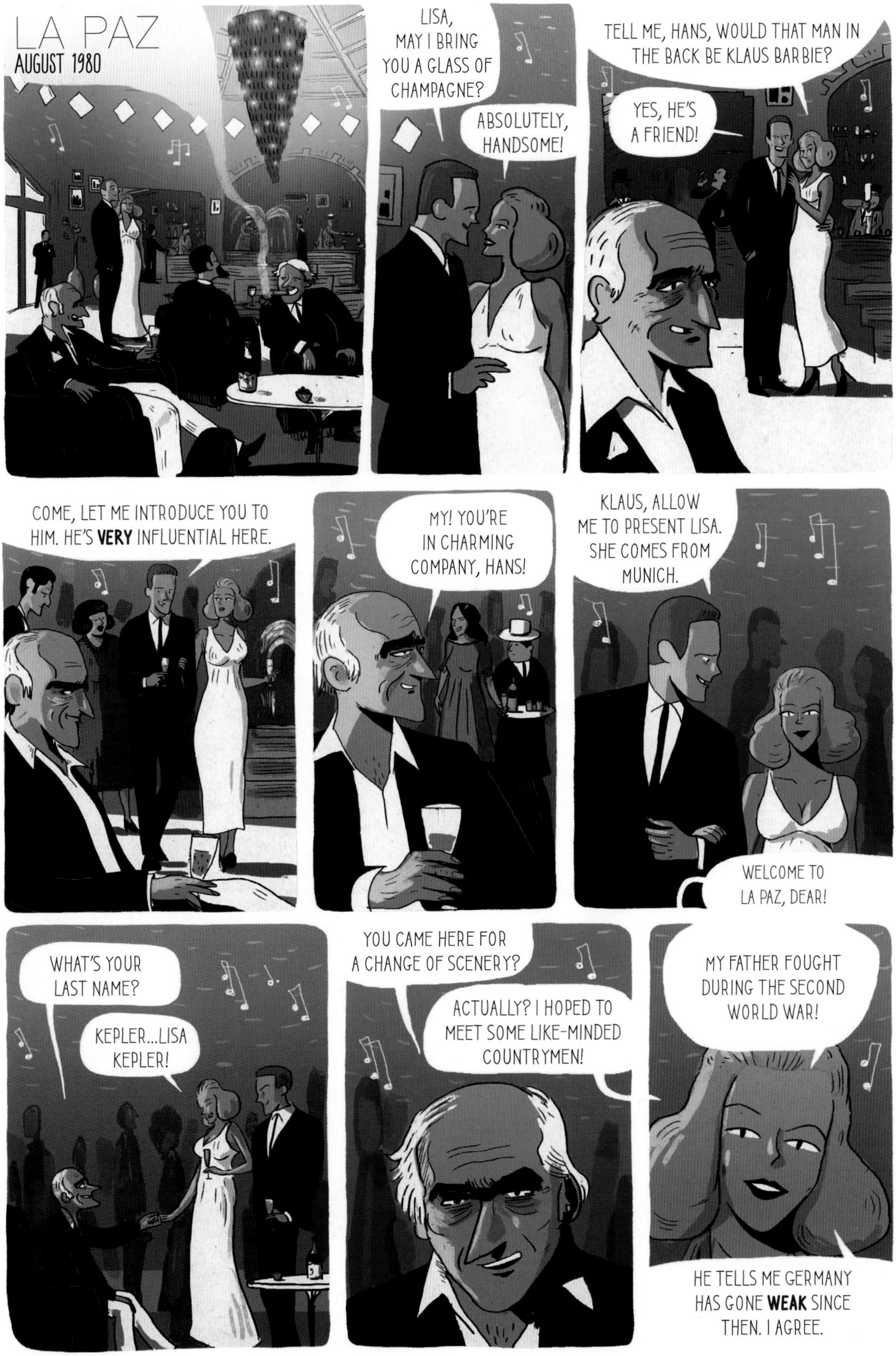
LA PAZ
AUGUST 1980
LISA, MAY I BRING YOU A GLASS OF CHAMPAGNE?
ABSOLUTELY, HANDSOME!
TELL ME, HANS, WOULD THAT MAN IN THE BACK BE KLAUS BARBIE?
YES, HE'S A FRIEND!
COME, LET ME INTRODUCE YOU TO HIM. HE'S **VERY** INFLUENTIAL HERE.
MY! YOU'RE IN CHARMING COMPANY, HANS!
KLAUS, ALLOW ME TO PRESENT LISA. SHE COMES FROM MUNICH.
WELCOME TO LA PAZ, DEAR!
WHAT'S YOUR LAST NAME?
KEPLER...LISA KEPLER!
YOU CAME HERE FOR A CHANGE OF SCENERY?
ACTUALLY? I HOPED TO MEET SOME LIKE-MINDED COUNTRYMEN!
MY FATHER FOUGHT DURING THE SECOND WORLD WAR!
HE TELLS ME GERMANY HAS GONE **WEAK** SINCE THEN. I AGREE.

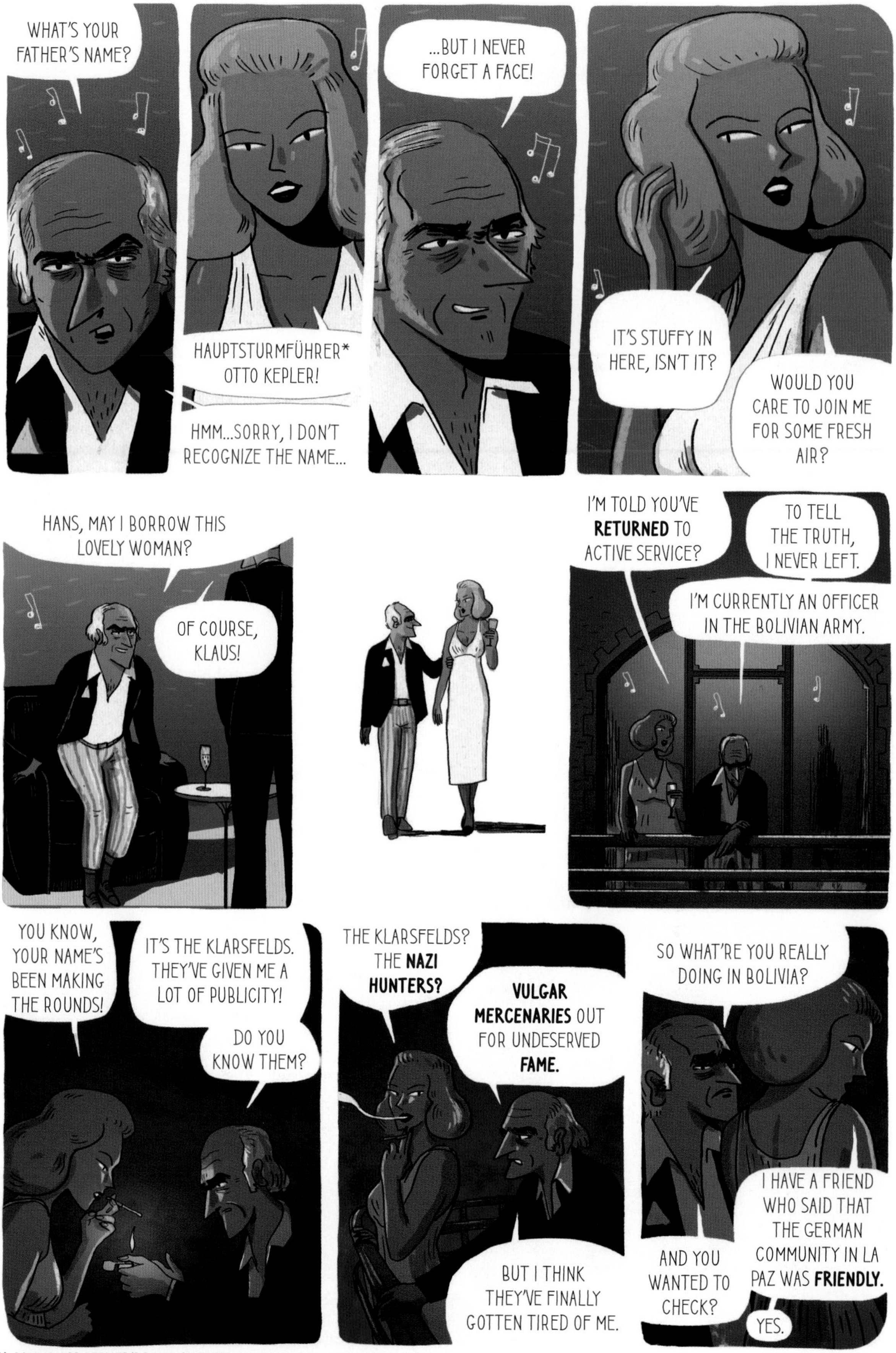

WHAT'S YOUR FATHER'S NAME?
HAUPTSTURMFÜHRER* OTTO KEPLER!
HMM...SORRY, I DON'T RECOGNIZE THE NAME...
...BUT I NEVER FORGET A FACE!
IT'S STUFFY IN HERE, ISN'T IT?
WOULD YOU CARE TO JOIN ME FOR SOME FRESH AIR?
HANS, MAY I BORROW THIS LOVELY WOMAN?
OF COURSE, KLAUS!
I'M TOLD YOU'VE **RETURNED** TO ACTIVE SERVICE?
TO TELL THE TRUTH, I NEVER LEFT.
I'M CURRENTLY AN OFFICER IN THE BOLIVIAN ARMY.
YOU KNOW, YOUR NAME'S BEEN MAKING THE ROUNDS!
IT'S THE KLARSFELDS. THEY'VE GIVEN ME A LOT OF PUBLICITY!
DO YOU KNOW THEM?
THE KLARSFELDS? THE **NAZI HUNTERS?**
VULGAR MERCENARIES OUT FOR UNDESERVED **FAME.**
BUT I THINK THEY'VE FINALLY GOTTEN TIRED OF ME.
SO WHAT'RE YOU REALLY DOING IN BOLIVIA?
I HAVE A FRIEND WHO SAID THAT THE GERMAN COMMUNITY IN LA PAZ WAS **FRIENDLY.**
AND YOU WANTED TO CHECK?
YES.

*A COMMON SS OFFICER'S RANK, BETWEEN MAJOR AND LIEUTENANT

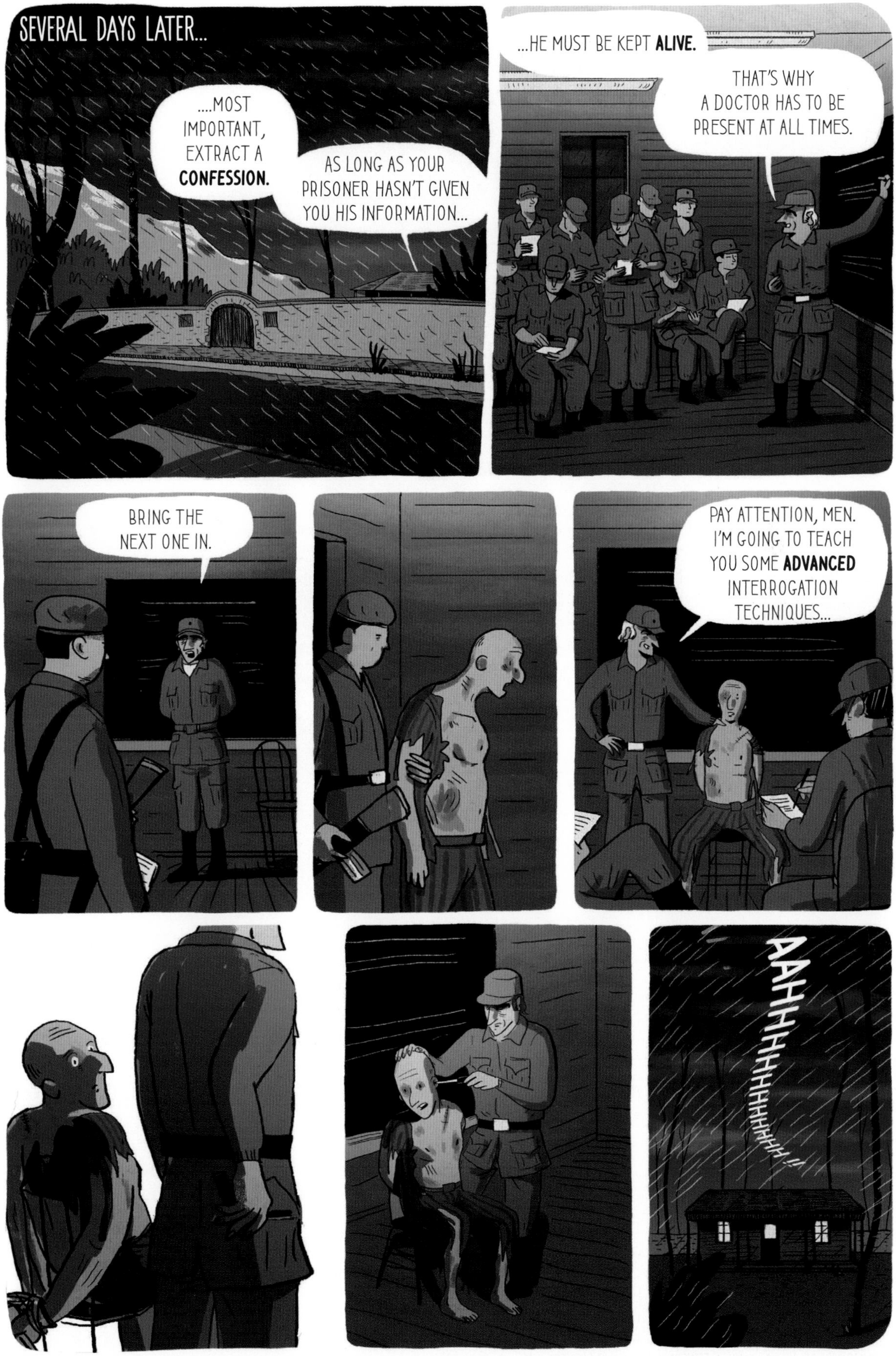
SEVERAL DAYS LATER...
....MOST IMPORTANT, EXTRACT A **CONFESSION.**
AS LONG AS YOUR PRISONER HASN'T GIVEN YOU HIS INFORMATION...
...HE MUST BE KEPT **ALIVE.**
THAT'S WHY A DOCTOR HAS TO BE PRESENT AT ALL TIMES.
BRING THE NEXT ONE IN.
PAY ATTENTION, MEN. I'M GOING TO TEACH YOU SOME **ADVANCED** INTERROGATION TECHNIQUES...
AAHHHHHHHHHHHHHH!!

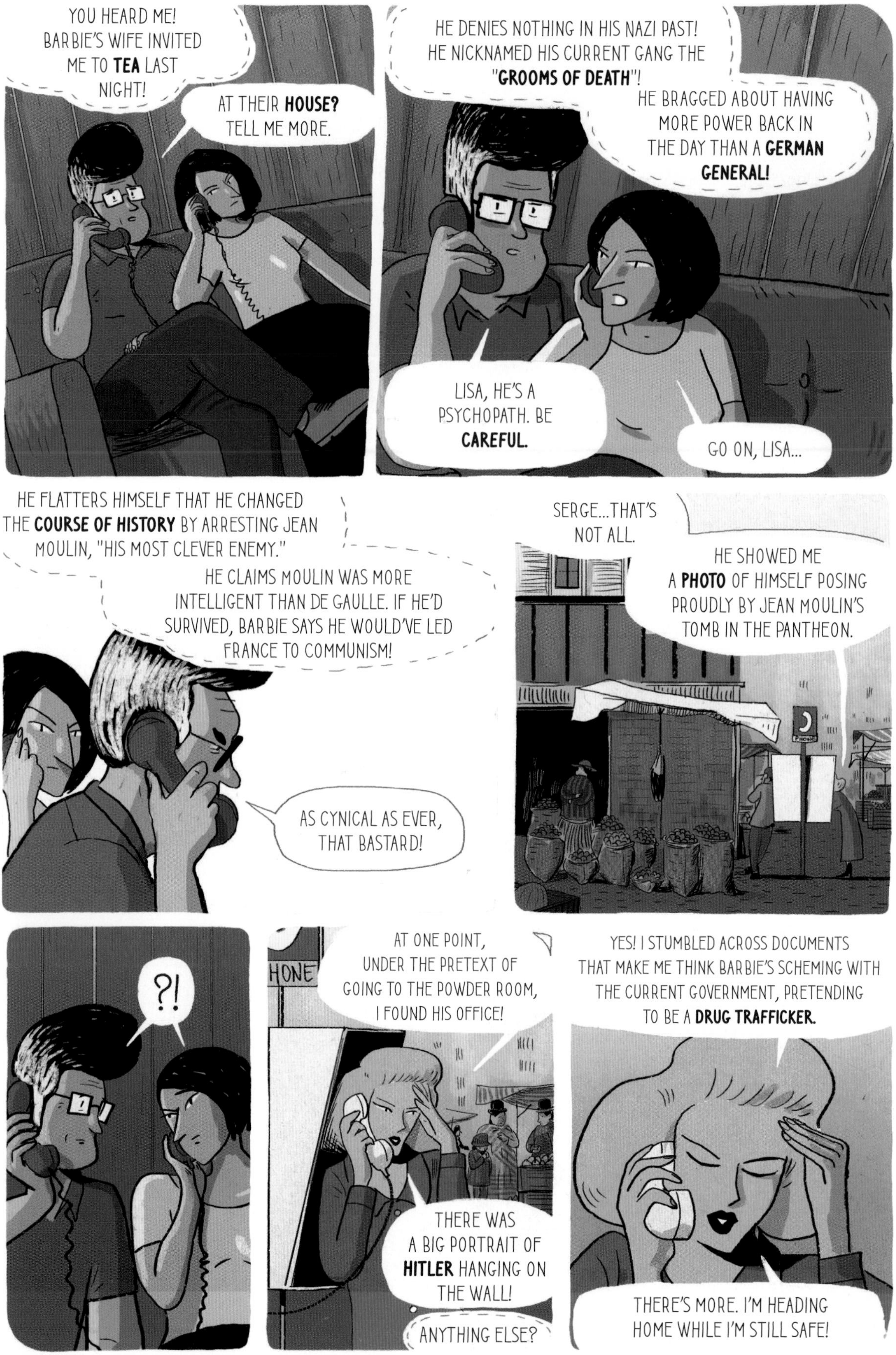

YOU HEARD ME! BARBIE'S WIFE INVITED ME TO **TEA** LAST NIGHT!
AT THEIR **HOUSE?** TELL ME MORE.
HE DENIES NOTHING IN HIS NAZI PAST! HE NICKNAMED HIS CURRENT GANG THE "**GROOMS OF DEATH**"!
HE BRAGGED ABOUT HAVING MORE POWER BACK IN THE DAY THAN A **GERMAN GENERAL!**
LISA, HE'S A PSYCHOPATH. BE **CAREFUL.**
GO ON, LISA...
HE FLATTERS HIMSELF THAT HE CHANGED THE **COURSE OF HISTORY** BY ARRESTING JEAN MOULIN, "HIS MOST CLEVER ENEMY."
HE CLAIMS MOULIN WAS MORE INTELLIGENT THAN DE GAULLE. IF HE'D SURVIVED, BARBIE SAYS HE WOULD'VE LED FRANCE TO COMMUNISM!
AS CYNICAL AS EVER, THAT BASTARD!
SERGE...THAT'S NOT ALL.
HE SHOWED ME A **PHOTO** OF HIMSELF POSING PROUDLY BY JEAN MOULIN'S TOMB IN THE PANTHEON.
PHONE
?!
HONE
AT ONE POINT, UNDER THE PRETEXT OF GOING TO THE POWDER ROOM, I FOUND HIS OFFICE!
THERE WAS A BIG PORTRAIT OF **HITLER** HANGING ON THE WALL!
ANYTHING ELSE?
YES! I STUMBLED ACROSS DOCUMENTS THAT MAKE ME THINK BARBIE'S SCHEMING WITH THE CURRENT GOVERNMENT, PRETENDING TO BE A **DRUG TRAFFICKER.**
THERE'S MORE. I'M HEADING HOME WHILE I'M STILL SAFE!

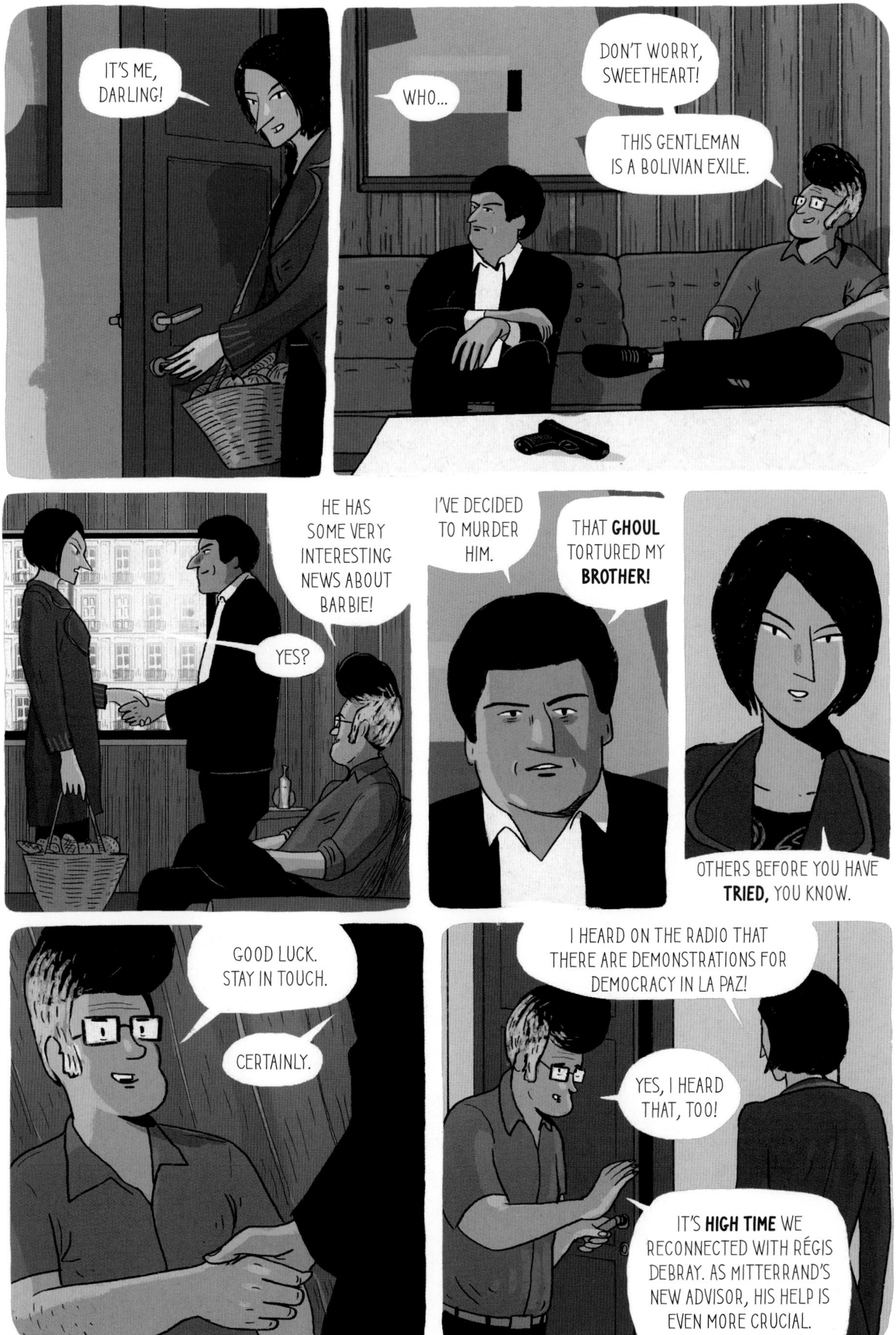
IT'S ME, DARLING!
WHO...
DON'T WORRY, SWEETHEART!
THIS GENTLEMAN IS A BOLIVIAN EXILE.
HE HAS SOME VERY INTERESTING NEWS ABOUT BARBIE!
YES?
I'VE DECIDED TO MURDER HIM.
THAT **GHOUL** TORTURED MY **BROTHER!**
OTHERS BEFORE YOU HAVE **TRIED,** YOU KNOW.
GOOD LUCK. STAY IN TOUCH.
CERTAINLY.
I HEARD ON THE RADIO THAT THERE ARE DEMONSTRATIONS FOR DEMOCRACY IN LA PAZ!
YES, I HEARD THAT, TOO!
IT'S **HIGH TIME** WE RECONNECTED WITH RÉGIS DEBRAY. AS MITTERRAND'S NEW ADVISOR, HIS HELP IS EVEN MORE CRUCIAL.

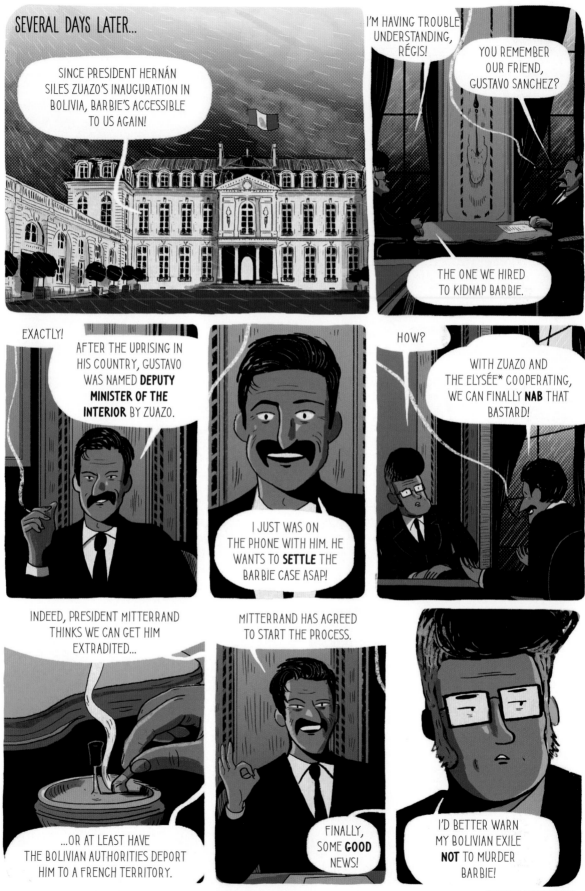

SEVERAL DAYS LATER...

SINCE PRESIDENT HERNÁN SILES ZUAZO'S INAUGURATION IN BOLIVIA, BARBIE'S ACCESSIBLE TO US AGAIN!

I'M HAVING TROUBLE UNDERSTANDING, RÉGIS!

YOU REMEMBER OUR FRIEND, GUSTAVO SANCHEZ?

THE ONE WE HIRED TO KIDNAP BARBIE.

EXACTLY!

AFTER THE UPRISING IN HIS COUNTRY, GUSTAVO WAS NAMED **DEPUTY MINISTER OF THE INTERIOR** BY ZUAZO.

I JUST WAS ON THE PHONE WITH HIM. HE WANTS TO **SETTLE** THE BARBIE CASE ASAP!

HOW?

WITH ZUAZO AND THE ELYSÉE* COOPERATING, WE CAN FINALLY **NAB** THAT BASTARD!

INDEED, PRESIDENT MITTERRAND THINKS WE CAN GET HIM EXTRADITED...

MITTERRAND HAS AGREED TO START THE PROCESS.

...OR AT LEAST HAVE THE BOLIVIAN AUTHORITIES DEPORT HIM TO A FRENCH TERRITORY.

FINALLY, SOME **GOOD** NEWS!

I'D BETTER WARN MY BOLIVIAN EXILE **NOT** TO MURDER BARBIE!

*FRENCH GOVERNMENT

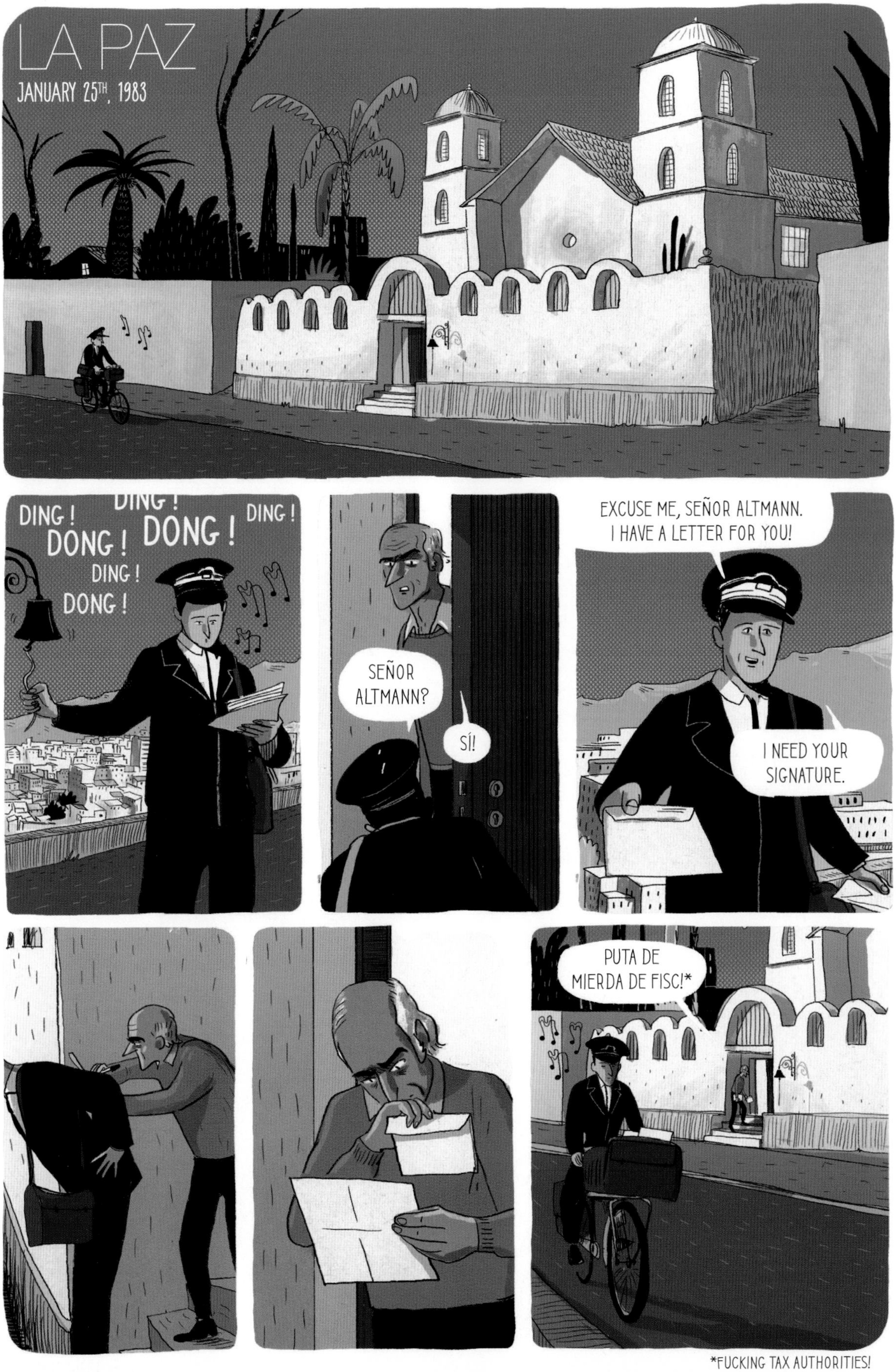
LA PAZ
JANUARY 25TH, 1983
DING! DONG! DING! DONG! DING! DONG! DING!
SEÑOR ALTMANN?
SÍ!
EXCUSE ME, SEÑOR ALTMANN. I HAVE A LETTER FOR YOU!
I NEED YOUR SIGNATURE.
PUTA DE MIERDA DE FISC!*
*FUCKING TAX AUTHORITIES!

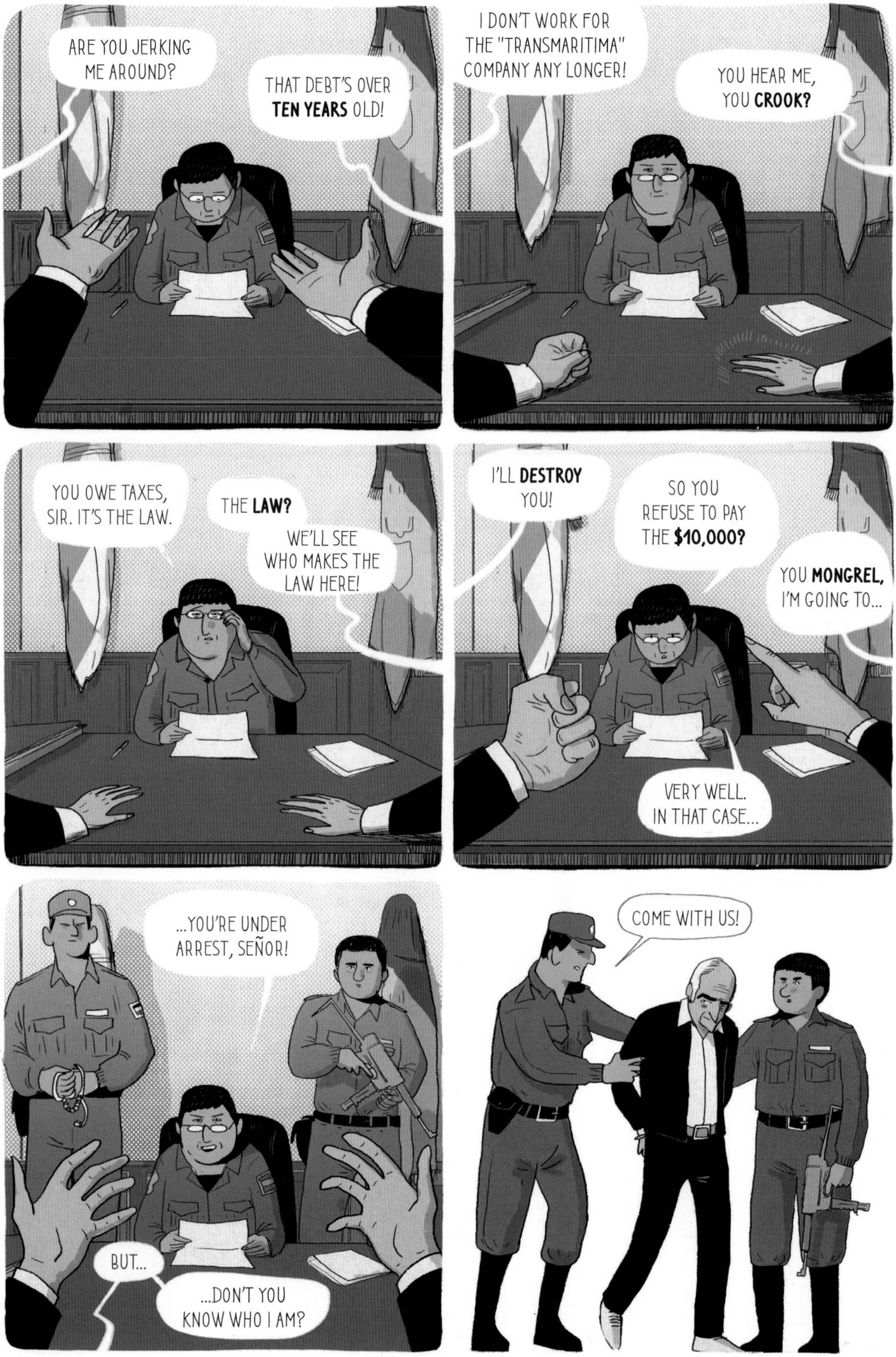
ARE YOU JERKING ME AROUND?
THAT DEBT'S OVER **TEN YEARS** OLD!
I DON'T WORK FOR THE "TRANSMARITIMA" COMPANY ANY LONGER!
YOU HEAR ME, YOU **CROOK?**
YOU OWE TAXES, SIR. IT'S THE LAW.
THE **LAW?**
WE'LL SEE WHO MAKES THE LAW HERE!
I'LL **DESTROY** YOU!
SO YOU REFUSE TO PAY THE **$10,000?**
YOU **MONGREL,** I'M GOING TO...
VERY WELL. IN THAT CASE...
...YOU'RE UNDER ARREST, SEÑOR!
BUT...
...DON'T YOU KNOW WHO I AM?
COME WITH US!

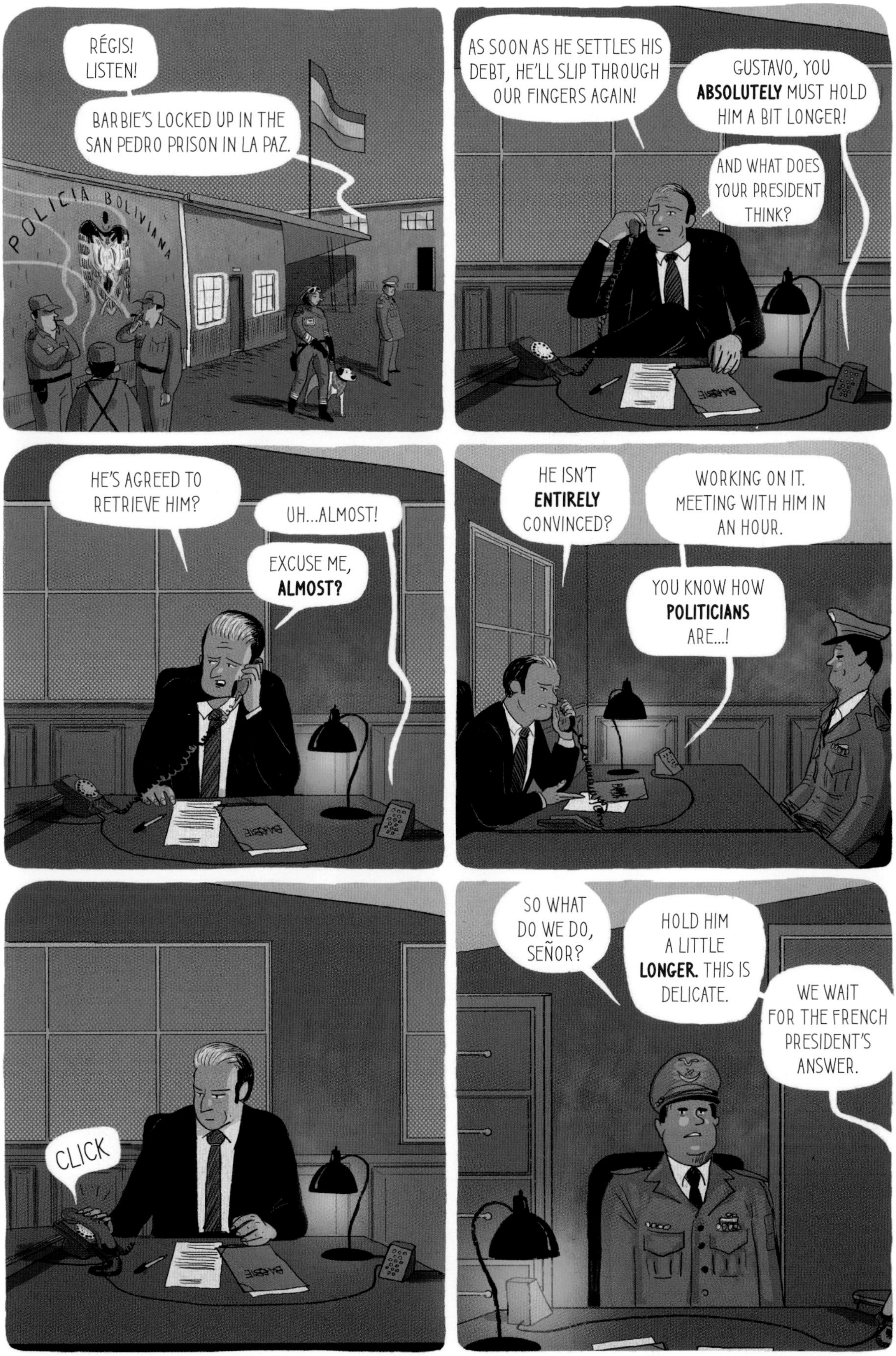
RÉGIS! LISTEN!
BARBIE'S LOCKED UP IN THE SAN PEDRO PRISON IN LA PAZ.
POLICIA BOLIVIANA
AS SOON AS HE SETTLES HIS DEBT, HE'LL SLIP THROUGH OUR FINGERS AGAIN!
GUSTAVO, YOU **ABSOLUTELY** MUST HOLD HIM A BIT LONGER!
AND WHAT DOES YOUR PRESIDENT THINK?
BARBIE
HE'S AGREED TO RETRIEVE HIM?
UH...ALMOST!
EXCUSE ME, **ALMOST?**
BARBIE
HE ISN'T **ENTIRELY** CONVINCED?
WORKING ON IT. MEETING WITH HIM IN AN HOUR.
YOU KNOW HOW **POLITICIANS** ARE...!
CLICK
BARBIE
SO WHAT DO WE DO, SEÑOR?
HOLD HIM A LITTLE **LONGER.** THIS IS DELICATE.
WE WAIT FOR THE FRENCH PRESIDENT'S ANSWER.

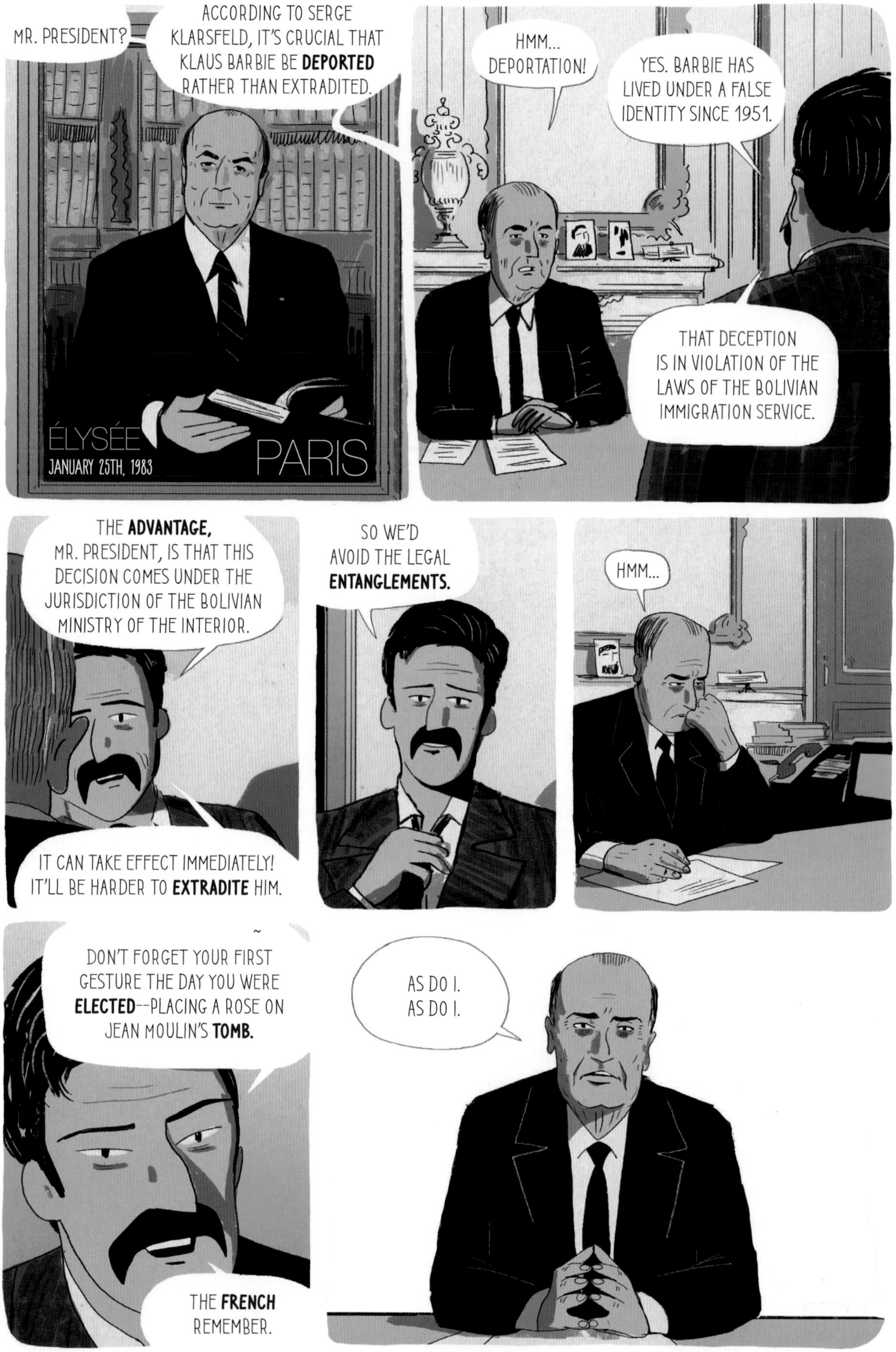
MR. PRESIDENT?
ACCORDING TO SERGE KLARSFELD, IT'S CRUCIAL THAT KLAUS BARBIE BE **DEPORTED** RATHER THAN EXTRADITED.
ÉLYSÉE
JANUARY 25TH, 1983
PARIS
HMM... DEPORTATION!
YES. BARBIE HAS LIVED UNDER A FALSE IDENTITY SINCE 1951.
THAT DECEPTION IS IN VIOLATION OF THE LAWS OF THE BOLIVIAN IMMIGRATION SERVICE.
THE **ADVANTAGE,** MR. PRESIDENT, IS THAT THIS DECISION COMES UNDER THE JURISDICTION OF THE BOLIVIAN MINISTRY OF THE INTERIOR.
IT CAN TAKE EFFECT IMMEDIATELY! IT'LL BE HARDER TO **EXTRADITE** HIM.
SO WE'D AVOID THE LEGAL **ENTANGLEMENTS.**
HMM...
DON'T FORGET YOUR FIRST GESTURE THE DAY YOU WERE **ELECTED**--PLACING A ROSE ON JEAN MOULIN'S **TOMB.**
THE **FRENCH** REMEMBER.
AS DO I. AS DO I.

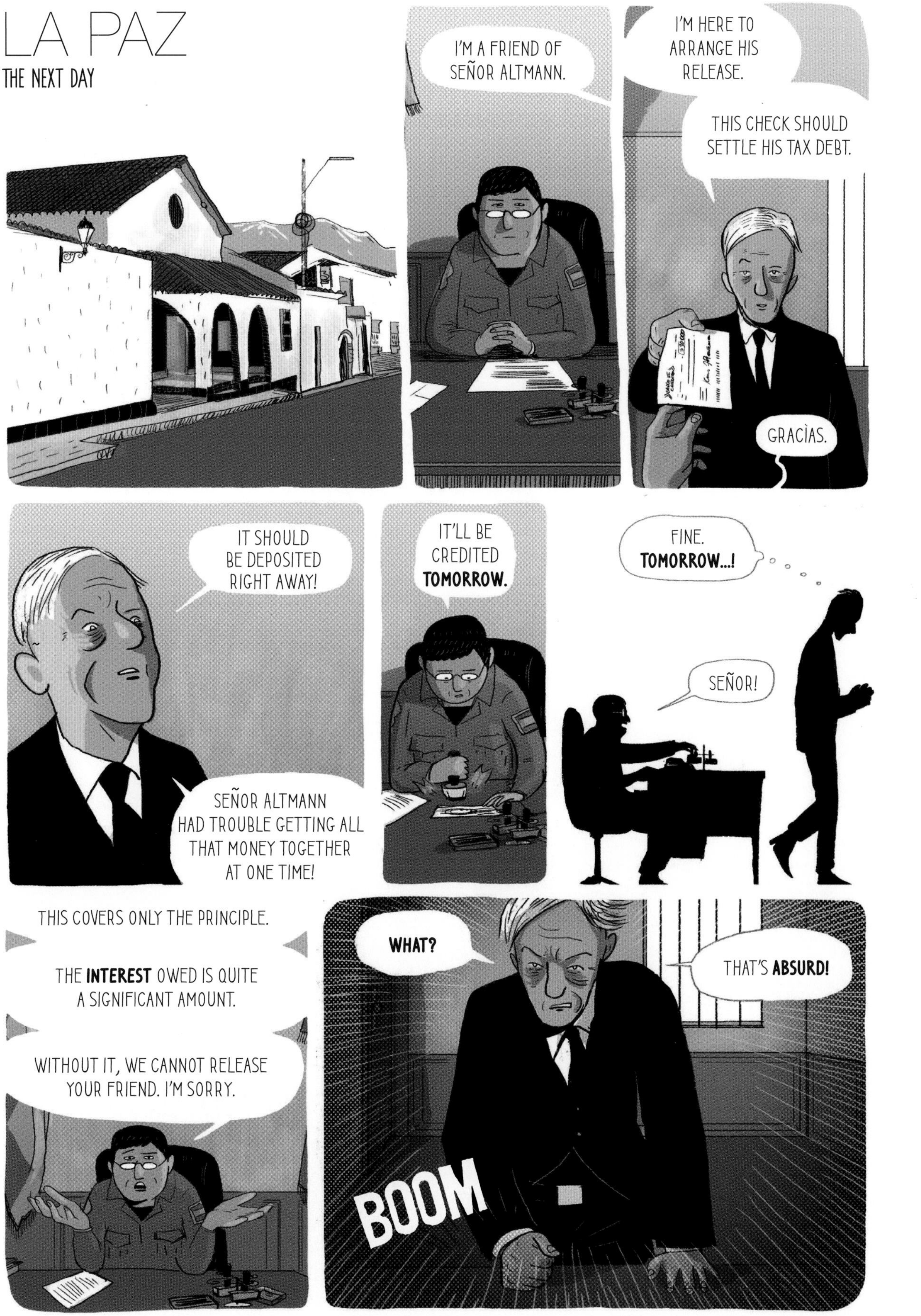
LA PAZ
THE NEXT DAY
I'M A FRIEND OF SEÑOR ALTMANN.
I'M HERE TO ARRANGE HIS RELEASE.
THIS CHECK SHOULD SETTLE HIS TAX DEBT.
GRACÌAS.
IT SHOULD BE DEPOSITED RIGHT AWAY!
SEÑOR ALTMANN HAD TROUBLE GETTING ALL THAT MONEY TOGETHER AT ONE TIME!
IT'LL BE CREDITED **TOMORROW.**
FINE. **TOMORROW...!**
SEÑOR!
THIS COVERS ONLY THE PRINCIPLE.
THE **INTEREST** OWED IS QUITE A SIGNIFICANT AMOUNT.
WITHOUT IT, WE CANNOT RELEASE YOUR FRIEND. I'M SORRY.
WHAT?
THAT'S **ABSURD!**
BOOM

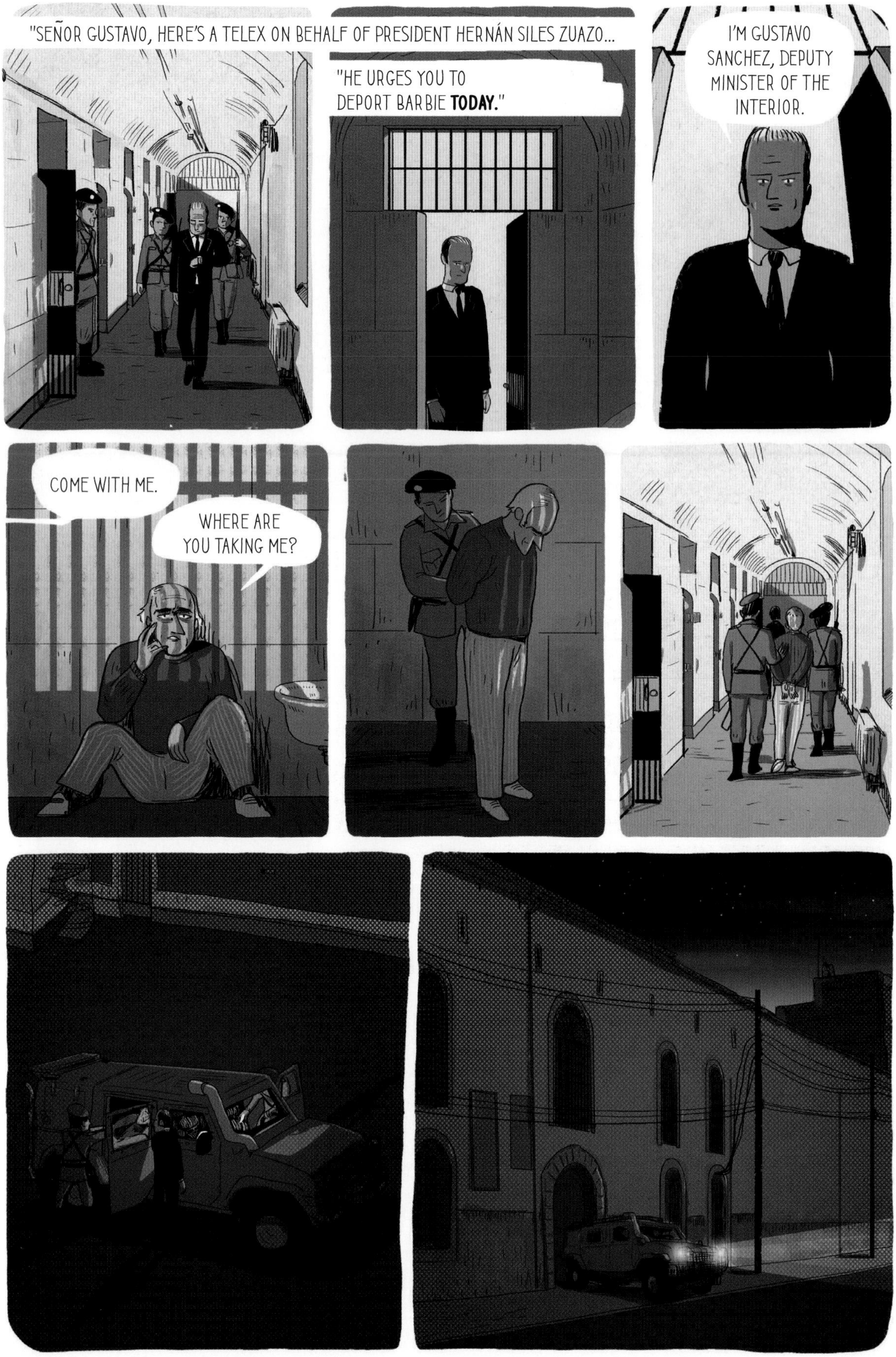
"SEÑOR GUSTAVO, HERE'S A TELEX ON BEHALF OF PRESIDENT HERNÁN SILES ZUAZO...
"HE URGES YOU TO DEPORT BARBIE **TODAY.**"
I'M GUSTAVO SANCHEZ, DEPUTY MINISTER OF THE INTERIOR.
COME WITH ME.
WHERE ARE YOU TAKING ME?

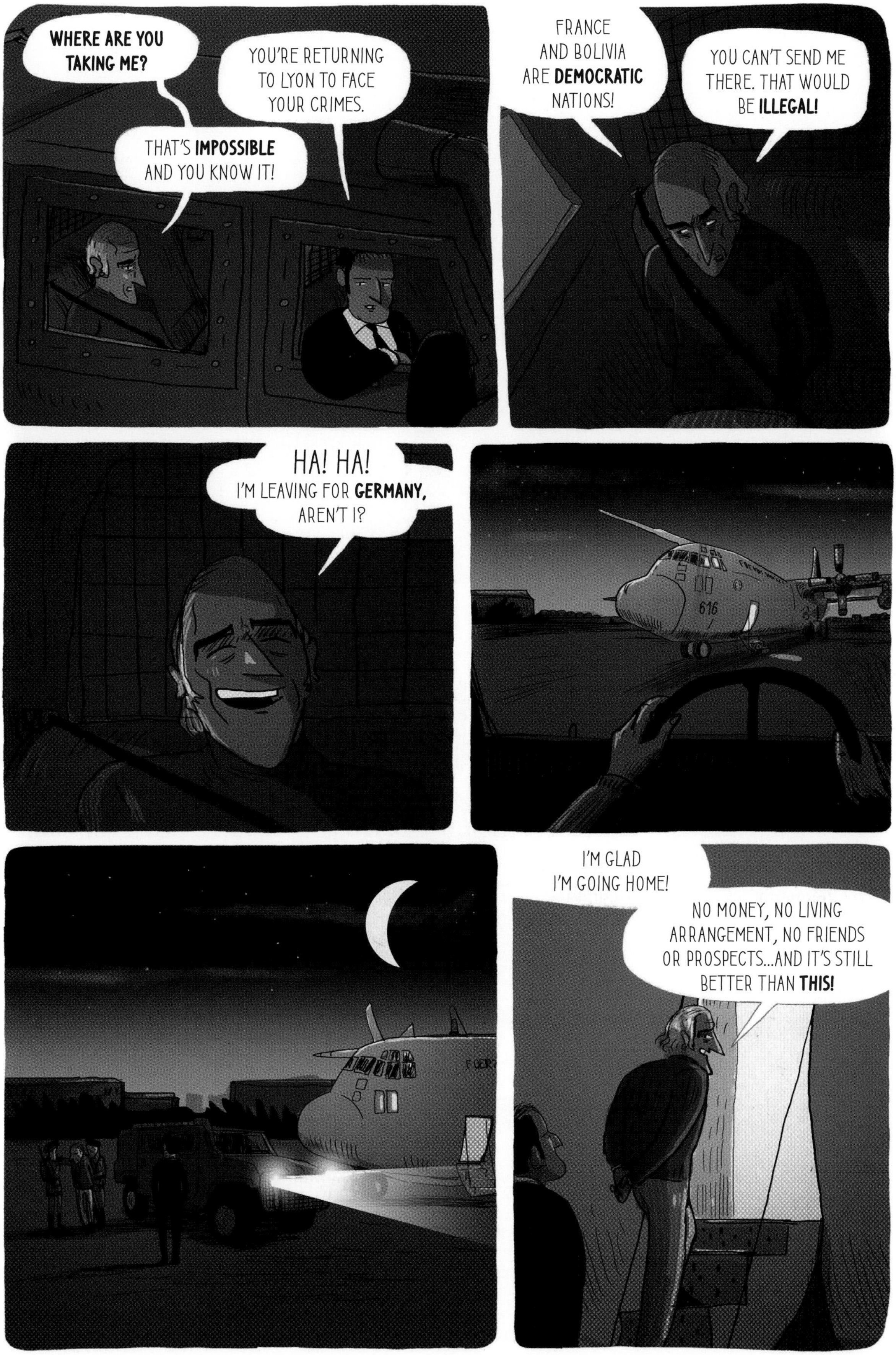

WHERE ARE YOU TAKING ME?
YOU'RE RETURNING TO LYON TO FACE YOUR CRIMES.
THAT'S **IMPOSSIBLE** AND YOU KNOW IT!
FRANCE AND BOLIVIA ARE **DEMOCRATIC** NATIONS!
YOU CAN'T SEND ME THERE. THAT WOULD BE **ILLEGAL!**
HA! HA!
I'M LEAVING FOR **GERMANY,** AREN'T I?
616
I'M GLAD I'M GOING HOME!
NO MONEY, NO LIVING ARRANGEMENT, NO FRIENDS OR PROSPECTS...AND IT'S STILL BETTER THAN **THIS!**

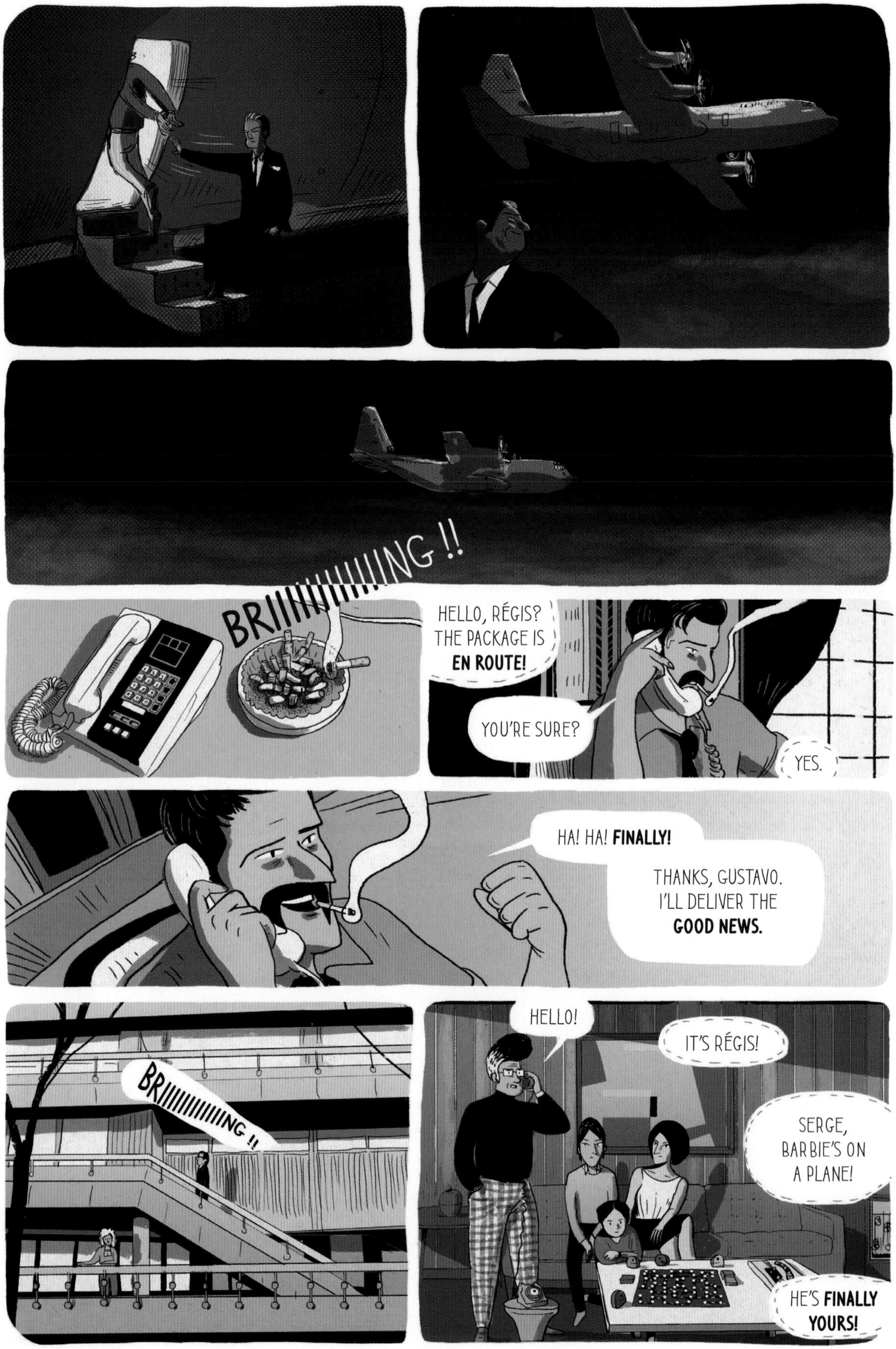
BRIIIIIIIIIIIIIIING !!
HELLO, RÉGIS? THE PACKAGE IS EN ROUTE!
YOU'RE SURE?
YES.
HA! HA! FINALLY!
THANKS, GUSTAVO. I'LL DELIVER THE GOOD NEWS.
BRIIIIIIIIIIIING !!
HELLO!
IT'S RÉGIS!
SERGE, BARBIE'S ON A PLANE!
HE'S FINALLY YOURS!

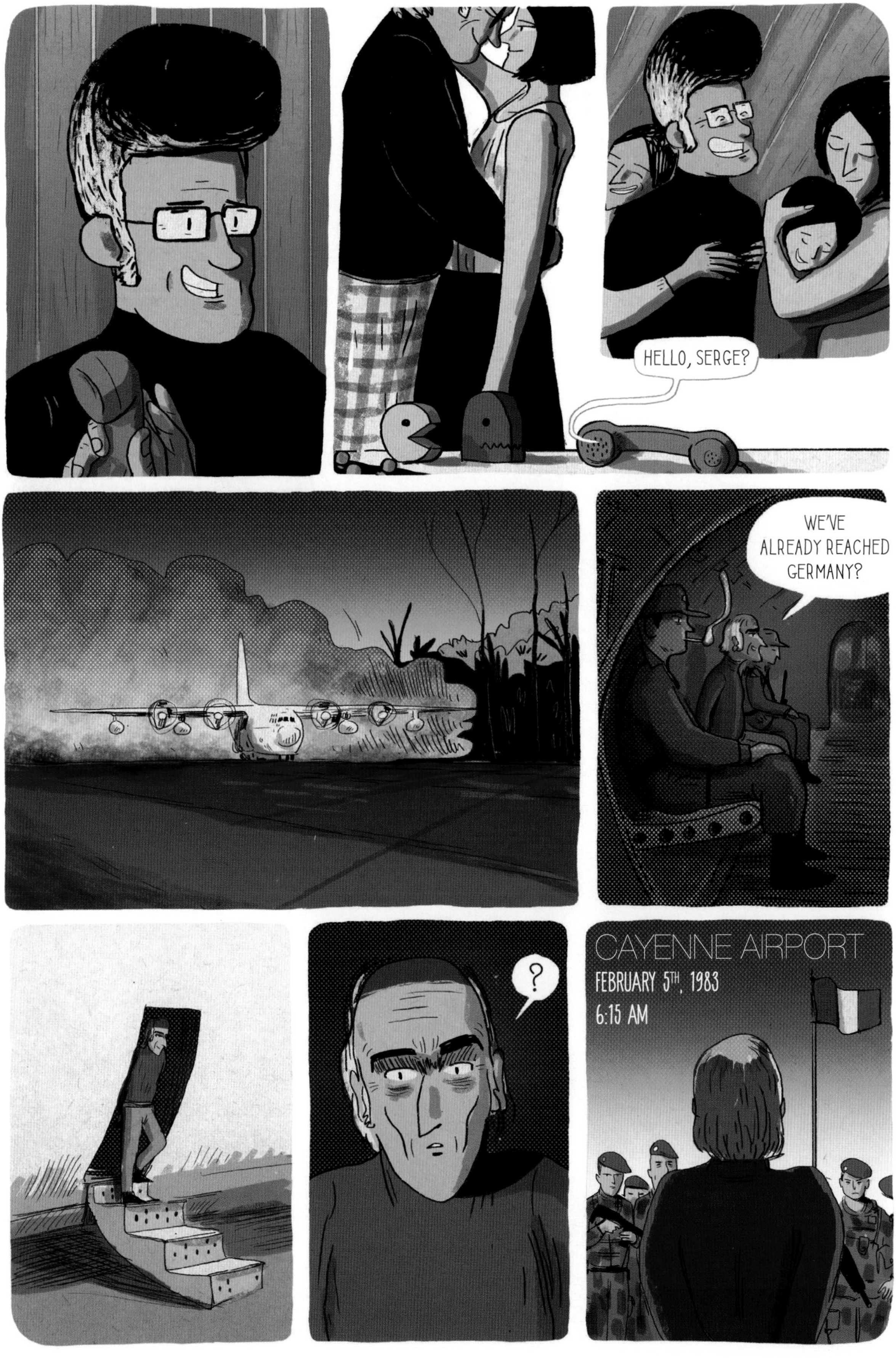
HELLO, SERGE?
WE'VE ALREADY REACHED GERMANY?
?
CAYENNE AIRPORT
FEBRUARY 5TH, 1983
6:15 AM

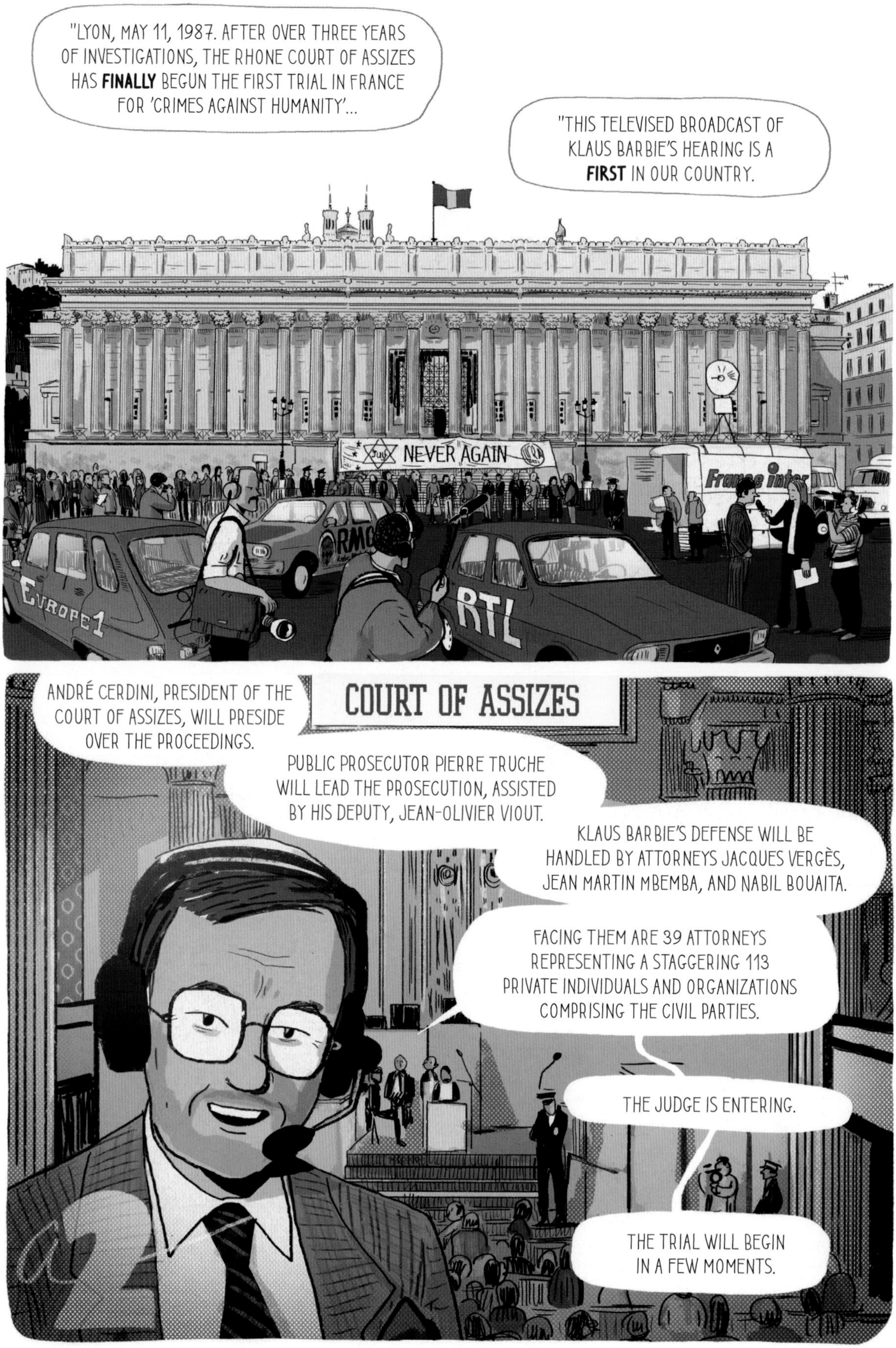
"LYON, MAY 11, 1987. AFTER OVER THREE YEARS OF INVESTIGATIONS, THE RHONE COURT OF ASSIZES HAS **FINALLY** BEGUN THE FIRST TRIAL IN FRANCE FOR 'CRIMES AGAINST HUMANITY'...
"THIS TELEVISED BROADCAST OF KLAUS BARBIE'S HEARING IS A **FIRST** IN OUR COUNTRY.
NEVER AGAIN
EUROPE 1
RTL
France inter
COURT OF ASSIZES
ANDRÉ CERDINI, PRESIDENT OF THE COURT OF ASSIZES, WILL PRESIDE OVER THE PROCEEDINGS.
PUBLIC PROSECUTOR PIERRE TRUCHE WILL LEAD THE PROSECUTION, ASSISTED BY HIS DEPUTY, JEAN-OLIVIER VIOUT.
KLAUS BARBIE'S DEFENSE WILL BE HANDLED BY ATTORNEYS JACQUES VERGÈS, JEAN MARTIN MBEMBA, AND NABIL BOUAITA.
FACING THEM ARE 39 ATTORNEYS REPRESENTING A STAGGERING 113 PRIVATE INDIVIDUALS AND ORGANIZATIONS COMPRISING THE CIVIL PARTIES.
THE JUDGE IS ENTERING.
THE TRIAL WILL BEGIN IN A FEW MOMENTS.

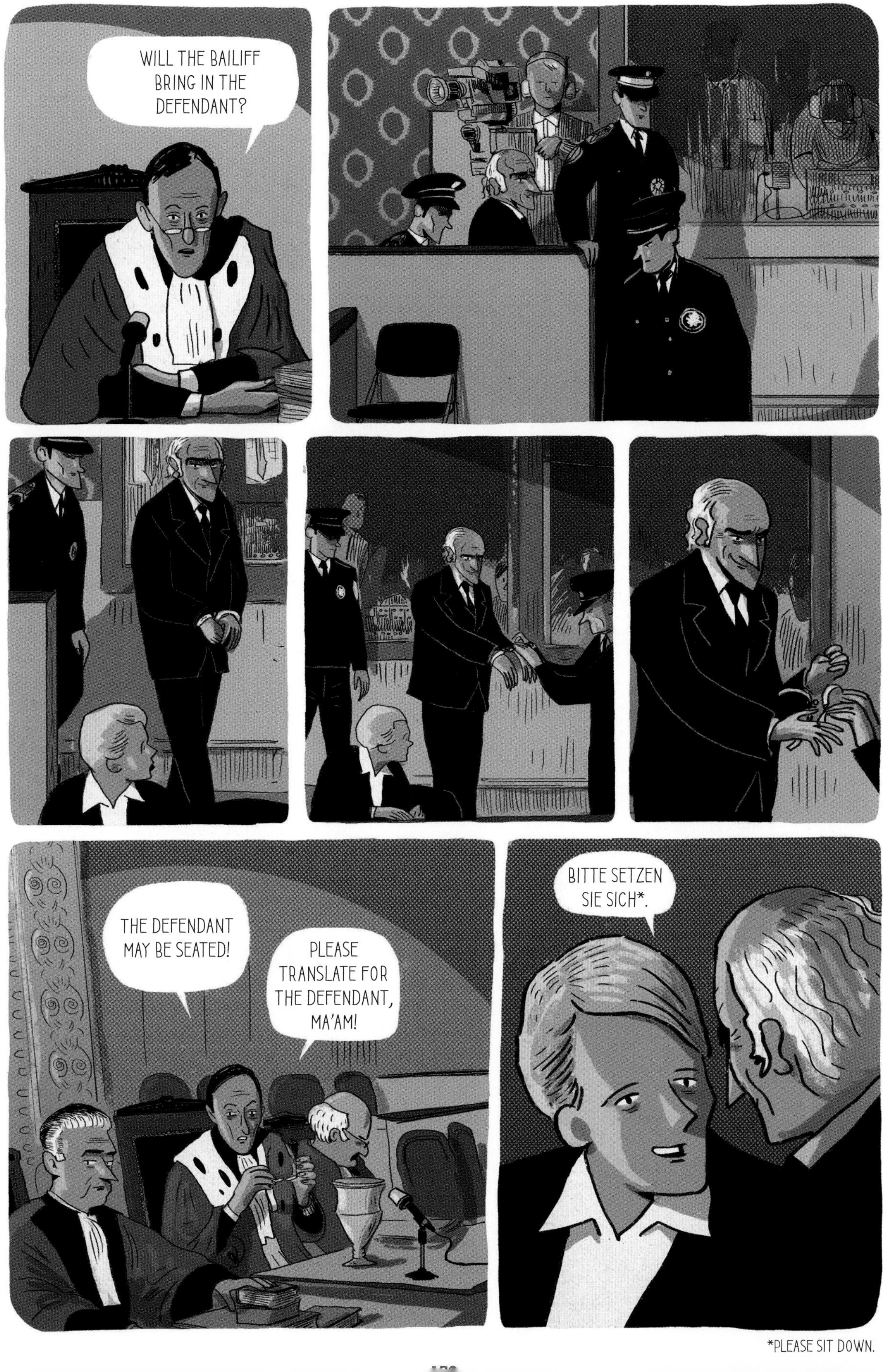
WILL THE BAILIFF BRING IN THE DEFENDANT?
THE DEFENDANT MAY BE SEATED!
PLEASE TRANSLATE FOR THE DEFENDANT, MA'AM!
BITTE SETZEN SIE SICH*.

*PLEASE SIT DOWN.

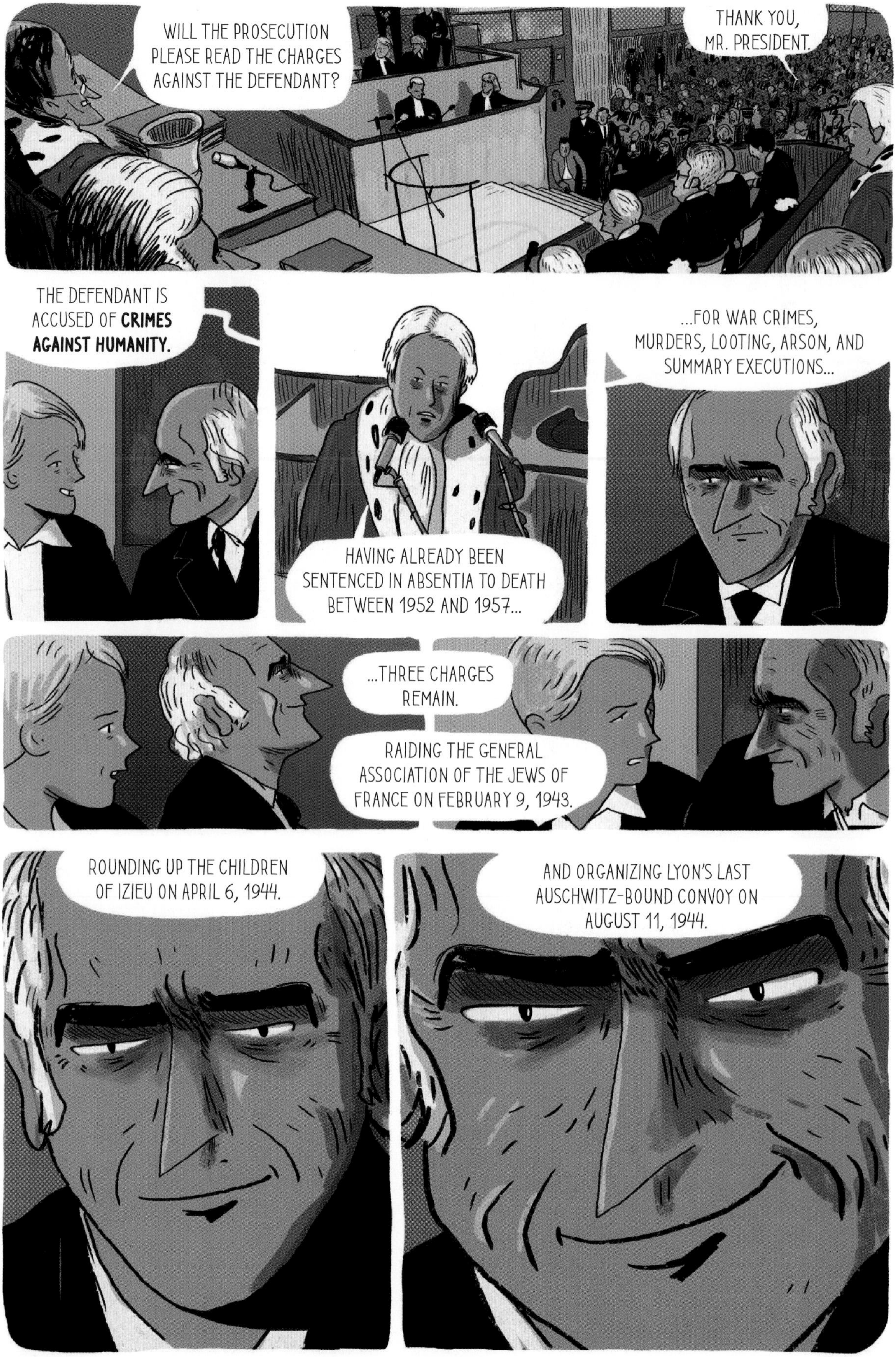
WILL THE PROSECUTION PLEASE READ THE CHARGES AGAINST THE DEFENDANT?
THANK YOU, MR. PRESIDENT.
THE DEFENDANT IS ACCUSED OF **CRIMES AGAINST HUMANITY.**
HAVING ALREADY BEEN SENTENCED IN ABSENTIA TO DEATH BETWEEN 1952 AND 1957...
...FOR WAR CRIMES, MURDERS, LOOTING, ARSON, AND SUMMARY EXECUTIONS...
...THREE CHARGES REMAIN.
RAIDING THE GENERAL ASSOCIATION OF THE JEWS OF FRANCE ON FEBRUARY 9, 1943.
ROUNDING UP THE CHILDREN OF IZIEU ON APRIL 6, 1944.
AND ORGANIZING LYON'S LAST AUSCHWITZ-BOUND CONVOY ON AUGUST 11, 1944.

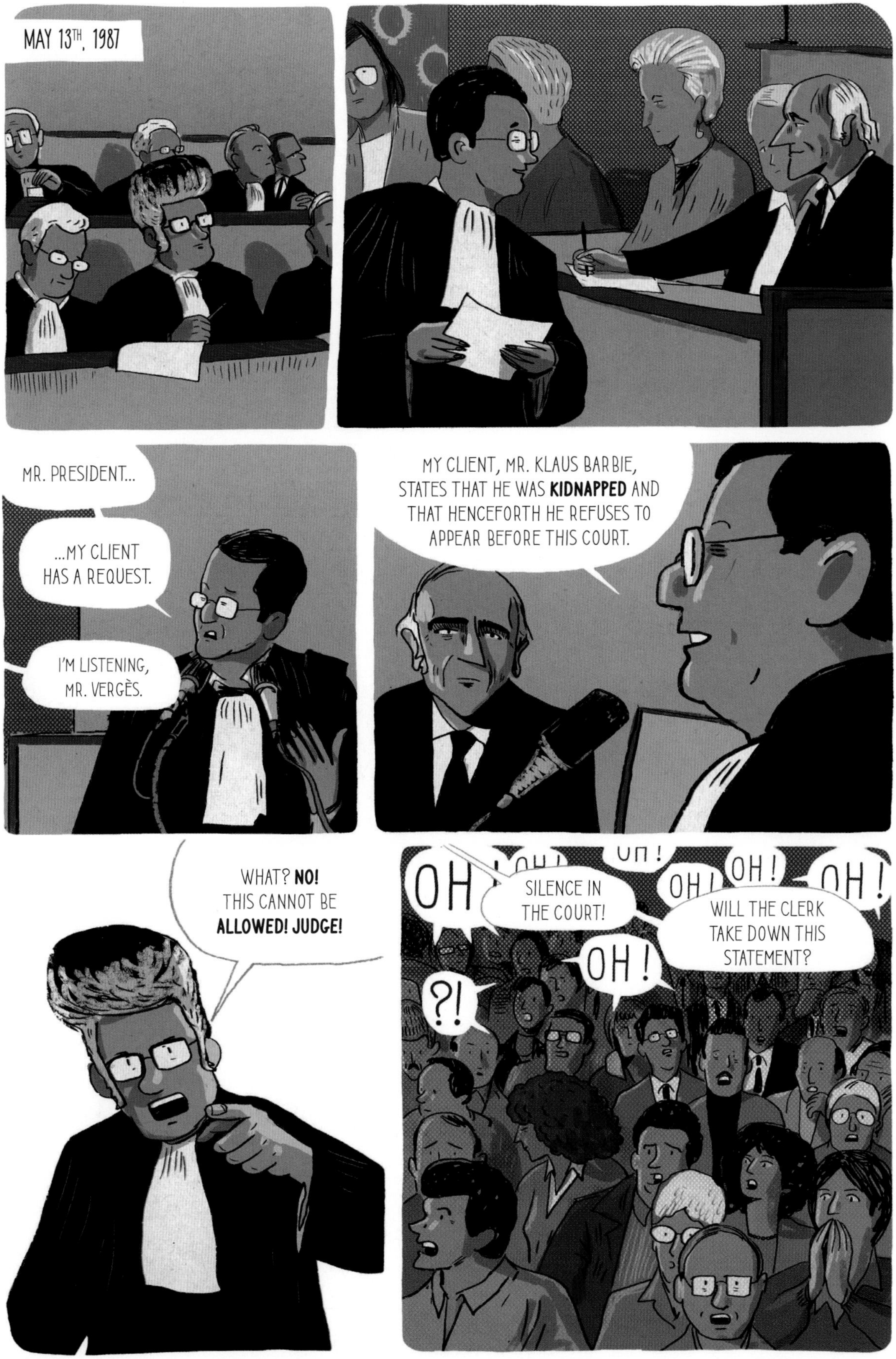

MAY 13TH, 1987
MR. PRESIDENT...
...MY CLIENT HAS A REQUEST.
I'M LISTENING, MR. VERGÈS.
MY CLIENT, MR. KLAUS BARBIE, STATES THAT HE WAS **KIDNAPPED** AND THAT HENCEFORTH HE REFUSES TO APPEAR BEFORE THIS COURT.
WHAT? **NO!** THIS CANNOT BE **ALLOWED! JUDGE!**
OH!
OH!
SILENCE IN THE COURT!
OH!
OH!
OH!
WILL THE CLERK TAKE DOWN THIS STATEMENT?
OH!
?!

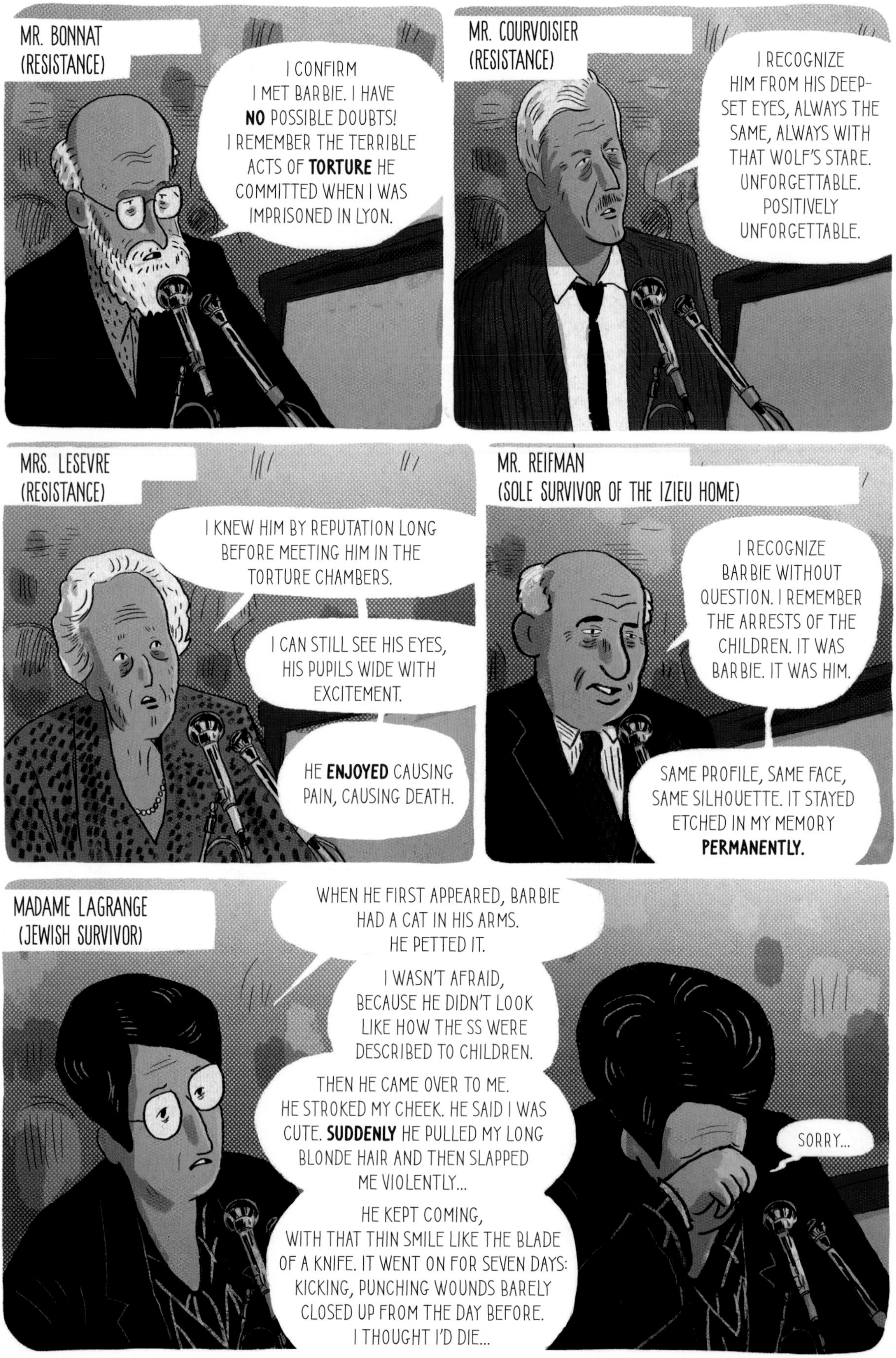
MR. BONNAT (RESISTANCE)
I CONFIRM I MET BARBIE. I HAVE **NO** POSSIBLE DOUBTS! I REMEMBER THE TERRIBLE ACTS OF **TORTURE** HE COMMITTED WHEN I WAS IMPRISONED IN LYON.
MR. COURVOISIER (RESISTANCE)
I RECOGNIZE HIM FROM HIS DEEP-SET EYES, ALWAYS THE SAME, ALWAYS WITH THAT WOLF'S STARE. UNFORGETTABLE. POSITIVELY UNFORGETTABLE.
MRS. LESEVRE (RESISTANCE)
I KNEW HIM BY REPUTATION LONG BEFORE MEETING HIM IN THE TORTURE CHAMBERS.
I CAN STILL SEE HIS EYES, HIS PUPILS WIDE WITH EXCITEMENT.
HE **ENJOYED** CAUSING PAIN, CAUSING DEATH.
MR. REIFMAN (SOLE SURVIVOR OF THE IZIEU HOME)
I RECOGNIZE BARBIE WITHOUT QUESTION. I REMEMBER THE ARRESTS OF THE CHILDREN. IT WAS BARBIE. IT WAS HIM.
SAME PROFILE, SAME FACE, SAME SILHOUETTE. IT STAYED ETCHED IN MY MEMORY **PERMANENTLY.**
MADAME LAGRANGE (JEWISH SURVIVOR)
WHEN HE FIRST APPEARED, BARBIE HAD A CAT IN HIS ARMS. HE PETTED IT.
I WASN'T AFRAID, BECAUSE HE DIDN'T LOOK LIKE HOW THE SS WERE DESCRIBED TO CHILDREN.
THEN HE CAME OVER TO ME. HE STROKED MY CHEEK. HE SAID I WAS CUTE. **SUDDENLY** HE PULLED MY LONG BLONDE HAIR AND THEN SLAPPED ME VIOLENTLY...
HE KEPT COMING, WITH THAT THIN SMILE LIKE THE BLADE OF A KNIFE. IT WENT ON FOR SEVEN DAYS: KICKING, PUNCHING WOUNDS BARELY CLOSED UP FROM THE DAY BEFORE. I THOUGHT I'D DIE...
SORRY...

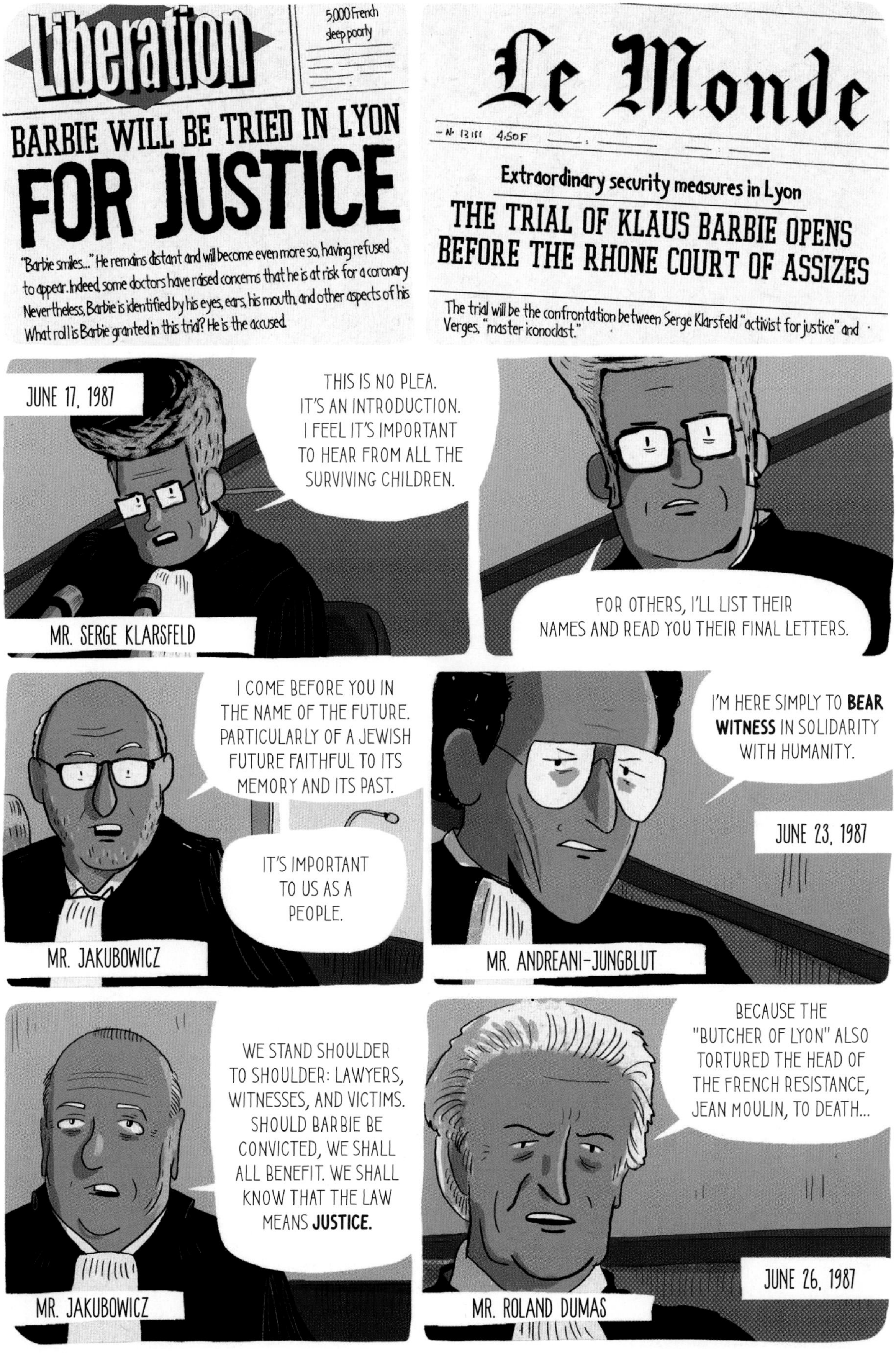

Liberation
5,000 French sleep poorly
BARBIE WILL BE TRIED IN LYON
FOR JUSTICE
"Barbie smiles..." He remains distant and will become even more so, having refused to appear. Indeed, some doctors have raised concerns that he is at risk for a coronary Nevertheless, Barbie is identified by his eyes, ears, his mouth, and other aspects of his What roll is Barbie granted in this trial? He is the accused.
Le Monde
Extraordinary security measures in Lyon
THE TRIAL OF KLAUS BARBIE OPENS BEFORE THE RHONE COURT OF ASSIZES
The trial will be the confrontation between Serge Klarsfeld "activist for justice" and Verges, "master iconoclast."
JUNE 17, 1987
THIS IS NO PLEA. IT'S AN INTRODUCTION. I FEEL IT'S IMPORTANT TO HEAR FROM ALL THE SURVIVING CHILDREN.
MR. SERGE KLARSFELD
FOR OTHERS, I'LL LIST THEIR NAMES AND READ YOU THEIR FINAL LETTERS.
I COME BEFORE YOU IN THE NAME OF THE FUTURE. PARTICULARLY OF A JEWISH FUTURE FAITHFUL TO ITS MEMORY AND ITS PAST.
IT'S IMPORTANT TO US AS A PEOPLE.
MR. JAKUBOWICZ
I'M HERE SIMPLY TO **BEAR WITNESS** IN SOLIDARITY WITH HUMANITY.
JUNE 23, 1987
MR. ANDREANI-JUNGBLUT
WE STAND SHOULDER TO SHOULDER: LAWYERS, WITNESSES, AND VICTIMS. SHOULD BARBIE BE CONVICTED, WE SHALL ALL BENEFIT. WE SHALL KNOW THAT THE LAW MEANS **JUSTICE.**
MR. JAKUBOWICZ
BECAUSE THE "BUTCHER OF LYON" ALSO TORTURED THE HEAD OF THE FRENCH RESISTANCE, JEAN MOULIN, TO DEATH...
JUNE 26, 1987
MR. ROLAND DUMAS

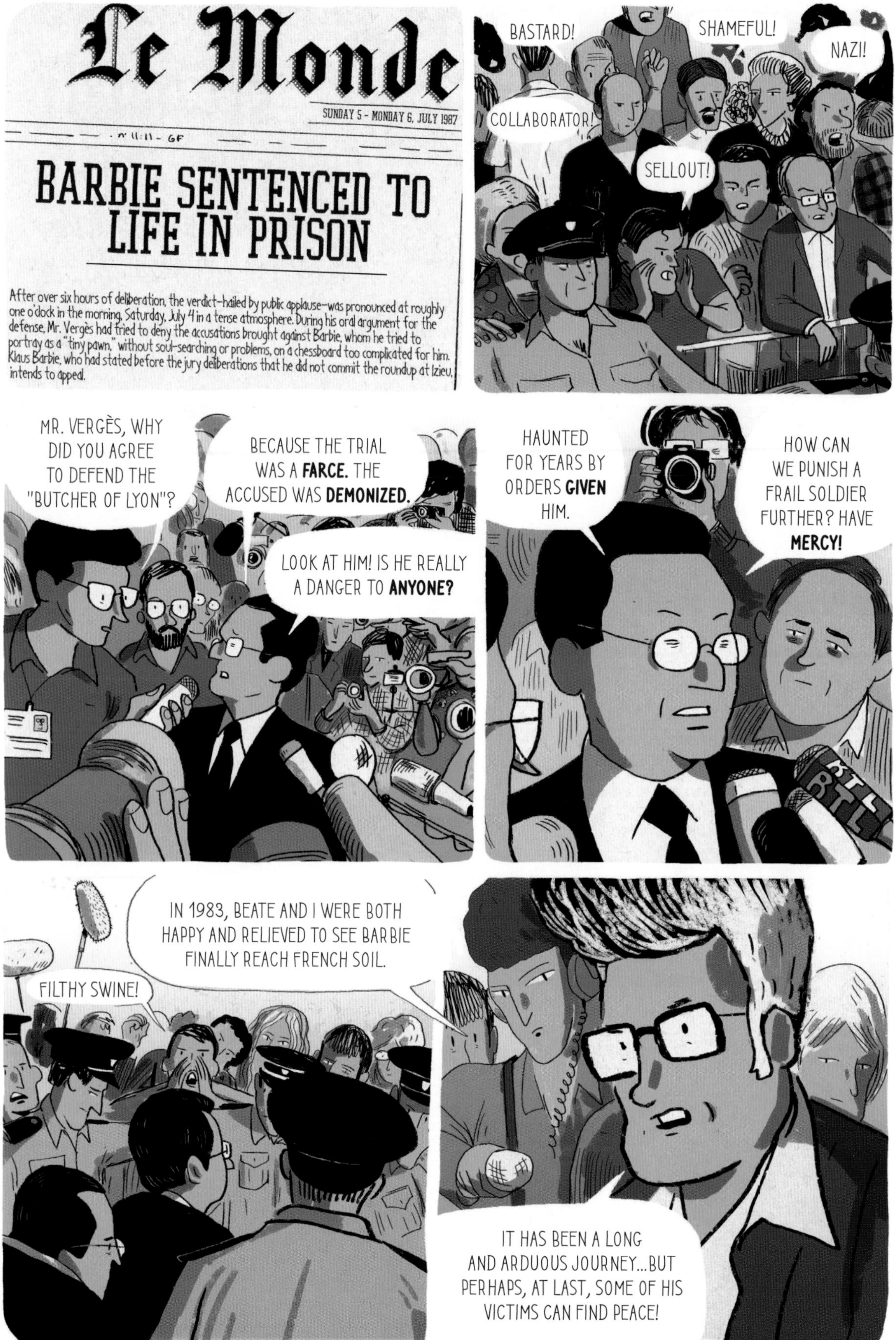
Le Monde
SUNDAY 5 - MONDAY 6, JULY 1987
BARBIE SENTENCED TO LIFE IN PRISON
After over six hours of deliberation, the verdict—hailed by public applause—was pronounced at roughly one o'clock in the morning, Saturday, July 4 in a tense atmosphere. During his oral argument for the defense, Mr. Vergès had tried to deny the accusations brought against Barbie, whom he tried to portray as a "tiny pawn," without soul-searching or problems, on a chessboard too complicated for him. Klaus Barbie, who had stated before the jury deliberations that he did not commit the roundup at Izieu, intends to appeal.
BASTARD!
SHAMEFUL!
NAZI!
COLLABORATOR!
SELLOUT!
MR. VERGÈS, WHY DID YOU AGREE TO DEFEND THE "BUTCHER OF LYON"?
BECAUSE THE TRIAL WAS A FARCE. THE ACCUSED WAS DEMONIZED.
LOOK AT HIM! IS HE REALLY A DANGER TO ANYONE?
HAUNTED FOR YEARS BY ORDERS GIVEN HIM.
HOW CAN WE PUNISH A FRAIL SOLDIER FURTHER? HAVE MERCY!
RTL
IN 1983, BEATE AND I WERE BOTH HAPPY AND RELIEVED TO SEE BARBIE FINALLY REACH FRENCH SOIL.
FILTHY SWINE!
IT HAS BEEN A LONG AND ARDUOUS JOURNEY...BUT PERHAPS, AT LAST, SOME OF HIS VICTIMS CAN FIND PEACE!

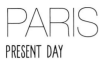

PARIS

PRESENT DAY

SO VERGÈS TRIED TO ARGUE THAT BARBIE'S ACTIONS WERE NO WORSE THAN THE SUPPOSEDLY ORDINARY ACTIONS OF COLONIALISTS WORLDWIDE, AND THAT HIS TRIAL WAS TANTAMOUNT TO SELECTIVE PROSECUTION.

BUT BY SETTING A JUDICIAL AND HISTORIC PRECEDENT, THE BARBIE CASE CAME TO DEFINE SPECIFICALLY WHAT THE ACCUSATION "CRIMES AGAINST HUMANITY" REALLY MEANT. IT LAID BARE BEFORE AN ENRAGED PUBLIC, IN HORRIFIC DETAIL, THE ATROCITIES THAT THE NAZIS HAD COMMITTED.

THE COURT REJECTED THE DEFENSE'S ARGUMENT. ON JULY 4TH 1987, BARBIE WAS CONVICTED AND SENTENCED TO LIFE IMPRISONMENT. THE HIGHLY PUBLICIZED VERDICT MEANT THAT THIS TRIAL--BY RENDERING JUSTICE TO THE VICTIMS OF THE BUTCHER OF LYON--RAISED AWARENESS OF OUR CAUSE TO THE FRENCH AND TO INTERNATIONAL SOCIETY.

BARBIE AND HIS ATTORNEYS NEVER REACHED ANY SUCCESSFUL APPEAL.

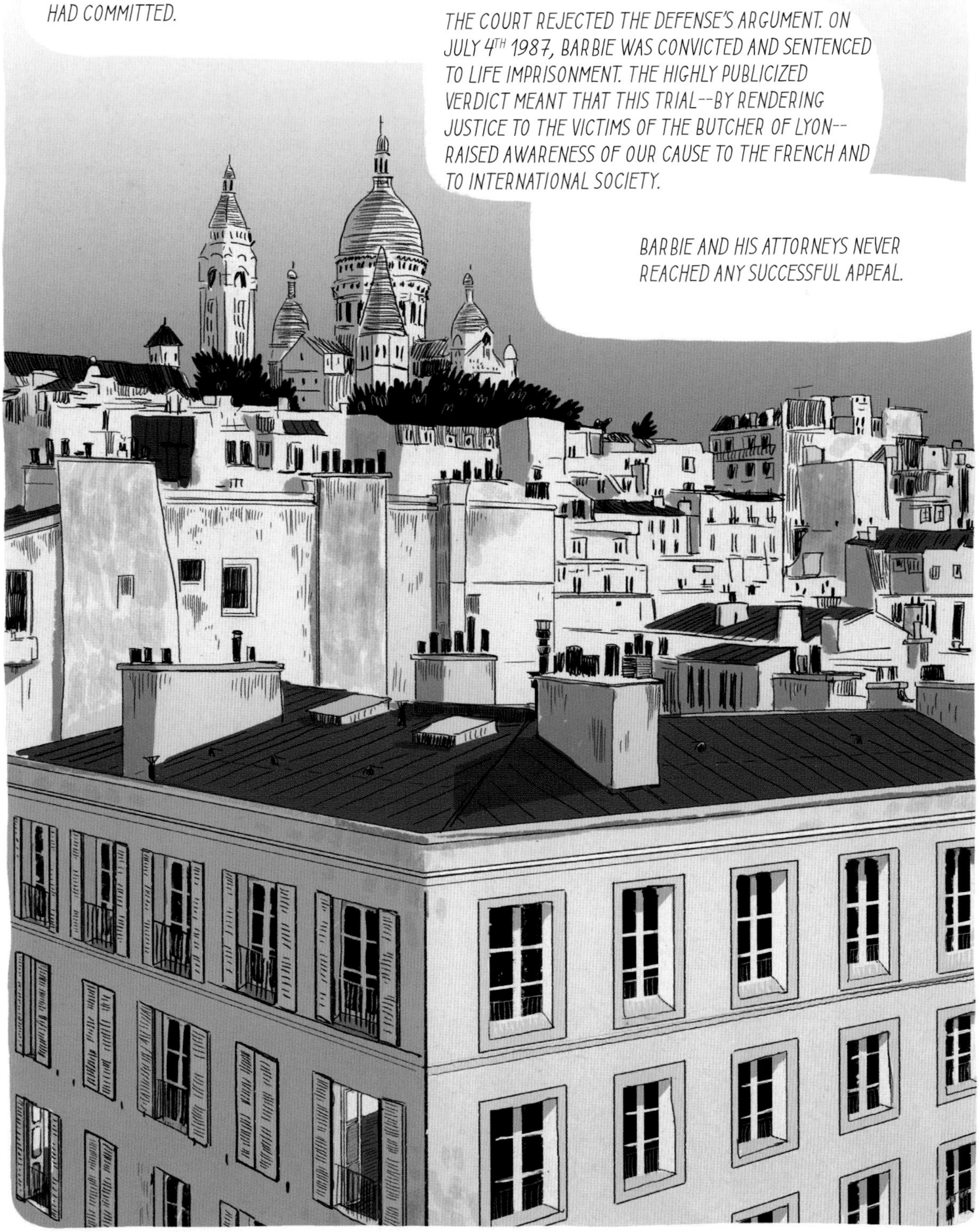

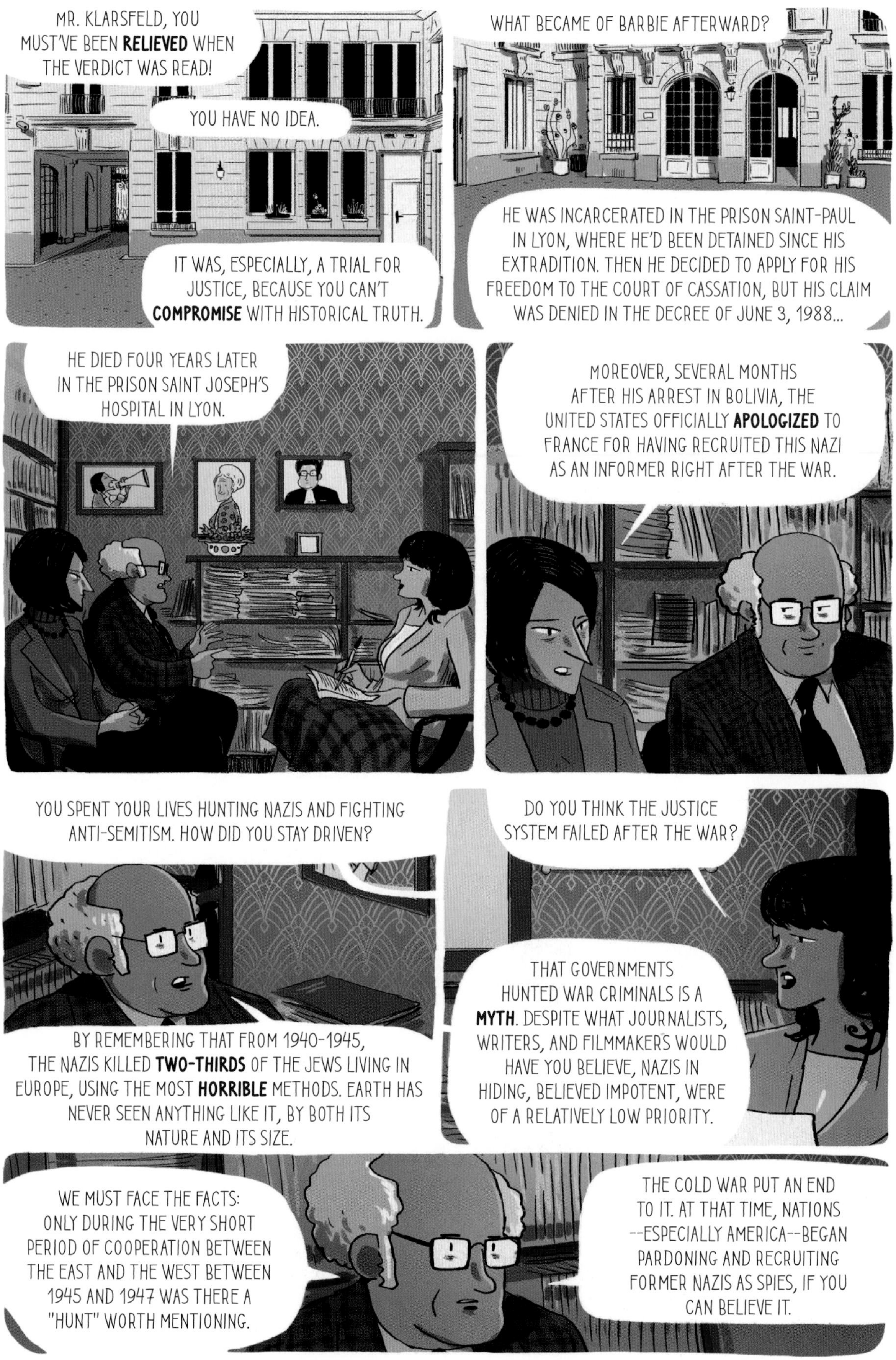

MR. KLARSFELD, YOU MUST'VE BEEN **RELIEVED** WHEN THE VERDICT WAS READ!
YOU HAVE NO IDEA.
IT WAS, ESPECIALLY, A TRIAL FOR JUSTICE, BECAUSE YOU CAN'T **COMPROMISE** WITH HISTORICAL TRUTH.
WHAT BECAME OF BARBIE AFTERWARD?
HE WAS INCARCERATED IN THE PRISON SAINT-PAUL IN LYON, WHERE HE'D BEEN DETAINED SINCE HIS EXTRADITION. THEN HE DECIDED TO APPLY FOR HIS FREEDOM TO THE COURT OF CASSATION, BUT HIS CLAIM WAS DENIED IN THE DECREE OF JUNE 3, 1988...
HE DIED FOUR YEARS LATER IN THE PRISON SAINT JOSEPH'S HOSPITAL IN LYON.
MOREOVER, SEVERAL MONTHS AFTER HIS ARREST IN BOLIVIA, THE UNITED STATES OFFICIALLY **APOLOGIZED** TO FRANCE FOR HAVING RECRUITED THIS NAZI AS AN INFORMER RIGHT AFTER THE WAR.
YOU SPENT YOUR LIVES HUNTING NAZIS AND FIGHTING ANTI-SEMITISM. HOW DID YOU STAY DRIVEN?
BY REMEMBERING THAT FROM 1940-1945, THE NAZIS KILLED **TWO-THIRDS** OF THE JEWS LIVING IN EUROPE, USING THE MOST **HORRIBLE** METHODS. EARTH HAS NEVER SEEN ANYTHING LIKE IT, BY BOTH ITS NATURE AND ITS SIZE.
DO YOU THINK THE JUSTICE SYSTEM FAILED AFTER THE WAR?
THAT GOVERNMENTS HUNTED WAR CRIMINALS IS A **MYTH**. DESPITE WHAT JOURNALISTS, WRITERS, AND FILMMAKERS WOULD HAVE YOU BELIEVE, NAZIS IN HIDING, BELIEVED IMPOTENT, WERE OF A RELATIVELY LOW PRIORITY.
WE MUST FACE THE FACTS: ONLY DURING THE VERY SHORT PERIOD OF COOPERATION BETWEEN THE EAST AND THE WEST BETWEEN 1945 AND 1947 WAS THERE A "HUNT" WORTH MENTIONING.
THE COLD WAR PUT AN END TO IT. AT THAT TIME, NATIONS --ESPECIALLY AMERICA--BEGAN PARDONING AND RECRUITING FORMER NAZIS AS SPIES, IF YOU CAN BELIEVE IT.

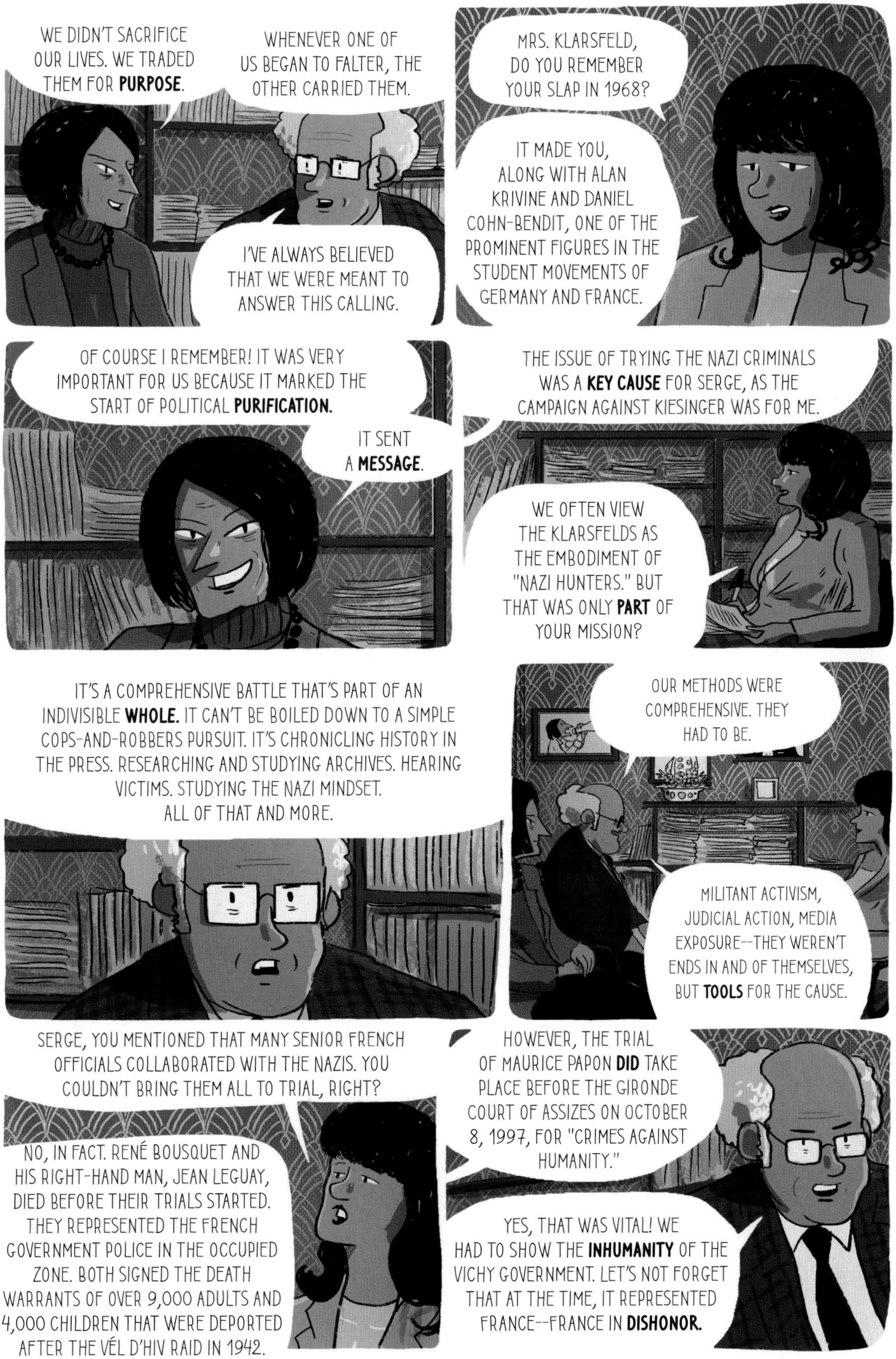
WE DIDN'T SACRIFICE OUR LIVES. WE TRADED THEM FOR PURPOSE.
WHENEVER ONE OF US BEGAN TO FALTER, THE OTHER CARRIED THEM.
I'VE ALWAYS BELIEVED THAT WE WERE MEANT TO ANSWER THIS CALLING.
MRS. KLARSFELD, DO YOU REMEMBER YOUR SLAP IN 1968?
IT MADE YOU, ALONG WITH ALAN KRIVINE AND DANIEL COHN-BENDIT, ONE OF THE PROMINENT FIGURES IN THE STUDENT MOVEMENTS OF GERMANY AND FRANCE.
OF COURSE I REMEMBER! IT WAS VERY IMPORTANT FOR US BECAUSE IT MARKED THE START OF POLITICAL PURIFICATION.
IT SENT A MESSAGE.
THE ISSUE OF TRYING THE NAZI CRIMINALS WAS A KEY CAUSE FOR SERGE, AS THE CAMPAIGN AGAINST KIESINGER WAS FOR ME.
WE OFTEN VIEW THE KLARSFELDS AS THE EMBODIMENT OF "NAZI HUNTERS." BUT THAT WAS ONLY PART OF YOUR MISSION?
IT'S A COMPREHENSIVE BATTLE THAT'S PART OF AN INDIVISIBLE WHOLE. IT CAN'T BE BOILED DOWN TO A SIMPLE COPS-AND-ROBBERS PURSUIT. IT'S CHRONICLING HISTORY IN THE PRESS. RESEARCHING AND STUDYING ARCHIVES. HEARING VICTIMS. STUDYING THE NAZI MINDSET. ALL OF THAT AND MORE.
OUR METHODS WERE COMPREHENSIVE. THEY HAD TO BE.
MILITANT ACTIVISM, JUDICIAL ACTION, MEDIA EXPOSURE--THEY WEREN'T ENDS IN AND OF THEMSELVES, BUT TOOLS FOR THE CAUSE.
SERGE, YOU MENTIONED THAT MANY SENIOR FRENCH OFFICIALS COLLABORATED WITH THE NAZIS. YOU COULDN'T BRING THEM ALL TO TRIAL, RIGHT?
NO, IN FACT. RENÉ BOUSQUET AND HIS RIGHT-HAND MAN, JEAN LEGUAY, DIED BEFORE THEIR TRIALS STARTED. THEY REPRESENTED THE FRENCH GOVERNMENT POLICE IN THE OCCUPIED ZONE. BOTH SIGNED THE DEATH WARRANTS OF OVER 9,000 ADULTS AND 4,000 CHILDREN THAT WERE DEPORTED AFTER THE VÉL D'HIV RAID IN 1942.
HOWEVER, THE TRIAL OF MAURICE PAPON DID TAKE PLACE BEFORE THE GIRONDE COURT OF ASSIZES ON OCTOBER 8, 1997, FOR "CRIMES AGAINST HUMANITY."
YES, THAT WAS VITAL! WE HAD TO SHOW THE INHUMANITY OF THE VICHY GOVERNMENT. LET'S NOT FORGET THAT AT THE TIME, IT REPRESENTED FRANCE--FRANCE IN DISHONOR.

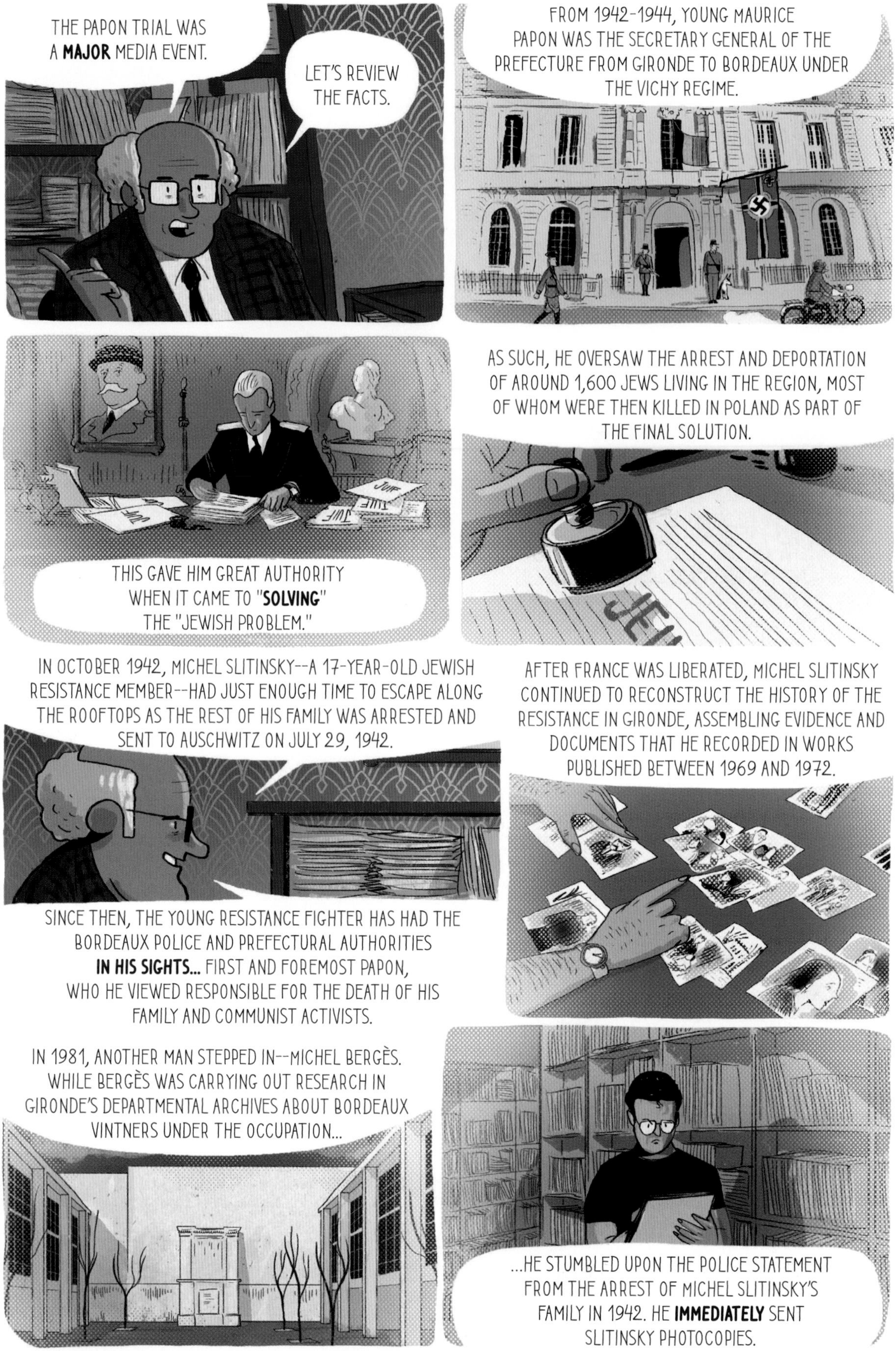
THE PAPON TRIAL WAS A **MAJOR** MEDIA EVENT.
LET'S REVIEW THE FACTS.
FROM 1942-1944, YOUNG MAURICE PAPON WAS THE SECRETARY GENERAL OF THE PREFECTURE FROM GIRONDE TO BORDEAUX UNDER THE VICHY REGIME.
JUIF
THIS GAVE HIM GREAT AUTHORITY WHEN IT CAME TO "**SOLVING**" THE "JEWISH PROBLEM."
AS SUCH, HE OVERSAW THE ARREST AND DEPORTATION OF AROUND 1,600 JEWS LIVING IN THE REGION, MOST OF WHOM WERE THEN KILLED IN POLAND AS PART OF THE FINAL SOLUTION.
IN OCTOBER 1942, MICHEL SLITINSKY--A 17-YEAR-OLD JEWISH RESISTANCE MEMBER--HAD JUST ENOUGH TIME TO ESCAPE ALONG THE ROOFTOPS AS THE REST OF HIS FAMILY WAS ARRESTED AND SENT TO AUSCHWITZ ON JULY 29, 1942.
SINCE THEN, THE YOUNG RESISTANCE FIGHTER HAS HAD THE BORDEAUX POLICE AND PREFECTURAL AUTHORITIES **IN HIS SIGHTS...** FIRST AND FOREMOST PAPON, WHO HE VIEWED RESPONSIBLE FOR THE DEATH OF HIS FAMILY AND COMMUNIST ACTIVISTS.
AFTER FRANCE WAS LIBERATED, MICHEL SLITINSKY CONTINUED TO RECONSTRUCT THE HISTORY OF THE RESISTANCE IN GIRONDE, ASSEMBLING EVIDENCE AND DOCUMENTS THAT HE RECORDED IN WORKS PUBLISHED BETWEEN 1969 AND 1972.
IN 1981, ANOTHER MAN STEPPED IN--MICHEL BERGÈS. WHILE BERGÈS WAS CARRYING OUT RESEARCH IN GIRONDE'S DEPARTMENTAL ARCHIVES ABOUT BORDEAUX VINTNERS UNDER THE OCCUPATION...
...HE STUMBLED UPON THE POLICE STATEMENT FROM THE ARREST OF MICHEL SLITINSKY'S FAMILY IN 1942. HE **IMMEDIATELY** SENT SLITINSKY PHOTOCOPIES.

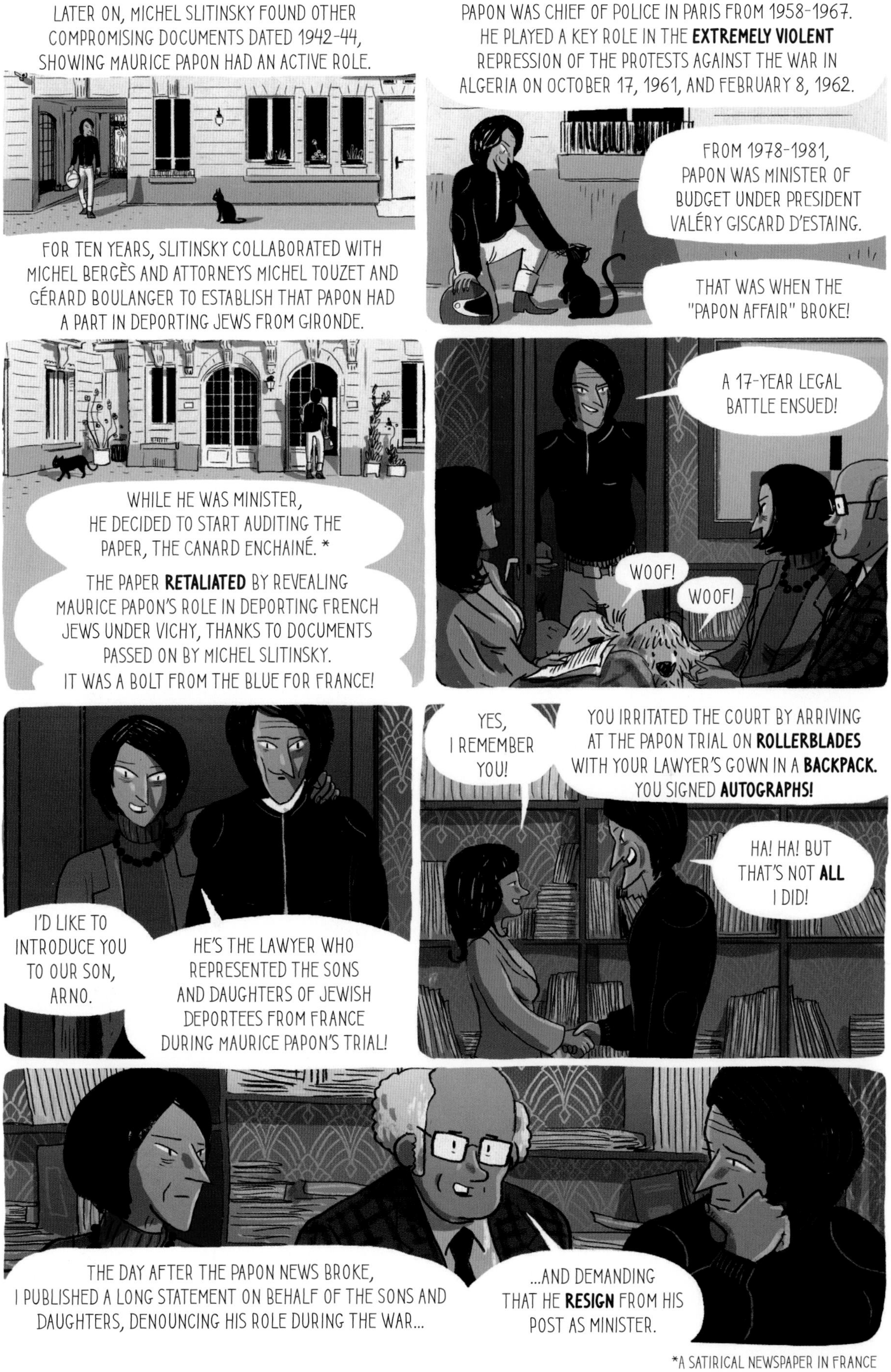
LATER ON, MICHEL SLITINSKY FOUND OTHER COMPROMISING DOCUMENTS DATED 1942-44, SHOWING MAURICE PAPON HAD AN ACTIVE ROLE.
FOR TEN YEARS, SLITINSKY COLLABORATED WITH MICHEL BERGÈS AND ATTORNEYS MICHEL TOUZET AND GÉRARD BOULANGER TO ESTABLISH THAT PAPON HAD A PART IN DEPORTING JEWS FROM GIRONDE.
PAPON WAS CHIEF OF POLICE IN PARIS FROM 1958-1967. HE PLAYED A KEY ROLE IN THE **EXTREMELY VIOLENT** REPRESSION OF THE PROTESTS AGAINST THE WAR IN ALGERIA ON OCTOBER 17, 1961, AND FEBRUARY 8, 1962.
FROM 1978-1981, PAPON WAS MINISTER OF BUDGET UNDER PRESIDENT VALÉRY GISCARD D'ESTAING.
THAT WAS WHEN THE "PAPON AFFAIR" BROKE!
WHILE HE WAS MINISTER, HE DECIDED TO START AUDITING THE PAPER, THE CANARD ENCHAINÉ. *
THE PAPER **RETALIATED** BY REVEALING MAURICE PAPON'S ROLE IN DEPORTING FRENCH JEWS UNDER VICHY, THANKS TO DOCUMENTS PASSED ON BY MICHEL SLITINSKY. IT WAS A BOLT FROM THE BLUE FOR FRANCE!
A 17-YEAR LEGAL BATTLE ENSUED!
WOOF!
WOOF!
I'D LIKE TO INTRODUCE YOU TO OUR SON, ARNO.
HE'S THE LAWYER WHO REPRESENTED THE SONS AND DAUGHTERS OF JEWISH DEPORTEES FROM FRANCE DURING MAURICE PAPON'S TRIAL!
YES, I REMEMBER YOU!
YOU IRRITATED THE COURT BY ARRIVING AT THE PAPON TRIAL ON **ROLLERBLADES** WITH YOUR LAWYER'S GOWN IN A **BACKPACK.** YOU SIGNED **AUTOGRAPHS!**
HA! HA! BUT THAT'S NOT **ALL** I DID!
THE DAY AFTER THE PAPON NEWS BROKE, I PUBLISHED A LONG STATEMENT ON BEHALF OF THE SONS AND DAUGHTERS, DENOUNCING HIS ROLE DURING THE WAR...
...AND DEMANDING THAT HE **RESIGN** FROM HIS POST AS MINISTER.

*A SATIRICAL NEWSPAPER IN FRANCE

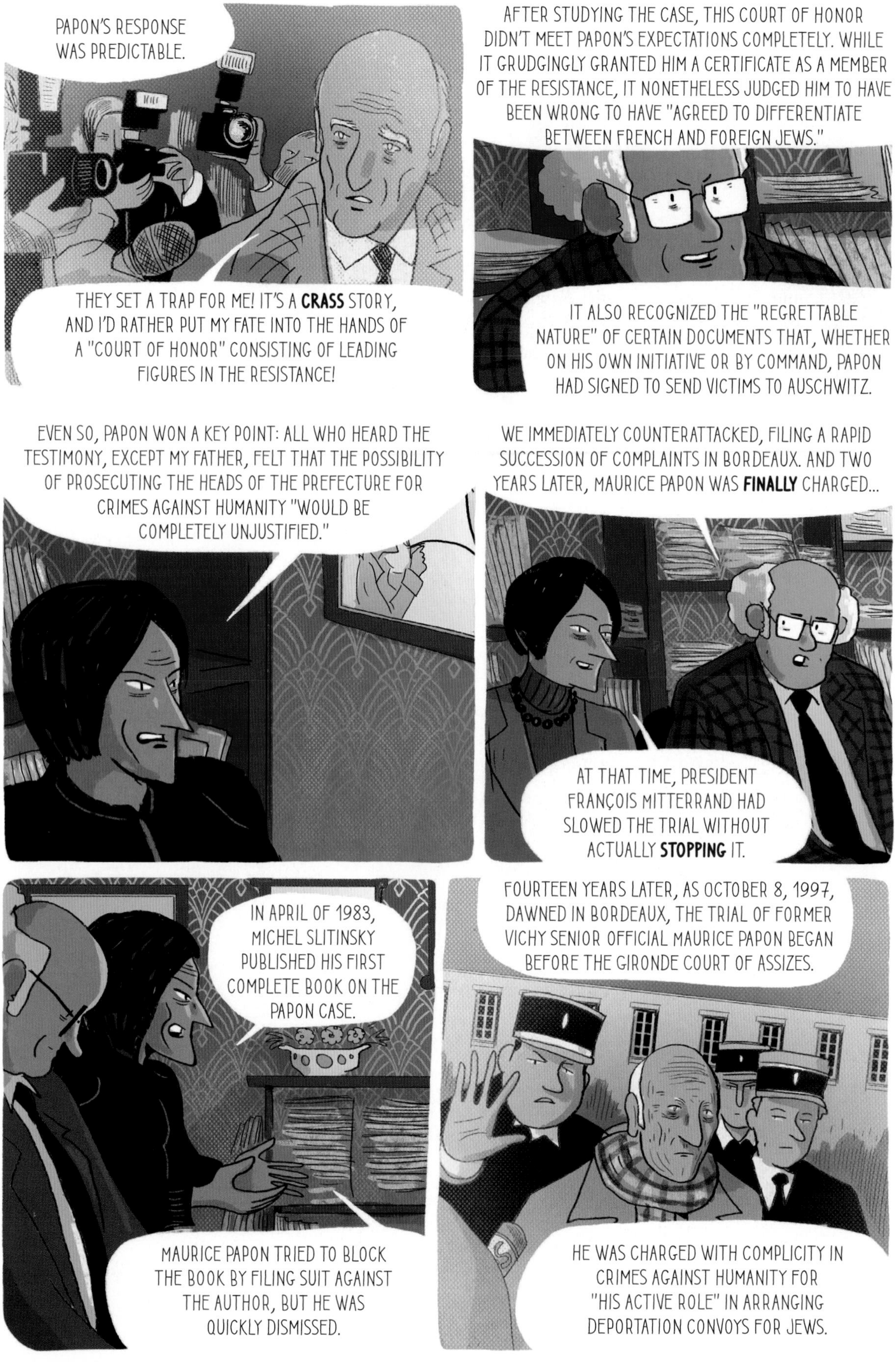
PAPON'S RESPONSE WAS PREDICTABLE.
THEY SET A TRAP FOR ME! IT'S A **CRASS** STORY, AND I'D RATHER PUT MY FATE INTO THE HANDS OF A "COURT OF HONOR" CONSISTING OF LEADING FIGURES IN THE RESISTANCE!
AFTER STUDYING THE CASE, THIS COURT OF HONOR DIDN'T MEET PAPON'S EXPECTATIONS COMPLETELY. WHILE IT GRUDGINGLY GRANTED HIM A CERTIFICATE AS A MEMBER OF THE RESISTANCE, IT NONETHELESS JUDGED HIM TO HAVE BEEN WRONG TO HAVE "AGREED TO DIFFERENTIATE BETWEEN FRENCH AND FOREIGN JEWS."
IT ALSO RECOGNIZED THE "REGRETTABLE NATURE" OF CERTAIN DOCUMENTS THAT, WHETHER ON HIS OWN INITIATIVE OR BY COMMAND, PAPON HAD SIGNED TO SEND VICTIMS TO AUSCHWITZ.
EVEN SO, PAPON WON A KEY POINT: ALL WHO HEARD THE TESTIMONY, EXCEPT MY FATHER, FELT THAT THE POSSIBILITY OF PROSECUTING THE HEADS OF THE PREFECTURE FOR CRIMES AGAINST HUMANITY "WOULD BE COMPLETELY UNJUSTIFIED."
WE IMMEDIATELY COUNTERATTACKED, FILING A RAPID SUCCESSION OF COMPLAINTS IN BORDEAUX. AND TWO YEARS LATER, MAURICE PAPON WAS **FINALLY** CHARGED...
AT THAT TIME, PRESIDENT FRANÇOIS MITTERRAND HAD SLOWED THE TRIAL WITHOUT ACTUALLY **STOPPING** IT.
IN APRIL OF 1983, MICHEL SLITINSKY PUBLISHED HIS FIRST COMPLETE BOOK ON THE PAPON CASE.
MAURICE PAPON TRIED TO BLOCK THE BOOK BY FILING SUIT AGAINST THE AUTHOR, BUT HE WAS QUICKLY DISMISSED.
FOURTEEN YEARS LATER, AS OCTOBER 8, 1997, DAWNED IN BORDEAUX, THE TRIAL OF FORMER VICHY SENIOR OFFICIAL MAURICE PAPON BEGAN BEFORE THE GIRONDE COURT OF ASSIZES.
HE WAS CHARGED WITH COMPLICITY IN CRIMES AGAINST HUMANITY FOR "HIS ACTIVE ROLE" IN ARRANGING DEPORTATION CONVOYS FOR JEWS.

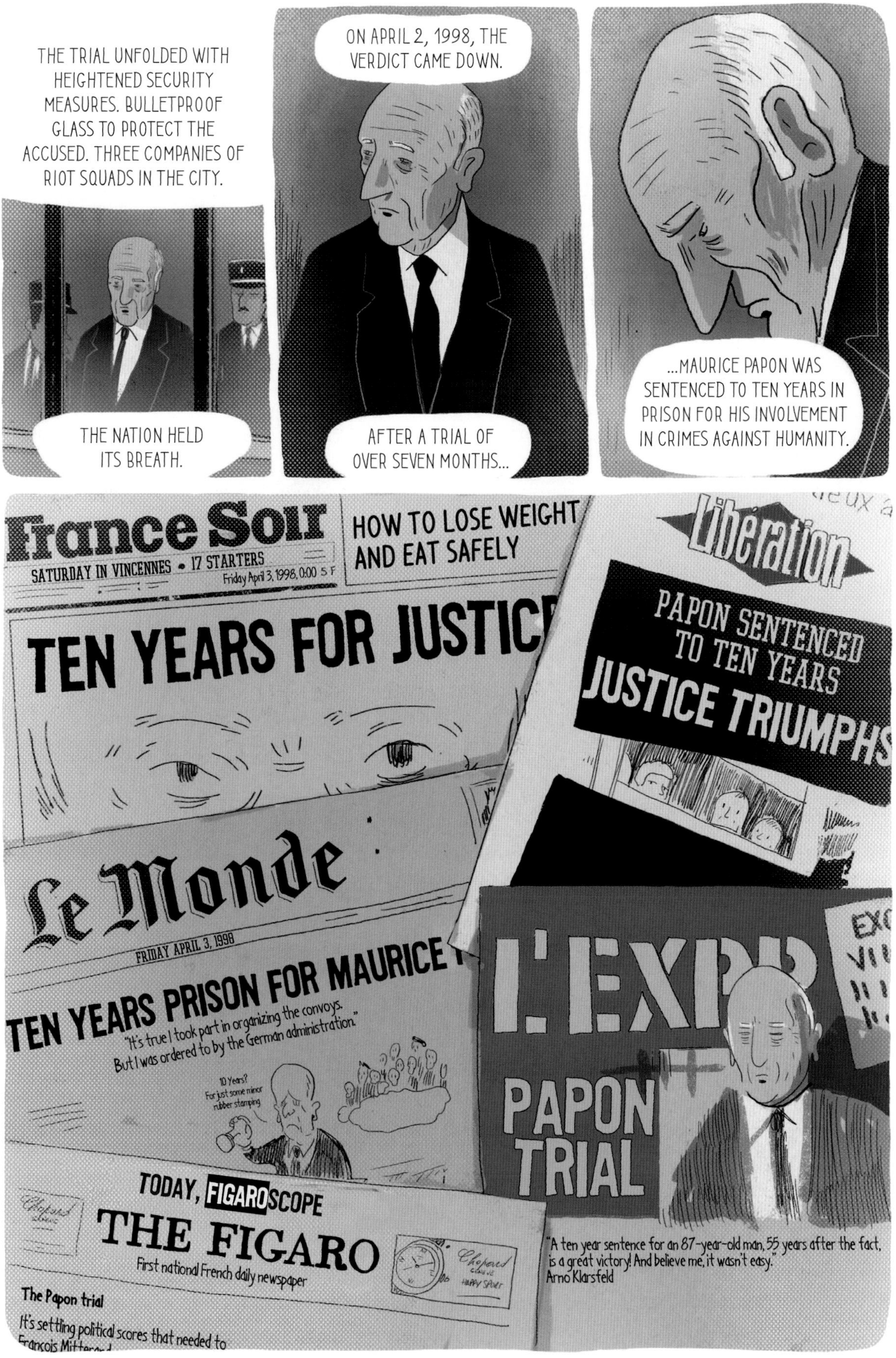
THE TRIAL UNFOLDED WITH HEIGHTENED SECURITY MEASURES. BULLETPROOF GLASS TO PROTECT THE ACCUSED. THREE COMPANIES OF RIOT SQUADS IN THE CITY.
THE NATION HELD ITS BREATH.
ON APRIL 2, 1998, THE VERDICT CAME DOWN.
AFTER A TRIAL OF OVER SEVEN MONTHS...
...MAURICE PAPON WAS SENTENCED TO TEN YEARS IN PRISON FOR HIS INVOLVEMENT IN CRIMES AGAINST HUMANITY.
France Soir
SATURDAY IN VINCENNES • 17 STARTERS
Friday April 3, 1998, 0.00 5 F
HOW TO LOSE WEIGHT AND EAT SAFELY
TEN YEARS FOR JUSTIC
Libération
PAPON SENTENCED TO TEN YEARS
JUSTICE TRIUMPHS
Le Monde
FRIDAY APRIL 3, 1998
TEN YEARS PRISON FOR MAURICE
"It's true I took part in organizing the convoys. But I was ordered to by the German administration."
10 Years? For just some minor rubber stamping
L'EXPR
PAPON TRIAL
"A ten year sentence for an 87-year-old man, 55 years after the fact, is a great victory! And believe me, it wasn't easy."
Arno Klarsfeld
TODAY, FIGAROSCOPE
THE FIGARO
First national French daily newspaper
The Papon trial
It's settling political scores that needed to

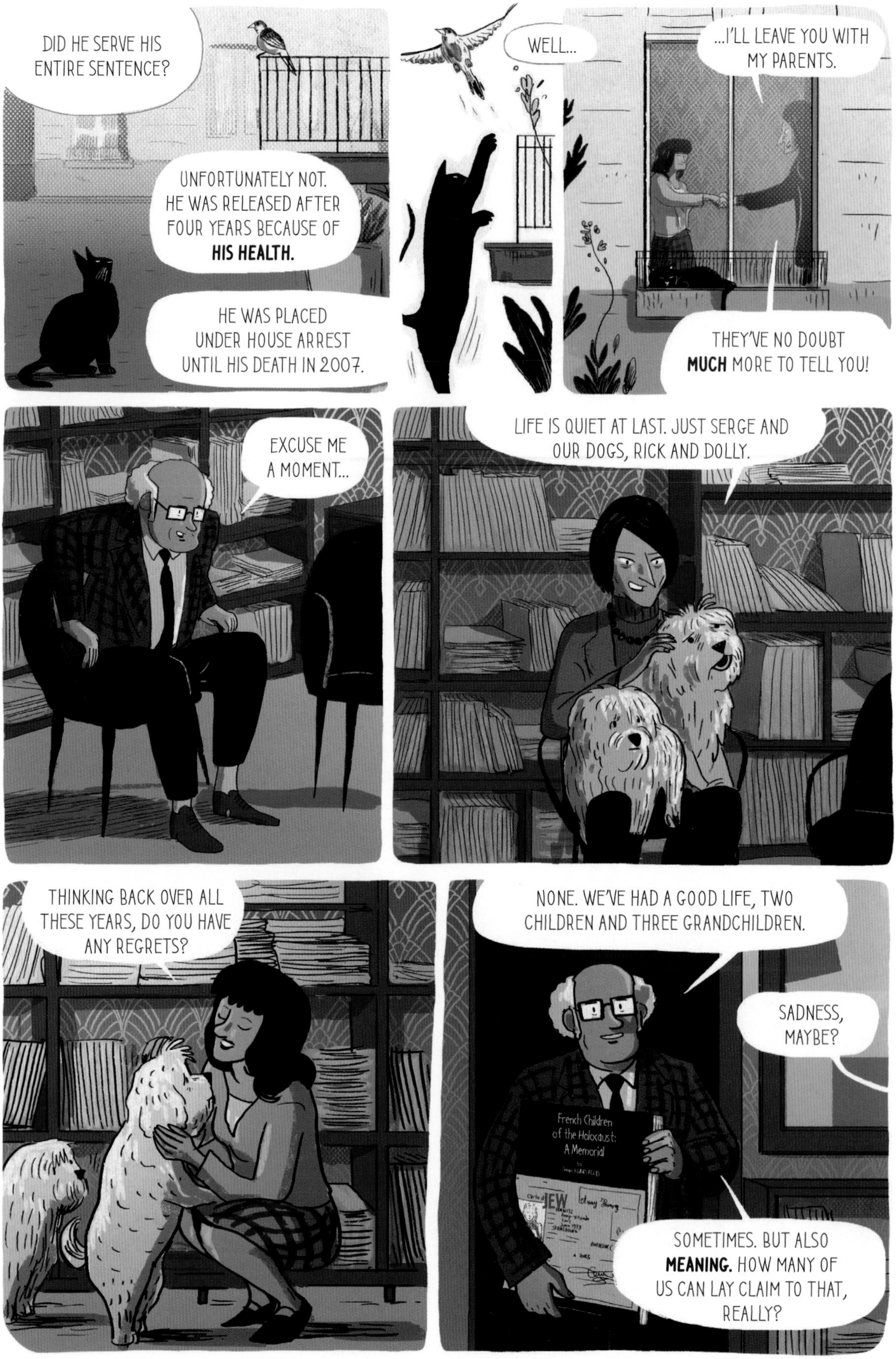
DID HE SERVE HIS ENTIRE SENTENCE?
UNFORTUNATELY NOT. HE WAS RELEASED AFTER FOUR YEARS BECAUSE OF **HIS HEALTH.**
HE WAS PLACED UNDER HOUSE ARREST UNTIL HIS DEATH IN 2007.
WELL...
...I'LL LEAVE YOU WITH MY PARENTS.
THEY'VE NO DOUBT **MUCH** MORE TO TELL YOU!
EXCUSE ME A MOMENT...
LIFE IS QUIET AT LAST. JUST SERGE AND OUR DOGS, RICK AND DOLLY.
THINKING BACK OVER ALL THESE YEARS, DO YOU HAVE ANY REGRETS?
NONE. WE'VE HAD A GOOD LIFE, TWO CHILDREN AND THREE GRANDCHILDREN.
SADNESS, MAYBE?
French Children of the Holocaust: A Memorial
SOMETIMES. BUT ALSO **MEANING.** HOW MANY OF US CAN LAY CLAIM TO THAT, REALLY?

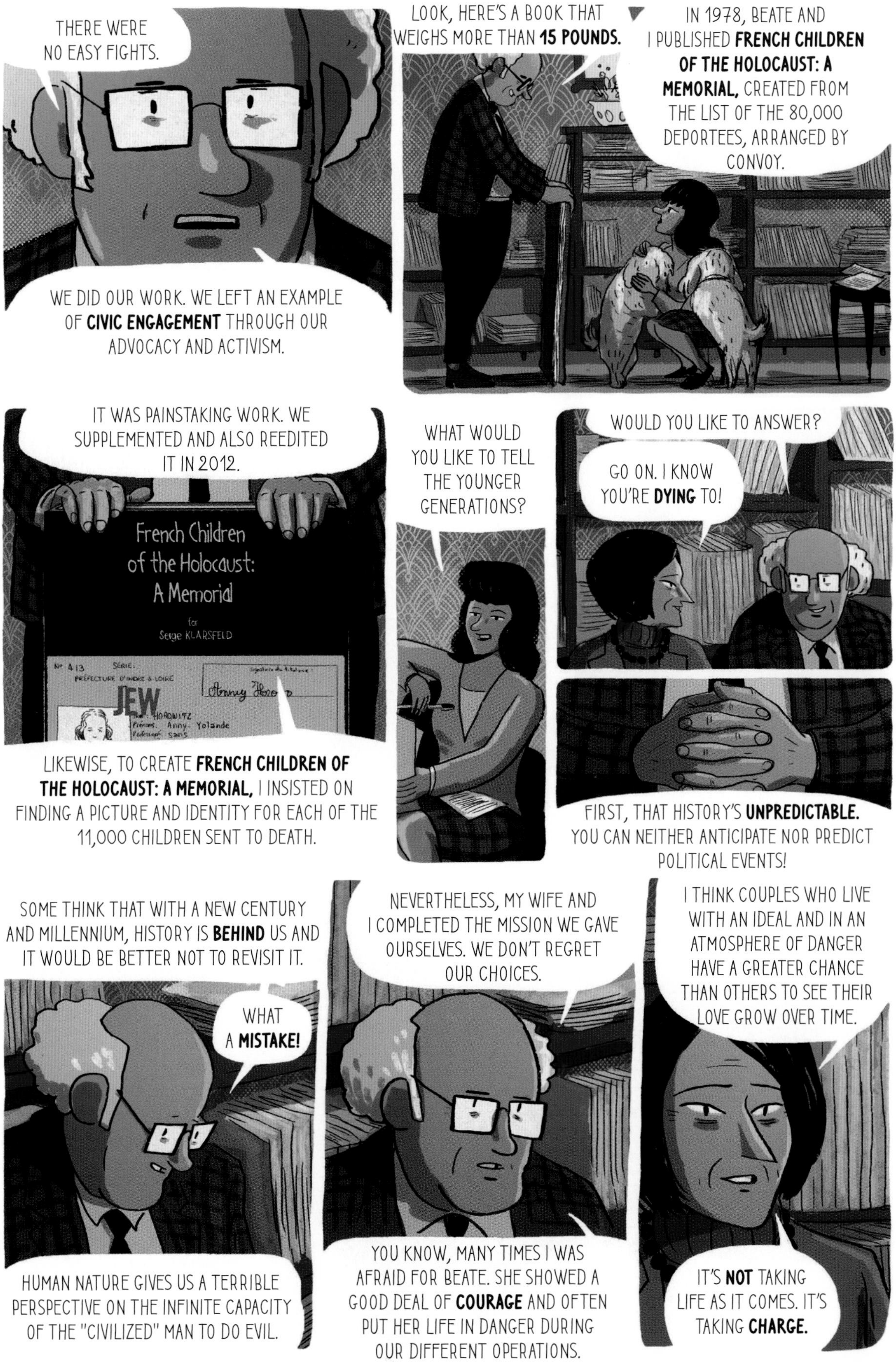
THERE WERE NO EASY FIGHTS.
WE DID OUR WORK. WE LEFT AN EXAMPLE OF **CIVIC ENGAGEMENT** THROUGH OUR ADVOCACY AND ACTIVISM.
LOOK, HERE'S A BOOK THAT WEIGHS MORE THAN **15 POUNDS.**
IN 1978, BEATE AND I PUBLISHED **FRENCH CHILDREN OF THE HOLOCAUST: A MEMORIAL,** CREATED FROM THE LIST OF THE 80,000 DEPORTEES, ARRANGED BY CONVOY.
IT WAS PAINSTAKING WORK. WE SUPPLEMENTED AND ALSO REEDITED IT IN 2012.
French Children of the Holocaust: A Memorial
for Serge KLARSFELD
JEW
LIKEWISE, TO CREATE **FRENCH CHILDREN OF THE HOLOCAUST: A MEMORIAL,** I INSISTED ON FINDING A PICTURE AND IDENTITY FOR EACH OF THE 11,000 CHILDREN SENT TO DEATH.
WHAT WOULD YOU LIKE TO TELL THE YOUNGER GENERATIONS?
WOULD YOU LIKE TO ANSWER?
GO ON. I KNOW YOU'RE **DYING** TO!
FIRST, THAT HISTORY'S **UNPREDICTABLE.** YOU CAN NEITHER ANTICIPATE NOR PREDICT POLITICAL EVENTS!
SOME THINK THAT WITH A NEW CENTURY AND MILLENNIUM, HISTORY IS **BEHIND** US AND IT WOULD BE BETTER NOT TO REVISIT IT.
WHAT A **MISTAKE!**
HUMAN NATURE GIVES US A TERRIBLE PERSPECTIVE ON THE INFINITE CAPACITY OF THE "CIVILIZED" MAN TO DO EVIL.
NEVERTHELESS, MY WIFE AND I COMPLETED THE MISSION WE GAVE OURSELVES. WE DON'T REGRET OUR CHOICES.
YOU KNOW, MANY TIMES I WAS AFRAID FOR BEATE. SHE SHOWED A GOOD DEAL OF **COURAGE** AND OFTEN PUT HER LIFE IN DANGER DURING OUR DIFFERENT OPERATIONS.
I THINK COUPLES WHO LIVE WITH AN IDEAL AND IN AN ATMOSPHERE OF DANGER HAVE A GREATER CHANCE THAN OTHERS TO SEE THEIR LOVE GROW OVER TIME.
IT'S **NOT** TAKING LIFE AS IT COMES. IT'S TAKING **CHARGE.**

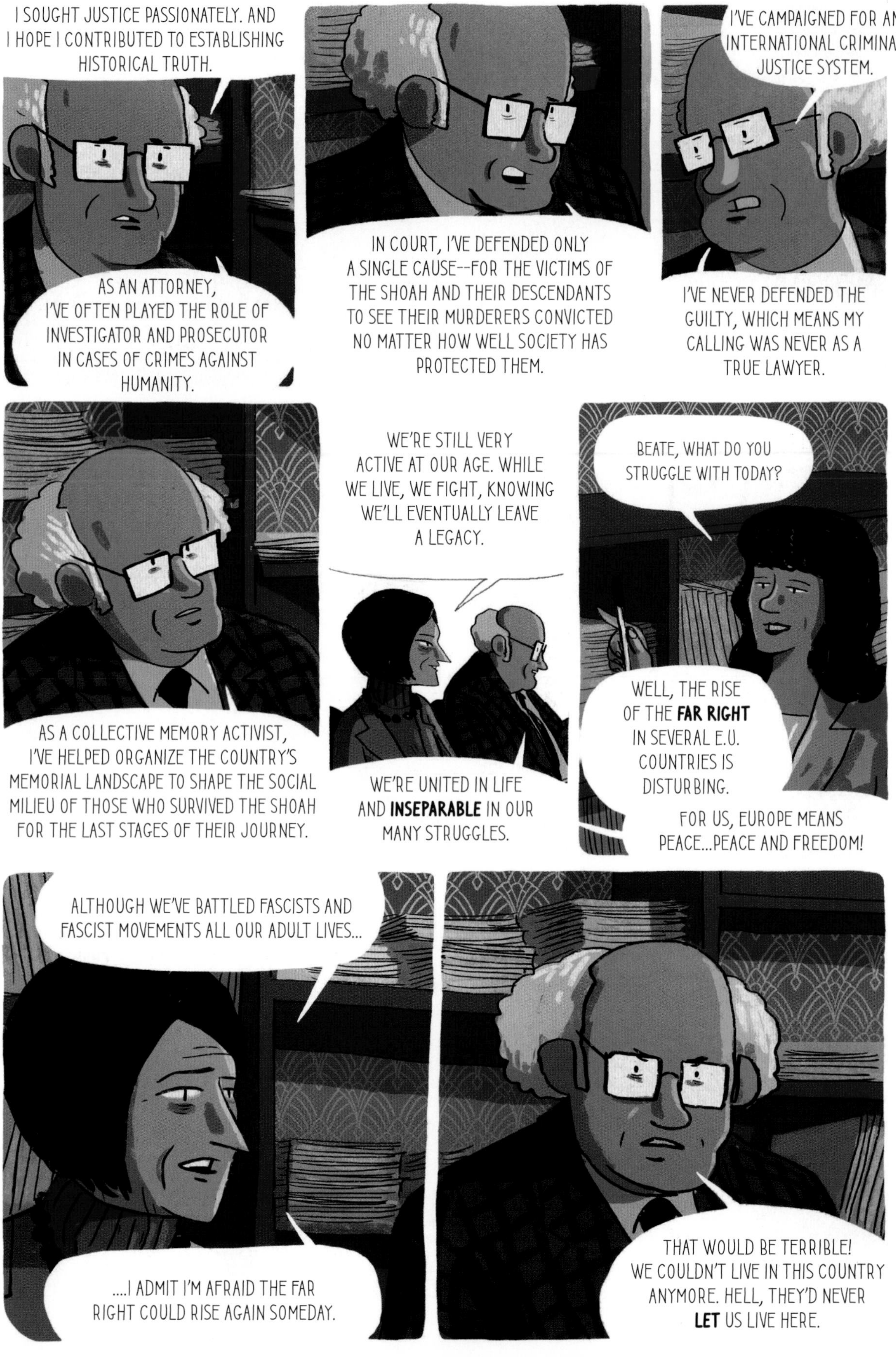

I SOUGHT JUSTICE PASSIONATELY. AND I HOPE I CONTRIBUTED TO ESTABLISHING HISTORICAL TRUTH.
AS AN ATTORNEY, I'VE OFTEN PLAYED THE ROLE OF INVESTIGATOR AND PROSECUTOR IN CASES OF CRIMES AGAINST HUMANITY.
IN COURT, I'VE DEFENDED ONLY A SINGLE CAUSE--FOR THE VICTIMS OF THE SHOAH AND THEIR DESCENDANTS TO SEE THEIR MURDERERS CONVICTED NO MATTER HOW WELL SOCIETY HAS PROTECTED THEM.
I'VE CAMPAIGNED FOR AN INTERNATIONAL CRIMINAL JUSTICE SYSTEM.
I'VE NEVER DEFENDED THE GUILTY, WHICH MEANS MY CALLING WAS NEVER AS A TRUE LAWYER.
AS A COLLECTIVE MEMORY ACTIVIST, I'VE HELPED ORGANIZE THE COUNTRY'S MEMORIAL LANDSCAPE TO SHAPE THE SOCIAL MILIEU OF THOSE WHO SURVIVED THE SHOAH FOR THE LAST STAGES OF THEIR JOURNEY.
WE'RE STILL VERY ACTIVE AT OUR AGE. WHILE WE LIVE, WE FIGHT, KNOWING WE'LL EVENTUALLY LEAVE A LEGACY.
WE'RE UNITED IN LIFE AND **INSEPARABLE** IN OUR MANY STRUGGLES.
BEATE, WHAT DO YOU STRUGGLE WITH TODAY?
WELL, THE RISE OF THE **FAR RIGHT** IN SEVERAL E.U. COUNTRIES IS DISTURBING.
FOR US, EUROPE MEANS PEACE...PEACE AND FREEDOM!
ALTHOUGH WE'VE BATTLED FASCISTS AND FASCIST MOVEMENTS ALL OUR ADULT LIVES...
....I ADMIT I'M AFRAID THE FAR RIGHT COULD RISE AGAIN SOMEDAY.
THAT WOULD BE TERRIBLE! WE COULDN'T LIVE IN THIS COUNTRY ANYMORE. HELL, THEY'D NEVER **LET** US LIVE HERE.

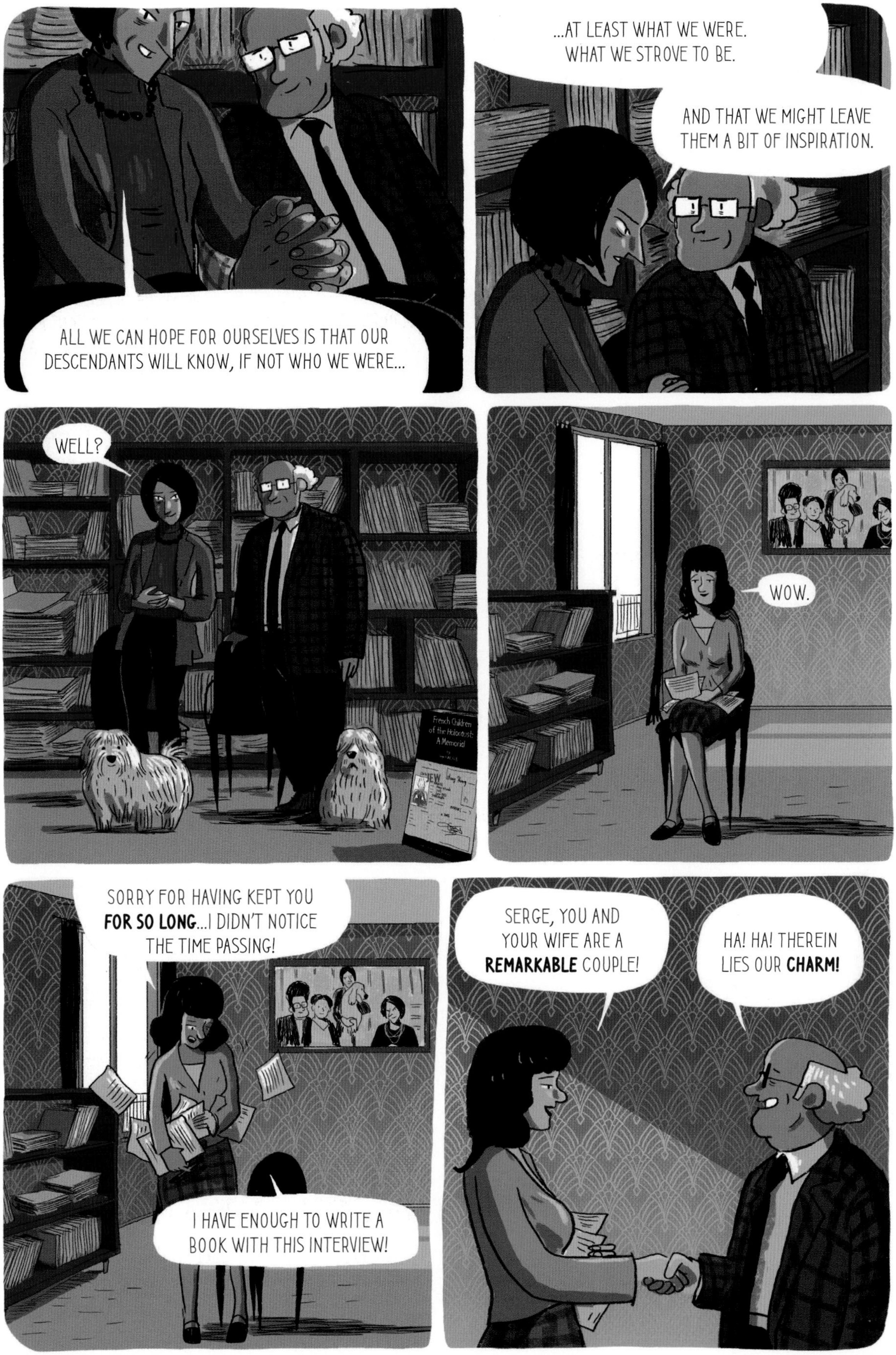
ALL WE CAN HOPE FOR OURSELVES IS THAT OUR DESCENDANTS WILL KNOW, IF NOT WHO WE WERE...
...AT LEAST WHAT WE WERE. WHAT WE STROVE TO BE.
AND THAT WE MIGHT LEAVE THEM A BIT OF INSPIRATION.
WELL?
French Children of the Holocaust: A Memorial
WOW.
SORRY FOR HAVING KEPT YOU **FOR SO LONG**...I DIDN'T NOTICE THE TIME PASSING!
I HAVE ENOUGH TO WRITE A BOOK WITH THIS INTERVIEW!
SERGE, YOU AND YOUR WIFE ARE A **REMARKABLE** COUPLE!
HA! HA! THEREIN LIES OUR **CHARM!**

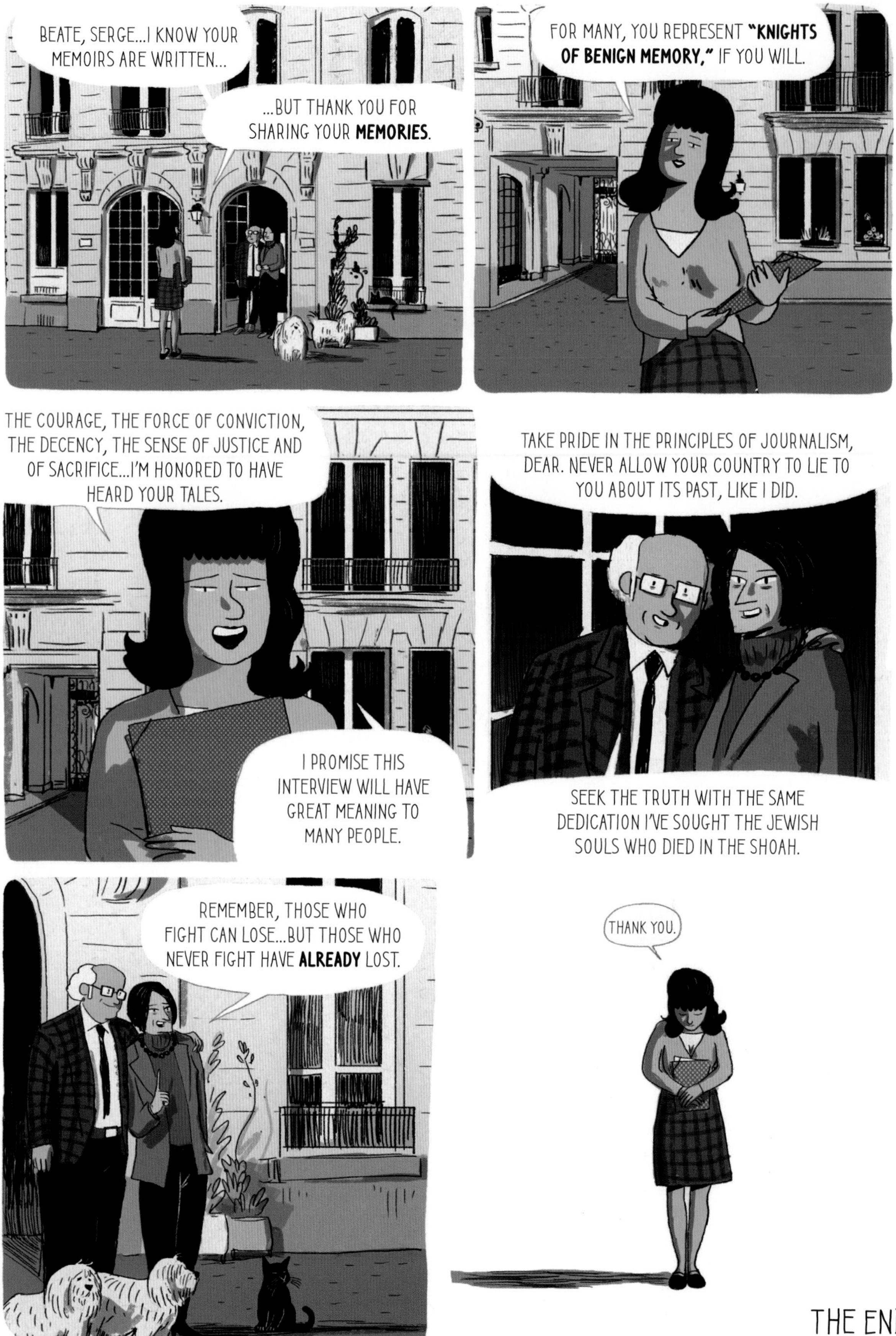
BEATE, SERGE...I KNOW YOUR MEMOIRS ARE WRITTEN...
...BUT THANK YOU FOR SHARING YOUR **MEMORIES**.
FOR MANY, YOU REPRESENT **"KNIGHTS OF BENIGN MEMORY,"** IF YOU WILL.
THE COURAGE, THE FORCE OF CONVICTION, THE DECENCY, THE SENSE OF JUSTICE AND OF SACRIFICE...I'M HONORED TO HAVE HEARD YOUR TALES.
I PROMISE THIS INTERVIEW WILL HAVE GREAT MEANING TO MANY PEOPLE.
TAKE PRIDE IN THE PRINCIPLES OF JOURNALISM, DEAR. NEVER ALLOW YOUR COUNTRY TO LIE TO YOU ABOUT ITS PAST, LIKE I DID.
SEEK THE TRUTH WITH THE SAME DEDICATION I'VE SOUGHT THE JEWISH SOULS WHO DIED IN THE SHOAH.
REMEMBER, THOSE WHO FIGHT CAN LOSE...BUT THOSE WHO NEVER FIGHT HAVE **ALREADY** LOST.
THANK YOU.

THE END
03/09/2020

PHOTO ALBUM

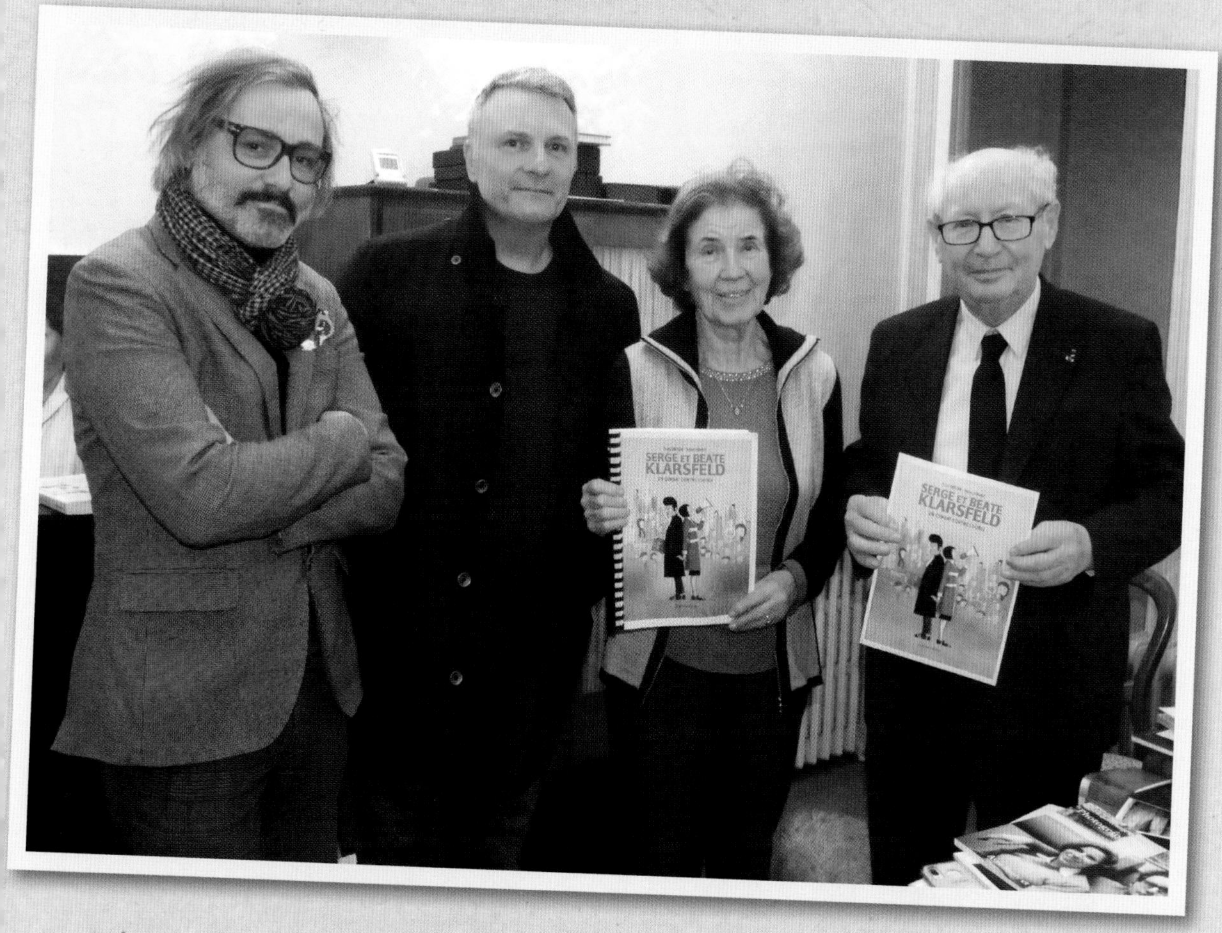
SERGE ET BEATE KLARSFELD
SERGE ET BEATE KLARSFELD

Artist Sylvain Dorange and writer Pascal Bresson, the authors of the graphic novel, with Beate and Serge Klarsfield, 2020.

THE CHILDHOOD

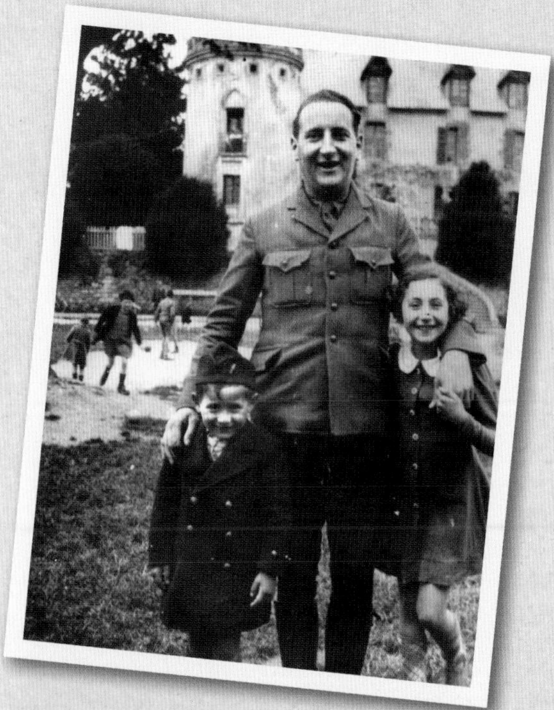

Serge, his father, and his sister after he escaped, 1941. (Klarsfeld Private Collection)

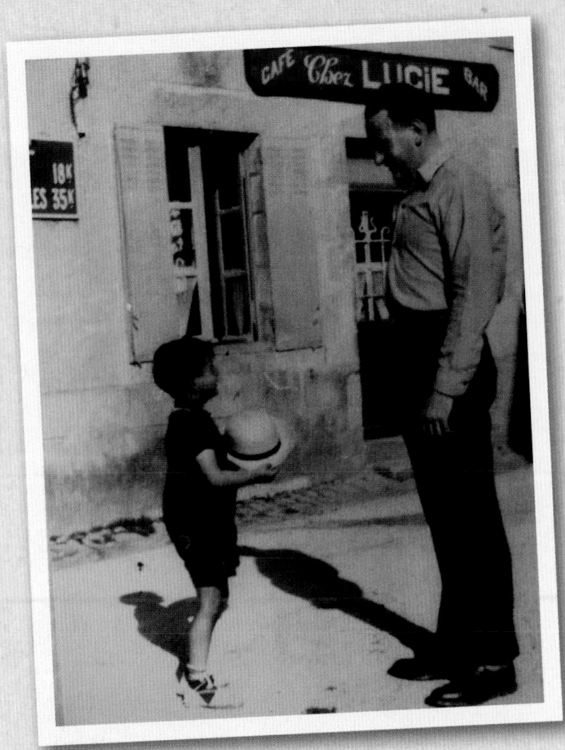
CAFE
Chez LUCIE
BAR

Serge and his father in the Creuse, 1941. (Klarsfeld Private Collection)

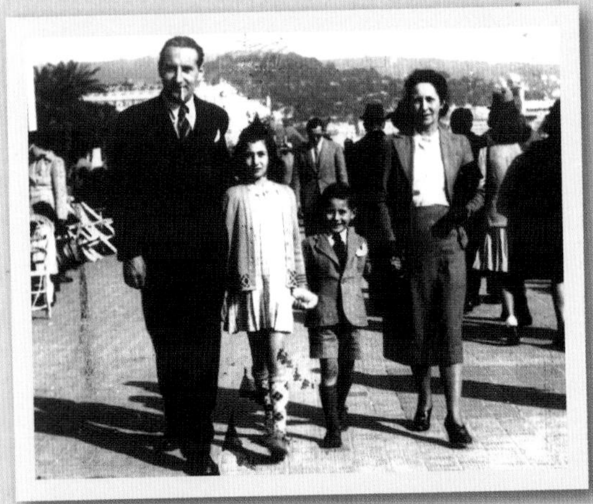

The Klarsfeld Family, 1943. (Klarsfeld Private Collection)

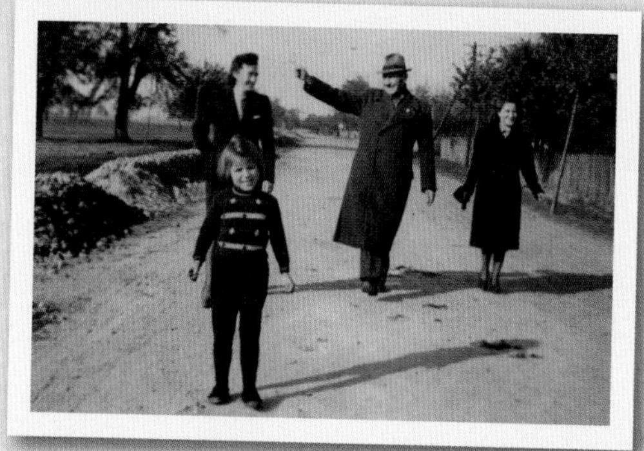

Beate and her family in Lodz, 1943. (Klarsfeld Private Collection)

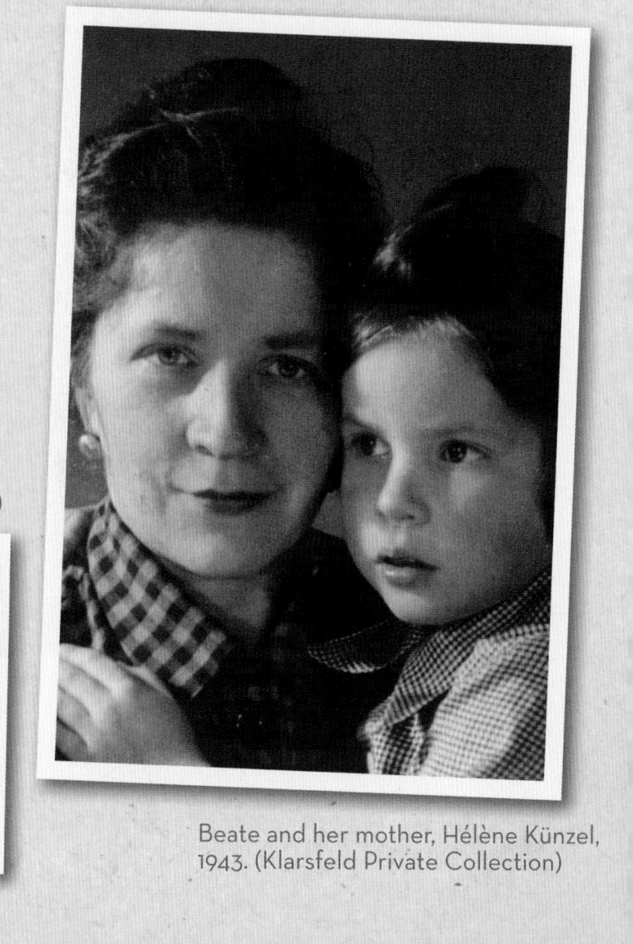

Beate and her mother, Hélène Künzel, 1943. (Klarsfeld Private Collection)

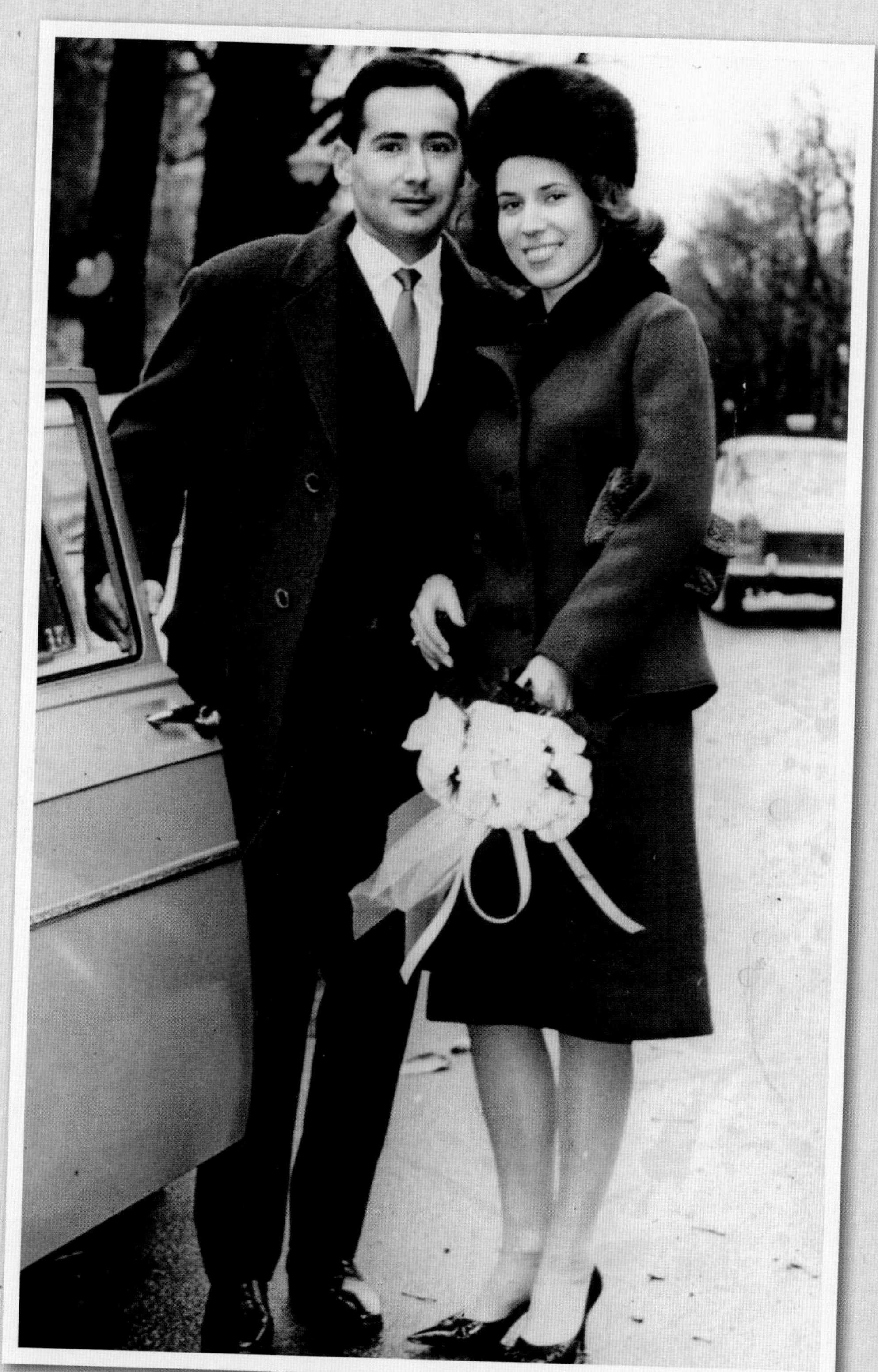

Beate and Serge Klarsfeld's wedding, 1963. (Klarsfeld Private Collection)

THE FAMILY

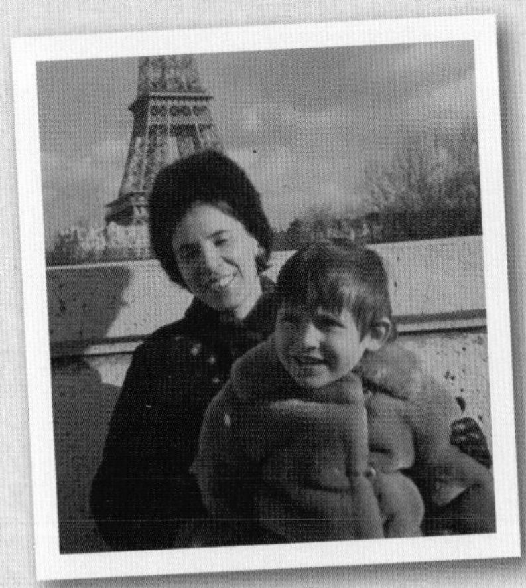

Beate and Arno in Paris, 1968. (Mémorial de la Shoah & Klarsfeld Private Collection)

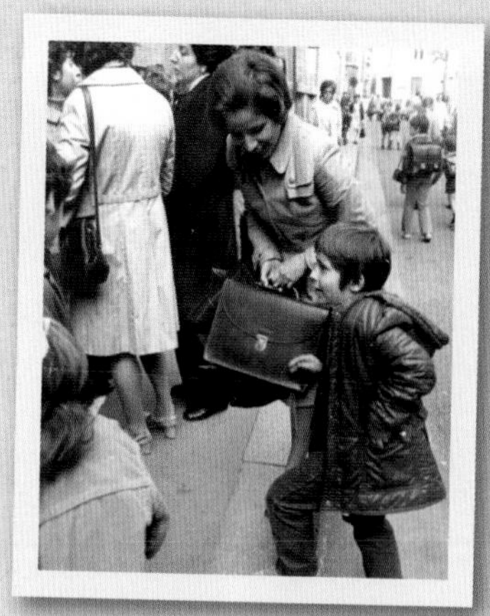

Beate and Arno going to school, circa 1970. (Klarsfeld Private Collection)

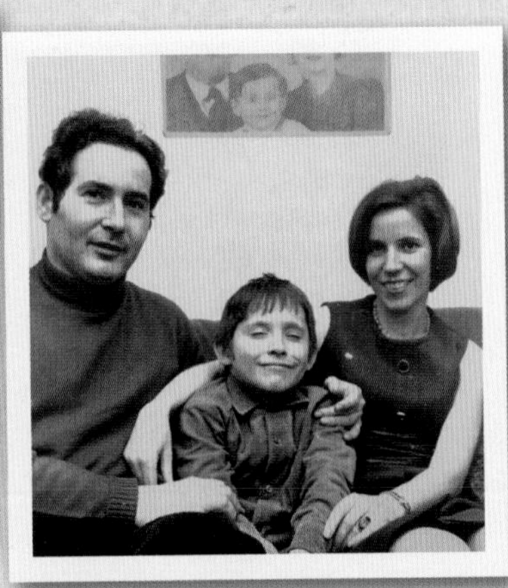

Serge, Arno and Beate, circa 1970. (Klarsfeld Private Collection)

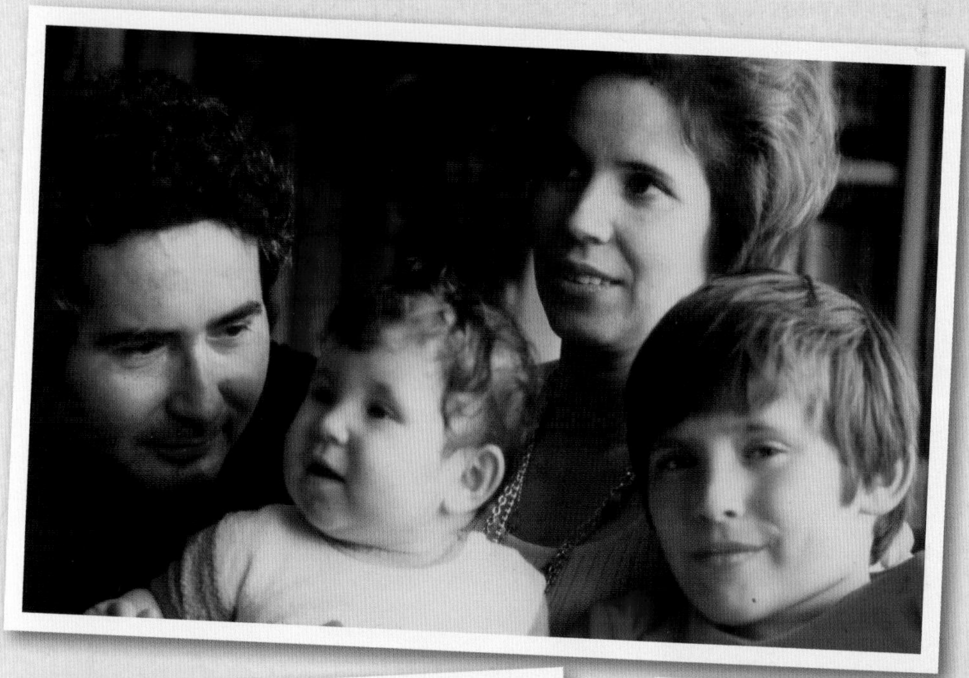

Lida's birth, 1973. (Mémorial de la Shoah & Klarsfeld Private Collection)

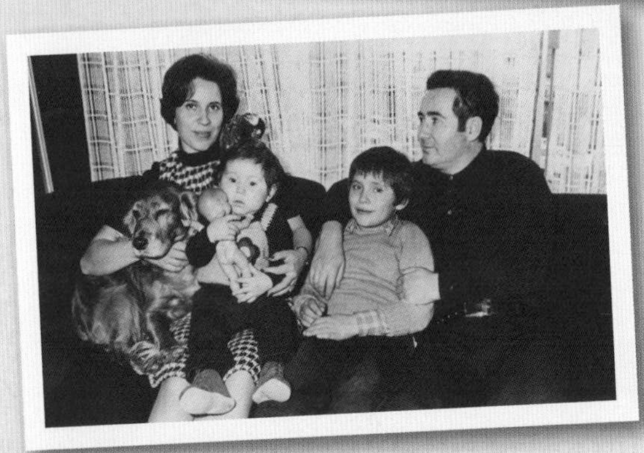

Klarsfeld Family, 1976. (Klarsfeld Private Collection)

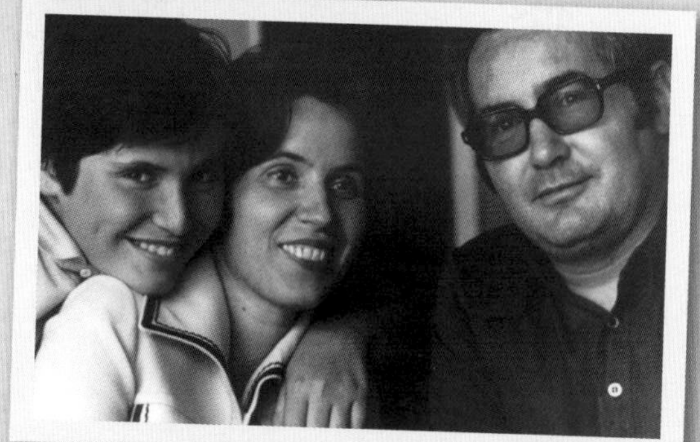

Arno, Beate and Serge, January 1979. (Klarsfeld Private Collection, ©Elie Kagan)

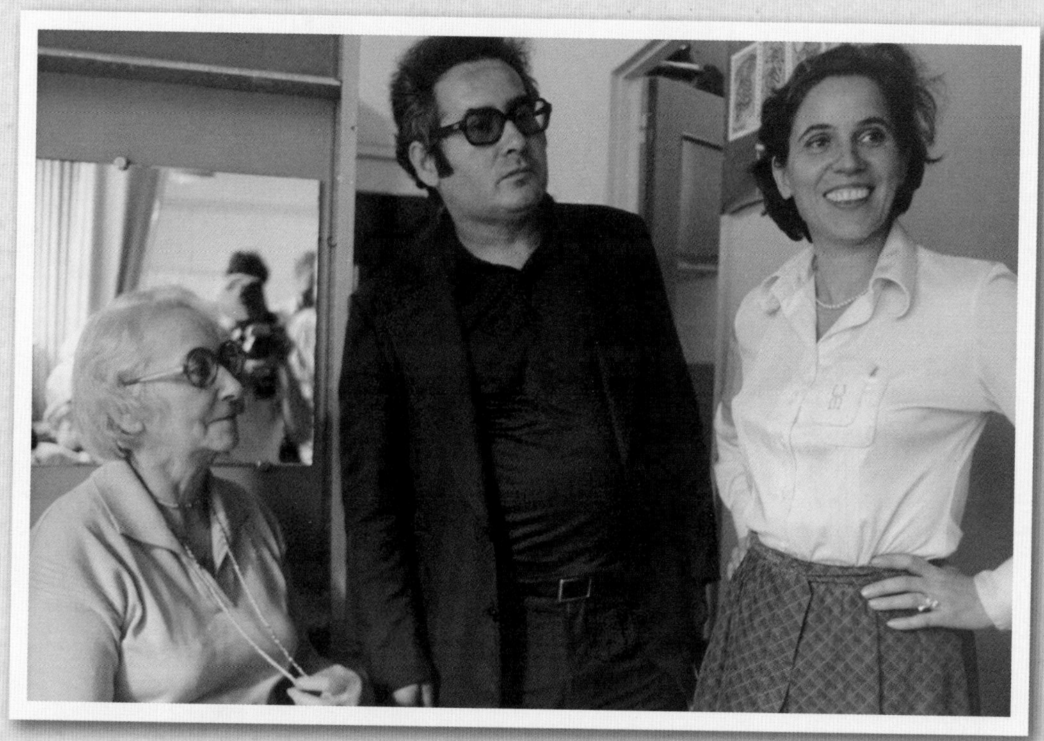

Serge's mother, Raïssa, Serge, and Beate, 1979.
(Klarsfeld Private Collection, © Elie Kagan)

BEATE AND HER PETS

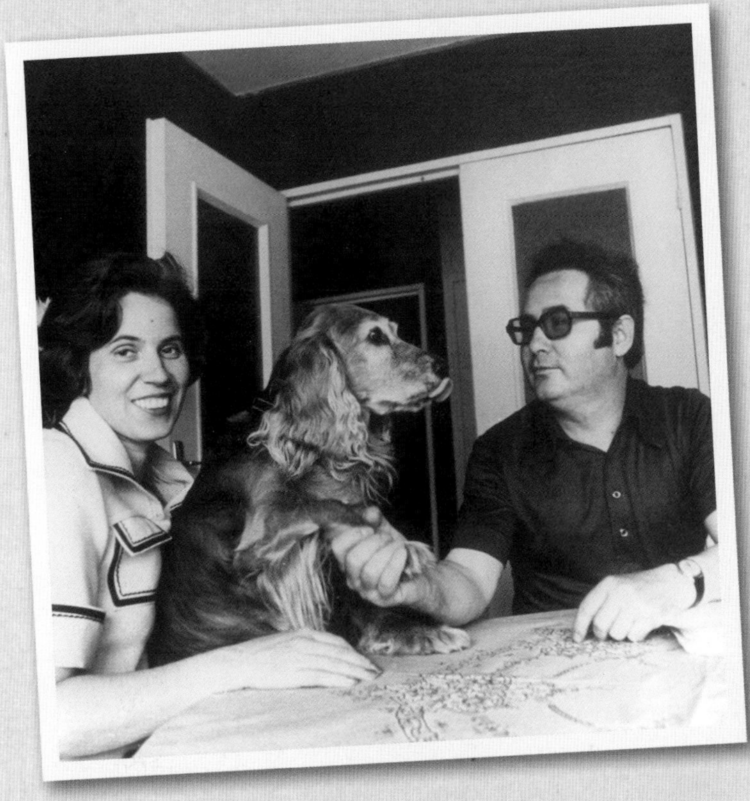

Beate, Serge and Pétia, their cocker-spaniel, 1970s.
(Klarsfeld Private Collection, © Elie Kagan)

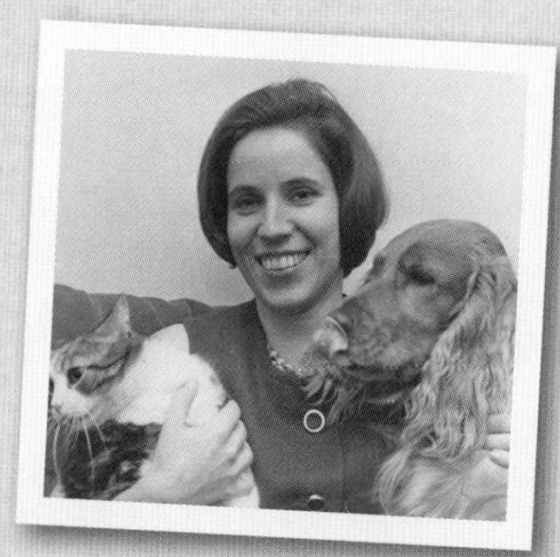

Beate and her pets, 1970s.
(Klarsfeld Private Collection)

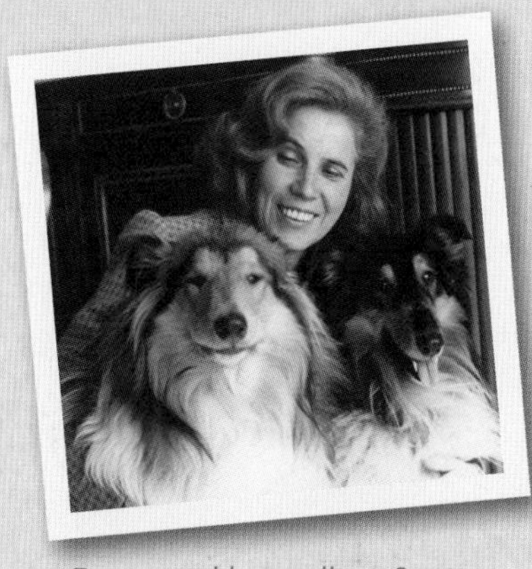

Beate and her collies, Scott and Flynn, circa 1985.
(Klarsfeld Private Collection)

THE 1960s AND THE FIGHT AGAINST THE CHANCELLOR, KIESINGER

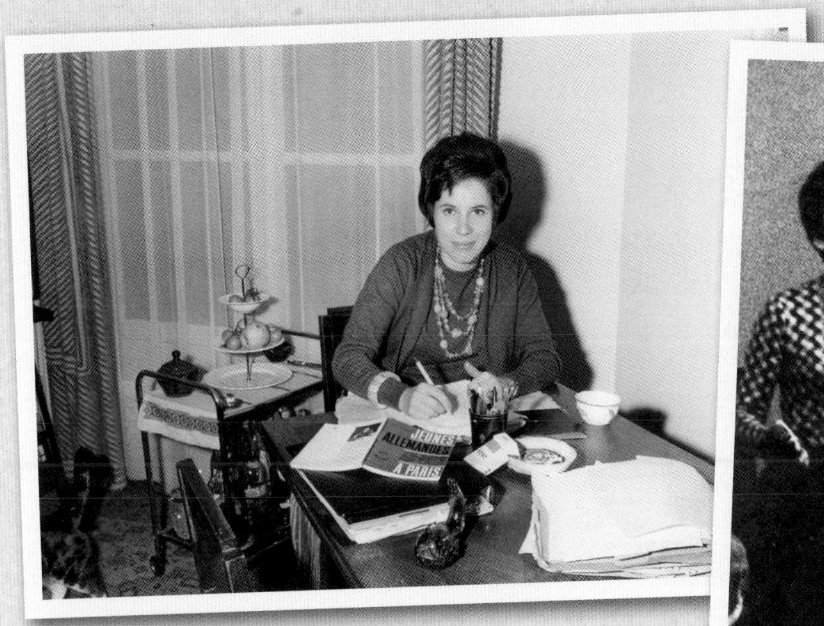

JEUNES ALLEMANDES
A PARIS

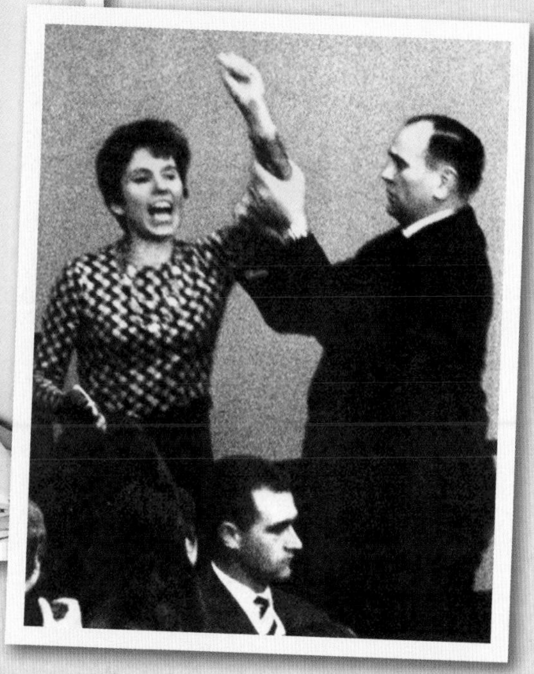

Beate and her book *Young Au-Pair Germans in Paris*, 1964. (Klarsfeld Private Collection, © Dalmas - Sipa Presse)

Beate yells "Nazi" at the German Bundestag, April 2nd 1968. (Klarsfeld Private Collection)

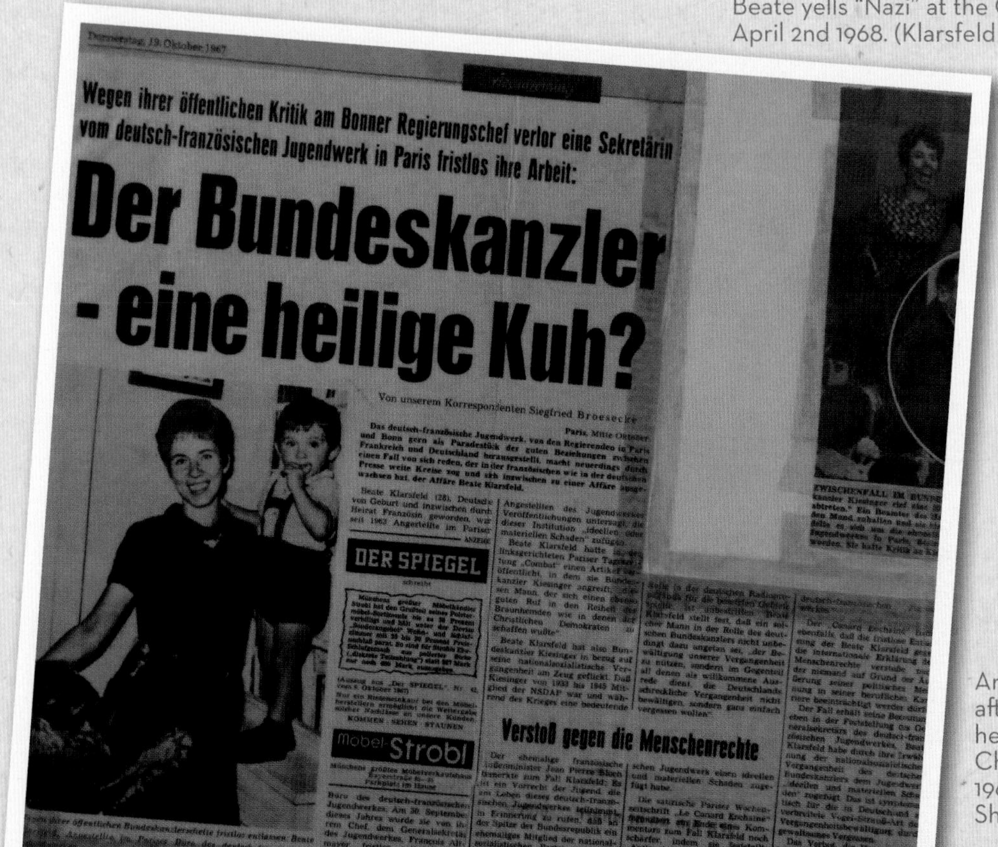

Donnerstag, 19. Oktober 1967

Wegen ihrer öffentlichen Kritik am Bonner Regierungschef verlor eine Sekretärin vom deutsch-französischen Jugendwerk in Paris fristlos ihre Arbeit:

Der Bundeskanzler - eine heilige Kuh?

Von unserem Korrespondenten Siegfried Broesecke

Paris, Mitte Oktober

Das deutsch-französische Jugendwerk, von den Regierenden in Paris und Bonn gern als Paradestück der guten Beziehungen zwischen Frankreich und Deutschland herausgestellt, macht neuerdings durch einen Fall von sich reden, der in der französischen wie in der deutschen Presse weite Kreise zog und sich inzwischen zu einer Affäre ausgewachsen hat, der Affäre Beate Klarsfeld.

Beate Klarsfeld (28), Deutsche von Geburt und inzwischen durch Heirat Französin geworden, war seit 1963 Angestellte im Pariser ...

... Angestellten des Jugendwerkes Veröffentlichungen untersagt, die dieser Institution „ideellen oder materiellen Schaden" zufügen.

Beate Klarsfeld hatte in der linksgerichteten Pariser Tageszeitung „Combat" einen Artikel veröffentlicht, in dem sie Bundeskanzler Kiesinger angreift ...

DER SPIEGEL

Verstoß gegen die Menschenrechte

Möbel-Strobl

KOMMEN · SEHEN · STAUNEN

ZWISCHENFALL IM BUNDESTAG

An article about Beate after she was fired from her job for denouncing Chancellor Kiesinger, 1967. (Mémorial de la Shoah Collection)

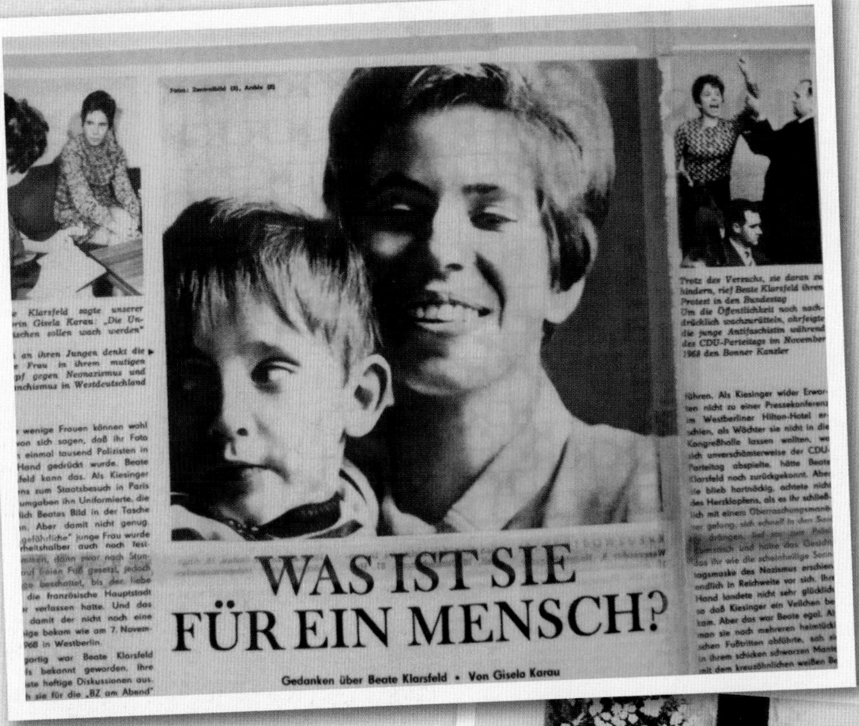

Foto: Zentralbild (2), Archiv (2)

... Klarsfeld sagte unserer ...rin Gisela Karau: „Die Un...ischen sollen wach werden"

... an ihren Jungen denkt die ...e Frau in ihrem mutigen ...pf gegen Neonazismus und ...nchismus in Westdeutschland

... wenige Frauen können wohl von sich sagen, daß ihr Foto ... einmal tausend Polizisten in ... Hand gedrückt wurde. Beate ...feld kann das. Als Kiesinger ...ns zum Staatsbesuch in Paris ... umgaben ihn Uniformierte, die ...lich Beates Bild in der Tasche ...n. Aber damit nicht genug. ...gefährliche" junge Frau wurde ...rheitshalber auch noch fest... ... die französische Hauptstadt ...r verlassen hatte. Und das ... damit der nicht noch eine ...ige bekam wie am 7. Novem...968 in Westberlin.

...gartig war Beate Klarsfeld ...ls bekannt geworden. Ihre ...ste heftige Diskussionen aus. ...h sie für die „BZ am Abend"

WAS IST SIE FÜR EIN MENSCH?

Gedanken über Beate Klarsfeld • Von Gisela Karau

Trotz des Versuchs, sie daran zu hindern, rief Beate Klarsfeld ihren Protest in den Bundestag

Um die Öffentlichkeit noch nachdrücklich wachzurütteln, ohrfeigte die junge Antifaschistin während des CDU-Parteitags im November 1968 den Bonner Kanzler

...führen. Als Kiesinger wider Erwar...ten nicht zu einer Pressekonferenz im Westberliner Hilton-Hotel er...schien, als Wächter sie nicht in die Kongreßhalle lassen wollten, wo sich unverschämterweise der CDU-Parteitag abspielte, hätte Beate Klarsfeld noch zurückgekonnt. Aber sie blieb hartnäckig, achtete nicht des Herzklopfens, als es ihr schließ...lich mit einem Überraschungsmanö... ... ...sagsmaske des Nazismus erschien... endlich in Reichweite vor sich. Ihre Hand landete nicht sehr glücklich, so daß Kiesinger ein Veilchen be...kam. Aber das war Beate egal. Al... man sie nach mehreren heimtück...ischen Fußtritten abführte, sah si... in ihrem schicken schwarzen Mante... mit dem kreuzähnlichen weißen Br...

Article about Beate's actions at the Bundestag, 1968. (Mémorial de la Shoah Collection)

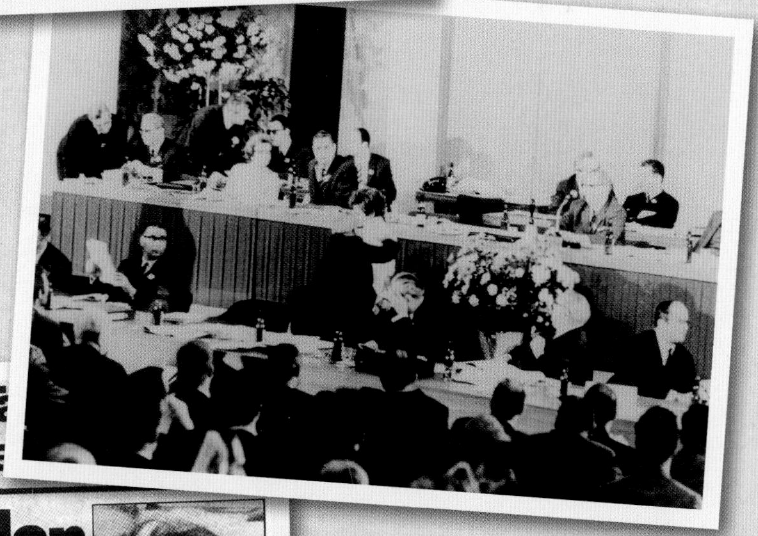

The slap inflicted upon the German Chancellor, Kiesinger, November 7, 1968. (Mémorial de la Shoah Collection, photo DR)

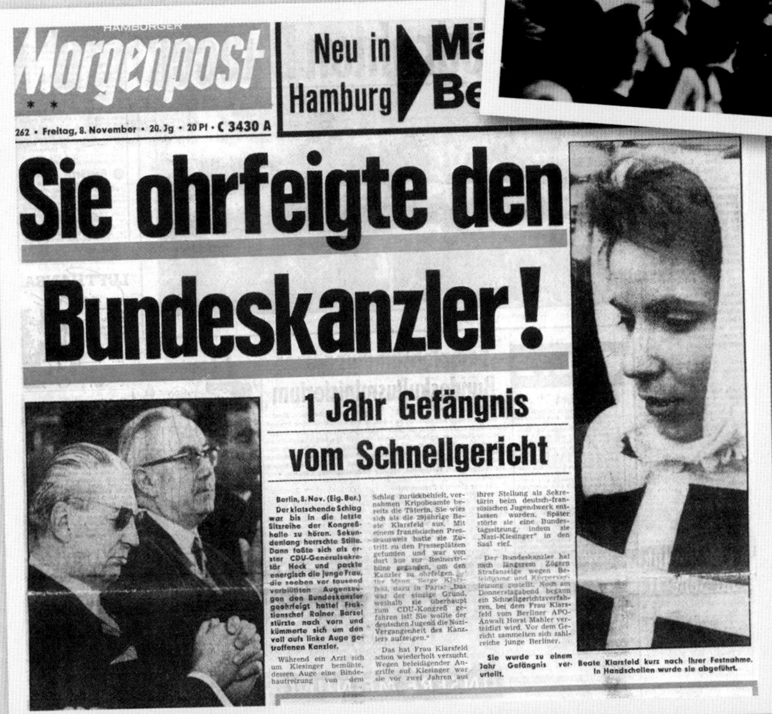

HAMBURGER **Morgenpost**

Neu in Hamburg Mä... Be...

262 • Freitag, 8. November • 20. Jg • 20 Pf • C 3430 A

Sie ohrfeigte den Bundeskanzler!

1 Jahr Gefängnis vom Schnellgericht

Berlin, 8. Nov. (Eig. Ber.) Der klatschende Schlag war bis in die letzte Sitzreihe der Kongreßhalle zu hören. Sekundenlang herrschte Stille. Dann faßte sich als erster CDU-Generalsekretär Heck und packte energisch die junge Frau, die soeben vor tausend verblüfften Augenzeugen den Bundeskanzler geohrfeigt hatte! Fraktionschef Rainer Barzel stürzte nach vorn und kümmerte sich um den voll aufs linke Auge getroffenen Kanzler.

Während ein Arzt sich um Kiesinger bemühte, dessen Auge eine Bindehautreizung von dem Schlag zurückbehielt, vernahmen Kripobeamte bereits die Täterin. Sie wies sich als die 29jährige Beate Klarsfeld aus. Mit einem französischen Presseausweis hatte sie Zutritt zu den Presseplätzen gefunden und war von dort aus zur Rednertribüne gegangen, um den Kanzler zu ohrfeigen. Ihr Mann, Serge Klarsfeld, dazu in Paris: „Das war der einzige Grund, weshalb sie überhaupt zum CDU-Kongreß gefahren ist! Sie wollte der deutschen Jugend die Nazi-Vergangenheit des Kanzlers aufzeigen."

Das hat Frau Klarsfeld schon wiederholt versucht. Wegen beleidigender Angriffe auf Kiesinger war sie vor zwei Jahren aus ihrer Stellung als Sekretärin beim deutsch-französischen Jugendwerk entlassen worden. Später störte sie eine Bundestagssitzung, indem sie „Nazi-Kiesinger" in den Saal rief.

Der Bundeskanzler hat nach längerem Zögern Strafanzeige wegen Beleidigung und Körperverletzung gestellt. Noch am Donnerstagabend begann ein Schnellgerichtsverfahren, bei dem Frau Klarsfeld vom Berliner APO-Anwalt Horst Mahler verteidigt wird. Vor dem Gericht sammelten sich zahlreiche junge Berliner.

Sie wurde zu einem Jahr Gefängnis verurteilt.

Beate Klarsfeld kurz nach ihrer Festnahme. In Handschellen wurde sie abgeführt.

Coverage of the slap in the German newspapers, November 8, 1968. (Klarsfeld Private Collection)

THE 1970s AND THE HUNT FOR THE FIRST NAZIS TO GO ON TRIAL

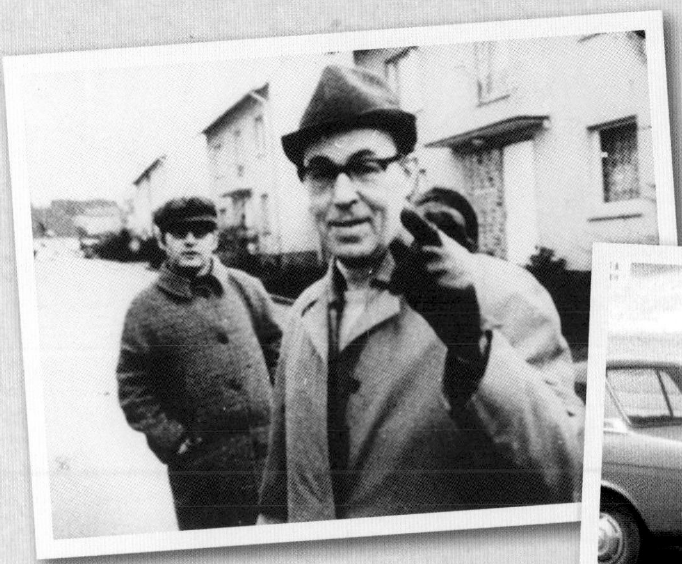

Herbert Haegen when he is exposed by Beate and Serge, 1971. (Klarsfeld Private Collection)

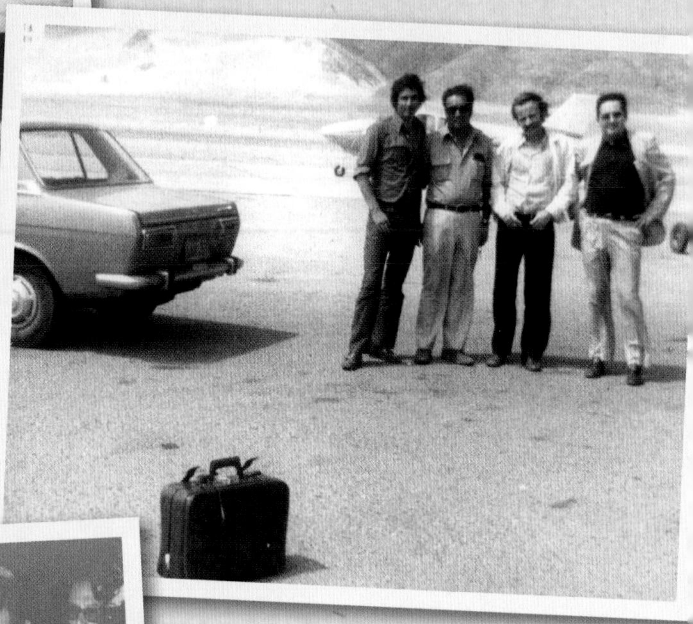

Serge, Régis Debray, and their Bolivian conspirators ready to capture Klaus Barbie, 1972. (Klarsfeld Private Collection)

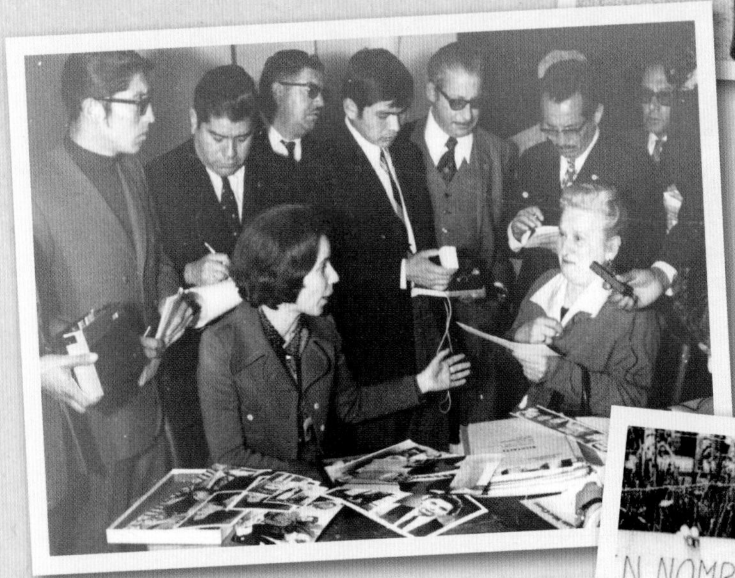

Beate Klarsfeld and Itta-Rosa Halaunbrenner with Bolivian journalists, February 1972. (Klarsfeld Private Collection)

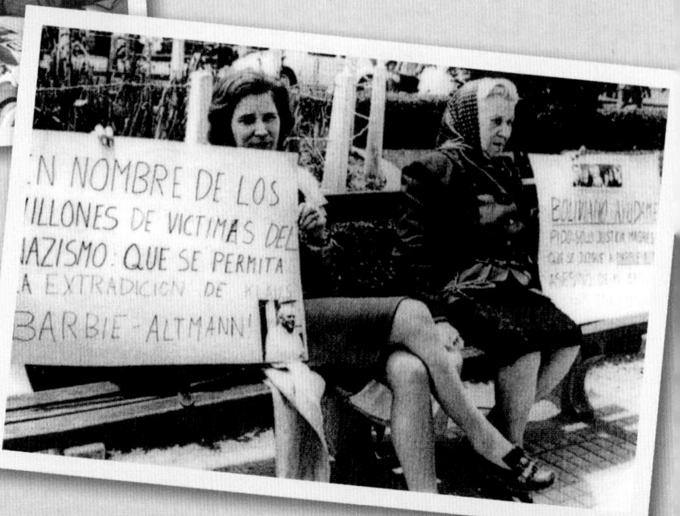
N NOMBRE DE LOS
ILLONES DE VICTIMAS DEL
AZISMO: QUE SE PERMITA
A EXTRADICION DE
BARBIE - ALTMANN!

Beate Klarsfeld and Itta-Rosa Halaunbrenner in front of Klaus Barbie's office in Bolivia, March 6, 1972. (Klarsfeld Private Collection)

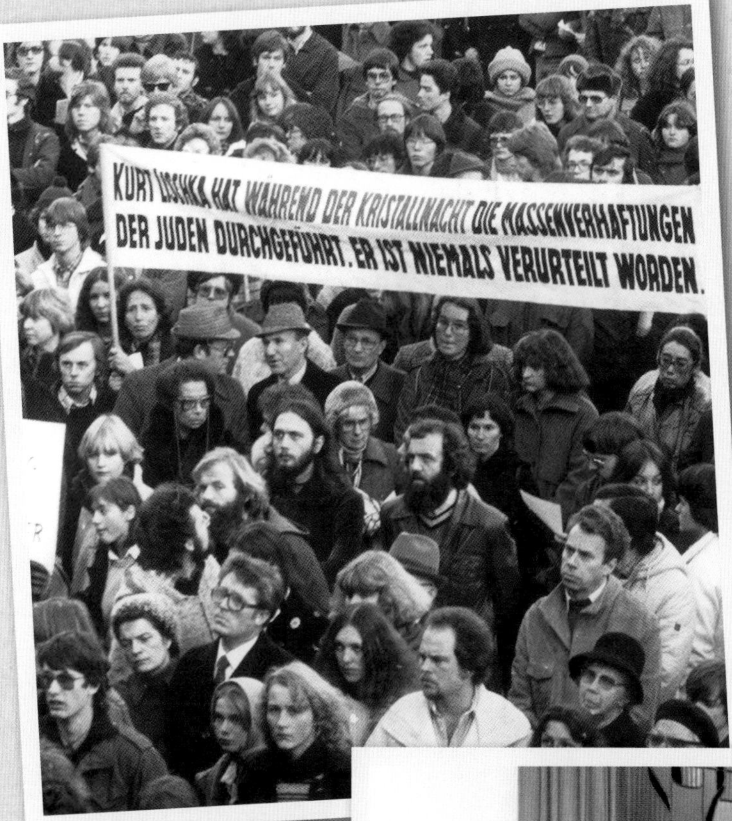
KURT LISCHKA HAT WÄHREND DER KRISTALLNACHT DIE MASSENVERHAFTUNGEN
DER JUDEN DURCHGEFÜHRT. ER IST NIEMALS VERURTEILT WORDEN.

March during the Lischka, Heinrichsohn and Hagen Trial in Cologne, October 1979. (Klarsfeld Private Collection, © Elie Kagan)

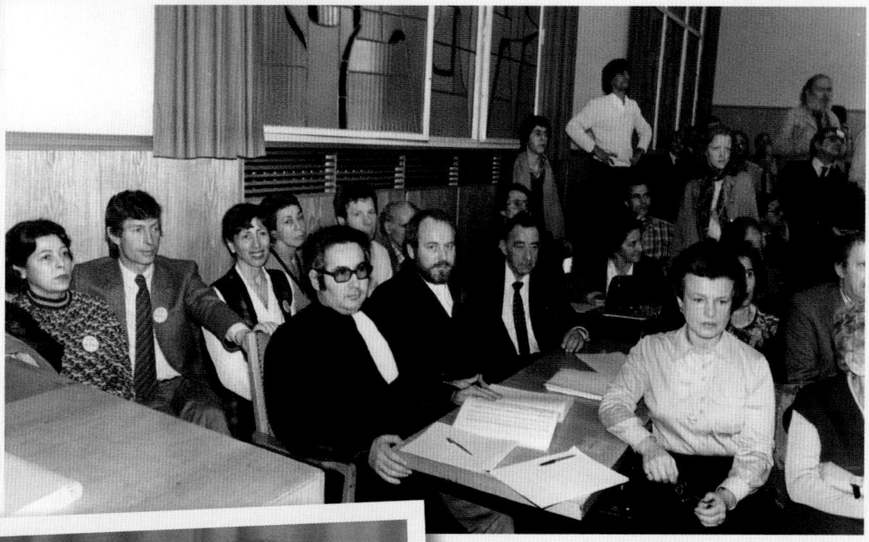

Serge at the Lischka, Heinrichsohn and Hagen Trial in Cologne, 1979. (Klarsfeld Private Collection, © Daniel Franck)

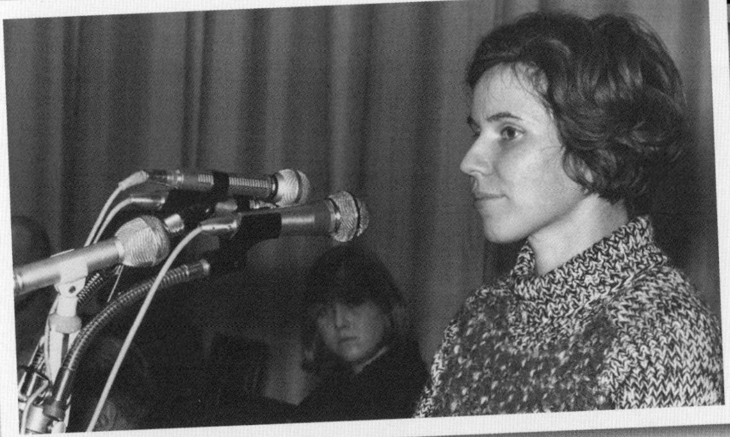

Beate at a conference, 1970s. (Klarsfeld Private Collection, © Daniel Franck)

THE 1980s–1990s AND THE FIGHT TO TRY, CHARGE AND DEPORT THE PEOPLE RESPONSIBLE FOR THE SHOAH IN FRANCE

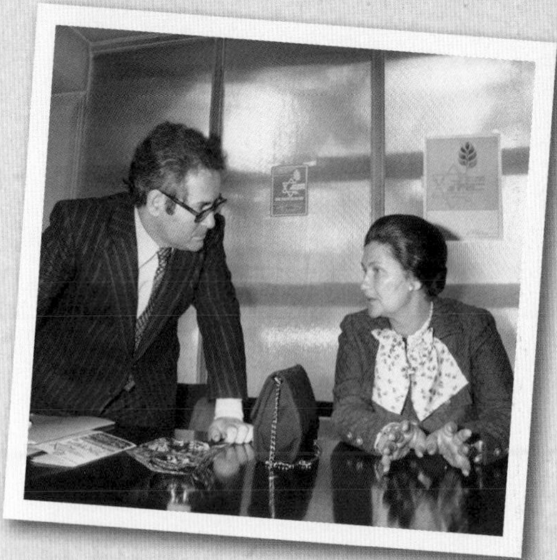

Serge Klarsfeld and Simone Veil, 1981.
(Klarsfeld Private Collection)

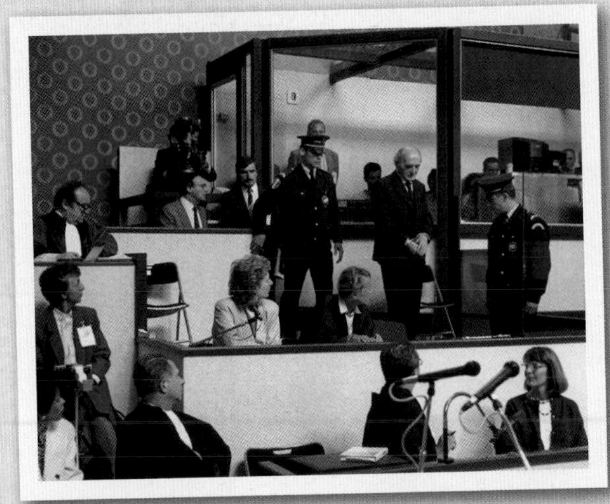

Klaus Barbie and his lawyer, Jacques Vergès, during his trial in Lyon, 1987.
(Progrès de Lyon)

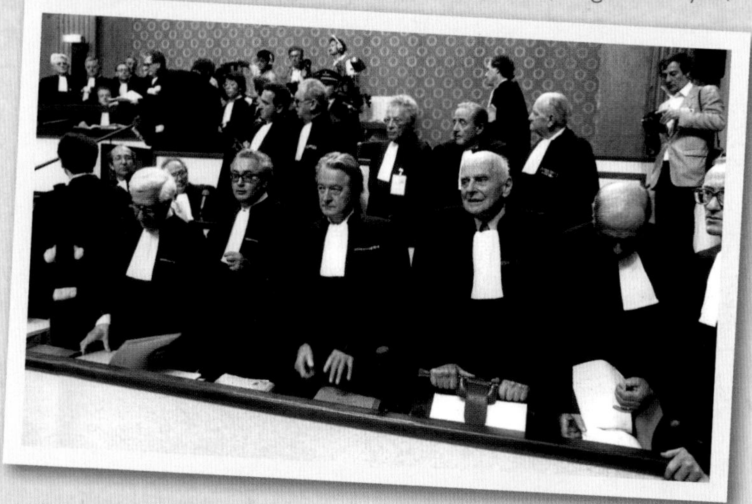

The counsel for the prosecution (in particular, Serge and Roland Dumas) during the Barbie trial, 1987. (All rights reserved - BM in Lyon)

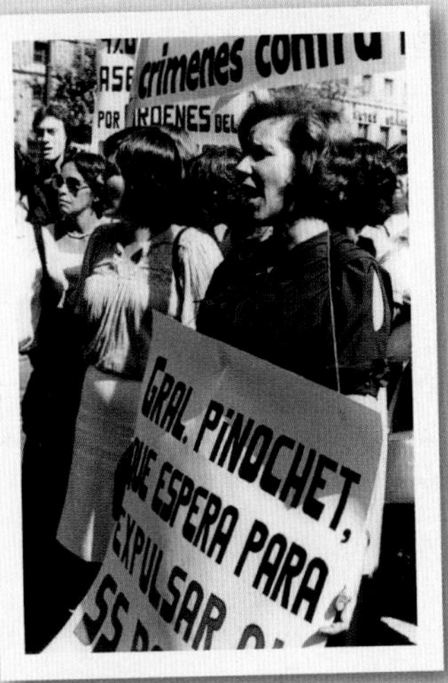
GRAL. PINOCHET,
EXPULSAR

Beate in Chili marching for the deportation of former SS, 1984.
(Mémorial de la Shoah & Klarsfeld Private Collection)

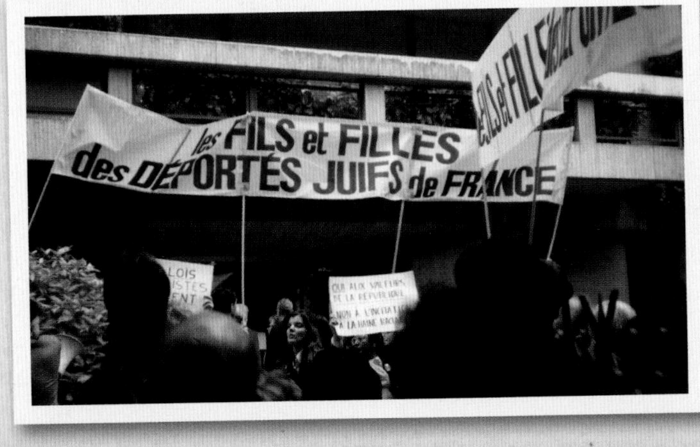
les FILS et FILLES
des DÉPORTÉS JUIFS de FRANCE

March of the Sons and Daughters of French Jewish Deportees in front of René Bousquet's home, 1984.
(Mémorial de la Shoah & Klarsfeld Private Collection)

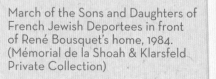

THE 2000s AND THE TRIALS OF PAPON AND ALOÏS BRUNNER

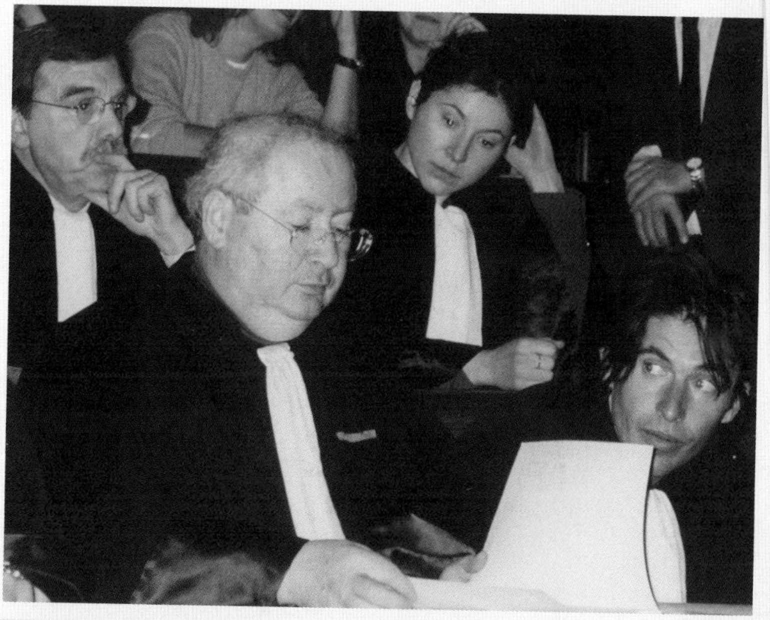

Lida, Serge, and Arno at the trial in absentia of Aloïs Brunner, March 2001. (Mémorial de la Shoah & Klarsfeld Private Collection)

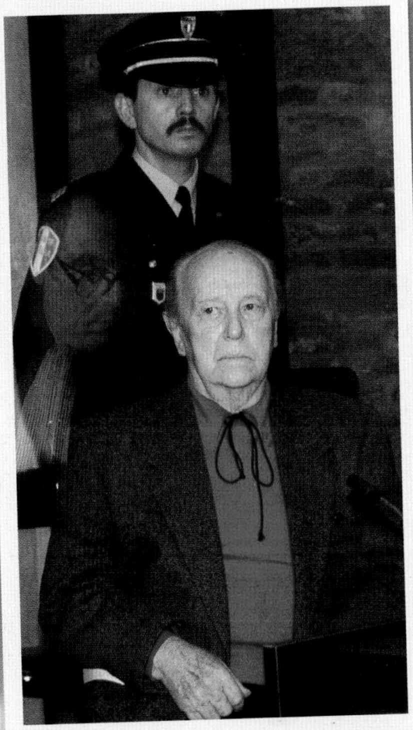

Paul Touvier at his trial, 1994. (Mémorial de la Shoah Collection)

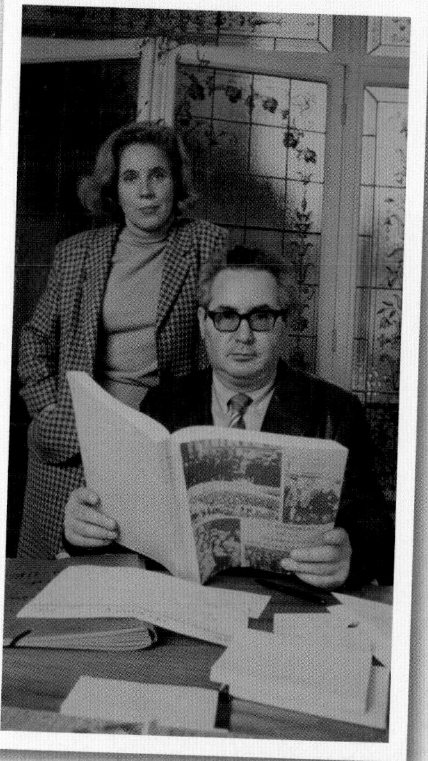

Beate and Serge holding an edition of the *Mémorial of the Jewish Deportees of France*, 1985. (Klarsfeld Private Collection)

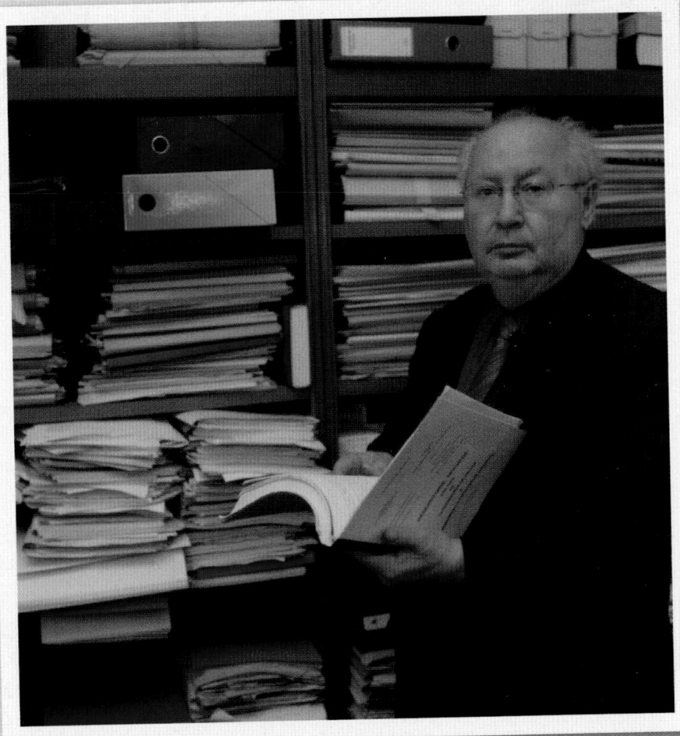

Serge and his archives, 2000s. (Klarsfeld Private Collection)

TODAY

Luigi in Lida's arms, Beate, Serge, Arno, Carlo Comporting, Lida's spouse, and Emma, their daughter, during the presentation of the Légion d'Honneur in recognition of Beate and Serge by the president François Hollande, July 2014.

Beate and Serge at the Children's Memorial in the Mémorial de la Shoah, which features 3,000 photographs of deported Jewish children, 2011.
(© Joël Saget - All rights reserved)